Volume Two

Xlib Reference Manual

---

for Version 11 of the
X Window System

edited by Adrian Nye

O'Reilly & Associates, Inc.

Revision and Printing History

August 1988:   First Printing.
November 1988: Second Printing. Minor revisions.
May 1989:   Third Printing. Release 3 updates added. Minor revisions.
April 1990:   Second Edition covers Release 3 and Release 4. Major revisions.

Small Print

The X Window System Series

The books in the X Window System Series are based in part on the original MIT X Window System documentation, but are far more comprehensive, easy to use, and are loaded with examples, tutorials and helpful hints. Over 20 major computer vendors recommend or license volumes in the series. In short, these are the definitive guides to the X Window System.

Volume 0:
X Protocol Reference Manual

A complete programmer's reference to the X Network Protocol, the language of communication between the X server and the X clients. 418 pages, $30.00.

Volumes 1 and 2:
Xlib Programming Manual
Xlib Reference Manual

Complete guide and reference to programming with the X library (Xlib), the lowest level of programming interface to X. 659 and 723 pages. $60.00 for the set, or $34.95 each.

Volume 3:
X Window System User's Guide

Describes window system concepts and the most common client applications available for X, Release 4. Includes complete explanation of the new window manager, *twm*, and a chapter on Motif. For experienced users, later chapters explain customizing the X environment. Useful with either Release 3 or Release 4. 586 pages. $30.00.

Volumes 4 and 5:
X Toolkit Intrinsics Programming Manual
X Toolkit Intrinsics Reference Manual

Complete guides to programming with the X Toolkit. The *Programming Manual* provides concepts and examples for using widgets and for the more complex task of writing new widgets. The *Reference Manual* provides reference pages for Xt functions, and Xt and Athena widgets. 582 and 545 pages. $55.00 for the set, or $30.00 each.

Volume 7:
XView Programming Manual

XView is an easy-to-use toolkit that is not just for Sun developers. It is available on MIT's R4 tape and System V Release 4, as well as being a part of Sun's Open Windows package. This manual provides complete information on XView, from concepts to creating applications to reference pages. 566 pages. $30.00.

For orders or a free catalog of all our books, please contact us.

O'Reilly & Associates, Inc.

Creators and Publishers of Nutshell Handbooks
632 Petaluma Avenue, Sebastapol, CA 95472
email: uunet!ora!nuts · 1-800-338-6887 · in CA 1-800-533-6887 · or 1-707-829-0515

Table of Contents

Preface

About This Manual

This manual describes the X library, the C Language programming interface to Version 11 of the X Window System. The X library, known as Xlib, is the lowest level of programming interface to X. This library enables a programmer to write applications with an advanced user interface based on windows on the screen, with complete network transparency, that will run without changes on many types of workstations and personal computers.

Xlib is powerful enough to write effective applications without additional programming tools and is necessary for certain tasks even in applications written with higher-level "toolkits."

There are a number of these toolkits for X programming, the most notable being the DEC/MIT toolkit Xt, the Andrew toolkit developed by IBM and Carnegie-Mellon University, and the InterViews toolkit from Stanford. These toolkits are still evolving, and only Xt is currently part of the X standard. Toolkits simplify the process of application writing considerably, providing a number of *widgets* that implement menus, command buttons, and other common features of the user interface.

This manual does not describe Xt or any other toolkit. That is done in Volumes Four, Five, and Six of our X Window System series. Nonetheless, much of the material described in this book is helpful for understanding and using the toolkits, since the toolkits themselves are written using Xlib and allow Xlib code to be intermingled with toolkit code.

Summary of Contents

This manual is divided into two volumes. This is the second volume, the *Xlib Reference Manual*. It includes reference pages for each of the Xlib functions (organized alphabetically), a permuted index, and numerous appendices and quick reference aids.

The first volume, the *Xlib Programming Manual*, provides a conceptual introduction to Xlib, including tutorial material and numerous programming examples. Arranged by task or topic, each chapter brings together a group of Xlib functions, describes the conceptual foundation they are based on, and illustrates how they are most often used in writing applications (or, in the case of the last chapter, in writing window managers). Volume One is structured so as to be useful as a tutorial and also as a task-oriented reference.

Volume One and Volume Two are designed to be used together. To get the most out of the examples in Volume One, you will need the exact calling sequences of each function from Volume Two. To understand fully how to use each of the functions described in Volume Two, all but the most experienced X "hacker" will need the explanation and examples in Volume One.

Both volumes include material from the original Xlib and X11 Protocol documentation provided by MIT, as well as from other documents provided on the MIT release tape. We have done our best to incorporate all of the useful information from the MIT documentation, to correct references we found to be in error, to reorganize and present it in a more useful form, and to supplement it with conceptual material, tutorials, reference aids, and examples. In other words, this manual is not only a replacement but is a superset of the MIT documentation.

Those of you familiar with the MIT documentation will recognize that each reference page in Volume Two includes the detailed description of the routine found in Gettys, Newman, and Scheifler's *Xlib–C Language X Interface*, plus, in many cases, additional text that clarifies ambiguities and describes the context in which the routine would be used. We have also added cross references to related reference pages and to where additional information can be found in Volume One.

How to Use This Manual

Volume Two is designed to make it as easy and fast as possible to look up virtually any fact about Xlib. It includes a permuted index, reference pages for each library function, appendices that cover macros, structures, function groups, events, fonts, colors, cursors, keysyms, and errors, and at-a-glance tables for the graphics context and window attributes.

The permuted index is the standard UNIX way of finding a particular function name given a keyword. By looking up a word in the second column that you think describes the function you are looking for, you can find the group of functions that have that word in their description lines. The description line also appears at the top of each reference page. Once you have found the routine you are looking for, you can look for its reference page.

The reference pages themselves provide all the details necessary for calling each routine, including its arguments, returned values, definitions of the structure types of arguments and returned values, and the errors it may generate. Many of the pages also give hints about how the routine is used in the context of other routines. This is the part of this volume you will use the most.

Appendix A, *Function Group Summary*, groups the routines according to function, and provides brief descriptions. You'll find it useful to have in one place a description of related routines, so their differences can be noted and the appropriate one chosen.

Appendix B, *Error Messages and Protocol Requests*, describes the errors that Xlib routines can generate. When an error is handled by the default error handler, one of these messages is printed. Also printed is the X Protocol request that caused the error. Since Protocol requests do not map directly to Xlib routines, this appendix provides a table with which you can find out which Xlib routine in your code caused the error.

Appendix C, *Macros*, describes the macros that access members of the `Display` structure, classify keysyms, and convert resource manager types.

Appendix D, *ColorCaEE*, presents the standard color database. The color names in this database should be available on all servers, though the corresponding RGB values may have been modified to account for screen variations.

Appendix E, *Event Reference*, describes each event type and structure, in a reference page format. This is an invaluable reference for event programming.

Appendix F, *Structure Reference*, describes all structures used by Xlib except the event structures described in Appendix E, including which routines use each structure.

Appendix G, *Symbol Reference*, lists in alphabetical order and describes all of the symbols defined in Xlib include files.

Appendix H, *Keysym Reference*, lists and describes each character in the standard keysym families, used for translating keyboard events. The characters for English and foreign language keysyms are shown where possible.

Appendix I, *The Cursor Font*, describes the standard cursor font, including a illustration of the font shapes.

Appendix J, *The Xmu Library*, provides reference pages for each function in the miscellaneous utilities library. This library is provided with the standard X distribution and is very useful when programming with Xlib.

Finally, Volume Two concludes with at-a-glance charts that help in setting the graphics context (GC) and the window attributes.

Example Programs

The example programs in this book are on the X11 Release 4 distribution in the contributed section. There are many ways of getting this distribution; most are described in Appendix H.

The example programs are also available free from UUNET (that is, free except for UUNET's usual connect-time charges). If you have access to UUNET, you can retrieve the source code using *uucp* or *ftp*. For *uucp*, find a machine with direct access to UUNET and type the following command:

```
uucp uunet\!~uucp/nutshell/Xlib/xlibprgs.tar.Z yourhost\!~/yourname/
```

The backslashes can be omitted if you use the Bourne shell (*sh*) instead of *csh*. The file should appear some time later (up to a day or more) in the directory */usr/spool/uucp-public/yourname*.

To use *ftp*, *ftp* to *uunet.uu.net* and use *anonymous* as your user name and *guest* as your password. Then type the following:

```
cd /nutshell/Xlib
binary  (you must specify binary transfer for compressed files)
get xlibprgs.tar.Z
bye
```

The file is a compressed shell archive. To restore the files once you have retrieved the archive, type:

```
uncompress xlibprgs.tar
sh xlibprgs.tar
```

The example programs are also available free by *ftp* from *expo.lcs.mit.edu*. The directory containing the examples is *contrib/examples/OReilly/Xlib*.

The examples will be installed in subdirectories under the current directory, one for each chapter in the book. Imakefiles are included. (Imakefiles are used with *imake*, a program supplied with the X11 distribution that generates proper Makefiles on a wide variety of systems.)

Assumptions

Readers should be proficient in the C programming language, although examples are provided for infrequently used features of the language that are necessary or useful when programming with X. In addition, general familiarity with the principles of raster graphics will be helpful.

Font Conventions Used in This Manual

Italic is used for:

- UNIX pathnames, filenames, program names, user command names, and options for user commands.

- New terms where they are defined.

`Typewriter Font` is used for:

- Anything that would be typed verbatim into code, such as examples of source code and text on the screen.

- The contents of include files, such as structure types, structure members, symbols (defined constants and bit flags), and macros.

- Xlib functions.

- Names of subroutines of the example programs.

`Italic Typewriter Font` is used for:

- Arguments to Xlib functions, since they could be typed in code as shown but are arbitrary.

Helvetica Italics are used for:

- Titles of examples, figures, and tables.

Boldface is used for:

- Chapter and section headings.

Related Documents

The C Programming Language by B. W. Kernighan and D. M. Ritchie

The following documents are included on the X11 source tape:

> *Xt Toolkit Intrinsics* by Joel McCormack, Paul Asente, and Ralph Swick
> *Xt Toolkit Widgets* by Ralph Swick and Terry Weissman
> *Xlib–C Language X Interface* by Jim Gettys, Ron Newman, and Robert Scheifler
> *X Window System Protocol, Version 11* by Robert Scheifler

The following books on the X Window System are available from O'Reilly and Associates, Inc.:

> Volume Zero — *X Protocol Reference Manual*
> Volume Three — *X Window System User's Guide*
> Volume Four — *X Toolkit Intrinsics Programming Manual*
> Volume Five — *X Toolkit Intrinsics Reference Manual*
> Volume Six — *X Toolkit Widgets Reference Manual* (available summer 1990)
> Volume Seven — *XView Programmer's Guide*

Requests for Comments

Please write to tell us about any flaws you find in this manual or how you think it could be improved, to help us provide you with the best documentation possible.

Our U.S. mail address, e-mail address, and telephone number are as follows:

O'Reilly and Associates, Inc.
632 Petaluma Avenue
Sebastopol, CA 95472
(800) 338-6887

UUCP: uunet!ora!adrian   ARPA: adrian@ora.UU.NET

Bulk Sales Information

This manual is being resold as the official X Window System documentation by many workstation manufacturers. For information on volume discounts for bulk purchase, call Linda Walsh at O'Reilly and Associates, Inc., at 617-354-5800, or send e-mail to linda@ora.com.

For companies requiring extensive customization of the book, source licensing terms are also available.

Acknowledgements

The information contained in this manual is based in part on *Xlib–C Language X Interface*, written by Jim Gettys, Ron Newman, and Robert Scheifler, and the *X Window System Protocol, Version 11*, by Robert Scheifler (with many contributors). The X Window System software and these documents were written under the auspices of Project Athena at MIT. In addition, this manual includes material from Oliver Jones' Xlib tutorial presentation, which was given at the MIT X Conference in January 1988, and from David Rosenthal's *Inter-Client Communication Conventions Manual*.

I would like to thank the people who helped this book come into being. It was Tim O'Reilly who originally sent me out on a contract to write a manual for X Version 10 for a workstation manufacturer and later to another company to write a manual for X Version 11, from which this book began. I have learned most of what I know about computers and technical writing while working for Tim. For this book, he acted as an editor, he helped me reorganize several chapters, he worked on the *Color* and *Managing User Preferences* chapters when time was too short for me to do it, and he kept my spirits up through this long project. While I was concentrating on the details, his eye was on the overall presentation, and his efforts improved the book enormously.

This book would not be as good (and we might still be working on it) had it not been for Daniel Gilly. Daniel was my production assistant for critical periods in the project. He dealt with formatting issues, checked for consistent usage of terms and noticed irregularities in content, and edited files from written corrections by me and by others. His job was to take as much of the work off me as possible, and with his technical skill and knowledge of UNIX, he did that very well.

This manual has benefitted from the work and assistance of the entire staff of O'Reilly and Associates, Inc. Susan Willing was responsible for graphics and design, and she proofed many drafts of the book; Linda Mui tailored the troff macros to the design by Sue Willing and myself and was invaluable in the final production process; John Strang figured out the resource manager and wrote the original section on that topic; Karen Cakebread edited a draft of the manual and established some conventions for terms and format. Peter Mui executed the "at-a-glance" tables for the inside back cover; Tom Scanlon entered written edits and performed copy fitting; Donna Woonteiler wrote the index of the book, Valerie Quercia, Tom Van Raalte, and Linda Walsh all contributed in some small ways; and Cathy Brennan, Suzanne Van Hove, and Jill Berlin fielded many calls from people interested in the X manual and saved me all the time that would have taken. Ruth Terry, Lenny Muellner, and Donna

Woonteiler produced the Second Edition, with graphics done by Chr. thanks to everyone at O'Reilly and Associates for putting up with my terminal hogging, lugging X books around, recycling paper, and for gen. what they do and good-natured to boot.

Many people sent in corrections for this Second Edition of the manual. T. were most noteworthy were Jane-Na Chang of NEC, Jonathan Saunders of Security Systems Inc., Saundra Miller, and Russell Ferriday.

I would also like to thank the people from other companies that reviewed the book or otherwise made this project possible: John Posner, Barry Kingsbury, Jeff MacMann and Jeffrey Vroom of Stellar Computer; Oliver Jones of Apollo Computer; Sam Black, Jeff Graber, and Janet Egan of Masscomp; Al Tabayoyon, Paul Shearer, and many others from Tektronix; Robert Scheifler and Jim Fulton of the X Consortium (who helped with the *Color* and *Managing User Preferences* chapters), and Peter Winston II and Aub Harden of Integrated Computer Solutions. Despite the efforts of the reviewers and everyone else, any errors that remain are my own.

— *Adrian Nye*

Permuted Index

How to Use the Permuted Index

The permuted index takes the brief descriptive string from the title of each command page and rotates (permutes) the string so that each keyword will at one point start the *second*, or center, column of the line. The beginning and end of the original string are indicated by a slash when they are in other than their original position; if the string is too long, it is truncated.

To find the command you want, simply scan down the middle of the page, looking for a keyword of interest on the right side of the blank gutter. Once you find the keyword you want, you can read (with contortions) the brief description of the command that makes up the entry. If things still look promising, you can look all the way over to the right for the name of the relevant command page.

The Permuted Index

for string and font metrics of a	16-bit character string /server	XQueryTextExtents16
/get string and font metrics of a	16-bit character string, locally	XTextExtents16
/get the width in pixels of a	16-bit character string, locally	XTextWidth16
XDrawImageString16: draw	16-bit image text characters	XDrawImageString16
XDrawText16: draw	16-bit polytext strings	XDrawText16
/get the width in pixels of an	8-bit character string, locally	XTextWidth
XDrawImageString: draw	8-bit image text characters	XDrawImageString
XDrawText: draw	8-bit polytext strings	XDrawText
only XDrawString: draw an	8-bit text string, foreground	XDrawString
/disable or enable	access control	XSetAccessControl
XAddHost: add a host to the	access control list	XAddHost
add multiple hosts to the	access control list XAddHosts:	XAddHosts
/remove a host from the	access control list	XRemoveHost
/remove multiple hosts from the	access control list	XRemoveHosts
deny/ XEnableAccessControl: use	access control list to allow or	XEnableAccessControl
XDisableAccessControl: allow	access from any host	XDisableAccessControl
/obtain a list of hosts having	access to this display	XListHosts
XActivateScreenSaver:	activate screen blanking	XActivateScreenSaver
release the keyboard from an	active grab XUngrabKeyboard:	XUngrabKeyboard
release the pointer from an	active grab XUngrabPointer:	XUngrabPointer
/change the parameters of an	active pointer grab	XChangeActivePointerGrab
pixel value in an/ XAddPixel:	add a constant value to every	XAddPixel
list XAddHost:	add a host to the access control	XAddHost

Xlib Reference Manual

a location within/ XGetSubImage: copy a rectangle in drawable to .... XGetSubImage
drawable into a/ XCopyPlane: copy a single plane of a .... XCopyPlane
XCopyArea: copy an area of a drawable .... XCopyArea
XLookupKeysym: get the keysym corresponding to a keycode in/ .... XLookupKeysym
XSaveContext: save a data value corresponding to a window and/ .... XSaveContext
format/ XCreateBitmapFromData: create a bitmap from X11 bitmap .... XCreateBitmapFromData
XCreateColormap: create a colormap. .... XCreateColormap
XCreateGlyphCursor: create a cursor from font glyphs .... XCreateGlyphCursor
standard/ XCreateFontCursor: create a cursor from the .... XCreateFontCursor
XCreatePixmapCursor: create a cursor from two bitmaps .... XCreatePixmapCursor
XrmGetStringDatabase: create a database from a string .... XrmGetStringDatabase
mapping/ XNewModifiermap: create a keyboard modifier .... XNewModifiermap
(X10) XCreateAssocTable: create a new association table .... XCreateAssocTable
graphics/ XUniqueContext: create a new context ID (not .... XUniqueContext
XCreateRegion: create a new empty region .... XCreateRegion
for a given screen/ XCreateGC: create a new graphics context .... XCreateGC
XCreatePixmap: create a pixmap .... XCreatePixmap
XCreatePixmapFromBitmapData: create a pixmap with depth from/ .... XCreatePixmapFromBitmapData
an image XSubImage: create a subimage from part of .... XSubImage
attributes XCreateWindow: create a window and set .... XCreateWindow
association table XMakeAssoc: create an entry in an .... XMakeAssoc
window XCreateSimpleWindow: create an unmapped InputOutput .... XCreateSimpleWindow
XGetWindowAttributes: obtain the current attributes of window .... XGetWindowAttributes
context XSetFont: set the current font in a graphics .... XSetFont
XGetFontPath: get the current font search path .... XGetFontPath
XGetGeometry: obtain the current geometry of drawable .... XGetGeometry
XGetInputFocus: return the current keyboard focus window .... XGetInputFocus
/obtain a list of the current keyboard preferences .... XGetKeyboardControl
XQueryPointer: get the current pointer location .... XQueryPointer
XGetPointerControl: get the current pointer preferences .... XGetPointerControl
XGetScreenSaver: get the current screen saver parameters .... XGetScreenSaver
/obtain a bit vector for the current state of the keyboard .... XQueryKeymap
XFreeCursor: release a cursor .... XFreeCursor
change the color of a cursor XRecolorCursor: .... XRecolorCursor
a cursor from the standard cursor font /create .... XCreateFontCursor
XUndefineCursor: disassociate a cursor from a window .... XUndefineCursor
XCreateGlyphCursor: create a cursor from font glyphs .... XCreateGlyphCursor
XCreateFontCursor: create a cursor from the standard cursor/ .... XCreateFontCursor
XCreatePixmapCursor: create a cursor from two bitmaps .... XCreatePixmapCursor
get the closest supported cursor sizes XQueryBestCursor: .... XQueryBestCursor
/obtain the "best" supported cursor, tile, or stipple size .... XQueryBestSize
XDefineCursor: assign a cursor to a window .... XDefineCursor
X10) XDraw: draw a polyline or curve between vertex list (from .... XDraw
X10) /draw a filled polygon or curve from vertex list (from .... XDrawFilled
XFetchBuffer: return data from a cut buffer .... XFetchBuffer
XStoreBuffer: store data in a cut buffer .... XStoreBuffer
XFetchBytes: return data from cut buffer 0 .... XFetchBytes
XStoreBytes: store data in cut buffer 0 .... XStoreBytes
XRotateBuffers: rotate the cut buffers .... XRotateBuffers
/set a pattern of line dashes in a graphics context .... XSetDashes
a bitmap from X11 bitmap format data /create .... XCreateBitmapFromData
a pixmap with depth from bitmap data. /create .... XCreatePixmapFromBitmapData
specified/ /free the in-memory data associated with the .... XFreeStringList
XFetchBuffer: return data from a cut buffer .... XFetchBuffer
XLookUpAssoc: obtain data from an association table .... XLookUpAssoc
XFetchBytes: return data from cut buffer 0 .... XFetchBytes
(not graphics/ XFindContext: get data from the context manager .... XFindContext
XStoreBuffer: store data in a cut buffer .... XStoreBuffer

XGetIconName: get the name to be displayed in an icon .... XGetIconName
next event that matches mask; don't wait /remove the .... XCheckMaskEvent
queue that matches event type; don't wait /the next event in .... XCheckTypedEvent
passed window and passed mask; don't wait /event matching both .... XCheckWindowEvent
stacking order of children up or down /circulate the .... XCirculateSubwindows
/change the close down mode of a client .... XSetCloseDownMode
characters XDrawImageString16: draw 16-bit image text XDrawImageString16
XDrawText16: draw 16-bit polytext strings XDrawText16
XDrawImageString: draw 8-bit image text characters .... XDrawImageString
XDrawText: draw 8-bit polytext strings .... XDrawText
from vertex list/ XDrawFilled: draw a filled polygon or curve .... XDrawFilled
XDrawLine: draw a line between two points .... XDrawLine
XDrawPoint: draw a point .... XDrawPoint
vertex list (from X10) XDraw: draw a polyline or curve between .... XDraw
foreground only XDrawString: draw an 8-bit text string, ... XDrawString
rectangle XDrawArc: draw an arc fitting inside a .... XDrawArc
pixmap XPutImage: draw an image on a window or .... XPutImage
XDrawRectangle: draw an outline of a rectangle .... XDrawRectangle
XDrawArcs: draw multiple arcs .... XDrawArcs
XDrawLines: draw multiple connected lines. .... XDrawLines
XDrawSegments: draw multiple disjoint lines .... XDrawSegments
XDrawPoints: draw multiple points. .... XDrawPoints
rectangles XDrawRectangles: draw the outlines of multiple .... XDrawRectangles
XDrawString16: draw two-byte text strings XDrawString16
XCopyArea: copy an area of a drawable .... XCopyArea
with the depth of the specified drawable /for a given screen .... XCreateGC
obtain the current geometry of drawable XGetGeometry: .... XGetGeometry
depth./ /copy a single plane of a drawable into a drawable with .... XCopyPlane
contents of a rectangle from drawable into an image /place .... XGetImage
the/ /copy a rectangle in drawable to a location within .... XGetSubImage
/plane of a drawable into a drawable with depth, applying/ .... XCopyPlane
XSetLineAttributes: set the line drawing components in a graphics/ .... XSetLineAttributes
determine if a region is empty XEmptyRegion: .... XEmptyRegion
XCreateRegion: create a new empty region .... XCreateRegion
XSetAccessControl: disable or enable access control .... XSetAccessControl
synchronization/ XSynchronize: enable or disable .... XSynchronize
generate the smallest rectangle enclosing a region XClipBox: .... XClipBox
XClearWindow: clear an entire window .... XClearWindow
XDeleteContext: delete a context entry for a given window and/ .... XDeleteContext
XDeleteAssoc: delete an entry from an association table. .... XDeleteAssoc
structure /delete an entry from an XModifierKeymap .... XDeleteModifiermapEntry
XMakeAssoc: create an entry in an association table .... XMakeAssoc
structure /add a new entry to an XModifierKeymap .... XInsertModifiermapEntry
/values of a read/write colormap entry to the closest possible/ .... XStoreColor
obtain a description of error code XGetErrorText: .... XGetErrorText
/obtain error messages from the error database .... XGetErrorDatabaseText
XSetErrorHandler: set a nonfatal error event handler .... XSetErrorHandler
XGetErrorDatabaseText: obtain error messages from the error/ .... XGetErrorDatabaseText
/and wait for all events and errors to be processed by the/ .... XSync
modifier keys (Shift, Control, etc.) /obtain a mapping of .... XGetModifierMapping
as modifiers (Shift, Control, etc.) /set keycodes to be used .... XSetModifierMapping
the event queue for a matching event XCheckIfEvent: check .... XCheckIfEvent
XSendEvent: send an event .... XSendEvent
XPutBackEvent: push an event back on the input queue .... XPutBackEvent
set a nonfatal error event handler XSetErrorHandler: .... XSetErrorHandler
window /return the next event in queue matching type and .... XCheckTypedWindowEvent
event type;/ /return the next event in queue that matches .... XCheckTypedEvent
procedure/ XPeekIfEvent: get an event matched by predicate .... XPeekIfEvent

with the specified string list /in-memory data associated .... XFreeStringList
a host from the access control list XRemoveHost: remove .... XRemoveHost
hosts from the access control list /remove multiple .... XRemoveHosts
to a binding list and a quark list /convert a key string .... XrmStringToBindingQuarkList
convert a key string to a quark list XrmStringToQuarkList: .... XrmStringToQuarkList
a key string to a binding list and a quark list /convert .... XrmStringToBindingQuarkList
/search prepared list for a given resource .... XrmQGetSearchResource
/get the property list for a window .... XListProperties
polyline or curve between vertex list (from X10) XDraw: draw a .... XDraw
polygon or curve from vertex list (from X10) /draw a filled .... XDrawFilled
XListExtensions: return a list of all extensions to X/ .... XListExtensions
root XQueryTree: return a list of children, parent, and .... XQueryTree
XrmQGetSearchList: return a list of database levels .... XrmQGetSearchList
this/ XListHosts: obtain a list of hosts having access to .... XListHosts
XListInstalledColormaps: get a list of installed colormaps .... XListInstalledColormaps
/free memory allocated for a list of installed extensions .... XFreeExtensionList
in a graphics context to a list of rectangles /clip_mask .... XSetClipRectangles
XTextProperty/ /obtain a list of strings from a specified .... XTextPropertyToStringList
XTextProperty/ /set the specified list of strings to an .... XStringListToTextProperty
XListFonts: return a list of the available font names .... XListFonts
XGetKeyboardControl: obtain a list of the current keyboard/ .... XGetKeyboardControl
requests /use access control list to allow or deny connection .... XEnableAccessControl
structure XLoadQueryFont: load a font and fill information .... XLoadQueryFont
loaded; get font ID XLoadFont: load a font if not already .... XLoadFont
command line/ XrmParseCommand: load a resource database from .... XrmParseCommand
return information about a loaded font XQueryFont: .... XQueryFont
the names and information about loaded fonts /obtain .... XListFontsWithInfo
load a font if not already loaded; get font ID XLoadFont: .... XLoadFont
get string and font metrics locally XTextExtents: .... XTextExtents
of a 16-bit character string, locally /string and font metrics XTextExtents16
of an 8-bit character string, locally /get the width in pixels .... XTextWidth
of a 16-bit character string, locally /get the width in pixels XTextWidth16
get the current pointer location XQueryPointer: .... XQueryPointer
/a rectangle in drawable to a location within the pre-existing/ .... XGetSubImage
/set the foreground, background, logical function, and plane mask/ .... XSetState
XSetFunction: set the bitwise logical operation in a graphics/ .... XSetFunction
color name or/ XParseColor: look up RGB values from ASCII .... XParseColor
order XLowerWindow: lower a window in the stacking .... XLowerWindow
initialize the resource manager XrmInitialize: .... XrmInitialize
set of properties for the window manager /set the minimum .... XSetStandardProperties
name to a window for the window manager XStoreName: assign a .... XStoreName
XGetWMHints: read the window manager hints property .... XGetWMHints
XSetWMHints: set a window manager hints property .... XSetWMHints
/get data from the context manager (not graphics context) .... XFindContext
/set a window's standard window manager properties .... XSetWMProperties
keysym, and/ XLookupString: map a key event to ASCII string, ... XLookupString
XMapWindow: map a window .... XMapWindow
siblings XMapRaised: map a window on top of its .... XMapRaised
XMapSubwindows: map all subwindows of window .... XMapSubwindows
change the keyboard mapping XChangeKeyboardMapping: ... XChangeKeyboardMapping
get the pointer button mapping XGetPointerMapping: .... XGetPointerMapping
set the pointer button mapping XSetPointerMapping: .... XSetPointerMapping
/read keycode-keysym mapping from server into Xlib .... XRefreshKeyboardMapping
XGetModifierMapping: obtain a mapping of modifier keys (Shift,/ .... XGetModifierMapping
and free a keyboard modifier mapping structure /destroy .... XFreeModifiermap
/create a keyboard modifier mapping structure .... XNewModifiermap
the next event that matches mask XMaskEvent: remove .... XMaskEvent
event that matches the specified mask and window /remove the next .... XWindowEvent

the next event that matches mask; don't wait /remove .... XCheckMaskEvent
both passed window and passed mask; don't wait /event matching .... XCheckWindowEvent
XSetPlaneMask: set the plane mask in a graphics context .... XSetPlaneMask
/logical function, and plane mask in a graphics context .... XSetState
/information structures that match the specified template .... XGetVisualInfo
XPeekIfEvent: get an event matched by predicate procedure/ .... XPeekIfEvent
XIfEvent: wait for event matched in predicate procedure .... XIfEvent
/the next event in queue that matches event type; don't wait .... XCheckTypedEvent
remove the next event that matches mask XMaskEvent: .... XMaskEvent
/remove the next event that matches mask; don't wait .... XCheckMaskEvent
/the visual information that matches the desired depth and/ .... XMatchVisualInfo
/remove the next event that matches the specified mask and/ .... XWindowEvent
passed/ /remove the next event matching both passed window and .... XCheckWindowEvent
check the event queue for a matching event XCheckIfEvent: .... XCheckIfEvent
/return the next event in queue matching type and window .... XCheckTypedWindowEvent
function XFree: free specified memory allocated by an Xlib .... XFree
XFreeFontPath: free the memory allocated by XGetFontPath .... XFreeFontPath
XFreeFontNames: free the memory allocated by XListFonts. .... XFreeFontNames
XFreeFontInfo: free the memory allocated by/ .... XFreeFontInfo
XFreeExtensionList: free memory allocated for a list of/ .... XFreeExtensionList
XDestroyAssocTable: free the memory allocated for an/ .... XDestroyAssocTable
XDestroyImage: deallocate memory associated with an image .... XDestroyImage
XCreateImage: allocate memory for an XImage structure .... XCreateImage
Xpermalloc: allocate memory never to be freed .... Xpermalloc
database/ XrmMergeDatabases: merge the contents of one .... XrmMergeDatabases
／obtain error messages from the error database .... XGetErrorDatabaseText
the server for string and font metrics /query .... XQueryTextExtents
get string and font metrics locally XTextExtents: .... XTextExtents
/the server for string and font metrics of a 16-bit character/ XQueryTextExtents16
string,/ /get string and font metrics of a 16-bit character XTextExtents16
XSetStandardProperties: set the minimum set of properties for/ .... XSetStandardProperties
XSetArcMode: set the arc mode in a graphics context .... XSetArcMode
/set the subwindow mode in a graphics context .... XSetSubwindowMode
/change the close down mode of a client .... XSetCloseDownMode
etc.) /obtain a mapping of modifier keys (Shift, Control, ... XGetModifierMapping
/destroy and free a keyboard modifier mapping structure .... XFreeModifiermap
/create a keyboard modifier mapping structure .... XNewModifiermap
/set keycodes to be used as modifiers (Shift, Control, etc.) .... XSetModifierMapping
/get events from pointer motion history buffer .... XGetMotionEvents
XMoveWindow: move a window .... XMoveWindow
point on the/ XWarpPointer: move the pointer to another .... XWarpPointer
XDrawArcs: draw multiple arcs .... XDrawArcs
XFillArcs: fill multiple arcs .... XFillArcs
XDrawLines: draw multiple connected lines. .... XDrawLines
XDrawSegments: draw multiple disjoint lines .... XDrawSegments
control/ XRemoveHosts: remove multiple hosts from the access .... XRemoveHosts
control list XAddHosts: add multiple hosts to the access .... XAddHosts
XDrawPoints: draw multiple points. .... XDrawPoints
/draw the outlines of multiple rectangles .... XDrawRectangles
XFillRectangles: fill multiple rectangular areas .... XFillRectangles
a read-only colorcell from color name XAllocNamedColor: allocate .... XAllocNamedColor
RGB values from color name /closest hardware-supported .... XLookupColor
a read/write colorcell by color name /set RGB values of .... XStoreNamedColor
/get a resource value using name and class as quarks .... XrmQGetResource
/get a resource from name and class as strings .... XrmGetResource
database using a quark resource name and string value /to a .... XrmQPutStringResource
with separate resource name and value /specification .... XrmPutStringResource
atom XGetAtomName: get a string name for a property given its .... XGetAtomName

/up RGB values from ASCII color	name or translate hexadecimal/	.... XParseColor
an atom for a given property	name string XInternAtom: return	.... XInternAtom
/convert a keysym	name string to a keysym	.... XStringToKeysym
manager XStoreName: assign a	name to a window for the window	.... XStoreName
window's/ XSetIconName: set the	name to be displayed in a	.... XSetIconName
XGetIconName: get the	name to be displayed in an icon	.... XGetIconName
XDisplayName: report the display	name (when connection to a/	.... XDisplayName
XFetchName: get a window's	name (XA_WM_NAME property)	.... XFetchName
a list of the available font	names XListFonts: return	.... XListFonts
XListFontsWithInfo: obtain the	names and information about/	.... XListFontsWithInfo
Xpermalloc: allocate memory	never to be freed	.... Xpermalloc
XCreateAssocTable: create a	new association table (X10)	.... XCreateAssocTable
/copy a colormap and return a	new colormap ID	.... XCopyColormapAndFree
XUniqueContext: create a	new context ID (not graphics/	.... XUniqueContext
XCreateRegion: create a	new empty region	.... XCreateRegion
XInsertModifiermapEntry: add a	new entry to an XModifierKeymap/	.... XInsertModifiermapEntry
screen with/ XCreateGC: create a	new graphics context for a given	.... XCreateGC
XrmUniqueQuark: allocate a	new quark	.... XrmUniqueQuark
type and window /return the	next event in queue matching	.... XCheckTypedWindowEvent
XCheckTypedEvent: return the	next event in queue that matches/	.... XCheckTypedEvent
XCheckWindowEvent: remove the	next event matching both passed/	.... XCheckWindowEvent
XNextEvent: get the	next event of any type or window	.... XNextEvent
XMaskEvent: remove the	next event that matches mask	.... XMaskEvent
XCheckMaskEvent: remove the	next event that matches mask;/	.... XCheckMaskEvent
XWindowEvent: remove the	next event that matches the/	.... XWindowEvent
XSetErrorHandler: set a	nonfatal error event handler	.... XSetErrorHandler
/allocate read/write	(nonshareable) color planes	.... XAllocColorPlanes
/allocate read/write	(nonshared) colorcells	.... XAllocColorCells
the server XNoOp: send a	NoOp to exercise connection with	.... XNoOp
/hints property of a window in	normal state (not zoomed or/	.... XGetNormalHints
/hints property of a window in	normal state (not zoomed or/	.... XSetNormalHints
a colormap; install default if	not already installed /uninstall	.... XUninstallColormap
XLoadFont: load a font if	not already loaded; get font ID	.... XLoadFont
data from the context manager	(not graphics context) /get	.... XFindContext
/to a window and context type	(not graphics context)	.... XSaveContext
/create a new context ID	(not graphics context)	.... XUniqueContext
/of a window in normal state	(not zoomed or iconified)	.... XGetNormalHints
/of a window in normal state	(not zoomed or iconified)	.... XSetNormalHints
queue XEventsQueued: check the	number of events in the event	.... XEventsQueued
/request buffer and return the	number of pending input events	.... XPending
current state of/ XQueryKeymap:	obtain a bit vector for the	.... XQueryKeymap
code XGetErrorText:	obtain a description of error	.... XGetErrorText
access to this/ XListHosts:	obtain a list of hosts having	.... XListHosts
XTextPropertyToStringList:	obtain a list of strings from a/	.... XTextPropertyToStringList
keyboard/ XGetKeyboardControl:	obtain a list of the current	.... XGetKeyboardControl
keys/ XGetModifierMapping:	obtain a mapping of modifier	.... XGetModifierMapping
an image XGetPixel:	obtain a single pixel value from	.... XGetPixel
information XWMGeometry:	obtain a window's geometry	.... XWMGeometry
from Xlib's GC/ XGetGCValues:	obtain components of a given GC	.... XGetGCValues
table XLookUpAssoc:	obtain data from an association	.... XLookUpAssoc
error/ XGetErrorDatabaseText:	obtain error messages from the	.... XGetErrorDatabaseText
of colorcells XQueryColors:	obtain RGB values for an array	.... XQueryColors
property/ XGetWindowProperty:	obtain the atom type and	.... XGetWindowProperty
cursor, tile,/ XQueryBestSize:	obtain the "best" supported	.... XQueryBestSize
window XGetWindowAttributes:	obtain the current attributes of	.... XGetWindowAttributes
drawable XGetGeometry:	obtain the current geometry of	.... XGetGeometry
fill tile shape XQueryBestTile:	obtain the fastest supported	.... XQueryBestTile
stipple/ XQueryBestStipple:	obtain the fastest supported	.... XQueryBestStipple

ID) associated/ XGContextFromGC:	obtain the GContext (resource	XGContextFromGC
about/ XListFontsWithInfo:	obtain the names and information	XListFontsWithInfo
keycodes for/ XDisplayKeycodes:	obtain the range of legal	XDisplayKeycodes
for a specified/ XQueryColor:	obtain the RGB values and flags	XQueryColor
formats for/ XListPixmapFormats:	obtain the supported pixmap	XListPixmapFormats
Visual XVisualIDFromVisual:	obtain the visual ID from a	XVisualIDFromVisual
that matches/ XMatchVisualInfo:	obtain the visual information	XMatchVisualInfo
structure/ XGetRGBColormaps:	obtain the XStandardColormap	XGetRGBColormaps
turn the screen saver on or	off XForceScreenSaver:	XForceScreenSaver
keys XAutoRepeatOff: turn	off the keyboard auto-repeat	XAutoRepeatOff
two regions have the same size,	offset, and shape /determine if	XEqualRegion
XOffsetRegion: change	offset of a region	XOffsetRegion
an 8-bit text string, foreground	only XDrawString: draw	XDrawString
/set the bitwise logical	operation in a graphics context	XSetFunction
XGetDefault: extract an	option value from the resource/	XGetDefault
child to the top of the stacking	order /circulate the bottom	XCirculateSubwindowsDown
to the bottom of the stacking	order /circulate the top child	XCirculateSubwindowsUp
size, border width, or stacking	order /the window position,	XConfigureWindow
lower a window in the stacking	order XLowerWindow:	XLowerWindow
to the top of the stacking	order /raise a window	XRaiseWindow
/circulate the stacking	order of children up or down	XCirculateSubwindows
/change the stacking	order of siblings	XRestackWindows
XSetClipOrigin: set the clip	origin in a graphics context	XSetClipOrigin
/set the tile/stipple	origin in a graphics context	XSetTSOrigin
XDrawRectangle: draw an	outline of a rectangle	XDrawRectangle
XDrawRectangles: draw the	outlines of multiple rectangles	XDrawRectangles
XGetSelectionOwner: return the	owner of a selection	XGetSelectionOwner
XSetSelectionOwner: set the	owner of a selection	XSetSelectionOwner
get the current screen saver	parameters XGetScreenSaver:	XGetScreenSaver
grab /change the	parameters of an active pointer	XChangeActivePointerGrab
XSetScreenSaver: set the	parameters of the screen saver	XSetScreenSaver
between another window and its	parent /insert a window	XReparentWindow
return a list of children,	parent, and root XQueryTree:	XQueryTree
create a subimage from	part of an image XSubImage:	XSubImage
matching both passed window and	passed mask; don't wait /event	XCheckWindowEvent
/the next event matching both	passed window and passed mask;/	XCheckWindowEvent
release a button from a	passive grab XUngrabButton:	XUngrabButton
XUngrabKey: release a key from a	passive grab	XUngrabKey
get the current font search	path XGetFontPath:	XGetFontPath
set the font search	path XSetFontPath:	XSetFontPath
graphics/ XSetDashes: set a	pattern of line dashes in a	XSetDashes
buffer and return the number of	pending input events /request	XPending
repaint/ /change a window border	pixel value attribute and	XSetWindowBorder
window /set the background	pixel value attribute of a	XSetWindowBackground
XGetPixel: obtain a single	pixel value from an image	XGetPixel
context /set the background	pixel value in a graphics	XSetBackground
context /set the foreground	pixel value in a graphics	XSetForeground
/add a constant value to every	pixel value in an image	XAddPixel
XPutPixel: set a	pixel value in an image	XPutPixel
a drawable with depth, applying	pixel values /of a drawable into	XCopyPlane
XTextWidth16: get the width in	pixels of a 16-bit character/	XTextWidth16
XTextWidth: get the width in	pixels of an 8-bit character/	XTextWidth
XCreatePixmap: create a	pixmap	XCreatePixmap
draw an image on a window or	pixmap XPutImage:	XPutImage
server /obtain the supported	pixmap formats for a given	XListPixmapFormats
XFreePixmap: free a	pixmap ID	XFreePixmap
XSetClipMask: set clip_mask	pixmap in a graphics context	XSetClipMask
data. /create a	pixmap with depth from bitmap	XCreatePixmapFromBitmapData

from drawable into/ XGetImage: place contents of a rectangle .... XGetImage

XSetPlaneMask: set the plane mask in a graphics context .... XSetPlaneMask

/logical function, and plane mask in a graphics context .... XSetState

XCopyPlane: copy a single plane of a drawable into a/ .... XCopyPlane

read/write (nonshareable) color planes /allocate .... XAllocColorPlanes

free colormap cells or planes XFreeColors: .... XFreeColors

XDrawPoint: draw a point .... XDrawPoint

XPointInRegion: determine if a point is inside a region .... XPointInRegion

/move the pointer to another point on the screen .... XWarpPointer

XGrabPointer: grab the pointer .... XGrabPointer

XGrabButton: grab a pointer button .... XGrabButton

XGetPointerMapping: get the pointer button mapping .... XGetPointerMapping

XSetPointerMapping: set the pointer button mapping .... XSetPointerMapping

/the behavior of keyboard and pointer events when these/ .... XAllowEvents

XUngrabPointer: release the pointer from an active grab .... XUngrabPointer

the parameters of an active pointer grab /change .... XChangeActivePointerGrab

XQueryPointer: get the current pointer location .... XQueryPointer

/get events from pointer motion history buffer .... XGetMotionEvents

/change the pointer preferences .... XChangePointerControl

/get the current pointer preferences .... XGetPointerControl

screen XWarpPointer: move the pointer to another point on the .... XWarpPointer

draw a line between two points XDrawLine: .... XDrawLine

XDrawPoints: draw multiple points. .... XDrawPoints

generate a region from points XPolygonRegion: .... XPolygonRegion

XFillPolygon: fill a polygon .... XFillPolygon

list/ XDrawFilled: draw a filled polygon or curve from vertex .... XDrawFilled

list (from X10) XDraw: draw a polyline or curve between vertex .... XDraw

XDrawText: draw 8-bit polytext strings .... XDrawText

XDrawText16: draw 16-bit polytext strings XDrawText16

window/ XParseGeometry: generate position and size from standard .... XParseGeometry

/change the size and position of a window .... XMoveResizeWindow

stacking/ /change the window position, size, border width, or .... XConfigureWindow

/colormap entry to the closest possible hardware color .... XStoreColor

/colorcells to the closest possible hardware colors .... XStoreColors

wait for event matched in predicate procedure XIfEvent: .... XIfEvent

/get an event matched by predicate procedure without/ .... XPeekIfEvent

to a location within the pre-existing image /in drawable .... XGetSubImage

/change the pointer preferences .... XChangePointerControl

a list of the current keyboard preferences /obtain .... XGetKeyboardControl

get the current pointer preferences XGetPointerControl: .... XGetPointerControl

/change the keyboard preferences such as key click .... XChangeKeyboardControl

XGetIconSizes: get preferred icon sizes .... XGetIconSizes

XrmQGetSearchResource: search prepared list for a given/ .... XrmQGetSearchResource

for event matched in predicate procedure XIfEvent: wait .... XIfEvent

/an event matched by predicate procedure without removing it/ .... XPeekIfEvent

for all events and errors to be processed by the server /wait .... XSync

display /disconnect a client program from an X server and .... XCloseDisplay

XOpenDisplay: connect a client program to an X server .... XOpenDisplay

read one of a window's text properties XGetTextProperty: .... XGetTextProperty

set one of a window's text properties XSetTextProperty: .... XSetTextProperty

window's standard window manager properties /set a .... XSetWMProperties

/rotate properties in the properties array .... XRotateWindowProperties

manager /set the minimum set of properties for the window .... XSetStandardProperties

XRotateWindowProperties: rotate properties in the properties/ .... XRotateWindowProperties

XDeleteProperty: delete a window property .... XDeleteProperty

get a window's name (XA_WM_NAME property) XFetchName: .... XFetchName

associated with the specified property /structure .... XGetRGBColormaps

get the standard colormap property XGetStandardColormap: .... XGetStandardColormap

server/ XRefreshKeyboardMapping:	read keycode-keysym mapping from	XRefreshKeyboardMapping
properties XGetTextProperty:	read one of a window's text	XGetTextProperty
a zoomed window XGetZoomHints:	read the size hints property of	XGetZoomHints
property XGetWMHints:	read the window manager hints	XGetWMHints
XAllocNamedColor: allocate a	read-only colorcell from color/	XAllocNamedColor
closest/ XAllocColor: allocate a	read-only colormap cell with	XAllocColor
name /set RGB values of a	read/write colorcell by color	XStoreNamedColor
/set or change the RGB values of	read/write colorcells to the/	XStoreColors
/or change the RGB values of a	read/write colormap entry to the/	XStoreColor
XAllocColorPlanes: allocate	read/write (nonshareable) color/	XAllocColorPlanes
XAllocColorCells: allocate	read/write (nonshared)/	XAllocColorCells
client XRebindKeysym:	rebind a keysym to a string for	XRebindKeysym
that a top-level window be	reconfigured /request	XReconfigureWMWindow
draw an arc fitting inside a	rectangle XDrawArc:	XDrawArc
draw an outline of a	rectangle XDrawRectangle:	XDrawRectangle
XClipBox: generate the smallest	rectangle enclosing a region	XClipBox
XGetImage: place contents of a	rectangle from drawable into an/	XGetImage
location/ XGetSubImage: copy a	rectangle in drawable to a	XGetSubImage
XRectInRegion: determine if a	rectangle resides in a region	XRectInRegion
XUnionRectWithRegion: add a	rectangle to a region	XUnionRectWithRegion
draw the outlines of multiple	rectangles XDrawRectangles:	XDrawRectangles
a graphics context to a list of	rectangles /change clip_mask in	XSetClipRectangles
XFillRectangle: fill a	rectangular area	XFillRectangle
XClearArea: clear a	rectangular area in a window	XClearArea
XFillRectangles: fill multiple	rectangular areas	XFillRectangles
region XShrinkRegion:	reduce or expand the size of a	XShrinkRegion
smallest rectangle enclosing a	region XClipBox: generate the	XClipBox
create a new empty	region XCreateRegion:	XCreateRegion
storage associated with a	region /deallocate	XDestroyRegion
change offset of a	region XOffsetRegion:	XOffsetRegion
determine if a point is inside a	region XPointInRegion:	XPointInRegion
if a rectangle resides in a	region XRectInRegion: determine	XRectInRegion
context to the specified	region /of the graphics	XSetRegion
reduce or expand the size of a	region XShrinkRegion:	XShrinkRegion
add a rectangle to a	region XUnionRectWithRegion:	XUnionRectWithRegion
XSubtractRegion: subtract one	region from another	XSubtractRegion
XPolygonRegion: generate a	region from points	XPolygonRegion
XEmptyRegion: determine if a	region is empty	XEmptyRegion
compute the intersection of two	regions XIntersectRegion:	XIntersectRegion
compute the union of two	regions XUnionRegion:	XUnionRegion
union and intersection of two	regions /difference between the	XXorRegion
XEqualRegion: determine if two	regions have the same size,/	XEqualRegion
grab XUngrabButton:	release a button from a passive	XUngrabButton
XFreeCursor:	release a cursor	XFreeCursor
grab XUngrabKey:	release a key from a passive	XUngrabKey
active grab XUngrabKeyboard:	release the keyboard from an	XUngrabKeyboard
active grab XUngrabPointer:	release the pointer from an	XUngrabPointer
XUngrabServer:	release the server from grab	XUngrabServer
/destroy a client or its	remaining resources	XKillClient
control list XRemoveHost:	remove a host from the access	XRemoveHost
client's/ XChangeSaveSet: add or	remove a subwindow from the	XChangeSaveSet
client's/ XRemoveFromSaveSet:	remove a window from the	XRemoveFromSaveSet
access control/ XRemoveHosts:	remove multiple hosts from the	XRemoveHosts
both passed/ XCheckWindowEvent:	remove the next event matching	XCheckWindowEvent
matches mask XMaskEvent:	remove the next event that	XMaskEvent
matches mask;/ XCheckMaskEvent:	remove the next event that	XCheckMaskEvent
matches the/ XWindowEvent:	remove the next event that	XWindowEvent
XPeekEvent: get an event without	removing it from the queue	XPeekEvent

/by predicate procedure without removing it from the queue .... XPeekIfEvent
border pixel value attribute and repaint the border /a window .... XSetWindowBorder
window border tile attribute and repaint the border /change a .... XSetWindowBorderPixmap
connection to a/ XDisplayName: report the display name (when .... XDisplayName
number of/ XPending: flush the request buffer and return the .... XPending
events and/ XSync: flush the request buffer and wait for all .... XSync
queued/ XFlush: flush the request buffer (display all .... XFlush
be iconified XIconifyWindow: request that a top-level window .... XIconifyWindow
be/ XReconfigureWMWindow: request that a top-level window .... XReconfigureWMWindow
be withdrawn XWithdrawWindow: request that a top-level window .... XWithdrawWindow
list to allow or deny connection requests /use access control .... XEnableAccessControl
buffer (display all queued requests) /flush the request .... XFlush
XResetScreenSaver: reset the screen saver .... XResetScreenSaver
/determine if a rectangle resides in a region .... XRectInRegion
search prepared list for a given resource XrmQGetSearchResource: .... XrmQGetSearchResource
extract an option value from the resource database XGetDefault: .... XGetDefault
XrmDestroyDatabase: destroy a resource database. .... XrmDestroyDatabase
a resource specification to a resource database /add .... XrmPutLineResource
a resource specification into a resource database /store .... XrmPutResource
line/ XrmParseCommand: load a resource database from command .... XrmParseCommand
XrmPutFileDatabase: store a resource database in a file .... XrmPutFileDatabase
strings XrmGetResource: get a resource from name and class as .... XrmGetResource
the/ /obtain the GContext (resource ID) associated with .... XGContextFromGC
XrmInitialize: initialize the resource manager .... XrmInitialize
/to a database using a quark resource name and string value .... XrmQPutStringResource
/specification with separate resource name and value .... XrmPutStringResource
XrmQPutResource: store a resource specification into a/ .... XrmQPutResource
XrmPutResource: store a resource specification into a/ .... XrmPutResource
XrmQPutStringResource: add a resource specification to a/ .... XrmQPutStringResource
XrmPutLineResource: add a resource specification to a/ .... XrmPutLineResource
XrmPutStringResource: add a resource specification with/ .... XrmPutStringResource
class as/ XrmQGetResource: get a resource value using name and .... XrmQGetResource
a client or its remaining resources XKillClient: destroy .... XKillClient
and pointer events when these resources are grabbed /keyboard .... XAllowEvents
XrmGetFileDatabase: retrieve a database from a file .... XrmGetFileDatabase
to X supported/ XListExtensions: return a list of all extensions .... XListExtensions
parent, and root XQueryTree: return a list of children, ... XQueryTree
XrmQGetSearchList: return a list of database levels .... XrmQGetSearchList
font names XListFonts: return a list of the available .... XListFonts
/copy a colormap and return a new colormap ID .... XCopyColormapAndFree
property name/ XInternAtom: return an atom for a given .... XInternAtom
XFetchBuffer: return data from a cut buffer .... XFetchBuffer
XFetchBytes: return data from cut buffer 0 .... XFetchBytes
loaded font XQueryFont: return information about a .... XQueryFont
XGetKeyboardMapping: return symbols for keycodes .... XGetKeyboardMapping
focus window XGetInputFocus: return the current keyboard .... XGetInputFocus
XCheckTypedWindowEvent: return the next event in queue/ .... XCheckTypedWindowEvent
that matches/ XCheckTypedEvent: return the next event in queue .... XCheckTypedEvent
/flush the request buffer and return the number of pending/ .... XPending
XGetSelectionOwner: return the owner of a selection .... XGetSelectionOwner
XLookupColor: get database RGB values and closest/ .... XLookupColor
XQueryColor: obtain the RGB values and flags for a/ .... XQueryColor
colorcells XQueryColors: obtain RGB values for an array of .... XQueryColors
or/ XParseColor: look up RGB values from ASCII color name .... XParseColor
/and closest hardware-supported RGB values from color name .... XLookupColor
colorcell/ XStoreNamedColor: set RGB values of a read/write .... XStoreNamedColor
XStoreColor: set or change the RGB values of a read/write/ .... XStoreColor
XStoreColors: set or change the RGB values of read/write/ .... XStoreColors

in/ XGetNormalHints: get the	size hints property of a window	XGetNormalHints
in/ XSetNormalHints: set the	size hints property of a window	XSetNormalHints
window XGetZoomHints: read the	size hints property of a zoomed	XGetZoomHints
window XSetZoomHints: set the	size hints property of a zoomed	XSetZoomHints
reduce or expand the	size of a region XShrinkRegion:	XShrinkRegion
/if two regions have the same	size, offset, and shape	XEqualRegion
get preferred icon	sizes XGetIconSizes:	XGetIconSizes
get the closest supported cursor	sizes XQueryBestCursor:	XQueryBestCursor
region XClipBox: generate the	smallest rectangle enclosing a	XClipBox
using quarks /store a resource	specification into a database	XrmQPutResource
XrmPutResource: store a resource	specification into a resource/	XrmPutResource
using a quark/ /add a resource	specification to a database	XrmQPutStringResource
database /add a resource	specification to a resource	XrmPutLineResource
resource name/ /add a resource	specification with separate	XrmPutStringResource
the RGB values and flags for a	specified colorcell /obtain	XQueryColor
screen with the depth of the	specified drawable /for a given	XCreateGC
/ID) associated with the	specified graphics context	XGContextFromGC
XTextProperty structure /set the	specified list of strings to an	XStringListToTextProperty
/the next event that matches the	specified mask and window	XWindowEvent
Xlib function XFree: free	specified memory allocated by an	XFree
/structure associated with the	specified property	XGetRGBColormaps
of the graphics context to the	specified region /set clip_mask	XSetRegion
data associated with the	specified string list /in-memory	XFreeStringList
structures that match the	specified template /information	XGetVisualInfo
/obtain a list of strings from a	specified XTextProperty/	XTextPropertyToStringList
bottom child to the top of the	stacking order /circulate the	XCirculateSubwindowsDown
top child to the bottom of the	stacking order /circulate the	XCirculateSubwindowsUp
position, size, border width, or	stacking order /the window	XConfigureWindow
lower a window in the	stacking order XLowerWindow:	XLowerWindow
raise a window to the top of the	stacking order XRaiseWindow:	XRaiseWindow
down /circulate the	stacking order of children up or	XCirculateSubwindows
XRestackWindows: change the	stacking order of siblings	XRestackWindows
XGetStandardColormap: get the	standard colormap property	XGetStandardColormap
XSetStandardColormap: change the	standard colormap property	XSetStandardColormap
/create a cursor from the	standard cursor font	XCreateFontCursor
/generate position and size from	standard window geometry string	XParseGeometry
XSetWMProperties: set a window's	standard window manager/	XSetWMProperties
/property of a window in normal	state (not zoomed or iconified)	XGetNormalHints
/property of a window in normal	state (not zoomed or iconified)	XSetNormalHints
a bit vector for the current	state of the keyboard /obtain	XQueryKeymap
XSetStipple: set the	stipple in a graphics context	XSetStipple
/obtain the fastest supported	stipple shape	XQueryBestStipple
supported cursor, tile, or	stipple size /the "best"	XQueryBestSize
XDestroyRegion: deallocate	storage associated with a region	XDestroyRegion
/unload a font and free	storage for the font structure	XFreeFont
file XrmPutFileDatabase:	store a resource database in a	XrmPutFileDatabase
into a/ XrmQPutResource:	store a resource specification	XrmQPutResource
into a resource/ XrmPutResource:	store a resource specification	XrmPutResource
XStoreBuffer:	store data in a cut buffer	XStoreBuffer
XStoreBytes:	store data in cut buffer 0	XStoreBytes
atom for a given property name	string XInternAtom: return an	XInternAtom
convert a keysym symbol to a	string XKeysymToString:	XKeysymToString
from standard window geometry	string /position and size	XParseGeometry
metrics of a 16-bit character	string /for string and font	XQueryTextExtents16
create a database from a	string XrmGetStringDatabase:	XrmGetStringDatabase
convert a quark to a	string XrmQuarkToString:	XrmQuarkToString
/geometry given user geometry	string and default geometry	XGeometry
/query the server for	string and font metrics	XQueryTextExtents

XSynchronize: enable or disable synchronization for debugging .... XSynchronize
another /change the coordinate system from one window to .... XTranslateCoordinates
an entry from an association table. XDeleteAssoc: delete .... XDeleteAssoc
allocated for an association table. /free the memory .... XDestroyAssocTable
obtain data from an association table XLookUpAssoc: .... XLookUpAssoc
an entry in an association table XMakeAssoc: create .... XMakeAssoc
create a new association table (X10) XCreateAssocTable: .... XCreateAssocTable
that match the specified template /information structures .... XGetVisualInfo
/draw 8-bit image text characters .... XDrawImageString
/draw 16-bit image text characters XDrawImageString16
/read one of a window's text properties .... XGetTextProperty
/set one of a window's text properties .... XSetTextProperty
XDrawString: draw an 8-bit text string, foreground only .... XDrawString
XDrawString16: draw two-byte text strings XDrawString16
border /change a window border tile attribute and repaint the .... XSetWindowBorderPixmap
/change the background tile attribute of a window .... XSetWindowBackgroundPixmap
XSetTile: set the fill tile in a graphics context .... XSetTile
the "best" supported cursor, tile, or stipple size /obtain .... XQueryBestSize
the fastest supported fill tile shape /obtain .... XQueryBestTile
graphics/ XSetTSOrigin: set the tile/stipple origin in a .... XSetTSOrigin
stacking order /circulate the top child to the bottom of the .... XCirculateSubwindowsUp
XMapRaised: map a window on top of its siblings .... XMapRaised
/the bottom child to the top of the stacking order .... XCirculateSubwindowsDown
/raise a window to the top of the stacking order .... XRaiseWindow
XIconifyWindow: request that a top-level window be iconified .... XIconifyWindow
/request that a top-level window be reconfigured .... XReconfigureWMWindow
XWithdrawWindow: request that a top-level window be withdrawn .... XWithdrawWindow
values from ASCII color name or translate hexadecimal value /RGB .... XParseColor
auto-repeat/ XAutoRepeatOff: turn off the keyboard .... XAutoRepeatOff
keys XAutoRepeatOn: turn on the keyboard auto-repeat .... XAutoRepeatOn
XForceScreenSaver: turn the screen saver on or off .... XForceScreenSaver
/create a cursor from two bitmaps .... XCreatePixmapCursor
XDrawLine: draw a line between two points .... XDrawLine
compute the intersection of two regions XIntersectRegion: .... XIntersectRegion
compute the union of two regions XUnionRegion: .... XUnionRegion
the union and intersection of two regions /difference between .... XXorRegion
XEqualRegion: determine if two regions have the same size,/ .... XEqualRegion
XDrawString16: draw two-byte text strings XDrawString16
entry for a given window and type /delete a context .... XDeleteContext
window /obtain the atom type and property format for a .... XGetWindowProperty
the next event in queue matching type and window /return .... XCheckTypedWindowEvent
in queue that matches event type; don't wait /the next event .... XCheckTypedEvent
/to a window and context type (not graphics context) .... XSaveContext
get the next event of any type or window XNextEvent: .... XNextEvent
/read any property of type XA_SIZE_HINTS .... XGetSizeHints
/set the value of any property of type XA_SIZE_HINTS .... XSetSizeHints
XSelectInput: select the event types to be sent to a window .... XSelectInput
default if/ XUninstallColormap: uninstall a colormap; install .... XUninstallColormap
/the difference between the union and intersection of two/ .... XXorRegion
XUnionRegion: compute the union of two regions .... XUnionRegion
XUnloadFont: unload a font. .... XUnloadFont
for the font/ XFreeFont: unload a font and free storage .... XFreeFont
XUnmapWindow: unmap a window .... XUnmapWindow
window XUnmapSubwindows: unmap all subwindows of a given .... XUnmapSubwindows
all subwindows. XDestroyWindow: unmap and destroy a window and .... XDestroyWindow
XCreateSimpleWindow: create an unmapped InputOutput window .... XCreateSimpleWindow
/calculate window geometry given user geometry string and default/ .... XGeometry
/specification to a database using a quark resource name and/ .... XrmQPutStringResource

get the property list for a	window	XListProperties: .... XListProperties
map all subwindows of	window	XMapSubwindows: .... XMapSubwindows
XMapWindow: map a	window	.... XMapWindow
the size and position of a	window	/change .... XMoveResizeWindow
XMoveWindow: move a	window	.... XMoveWindow
the next event of any type or	window	XNextEvent: get .... XNextEvent
the event types to be sent to a	window	XSelectInput: select .... XSelectInput
the XA_WM_CLASS property of a	window	XSetClassHint: set .... XSetClassHint
set the keyboard focus	window	XSetInputFocus: .... XSetInputFocus
property for a	window	/the XA_WM_TRANSIENT_FOR XSetTransientForHint
pixel value attribute of a	window	/set the background .... XSetWindowBackground
background tile attribute of a	window	/change the .... XSetWindowBackgroundPixmap
change the border width of a	window	XSetWindowBorderWidth: .... XSetWindowBorderWidth
set the colormap attribute for a	window	XSetWindowColormap: .... XSetWindowColormap
size hints property of a zoomed	window	XSetZoomHints: set the .... XSetZoomHints
disassociate a cursor from a	window	XUndefineCursor: .... XUndefineCursor
unmap all subwindows of a given	window	XUnmapSubwindows: .... XUnmapSubwindows
XUnmapWindow: unmap a	window	.... XUnmapWindow
matches the specified mask and	window	/the next event that .... XWindowEvent
/unmap and destroy a	window	and all subwindows. .... XDestroyWindow
/a data value corresponding to a	window	and context type (not/ .... XSaveContext
/insert a window between another	window	and its parent .... XReparentWindow
/next event matching both passed	window	and passed mask; don't/ .... XCheckWindowEvent
XCreateWindow: create a	window	and set attributes .... XCreateWindow
a context entry for a given	window	and type /delete .... XDeleteContext
XChangeWindowAttributes: set	window	attributes .... XChangeWindowAttributes
/request that a top-level	window	be iconified .... XIconifyWindow
/request that a top-level	window	be reconfigured .... XReconfigureWMWindow
/request that a top-level	window	be withdrawn .... XWithdrawWindow
and/ XReparentWindow: insert a	window	between another window .... XReparentWindow
XSetWindowBorder: change a	window	border pixel value/ .... XSetWindowBorder
XSetWindowBorderPixmap: change a	window	border tile attribute and/ .... XSetWindowBorderPixmap
XStoreName: assign a name to a	window	for the window manager .... XStoreName
XRemoveFromSaveSet: remove a	window	from the client's/ .... XRemoveFromSaveSet
geometry/ XGeometry: calculate	window	geometry given user .... XGeometry
position and size from standard	window	geometry string /generate .... XParseGeometry
/get the size hints property of a	window	in normal state (not/ .... XGetNormalHints
/set the size hints property of a	window	in normal state (not/ .... XSetNormalHints
XLowerWindow: lower a	window	in the stacking order .... XLowerWindow
set of properties for the	window	manager /set the minimum .... XSetStandardProperties
a name to a window for the	window	manager /assign .... XStoreName
XGetWMHints: read the	window	manager hints property .... XGetWMHints
XSetWMHints: set a	window	manager hints property .... XSetWMHints
/set a window's standard	window	manager properties .... XSetWMProperties
XMapRaised: map a	window	on top of its siblings .... XMapRaised
XPutImage: draw an image on a	window	or pixmap .... XPutImage
XConfigureWindow: change the	window	position, size, border/ .... XConfigureWindow
XDeleteProperty: delete a	window	property .... XDeleteProperty
the coordinate system from one	window	to another /change .... XTranslateCoordinates
XAddToSaveSet: add a	window	to the client's save-set .... XAddToSaveSet
stacking/ XRaiseWindow: raise a	window	to the top of the .... XRaiseWindow
XWMGeometry: obtain a	window	's geometry information .... XWMGeometry
the name to be displayed in a	window	's icon XSetIconName: set .... XSetIconName
property) XFetchName: get a	window	's name (XA_WM_NAME .... XFetchName
XResizeWindow: change a	window	's size .... XResizeWindow
XSetWMProperties: set a	window	's standard window manager/ ..... XSetWMProperties
XGetTextProperty: read one of a	window	's text properties .... XGetTextProperty
XSetTextProperty: set one of a	window	's text properties .... XSetTextProperty

This page describes the format of each reference page in this volume.

Name

XFunctionName — brief description of the function.

Synopsis

The Synopsis section presents the calling syntax for the routine, including the declarations of the arguments and return type. For example:

```
returntype XFunctionName(arg1, arg2, arg3);
      type1 arg1;
      type2 *arg2;               /* RETURN */
      type3 *arg3;               /* SEND and RETURN */
```

The return type `Status` is of type `int`; it returns either `True` or `False` to indicate whether the routine was successful.

Arguments

The Arguments section describes each of the arguments used by the function. There are three sorts of arguments: arguments that specify data to the function, arguments that return data from the function, and arguments that do both. An example of each type is shown below:

arg1   Specifies information for `XFunctionName`. The description of arguments that pass data to the function always begins with the word "Specifies," as shown in this example.

arg2   Returns a pointer to data to be filled in by `XFunctionName`. The description of arguments that return data from the function always begins with the word "Returns."

arg3   Specifies information for `XFunctionName`, and returns data from the function. The description of arguments that both pass data to the function and return data from the function uses both the words "Specifies" and "Returns."

Availability

The Availability section specifies that a given function is only available in Release 4 and later releases. If there is no Availability section, the function is available prior to Release 4.

Description

The Description section describes what the function does, what it returns, and what events or side-effects it causes. It also contains miscellaneous information such as examples of usage, special error cases, and pointers to related information in both volumes of this manual.

Structures

The Structures section contains the C definitions of the X-specific data types used by `FunctionName` as arguments or return values. It also contains definitions of important constants used by the function. Additional structures not shown can be found in Appendix F, *Structure Reference*.

Errors

The general description of the error types is contained in Appendix B, *Error Messages and Protocol Requests*. Some functions generate errors due to function-specific interpretation of arguments. Where appropriate, these function-specific causes have been listed along with the error event types they generate.

Related Commands

The Related Commands section lists the Xlib functions and macros related to XFunction-Name.

XActivateScreenSaver

Name

XActivateScreenSaver — activate screen blanking.

Synopsis

```
XActivateScreenSaver(display)
    Display *display;
```

Arguments

display   Specifies a connection to an X server; returned from XOpenDisplay.

Description

XActivateScreenSaver turns on the screen saver using the parameters set with XSet-ScreenSaver. The screen saver blanks the screen or makes random changes to the display in order to save the phosphors from burnout when the screen is left unattended for an extended period of time. The interval that the server will wait before starting screen save activity can be set with XSetScreenSaver. Exactly how the screen saver works is server-dependent.

For more information on the screen saver, see Volume One, Chapter 13, *Other Programming Techniques*.

Related Commands

XForceScreenSaver, XGetScreenSaver, XResetScreenSaver, XSetScreen-Saver.

Name

XAddHost — add a host to the access control list.

Synopsis

```
XAddHost (display, host)
    Display *display;
    XHostAddress *host;
```

Arguments

display   Specifies a connection to an X server; returned from XOpenDisplay.

host   Specifies the network address of the host machine to be added.

Description

XAddHost adds the specified host to the access control list for the server specified by *display*. The access control list is a primitive security feature that allows access to the server only by other machines listed in a file on the machine running the server. On UNIX-based systems, this file is called */etc/X?.hosts*, where *?* is the number of the server.

The application that calls XAddHost and the server whose list is being updated must be running on the same host machine.

The address data must be a valid address for the type of network in which the server operates, as specified in the family member. Internet, DECnet and ChaosNet networks are currently supported.

For TCP/IP, the address should be in network byte order. For the DECnet family, the server performs no automatic swapping on the address bytes. A Phase IV address is two bytes long. The first byte contains the least significant eight bits of the node number. The second byte contains the most significant two bits of the node number in the least significant two bits of the byte, and the area in the most significant six bits of the byte.

For more information on access control, see Volume One, Chapter 13, *Other Programming Techniques*.

Structures

```
typedef struct {
    int family;              /* for example FamilyInternet */
    int length;              /* length of address, in bytes */
    char *address;           /* pointer to where to find the bytes */
} XHostAddress;

/* The following constants for family member */
#define FamilyInternet      0
#define FamilyDECnet        1
#define FamilyChaos         2
```

Errors

BadAccess
BadValue

Related Commands

XAddHosts, XDisableAccessControl, XEnableAccessControl, XListHosts,
XRemoveHost, XRemoveHosts, XSetAccessControl.

XAddHosts

Xlib – Host Access –

Name

XAddHosts — add multiple hosts to the access control list.

Synopsis

```
XAddHosts(display, hosts, num_hosts)
    Display *display;
    XHostAddress *hosts;
    int num_hosts;
```

Arguments

display   Specifies a connection to an X server; returned from XOpenDisplay.

hosts   Specifies each host that is to be added.

num_hosts   Specifies the number of hosts that are to be added.

Description

XAddHosts adds each specified host to the access control list for the server specified by *display*. The access control list is a primitive security feature that allows access to the server only by other machines listed in a file on the machine running the server. On UNIX systems, this file is */etc/X?.hosts*, where *?* is the number of the display.

The application that calls XAddHosta and the server whose list is being updated must be running on the same host machine.

The address data must be a valid address for the type of network in which the server operates, as specified by the family member. Internet, DECnet and ChaosNet networks are currently supported.

For TCP/IP, the address should be in network byte order. For the DECnet family, the server performs no automatic swapping on the address bytes. A Phase IV address is two bytes long. The first byte contains the least significant eight bits of the node number. The second byte contains the most significant two bits of the node number in the least significant two bits of the byte, and the area in the most significant six bits of the byte.

For more information on access control, see Volume One, Chapter 13, *Other Programming Techniques*.

Structures

```
typedef struct {
    int family;             /* for example Family Internet */
    int length;             /* length of address, in bytes */
    char *address;          /* pointer to where to find the bytes */
} XHostAddress;

/* The following constants for family member */
#define FamilyInternet      0
#define FamilyDECnet        1
#define FamilyChaos         2
```

Errors
```
BadAccess
BadValue
```

Related Commands
```
XAddHost, XDisableAccessControl, XEnableAccessControl, XListHosts,
XRemoveHost, XRemoveHosts, XSetAccessControl.
```

Name

XAddPixel — add a constant value to every pixel value in an image.

Synopsis

```
XAddPixel(ximage, value)
    XImage *ximage;
    unsigned long value;
```

Arguments

ximage   Specifies a pointer to the image to be modified.

value   Specifies the constant value that is to be added. Valid pixel value ranges
              depend on the visual used to create the image. If this value added to the
              existing value causes an overflow, extra bits in the result are truncated.

Description

XAddPixel adds a constant value to every pixel value in an image. This function is useful
when you have a base pixel value derived from the allocation of color resources and need to
manipulate an image so that the pixel values are in the same range.

For more information on images, see Volume One, Chapter 6, *Drawing Graphics and Text*.

Structures

```
typedef struct _XImage {
    int width, height;              /* size of image */
    int xoffset;                    /* number of pixels offset in X direction */
    int format;                     /* XYBitmap, XYPixmap, ZPixmap */
    char *data;                     /* pointer to image data */
    int byte_order;                 /* data byte order, LSBFirst, MSBFirst */
    int bitmap_unit;                /* quantity of scan line 8, 16, 32 */
    int bitmap_bit_order;           /* LSBFirst, MSBFirst */
    int bitmap_pad;                 /* 8, 16, 32 either XY or ZPixmap */
    int depth;                      /* depth of image */
    int bytes_per_line;             /* accelerator to next line */
    int bits_per_pixel;             /* bits per pixel (ZPixmap) */
    unsigned long red_mask;         /* bits in z arrangment */
    unsigned long green_mask;
    unsigned long blue_mask;
    char *obdata;                   /* hook for object routines to hang on */
    struct funcs {                  /* image manipulation routines */
    struct _XImage *(*create_image)();
    int (*destroy_image)();
    unsigned long (*get_pixel)();
    int (*put_pixel)();
    struct _XImage *(*sub_image)();
    int (*add_pixel)();
    } f;
} XImage;
```

Related Commands

ImageByteOrder, XCreateImage, XDestroyImage, XGetImage, XGetPixel,
XGetSubImage, XPutImage, XPutPixel, XSubImage.

XAddToSaveSet

Name

XAddToSaveSet — add a window to the client's save-set.

Synopsis

```
XAddToSaveSet (display, w)
    Display *display;
    Window w;
```

Arguments

display   Specifies a connection to an X server; returned from XOpenDisplay.

w   Specifies the ID of the window you want to add to the client's save-set.

Description

XAddToSaveSet adds the specified window to the client's save-set.

The save-set is a safety net for windows that have been reparented by the window manager, usually to provide a titlebar or other decorations for each application. When the window manager dies unexpectedly, the windows in the save-set are reparented to their closest living ancestor, so that they remain alive. See Volume One, Chapter 13, *Other Programming Techniques*, for more information about save-sets.

Use XRemoveFromSaveSet to remove a window from the client's save-set.

Errors

BadMatch   *w* not created by some other client.

BadWindow

Related Commands

XChangeSaveSet, XRemoveFromSaveSet.

XAllocClassHint

Name

XAllocClassHint — allocate an `XClassHint` structure.

Synopsis

```
XClassHint *XAllocClassHint()
```

Availability

Release 4 and later.

Description

XAllocClassHint allocates and returns a pointer to an `XClassHint` structure, for use in calling `XSetWMProperties`, `XGetClassHint`, or `XSetClassHint`. Note that the pointer fields in the `XClassHint` structure are initially set to NULL. If insufficient memory is available, XAllocClassHint returns NULL. To free the memory allocated to this structure, use XFree.

The purpose of this function is to avoid compiled-in structure sizes, so that object files will be binary compatible with later releases that may have new members added to structures.

For more information, see Volume One, Chapter 10, *Interclient Communication*.

Structures

```
typedef struct {
    char *res_name;
    char *res_class;
} XClassHint;
```

Related Commands

XGetClassHint, XSetClassHint, XSetWMProperties.

XAllocColor

Name

XAllocColor — allocate a read-only colormap cell with closest hardware-supported color.

Synopsis

```
Status XAllocColor(display, cmap, colorcell_def)
    Display *display;
    Colormap cmap;
    XColor *colorcell_def; /* SENDs and RETURNs */
```

Arguments

display   Specifies a connection to an X server; returned from XOpenDisplay.

cmap   Specifies the ID of the colormap in which the colorcell is to be allocated.

colorcell_def
              Specifies desired RGB values, and also returns the pixel value and the RGB values actually used in the colormap.

Description

XAllocColor returns in the XColor structure the pixel value of a read-only (shareable) colorcell with the closest RGB values available in cmap. XAllocColor also returns the red, green, and blue values actually used.

If the display hardware has an immutable hardware colormap, the entire colormap will be read-only, and the closest cell that exists will be returned. Otherwise, the colormap is read/write, and may have some read/write cells, some read-only cells, and some unallocated cells. If a read-only cell exists that matches the requested RGB values, that cell is returned. If no matching cell exists but there are unallocated cells, a cell is allocated to match the specified RGB values. If no matching cell exists and there are no unallocated cells, XAllocColor returns a Status of zero (in read/write colormaps, it does not return the closest available read-only colorcell that has already been allocated). If it succeeds, XAllocColor returns nonzero.

Note that colorcell_def stores both the requested color when XAllocColor is called and the result when XAllocColor returns.

XAllocColor does not use or affect the flags member of the XColor structure.

For more information, see Volume One, Chapter 7, *Color*.

Structures

```
typedef struct {
    unsigned long pixel;
    unsigned short red, green, blue;
    char flags;                        /* DoRed, DoGreen, DoBlue */
    char pad;
} XColor;
```

Errors

```
BadColormap
```

Related Commands

`BlackPixel`, `WhitePixel`, `XAllocColorCells`, `XAllocColorPlanes`, `XAlloc-`
`NamedColor`, `XFreeColors`, `XLookupColor`, `XParseColor`, `XQueryColor`,
`XQueryColors`, `XStoreColor`, `XStoreColors`, `XStoreNamedColor`.

XAllocColorCells

Name

XAllocColorCells — allocate read/write (nonshared) colorcells.

Synopsis

```
Status XAllocColorCells(display, cmap, contig, plane_masks,
        nplanes, pixels, ncolors)
    Display *display;
    Colormap cmap;
    Bool contig;
    unsigned long plane_masks[nplanes]; /* RETURN */
    unsigned int nplanes;
    unsigned long pixels[ncolors];      /* RETURN pixel values */
    unsigned int ncolors;
```

Arguments

display	Specifies a connection to an X server; returned from `XOpenDisplay`.
cmap	Specifies the ID of the colormap in which the colorcell is to be allocated.
contig	Specifies a boolean value. Pass `True` if the planes must be contiguous or `False` if the planes need not be contiguous.
plane_mask	Returns an array of plane masks.
nplanes	Specifies the number of plane masks returned in the plane masks array. Must be nonnegative.
pixels	Returns an array of pixel values.
ncolors	Specifies the number of pixel values returned in the *pixels* array. Must be positive.

Description

`XAllocColorCells` allocates read/write colorcells in a read/write colormap. If `ncolors` and `nplanes` are requested, then `ncolors` pixels and `nplanes` plane masks are returned. No mask will have any bits in common with any other mask, or with any of the pixels. By ORing together each of the `pixels` with any combination of the `plane_masks`, `ncolors`$*2^{(nplanes)}$ distinct pixels can be produced. For `GrayScale` or `PseudoColor`, each mask will have exactly one bit, and for `DirectColor` each will have exactly three bits. If *contig* is `True`, then if all plane masks are ORed together, a single contiguous set of bits will be formed for `GrayScale` or `PseudoColor` and three contiguous sets of bits (one within each pixel subfield) for `DirectColor`. The RGB values of the allocated entries are undefined until set with `XStoreColor`, `XStoreColors`, or `XStoreNamedColor`.

`Status` is zero on failure, and nonzero on success.

For more information, see Volume One, Chapter 7, *Color*.

Errors

    BadColormap

    BadValue   *nplanes* is negative.
                    ncolors is not positive.

Related Commands

    BlackPixel, WhitePixel, XAllocColor, XAllocColorPlanes, XAllocNamed-
    Color, XFreeColors, XLookupColor, XParseColor, XQueryColor, XQuery-
    Colors, XStoreColor, XStoreColors, XStoreNamedColor.

XAllocColorPlanes

Name

XAllocColorPlanes — allocate read/write (nonshareable) color planes.

Synopsis

```
Status XAllocColorPlanes(display, cmap, contig, pixels, ncolors,
        nreds, ngreens, nblues, rmask, gmask, bmask)
    Display *display;
    Colormap cmap;
    Bool contig;
    unsigned long pixels[ncolors];          /* RETURN */
    int ncolors;
    int nreds, ngreens, nblues;
    unsigned long *rmask, *gmask, *bmask;  /* RETURN */
```

Arguments

display   Specifies a connection to an X server; returned from XOpenDisplay.

cmap   Specifies the ID of the colormap to be used.

contig   Specifies a boolean value. Pass True if the planes must be contiguous or
            False if the planes do not need to be contiguous.

pixels   Returns an array of pixel values.

ncolors   Specifies the number of pixel values returned in the pixels array. Must be posi-
            tive.

nreds   Specify the number of red, green, and blue planes (shades). Must be nonnega-
ngreens   tive.
nblues

rmask   Return bit masks for the red, green, and blue planes.
gmask
bmask

Description

If *ncolors*, *nreds*, *ngreens*, and *nblues* are requested, then *ncolors* pixels are
returned, and the masks have *nreds*, *ngreens*, and *nblues* bits set to 1 respectively.
Unique pixel values are generated by by ORing together subsets of masks with each item in the
pixels list (*pixels* does not by itself contain pixel values). In doing this, note that
$ncolors*(2^{(nreds+ngreens+nblues)})$ distinct pixel values are allocated.

If *contig* is True, then each mask will have a contiguous set of bits. No mask will have any
bits in common with any other mask, or with any of the *pixels*. For DirectColor, each
mask will lie within the corresponding pixel subfield.

Note, however, that there are actually only $ncolors*(2^{nreds})$ independent red entries,
$ncolors*(2^{ngreens})$ independent green entries, and $ncolors*(2^{nblues})$ independent blue
entries in the colormap. This is true even for PseudoColor. This does not cause problems,
though, because when the colormap entry for a pixel value is changed using XStoreColors

or XStoreNamedColor, the pixel is decomposed according to *rmask*, *gmask*, and *bmask* and the corresponding pixel subfield entries are updated.

Status is zero on failure, and nonzero on success.

For more information, see Volume One, Chapter 7, *Color*.

Errors
BadColormap

BadValue   *ncolors* is not positive.
                  At least one of *nreds*, *ngreens*, *nblues* is negative.

Related Commands
BlackPixel, WhitePixel, XAllocColor, XAllocColorCells, XAllocNamed-Color, XFreeColors, XLookupColor, XParseColor, XQueryColor, XQuery-Colors, XStoreColor, XStoreColors, XStoreNamedColor.

XAllocIconSize

Name

XAllocIconSize — allocate an XIconSize structure.

Synopsis

```
XIconSize *XAllocIconSize()
```

Availability

Release 4 and later.

Description

XAllocIconSize allocates and returns a pointer to an XIconSize structure, for use in calling XGetIconSizes or XSetIconSizes. Note that all fields in the XIconSize structure are initially set to zero. If insufficient memory is available, XAllocIconSize returns NULL. To free the memory allocated to this structure, use XFree.

The purpose of this function is to avoid compiled-in structure sizes, so that object files will be binary compatible with later releases that may have new members added to structures.

For more information, see Volume One, Chapter 10, *Interclient Communication*.

Structures

```
typedef struct {
    int min_width, min_height;
    int max_width, max_height;
    int width_inc, height_inc;
} XIconSize;
```

Related Commands

XGetIconSizes, XSetIconSizes.

XAllocNamedColor

Name

XAllocNamedColor — allocate a read-only colorcell from color name.

Synopsis

```
Status XAllocNamedColor(display, cmap, colorname,
        colorcell_def, rgb_db_def)
    Display *display;
    Colormap cmap;
    char *colorname;
    XColor *colorcell_def;      /* RETURN */
    XColor *rgb_db_def;         /* RETURN */
```

Arguments

display   Specifies a connection to an X server; returned from XOpenDisplay.

cmap   Specifies the ID of the colormap in which the colorcell will be allocated.

colorname   Specifies the color name string (for example, "red") you want. Upper or lower case does not matter. The string should be in ISO LATIN-1 encoding, which means that the first 128 character codes are ASCII, and the second 128 character codes are for special characters needed in western languages other than English.

colorcell_def

Returns the pixel value and RGB values actually used in the colormap. This is the closest color supported by the hardware.

rgb_db_def   Returns the exact RGB values from the database corresponding to the *colorname* supplied.

Description

XAllocNamedColor determines the RGB values for the specified *colorname* from the color database, and then allocates a read-only colorcell with the closest color available, as described under XAllocColor. Both the 'exact' database definition of the color, and the color actually allocated are returned. If the colormap is not full, the RGB values allocated are the closest supported by the hardware. If the colormap is full, and is a StaticColor, DirectColor, or StaticGray visual class, XAllocNamedColor returns the closest read-only colorcell already allocated, and does not actually create or set any new colorcell. If the colormap is full and is a PseudoColor, TrueColor, or GrayScale visual class, XAllocNamedColor fails and returns zero.

XAllocNamedColor returns a Status of zero if *colorname* was not found in the database or if the color could not be allocated. The function returns nonzero when it succeeds.

For more information, see Volume One, Chapter 7, *Color*.

Errors

    BadColormap
    BadName

Structures

    typedef struct {
        unsigned long pixel;
        unsigned short red, green, blue;
        char flags;   /* DoRed, DoGreen, DoBlue */
        char pad;
    } XColor;

Related Commands

    BlackPixel, WhitePixel, XAllocColor, XAllocColorCells, XAllocColor-
    Planes, XFreeColors, XLookupColor, XParseColor, XQueryColor, XQuery-
    Colors, XStoreColor, XStoreColors, XStoreNamedColor.

XAllocSizeHints

Name

XAllocSizeHints — allocate an XSizeHints structure.

Synopsis

```
XSizeHints *XAllocSizeHints()
```

Availability

Release 4 and later.

Description

XAllocSizeHints allocates and returns a pointer to an XSizeHints structure, for use in calling XSetWMProperties, XSetWMNormalHints, or XGetWMNormalHints. Note that all fields in the XSizeHints structure are initially set to zero. If insufficient memory is available, XAllocSizeHints returns NULL. To free the memory allocated to this structure, use XFree.

The purpose of this function is to avoid compiled-in structure sizes, so that object files will be binary compatible with later releases that may have new members added to structures.

For more information, see Volume One, Chapter 10, *Interclient Communication*.

Structures

```
typedef struct {
    long flags;       /* marks which fields in this structure are defined */
    int x, y;         /* Obsolete */
    int width, height;  /* Obsolete */
    int min_width, min_height;
    int max_width, max_height;
    int width_inc, height_inc;
    struct {
        int x;        /* numerator */
        int y;        /* denominator */
    } min_aspect, max_aspect;
    int base_width, base_height;
    int win_gravity;
} XSizeHints;
```

Related Commands

XGetWMNormalHints, XSetWMNormalHints, XSetWMProperties.

XAllocStandardColormap

Name
XAllocStandardColormap — allocate an XStandardColormap structure.

Synopsis
```
XStandardColormap *XAllocStandardColormap()
```

Availability
Release 4 and later.

Description
XAllocStandardColormap allocates and returns a pointer to an XStandardColormap structure for use in calling XGetRGBColormaps or XSetRGBColormaps. Note that all fields in the XStandardColormap structure are initially set to zero. If insufficient memory is available, XAllocStandardColormap returns NULL. To free the memory allocated to this structure, use XFree.

The purpose of this function is to avoid compiled-in structure sizes, so that object files will be binary compatible with later releases that may have new members added to structures.

For more information, see Volume One, Chapter 7, *Color*.

Structures
```
/* value for killid field */

#define   ReleaseByFreeingColormap     ( (XID) 1L)

typedef struct {
    Colormap colormap;
    unsigned long red_max;
    unsigned long red_mult;
    unsigned long green_max;
    unsigned long green_mult;
    unsigned long blue_max;
    unsigned long blue_mult;
    unsigned long base_pixel;
    VisualID visualid;
    XID killid;
} XStandardColormap;
```

Related Commands
XGetRGBColormaps, XSetRGBColormaps.

XAllocWMHints

Name

XAllocWMHints — allocate an XWMHints structure.

Synopsis

```
XWMHints *XAllocWMHints()
```

Availability

Release 4 and later.

Description

The XAllocWMHints function allocates and returns a pointer to an XWMHints structure, for use in calling XSetWMProperties, XSetWMHints, or XGetWMHints. Note that all fields in the XWMHints structure are initially set to zero. If insufficient memory is available, XAllocWMHints returns NULL. To free the memory allocated to this structure, use XFree.

The purpose of this function is to avoid compiled-in structure sizes, so that object files will be binary compatible with later releases that may have new members added to structures.

For more information, see Volume One, Chapter 10, *Interclient Communication*.

Structures

```
typedef struct {
    long flags;            /* marks which fields in this structure are defined */
    Bool input;            /* does this application rely on the window manager
                              to get keyboard input? */
    int initial_state;     /* see below */
    Pixmap icon_pixmap;    /* pixmap to be used as icon */
    Window icon_window;    /* window to be used as icon */
    int icon_x, icon_y;    /* initial position of icon */
    Pixmap icon_mask;      /* pixmap to be used as mask for icon_pixmap */
    XID window_group;      /* id of related window group */
    /* this structure may be extended in the future */
} XWMHints;
```

Related Commands

XGetWMHints, XSetWMHints, XSetWMProperties.

Name

XAllowEvents — control the behavior of keyboard and pointer events when these resources are grabbed.

Synopsis

```
XAllowEvents(display, event_mode, time)
    Display *display;
    int event_mode;
    Time time;
```

Arguments

display   Specifies a connection to an X server; returned from XOpenDisplay.

event_mode   Specifies the event mode. Pass one of these constants: AsyncPointer, SyncPointer, AsyncKeyboard, SyncKeyboard, ReplayPointer, ReplayKeyboard, AsyncBoth, or SyncBoth.

time   Specifies the time when the grab should take place. Pass either a timestamp, expressed in milliseconds, or the constant CurrentTime.

Description

XAllowEvents releases the events queued in the server since the last XAllowEvents call for the same device and by the same client. Events are queued in the server (not released to Xlib to propagate into Xlib's queues) only when the client has caused a device to "freeze" (by grabbing the device with mode GrabModeSync). The request has no effect if *time* is earlier than the last-grab time or later than the current server time.

The *event_mode* argument controls what device events are released for and just how and when they are released. The *event_mode* is interpreted as follows:

AsyncPointer   If XAllowEvents is called with AsyncPointer while the pointer is frozen by the client, pointer event processing resumes normally, even if the pointer is frozen twice by the client on behalf of two separate grabs. AsyncPointer has no effect if the pointer is not frozen by the client, but the pointer need not be grabbed by the client.

AsyncKeyboard   If XAllowEvents is called with AsyncKeyboard while the keyboard is frozen by the client, keyboard event processing resumes normally, even if the keyboard is frozen twice by the client on behalf of two separate grabs. AsyncKeyboard has no effect if the keyboard is not frozen by the client, but the keyboard need not be grabbed by the client.

SyncPointer   If XAllowEvents is called with SyncPointer while the pointer is frozen by the client, normal pointer event processing continues until the next ButtonPress or ButtonRelease event is reported to the client. At this time, the pointer again appears to freeze. However, if the reported event causes the pointer grab to be released, then the pointer does not freeze, which is the case when an automatic grab is released by a `ButtonRelease` or when `XGrab-Button` or `XGrabKey` has been called and the specified key or button is released. `SyncPointer` has no effect if the pointer is not frozen or not grabbed by the client.

`SyncKeyboard`   If `XAllowEvents` is called with `SyncKeyboard` while the keyboard is frozen by the client, normal keyboard event processing continues until the next `KeyPress` or `KeyRelease` event is reported to the client. At this time, the keyboard again appears to freeze. However, if the reported event causes the keyboard grab to be released, then the keyboard does not freeze, which is the case when an automatic grab is released by a `ButtonRelease` or when `XGrabButton` or `XGrabKey` has been called and the specified key or button is released. `SyncKeyboard` has no effect if the keyboard is not frozen or not grabbed by the client.

`ReplayPointer`   This symbol has an effect only if the pointer is grabbed by the client and thereby frozen as the result of an event. In other words, `XGrabButton` must have been called and the selected button/key combination pressed, or an automatic grab (initiated by a `Button-Press`) must be in effect, or a previous `XAllowEvents` must have been called with mode `SyncPointer`. If the `pointer_mode` of the `XGrabPointer` was `GrabModeSync`, then the grab is released and the releasing event is processed as if it had occurred after the release, ignoring any passive grabs at or above in the hierarchy (towards the root) on the grab-window of the grab just released.

`ReplayKeyboard`   This symbol has an effect only if the keyboard is grabbed by the client and if the keyboard is frozen as the result of an event. In other words, `XGrabKey` must have been called and the selected key combination pressed, or a previous `XAllowEvents` must have been called with mode `SyncKeyboard`. If the `pointer_mode` or `keyboard_mode` of the `XGrabKey` was `GrabModeSync`, then the grab is released and the releasing event is processed as if it had occurred after the release, ignoring any passive grabs at or above in the hierarchy (towards the root).

`SyncBoth`   `SyncBoth` has the effect described for both `SyncKeyboard` and `SyncPointer`. `SyncBoth` has no effect unless both pointer and keyboard are frozen by the client. If the pointer or keyboard is frozen twice by the client on behalf of two separate grabs, `SyncBoth` "thaws" for both (but a subsequent freeze for `SyncBoth` will only freeze each device once).

`AsyncBoth`   `AsyncBoth` has the effect described for both `AsyncKeyboard` and `AsyncPointer`. `AsyncBoth` has no effect unless both pointer and keyboard are frozen by the client. If the pointer and the keyboard were frozen by the client, or if both are frozen twice by two separate grabs, event processing (for both devices) continues normally. If a device is frozen twice by the client on behalf of the two separate grabs, `AsyncBoth` releases events for both.

`AsyncPointer`, `SyncPointer`, and `ReplayPointer` have no effect on the processing of keyboard events. `AsyncKeyboard`, `SyncKeyboard`, and `ReplayKeyboard` have no effect on the processing of pointer events.

It is possible for both a pointer grab and a keyboard grab (by the same or different clients) to be active simultaneously. If a device is frozen on behalf of either grab, no event processing is performed for the device. It is also possible for a single device to be frozen because of both grabs. In this case, the freeze must be released on behalf of both grabs before events will be released.

For more information on event handling, see Volume One, Chapter 9, *The Keyboard and Pointer*.

Errors

`BadValue`   Invalid mode constant.

Related Commands

`QLength`, `XCheckIfEvent`, `XCheckMaskEvent`, `XCheckTypedEvent`, `XCheck-`
`TypedWindowEvent`, `XCheckWindowEvent`, `XEventsQueued`, `XGetInputFocus`,
`XGetMotionEvents`, `XIfEvent`, `XMaskEvent`, `XNextEvent`, `XPeekEvent`, `XPeek-`
`IfEvent`, `XPending`, `XPutBackEvent`, `XSelectInput`, `XSendEvent`, `XSetInput-`
`Focus`, `XSynchronize`, `XWindowEvent`.

XAutoRepeatOff

Name

XAutoRepeatOff — turn off the keyboard auto-repeat keys.

Synopsis

```
XAutoRepeatOff(display)
    Display *display;
```

Arguments

display   Specifies a connection to an X server; returned from XOpenDisplay.

Description

XAutoRepeatOff turns off auto-repeat for the keyboard. It sets the keyboard so that holding any non-modal key down will not result in multiple events.

Related Commands

XAutoRepeatOn, XBell, XChangeKeyboardControl, XGetDefault, XGet-KeyboardControl, XGetPointerControl.

XAutoRepeatOn

Name

XAutoRepeatOn — turn on the keyboard auto-repeat keys.

Synopsis

```
XAutoRepeatOn (display)
    Display *display;
```

Arguments

display   Specifies a connection to an X server; returned from XOpenDisplay.

Description

XAutoRepeatOn sets the keyboard to auto-repeat; that is, holding any non-modal key down
will result in multiple KeyPress and KeyRelease event pairs with the same keycode
member. Keys such as Shift Lock will still not repeat.

Related Commands

XAutoRepeatOff, XBell, XChangeKeyboardControl, XGetDefault, XGet-
KeyboardControl, XGetPointerControl.

Name

XBell — ring the bell (Control G).

Synopsis

```
XBell(display, percent)
    Display *display;
    int percent;
```

Arguments

display   Specifies a connection to an X server; returned from XOpenDisplay.

percent   Specifies the volume for the bell, relative to the base volume set with XChangeKeyboardControl. Possible values are –100 (off), through 0 (base volume), to 100 (loudest) inclusive.

Description

Rings the bell on the keyboard at a volume relative to the base volume, if possible. *percent* can range from –100 to 100 inclusive (else a BadValue error). The volume at which the bell is rung when *percent* is nonnegative is:

```
volume = base - [(base * percent) / 100] + percent
```

and when *percent* is negative:

```
volume = base + [(base * percent) / 100]
```

To change the base volume of the bell, set the bell_percent variable of XChange-KeyboardControl.

Errors

BadValue   *percent* < –100 or *percent* > 100.

Related Commands

XAutoRepeatOff, XAutoRepeatOn, XChangeKeyboardControl, XGetDefault, XGetKeyboardControl, XGetPointerControl.

Name

XChangeActivePointerGrab — change the parameters of an active pointer grab.

Synopsis

```
XChangeActivePointerGrab(display, event_mask, cursor, time)
        Display *display;
        unsigned int event_mask;
        Cursor cursor;
        Time time;
```

Arguments

display   Specifies a connection to an X server; returned from XOpenDisplay.

event_mask   Specifies which pointer events are reported to the client. This mask is the bit-wise OR of one or more of these pointer event masks: ButtonPressMask, ButtonReleaseMask, EnterWindowMask, LeaveWindowMask, PointerMotionMask, PointerMotionHintMask, Button1-MotionMask, Button2MotionMask, Button3MotionMask, Button4MotionMask, Button5MotionMask, ButtonMotionMask, KeymapStateMask.

cursor   Specifies the cursor that is displayed. A value of None will keep the current cursor.

time   Specifies the time when the grab should take place. Pass either a timestamp, expressed in milliseconds, or the constant CurrentTime.

Description

XChangeActivePointerGrab changes the characteristics of an active pointer grab, if the specified time is no earlier than the last pointer grab time and no later than the current X server time. XChangeActivePointerGrab has no effect on the passive parameters of XGrab-Button, or the automatic grab that occurs between ButtonPress and ButtonRelease.

event_mask is always augmented to include ButtonPress and ButtonRelease.

For more information on pointer grabbing, see Volume One, Chapter 9, *The Keyboard and Pointer*.

Errors

BadCursor

BadValue   The *event_mask* argument is invalid.

Related Commands

XChangePointerControl, XGetPointerControl, XGetPointerMapping, XGrabPointer, XQueryPointer, XSetPointerMapping, XUngrabPointer, XWarpPointer.

XChangeGC

Name

XChangeGC — change the components of a given graphics context.

Synopsis

```
XChangeGC(display, gc, valuemask, values)
    Display *display;
    GC gc;
    unsigned long valuemask;
    XGCValues *values;
```

Arguments

display   Specifies a connection to an X server; returned from XOpenDisplay.

gc   Specifies the graphics context.

valuemask   Specifies the components in the graphics context that you want to change. This argument is the bitwise OR of one or more of the GC component masks.

values   Specifies a pointer to the XGCValues structure.

Description

XChangeGC changes any or all of the components of a GC. The valuemask specifies which components are to be changed; it is made by combining any number of the mask symbols listed in the Structures section using bitwise OR (|). The values structure contains the values to be set. These two arguments operate just like they do in XCreateGC. Changing the clip_mask overrides any previous XSetClipRectangles request for this GC. Changing the dash_offset or dash_list overrides any previous XSetDashes request on this GC.

Since consecutive changes to the same GC are buffered, there is no performance advantage to using this routine over the routines that set individual members of the GC.

Even if an error occurs, a subset of the components may have already been altered.

For more information, see Volume One, Chapter 5, *The Graphics Context*, and Chapter 6, *Drawing Graphics and Text*.

Structures

```
typedef struct {
    int function;              /* logical operation */
    unsigned long plane_mask;  /* plane mask */
    unsigned long foreground;  /* foreground pixel */
    unsigned long background;  /* background pixel */
    int line_width;            /* line width */
    int line_style;            /* LineSolid, LineOnOffDash, LineDoubleDash */
    int cap_style;             /* CapNotLast, CapButt, CapRound, CapProjecting */
    int join_style;            /* JoinMiter, JoinRound, JoinBevel */
    int fill_style;            /* FillSolid, FillTiled, FillStippled */
    int fill_rule;             /* EvenOddRule, WindingRule */
    int arc_mode;              /* ArcChord, ArcPieSlice */
    Pixmap tile;               /* tile pixmap for tiling operations */
    Pixmap stipple;            /* stipple 1 plane pixmap for stipping */
    int ts_x_origin;           /* offset for tile or stipple operations */
```

```
        int ts_y_origin;
        Font font;                  /* default text font for text operations */
        int subwindow_mode;         /* ClipByChildren, IncludeInferiors */
        Bool graphics_exposures;    /* generate events on XCopy, Area, XCopyPlane*/
        int clip_x_origin;          /* origin for clipping */
        int clip_y_origin;
        Pixmap clip_mask;           /* bitmap clipping; other calls for rects */
        int dash_offset;            /* patterned/dashed line information */
        char dashes;
} XGCValues;

#define GCFunction              (1L<<0)
#define GCPlaneMask             (1L<<1)
#define GCForeground            (1L<<2)
#define GCBackground            (1L<<3)
#define GCLineWidth             (1L<<4)
#define GCLineStyle             (1L<<5)
#define GCCapStyle              (1L<<6)
#define GCJoinStyle             (1L<<7)
#define GCFillStyle             (1L<<8)
#define GCFillRule              (1L<<9)
#define GCTile                  (1L<<10)
#define GCStipple               (1L<<11)
#define GCTileStipXOrigin       (1L<<12)
#define GCTileStipYOrigin       (1L<<13)
#define GCFont                  (1L<<14)
#define GCSubwindowMode         (1L<<15)
#define GCGraphicsExposures     (1L<<16)
#define GCClipXOrigin           (1L<<17)
#define GCClipYOrigin           (1L<<18)
#define GCClipMask              (1L<<19)
#define GCDashOffset            (1L<<20)
#define GCDashList              (1L<<21)
#define GCArcMode               (1L<<22)
```

Errors

```
BadAlloc
BadFont
BadGC
BadMatch
BadPixmap
BadValue
```

Related Commands

DefaultGC, XCopyGC, XCreateGC, XFreeGC, XGContextFromGC, XGetGCValues, XSetArcMode, XSetBackground, XSetClipMask, XSetClipOrigin, XSetClip-Rectangles, XSetDashes, XSetFillRule, XSetFillStyle, XSetForeground, XSetFunction, XSetGraphicsExposures, XSetLineAttributes, XSetPlane-Mask, XSetRegion, XSetState, XSetStipple, XSetSubwindowMode, XSet-TSOrigin.

XChangeKeyboardControl

Name

XChangeKeyboardControl — change the keyboard preferences such as key click.

Synopsis

```
XChangeKeyboardControl(display, value_mask, values)
    Display *display;
    unsigned long value_mask;
    XKeyboardControl *values;
```

Arguments

display   Specifies a connection to an X server; returned from XOpenDisplay.

value_mask   Specifies a mask composed of ORed symbols from the table shown in the Structures section below, specifying which fields to set.

values   Specifies the settings for the keyboard preferences.

Description

XChangeKeyboardControl sets user preferences such as key click, bell volume and duration, light state, and keyboard auto-repeat. Changing some or all these settings may not be possible on all servers.

The value_mask argument specifies which values are to be changed; it is made by combining any number of the mask symbols listed in the Structures section using bitwise OR (|).

The values structure contains the values to be set, as follows:

key_click_percent sets the volume for key clicks between 0 (off) and 100 (loud) inclusive. Setting to –1 restores the default.

bell_percent sets the base volume for the bell between 0 (off) and 100 (loud) inclusive. Setting to –1 restores the default.

bell_pitch sets the pitch (specified in Hz) of the bell. Setting to –1 restores the default.

bell_duration sets the duration (specified in milliseconds) of the bell. Setting to -1 restores the default.

led_mode is either LedModeOn or LedModeOff. led is a number between 1 and 32 inclusive that specifies which light's state is to be changed. If both led_mode and led are specified, then the state of the LED specified in led is changed to the state specified in led_mode. If only led_mode is specified, then all the LEDs assume the value specified by led_mode.

auto_repeat_mode is either AutoRepeatModeOn, AutoRepeatModeOff, or AutoRepeatModeDefault. key is a keycode between 7 and 255 inclusive. If both auto_repeat_mode and key are specified, then the auto-repeat mode of the key specified by key is set as specified by auto_repeat_mode. If only auto_repeat_mode is specified, then the global auto repeat mode for the entire keyboard is changed, without affecting the settings for each key. If the auto_repeat_mode is AutoRepeatModeDefault for either case, the key or the entire keyboard is returned to its default setting for the server, which is normally to have all non-modal keys repeat.

When a key is being used as a modifier key, it does not repeat regardless of the individual or global auto repeat mode.

The order in which the changes are performed is server-dependent, and some may be completed when another causes an error.

For more information on user preferences, see Volume One, Chapter 9, *The Keyboard and Pointer.*

Structures

```
/* masks for ChangeKeyboardControl */

#define KBKeyClickPercent      (1L<<0)
#define KBBellPercent          (1L<<1)
#define KBBellPitch            (1L<<2)
#define KBBellDuration         (1L<<3)
#define KBLed                  (1L<<4)
#define KBLedMode              (1L<<5)
#define KBKey                  (1L<<6)
#define KBAutoRepeatMode       (1L<<7)


/* structure for ChangeKeyboardControl */

typedef struct {
    int key_click_percent;
    int bell_percent;
    int bell_pitch;
    int bell_duration;
    int led;
    int led_mode;              /* LedModeOn or LedModeOff */
    int key;
    int auto_repeat_mode;      /* AutoRepeatModeOff, AutoRepeatModeOn,
                                  AutoRepeatModeDefault */
} XKeyboardControl;
```

Errors

BadMatch   *values*.key specified but *values*.auto.repeat.mode not specified.
                values.led specified but *values*.led_mode not specified.

BadValue   *values*.key_click_percent < *-1*.
                values.bell_percent < *-1*.
                values.bell_pitch < *-1*.
                values.bell_duration < *-1*.

Related Commands

XAutoRepeatOff, XAutoRepeatOn, XBell, XGetDefault, XGetKeyboard-
Control, XGetPointerControl.

Name

XChangeKeyboardMapping — change the keyboard mapping.

Synopsis

```
XChangeKeyboardMapping(display, first_code, keysyms_per_code,
        keysyms, num_codes)
    Display *display;
    int first_keycode;
    int keysyms_per_keycode;
    KeySym *keysyms;
    int num_keycodes;
```

Arguments

display   Specifies a connection to an X server; returned from XOpenDisplay.

first_keycode
          Specifies the first keycode that is to be changed.

keysyms_per_keycode
          Specifies the number of keysyms that the caller is supplying for each keycode.

keysyms   Specifies a pointer to the list of keysyms.

num_keycodes
          Specifies the number of keycodes that are to be changed.

Description

Starting with *first_keycode*, XChangeKeyboardMapping defines the keysyms for the specified number of keycodes. The symbols for keycodes outside this range remain unchanged. The number of elements in the *keysyms* list must be a multiple of *keysyms_per_keycode* (else a BadLength error). The specified *first_keycode* must be greater than or equal to min_keycode supplied at connection setup and stored in the display structure (else a Bad-Value error). In addition, the following expression must be less than or equal to max_keycode field of the Display structure (else a BadValue error):

```
max_keycode >= first_keycode + (num_keycodes / keysyms_per_keycode) - 1
```

The keysym number *N* (counting from 0) for keycode *K* has an index in the *keysyms* array (counting from 0) of the following (in keysyms):

```
index = (K - first_keycode) * keysyms_per_keycode + N
```

The specified *keysyms_per_keycode* can be chosen arbitrarily by the client to be large enough to hold all desired symbols. A special keysym value of NoSymbol should be used to fill in unused elements for individual keycodes. It is legal for NoSymbol to appear in nontrailing positions of the effective list for a keycode.

XChangeKeyboardMapping generates a MappingNotify event, sent to this and all other clients, since the keycode to keysym mapping is global to all clients.

Errors

BadAlloc

BadValue   *first.keycode* less than *display*->min_keycode.
                display->max_keycode exceeded (see above).

Related Commands

XDeleteModifiermapEntry, XFreeModifiermap, XGetKeyboardMapping,
XGetModifierMapping, XInsertModifiermapEntry, XKeycodeToKeysym,
XKeysymToKeycode, XKeysymToString, XLookupKeysym, XLookupString,
XNewModifierMap, XQueryKeymap, XRebindKeySym, XRefreshKeyboard-
Mapping, XSetModifierMapping, XStringToKeysym.

XChangePointerControl

Name

XChangePointerControl — change the pointer preferences.

Synopsis

```
XChangePointerControl(display, do_accel, do_threshold,
        accel_numerator, accel_denominator, threshold)
    Display *display;
    Bool do_accel, do_threshold;
    int accel_numerator, accel_denominator;
    int threshold;
```

Arguments

display   Specifies a connection to an X server; returned from XOpenDisplay.

do_accel   Specifies a boolean value that controls whether the values for the accel_numerator or accel_denominator are set. You can pass one of these constants: True or False.

do_threshold

Specifies a boolean value that controls whether the value for the threshold is set. You can pass one of these constants: True or False.

accel_numerator

Specifies the numerator for the acceleration multiplier.

accel_denominator

Specifies the denominator for the acceleration multiplier.

threshold   Specifies the acceleration threshold.

Description

XChangePointerControl defines how the pointing device functions. The acceleration is a fraction (*accel_numerator/accel_denominator*) which specifies how many times faster than normal the sprite on the screen moves for a given pointer movement. Acceleration takes effect only when a particular pointer motion is greater than *threshold* pixels at once, and only applies to the motion beyond *threshold* pixels. The values for *do_accel* and *do_threshold* must be nonzero for the pointer values to be set; otherwise, the parameters will be unchanged. Setting any of the last three arguments to –1 restores the default for that argument.

The fraction may be rounded arbitrarily by the server.

Errors

BadValue   *accel_denominator* is 0.

                   Negative value for *do_accel* or *do_threshold*.

Related Commands

    XChangeActivePointerGrab, XGetPointerControl, XGetPointerMapping,
    XGrabPointer, XQueryPointer, XSetPointerMapping, XUngrabPointer,
    XWarpPointer.

XChangeProperty

Name

XChangeProperty — change a property associated with a window.

Synopsis

```
XChangeProperty(display, w, property, type, format, mode,
        data, nelements)
    Display *display;
    Window w;
    Atom property, type;
    int format;
    int mode;
    unsigned char *data;
    int nelements;
```

Arguments

display	Specifies a connection to an X server; returned from XOpenDisplay.
w	Specifies the ID of the window whose property you want to change.
property	Specifies the property atom.
type	Specifies the type of the property. X does not interpret the type, but simply passes it back to an application that later calls XGetProperty.
format	Specifies whether the data should be viewed as a list of 8-bit, 16-bit, or 32-bit quantities. This information allows the X server to correctly perform byte-swap operations as necessary. If the format is 16-bit or 32-bit, you must explicitly cast your data pointer to a (*char **) in the call to XChange-Property. Possible values are 8, 16, and 32.
mode	Specifies the mode of the operation. Possible values are PropMode-Replace, PropModePrepend, PropModeAppend, or no value.
data	Specifies the property data.
nelements	Specifies the number of elements in the property.

Description

XChangeProperty changes a property and generates PropertyNotify events if they have been selected.

XChangeProperty does the following according to the *mode* argument:

- PropModeReplace

    Discards the previous property value and stores the new data.

- PropModePrepend

    Inserts the data before the beginning of the existing data. If the property is undefined, it is treated as defined with the correct type and format with zero-length data. *type* and *format* arguments must match the existing property value; otherwise a BadMatch error occurs.

- PropModeAppend

    Appends the data onto the end of the existing data. If the property is undefined, it is treated as defined with the correct type and format with zero-length data. *type* and *format* arguments must match the existing property value; otherwise a BadMatch error occurs.

The property may remain defined even after the client which defined it exits. The property becomes undefined only if the application calls XDeleteProperty, destroys the specified window, or closes the last connection to the X server.

The maximum size of a property is server-dependent and can vary dynamically if the server has insufficient memory.

For more information, see Volume One, Chapter 10, *Interclient Communication*.

Errors
    BadAlloc
    BadAtom
    BadMatch
    BadValue
    BadWindow

Related Commands
    XDeleteProperty, XGetAtomName, XGetFontProperty, XGetWindowProperty,
    XInternAtom, XListProperties, XRotateWindowProperties, XSetStandard-
    Properties.

Name

XChangeSaveSet — add or remove a subwindow from the client's save-set.

Synopsis

```
XChangeSaveSet(display, w, change_mode)
    Display *display;
    Window w;
    int change_mode;
```

Arguments

display   Specifies a connection to an X server; returned from XOpenDisplay.

w   Specifies the ID of the window whose children you want to add or remove from the client's save-set; it must have been created by some other client.

change_mode Specifies the mode. Pass one of these constants: SetModeInsert (adds the window to this client's save-set) or SetModeDelete (deletes the window from this client's save-set).

Description

XChangeSaveSet adds or deletes windows from a client's save-set. This client is usually the window manager.

The save-set of the window manager is a list of other client's top-level windows which have been reparented. If the window manager dies unexpectedly, these top-level application windows are children of a window manager window and therefore would normally be destroyed. The save-set prevents this by automatically reparenting the windows listed in the save-set to their closest existing ancestor, and then remapping them.

Windows are removed automatically from the save-set by the server when they are destroyed.

For more information on save-sets, see Volume One, Chapter 13, *Other Programming Techniques*.

Errors

BadMatch   *w* not created by some other client.

BadValue

BadWindow

Related Commands

XAddToSaveSet, XRemoveFromSaveSet.

XChangeWindowAttributes

Name

XChangeWindowAttributes — set window attributes.

Synopsis

```
XChangeWindowAttributes(display, w, valuemask, attributes)
    Display *display;
    Window w;
    unsigned long valuemask;
    XSetWindowAttributes *attributes;
```

Arguments

display   Specifies a connection to an X server; returned from XOpenDisplay.

w   Specifies the window ID.

valuemask   Specifies which window attributes are defined in the attributes argument. The mask is made by combining the appropriate mask symbols listed in the Structures section using bitwise OR (|). If valuemask is zero, the rest is ignored, and attributes is not referenced. The values and restrictions are the same as for XCreateWindow.

attributes   Window attributes to be changed. The valuemask indicates which members in this structure are referenced.

Description

XChangeWindowAttributes changes any or all of the window attributes that can be changed. For descriptions of the window attributes, see Volume One, Chapter 4, *Window Attributes*.

Changing the background does not cause the window contents to be changed immediately–not until the next Expose event or XClearWindow call. Drawing into the pixmap that was set as the background pixmap attribute has an undefined effect on the window background. The server may or may not make a copy of the pixmap. Setting the border causes the border to be repainted immediately. Changing the background of a root window to None or Parent-Relative restores the default background pixmap. Changing the border of a root window to CopyFromParent restores the default border pixmap.

Changing the win_gravity does not affect the current position of the window. Changing the backing_store of an obscured window to WhenMapped or Always may have no immediate effect. Also changing the backing_planes, backing_pixel, or save_under of a mapped window may have no immediate effect.

Multiple clients can select input on the same window; the event_mask attributes passed are disjoint. When an event is generated it will be reported to all interested clients. Therefore, the setting of the event_mask attribute by one client will not affect the event_mask of others on the same window. However, at most, one client at a time can select each of SubstructureRedirectMask, ResizeRedirectMask, and ButtonPressMask on any one window. If a client attempts to select on SubstructureRedirectMask, Resize-

RedirectMask, or ButtonPressMask and some other client has already selected it on the same window, the X server generates a BadAccess error.

There is only one do_not_propagate_mask for a window, not one per client.

Changing the colormap attribute of a window generates a ColormapNotify event. Changing the colormap attribute of a visible window may have no immediate effect on the screen (because the colormap may not be installed until the window manager calls XInstall-Colormap).

Changing the cursor of a root window to None restores the default cursor.

For more information, see Volume One, Chapter 2, *X Concepts*, and Chapter 4, *Window Attributes*.

Structures

```
/*
 * Data structure for setting window attributes.
 */
typedef struct {
    Pixmap background_pixmap;        /* pixmap, None, or ParentRelative */
    unsigned long background_pixel;  /* background pixel */
    Pixmap border_pixmap;            /* pixmap, None, or CopyFromParent */
    unsigned long border_pixel;      /* border pixel value */
    int bit_gravity;                 /* one of bit gravity values */
    int win_gravity;                 /* one of the window gravity values */
    int backing_store;               /* NotUseful, WhenMapped, Always */
    unsigned long backing_planes;    /* planes to be preseved if possible */
    unsigned long backing_pixel;     /* value to use in restoring planes */
    Bool save_under;                 /* should bits under be saved (popups) */
    long event_mask;                 /* set of events that should be saved */
    long do_not_propagate_mask;      /* set of events that should not propagate */
    Bool override_redirect;          /* override redirected config request */
    Colormap colormap;               /* colormap to be associated with window */
    Cursor cursor;                   /* cursor to be displayed (or None) */
} XSetWindowAttributes;

/* Definitions for valuemask argument of CreateWindow and ChangeWindowAttributes */

#define CWBackPixmap        (1L<<0)
#define CWBackPixel         (1L<<1)
#define CWBorderPixmap      (1L<<2)
#define CWBorderPixel       (1L<<3)
#define CWBitGravity        (1L<<4)
#define CWWinGravity        (1L<<5)
#define CWBackingStore      (1L<<6)
#define CWBackingPlanes     (1L<<7)
#define CWBackingPixel      (1L<<8)
#define CWOverrideRedirect  (1L<<9)
#define CWSaveUnder         (1L<<10)
#define CWEventMask         (1L<<11)
#define CWDontPropagate     (1L<<12)
#define CWColormap          (1L<<13)
#define CWCursor            (1L<<14)
```

Errors
    BadAccess
    BadColormap
    BadCursor
    BadMatch
    BadPixmap
    BadValue
    BadWindow

Related Commands
    XGetGeometry, XGetWindowAttributes, XSetWindowBackground, XSet-
    WindowBackgroundPixmap, XSetWindowBorder, XSetWindowBorderPixmap.

XCheckIfEvent

Name

XCheckIfEvent — check the event queue for a matching event.

Synopsis

```
Bool XCheckIfEvent (display, event, predicate, arg)
    Display *display;
    XEvent *event;                 /* RETURN */
    Bool (*predicate) () ;
    char *arg;
```

Arguments

display   Specifies a connection to an X server; returned from XOpenDisplay.

event   Returns the matched event.

predicate   Specifies the procedure that is called to determine if the next event matches your criteria.

arg   Specifies the user-specified argument that will be passed to the predicate procedure.

Description

XCheckIfEvent returns the next event in the queue that is matched by the specified predicate procedure. If found, that event is removed from the queue, and True is returned. If no match is found, XCheckIfEvent returns False and flushes the request buffer. No other events are removed from the queue. Later events in the queue are not searched.

The predicate procedure is called with the arguments display, event, and arg.

For more information, see Volume One, Chapter 8, *Events*.

Related Commands

QLength, XAllowEvents, XCheckMaskEvent, XCheckTypedEvent, XCheck-
TypedWindowEvent, XCheckWindowEvent, XEventsQueued, XGetInputFocus,
XGetMotionEvents, XIfEvent, XMaskEvent, XNextEvent, XPeekEvent, XPeek-
IfEvent, XPending, XPutBackEvent, XSelectInput, XSendEvent, XSetInput-
Focus, XSynchronize, XWindowEvent.

Name

XCheckMaskEvent — remove the next event that matches mask; don't wait.

Synopsis

```
Bool XCheckMaskEvent(display, event_mask, event)
    Display *display;
    long event_mask;
    XEvent *event;                  /* RETURN */
```

Arguments

display   Specifies a connection to an X server; returned from XOpenDisplay.

event_mask   Specifies the event types to be returned. See list under XSelectInput.

event   Returns a copy of the matched event's XEvent structure.

Description

XCheckMaskEvent removes the next event in the queue that matches the passed mask. The event is copied into an XEvent supplied by the caller and XCheckMaskEvent returns True. Other events earlier in the queue are not discarded. If no such event has been queued, XCheckMaskEvent flushes the request buffer and immediately returns False, without waiting.

For more information, see Volume One, Chapter 8, *Events*.

Related Commands

QLength, XAllowEvents, XCheckIfEvent, XCheckTypedEvent, XCheckTyped-WindowEvent, XCheckWindowEvent, XEventsQueued, XGetInputFocus, XGet-MotionEvents, XIfEvent, XMaskEvent, XNextEvent, XPeekEvent, XPeek-IfEvent, XPending, XPutBackEvent, XSelectInput, XSendEvent, XSetInput-Focus, XSynchronize, XWindowEvent.

XCheckTypedEvent

Name

XCheckTypedEvent — return the next event in queue that matches event type; don't wait.

Synopsis

```
Bool XCheckTypedEvent(display, event_type, report)
    Display *display;
    int event_type;
    XEvent *report;                 /* RETURN */
```

Arguments

display   Specifies a connection to an X server; returned from XOpenDisplay.

event_type   Specifies the event type to be compared.

report   Returns a copy of the matched event structure.

Description

XCheckTypedEvent searches first the event queue, then the events available on the server connection, for the specified event_type. If there is a match, it returns the associated event structure. Events searched but not matched are not discarded. XCheckTypedEvent returns True if the event is found. If the event is not found, XCheckTypedEvent flushes the request buffer and returns False.

This command is similar to XCheckMaskEvent, but it searches through the queue instead of inspecting only the last item on the queue. It also matches only a single event type instead of multiple event types as specified by a mask.

For more information, see Volume One, Chapter 8, *Events*.

Related Commands

QLength, XAllowEvents, XCheckIfEvent, XCheckMaskEvent, XCheckTyped-WindowEvent, XCheckWindowEvent, XEventsQueued, XGetInputFocus, XGet-MotionEvents, XIfEvent, XMaskEvent, XNextEvent, XPeekEvent, XPeek-IfEvent, XPending, XPutBackEvent, XSelectInput, XSendEvent, XSetInput-Focus, XSynchronize, XWindowEvent.

Name

XCheckTypedWindowEvent — return the next event in queue matching type and window.

Synopsis

```
Bool XCheckTypedWindowEvent(display, w, event_type, report)
    Display *display;
    Window w;
    int event_type;
    XEvent *report;               /* RETURN */
```

Arguments

display   Specifies a connection to an X server; returned from XOpenDisplay.

w   Specifies the window ID.

event_type   Specifies the event type to be compared.

report   Returns the matched event's associated structure into this client-supplied structure.

Description

XCheckTypedWindowEvent searches first the event queue, then any events available on the server connection, for an event that matches the specified window and the specified event type. Events searched but not matched are not discarded.

XCheckTypedWindowEvent returns True if the event is found; it flushes the request buffer and returns False if the event is not found.

For more information, see Volume One, Chapter 8, *Events*.

Related Commands

QLength, XAllowEvents, XCheckIfEvent, XCheckMaskEvent, XCheckTyped-
Event, XCheckWindowEvent, XEventsQueued, XGetInputFocus, XGetMotion-
Events, XIfEvent, XMaskEvent, XNextEvent, XPeekEvent, XPeekIfEvent,
XPending, XPutBackEvent, XSelectInput, XSendEvent, XSetInputFocus,
XSynchronize, XWindowEvent.

XCheckWindowEvent

Name

XCheckWindowEvent — remove the next event matching both passed window and passed mask; don't wait.

Synopsis

```
Bool XCheckWindowEvent(display, w, event_mask, event)
    Display *display;
    Window w;
    long event_mask;
    XEvent *event;              /* RETURN */
```

Arguments

display   Specifies a connection to an X server; returned from XOpenDisplay.

w   Specifies the window ID. The event must match both the passed window and the passed event mask.

event_mask   Specifies the event mask. See XSelectInput for a list of mask elements.

event   Returns the XEvent structure.

Description

XCheckWindowEvent removes the next event in the queue that matches both the passed window and the passed mask. If such an event exists, it is copied into an XEvent supplied by the caller. Other events earlier in the queue are not discarded.

If a matching event is found, XCheckWindowEvent returns True. If no such event has been queued, it flushes the request buffer and returns False, without waiting.

For more information, see Volume One, Chapter 8, *Events*.

Related Commands

QLength, XAllowEvents, XCheckIfEvent, XCheckMaskEvent, XCheckTyped-Event, XCheckTypedWindowEvent, XEventsQueued, XGetInputFocus, XGet-MotionEvents, XIfEvent, XMaskEvent, XNextEvent, XPeekEvent, XPeek-IfEvent, XPending, XPutBackEvent, XSelectInput, XSendEvent, XSetInput-Focus, XSynchronize, XWindowEvent.

XCirculateSubwindows

Name

XCirculateSubwindows — circulate the stacking order of children up or down.

Synopsis

```
XCirculateSubwindows(display, w, direction)
    Display *display;
    Window w;
    int direction;
```

Arguments

display   Specifies a connection to an X server; returned from XOpenDisplay.

w   Specifies the window ID of the parent of the subwindows to be circulated.

direction   Specifies the direction (up or down) that you want to circulate the children. Pass either RaiseLowest or LowerHighest.

Description

XCirculateSubwindows circulates the children of the specified window in the specified direction, either RaiseLowest or LowerHighest. If some other client has selected SubstructureRedirectMask on the specified window, then a CirculateRequest event is generated, and no further processing is performed. If you specify RaiseLowest, this function raises the lowest mapped child (if any) that is occluded by another child to the top of the stack. If you specify LowerHighest, this function lowers the highest mapped child (if any) that occludes another child to the bottom of the stack. Exposure processing is performed on formerly obscured windows.

For more information, see Volume One, Chapter 14, *Window Management*.

Errors

BadValue
BadWindow

Related Commands

XCirculateSubwindowsDown, XCirculateSubwindowsUp, XConfigureWindow, XLowerWindow, XMoveResizeWindow, XMoveWindow, XQueryTree, XRaise-Window, XReparentWindow, XResizeWindow, XRestackWindows.

XCirculateSubwindowsDown

Name

XCirculateSubwindowsDown — circulate the bottom child to the top of the stacking order.

Synopsis

```
XCirculateSubwindowsDown(display, w)
    Display *display;
    Window w;
```

Arguments

display   Specifies a connection to an X server; returned from XOpenDisplay.

w   Specifies the window ID of the parent of the windows to be circulated.

Description

XCirculateSubwindowsDown lowers the highest mapped child of the specified window that partially or completely obscures another child. The lowered child goes to the bottom of the stack. Completely unobscured children are not affected.

This function generates exposure events on any window formerly obscured. Repeated executions lead to round-robin lowering. This is equivalent to XCirculateSubwindows (*display*, *w*, LowerHighest).

If some other client has selected SubstructureRedirectMask on the window, then a CirculateRequest event is generated, and no further processing is performed. This allows the window manager to intercept this request when *w* is the root window. Usually, only the window manager will call this on the root window.

For more information, see Volume One, Chapter 14, *Window Management*.

Errors

BadWindow

Related Commands

XCirculateSubwindows, XCirculateSubwindowsUp, XConfigureWindow, XLowerWindow, XMoveResizeWindow, XMoveWindow, XQueryTree, XRaise-Window, XReparentWindow, XResizeWindow, XRestackWindows.

Name

XCirculateSubwindowsUp — circulate the top child to the bottom of the stacking order.

Synopsis

```
XCirculateSubwindowsUp(display, w)
    Display *display;
    Window w;
```

Arguments

display   Specifies a connection to an X server; returned from XOpenDisplay.

w   Specifies the window ID of the parent of the windows to be circulated.

Description

XCirculateSubwindowsUp raises the lowest mapped child of the specified window that is partially or completely obscured by another child. The raised child goes to the top of the stack. Completely unobscured children are not affected. This generates exposure events on the raised child (and its descendents, if any). Repeated executions lead to round robin-raising. This is equivalent to XCirculateSubwindows (*display*, *w*, RaiseLowest).

If some other client has selected SubstructureRedirectMask on the window, then a CirculateRequest event is generated, and no further processing is performed. This allows the window manager to intercept this request when *w* is the root window. Usually, only the window manager will call this on the root window.

For more information, see Volume One, Chapter 14, *Window Management*.

Errors

BadWindow

Related Commands

XCirculateSubwindows, XCirculateSubwindowsDown, XConfigureWindow, XLowerWindow, XMoveResizeWindow, XMoveWindow, XQueryTree, XRaise-Window, XReparentWindow, XResizeWindow, XRestackWindows.

Name

XClearArea — clear a rectangular area in a window.

Synopsis

```
XClearArea(display, w, x, y, width, height, exposures)
    Display *display;
    Window w;
    int x, y;
    unsigned int width, height;
    Bool exposures;
```

Arguments

display   Specifies a connection to an X server; returned from XOpenDisplay.

w   Specifies the ID of an InputOutput window.

x   Specify the x and y coordinates of the upper-left corner of the rectangle to be
y   cleared, relative to the origin of the window.

width   Specify the dimensions in pixels of the rectangle to be cleared.
height

exposures Specifies whether exposure events are generated. Must be either True or
           False.

Description

XClearArea clears a rectangular area in a window.

If width is zero, the window is cleared from x to the right edge of the window. If height is
zero, the window is cleared from y to the bottom of the window. See figure above..

If the window has a defined background tile or it is ParentRelative, the rectangle is tiled
with a plane_mask of all 1's, a function of GXcopy, and a subwindow_mode of
ClipByChildren. If the window has background None, the contents of the window are not
changed. In either case, if exposures is True, then one or more exposure events are generated for regions of the rectangle that are either visible or are being retained in a backing store.

For more information, see Volume One, Chapter 6, *Drawing Graphics and Text.*

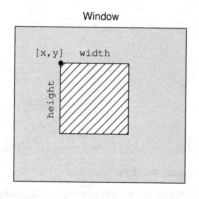

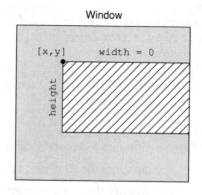

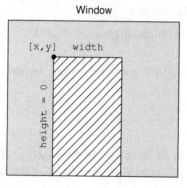

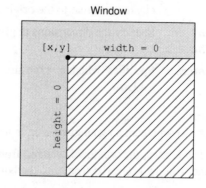

Errors

BadMatch   Window is an `InputOnly` class window.

BadValue

BadWindow

Related Commands

XClearWindow, XCopyArea, XCopyPlane, XDraw, XDrawArc, XDrawArcs, XDraw-
Filled, XDrawLine, XDrawLines, XDrawPoint, XDrawPoints, XDrawRectangle,
XDrawRectangles, XDrawSegments, XFillArc, XFillArcs, XFillPolygon,
XFillRectangle, XFillRectangles.

XClearWindow

Name

XClearWindow — clear an entire window.

Synopsis

```
XClearWindow(display, w)
    Display *display;
    Window w;
```

Arguments

display	Specifies a connection to an X server; returned from XOpenDisplay.
w	Specifies the ID of the window to be cleared.

Description

XClearWindow clears a window, but does not cause exposure events. This function is equivalent to XClearArea(display, w, 0, 0, 0, 0, False).

If the window has a defined background tile or it is ParentRelative, the rectangle is tiled with a plane_mask of all 1's and function of GXcopy. If the window has background None, the contents of the window are not changed.

For more information, see Volume One, Chapter 6, *Drawing Graphics and Text*.

Errors

BadMatch	If w is an InputOnly class window.
BadValue	
BadWindow	

Related Commands

XClearArea, XCopyArea, XCopyPlane, XDraw, XDrawArc, XDrawArcs, XDrawFilled, XDrawLine, XDrawLines, XDrawPoint, XDrawPoints, XDrawRectangle, XDrawRectangles, XDrawSegments, XFillArc, XFillArcs, XFillPolygon, XFillRectangle, XFillRectangles.

Name

XClipBox — generate the smallest rectangle enclosing a region.

Synopsis

```
XClipBox(r, rect)
    Region r;
    XRectangle *rect;              /* RETURN */
```

Arguments

r   Specifies the region.

rect   Returns the smallest rectangle enclosing region r.

Description

XClipBox returns the smallest rectangle that encloses the given region.

For more information, see Volume One, Chapter 6, *Drawing Graphics and Text*.

Structures

Region is a pointer to an opaque structure type.

Related Commands

XCreateRegion, XDestroyRegion, XEmptyRegion, XEqualRegion,
XIntersectRegion, XOffsetRegion, XPointInRegion, XPolygonRegion,
XRectInRegion, XSetRegion, XShrinkRegion, XSubtractRegion, XUnion-
RectWithRegion, XUnionRegion, XXorRegion.

XCloseDisplay

Name

XCloseDisplay — disconnect a client program from an X server and display.

Synopsis

```
XCloseDisplay(display)
    Display *display;
```

Arguments

display   Specifies a connection to an X server; returned from XOpenDisplay.

Description

XCloseDisplay closes the connection between the current client and the X server specified by the Display argument.

The XCloseDisplay routine destroys all windows, resource IDs (Window, Font, Pixmap, Colormap, Cursor, and GContext), or other resources (GCs) that the client application has created on this display, unless the close down mode of the client's resources has been changed by XSetCloseDownMode. Therefore, these windows, resource IDs, and other resources should not be referenced again. In addition, this routine discards any requests that have been buffered but not yet sent to the server.

Although these operations automatically (implicitly) occur when a process exits under UNIX, you should call XCloseDisplay anyway.

For more information, see Volume One, Chapter 3, *Basic Window Program*.

Related Commands

DefaultScreen, XFree, XNoOp, XOpenDisplay.

XConfigureWindow

Name

XConfigureWindow — change the window position, size, border width, or stacking order.

Synopsis

```
XConfigureWindow(display, w, value_mask, values)
    Display *display;
    Window w;
    unsigned int value_mask;
    XWindowChanges *values;
```

Arguments

display   Specifies a connection to an X server; returned from XOpenDisplay.

w   Specifies the ID of the window to be reconfigured.

value_mask   Specifies which values are to be set using information in the values struc-
                 ture. *value_mask* is the bitwise OR of any number of symbols listed in the
                 Structures section below.

values   Specifies a pointer to the XWindowChanges structure containing new confi-
                 guration information. See the Structures section below.

Description

XConfigureWindow changes the window position, size, border width, and/or the stacking
order. If selected, a ConfigureNotify event is generated to announce any changes.

If the window to be reconfigured is a top-level window, there will be interaction with the window manager if the override_redirect attribute of the window is False. In this case,
the X server sends a ConfigureRequest event to the window manager and does not reconfigure the window. The window manager receives this event and then makes the decision
whether to allow the application to reconfigure its window. The client should wait for the
ConfigureNotify event to find out the size and position of the window.

In Release 4, XReconfigureWMWindow should be used instead of XConfigureWindow
for top-level windows. This routine handles restacking of top-level windows properly.

If a window's size actually changes, the window's subwindows may move according to their
window gravity. If they do, GravityNotify events will be generated for them. Depending
on the window's bit gravity, the contents of the window also may be moved. See Volume One,
Chapter 4, *Window Attributes* for further information.

Exposure processing is performed on formerly obscured windows, including the window itself
and its inferiors, if regions of them were obscured but afterward are not. As a result of increas-
ing the width or height, exposure processing is also performed on any new regions of the window and any regions where window contents are lost.

The members of XWindowChanges that you specify in *values* are:

x y	Specify the x and y coordinates of the upper-left outer corner of the window relative to the parent's origin.
width *height*	Specify the inside size of the window in pixels, not including the border. These arguments must be positive.

border_width
Specifies the width of the border in pixels.

sibling	Specifies the sibling window for stacking operations. If not specified, no change in the stacking order will be made. If specified, stack_mode must also be specified.
stack_mode	The stack mode can be any of these constants: Above, Below, TopIf, BottomIf, or Opposite.

The computation for the BottomIf, TopIf, and Opposite stacking modes is performed with respect to window *w*'s final size and position (as controlled by the other arguments to XConfigureWindow, not its initial position.) It is an error if *sibling* is specified without *stack_mode*. If *sibling* and *stack_mode* are specified, the window is restacked as follows:

Stacking Flag	Position
Above	*w* is placed just above *sibling*
Below	*w* is placed just below *sibling*
TopIf	if *sibling* obscures *w*, then *w* is placed at the top of the stack
BottomIf	if *w* obscures *sibling*, then *w* is placed at the bottom of the stack
Opposite	if *sibling* occludes *w*, then *w* is placed at the top of the stack. If *w* occludes *sibling*, then *w* is placed at the bottom of the stack. If *w* and *sibling* do not overlap, no change is made.

If a stack_mode is specified but no sibling is specified, the window is restacked as follows:

Stacking Flag	Position
Above	*w* is placed at the top of the stack
Below	*w* is placed at the bottom of the stack
TopIf	if any sibling obscures *w*, then *w* is placed at the top of the stack
BottomIf	if *w* obscures any sibling, then window is placed at the bottom of the stack
Opposite	if any sibling occludes *w*, then *w* is placed at the top of the stack, else if *w* occludes any sibling, then *w* is placed at the bottom of the stack

Under Release 4, use XReconfigureWMWindow to configure a top-level window.

Structures

```
typedef struct {
    int x, y;
    int width, height;
    int border_width;
    Window sibling;
    int stack_mode;
} XWindowChanges;

/* ConfigureWindow structure */
/* ChangeWindow value bits definitions for valuemask */
#define CWX             (1<<0)
#define CWY             (1<<1)
#define CWWidth         (1<<2)
#define CWHeight        (1<<3)
#define CWBorderWidth   (1<<4)
#define CWSibling       (1<<5)
#define CWStackMode     (1<<6)
```

Errors

BadMatch   Attempt to set any invalid attribute of InputOnly window.
sibling specified without a *stack_mode*.
The *sibling* window is not actually a sibling.

BadValue   *width* or *height* is 0.

BadWindow

Related Commands

XCirculateSubwindows, XCirculateSubwindowsDown, XCirculate-
SubwindowsUp, XLowerWindow, XMoveResizeWindow, XMoveWindow, XQuery-
Tree, XReconfigureWMWindow, XRaiseWindow, XReparentWindow, XResize-
Window, XRestackWindows.

Name

XConvertSelection — use the value of a selection.

Synopsis

```
XConvertSelection(display, selection, target, property,
        requestor, time)
    Display *display;
    Atom selection, target;
    Atom property;                  /* may be None */
    Window requestor;
    Time time;
```

Arguments

display   Specifies a connection to an X server; returned from XOpenDisplay.

selection   Specifies the selection atom. XA_PRIMARY and XA_SECONDARY are the standard selection atoms.

target   Specifies the atom of the type property that specifies the desired format for the data.

property   Specifies the property in which the requested data is to be placed. None is also valid, but current conventions specify that the requestor is in a better position to select a property than the selection owner.

requestor   Specifies the requesting window.

time   Specifies the time when the conversion should take place. Pass either a timestamp, expressed in milliseconds, or the constant CurrentTime.

Description

XConvertSelection causes a SelectionRequest event to be sent to the current selection owner if there is one, specifying the property to store the data in (*selection*), the format to convert that data into before storing it (*target*), the property to place the information in (*property*), the window that wants the information (*requestor*), and the time to make the conversion (*time*).

The selection owner responds by sending a SelectionNotify event, which confirms the selected atom and type. If no owner for the specified selection exists, or if the owner could not convert to the type specified by requestor, the X server generates or the owner sends a SelectionNotify event to the *requestor* with property None. Whether or not the owner exists, the arguments are passed unchanged. See Volume One, Chapter 10, *Interclient Communication*, for a description of selection events and selection conventions.

Errors

BadAtom
BadWindow

Related Commands

XGetSelectionOwner, XSetSelectionOwner.

XCopyArea

Name

XCopyArea — copy an area of a drawable.

Synopsis

```
XCopyArea (display, src, dest, gc, src_x, src_y, width,
        height,  dest_x, dest_y)
    Display *display;
    Drawable src, dest;
    GC gc;
    int src_x, src_y;
    unsigned int width, height;
    int dest_x, dest_y;
```

Arguments

display	Specifies a connection to an X server; returned from XOpenDisplay.
src dest	Specify the source and destination rectangles to be combined. src and dest must have the same root and depth.
gc	Specifies the graphics context.
src_x src_y	Specify the x and y coordinates of the upper-left corner of the source rectangle relative to the origin of the source drawable.
width height	Specify the dimensions in pixels of both the source and destination rectangles.
dest_x dest_y	Specify the x and y coordinates within the destination window.

Description

XCopyArea combines the specified rectangle of src with the specified rectangle of dest. src and dest must have the same root and depth.

If regions of the source rectangle are obscured and have not been retained in backing_store, or if regions outside the boundaries of the source drawable are specified, then those regions are not copied. Instead, the following occurs on all corresponding destination regions that are either visible or are retained in backing_store. If dest is a window with a background other than None, the corresponding regions of the destination are tiled (with plane_mask of all 1's and function GXcopy) with that background. Regardless of tiling, if the destination is a window and graphics_exposures in gc is True, then Graphics-Expose events for all corresponding destination regions are generated. If graphics_exposures is True but no regions are exposed, then a NoExpose event is generated.

If regions of the source rectangle are not obscured and graphics_exposures is False, one NoExpose event is generated on the destination.

XCopyArea uses these graphics context components: `function`, `plane_mask`, `subwindow_mode`, `graphics_exposures`, `clip_x_origin`, `clip_y_origin`, and `clip_mask`.

Errors

BadDrawable

BadGC

BadMatch   The *src* and *dest* rectangles do not have the same root and depth.

Related Commands

XClearArea, XClearWindow, XCopyPlane, XDraw, XDrawArc, XDrawArcs, XDrawFilled, XDrawLine, XDrawLines, XDrawPoint, XDrawPoints, XDraw-Rectangle, XDrawRectangles, XDrawSegments, XFillArc, XFillArcs, XFill-Polygon, XFillRectangle, XFillRectangles.

XCopyColormapAndFree

Name

XCopyColormapAndFree — copy a colormap and return a new colormap ID.

Synopsis

```
Colormap XCopyColormapAndFree(display, cmap)
    Display *display;
    Colormap cmap;
```

Arguments

display	Specifies a connection to an X server; returned from XOpenDisplay.
cmap	Specifies the colormap you are moving out of.

Description

XCopyColormapAndFree is used to obtain a new virtual colormap when allocating color-cells out of a previous colormap has failed due to resource exhaustion (that is, too many cells or planes were in use in the original colormap).

XCopyColormapAndFree moves all of the client's existing allocations from *cmap* to the returned Colormap and frees those entries in *cmap*. The visual type and screen for the new colormap is the same as for the old.

If *cmap* was created by the client with the *alloc* argument set to AllocAll, the new colormap is also created with AllocAll, all color values for all entries are copied from *cmap*, and then all entries in *cmap* are freed.

If *cmap* was created by the client with AllocNone, the allocations to be moved are all those pixels and planes that have been allocated by the client using XAllocColor, XAlloc-NamedColor, XAllocColorCells, or XAllocColorPlanes and that have not been freed since they were allocated. Values in other entries of the new Colormap are undefined.

For more information, see Volume One, Chapter 7, *Color*.

Errors

```
BadAlloc
BadColormap
```

Related Commands

DefaultColormap, DisplayCells, XCreateColormap, XFreeColormap, XGet-StandardColormap, XInstallColormap, XListInstalledColormaps, XSet-StandardColormap, XSetWindowColormap, XUninstallColormap.

Name

XCopyGC — copy a graphics context.

Synopsis

```
XCopyGC(display, src, valuemask, dest)
    Display *display;
    GC src, dest;
    unsigned long valuemask;
```

Arguments

display   Specifies a connection to an X server; returned from XOpenDisplay.

src   Specifies the components of the source graphics context.

valuemask   Specifies the components in the source GC structure to be copied into the des-
             tination GC. valuemask is made by combining any number of the mask
             symbols listed in the Structures section using bitwise OR (|).

dest   Specifies the destination graphics context.

Description

XCopyGC copies the selected elements of one graphics context to another. See Volume One,
Chapter 5, *The Graphics Context*, for a description of the graphics context.

Structures

The GC structure contains the following elements:

```
/*
 * Data structure for setting graphics context.
 */
typedef struct {
    int function;              /* logical operation */
    unsigned long plane_mask;  /* plane mask */
    unsigned long foreground;  /* foreground pixel */
    unsigned long background;  /* background pixel */
    int line_width;            /* line width */
    int line_style;            /* Solid, OnOffDash, DoubleDash */
    int cap_style;             /* NotLast, Butt, Round, Projecting */
    int join_style;            /* Miter, Round, Bevel */
    int fill_style;            /* Solid, Tiled, Stippled */
    int fill_rule;             /* EvenOdd, Winding */
    int arc_mode;              /* PieSlice */
    Pixmap tile;               /* tile pixmap for tiling operations */
    Pixmap stipple;            /* stipple 1 plane pixmap for stipping */
    int ts_x_origin;           /* offset for tile or stipple operations */
    int ts_y_origin;
    Font font;                 /* default text font for text operations */
    int subwindow_mode;        /* ClipByChildren, IncludeInferiors */
    Bool graphics_exposures;   /* boolean, should exposures be generated */
    int clip_x_origin;         /* origin for clipping */
```

```
    int clip_y_origin;
    Pixmap clip_mask;              /* bitmap clipping; other calls for rects */
    int dash_offset;               /* patterned/dashed line information */
    char dashes;
} XGCValues;

#define GCFunction           (1L<<0)
#define GCPlaneMask          (1L<<1)
#define GCForeground         (1L<<2)
#define GCBackground         (1L<<3)
#define GCLineWidth          (1L<<4)
#define GCLineStyle          (1L<<5)
#define GCCapStyle           (1L<<6)
#define GCJoinStyle          (1L<<7)
#define GCFillStyle          (1L<<8)
#define GCFillRule           (1L<<9)
#define GCTile               (1L<<10)
#define GCStipple            (1L<<11)
#define GCTileStipXOrigin    (1L<<12)
#define GCTileStipYOrigin    (1L<<13)
#define GCFont               (1L<<14)
#define GCSubwindowMode      (1L<<15)
#define GCGraphicsExposures  (1L<<16)
#define GCClipXOrigin        (1L<<17)
#define GCClipYOrigin        (1L<<18)
#define GCClipMask           (1L<<19)
#define GCDashOffset         (1L<<20)
#define GCDashList           (1L<<21)
#define GCArcMode            (1L<<22)
```

Errors

BadAlloc
BadGC
BadMatch   *src* and *dest* do not have the same root and depth.

Related Commands

DefaultGC, XChangeGC, XCreateGC, XFreeGC, XGContextFromGC, XGet-
GCValues, XSetArcMode, XSetBackground, XSetClipMask, XSetClipOrigin,
XSetClipRectangles, XSetDashes, XSetFillRule, XSetFillStyle, XSet-
Foreground, XSetFunction, XSetGraphicsExposures, XSetLineAttributes,
XSetPlaneMask, XSetState, XSetStipple, XSetSubwindowMode, XSet-
TSOrigin.

Name

XCopyPlane — copy a single plane of a drawable into a drawable with depth, applying pixel values.

Synopsis

```
XCopyPlane(display, src, dest, gc, src_x, src_y, width,
        height, dest_x, dest_y, plane)
    Display *display;
    Drawable src, dest;
    GC gc;
    int src_x, src_y;
    unsigned int width, height;
    int dest_x, dest_y;
    unsigned long plane;
```

Arguments

display   Specifies a connection to an X server; returned from XOpenDisplay.

src
dest   Specify the source and destination drawables.

gc   Specifies the graphics context.

src_x
src_y   Specify the x and y coordinates of the upper-left corner of the source rectangle relative to the origin of the drawable.

width
height   Specify the width and height in pixels. These are the dimensions of both the source and destination rectangles.

dest_x
dest_y   Specify the x and y coordinates at which the copied area will be placed relative to the origin of the destination drawable.

plane   Specifies the source bit-plane. You must set exactly one bit, and the bit must specify a plane that exists in src.

Description

XCopyPlane copies a single plane of a rectangle in the source into the entire depth of a corresponding rectangle in the destination. The plane of the source drawable and the foreground/background pixel values in gc are combined to form a pixmap of the same depth as the destination drawable, and the equivalent of an XCopyArea is performed, with all the same exposure semantics.

XCopyPlane uses these graphics context components: function, plane_mask, foreground, background, subwindow_mode, graphics_exposures, clip_x_origin, clip_y_origin, and clip_mask.

The src and dest drawables must have the same root, but need not have the same depth.

For more information, see Volume One, Chapter 5, *The Graphics Context*.

Errors

BadDrawable

BadGC

BadMatch   *src* and *dest* do not have the same root.

BadValue   *plane* does not have exactly one bit set, or bit specified in *plane* is not a plane in *src*.

Related Commands

XClearArea, XClearWindow, XCopyArea, XDraw, XDrawArc, XDrawArcs, XDraw-
Filled, XDrawLine, XDrawLines, XDrawPoint, XDrawPoints, XDrawRectangle,
XDrawRectangles, XDrawSegments, XFillArc, XFillArcs, XFillPolygon,
XFillRectangle, XFillRectangles.

Name

XCreateAssocTable — create a new association table (X10).

Synopsis

```
XAssocTable *XCreateAssocTable(size)
    int size;
```

Arguments

size   Specifies the number of buckets in the hashed association table.

Description

XCreateAssocTable creates an association table, which allows you to associate your own structures with X resources in a fast lookup table. This function is provided for compatibility with X Version 10. To use it you must include the file <X11/X10.h> and link with the library -loldX.

The size argument specifies the number of buckets in the hash system of XAssocTable. For reasons of efficiency the number of buckets should be a power of two. Some size suggestions might be: use 32 buckets per 100 objects; a reasonable maximum number of object per buckets is 8.

If there is an error allocating memory for the XAssocTable, a NULL pointer is returned.

For more information on association tables, see Volume One, Appendix B, *X10 Compatibility*.

Structures

```
typedef struct {
    XAssoc *buckets;      /* pointer to first bucket in array */
    int size;             /* table size (number of buckets) */
} XAssocTable;
```

Related Commands

XDeleteAssoc, XDestroyAssocTable, XLookUpAssoc, XMakeAssoc.

XCreateBitmapFromData

Name

XCreateBitmapFromData — create a bitmap from X11 bitmap format data.

Synopsis

```
Pixmap XCreateBitmapFromData(display, drawable, data,
        width, height)
    Display *display;
    Drawable drawable;
    char *data;
    unsigned int width, height;
```

Arguments

display	Specifies a connection to an X server; returned from XOpenDisplay.
drawable	Specifies a drawable. This determines which screen to create the bitmap on.
data	Specifies the bitmap data, in X11 bitmap file format.
width *height*	Specify the dimensions in pixels of the created bitmap. If smaller than the bitmap data, the upper-left corner of the data is used.

Description

XCreateBitmapFromData creates a single-plane pixmap from an array of hexadecimal data. This data may be defined in the program or included. The bitmap data must be in X version 11 format as shown below (it cannot be in X10 format). The following format is assumed for the data, where the variables are members of the XImage structure described in Volume One, Chapter 6, *Drawing Graphics and Text*:

```
format=XYPixmap
bit_order=LSBFirst
byte_order=LSBFirst
bitmap_unit=8
bitmap_pad=8
xoffset=0
no extra bytes per line
```

XCreateBitmapFromData creates an image with the specified data and copies it into the created pixmap. The following is an example of creating a bitmap:

```
#define gray_width 16
#define gray_height 16
#define gray_x_hot 8
#define gray_y_hot 8
static char gray_bits[] = {
    0xf8, 0x1f, 0xe3, 0xc7, 0xcf, 0xf3, 0x9f, 0xf9,
    0xbf, 0xfd, 0x33, 0xcc, 0x7f, 0xfe, 0x7f, 0xfe,
```

```
        0x7e, 0x7e, 0x7f, 0xfe, 0x37, 0xec, 0xbb, 0xdd,
        0x9c, 0x39, 0xcf, 0xf3, 0xe3, 0xc7, 0xf8, 0x1f};

    Pixmap XCreateBitmapFromData(display, window, gray_bits,
        gray_width, gray_height);
```

If the call could not create a pixmap of the requested size on the server, XCreateBitmap-FromData returns 0 (zero), and the server generates a BadAlloc error. If the requested depth is not supported on the screen of the specified drawable, the server generates a Bad-Match error.

The user should free the bitmap using XFreePixmap when it is no longer needed.

For more information, see Volume One, Chapter 6, *Drawing Graphics and Text*.

Errors

BadAlloc   Server has insufficient memory to create bitmap.

BadDrawable

BadValue   Specified bitmap dimensions are zero.

Related Commands

XCreatePixmap, XCreatePixmapFromBitmapData, XCreatePixmapFrom-BitmapData, XFreePixmap, XQueryBestSize, XQueryBestStipple, XQuery-BestTile, XReadBitmapFile, XSetTile, XSetWindowBackgroundPixmap, XSetWindowBorderPixmap, XWriteBitmapFile.

XCreateColormap

Name

XCreateColormap — create a colormap.

Synopsis

```
Colormap XCreateColormap(display, w, visual, alloc)
    Display *display;
    Window w;
    Visual *visual;
    int alloc;
```

Arguments

display   Specifies a connection to an X server; returned from XOpenDisplay.

w   Specifies a window ID. The colormap created will be associated with the same screen as the window.

visual   Specifies a pointer to the Visual structure for the colormap. The visual class and depth must be supported by the screen.

alloc   Specifies how many colormap entries to allocate. Pass either AllocNone or AllocAll.

Description

XCreateColormap creates a colormap of the specified visual type and allocates either none or all of its entries, and returns the colormap ID.

It is legal to specify any visual class in the structure pointed to by the *visual* argument. If the class is StaticColor, StaticGray, or TrueColor, the colorcells will have pre-allocated read-only values defined by the individual server but unspecified by the X11 protocol. In these cases, *alloc* must be specified as AllocNone (else a BadMatch error).

For the other visual classes, PseudoColor, DirectColor, and GrayScale, you can pass either AllocAll or AllocNone to the *alloc* argument. If you pass AllocNone, the colormap has no allocated entries. This allows your client programs to allocate read-only colorcells with XAllocColor or read/write cells with XAllocColorCells, Alloc-ColorPlanes and XStoreColors. If you pass the constant AllocAll, the entire colormap is allocated writable (all the entries are read/write, nonshareable and have undefined initial RGB values), and the colors can be set with XStoreColors. However, you cannot free these entries with XFreeColors, and no relationships between the entries are defined.

If the visual class is PseudoColor or GrayScale and *alloc* is AllocAll, this function simulates a call to the function XAllocColor cells returning all pixel values from 1 to (map_entries - 1). For a visual class of DirectColor, the processing for AllocAll simulates a call to the function XAllocColorPlanes, returning a pixel value of 0 and mask values the same as the red_mask, green_mask, and blue_mask members in *visual*.

The *visual* argument should be as returned from the DefaultVisual macro, XMatch-VisualInfo, or XGetVisualInfo.

If the hardware colormap on the server is immutable, and therefore there is no possibility that a virtual colormap could ever be installed, XCreateColormap returns the default colormap. Code should check the returned ID against the default colormap to catch this situation.

For more information on creating colormaps, see Volume One, Chapter 7, *Color*.

Errors

BadAlloc

BadMatch   Didn't use AllocNone for StaticColor, StaticGray, or True-Color.
          visual type not supported on screen.

BadValue

BadWindow

Related Commands

DefaultColormap, DisplayCells, XCopyColormapAndFree, XFreeColormap, XGetStandardColormap, XInstallColormap, XListInstalledColormaps, XSetStandardColormap, XSetWindowColormap, XUninstallColormap.

XCreateFontCursor

Name

XCreateFontCursor — create a cursor from the standard cursor font.

Synopsis

```
#include <X11/cursorfont.h>
Cursor XCreateFontCursor(display, shape)
    Display *display;
    unsigned int shape;
```

Arguments

display   Specifies a connection to an X server; returned from XOpenDisplay.

shape   Specifies which character in the standard cursor font should be used for the cursor.

Description

X provides a set of standard cursor shapes in a special font named "cursor." Programs are encouraged to use this interface for their cursors, since the font can be customized for the individual display type and shared between clients.

The hotspot comes from the information stored in the font. The initial colors of the cursor are black for the foreground and white for the background. XRecolorCursor can be used to change the colors of the cursor to those desired.

For more information about cursors and their shapes in fonts, see Appendix I, *The Cursor Font*.

Errors

BadAlloc

BadFont

BadValue   The *shape* argument does not specify a character in the standard cursor font.

Related Commands

XCreateGlyphCursor, XCreatePixmapCursor, XDefineCursor, XFreeCursor,
XQueryBestCursor, XQueryBestSize, XRecolorCursor, XUndefineCursor.

Name

XCreateGC — create a new graphics context for a given screen with the depth of the specified drawable.

Synopsis

```
GC XCreateGC(display, drawable, valuemask, values)
    Display *display;
    Drawable drawable;
    unsigned long valuemask;
    XGCValues *values;
```

Arguments

display   Specifies a connection to an X server; returned from `XOpenDisplay`.

drawable   Specifies a drawable. The created GC can only be used to draw in drawables of the same depth as this *drawable*.

valuemask   Specifies which members of the GC are to be set using information in the *values* structure. *valuemask* is made by combining any number of the mask symbols listed in the Structures section.

values   Specifies a pointer to an `XGCValues` structure which will provide components for the new GC.

Description

`XCreateGC` creates a new graphics context resource in the server. The returned GC can be used in subsequent drawing requests, but only on drawables on the same screen and of the same depth as the drawable specified in the *drawable* argument.

The specified components of the new graphics context in *valuemask* are set to the values passed in the *values* argument. Unset components default as follows:

Component	Value
plane_mask	all 1's
foreground	0
background	1
line_width	0
line_style	LineSolid
cap_style	CapButt
join_style	JoinMiter
fill_style	FillSolid
fill_rule	EvenOddRule
arc_mode	ArcPieSlice
tile	Pixmap filled with foreground pixel
stipple	Pixmap filled with 1's

Component	Value
ts_x_origin	0
ts_y_origin	0
font	(implementation dependent)
subwindow_mode	ClipByChildren
graphics_exposures	True
clip_x_origin	0
clip_y_origin	0
clip_mask	None
dash_offset	0
dash_list	4 (i.e., the list [4, 4])

An application should minimize the number of GCs it creates, because some servers cache a limited number of GCs in the display hardware, and can attain better performance with a small number of GCs.

For more information, see Volume One, Chapter 5, *The Graphics Context*.

Errors

BadAlloc   Server could not allocate memory for GC.

BadDrawable   Specified drawable is invalid.

BadFont   Font specified for *font* component of GC has not been loaded.

BadMatch   Pixmap specified for *tile* component has different depth or is on different screen from the specified drawable. Or pixmap specified for stipple or clip_mask component has depth other than 1.

BadPixmap   Pixmap specified for *tile*, *stipple*, or clip_mask components is invalid.

BadValue   Values specified for *function*, line_style, cap_style, join_style, fill_style, fill_rule, subwindow_mode, graphics_exposures, dashes, or arc_mode are invalid, or invalid mask specified for *valuemask* argument.

Structures

```
typedef struct {
    int function;               /* logical operation */
    unsigned long plane_mask;   /* plane mask */
    unsigned long foreground;   /* foreground pixel */
    unsigned long background;   /* background pixel */
    int line_width;             /* line width */
    int line_style;             /* LineSolid, LineOnOffDash, LineDoubleDash */
    int cap_style;              /* CapNotLast, CapButt, CapRound, CapProjecting */
    int join_style;             /* JoinMiter, JoinRound, JoinBevel */
    int fill_style;             /* FillSolid, FillTiled, FillStippled */
    int fill_rule;              /* EvenOddRule, WindingRule */
```

```
    int arc_mode;                /* ArcPieSlice, ArcChord */
    Pixmap tile;                 /* tile pixmap for tiling operations */
    Pixmap stipple;              /* stipple 1 plane pixmap for stipping */
    int ts_x_origin;             /* offset for tile or stipple operations */
    int ts_y_origin;
    Font font;                   /* default text font for text operations */
    int subwindow_mode;          /* ClipByChildren, IncludeInferiors */
    Bool graphics_exposures;     /* generate events on XCopyArea, XCopyPlane */
    int clip_x_origin;           /* origin for clipping */
    int clip_y_origin;
    Pixmap clip_mask;            /* bitmap clipping; other calls for rects */
    int dash_offset;             /* patterned/dashed line information */
    char dashes;
} XGCValues;

#define GCFunction              (1L<<0)
#define GCPlaneMask             (1L<<1)
#define GCForeground            (1L<<2)
#define GCBackground            (1L<<3)
#define GCLineWidth             (1L<<4)
#define GCLineStyle             (1L<<5)
#define GCCapStyle              (1L<<6)
#define GCJoinStyle             (1L<<7)
#define GCFillStyle             (1L<<8)
#define GCFillRule              (1L<<9)
#define GCTile                  (1L<<10)
#define GCStipple               (1L<<11)
#define GCTileStipXOrigin       (1L<<12)
#define GCTileStipYOrigin       (1L<<13)
#define GCFont                  (1L<<14)
#define GCSubwindowMode         (1L<<15)
#define GCGraphicsExposures     (1L<<16)
#define GCClipXOrigin           (1L<<17)
#define GCClipYOrigin           (1L<<18)
#define GCClipMask              (1L<<19)
#define GCDashOffset            (1L<<20)
#define GCDashList              (1L<<21)
#define GCArcMode               (1L<<22)
```

Related Commands

DefaultGC, XChangeGC, XCopyGC, XFreeGC, XGContextFromGC, XGetGCValues,
XSetArcMode, XSetBackground, XSetClipMask, XSetClipOrigin, XSetClip-
Rectangles, XSetDashes, XSetFillRule, XSetFillStyle, XSetForeground,
XSetFunction, XSetGraphicsExposures, XSetLineAttributes, XSetPlane-
Mask, XSetState, XSetStipple, XSetSubwindowMode, XSetTSOrigin.

Name

XCreateGlyphCursor — create a cursor from font glyphs.

Synopsis

```
Cursor XCreateGlyphCursor(display, source_font, mask_font,
        source_char, mask_char, foreground_color, back-
        ground_color)
    Display *display;
    Font source_font, mask_font;
    unsigned int source_char, mask_char;
    XColor *foreground_color;
    XColor *background_color;
```

Arguments

display   Specifies a connection to an X server; returned from XOpenDisplay.

source_font Specifies the font from which a character is to be used for the cursor.

mask_font   Specifies the mask font. Optional; specify 0 if not needed.

source_char Specifies the index into the cursor shape font.

mask_char   Specifies the index into the mask shape font. Optional; specify 0 if not needed.

foreground_color
        Specifies the red, green, and blue (RGB) values for the foreground.

background_color
        Specifies the red, green, and blue (RGB) values for the background.

Description

XCreateGlyphCursor is similar to XCreatePixmapCursor, but the source and mask bitmaps are obtained from separate font characters, perhaps in separate fonts. The mask font and character are optional. If *mask_char* is not specified, all pixels of the source are displayed.

The x offset for the hotspot of the created cursor is the left-bearing for the source character, and the y offset is the ascent, each measured from the upper-left corner of the bounding rectangle of the character.

The origins of the source and mask (if it is defined) characters are positioned coincidently and define the hotspot. The source and mask need not have the same bounding box metrics, and there is no restriction on the placement of the hotspot relative to the bounding boxes.

Note that *source_char* and *mask_char* are of type unsigned int, not of type XChar2b. For two-byte matrix fonts, *source_char* and *mask_char* should be formed with the byte1 member in the most significant byte and the byte2 member in the least significant byte.

You can free the fonts with XFreeFont if they are no longer needed after creating the glyph cursor.

For more information on fonts and cursors, see Volume One, Chapter 6, *Drawing Graphics and Text*.

Structures
```
typedef struct {
    unsigned long pixel;
    unsigned short red, green, blue;
    char flags;                        /* DoRed, DoGreen, DoBlue */
    char pad;
} XColor;
```

Errors
BadAlloc

BadFont

BadValue   *source_char* not defined in *source_font*.
             mask_char not defined in *mask_font* (if *mask_font* defined).

Related Commands
XCreateFontCursor, XCreatePixmapCursor, XDefineCursor, XFreeCursor, XQueryBestCursor, XQueryBestSize, XRecolorCursor, XUndefineCursor.

XCreateImage

Name

XCreateImage — allocate memory for an XImage structure.

Synopsis

```
#include <X11/Xutil.h>
XImage *XCreateImage(display, visual, depth, format, offset,
        data, width, height, bitmap_pad, bytes_per_line)
    Display *display;
    Visual *visual;
    unsigned int depth;
    int format;
    int offset;
    char *data;
    unsigned int width;
    unsigned int height;
    int bitmap_pad;
    int bytes_per_line;
```

Arguments

display   Specifies a connection to an X server; returned from XOpenDisplay.

visual   Specifies a pointer to a visual that should match the visual of the window the image is to be displayed in.

depth   Specifies the depth of the image.

format   Specifies the format for the image. Pass one of these constants: XYPixmap, or ZPixmap.

offset   Specifies the number of pixels beyond the beginning of the data (pointed to by data) where the image actually begins. This is useful if the image is not aligned on an even addressable boundary.

data   Specifies a pointer to the image data.

width   Specify the width and height in pixels of the image.
height

bitmap_pad   Specifies the quantum of a scan line. In other words, the start of one scan line is separated in client memory from the start of the next scan line by an integer multiple of this many bits. You must pass one of these values: 8, 16, or 32.

bytes_per_line

     Specifies the number of bytes in the client image between the start of one scan line and the start of the next. If you pass a value of 0 here, Xlib assumes that the scan lines are contiguous in memory and thus calculates the value of bytes_per_line itself.

Description

XCreateImage allocates the memory needed for an XImage structure for the specified display and visual.

This function does not allocate space for the image itself. It initializes the structure with byte order, bit order, and bitmap unit values, and returns a pointer to the XImage structure. The red, green, and blue mask values are defined for ZPixmap format images only and are derived from the Visual structure passed in.

For a description of images, see Volume One, Chapter 6, *Drawing Graphics and Text*.

Related Commands

ImageByteOrder, XAddPixel, XDestroyImage, XGetImage, XGetPixel, XGet-
SubImage, XPutImage, XPutPixel, XSubImage.

XCreatePixmap

Name
XCreatePixmap — create a pixmap.

Synopsis
```
Pixmap XCreatePixmap(display, drawable, width, height, depth)
    Display *display;
    Drawable drawable;
    unsigned int width, height;
    unsigned int depth;
```

Arguments

display   Specifies a connection to an X server; returned from `XOpenDisplay`.

drawable   Specifies the drawable. May be an `InputOnly` window.

width   Specify the width and height in pixels of the pixmap. The values must be
height   nonzero.

depth   Specifies the depth of the pixmap. The depth must be supported by the screen
of the specified drawable. (Use `XListDepths` if in doubt.)

Description

`XCreatePixmap` creates a *pixmap* resource and returns its pixmap ID. The initial contents of the pixmap are undefined.

The server uses the *drawable* argument to determine which screen the pixmap is stored on. The pixmap can only be used on this screen. The pixmap can only be drawn drawn into with GCs of the same depth, and can only be copied to drawables of the same depth, except in `XCopyPlane`.

A bitmap is a single-plane pixmap. There is no separate bitmap type in X Version 11.

Pixmaps should be considered a precious resource, since many servers have limits on the amount of off-screen memory available.

For more information, see Volume One, Chapter 6, *Drawing Graphics and Text*.

Errors

`BadAlloc`

`BadDrawable`

`BadValue`   *width* or *height* is 0.
                 depth is not supported on screen.

Related Commands

`XCreateBitmapFromData`, `XCreatePixmapFromBitmapData`, `XFreePixmap`, `XListDepths`, `XListPixmapFormat`, `XQueryBestCursor`, `XQueryBestSize`, `XQueryBestStipple`, `XQueryBestTile`, `XReadBitmapFile`, `XSetTile`, `XSetWindowBackgroundPixmap`, `XSetWindowBorderPixmap`, `XWriteBitmapFile`.

Name

XCreatePixmapCursor — create a cursor from two bitmaps.

Synopsis

```
Cursor XCreatePixmapCursor(display, source, mask,
        foreground_color, background_color, x_hot, y_hot)
    Display *display;
    Pixmap source;
    Pixmap mask;
    XColor *foreground_color;
    XColor *background_color;
    unsigned int x_hot, y_hot;
```

Arguments

display   Specifies a connection to an X server; returned from XOpenDisplay.

source   Specifies the shape of the source cursor. A pixmap of depth 1.

mask   Specifies the bits of the cursor that are to be displayed (the mask or stipple). A pixmap of depth 1.

foreground_color
                 Specifies the red, green, and blue (RGB) values for the foreground.

background_color
                 Specifies the red, green, and blue (RGB) values for the background.

x_hot   Specify the coordinates of the cursor's hotspot relative to the source's origin.
y_hot   Must be a point within the source.

Description

XCreatePixmapCursor creates a cursor and returns a cursor ID. Foreground and background RGB values must be specified using foreground_color and background_color, even if the server only has a monochrome screen. The foreground_color is used for the 1 bits in the source, and the background is used for the 0 bits. Both source and mask (if specified) must have depth 1, but can have any root. The mask pixmap defines the shape of the cursor; that is, the 1 bits in the mask define which source pixels will be displayed. If no mask is given, all pixels of the source are displayed. The mask, if present, must be the same size as the source.

The pixmaps can be freed immediately if no further explicit references to them are to be made.

For more information on cursors, see Volume One, Chapter 6, *Drawing Graphics and Text*.

Structures

```
typedef struct {
    unsigned long pixel;
    unsigned short red, green, blue;
    char flags;                        /* DoRed, DoGreen, DoBlue */
```

```
        char pad;
    } XColor;
```

Errors

BadAlloc

BadMatch   Mask bitmap must be the same size as source bitmap.

BadPixmap

Related Commands

XCreateBitmapFromData, XDefineCursor, XCreateFontCursor, XCreate-
Pixmap, XCreatePixmapCursor, XFreeCursor, XFreePixmap, XQueryBest-
Cursor, XQueryBestCursor, XQueryBestSize, XQueryBestSize, XRead-
BitmapFile, XRecolorCursor, XUndefineCursor.

XCreatePixmapFromBitmapData

Name

XCreatePixmapFromBitmapData — create a pixmap with depth from bitmap data.

Synopsis

```
Pixmap XCreatePixmapFromBitmapData(display, drawable, data,
        width, height, fg, bg, depth)
    Display *display;
    Drawable drawable;
    char *data;
    unsigned int width, height;
    unsigned long fg, bg;
    unsigned int depth;
```

Arguments

display	Specifies a connection to an Display structure, returned from XOpen-Display.
drawable	Specifies a drawable ID which indicates which screen the pixmap is to be used on.
data	Specifies the data in bitmap format.
width *height*	Specify the width and height in pixels of the pixmap to create.
fg *bg*	Specify the foreground and background pixel values to use.
depth	Specifies the depth of the pixmap. Must be valid on the screen specified by *drawable*.

Description

XCreatePixmapFromBitmapData creates a pixmap of the given depth using bitmap data and foreground and background pixel values.

The following format for the data is assigned, where the variables are members of the XImage structure described in Volume One, Chapter 6, *Drawing Graphics and Text*:

```
format=XYPixmap
bit_order=LSBFirst
byte_order=LSBFirst
bitmap_unit=8
bitmap_pad=8
xoffset=0
no extra bytes per line
```

XCreatePixmapFromBitmapData creates an image from the data and uses XPutImage to place the data into the pixmap. For example:

```
#define gray_width 16
#define gray_height 16
#define gray_x_hot 8
#define gray_y_hot 8
static char gray_bits[] = {
    0xf8, 0x1f, 0xe3, 0xc7, 0xcf, 0xf3, 0x9f, 0xf9, 0xbf,
    0xfd, 0x33, 0xcc, 0x7f, 0xfe, 0x7f, 0xfe, 0x7e, 0x7e,
    0x7f, 0xfe, 0x37, 0xec, 0xbb, 0xdd, 0x9c, 0x39, 0xcf,
    0xf3, 0xe3, 0xc7, 0xf8, 0x1f};
unsigned long foreground, background;
unsigned int depth;

/* open display, determine colors and depth */

Pixmap XCreatePixmapFromBitmapData(display, window, gray_bits,
        gray_width, gray_height, foreground, background, depth);
```

If you want to use data of a different format, it is straightforward to write a routine that does this yourself, using images.

Pixmaps should be considered a precious resource, since many servers have limits on the amount of off-screen memory available.

Errors

```
BadAlloc
BadDrawable
```

BadValue   The *width* or *height* of pixmap are zero, or *depth* is not a valid depth on the screen specified by drawable.

Related Commands

XCreateBitmapFromData, XCreateFontCursor, XCreatePixmap, XCreate-PixmapCursor, XDefineCursor, XFreeCursor, XFreePixmap, XListPixmap-Formats, XQueryBestCursor, XQueryBestSize, XReadBitmapFile, XRecolor-Cursor, XUndefineCursor.

Name

XCreateRegion — create a new empty region.

Synopsis

```
Region XCreateRegion()
```

Description

XCreateRegion creates a new region of undefined size. XPolygonRegion can be used to create a region with a defined shape and size. Many of the functions that perform operations on regions can also create regions.

For a description of regions, see Volume One, Chapter 6, *Drawing Graphics and Text*.

Structures

Region is a pointer to an opaque structure type.

Related Commands

XClipBox, XDestroyRegion, XEmptyRegion, XEqualRegion, XIntersect-
Region, XOffsetRegion, XPointInRegion, XPolygonRegion, XRectInRegion,
XSetRegion, XShrinkRegion, XSubtractRegion, XUnionRectWithRegion,
XUnionRegion, XXorRegion.

XCreateSimpleWindow

Name

XCreateSimpleWindow — create an unmapped InputOutput window.

Synopsis

```
Window XCreateSimpleWindow(display, parent, x, y, width, height,
border_width, border, background)
    Display *display;
    Window parent;
    int x, y;
    unsigned int width, height, border_width;
    unsigned long border;
    unsigned long background;
```

Arguments

display   Specifies a pointer to the Display structure; returned from XOpenDisplay.

parent   Specifies the parent window ID. Must be an InputOutput window.

x   Specify the x and y coordinates of the upper-left pixel of the new window's
y   border relative to the origin of the parent (inside the parent window's border).

width   Specify the width and height, in pixels, of the new window. These are the
height   inside dimensions, not including the new window's borders, which are entirely
               outside of the window. Must be nonzero. Any part of the window that extends
               outside its parent window is clipped.

border_width
               Specifies the width, in pixels, of the new window's border.

border   Specifies the pixel value for the border of the window.

background   Specifies the pixel value for the background of the window.

Description

XCreateSimpleWindow creates an unmapped InputOutput subwindow of the specified
parent window. Use XCreateWindow if you want to set the window attributes while creating
a window. (After creation, XChangeWindowAttributes can be used.)

XCreateSimpleWindow returns the ID of the created window. The new window is placed
on top of the stacking order relative to its siblings. Note that the window is unmapped when it
is created—use MapWindow to display it. This function generates a XCreateNotify event.

The initial conditions of the window are as follows:

The window inherits its depth, class, and visual from its parent. All other window attributes
have their default values.

All properties have undefined values.

The new window will not have a cursor defined; the cursor will be that of the window's parent
until the cursor attribute is set with XDefineCursor or XChangeWindowAttributes.

If no background or border is specified, `CopyFromParent` is implied.

For more information, see Volume One, Chapter 2, *X Concepts*, and Volume One, Chapter 3, *Basic Window Program*.

Errors

`BadAlloc`

`BadMatch`

`BadValue`   *width* or *height* is zero.

`BadWindow`   Specified parent is an `InputOnly` window.

Related Commands

`XCreateWindow`, `XDestroySubwindows`, `XDestroyWindow`.

Name

XCreateWindow — create a window and set attributes.

Synopsis

```
Window XCreateWindow(display, parent, x, y, width, height,
        border_width, depth, class, visual, valuemask,
        attributes)
    Display *display;
    Window parent;
    int x, y;
    unsigned int width, height;
    unsigned int border_width;
    int depth;
    unsigned int class;
    Visual *visual
    unsigned long valuemask;
    XSetWindowAttributes *attributes;
```

Arguments

display	Specifies a connection to an X server; returned from XOpenDisplay.
parent	Specifies the parent window. Parent must be InputOutput if class of window created is to be InputOutput.
x y	Specify the x and y coordinates of the upper-left pixel of the new window's border relative to the origin of the parent (upper left inside the parent's border).
width height	Specify the width and height, in pixels, of the window. These are the new window's inside dimensions. These dimensions do not include the new window's borders, which are entirely outside of the window. Must be nonzero, otherwise the server generates a BadValue error.
border_width	Specifies the width, in pixels, of the new window's border. Must be 0 for InputOnly windows, otherwise a BadMatch error is generated.
depth	Specifies the depth of the window, which is less than or equal to the parent's depth. A depth of CopyFromParent means the depth is taken from the parent. Use XListDepths is choosing an unusual depth. The specified depth paired with the visual argument must be supported on the screen.
class	Specifies the new window's class. Pass one of these constants: Input-Output, InputOnly, or CopyFromParent.
visual	Specifies a connection to an visual structure describing the style of colormap to be used with this window. CopyFromParent is valid.
valuemask	Specifies which window attributes are defined in the attributes argument. If valuemask is 0, attributes is not referenced. This mask is the bitwise OR of the valid attribute mask bits listed in the Structures section below.

    attributes   Attributes of the window to be set at creation time should be set in this structure. The *valuemask* should have the appropriate bits set to indicate which attributes have been set in the structure.

Description

To create an unmapped subwindow for a specified parent window use XCreateWindow or XCreateSimpleWindow. XCreateWindow is a more general function that allows you to set specific window attributes when you create the window. If you do not want to set specific attributes when you create a window, use XCreateSimpleWindow, which creates a window that inherits its attributes from its parent. XCreateSimpleWindow creates only Input-Output windows that use the default depth and visual.

XCreateWindow returns the ID of the created window. XCreateWindow causes the X server to generate a CreateNotify event. The newly created window is placed on top of its siblings in the stacking order.

Extension packages may define other classes of windows.

The visual should be DefaultVisual or one returned by XGetVisualInfo or XMatchVisualInfo. The depth should be DefaultDepth, 1, or a depth returned by XListDepths. In current implementations of Xlib, if you specify a visual other than the one used by the parent, you must first find (using XGetRGBColormaps) or create a colormap matching this visual and then set the colormap window attribute in the *attributes* and *valuemask* arguments. Otherwise, you will get a BadMatch error.

For more information, see Volume One, Chapter 4, *Window Attributes*.

Structures

```
/*
 * Data structure for setting window attributes.
 */
typedef struct {
    Pixmap background_pixmap;          /* background or None or ParentRelative */
    unsigned long background_pixel;    /* background pixel */
    Pixmap border_pixmap;              /* border of the window */
    unsigned long border_pixel;        /* border pixel value */
    int bit_gravity;                   /* one of bit gravity values */
    int win_gravity;                   /* one of the window gravity values */
    int backing_store;                 /* NotUseful, WhenMapped, Always */
    unsigned long backing_planes;      /* planes to be preseved if possible */
    unsigned long backing_pixel;       /* value to use in restoring planes */
    Bool save_under;                   /* should bits under be saved (popups) */
    long event_mask;                   /* set of events that should be saved */
    long do_not_propagate_mask;        /* set of events that should not propagate */
    Bool override_redirect;            /* boolean value for override-redirect */
    Colormap colormap;                 /* colormap to be associated with window */
    Cursor cursor;                     /* cursor to be displayed (or None) */
} XSetWindowAttributes;
```

```
/* Definitions for valuemask argument */

#define CWBackPixmap            (1L<<0)
#define CWBackPixel             (1L<<1)
#define CWBorderPixmap          (1L<<2)
#define CWBorderPixel           (1L<<3)
#define CWBitGravity            (1L<<4)
#define CWWinGravity            (1L<<5)
#define CWBackingStore          (1L<<6)
#define CWBackingPlanes         (1L<<7)
#define CWBackingPixel          (1L<<8)
#define CWOverrideRedirect      (1L<<9)
#define CWSaveUnder             (1L<<10)
#define CWEventMask             (1L<<11)
#define CWDontPropagate         (1L<<12)
#define CWColormap              (1L<<13)
#define CWCursor                (1L<<14)
```

Errors

BadAlloc   Attribute besides win_gravity, event_mask, do_not_propagate_ mask, override_redirect or cursor specified for InputOnly window.

BadColormap   *depth* nonzero for InputOnly.

BadCursor   Parent of InputOutput is InputOnly.

BadMatch   *border_width* is nonzero for InputOnly.

BadPixmap   *depth* not supported on screen for InputOutput.

BadValue   *width* or *height* is 0.

BadWindow   *visual* not supported on screen.

Related Commands

XCreateSimpleWindow, XDestroySubwindows, XDestroyWindow, XList-Depths.

XDefineCursor

Name

XDefineCursor — assign a cursor to a window.

Synopsis

```
XDefineCursor(display, w, cursor)
    Display *display;
    Window w;
    Cursor cursor;
```

Arguments

display   Specifies a connection to an X server; returned from XOpenDisplay.

w   Specifies the ID of the window in which the cursor is to be displayed.

cursor   Specifies the cursor to be displayed when the pointer is in the specified window. Pass None to have the parent's cursor displayed in the window, or for the root window, to have the default cursor displayed.

Description

Sets the cursor attribute of a window, so that the specified cursor is shown whenever this window is visible and the pointer is inside. If XDefineCursor is not called, the parent's cursor is used by default.

For more information on available cursors, see Appendix I, *The Cursor Font*.

Errors

```
BadCursor
BadWindow
```

Related Commands

XCreateFontCursor, XCreateGlyphCursor, XCreatePixmapCursor, XFree-Cursor, XQueryBestCursor, XQueryBestSize, XRecolorCursor, XUndefine-Cursor.

Name

XDeleteAssoc — delete an entry from an association table.

Synopsis

```
XDeleteAssoc(display, table, x_id)
    Display *display;
    XAssocTable *table;
    XID x_id;
```

Arguments

display   Specifies a connection to an X server; returned from XOpenDisplay.

table   Specifies one of the association tables created by XCreateAssocTable.

x_id   Specifies the X resource ID of the association to be deleted.

Description

This function is provided for compatibility with X Version 10. To use it you must include the file *<X11/X10.h>* and link with the library *-loldX*.

XDeleteAssoc deletes an association in an XAssocTable keyed on its XID. Redundant deletes (and deletes of nonexistent XID's) are meaningless and cause no problems. Deleting associations in no way impairs the performance of an XAssocTable.

For more information on association tables, see Volume One, Appendix B, *X10 Compatibility*.

Structures

```
typedef struct {
    XAssoc *buckets;            /* pointer to first bucket in array */
    int size;                   /* table size (number of buckets) */
} XAssocTable;
```

Related Commands

XCreateAssocTable, XDestroyAssocTable, XLookUpAssoc, XMakeAssoc.

XDeleteContext

Name

XDeleteContext — delete a context entry for a given window and type.

Synopsis

```
int XDeleteContext(display, w, context)
    Display *display;
    Window w;
    XContext context;
```

Arguments

display   Specifies a connection to an X server; returned from XOpenDisplay.

w   Specifies the window with which the data is associated.

context   Specifies the context type to which the data belongs.

Description

XDeleteContext deletes the entry for the given window and type from the context data structure defined in *<X11/Xutil.h>*. This function returns XCNOENT if the context could not be found, or zero if it succeeds. XDeleteContext does not free the memory allocated for the data whose address was saved.

See Volume One, Chapter 13, *Other Programming Techniques*, for a description of context management.

Structures

```
typedef int XContext;
```

Related Commands

XFindContext, XSaveContext, XUniqueContext.

Name

XDeleteModifiermapEntry — delete an entry from an XModifierKeymap structure.

Synopsis

```
XModifierKeymap *XDeleteModifiermapEntry(modmap,
        keysym_entry, modifier)
    XModifierKeymap *modmap;
    KeyCode keysym_entry;
    int modifier;
```

Arguments

modmap   Specifies a pointer to an XModifierKeymap structure.

keysym_entry
                Specifies the keycode of the key to be deleted from modmap.

modifier   Specifies the modifier you no longer want mapped to the keycode specified in
                keysym_entry. This should be one of the constants: ShiftMapIndex,
                LockMapIndex, ControlMapIndex, Mod1MapIndex, Mod2Map-
                Index, Mod3MapIndex, Mod4MapIndex, or Mod5MapIndex.

Description

XDeleteModifiermapEntry returns an XModifierKeymap structure suitable for calling XSetModifierMapping, in which the specified keycode is deleted from the set of keycodes that is mapped to the specified modifier (like Shift or Control). XDelete-
ModifiermapEntry itself does not change the mapping.

This function is normally used by calling XGetModifierMapping to get a pointer to the
current XModifierKeymap structure for use as the modmap argument to XDelete-
ModifiermapEntry.

Note that the structure pointed to by modmap is freed by XDeleteModifiermapEntry. It
should not be freed or otherwise used by applications after this call.

For a description of the modifier map, see XSetModifierMapping.

Structures

```
typedef struct {
    int max_keypermod;      /* server's max number of keys per modifier */
    KeyCode *modifiermap;   /* an 8 by max_keypermod array of
                             * keycodes to be used as modifiers */
} XModifierKeymap;

#define ShiftMapIndex       0
#define LockMapIndex        1
#define ControlMapIndex     2
#define Mod1MapIndex        3
#define Mod2MapIndex        4
#define Mod3MapIndex        5
```

```
#define Mod4MapIndex        6
#define Mod5MapIndex        7
```

Related Commands

XFreeModifiermap, XGetKeyboardMapping, XGetModifierMapping,
XKeycodeToKeysym, XKeysymToKeycode, XKeysymToString, XLookupKeysym,
XLookupString, XNewModifiermap, XQueryKeymap, XRebindKeySym,
XRefreshKeyboardMapping, XSetModifierMapping, XStringToKeysym,
InsertModifiermapEntry.

Name

XDeleteProperty — delete a window property.

Synopsis

```
XDeleteProperty(display, w, property)
    Display *display;
    Window w;
    Atom property;
```

Arguments

display   Specifies a connection to an X server; returned from XOpenDisplay.

w   Specifies the ID of the window whose property you want to delete.

property   Specifies the atom of the property to be deleted.

Description

XDeleteProperty deletes a window property, so that it no longer contains any data. Its atom, specified by *property*, still exists after the call so that it can be used again later by any application to set the property once again. If the property was defined on the specified window, XDeleteProperty generates a PropertyNotify event.

See the introduction to properties in Volume One, Chapter 2, *X Concepts*, or more detailed information in Volume One, Chapter 10, *Interclient Communication*.

Errors

```
BadAtom
BadWindow
```

Related Commands

XChangeProperty, XGetAtomName, XGetFontProperty, XGetWindowProperty, XInternAtom, XListProperties, XRotateWindowProperties, XSetStandard-Properties.

XDestroyAssocTable

Name

XDestroyAssocTable — free the memory allocated for an association table.

Synopsis

```
XDestroyAssocTable(table)
    XAssocTable *table;
```

Arguments

table   Specifies the association table whose memory is to be freed.

Description

This function is provided for compatibility with X Version 10. To use it you must include the
file *<X11/X10.h>* and link with the library *-loldX*.

Using an XAssocTable after it has been destroyed will have unpredictable consequences.

For more information on association tables, see Volume One, Appendix B, *X10 Compatibility*.

Structures

```
typedef struct {
    XAssoc *buckets;          /* pointer to first bucket in array */
    int size;                 /* table size (number of buckets) */
} XAssocTable;
```

Related Commands

XCreateAssocTable, XDeleteAssoc, XLookUpAssoc, XMakeAssoc.

Name

XDestroyImage — deallocate memory associated with an image.

Synopsis

```
int XDestroyImage (ximage)
    XImage *ximage;
```

Arguments

ximage   Specifies a pointer to the image.

Description

XDestroyImage deallocates the memory associated with an XImage structure. This memory includes both the memory holding the XImage structure, and the memory holding the actual image data. (If the image data is statically allocated, the pointer to the data in the XImage structure must be set to zero before calling XDestroyImage.)

For more information on images, see Volume One, Chapter 6, *Drawing Graphics and Text*.

Related Commands

ImageByteOrder, XAddPixel, XCreateImage, XGetImage, XGetPixel, XGet-SubImage, XPutImage, XPutPixel, XSubImage.

XDestroyRegion

Name

XDestroyRegion — deallocate storage associated with a region.

Synopsis

```
XDestroyRegion(r)
    Region r;
```

Arguments

r   Specifies the region to be destroyed.

Description

XDestroyRegion frees the memory associated with a region and invalidates pointer r.

See Volume One, Chapter 6, *Drawing Graphics and Text*, for a description of regions.

Related Commands

XClipBox, XCreateRegion, XEmptyRegion, XEqualRegion, XIntersect-
Region, XOffsetRegion, XPointInRegion, XPolygonRegion, XRectInRegion,
XSetRegion, XShrinkRegion, XSubtractRegion, XUnionRectWithRegion,
XUnionRegion, XXorRegion.

XDestroySubwindows

Name

XDestroySubwindows — destroy all subwindows of a window.

Synopsis

```
XDestroySubwindows(display, w)
    Display *display;
    Window w;
```

Arguments

display   Specifies a connection to an X server; returned from XOpenDisplay.

w   Specifies the ID of the window whose subwindows are to be destroyed.

Description

This function destroys all descendants of the specified window (recursively), in bottom to top stacking order.

XDestroySubwindows generates exposure events on window w, if any mapped subwindows were actually destroyed. This is much more efficient than deleting many subwindows one at a time, since much of the work need only be performed once for all of the windows rather than for each window. It also saves multiple exposure events on the windows about to be destroyed. The subwindows should never again be referenced.

XCloseDisplay automatically destroys all windows that have been created by that client on the specified display (unless called after a fork system call).

Never call XDestroySubwindows with the window argument set to the root window! This will destroy all the applications on the screen, and if there is only one screen, often the server as well.

Errors

BadWindow

Related Commands

XCreateSimpleWindow, XCreateWindow, XDestroyWindow.

XDestroyWindow

Name

XDestroyWindow — unmap and destroy a window and all subwindows.

Synopsis

```
XDestroyWindow(display, window)
    Display *display;
    Window window;
```

Arguments

display   Specifies a connection to an X server; returned from XOpenDisplay.

window   Specifies the ID of the window to be destroyed.

Description

If *window* is mapped, an UnmapWindow request is performed automatically. The window and all inferiors (recursively) are then destroyed, and a DestroyNotify event is generated for each window. The ordering of the DestroyNotify events is such that for any given window, DestroyNotify is generated on all inferiors of the window before being generated on the window itself. The ordering among siblings and across subhierarchies is not otherwise constrained.

The windows should never again be referenced.

Destroying a mapped window will generate exposure events on other windows that were obscured by the windows being destroyed. XDestroyWindow may also generate EnterNotify events if *window* was mapped and contained the pointer.

No windows are destroyed if you try to destroy the root window.

Errors

BadWindow

Related Commands

XCreateSimpleWindow, XCreateWindow, XDestroySubwindows.

Name

XDisableAccessControl — allow access from any host.

Synopsis

```
XDisableAccessControl(display)
    Display *display;
```

Arguments

display   Specifies a connection to an X server; returned from XOpenDisplay.

Description

XDisableAccessControl instructs the server to allow access from clients on any host. This disables use of the host access list.

This routine can only be called from a client running on the same host as the server.

For more information on access control, see Volume One, Chapter 13, *Other Programming Techniques*.

Errors

BadAccess

Related Commands

XAddHost, XAddHosts, XEnableAccessControl, XListHosts, XRemoveHost, XRemoveHosts, XSetAccessControl.

Name

XDisplayKeycodes — obtain the range of legal keycodes for a server.

Synopsis

```
XDisplayKeycodes(display, min_keycodes, max_keycodes)
     Display *display;
     int *min_keycode, *max_keycode;  /* RETURN */
```

Arguments

display Specifies a connection to an X server; returned from XOpenDisplay.

min_keycode Returns the minimum keycode.

max_keycode Returns the maximum keycode.

Description

XDisplayKeycodes returns the *min_keycode* and *max_keycode* supported by the specified server. The minimum keycode returned is never less than 8, and the maximum keycode returned is never greater than 255. Not all keycodes in this range are required to have corresponding keys.

For more information, see Volume One, Chapter 9, *The Keyboard and Pointer*.

Related Commands

XKeycodeToKeysym, XKeysymToKeycode, XLookupString.

Name
XDisplayName — report the display name (when connection to a display fails).

Synopsis
```
char *XDisplayName(string)
    char *string;
```

Arguments
string   Specifies the character string.

Description
XDisplayName is normally used to report the name of the display the program attempted to open with XOpenDisplay. This is necessary because X error handling begins only after the connection to the server succeeds. If a NULL string is specified, XDisplayName looks in the DISPLAY environment variable and returns the display name that the user was requesting. Otherwise, XDisplayName returns its own argument. This makes it easier to report to the user precisely which server the program attempted to connect to.

For more information, see Volume One, Chapter 3, *Basic Window Program*.

Related Commands
XGetErrorDatabaseText, XGetErrorText, XSetAfterFunction, XSetError-
Handler, XSetIOErrorHandler, XSynchronize.

Name

XDraw — draw a polyline or curve between vertex list (from X10).

Synopsis

```
Status XDraw(display, drawable, gc, vlist, vcount)
    Display *display;
    Drawable drawable;
    GC gc;
    Vertex *vlist;
    int vcount;
```

Arguments

display   Specifies a connection to an X server; returned from XOpenDisplay.

drawable   Specifies the drawable.

gc   Specifies the graphics context.

vlist   Specifies a pointer to the list of vertices that indicates what to draw.

vcount   Specifies how many vertices are in vlist.

Description

This function is provided for compatibility with X Version 10. To use it you must include the file *<X11/X10.h>* and link with the library *-loldX*. Its performance is likely to be low.

XDraw draws an arbitrary polygon or curve. The figure drawn is defined by the specified list of vertices (vlist). The points are connected by lines as specified in the flags each the Vertex structure.

The Vertex structure contains an x,y coordinate and a bitmask called flags that specifies the drawing parameters.

The x and y elements of Vertex are the coordinates of the vertex that are relative to either the previous vertex (if VertexRelative is 1) or the upper-left inside corner of the drawable (if VertexRelative is 0). If VertexRelative is 0 the coordinates are said to be absolute. The first vertex must be an absolute vertex.

If the VertexDontDraw bit is 1, no line or curve is drawn from the previous vertex to this one. This is analogous to picking up the pen and moving to another place before drawing another line.

If the VertexCurved bit is 1, a spline algorithm is used to draw a smooth curve from the previous vertex, through this one, to the next vertex. Otherwise, a straight line is drawn from the previous vertex to this one. It makes sense to set VertexCurved to 1 only if a previous and next vertex are both defined (either explicitly in the array, or through the definition of a closed curve—see below.)

It is permissible for VertexDontDraw bits and VertexCurved bits to both be 1. This is useful if you want to define the previous point for the smooth curve, but you do not want an actual curve drawing to start until this point.

If `VertexStartClosed` bit is 1, then this point marks the beginning of a closed curve. This vertex must be followed later in the array by another vertex whose absolute coordinates are identical and which has `VertexEndClosed` bit of 1. The points in between form a cycle for the purpose of determining predecessor and successor vertices for the spline algorithm.

`XDraw` achieves the effects of the X10 `XDraw`, `XDrawDashed`, and `XDrawPatterned` functions.

`XDraw` uses the following graphics context components: `function`, `plane_mask`, `line_width`, `line_style`, `cap_style`, `join_style`, `fill_style`, `subwindow_mode`, `clip_x_origin`, `clip_y_origin`, and `clip_mask`. This function also uses these graphics context mode-dependent components: `foreground`, `background`, `tile`, `stipple`, `ts_x_origin`, `ts_y_origin`, `dash_offset`, and `dash_list`.

A `Status` of zero is returned on failure, and nonzero on success.

For more information, see Volume One, Appendix B, *X10 Compatibility*.

Structures

```
typedef struct _Vertex {
    short x,y;
    unsigned short flags;
} Vertex;

/* defined constants for use as flags */
#define VertexRelative      0x0001    /* else absolute */
#define VertexDontDraw      0x0002    /* else draw */
#define VertexCurved        0x0004    /* else straight */
#define VertexStartClosed   0x0008    /* else not */
#define VertexEndClosed     0x0010    /* else not */
```

Related Commands

`XClearArea`, `XClearWindow`, `XCopyArea`, `XCopyPlane`, `XDrawArc`, `XDrawArcs`, `XDrawFilled`, `XDrawLine`, `XDrawLines`, `XDrawPoint`, `XDrawPoints`, `XDrawRectangle`, `XDrawRectangles`, `XDrawSegments`, `XFillArc`, `XFillArcs`, `XFillPolygon`, `XFillRectangle`, `XFillRectangles`.

Name

XDrawArc — draw an arc fitting inside a rectangle.

Synopsis

```
XDrawArc(display, drawable, gc, x, y, width, height,
        angle1, angle2)
    Display *display;
    Drawable drawable;
    GC gc;
    int x, y;
    unsigned int width, height;
    int angle1, angle2;
```

Arguments

display   Specifies a connection to an X server; returned from XOpenDisplay.

drawable   Specifies the drawable.

gc   Specifies the graphics context.

x
y   Specify the x and y coordinates of the upper-left corner of the rectangle that contains the arc, relative to the origin of the specified drawable.

width
height   Specify the width and height in pixels of the major and minor axes of the arc.

angle1   Specifies the start of the arc relative to the three-o'clock position from the center. Angles are specified in 64ths of a degree (360 * 64 is a complete circle).

angle2   Specifies the end of the arc relative to the start of the arc. Angles are specified in 64ths of a degree (360 * 64 is a complete circle).

Description

XDrawArc draws a circular or elliptical arc. An arc is specified by a rectangle and two angles. The x and y coordinates are relative to the origin of the drawable, and define the upper-left corner of the rectangle. The center of the circle or ellipse is the center of the rectangle, and the major and minor axes are specified by the width and height, respectively. The angles are signed integers in 64ths of a degree, with positive values indicating counterclockwise motion and negative values indicating clockwise motion, truncated to a maximum of 360 degrees. The start of the arc is specified by *angle1* relative to the three-o'clock position from the center, and the path and extent of the arc is specified by *angle2* relative to the start of the arc.

By specifying one axis to be zero, a horizontal or vertical line is drawn (inefficiently).

Angles are computed based solely on the coordinate system and ignore the aspect ratio. In other words, if the bounding rectangle of the arc is not square and *angle1* is zero and *angle2* is (45x64), a point drawn from the center of the bounding box through the endpoint of the arc will not pass through the corner of the rectangle.

For any given arc, no pixel is drawn more than once, even if *angle2* is greater than *angle1* by more than 360 degrees.

XDrawArc uses these graphics context components: function, plane_mask, line_width, line_style, cap_style, join_style, fill_style, subwindow_ mode, clip_x_origin, clip_y_origin, and clip_mask. This function also uses these graphics context mode-dependent components: foreground, background, tile, stipple, ts_x_origin, ts_y_origin, dash_offset, and dash_list.

For more information, see Volume One, Chapter 6, *Drawing Graphics and Text.*

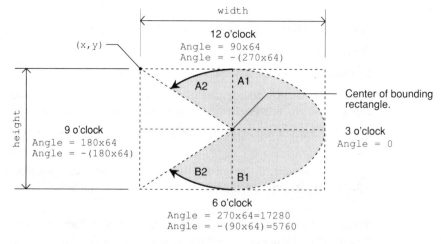

```
                              width
              |←──────────────────────────────→|
                        12 o'clock
                (x,y) ──   Angle = 90x64
                           Angle = -(270x64)

      ┌                                        ┐
      |                     ╲ A2 │ A1 ╱
      |                       ╲   │   ╱           Center of bounding
 h    |                    ───────┼──────         rectangle.
 e    |    9 o'clock         ╱    │    ╲
 i    |   Angle = 180x64   ─╱─────┼─────╲─      3 o'clock
 g    |   Angle = -(180x64) ╲     │     ╱        Angle = 0
 h    |                      ╲    │    ╱
 t    |                       ╲ B2│ B1╱
      └                                        ┘
                        6 o'clock
                   Angle = 270x64=17280
                   Angle = -(90x64)=5760
```

Example 1:
Arc from A1 to A2, Counterclockwise
A1 = 90 X 64
A2 = 45 X 64

Example 2:
Arc from B1 to B2, Clockwise
B1 = 270 X 64
B2 = -(45 X 64)

Errors

BadDrawable
BadGC
BadMatch

Related Commands

XClearArea, XClearWindow, XCopyArea, XCopyPlane, XDraw, XDrawArcs,
XDrawFilled, XDrawLine, XDrawLines, XDrawPoint, XDrawPoints, XDraw-
Rectangle, XDrawRectangles, XDrawSegments, XFillArc, XFillArcs, XFill-
Polygon, XFillRectangle, XFillRectangles.

Name

XDrawArcs — draw multiple arcs.

Synopsis

```
XDrawArcs(display, drawable, gc, arcs, narcs)
    Display *display;
    Drawable drawable;
    GC gc;
    XArc *arcs;
    int narcs;
```

Arguments

display   Specifies a connection to an X server; returned from XOpenDisplay.

drawable   Specifies the drawable.

gc   Specifies the graphics context.

arcs   Specifies a pointer to an array of arcs.

narcs   Specifies the number of arcs in the array.

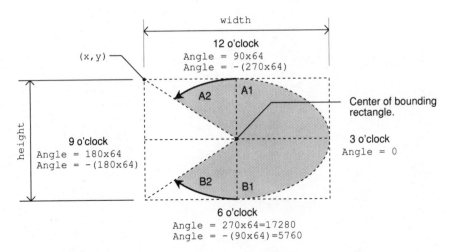

Description

This is the plural version of XDrawArc. See XDrawArc for details of drawing a single arc.

There is a limit to the number of arcs that can be drawn in a single call. It varies according to the server. To determine how many arcs you can draw in a single call, find out your server's maximum request size using XMaxRequestSize. Subtract 3 and divide by three: this is the maximum number of arcs you can draw in a single XDrawArcs call.

The arcs are drawn in the order listed in the *arcs* array.

By specifying one axis to be zero, a horizontal or vertical line can be drawn. Angles are computed based solely on the coordinate system, ignoring the aspect ratio.

For any given arc, no pixel is drawn more than once. If the last point in one arc coincides with the first point in the following arc, the two arcs will join correctly. If the first point in the first arc coincides with the last point in the last arc, the two arcs will join correctly. If two arcs join correctly and if line_width is greater than 0 and the arcs intersect, no pixel is drawn more than once. Otherwise, the intersecting pixels of intersecting arcs are drawn multiple times. Specifying an arc with one endpoint and a clockwise extent draws the same pixels as specifying the other endpoint and an equivalent counterclockwise extent, except as it affects joins.

XDrawArcs uses these graphics context components: function, plane_mask, line_width, line_style, cap_style, join_style, fill_style, subwindow_ mode, clip_x_origin, clip_y_origin, and clip_mask. This function also uses these graphics context mode-dependent components: foreground, background, tile, stipple, ts_x_origin, ts_y_origin, dash_offset, and dash_list.

The following is a technical explanation of the points drawn by XDrawArcs. For an arc specified as [x, y, width, height, angle1, angle2], the origin of the major and minor axes is at [x+(width/2), y+(height/2)], and the infinitely thin path describing the entire circle or ellipse intersects the horizontal axis at [x, y+(height/2)] and [x+width, y+(height/2)] and intersects the vertical axis at [x+(width/2),y] and [x+(width/2), y+height]. These coordinates can be fractional. That is, they are not truncated to discrete coordinates. The path should be defined by the ideal mathematical path. For a wide line with line width line_width, the bounding outlines for filling are given by the infinitely thin paths describing the arcs:

```
[x+dx/2, y+dy/2, width-dx, height-dy, angle1, angle2]
```

and

```
[x-line_width/2, y-line_width/2, width+line_width, height+line_width,
angle1, angle2]
```

where

```
dx=min(line_width,width)
dy=min(line_width,height)
```

If (height != width) the angles must be specified in the effectively skewed coordinate system of the ellipse (for a circle, the angles and coordinate systems are identical). The relationship between these angles and angles expressed in the normal coordinate system of the screen (as measured with a protractor) is as follows:

```
skewed-angle = atan(tan(normal-angle) * width/height) + adjust
```

The skewed-angle and normal-angle are expressed in radians (rather than in 64ths of a degree) in the range [0,2*PI], and where atan returns a value in the range [-PI/2,PI/2], and where adjust is:

```
0          for normal-angle in the range [0,PI/2]
PI         for normal-angle in the range [PI/2,(3*PI)/2]
2*PI       for normal-angle in the range [(3*PI)/2,2*PI]
```

For more information, see Volume One, Chapter 6, *Drawing Graphics and Text*.

Structures

```
typedef struct {
    short x, y;
    unsigned short width, height;
    short angle1, angle2;            /*  Start and end of arc, in */
                                     /*  64ths of degrees */
} XArc;
```

Errors

```
BadDrawable
BadGC
BadMatch
```

Related Commands

XClearArea, XClearWindow, XCopyArea, XCopyPlane, XDraw, XDrawArc, XDrawFilled, XDrawLine, XDrawLines, XDrawPoint, XDrawPoints, XDraw-Rectangle, XDrawRectangles, XDrawSegments, XFillArc, XFillArcs, XFill-Polygon, XFillRectangle, XFillRectangles.

XDrawFilled

Name

XDrawFilled — draw a filled polygon or curve from vertex list (from X10).

Synopsis

```
Status XDrawFilled(display, drawable, gc, vlist, vcount)
    Display *display;
    Drawable drawable;
    GC gc;
    Vertex *vlist;
    int vcount;
```

Arguments

display   Specifies a connection to an X server; returned from XOpenDisplay.

drawable   Specifies the drawable.

gc   Specifies the graphics context.

vlist   Specifies a pointer to the list of vertices.

vcount   Specifies how many vertices are in vlist.

Description

This function is provided for compatibility with X Version 10. To use it you must include the file *<X11/X10.h>* and link with the library *-loldX*. XDrawFilled achieves the effects of the X Version 10 XDrawTiled and XDrawFilled functions.

XDrawFilled draws arbitrary polygons or curves, according to the same rules as XDraw, and then fills them.

XDrawFilled uses the following graphics context components: function, plane_mask, line_width, line_style, cap_style, join_style, fill_style, subwindow_mode, clip_x_origin, clip_y_origin, and clip_mask. This function also uses these graphics context mode-dependent components: foreground, background, tile, stipple, ts_x_origin, ts_y_origin, dash_offset, dash_list, fill_style and fill_rule.

XDrawFilled returns a Status of zero on failure, and nonzero on success.

For more information, see Volume One, Appendix B, *X10 Compatibility*.

Related Commands

XClearArea, XClearWindow, XCopyArea, XCopyPlane, XDraw, XDrawArc, XDrawArcs, XDrawLine, XDrawLines, XDrawPoint, XDrawPoints, XDraw-Rectangle, XDrawRectangles, XDrawSegments, XFillArc, XFillArcs, XFill-Polygon, XFillRectangle, XFillRectangles.

Name

XDrawImageString — draw 8-bit image text characters.

Synopsis

```
XDrawImageString(display, drawable, gc, x, y, string, length)
    Display *display;
    Drawable drawable;
    GC gc;
    int x, y;
    char *string;
    int length;
```

Arguments

display   Specifies a connection to an X server; returned from XOpenDisplay.

drawable   Specifies the drawable.

gc   Specifies the graphics context.

x   Specify the x and y coordinates of the baseline starting position for the image

y   text character, relative to the origin of the specified drawable.

string   Specifies the character string.

length   Specifies the number of characters in the string argument.

Description

XDrawImageString draws a string, but unlike XDrawString it draws both the foreground and the background of the characters. It draws the characters in the foreground and fills the bounding box with the background.

XDrawImageString uses these graphics context components: plane_mask, foreground, background, font, subwindow_mode, clip_x_origin, clip_y_origin, and clip_mask. The function and fill_style defined in gc are ignored; the effective function is GXcopy and the effective fill_style is FillSolid.

XDrawImageString first fills a destination rectangle with the background pixel defined in gc, and then paints the text with the foreground pixel. The upper-left corner of the filled rectangle is at [x, y - font_ascent], the width is overall->width and the height is ascent + descent, where overall->width, ascent, and descent are as would be returned by XQueryTextExtents using gc and string.

For more information, see Volume One, Chapter 6, *Drawing Graphics and Text*, and Chapter 5, *The Graphics Context*.

Errors

BadDrawable
BadGC
BadMatch

Related Commands

XDrawImageString16, XDrawString, XDrawString16, XDrawText, XDraw-
Text16, XQueryTextExtents, XQueryTextExtents16, XTextExtents, XText-
Extents16, XTextWidth, XTextWidth16.

XDrawImageString16

Name

XDrawImageString16 — draw 16-bit image text characters.

Synopsis

```
XDrawImageString16(display, drawable, gc, x, y, string, length)
    Display *display;
    Drawable drawable;
    GC gc;
    int x, y;
    XChar2b *string;
    int length;
```

Arguments

display   Specifies a connection to an X server; returned from XOpenDisplay.

drawable   Specifies the drawable.

gc   Specifies the graphics context.

x   Specify the x and y coordinates of the baseline starting position for the image
y   text character, relative to the origin of the specified drawable.

string   Specifies the character string.

length   Specifies the number of characters in the string argument.

Description

XDrawImageString16 draws a string, but unlike XDrawString16 it draws both the foreground and the background of the characters. It draws the characters in the foreground and fills the bounding box with the background.

XDrawImageString16 uses these graphics context components: plane_mask, foreground, background, font, subwindow_mode, clip_x_origin, clip_y_origin, and clip_mask. The function and fill_style defined in gc are ignored; the effective function is GXcopy and the effective fill_style is FillSolid.

XDrawImageString16 first fills a destination rectangle with the background pixel defined in gc, and then paints the text with the foreground pixel. The upper-left corner of the filled rectangle is at [x, y - font_ascent], the width is overall->width and the height is ascent + descent, where overall->width, ascent, and descent are as would be returned by XQueryTextExtents16 using gc and string.

For more information, see Volume One, Chapter 6, *Drawing Graphics and Text*, and Chapter 5, *The Graphics Context*.

Structures

```
typedef struct {
    unsigned char byte1;
    unsigned char byte2;
} XChar2b;
```

Errors
    BadDrawable
    BadGC
    BadMatch

Related Commands

    XDrawImageString, XDrawString, XDrawString16, XDrawText, XDrawText16,
    XQueryTextExtents, XQueryTextExtents16, XTextExtents, XText-
    Extents16, XTextWidth, XTextWidth16.

XDrawLine

—Xlib – Drawing Primitives—

Name

XDrawLine — draw a line between two points.

Synopsis

```
XDrawLine(display, drawable, gc, x1, y1, x2, y2)
    Display *display;
    Drawable drawable;
    GC gc;
    int x1, y1, x2, y2;
```

Arguments

display   Specifies a connection to an X server; returned from XOpenDisplay.

drawable   Specifies the drawable.

gc   Specifies the graphics context.

x1   Specify the coordinates of the endpoints of the line relative to the drawable
y1   origin. XLine connects point (x1, y1) to point (x2, y2).
x2
y2

Description

XDrawLine uses the components of the specified graphics context to draw a line between two points in the specified drawable. No pixel is drawn more than once.

XDrawLine uses these graphics context components: function, plane_mask, line_width, line_style, cap_style, fill_style, subwindow_mode, clip_x_origin, clip_y_origin, and clip_mask. XDrawLine also uses these graphics context mode-dependent components: foreground, background, tile, stipple, ts_x_origin, ts_y_origin, dash_offset, and dash_list.

For more information, see Volume One, Chapter 6, *Drawing Graphics and Text*, and Chapter 5, *The Graphics Context*.

Errors

BadDrawable Specified drawable is invalid.

BadGC   Specified GC is invalid, or does not match the depth of drawable.

BadMatch   Specified drawable is an InputOnly window.

Related Commands

XClearArea, XClearWindow, XCopyArea, XCopyPlane, XDraw, XDrawArc, XDrawArcs, XDrawFilled, XDrawLines, XDrawPoint, XDrawPoints, XDrawRectangle, XDrawRectangles, XDrawSegments, XFillArc, XFillArcs, XFillPolygon, XFillRectangle, XFillRectangles.

154		Xlib Reference Manual

XDrawLines

Name

XDrawLines — draw multiple connected lines.

Synopsis

```
XDrawLines (display, drawable, gc, points, npoints, mode)
    Display *display;
    Drawable drawable;
    GC gc;
    XPoint *points;
    int npoints;
    int mode;
```

Arguments

display	Specifies a connection to an X server; returned from XOpenDisplay.
drawable	Specifies the drawable.
gc	Specifies the graphics context.
points	Specifies a pointer to an array of points.
npoints	Specifies the number of points in the array.
mode	Specifies the coordinate mode. Pass either CoordModeOrigin or CoordModePrevious.

Description

XDrawLines draws a series of lines joined end-to-end.

It draws lines connecting each point in the list (points array) to the next point in the list. The lines are drawn in the order listed in the points array. For any given line, no pixel is drawn more than once. If thin (zero line width) lines intersect, pixels will be drawn multiple times. If the first and last points coincide, the first and last lines will join correctly. If wide lines intersect, the intersecting pixels are drawn only once, as though the entire multiline request were a single filled shape.

There is a limit to the number of lines that can be drawn in a single call, that varies according to the server. To determine how many lines you can draw in a single call, you find out your server's maximum request size using XMaxRequestSize. Subtract 3 and divide by two, and this is the maximum number of lines you can draw in a single XDrawLines call.

The mode argument may have two values:

- CoordModeOrigin indicates that all points are relative to the drawable's origin.

- CoordModePrevious indicates that all points after the first are relative to the previous point. (The first point is always relative to the drawable's origin.)

XDrawLines uses the following components of the specified graphics context to draw multiple connected lines in the specified drawable: function, plane_mask, line_width, line_style, cap_style, join_style, fill_style, subwindow_mode, clip_x_origin, clip_y_ origin, and clip_mask. This function also uses these graphics context mode-dependent components: foreground, background, tile, stipple, ts_x_origin, ts_y_origin, dash_offset, and dash_list.

For more information, see Volume One, Chapter 6, *Drawing Graphics and Text*, and Chapter 5, *The Graphics Context*.

Structures
```
typedef struct {
    short x, y;
} XPoint;
```

Errors

BadDrawable	Specified drawable is invalid.
BadGC	Specified GC is invalid, or does not match the depth of drawable.
BadMatch	Specified drawable is an InputOnly window.
BadValue	Invalid coordinate_mode.

Related Commands

XClearArea, XClearWindow, XCopyArea, XCopyPlane, XDraw, XDrawArc, XDrawArcs, XDrawFilled, XDrawLine, XDrawPoint, XDrawPoints, XDraw-Rectangle, XDrawRectangles, XDrawSegments, XFillArc, XFillArcs, XFill-Polygon, XFillRectangle, XFillRectangles.

Name

XDrawPoint — draw a point.

Synopsis

```
XDrawPoint(display, drawable, gc, x, y)
    Display *display;
    Drawable drawable;
    GC gc;
    int x, y;
```

Arguments

display   Specifies a connection to an X server; returned from XOpenDisplay.

drawable   Specifies the drawable.

gc   Specifies the graphics context.

x   Specify the x and y coordinates of the point, relative to the origin of the draw-
y   able.

Description

XDrawPoint draws a single point into the specified drawable. XDrawPoint uses these graphics context components: function, plane_mask, foreground, subwindow_mode, clip_x_origin, clip_y_origin, and clip_mask. Use XDrawPoints to draw multiple points.

For more information, see Volume One, Chapter 6, *Drawing Graphics and Text*, and Chapter 5, *The Graphics Context*.

Errors

BadDrawable
BadGC
BadMatch

Related Commands

XClearArea, XClearWindow, XCopyArea, XCopyPlane, XDraw, XDrawArc, XDrawArcs, XDrawFilled, XDrawLine, XDrawLines, XDrawPoints, XDraw-Rectangle, XDrawRectangles, XDrawSegments, XFillArc, XFillArcs, XFill-Polygon, XFillRectangle, XFillRectangles.

XDrawPoints

Name

XDrawPoints — draw multiple points.

Synopsis

```
XDrawPoints(display, drawable, gc, points, npoints, mode)
    Display *display;
    Drawable drawable;
    GC gc;
    XPoint *points;
    int npoints;
    int mode;
```

Arguments

display	Specifies a connection to an X server; returned from XOpenDisplay.
drawable	Specifies the drawable.
gc	Specifies the graphics context.
points	Specifies a pointer to an array of XPoint structures containing the positions of the points.
npoints	Specifies the number of points to be drawn.
mode	Specifies the coordinate mode. CoordModeOrigin treats all coordinates as relative to the origin, while CoordModePrevious treats all coordinates after the first as relative to the previous point, while the first is still relative to the origin.

Description

XDrawPoints draws one or more points into the specified drawable.

There is a limit to the number of points that can be drawn in a single call, that varies according to the server. To determine how many points you can draw in a single call, you find out your server's maximum request size using XMaxRequestSize. Subtract 3 and this is the maximum number of points you can draw in a single XDrawPoints call.

XDrawPoints uses these graphics context components: function, plane_mask, foreground, subwindow_mode, clip_x_origin, clip_y_origin, and clip_mask.

For more information, see Volume One, Chapter 6, *Drawing Graphics and Text*, and Chapter 5, *The Graphics Context*.

Structures

```
typedef struct {
    short x, y;
} XPoint;
```

Errors
    BadDrawable
    BadGC
    BadMatch
    BadValue

Related Commands
    XClearArea, XClearWindow, XCopyArea, XCopyPlane, XDraw, XDrawArc,
    XDrawArcs, XDrawFilled, XDrawLine, XDrawLines, XDrawPoints, XDraw-
    Rectangle, XDrawRectangles, XDrawSegments, XFillArc, XFillArcs, XFill-
    Polygon, XFillRectangle, XFillRectangles.

XDrawRectangle

Name

XDrawRectangle — draw an outline of a rectangle.

Synopsis

```
XDrawRectangle(display, drawable, gc, x, y, width, height)
    Display *display;
    Drawable drawable;
    GC gc;
    int x, y;
    unsigned int width, height;
```

Arguments

display	Specifies a connection to an X server; returned from XOpenDisplay.
drawable	Specifies the drawable.
gc	Specifies the graphics context.
x y	Specify the x and y coordinates of the upper-left corner of the rectangle, relative to the drawable's origin.
width height	Specify the width and height in pixels. These dimensions define the outline of the rectangle.

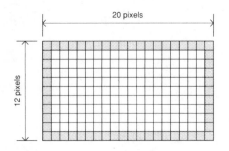
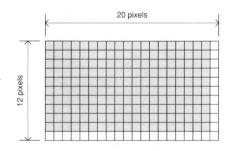

XDrawRectangle (display, drawable, gc, 0, 0, 19, 11);   XFillRectangle (display, drawable, gc, 0, 0, 19, 11);

Description

XDrawRectangle draws the outline of the rectangle by using the *x* and *y* coordinates, *width* and *height*, and graphics context you specify. Specifically, XDrawRectangle uses these graphics context components: function, plane_mask, line_width, line_style, cap_style, join_style, fill_style, subwindow_mode, clip_x_origin, clip_y_origin, and clip_mask. This function also uses these graphics context mode-dependent components: foreground, background, tile, stipple, ts_x_origin, ts_y_origin, dash_offset, and dash_list.

For the specified rectangle, no pixel is drawn more than once.

For more information, see Volume One, Chapter 6, *Drawing Graphics and Text*, and Chapter 5, *The Graphics Context*.

Structure

```
typedef struct {
    short x, y;
    unsigned short width, height;
} XRectangle;
```

Errors

BadDrawable
BadGC
BadMatch

Related Commands

XClearArea, XClearWindow, XCopyArea, XCopyPlane, XDraw, XDrawArc,
XDrawArcs, XDrawFilled, XDrawLine, XDrawLines, XDrawPoint, XDrawPoints,
XDrawRectangles, XDrawSegments, XFillArc, XFillArcs, XFillPolygon,
XFillRectangle, XFillRectangles.

XDrawRectangles

Name

XDrawRectangles — draw the outlines of multiple rectangles.

Synopsis

```
XDrawRectangles(display, drawable, gc, rectangles, nrectangles)
    Display *display;
    Drawable drawable;
    GC gc;
    XRectangle rectangles[];
    int nrectangles;
```

Arguments

display   Specifies a connection to an X server; returned from XOpenDisplay.

drawable   Specifies the drawable.

gc   Specifies the graphics context.

rectangles   Specifies a pointer to an array of rectangles containing position and size information.

nrectangles   Specifies the number of rectangles in the array.

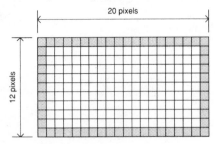

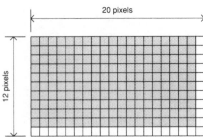

XDrawRectangle (display, drawable, gc, 0, 0, 19, 11);   XFillRectangle (display, drawable, gc, 0, 0, 19, 11);

Description

XDrawRectangles draws the outlines of the specified rectangles by using the position and size values in the array of rectangles. The x and y coordinates of each rectangle are relative to the drawable's origin, and define the upper-left corner of the rectangle.

The rectangles are drawn in the order listed. For any given rectangle, no pixel is drawn more than once. If rectangles intersect, pixels are drawn multiple times.

There is a limit to the number of rectangles that can be drawn in a single call. It varies according to the server. To determine how many rectangles you can draw in a single call, find out your server's maximum request size using XMaxRequestSize. Subtract 3 and divide by two. This is the maximum number of rectangles you can draw in a single XDraw-Rectangles call.

This function uses these graphics context components: function, plane_mask, line_width, line_style, cap_style, join_style, fill_style, subwin-dow_mode, clip_x_origin, clip_y_origin, and clip_mask. XDrawRectangles also uses these graphics context mode-dependent components: foreground, background, tile, stipple, ts_x_origin, ts_y_origin, dash_offset, and dash_list.

For more information, see Volume One, Chapter 6, *Drawing Graphics and Text*, and Chapter 5, *The Graphics Context*.

Structures
```
typedef struct {
    short x, y;
    unsigned short width, height;
} XRectangle;
```

Errors
BadDrawable
BadGC
BadMatch

Related Commands
XClearArea, XClearWindow, XCopyArea, XCopyPlane, XDraw, XDrawArc, XDrawArcs, XDrawFilled, XDrawLine, XDrawLines, XDrawPoint, XDrawPoints, XDrawRectangle, XDrawSegments, XFillArc, XFillArcs, XFillPolygon, XFillRectangle, XFillRectangles.

Name

XDrawSegments — draw multiple disjoint lines.

Synopsis

```
XDrawSegments(display, drawable, gc, segments, nsegments)
    Display *display;
    Drawable drawable;
    GC gc;
    XSegment *segments;
    int nsegments;
```

Arguments

display   Specifies a connection to an X server; returned from XOpenDisplay.

drawable   Specifies the drawable.

gc   Specifies the graphics context.

segments   Specifies a pointer to an array of line segments.

nsegments   Specifies the number of segments in the array.

Description

XDrawSegments draws multiple line segments into the specified drawable. Each line is specified by a pair of points, so the line may be connected or disjoint.

For each segment, XDrawSegments draws a line between (x1, y1) and (x2, y2). The lines are drawn in the order listed in segments. For any given line, no pixel is drawn more than once. If lines intersect, pixels will be drawn multiple times. The lines will be drawn separately, without regard to the join_style.

There is a limit to the number of segments that can be drawn in a single call. It varies according to the server. To determine how many segments you can draw in a single call, find out your server's maximum request size using XMaxRequestSize. Subtract 3 and divide by two. This is the maximum number of segments you can draw in a single XDrawSegments call.

XDrawSegments uses these graphics context components: function, plane_mask, line_width, line_style, cap_style, fill_style, subwindow_mode, clip_x_origin, clip_y_origin, and clip_mask. XDrawSegments also uses these graphics context mode-dependent components: foreground, background, tile, stipple, ts_x_origin, ts_y_origin, dash_offset, and dash_list.

For more information, see Volume One, Chapter 6, *Drawing Graphics and Text*, and Chapter 5, *The Graphics Context*.

Structures

```
typedef struct {
    short x1, y1, x2, y2;
} XSegment;
```

Errors

BadDrawable   Specified drawable is invalid.

BadGC   Specified GC is invalid, or does not match the depth of drawable.

BadMatch   Specified *drawable* is an InputOnly window.

Related Commands

XClearArea, XClearWindow, XCopyArea, XCopyPlane, XDraw, XDrawArc, XDrawArcs, XDrawFilled, XDrawLine, XDrawLines, XDrawPoint, XDrawPoints, XDrawRectangle, XDrawRectangles, XFillArc, XFillArcs, XFillPolygon, XFillRectangle, XFillRectangles.

Name

XDrawString — draw an 8-bit text string, foreground only.

Synopsis

```
XDrawString(display, drawable, gc, x, y, string, length)
    Display *display;
    Drawable drawable;
    GC gc;
    int x, y;
    char *string;
    int length;
```

Arguments

display   Specifies a connection to an X server; returned from XOpenDisplay.

drawable   Specifies the drawable.

gc   Specifies the graphics context.

x
y   Specify the x and y coordinates of the baseline starting position for the character, relative to the origin of the specified drawable.

string   Specifies the character string.

length   Specifies the number of characters in string.

Description

XDrawString draws the given string into a drawable using the foreground only to draw set bits in the font. It does not affect any other pixels in the bounding box for each character.

The y coordinate defines the baseline row of pixels while the x coordinate is the point from which lbearing, rbearing, and width are measured.

XDrawString uses these graphics context components: function, plane_mask, fill_style, font, subwindow_mode, clip_x_origin, clip_y_origin, and clip_mask. This function also uses these graphics context mode-dependent components: foreground, tile, stipple, ts_x_origin, and ts_y_origin. Each character image, as defined by the font in gc, is treated as an additional mask for a fill operation on the drawable.

For more information, see Volume One, Chapter 6, *Drawing Graphics and Text*, and Chapter 5, *The Graphics Context*.

Errors

BadDrawable
BadFont
BadGC
BadMatch

Related Commands

XDrawImageString, XDrawImageString16, XDrawString16, XDrawText,
XDrawText16, XQueryTextExtents, XQueryTextExtents16, XTextExtents,
XTextExtents16, XTextWidth, XTextWidth16.

Name

XDrawString16 — draw two-byte text strings.

Synopsis

```
XDrawString16(display, drawable, gc, x, y, string, length)
    Display *display;
    Drawable drawable;
    GC gc;
    int x, y;
    XChar2b *string;
    int length;
```

Arguments

display   Specifies a connection to an X server; returned from XOpenDisplay.

drawable   Specifies the drawable.

gc   Specifies the graphics context.

x   Specify the x and y coordinates of the baseline starting position for the char-
y   acter, relative to the origin of the specified drawable.

string   Specifies the character string. Characters are two bytes wide.

length   Specifies the number of characters in string.

Description

XDrawString16 draws a string in the foreground pixel value without drawing the surround-
ing pixels.

The y coordinate defines the baseline row of pixels while the x coordinate is the point from
which lbearing, rbearing, and width are measured. For more information on text
placement, see Volume One, Chapter 6, *Drawing Graphics and Text*.

XDrawString16 uses these graphics context components: function, plane_mask,
fill_style, font, subwindow_mode, clip_x_origin, clip_y_origin, and
clip_mask. This function also uses these graphics context mode-dependent components:
foreground, tile, stipple, ts_x_origin, and ts_y_origin. Each character
image, as defined by the font in gc, is treated as an additional mask for a fill operation on the
drawable.

For more information, see Volume One, Chapter 6, *Drawing Graphics and Text*, and Chapter 5,
The Graphics Context.

Structures

```
typedef struct {
    unsigned char byte1;
    unsigned char byte2;
} XChar2b;
```

Errors

    BadDrawable
    BadFont
    BadGC
    BadMatch

Related Commands

XDrawImageString, XDrawImageString16, XDrawString, XDrawText, XDraw-
Text16, XQueryTextExtents, XQueryTextExtents16, XTextExtents, XText-
Extents16, XTextWidth, XTextWidth16.

XDrawText

Name

XDrawText — draw 8-bit polytext strings.

Synopsis

```
XDrawText(display, drawable, gc, x, y, items, nitems)
    Display *display;
    Drawable drawable;
    GC gc;
    int x, y;
    XTextItem *items;
    int nitems;
```

Arguments

display	Specifies a connection to an X server; returned from XOpenDisplay.
drawable	Specifies the drawable.
gc	Specifies the graphics context.
x y	Specify the x and y coordinates of the baseline starting position for the initial string, relative to the origin of the specified drawable.
items	Specifies a pointer to an array of text items.
nitems	Specifies the number of text items in the items array.

Description

XDrawText is capable of drawing multiple strings on the same horizontal line and changing fonts between strings. Each XTextItem structure contains a string, the number of characters in the string, the delta offset from the starting position for the string, and the font. Each text item is processed in turn. The font in each XTextItem is stored in the specified GC and used for subsequent text. If the XTextItem.font is None, the font in the GC is used for drawing and is not changed. Switching between fonts with different drawing directions is permitted.

The delta in each XTextItem specifies the change in horizontal position before the string is drawn. The delta is always added to the character origin and is not dependent on the draw direction of the font. For example, if x = 40, y = 20, and items[0].delta = 8, the string specified by items[0].chars would be drawn starting at x = 48, y = 20. The delta for the second string begins at the rbearing of the last character in the first string. A negative delta would tend to overlay subsequent strings on the end of the previous string.

Only the pixels selected in the font are drawn (the background member of the GC is not used to fill the bounding box).

There is a limit to the number and size of strings that can be drawn in a single call, that varies according to the server. To determine how much text you can draw in a single call, you find out your server's maximum request size using XMaxRequestSize. Subtract four, and then subtract ((strlen(string) + 2) / 4) for each string. This is the maximum amount of text you can draw in a single XDrawText call.

170   Xlib Reference Manual

XDrawText uses the following elements in the specified GC: function, plane_mask, fill_style, font, subwindow_mode, clip_x_origin, clip_y_origin, and clip_mask. This function also uses these graphics context mode-dependent components: foreground, tile, stipple, ts_x_origin, and ts_y_origin.

For more information, see Volume One, Chapter 6, *Drawing Graphics and Text*, and Chapter 5, *The Graphics Context*.

Structures

```
typedef struct {
    char *chars;            /* pointer to string */
    int nchars;             /* number of characters */
    int delta;              /* delta between strings */
    Font font;              /* font to print it in, None don't change */
} XTextItem;
```

Errors

BadDrawable
BadFont
BadGC
BadMatch

Related Commands

XDrawImageString, XDrawImageString16, XDrawString, XDrawString16, XDrawText16, XQueryTextExtents, XQueryTextExtents16, XTextExtents, XTextExtents16, XTextWidth, XTextWidth16.

Name

XDrawText16 — draw 16-bit polytext strings.

Synopsis

```
XDrawText16(display, drawable, gc, x, y, items, nitems)
    Display *display;
    Drawable drawable;
    GC gc;
    int x, y;
    XTextItem16 *items;
    int nitems;
```

Arguments

display   Specifies a connection to an X server; returned from XOpenDisplay.

drawable   Specifies the drawable.

gc   Specifies the graphics context.

x   Specify the x and y coordinates of the baseline starting position for the initial
y   string, relative to the origin of the specified drawable.

items   Specifies a pointer to an array of text items using two-byte characters.

nitems   Specifies the number of text items in the array.

Description

XDrawText16 is capable of drawing multiple strings on the same horizontal line and changing fonts between strings. Each XTextItem structure contains a string, the number of characters in the string, the delta offset from the starting position for the string, and the font. Each
text item is processed in turn. The font in each XTextItem is stored in the specified GC and
used for subsequent text. If the XTextItem16.font is None, the font in the GC is used for
drawing and is not changed. Switching between fonts with different drawing directions is permitted.

The delta in each XTextItem specifies the change in horizontal position before the string is
drawn. The delta is always added to the character origin and is not dependent on the drawing
direction of the font. For example, if x = 40, y = 20, and items[0].delta = 8, the
string specified by items[0].chars would be drawn starting at x = 48, y = 20. The
delta for the second string begins at the rbearing of the last character in the first string. A
negative delta would tend to overlay subsequent strings on the end of the previous string.

Only the pixels selected in the font are drawn (the background member of the GC is not used
to fill the bounding box).

There is a limit to the number and size of strings that can be drawn in a single call, that varies
according to the server. To determine how much text you can draw in a single call, you find out
your server's maximum request size using XMaxRequestSize. Subtract four, and then subtract ((strlen(string) + 2) / 4) for each string. This is the maximum amount of
text you can draw in a single XDrawText16 call.

XDrawText16 uses the following elements in the specified GC: function, plane_mask, fill_style, font, subwindow_mode, clip_x_origin, clip_y_origin, and clip_mask. This function also uses these graphics context mode-dependent components: foreground, tile, stipple, ts_x_origin, and ts_y_origin.

Note that the chars member of the XTextItem16 structure is of type XChar2b, rather than of type char as it is in the XTextItem structure. For fonts defined with linear indexing rather than two-byte matrix indexing, the X server will interpret each member of the XChar2b structure as a 16-bit number that has been transmitted most significant byte first. In other words, the byte1 member of the XChar2b structure is taken as the most significant byte.

For more information, see Volume One, Chapter 6, *Drawing Graphics and Text*, and Chapter 5, *The Graphics Context*.

Structures
```
typedef struct {
    XChar2b *chars;        /* 2 byte characters */
    int nchars;            /* number of characters */
    int delta;             /* delta between strings */
    Font font;             /* font to print it in, None don't change */
} XTextItem16;

typedef struct {           /* normal 16 bit characters are two bytes */
    unsigned char byte1;
    unsigned char byte2;
} XChar2b;
```

Errors
```
BadDrawable
BadFont
BadGC
BadMatch
```

Related Commands
XDrawImageString, XDrawImageString16, XDrawString, XDrawString16, XDrawText, XQueryTextExtents, XQueryTextExtents16, XTextExtents, XTextExtents16, XTextWidth, XTextWidth16.

XEmptyRegion

Name

XEmptyRegion — determine if a region is empty.

Synopsis

```
Bool XEmptyRegion(r)
    Region r;
```

Arguments

r   Specifies the region to be checked.

Description

XEmptyRegion will return True if the specified region is empty, or False otherwise.

Structures

Region is a pointer to an opaque structure type.

Related Commands

XClipBox, XCreateRegion, XDestroyRegion, XEqualRegion, XIntersect-
Region, XOffsetRegion, XPointInRegion, XPolygonRegion, XRectInRegion,
XSetRegion, XShrinkRegion, XSubtractRegion, XUnionRectWithRegion,
XUnionRegion, XXorRegion.

XEnableAccessControl

Name

XEnableAccessControl — use access control list to allow or deny connection requests.

Synopsis

```
XEnableAccessControl(display)
    Display *display;
```

Arguments

display   Specifies a connection to an X server; returned from XOpenDisplay.

Description

XEnableAccessControl instructs the server to use the host access list to determine whether access should be granted to clients seeking a connection with the server.

By default, the host access list is used. If access has not been disabled with XDisable-AccessControl or XSetAccessControl, this routine does nothing.

This routine can only be called by clients running on the same host as the server.

For more information, see Volume One, Chapter 13, *Other Programming Techniques*.

Errors

BadAccess

Related Commands

XAddHost, XAddHosts, XDisableAccessControl, XListHosts, XRemoveHost, XRemoveHosts, XSetAccessControl.

XEqualRegion

Name

XEqualRegion — determine if two regions have the same size, offset, and shape.

Synopsis

```
Bool XEqualRegion(r1, r2)
    Region r1, r2;
```

Arguments

r1
r2   Specify the two regions you want to compare.

Description

XEqualRegion returns True if the two regions are identical; i.e., they have the same offset, size and shape, or False otherwise.

Regions are located using an offset from a point (the *region origin*) which is common to all regions. It is up to the application to interpret the location of the region relative to a drawable.

For more information, see Volume One, Chapter 6, *Drawing Graphics and Text*.

Structures

Region is a pointer to an opaque structure type.

Related Commands

XClipBox, XCreateRegion, XDestroyRegion, XEmptyRegion, XIntersect-Region, XOffsetRegion, XPointInRegion, XPolygonRegion, XRectInRegion, XSetRegion, XShrinkRegion, XSubtractRegion, XUnionRectWithRegion, XUnionRegion, XXorRegion.

Name

XEventsQueued — check the number of events in the event queue.

Synopsis

```
int XEventsQueued(display, mode)
    Display *display;
    int mode;
```

Arguments

display   Specifies a connection to a Display structure, returned from XOpen-Display.

mode   Specifies whether the request buffer is flushed if there are no events in Xlib's queue. You can specify one of these constants: QueuedAlready, QueuedAfterFlush, QueuedAfterReading.

Description

XEventsQueued checks whether events are queued. If there are events in Xlib's queue, the routine returns immediately to the calling routine. Its return value is the number of events regardless of mode.

mode specifies what happens if no events are found on Xlib's queue.

- If mode is QueuedAlready, and there are no events in the queue, XEvents-Queued returns zero (it does not flush the request buffer or attempt to read more events from the connection).

- If mode is QueuedAfterFlush, and there are no events in the queue, XEvents-Queued flushes the request buffer, attempts to read more events out of the application's connection, and returns the number read.

- If mode is QueuedAfterReading, and there are no events in the queue, XEventsQueued attempts to read more events out of the application's connection without flushing the request buffer and returns the number read.

Note that XEventsQueued always returns immediately without I/O if there are events already in the queue.

XEventsQueued with mode QueuedAfterFlush is identical in behavior to XPending. XEventsQueued with mode QueuedAlready is identical to the QLength macro (see Appendix C, *Macros*).

For more information, see Volume One, Chapter 8, *Events*.

Related Commands

QLength, XAllowEvents, XCheckIfEvent, XCheckMaskEvent, XCheckTyped-Event, XCheckTypedWindowEvent, XCheckWindowEvent, XGetInputFocus, XGetMotionEvents, XIfEvent, XMaskEvent, XNextEvent, XPeekEvent, XPeek-IfEvent, XPending, XPutBackEvent, XSelectInput, XSendEvent, XSetInput-Focus, XSynchronize, XWindowEvent.

Name

XFetchBuffer — return data from a cut buffer.

Synopsis

```
char *XFetchBuffer(display, nbytes, buffer)
    Display *display;
    int *nbytes;                  /* RETURN */
    int buffer;
```

Arguments

display   Specifies a connection to an X server; returned from XOpenDisplay.

nbytes   Returns the number of bytes in *buffer* returned by XFetchBuffer. If
             there is no data in the buffer, *nbytes is set to 0.

buffer   Specifies which buffer you want data from. Specify an integer from 0 to 7
             inclusive.

Description

XFetchBuffer returns data from one of the 8 buffers provided for interclient communication. If the buffer contains data, XFetchBuffer returns the number of bytes in *nbytes*, otherwise it returns NULL and sets *nbytes to 0. The appropriate amount of storage is allocated and the pointer returned; the client must free this storage when finished with it by calling XFree. Note that the cut buffer does not necessarily contain text, so it may contain embedded null bytes and may not terminate with a null byte.

Selections are preferred over cut buffers as a communication scheme.

For more information on cut buffers, see Volume One, Chapter 13, *Other Programming Techniques*.

Errors

BadValue   *buffer* not an integer between 0 and 7 inclusive.

Related Commands

XFetchBytes, XRotateBuffers, XStoreBuffer, XStoreBytes.

XFetchBytes

Name

XFetchBytes — return data from cut buffer 0.

Synopsis

```
char *XFetchBytes(display, nbytes)
    Display *display;
    int *nbytes;                    /* RETURN */
```

Arguments

display   Specifies a connection to an X server; returned from XOpenDisplay.

nbytes   Returns the number of bytes in the string returned by XFetchBytes. If there is no data in the buffer, *nbytes* is set to 0.

Description

XFetchBytes returns data from cut buffer 0 of the 8 buffers provided for interclient communication. If the buffer contains data, XFetchBytes returns the number of bytes in *nbytes*, otherwise it returns NULL and sets *nbytes* to 0. The appropriate amount of storage is allocated and the pointer returned; the client must free this storage when finished with it by calling XFree. Note that the cut buffer does not necessarily contain text, so it may contain embedded null bytes and may not terminate with a null byte.

Use XFetchBuffer to fetch data from any specified cut buffer.

Selections are preferred over cut buffers as a communication method.

For more information on cut buffers, see Volume One, Chapter 13, *Other Programming Techniques*.

Related Commands

XFetchBuffer, XRotateBuffers, XStoreBuffer, XStoreBytes.

Name

XFetchName — get a window's name (XA_WM_NAME property).

Synopsis

```
Status XFetchName(display, w, window_name)
    Display *display;
    Window w;
    char **window_name;          /* RETURN */
```

Arguments

display   Specifies a connection to an X server; returned from XOpenDisplay.

w   Specifies the ID of the window whose name you want a pointer set to.

window_name   Returns a pointer to the window name, which will be a null-terminated string. If the XA_WM_NAME property has not been set for this window, XFetchName sets *windowname* to NULL. When finished with it, a client can free the name string using XFree.

Description

XFetchName is superseded by XGetWMName in Release 4. XFetchName returns the current value of the XA_WM_NAME property for the specified window. XFetchName returns nonzero if it succeeds, and zero if the property has not been set for the argument window.

For more information, see Volume One, Chapter 10, *Interclient Communication*, and Chapter 14, *Window Management*.

Errors

BadWindow

Related Commands

XGetClassHint, XGetIconName, XGetIconSizes, XGetNormalHints, XGet-
SizeHints, XGetTransientForHint, XGetWMHints, XGetZoomHints, XSet-
ClassHint, XSetCommand, XSetIconName, XSetIconSizes, XSetNormalHints,
XSetSizeHints, XSetTransientForHint, XSetWMHints, XSetZoomHints,
XStoreName.

XFillArc

Name

XFillArc — fill an arc.

Synopsis

```
XFillArc(display, drawable, gc,  x, y, width, height,
         angle1, angle2)
    Display *display;
    Drawable drawable;
    GC gc;
    int x, y;
    unsigned int width, height;
    int angle1, angle2;
```

Arguments

display   Specifies a connection to an X server; returned from XOpenDisplay.

drawable   Specifies the drawable.

gc   Specifies the graphics context.

x
y   Specify the x and y coordinates of the upper-left corner of the bounding box containing the arc, relative to the origin of the drawable.

width
height   Specify the width and height in pixels. These are the major and minor axes of the arc.

angle1   Specifies the start of the arc relative to the three-o'clock position from the center. Angles are specified in 64ths of degrees.

angle2   Specifies the path and extent of the arc relative to the start of the arc. Angles are specified in 64ths of degrees.

Description

XFillArc draws a filled arc. The x, y, width, and height arguments specify the bounding box for the arc. See XDrawArc for the description of how this bounding box is used to compute the arc. Some, but not all, of the pixels drawn with XDrawArc will be drawn by XFill-Arc with the same arguments. See XFillRectangle for an example of the differences in pixels drawn by the draw and fill routines.

The arc forms one boundary of the area to be filled. The other boundary is determined by the arc_mode in the GC. If the arc_mode in the GC is ArcChord, the single line segment joining the endpoints of the arc is used. If ArcPieSlice, the two line segments joining the endpoints of the arc with the center point are used.

XFillArc uses these graphics context components: function, plane_mask, fill_style, arc_mode, subwindow_mode, clip_x_origin, clip_y_origin, and clip_mask. This function also uses these graphics context mode-dependent components: foreground, background, tile, stipple, ts_x_origin, and ts_y_ origin.

For more information, see Volume One, Chapter 6, *Drawing Graphics and Text*, and Chapter 5, *The Graphics Context*.

Errors

BadDrawable
BadGC
BadMatch

Related Commands

XClearArea, XClearWindow, XCopyArea, XCopyPlane, XDraw, XDrawArc,
XDrawArcs, XDrawFilled, XDrawLine, XDrawLines, XDrawPoint, XDrawPoints,
XDrawRectangle, XDrawRectangles, XDrawSegments, XFillArcs, XFill-
Polygon, XFillRectangle, XFillRectangles.

XFillArcs

Name

XFillArcs — fill multiple arcs.

Synopsis

```
XFillArcs(display, drawable, gc, arcs, narcs)
    Display *display;
    Drawable drawable;
    GC gc;
    XArc *arcs;
    int narcs;
```

Arguments

display   Specifies a connection to an X server; returned from XOpenDisplay.

drawable   Specifies the drawable.

gc   Specifies the graphics context.

arcs   Specifies a pointer to an array of arc definitions.

narcs   Specifies the number of arcs in the array.

Description

For each arc, XFillArcs fills the region closed by the specified arc and one or two line segments, depending on the arc_mode specified in the GC. It does not draw the complete outlines of the arcs, but some pixels may overlap.

The arc forms one boundary of the area to be filled. The other boundary is determined by the arc_mode in the GC. If the arc_mode in the GC is ArcChord, the single line segment joining the endpoints of the arc is used. If ArcPieSlice, the two line segments joining the endpoints of the arc with the center point are used. The arcs are filled in the order listed in the array. For any given arc, no pixel is drawn more than once. If filled arcs intersect, pixels will be drawn multiple times.

There is a limit to the number of arcs that can be filled in a single call, that varies according to the server. To determine how many arcs you can fill in a single call, you find out your server's maximum request size using XMaxRequestSize. Subtract 3 and divide by three, and this is the maximum number of arcs you can fill in a single XFillArcs call.

XFillArcs use these graphics context components: function, plane_mask, fill_style, arc_mode, subwindow_mode, clip_x_origin, clip_y_origin, and clip_mask. This function also uses these graphics context mode-dependent components: foreground, background, tile, stipple, ts_x_origin, and ts_y_origin.

For more information, see Volume One, Chapter 6, *Drawing Graphics and Text*, and Chapter 5, *The Graphics Context*.

Structures

```
typedef struct {
    short x, y;
    unsigned short width, height;
```

```
        short angle1, angle2;              /*  64ths of Degrees */
    } XArc;
```

Errors

    BadDrawable
    BadGC
    BadMatch

Related Commands

XClearArea, XClearWindow, XCopyArea, XCopyPlane, XDraw, XDrawArc,
XDrawArcs, XDrawFilled, XDrawLine, XDrawLines, XDrawPoint, XDrawPoints,
XDrawRectangle, XDrawRectangles, XDrawSegments, XFillArc, XFill-
Polygon, XFillRectangle, XFillRectangles.

Name

XFillPolygon — fill a polygon.

Synopsis

```
XFillPolygon(display, drawable, gc, points, npoints, shape, mode)
    Display *display;
    Drawable drawable;
    GC gc;
    XPoint *points;
    int npoints;
    int shape;
    int mode;
```

Arguments

display   Specifies a connection to an X server; returned from XOpenDisplay.

drawable   Specifies the drawable.

gc   Specifies the graphics context.

points   Specifies a pointer to an array of points.

npoints   Specifies the number of points in the array.

shape   Specifies an argument that helps the server to improve performance. Pass the last constant in this list that is valid for the polygon to be filled: Complex, Nonconvex, or Convex.

mode   Specifies the coordinate mode. Pass either CoordModeOrigin or Coord-ModePrevious.

Description

XFillPolygon fills the region closed by the specified path. Some but not all of the path itself will be drawn. The path is closed automatically if the last point in the list does not coincide with the first point. No pixel of the region is drawn more than once.

The *mode* argument affects the interpretation of the points that define the polygon:

- CoordModeOrigin indicates that all points are relative to the drawable's origin.

- CoordModePrevious indicates that all points after the first are relative to the previous point. (The first point is always relative to the drawable's origin.)

The *shape* argument allows the fill routine to optimize its performance given tips on the configuration of the area.

- Complex indicates the path may self-intersect. The fill_rule of the GC must be consulted to determine which areas are filled. See Volume One, Chapter 5, *The Graphics Context*, for a discussion of the fill rules EvenOddRule and WindingRule.

- Nonconvex indicates the path does not self-intersect, but the shape is not wholly convex. If known by the client, specifying Nonconvex instead of Complex may improve performance. If you specify Nonconvex for a self-intersecting path, the graphics results are undefined.

- Convex means that for every pair of points inside the polygon, the line segment connecting them does not intersect the path. This can improve performance even more, but if the path is not convex, the graphics results are undefined.

Contiguous coincident points in the path are not treated as self-intersection.

XFillPolygon uses these graphics context components when filling the polygon area: function, plane_mask, fill_style, fill_rule, subwindow_mode, clip_x_origin, clip_y_origin, and clip_mask. This function also uses these mode-dependent components of the GC: foreground, background, tile, stipple, ts_x_origin, and ts_y_origin.

For more information, see Volume One, Chapter 6, *Drawing Graphics and Text*, and Chapter 5, *The Graphics Context*.

Structures
```
typedef struct {
    short x, y;
} XPoint;
```

Errors
```
BadDrawable
BadGC
BadMatch
BadValue
```

Related Commands
XClearArea, XClearWindow, XCopyArea, XCopyPlane, XDraw, XDrawArc, XDrawArcs, XDrawFilled, XDrawLine, XDrawLines, XDrawPoint, XDrawPoints, XDrawRectangle, XDrawRectangles, XDrawSegments, XFillArc, XFillArcs, XFillRectangle, XFillRectangles.

XFillRectangle

Name

XFillRectangle — fill a rectangular area.

Synopsis

```
XFillRectangle(display, drawable, gc, x, y, width, height)
    Display *display;
    Drawable drawable;
    GC gc;
    int x, y;
    unsigned int width, height;
```

Arguments

display   Specifies a connection to an X server; returned from XOpenDisplay.

drawable   Specifies the drawable.

gc   Specifies the graphics context.

x   Specify the x and y coordinates of the upper-left corner of the rectangle, rela-
y   tive to the origin of the drawable.

width   Specify the dimensions in pixels of the rectangle to be filled.
height

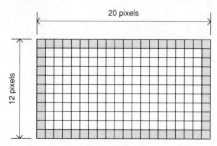
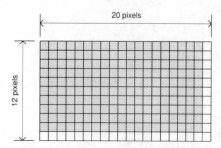

XDrawRectangle (display, drawable, gc, 0, 0, 19, 11);   XFillRectangle (display, drawable, gc, 0, 0, 19, 11);

Description

XFillRectangle fills the rectangular area in the specified drawable using the x and y coordinates, width and height dimensions, and graphics context you specify. XFill-
Rectangle draws some but not all of the path drawn by XDrawRectangle with the same
arguments.

XFillRectangle uses these graphics context components: function, plane_mask,
fill_style, subwindow_mode, clip_x_origin, clip_y_origin, and clip_
mask. This function also uses these graphics context components depending on the
fill_style: foreground, background tile, stipple, ts_x_origin, and
ts_y_origin.

For more information, see Volume One, Chapter 6, *Drawing Graphics and Text*, and Chapter 5,
The Graphics Context.

Errors

```
BadDrawable
BadGC
BadMatch
```

Related Commands

XClearArea, XClearWindow, XCopyArea, XCopyPlane, XDraw, XDrawArc,
XDrawArcs, XDrawFilled, XDrawLine, XDrawLines, XDrawPoint, XDrawPoints,
XDrawRectangle, XDrawRectangles, XDrawSegments, XFillArc, XFillArcs,
XFillPolygon, XFillRectangles.

Name

XFillRectangles — fill multiple rectangular areas.

Synopsis

```
XFillRectangles(display, drawable, gc, rectangles, nrectangles)
    Display *display;
    Drawable drawable;
    GC gc;
    XRectangle *rectangles;
    int nrectangles;
```

Arguments

display   Specifies a connection to an X server; returned from XOpenDisplay.

drawable   Specifies the drawable.

gc   Specifies the graphics context.

rectangles   Specifies a pointer to an array of rectangles.

nrectangles   Specifies the number of rectangles in the array.

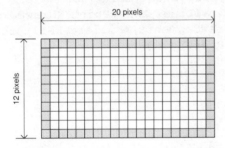

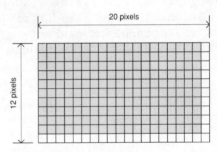

XDrawRectangle (display, drawable, gc, 0, 0, 19, 11);   XFillRectangle (display, drawable, gc, 0, 0, 19, 11);

Description

XFillRectangles fills multiple rectangular areas in the specified drawable using the graphics context.

The *x* and *y* coordinates of each rectangle are relative to the drawable's origin, and define the upper left corner of the rectangle. The rectangles are drawn in the order listed. For any given rectangle, no pixel is drawn more than once. If rectangles intersect, the intersecting pixels will be drawn multiple times.

There is a limit to the number of rectangles that can be filled in a single call, that varies according to the server. To determine how many rectangles you can fill in a single call, you find out your server's maximum request size using XMaxRequestSize. Subtract 3 and divide by two, and this is the maximum number of rectangles you can fill in a single XDraw-Rectangles call.

XFillRectangles uses these graphics context components: function, plane_mask, fill_style, subwindow_mode, clip_x_origin, clip_y_origin, and clip_ mask. This function also uses these graphics context components depending on the `fill_style`: foreground, background, tile, stipple, ts_x_origin, and ts_y_origin.

For more information, see Volume One, Chapter 6, *Drawing Graphics and Text*, and Chapter 5, *The Graphics Context*.

Structures
```
typedef struct {
    short x, y;
    unsigned short width, height;
} XRectangle;
```

Errors
```
BadDrawable
BadGC
BadMatch
```

Related Commands
XClearArea, XClearWindow, XCopyArea, XCopyPlane, XDraw, XDrawArc,
XDrawArcs, XDrawFilled, XDrawLine, XDrawLines, XDrawPoint, XDrawPoints,
XDrawRectangle, XDrawRectangles, XDrawSegments, XFillArc, XFillArcs,
XFillPolygon, XFillRectangle, XFillRectangles.

XFindContext

Name

XFindContext — get data from the context manager (not graphics context).

Synopsis

```
int XFindContext(display, w, context, data)
    Display *display;
    Window w;
    XContext context;
    caddr_t *data;                    /* RETURN */
```

Arguments

display   Specifies a connection to an X server; returned from XOpenDisplay.

w   Specifies the window with which the data is associated.

context   Specifies the context type to which the data corresponds.

data   Returns the data.

Description

XFindContext gets data that has been assigned to the specified window and context ID. The context manager is used to associate data with windows for use within an application.

This application should have called XUniqueContext to get a unique ID, and then XSave-Context to save the data into the array. The meaning of the data is indicated by the context ID, but is completely up to the client.

XFindContext returns XCNOENT (a nonzero error code) if the context could not be found and zero (0) otherwise.

For more information on the context manager, see Volume One, Chapter 13, *Other Programming Techniques*.

Structures

```
typedef int XContext;
```

Related Commands

XDeleteContext, XSaveContext, XUniqueContext.

XFlush

Name

XFlush — flush the request buffer (display all queued requests).

Synopsis

```
XFlush(display)
    Display *display;
```

Arguments

display   Specifies a connection to an X server; returned from XOpenDisplay.

Description

XFlush sends to the server ("flushes") all requests that have been buffered but not yet sent.

Flushing is done automatically when input is read if no matching events are in Xlib's queue (with XPending, XNextEvent, or XWindowEvent, etc.), or when a call is made that gets information from the server (such as XQueryPointer, XGetFontInfo) so XFlush is seldom needed. It is used when the buffer must be flushed before any of these calls are reached.

For more information, see Volume One, Chapter 2, *X Concepts*, and Chapter 3, *Basic Window Program*.

Related Commands

XSync.

XForceScreenSaver

Name

XForceScreenSaver — turn the screen saver on or off.

Synopsis

```
XForceScreenSaver(display, mode)
    Display *display;
    int mode;
```

Arguments

display   Specifies a connection to an X server; returned from XOpenDisplay.

mode   Specifies whether the screen saver is active or reset. The possible modes are: ScreenSaverActive or ScreenSaverReset.

Description

XForceScreenSaver resets or activates the screen saver.

If the specified mode is ScreenSaverActive and the screen saver currently is disabled, the screen saver is activated, even if the screen saver had been disabled by calling XSetScreenSaver with a timeout of zero (0). This means that the screen may go blank or have some random change take place to save the phosphors.

If the specified mode is ScreenSaverReset and the screen saver currently is enabled, the screen is returned to normal, the screen saver is deactivated and the activation timer is reset to its initial state (as if device input had been received). Expose events may be generated on all visible windows if the server cannot save the entire screen contents.

For more information on the screen saver, see Volume One, Chapter 13, *Other Programming Techniques*.

Errors

BadValue

Related Commands

XActivateScreenSaver, XGetScreenSaver, XResetScreenSaver, XSetScreenSaver.

XFree

Name

XFree — free specified memory allocated by an Xlib function.

Synopsis

```
XFree(data)
    caddr_t data;
```

Arguments

data   Specifies a pointer to the data that is to be freed.

Description

XFree is a general purpose routine for freeing memory allocated by Xlib calls.

Related Commands

DefaultScreen, XCloseDisplay, XNoOp, XOpenDisplay.

Name

XFreeColormap — delete a colormap and install the default colormap.

Synopsis

```
XFreeColormap(display, cmap)
    Display *display;
    Colormap cmap;
```

Arguments

display   Specifies a connection to an X server; returned from XOpenDisplay.

cmap   Specifies the colormap to delete.

Description

XFreeColormap destroys the specified colormap, unless it is the default colormap for a screen. That is, it not only uninstalls *cmap* from the hardware colormap if it is installed, but also frees the associated memory including the colormap ID.

XFreeColormap performs the following processing:

* If *cmap* is an installed map for a screen, it uninstalls the colormap and installs the default if not already installed.

* If *cmap* is defined as the colormap attribute for a window (by XCreateWindow or XChangeWindowAttributes), it changes the colormap attribute for the window to the constant None, generates a ColormapNotify event, and frees the colormap. The colors displayed with a colormap of None are server-dependent, since the default colormap is normally used.

For more information, see Volume One, Chapter 7, *Color*.

Errors

```
BadColormap
```

Related Commands

DefaultColormap, DisplayCells, XCopyColormapAndFree, XCreate-
Colormap, XGetStandardColormap, XInstallColormap, XListInstalled-
Colormaps, XSetStandardColormap, XSetWindowColormap, XUninstall-
Colormap.

XFreeColors

Xlib – Color Cells

Name

XFreeColors — free colormap cells or planes.

Synopsis

```
XFreeColors(display, cmap, pixels, npixels, planes)
    Display *display;
    Colormap cmap;
    unsigned long pixels[];
    int npixels;
    unsigned long planes;
```

Arguments

display   Specifies a connection to an X server; returned from XOpenDisplay.

cmap   Specifies the colormap.

pixels   Specifies an array of pixel values.

npixels   Specifies the number of pixels.

planes   Specifies the planes you want to free.

Description

XFreeColors frees the cells whose values are computed by ORing together subsets of the *planes* argument with each pixel value in the *pixels* array.

If the cells are read/write, they become available for reuse, unless they were allocated with XAllocColorPlanes, in which case all the related pixels may need to be freed before any become available.

If the cells were read-only, they become available only if this is the last client to have allocated those shared cells.

For more information, see Volume One, Chapter 7, *Color*.

Errors

BadAccess   Attempt to free a colorcell not allocated by this client (either unallocated or allocated by another client).

BadColormap

BadValue   A pixel value is not a valid index into *cmap*.

Note: if more than one pixel value is in error, the one reported is arbitrary.

Related Commands

BlackPixel, WhitePixel, XAllocColor, XAllocColorCells, XAllocColor-Planes, XAllocNamedColor, XLookupColor, XParseColor, XQueryColor, XQueryColors, XStoreColor, XStoreColors, XStoreNamedColor.

196   Xlib Reference Manual

Name

XFreeCursor — release a cursor.

Synopsis

```
XFreeCursor(display, cursor)
    Display *display;
    Cursor cursor;
```

Arguments

display   Specifies a connection to an X server; returned from XOpenDisplay.

cursor   Specifies the ID of the cursor to be affected.

Description

XFreeCursor deletes the association between the cursor ID and the specified cursor. The cursor storage is freed when all other clients have freed it. Windows with their cursor attribute set to this cursor will have this attribute set to None (which implies CopyFromParent). The specified cursor ID should not be referred to again.

Errors

BadCursor

Related Commands

XCreateFontCursor, XCreateGlyphCursor, XCreatePixmapCursor, XDefine-Cursor, XQueryBestCursor, XQueryBestSize, XRecolorCursor, XUndefine-Cursor.

Name

XFreeExtensionList — free memory allocated for a list of installed extensions.

Synopsis

```
XFreeExtensionList(list)
    char **list;
```

Arguments

list   Specifies a pointer to the list of extensions returned from XList-
     Extensions.

Description

XFreeExtensionList frees the memory allocated by XListExtensions.

For more information, see Volume One, Chapter 13, *Other Programming Techniques*.

Related Commands

XListExtensions, XQueryExtension.

XFreeFont

Name

XFreeFont — unload a font and free storage for the font structure.

Synopsis

```
XFreeFont (display, font_struct)
    Display *display;
    XFontStruct *font_struct;
```

Arguments

display   Specifies a connection to an X server; returned from XOpenDisplay.

font_struct Specifies the storage associated with the font.

Description

XFreeFont frees the memory allocated for the *font_struct* font information structure (XFontStruct) filled by XQueryFont or XLoadQueryFont. XFreeFont frees all storage associated with the *font_struct* argument. Neither the data nor the font should be referenced again.

The server unloads the font itself if no other client has loaded it.

For more information, see Volume One, Chapter 6, *Drawing Graphics and Text*.

Structures

```
typedef struct {
    XExtData *ext_data;              /* hook for extension to hang data */
    Font fid;                        /* Font ID for this font */
    unsigned direction;              /* hint about direction the font is painted */
    unsigned min_char_or_byte2;      /* first character */
    unsigned max_char_or_byte2;      /* last character */
    unsigned min_byte1;              /* first row that exists */
    unsigned max_byte1;              /* last row that exists */
    Bool all_chars_exist;            /* flag if all characters have nonzero size*/
    unsigned default_char;           /* char to print for undefined character */
    int n_properties;                /* how many properties there are */
    XFontProp *properties;           /* pointer to array of additional properties*/
    XCharStruct min_bounds;          /* minimum bounds over all existing char*/
    XCharStruct max_bounds;          /* minimum bounds over all existing char*/
    XCharStruct *per_char;           /* first_char to last_char information */
    int ascent;                      /* logical extent above baseline for spacing */
    int descent;                     /* logical descent below baseline for spacing */
} XFontStruct;
```

Errors

BadFont

Related Commands

XCreateFontCursor, XFreeFontInfo, XFreeFontNames, XFreeFontPath, XGetFontPath, XGetFontProperty, XListFonts, XListFontsWithInfo, XLoadFont, XLoadQueryFont, XQueryFont, XSetFont, XSetFontPath, XUnloadFont.

XFreeFontInfo

Name

XFreeFontInfo — free the memory allocated by XListFontsWithInfo.

Synopsis

```
XFreeFontInfo(names, info, actual_count)
    char **names;
    XFontStruct *info;
    int actual_count;
```

Arguments

names   Specifies a pointer to the list of font names that were returned by XList-FontsWithInfo.

info   Specifies a pointer to the list of font information that was returned by XListFontsWithInfo.

actual_count
                 Specifies the number of matched font names returned by XListFonts-WithInfo.

Description

XFreeFontInfo frees the list of font information structures allocated by XListFonts-WithInfo. It does not unload the specified fonts themselves.

Structures

```
typedef struct {
    XExtData *ext_data;            /* hook for extension to hang data */
    Font fid;                      /* Font ID for this font */
    unsigned direction;            /* hint about direction the font is painted */
    unsigned min_char_or_byte2;    /* first character */
    unsigned max_char_or_byte2;    /* last character */
    unsigned min_byte1;            /* first row that exists */
    unsigned max_byte1;            /* last row that exists */
    Bool all_chars_exist;          /* flag if all characters have nonzero size*/
    unsigned default_char;         /* char to print for undefined character */
    int n_properties;              /* how many properties there are */
    XFontProp *properties;         /* pointer to array of additional properties*/
    XCharStruct min_bounds;        /* minimum bounds over all existing char*/
    XCharStruct max_bounds;        /* minimum bounds over all existing char*/
    XCharStruct *per_char;         /* first_char to last_char information */
    int ascent;                    /* logical extent above baseline for spacing */
    int descent;                   /* logical descent below baseline for spacing */
} XFontStruct;
```

Related Commands

XCreateFontCursor, XFreeFont, XFreeFontNames, XGetFontPath, XGetFont-Property, XListFonts, XListFontsWithInfo, XLoadFont, XLoadQueryFont, XQueryFont, XSetFont, XSetFontPath, XUnloadFont.

Name

XFreeFontNames — free the memory allocated by XListFonts.

Synopsis

```
XFreeFontNames (list)
    char *list[];
```

Arguments

list   Specifies the array of font name strings to be freed.

Description

XFreeFontNames frees the array of strings returned by XListFonts.

Related Commands

XCreateFontCursor, XFreeFont, XFreeFontInfo, XFreeFontPath, XGetFont-Path, XGetFontProperty, XListFonts, XListFontsWithInfo, XLoadFont, XLoadQueryFont, XQueryFont, XSetFont, XSetFontPath, XUnloadFont.

Name

XFreeFontPath — free the memory allocated by XGetFontPath.

Synopsis

```
XFreeFontPath(list)
    char **list;
```

Arguments

list   Specifies an array of strings allocated by XGetFontPath.

Description

XFreeFontPath frees the data used by the array of pathnames returned by XGetFont-Path.

For more information, see Volume One, Chapter 6, *Drawing Graphics and Text*.

Related Commands

XCreateFontCursor, XFreeFont, XFreeFontInfo, XFreeFontNames, XGet-FontPath, XGetFontProperty, XListFonts, XListFontsWithInfo, XLoad-Font, XLoadQueryFont, XQueryFont, XSetFont, XSetFontPath, XUnloadFont.

XFreeGC

Name

XFreeGC — free a graphics context.

Synopsis

```
XFreeGC(display, gc)
    Display *display;
    GC gc;
```

Arguments

display   Specifies a connection to an X server; returned from XOpenDisplay.

gc   Specifies the graphics context to be freed.

Description

XFreeGC frees all memory associated with a graphics context, and removes the GC from the server and display hardware.

For more information, see Volume One, Chapter 5, *The Graphics Context*.

Errors

BadGC

Related Commands

DefaultGC, XChangeGC, XCopyGC, XCreateGC, XGContextFromGC, XSetArcMode, XSetBackground, XSetClipMask, XSetClipOrigin, XSetClipRectangles, XSetDashes, XSetFillRule, XSetFillStyle, XSetForeground, XSet-Function, XSetGraphicsExposures, XSetLineAttributes, XSetPlaneMask, XSetState, XSetStipple, XSetSubwindowMode, XSetTSOrigin.

Name
XFreeModifiermap — destroy and free a keyboard modifier mapping structure.

Synopsis
```
XFreeModifiermap(modmap)
    XModifierKeymap *modmap;
```

Arguments

modmap   Specifies a pointer to the XModifierKeymap structure to be freed.

Description

XFreeModifiermap frees an XModifierKeymap structure originally allocated by XNew-
ModifierMap or XGetModifierMapping.

For more information, see Volume One, Chapter 9, *The Keyboard and Pointer*.

Structures

```
typedef struct {
    int max_keypermod;      /* server's max number of keys per modifier */
    KeyCode *modifiermap;   /* an 8 by max_keypermod array of
                             * keycodes to be used as modifiers */
} XModifierKeymap;
```

Related Commands

XChangeKeyboardMapping, XDeleteModifiermapEntry, XGetKeyboard-
Mapping, XGetModifierMapping, XInsertModifiermapEntry, XKeycode-
ToKeysym, XKeysymToKeycode, XKeysymToString, XLookupKeysym, XLookup-
String, XNewModifierMap, XQueryKeymap, XRebindKeySym, XRefresh-
KeyboardMapping, XSetModifierMapping, XStringToKeysym.

Name

XFreePixmap — free a pixmap ID.

Synopsis

```
XFreePixmap(display, pixmap)
    Display *display;
    Pixmap pixmap;
```

Arguments

display   Specifies a connection to an X server; returned from XOpenDisplay.

pixmap   Specifies the pixmap whose ID should be freed.

Description

XFreePixmap disassociates a pixmap ID from its resource. If no other client has an ID for that resource, it is freed. The Pixmap should never be referenced again by this client. If it is, the ID will be unknown and a BadPixmap error will result.

Errors

BadPixmap

Related Commands

XCreateBitmapFromData, XCreatePixmap, XCreatePixmapFromBitmapData, XQueryBestSize, XQueryBestStipple, XQueryBestTile, XReadBitmapFile, XSetTile, XSetWindowBackgroundPixmap, XSetWindowBorderPixmap, XWriteBitmapFile.

XFreeStringList

Name

XFreeStringList — free the in-memory data associated with the specified string list.

Synopsis

```
void XFreeStringList(list)
      char **list;
```

Arguments

list   Specifies the list of strings to be freed.

Availability

Release 4 and later.

Description

XFreeStringList releases memory allocated by XTextPropertyToStringList.

Related Commands

XGetTextProperty, XSetTextProperty, XStringListToTextProperty, XTextPropertytoStringList.

XGContextFromGC

Name

XGContextFromGC — obtain the GContext (resource ID) associated with the specified graphics context.

Synopsis

```
GContext XGContextFromGC(gc)
    GC gc;
```

Arguments

gc   Specifies the graphics context of the desired resource ID.

Description

XGContextFromGC extracts the resource ID from the GC structure. The GC structure is Xlib's local cache of GC values and contains a field for the GContext ID. This function is essentially a macro that accesses this field, since the GC structure is intended to be opaque.

A GContext is needed to set a field of the XVisualInfo structure prior to calling XGet-VisualInfo.

Related Commands

DefaultGC, XChangeGC, XCopyGC, XCreateGC, XFreeGC, XSetArcMode, XSet-Background, XSetClipMask, XSetClipOrigin, XSetClipRectangles, XSet-Dashes, XSetFillRule, XSetFillStyle, XSetForeground, XSetFunction, XSetGraphicsExposures, XSetLineAttributes, XSetPlaneMask, XSetState, XSetStipple, XSetSubwindowMode, XSetTSOrigin.

Name

XGeometry — calculate window geometry given user geometry string and default geometry.

Synopsis

```
int XGeometry(display, screen, user_geom, default_geom, bwidth,
        fwidth, fheight, xadder, yadder, x, y, width, height)
    Display *display;
    int screen;
    char *user_geom, *default_geom;
    unsigned int bwidth;
    unsigned int fwidth, fheight;
    int xadder, yadder;
    int *x, *y, *width, *height;/* RETURN */
```

Arguments

display	Specifies a connection to an X server; returned from XOpenDisplay.
screen	Specifies which screen the window is on.
user_geom	Specifies the user or program supplied geometry string, perhaps incomplete.
default_geom	
	Specifies the default geometry string and must be complete.
bwidth	Specifies the border width.
fheight fwidth	Specify the font height and width in pixels (increment size).
xadder yadder	Specify additional interior padding in pixels needed in the window.
x y	Return the user-specified or default coordinates of the window.
width height	Return the window dimensions in pixels.

Description

XGeometry has been superseded by XWMGeometry as of Release 4.

XGeometry returns the position and size of a window given a user-supplied geometry (allowed to be partial) and a default geometry. Each user-supplied specification is copied into the appropriate returned argument, unless it is not present, in which case the default specification is used. The default geometry should be complete while the user-supplied one may not be.

XGeometry is useful for processing command line options and user preferences. These geometry strings are of the form:

```
=<width>x<height>{+-}<xoffset>{+-}<yoffset>
```

The "=" at the beginning of the string is now optional. (Items enclosed in <> are integers, and items enclosed in { } are a set from which one item is to be chosen. Note that the brackets should not appear in the actual string.)

The XGeometry return value is a bitmask that indicates which values were present in user_geom. This bitmask is composed of the exclusive OR of the symbols XValue, YValue, WidthValue, HeightValue, XNegative, or YNegative.

If the function returns either XValue or YValue, you should place the window at the requested position. The border width (bwidth), size of the width and height increments (typically fwidth and fheight), and any additional interior space (xadder and yadder) are passed in to make it easy to compute the resulting size.

Related Commands

XParseGeometry, XTranslateCoordinates, XWMGeometry.

XGetAtomName

Name

XGetAtomName — get a string name for a property given its atom.

Synopsis

```
char *XGetAtomName(display, atom)
    Display *display;
    Atom atom;
```

Arguments

display   Specifies a connection to an X server; returned from XOpenDisplay.

atom   Specifies the atom whose string name you want returned.

Description

An atom is a number identifying a property. Properties also have a string name. XGetAtom-Name returns the string name that was specified in the original call to XInternAtom that returned this atom, or, for predefined atoms, a string version of the symbolic constant without the XA_ is returned. If the specified atom is not defined, XGetAtomName returns NULL, and generates a BadAtom error.

For example, XGetAtomName returns "XA_WM_CLASS" (a string) when passed the prede-fined atom XA_WM_CLASS (a defined constant).

You should free the resulting string with XFree when it is no longer needed.

XInternAtom performs the inverse function, returning the atom given the string.

Errors

BadAtom

Related Commands

XChangeProperty, XDeleteProperty, XGetFontProperty, XGetWindow-Property, XInternAtom, XListProperties, XRotateWindowProperties, XSetStandardProperties.

210   Xlib Reference Manual

Name
XGetClassHint — get the XA_WM_CLASS property of a window.

Synopsis
```
Status XGetClassHint(display, w, class_hints)
    Display *display;
    Window w;
    XClassHint *class_hints;   /* RETURN */
```

Arguments
display   Specifies a connection to an X server; returned from XOpenDisplay.

w   Specifies the ID of the window for which the property is desired.

class_hints   Returns the XClassHints structure.

Description
XGetClassHint obtains the XA_WM_CLASS property for the specified window. This property stores the resource class and instance name, that the window manager uses to get any resource settings that may control how the window manager manages the application that set this property. XGetClassHint returns a Status of zero on failure, nonzero on success.

The XClassHint structure returned contains res_class, which is the name of the client such as "emacs", and res_name, which should be the first of the following that applies:

* command line option (*-rn name*)
* a specific environment variable (e.g., RESOURCE_NAME)
* the trailing component of argv[0] (after the last /)

To free res_name and res_class when finished with the strings, use XFree.

For more information on using hints, see Volume One, Chapter 10, *Interclient Communication*.

Structures
```
typedef struct {
    char *res_name;
    char *res_class;
} XClassHint;
```

Errors
BadWindow

Related Commands
XAllocClassHint, XFetchName, XGetIconName, XGetIconSizes, XGetNormal-Hints, XGetSizeHints, XGetTransientForHint, XGetWMHints, XGetZoom-Hints, XSetClassHint, XSetCommand, XSetIconName, XSetIconSizes, XSet-NormalHints, XSetSizeHints, XSetTransientForHint, XSetWMHints, XSet-ZoomHints, XStoreName, XSetWMProperties, XSetWMProperties.

Name

XGetDefault — extract an option value from the resource database.

Synopsis

```
char *XGetDefault(display, program, option)
    Display *display;
    char *program;
    char *option;
```

Arguments

display   Specifies a connection to an X server; returned from `XOpenDisplay`.

program   Specifies the program name to be looked for in the resource database. The program name is usually `argv[0]`, the first argument on the UNIX command line.

option   Specifies the option name or keyword. Lines containing both the *program* name and the *option* name, separated only by a period or asterisk, will be matched.

Description

`XGetDefault` returns a character string containing the user's default value for the specified *program* name and *option* name. `XGetDefault` returns `NULL` if no key can be found that matches *option* and *program*. For a description of the matching rules, see `XrmGetResource`.

The strings returned by `XGetDefault` are owned by Xlib and should not be modified or freed by the client.

Lines in the user's resource database look like this:

```
xterm.foreground:        #c0c0ff
xterm.geometry:          =81x28
xterm.saveLines:         256
xterm.font:              8x13
xterm.keyMapFile:        /usr/black/.keymap
xterm.activeIcon:        on
xmh.header.font          9x15
```

The portion on the left is known as a key; the portion on the right is the value. Upper or lower case is important in keys. The convention is to capitalize only the second and successive words in each option, if any.

Resource specifications are usually loaded into the `XA_RESOURCE_MANAGER` property on the root window at login. If no such property exists, a resource file in the user's home directory is loaded. On a UNIX-based system, this file is *$HOME/.Xdefaults*. After loading these defaults, `XGetDefault` merges additional defaults specified by the XENVIRONMENT environment variable. If XENVIRONMENT is defined, it contains a full path name for the additional resource file. If XENVIRONMENT is not defined, `XGetDefault` looks for *$HOME/.Xdefaults*-name, where *name* specifies the name of the machine on which the application is running.

The first invocation of XGetDefault reads and merges the various resource files into Xlib so that subsequent requests are fast. Therefore, changes to the resource files from the program will not be felt until the next invocation of the application.

For more information, see Volume One, Chapter 11, *Managing User Preferences*.

Related Commands

XAutoRepeatOff, XAutoRepeatOn, XBell, XChangeKeyboardControl, XGet-KeyboardControl, XGetPointerControl.

XGetErrorDatabaseText

Name

XGetErrorDatabaseText — obtain error messages from the error database.

Synopsis

```
XGetErrorDatabaseText (display, name, message,
        default_string, buffer, length)
    Display display;
    char *name, *message;
    char *default_string;
    char *buffer;                /* RETURN */
    int length;
```

Arguments

display   Specifies a connection to an X server; returned from `XOpenDisplay`.

name   Specifies the name of the application.

message   Specifies the type of the error message. One of `XProtoError`, `Xlib-Message`, or `XRequestMajor` (see Description below).

default_string
             Specifies the default error message.

buffer   Returns the error description.

length   Specifies the size of the return buffer.

Description

`XGetErrorDatabaseText` returns a message from the error message database. Given *name* and *message* as keys, `XGetErrorDatabaseText` uses the resource manager to look up a string and returns it in the buffer argument. Xlib uses this function internally to look up its error messages. On a UNIX-based system, the error message database is usually */usr/lib/X11/XErrorDB*.

The *name* argument should generally be the name of your application. The *message* argument should indicate which type of error message you want. Three predefined *message* types are used by Xlib to report errors:

- `XProtoError`
    The protocol error number is used as a string for the message argument.

- `XlibMessage`
    These are the message strings that are used internally by Xlib.

- `XRequestMajor`
    The major request protocol number is used for the message argument.

If no string is found in the error database, `XGetErrorDatabaseText` returns the `default_string` that you specify to the buffer.

The string in *buffer* will be of length *length*.

For more information, see Volume One, Chapter 3, *Basic Window Program*.

Related Commands

`XDisplayName`, `XGetErrorText`, `XSetAfterFunction`, `XSetErrorHandler`, `XSetIOErrorHandler`, `XSynchronize`.

XGetErrorText

Xlib – Error Handling

Name

XGetErrorText — obtain a description of error code.

Synopsis

```
XGetErrorText(display, code, buffer, length)
    Display *display;
    int code;
    char *buffer;                  /* RETURN */
    int length;
```

Arguments

display   Specifies a connection to an X server; returned from XOpenDisplay.

code   Specifies the error code for which you want to obtain a description.

buffer   Returns a pointer to the error description text.

length   Specifies the size of the buffer.

Description

XGetErrorText obtains textual descriptions of errors. XGetErrorText returns a pointer to a null-terminated string describing the specified error code with length length. This string is copied from static data and therefore may be freed. This routine allows extensions to the Xlib library to define their own error codes and error strings that can be accessed easily.

For more information, see Volume One, Chapter 3, *Basic Window Program*.

Related Commands

XDisplayName, XGetErrorDatabaseText, XSetAfterFunction, XSetError-Handler, XSetIOErrorHandler, XSynchronize.

216   *Xlib Reference Manual*

Name

XGetFontPath — get the current font search path.

Synopsis

```
char **XGetFontPath(display, npaths)
    Display *display;
    int *npaths;                    /* RETURN number of elements */
```

Arguments

display   Specifies a connection to an X server; returned from XOpenDisplay.

npaths   Returns the number of strings in the font path array.

Description

XGetFontPath allocates and returns an array of strings containing the search path for fonts. The data in the font path should be freed when no longer needed.

Related Commands

XCreateFontCursor, XFreeFont, XFreeFontInfo, XFreeFontNames, XFree-FontPath, XGetFontProperty, XListFonts, XListFontsWithInfo, XLoad-Font, XLoadQueryFont, XQueryFont, XSetFont, XSetFontPath, XUnloadFont.

XGetFontProperty

Name

XGetFontProperty — get a font property given its atom.

Synopsis

```
Bool XGetFontProperty(font_struct, atom, value)
    XFontStruct *font_struct;
    Atom atom;
    unsigned long *value;        /* RETURN */
```

Arguments

font_struct   Specifies the storage associated with the font.

atom   Specifies the atom associated with the property name you want returned.

value   Returns the value of the font property.

Description

XGetFontProperty returns the value of the specified font property, given the atom for that property. The function returns False if the atom was not defined, or True if was defined.

There are a set of predefined atoms for font properties which can be found in *<X11/Xatom.h>*. These atoms are listed and described in Volume One, Chapter 6, *Drawing Graphics and Text*. This set contains the standard properties associated with a font. The predefined font properties are likely but not guaranteed to be present for any given font.

See Volume One, Appendix I, *Logical Font Description Conventions*, for more information on font properties.

Structures

```
typedef struct {
    XExtData *ext_data;             /* hook for extension to hang data */
    Font fid;                       /* Font ID for this font */
    unsigned direction;             /* hint about direction the font is painted */
    unsigned min_char_or_byte2;     /* first character */
    unsigned max_char_or_byte2;     /* last character */
    unsigned min_byte1;             /* first row that exists */
    unsigned max_byte1;             /* last row that exists */
    Bool all_chars_exist;           /* flag if all characters have nonzero size*/
    unsigned default_char;          /* char to print for undefined character */
    int n_properties;               /* how many properties there are */
    XFontProp *properties;          /* pointer to array of additional properties*/
    XCharStruct min_bounds;         /* minimum bounds over all existing char*/
    XCharStruct max_bounds;         /* minimum bounds over all existing char*/
    XCharStruct *per_char;          /* first_char to last_char information */
    int ascent;                     /* logical extent above baseline for spacing */
    int descent;                    /* logical descent below baseline for spacing */
} XFontStruct;
```

Related Commands

XChangeProperty, XDeleteProperty, XGetAtomName, XGetWindowProperty, XInternAtom, XListProperties, XRotateWindowProperties, XSetStandardProperties.

Name

XGetGCValues — obtain components of a given GC from Xlib's GC cache.

Synopsis

```
Status XGetGCValues(display, gc, valuemask, values)
        Display *display;
        GC gc;
        unsigned long valuemask;
        XGCValues *values;              /* RETURN */
```

Arguments

display   Specifies a connection to an X server; returned from XOpenDisplay.

gc   Specifies the GC.

valuemask   Specifies which components in the GC are to be returned in the values argument. This argument is the bitwise inclusive OR of one or more of the valid GC component mask bits.

values   Returns the GC values in the specified XGCValues structure.

Availability

Release 4 and later.

Description

XGetGCValues returns the components specified by valuemask for the specified GC. Note that the clip mask and dash list (represented by the GCClipMask and GCDashList bits, respectively, in the valuemask) cannot be requested. If the valuemask contains a valid set of GC mask bits (any of those listed in the Structures section with the exception of GCClipMask and GCDashList) and no error occur, XGetGCValues sets the requested components in values and returns a nonzero status. Otherwise, it returns a zero status.

For more information, see Volume One, Chapter 5, *The Graphics Context*.

Structures

```
typedef struct {
    int function;                    /* logical operation */
    unsigned long plane_mask;        /* plane mask */
    unsigned long foreground;        /* foreground pixel */
    unsigned long background;        /* background pixel */
    int line_width;                  /* line width */
    int line_style;                  /* LineSolid, LineOnOffDash, LineDoubleDash */
    int cap_style;                   /* CapNotLast, CapButt, CapRound, CapProjecting */
    int join_style;                  /* JoinMiter, JoinRound, JoinBevel */
    int fill_style;                  /* FillSolid, FillTiled, FillStippled */
    int fill_rule;                   /* EvenOddRule, WindingRule */
    int arc_mode;                    /* ArcPieSlice, ArcChord */
    Pixmap tile;                     /* tile pixmap for tiling operations */
    Pixmap stipple;                  /* stipple 1 plane pixmap for stipping */
    int ts_x_origin;                 /* offset for tile or stipple operations */
```

```
        int ts_y_origin;
        Font font;                       /* default text font for text operations */
        int subwindow_mode;              /* ClipByChildren, IncludeInferiors */
        Bool graphics_exposures;         /* generate events on XCopyArea, XCopyPlane */
        int clip_x_origin;               /* origin for clipping */
        int clip_y_origin;
        Pixmap clip_mask;                /* bitmap clipping; other calls for rects */
        int dash_offset;                 /* patterned/dashed line information */
        char dashes;
} XGCValues;

#define GCFunction           (1L<<0)
#define GCPlaneMask          (1L<<1)
#define GCForeground         (1L<<2)
#define GCBackground         (1L<<3)
#define GCLineWidth          (1L<<4)
#define GCLineStyle          (1L<<5)
#define GCCapStyle           (1L<<6)
#define GCJoinStyle          (1L<<7)
#define GCFillStyle          (1L<<8)
#define GCFillRule           (1L<<9)
#define GCTile               (1L<<10)
#define GCStipple            (1L<<11)
#define GCTileStipXOrigin    (1L<<12)
#define GCTileStipYOrigin    (1L<<13)
#define GCFont               (1L<<14)
#define GCSubwindowMode      (1L<<15)
#define GCGraphicsExposures  (1L<<16)
#define GCClipXOrigin        (1L<<17)
#define GCClipYOrigin        (1L<<18)
#define GCClipMask           (1L<<19)   /* not valid in this call */
#define GCDashOffset         (1L<<20)
#define GCDashList           (1L<<21)   /* not valid in this call */
#define GCArcMode            (1L<<22)
```

Related Commands
XChangeGC, XCopyGC, XCreateGC.

XGetGeometry

Name
XGetGeometry — obtain the current geometry of drawable.

Synopsis
```
Status XGetGeometry(display, drawable, root, x, y,
        width, height, border_width, depth)
    Display *display;
    Drawable drawable;
    Window *root;                        /* RETURN */
    int *x, *y;                          /* RETURN */
    unsigned int *width, *height;        /* RETURN */
    unsigned int *border_width;          /* RETURN */
    unsigned int *depth;                 /* RETURN */
```

Arguments

display	Specifies a connection to an X server; returned from XOpenDisplay.
drawable	Specifies the drawable, either a window or a pixmap.
root	Returns the root window ID of the specified window.
x y	Return the coordinates of the upper-left pixel of the window's border, relative to its parent's origin. For pixmaps, these coordinates are always zero.
width height	Return the dimensions of the drawable. For a window, these return the inside size (not including the border).
border_width	Returns the borderwidth, in pixels, of the window's border, if the drawable is a window. Returns zero if the drawable is a pixmap.
depth	Returns the depth of the pixmap or window (bits per pixel for the object).

Description
This function gets the current geometry of a drawable, plus the ID of the root window of the screen the window is on.

XGetGeometry returns a Status of zero on failure, or nonzero on success.

Errors
BadDrawable

Related Commands
XConfigureWindow, XGetWindowAttributes, XMoveResizeWindow, XMove-Window, XResizeWindow.

XGetIconName

Name

XGetIconName — get the name to be displayed in an icon.

Synopsis

```
Status XGetIconName(display, w, icon_name)
    Display *display;
    Window w;
    char **icon_name;          /* RETURN */
```

Arguments

display   Specifies a connection to an X server; returned from XOpenDisplay.

w   Specifies the ID of the window whose icon name you want to learn.

icon_name   Returns a pointer to the name to be displayed in the window's icon. The name should be a null-terminated string. If a name hasn't been assigned to the window, XGetIconName sets this argument to NULL. When finished with it, a client must free the icon name string using XFree.

Description

XGetIconName is superseded by XGetWMIconName in Release 4. XGetIconName reads the icon name property of a window. This function is primarily used by window managers to get the name to be written in a window's icon when they need to display that icon.

XGetIconName returns a nonzero Status if it succeeds, and zero if no icon name has been set for the argument window.

For more information, see Volume One, Chapter 10, *Interclient Communication*.

Errors

BadWindow

Related Commands

XFetchName, XGetClassHint, XGetIconSizes, XGetNormalHints, XGetSize-Hints, XGetTransientForHint, XGetWMHints, XGetZoomHints, XSetClass-Hint, XSetCommand, XSetIconName, XSetIconSizes, XSetNormalHints, XSet-SizeHints, XSetTransientForHint, XSetWMHints, XSetZoomHints, XStore-Name.

XGetIconSizes

Name

XGetIconSizes — get preferred icon sizes.

Synopsis

```
Status XGetIconSizes(display, w, size_list, count)
    Display *display;
    Window w;
    XIconSize **size_list;      /* RETURN */
    int *count;                 /* RETURN */
```

Arguments

display   Specifies a connection to an X server; returned from XOpenDisplay.

w   Specifies the window ID (usually of the root window).

size_list   Returns a pointer to the size list.

count   Returns the number of items in the size list.

Description

XGetIconSizes reads the XA_WM_ICON_SIZE property that should be set by the window manager to specify its desired icon sizes. XGetIconSizes returns a Status of zero if a window manager has not set icon sizes, and a nonzero Status otherwise. This function should be called by all programs to find out what icon sizes are preferred by the window manager. The application should then use XSetWMHints to supply the window manager with an icon pixmap or window in one of the supported sizes. To free the data allocated in size_list, use XFree.

For more information, see Volume One, Chapter 10, *Interclient Communication*.

Structures

```
typedef struct {
    int min_width, min_height;
    int max_width, max_height;
    int width_inc, height_inc;
} XIconSize;

/* width_inc and height_inc provide the preferred
 * increment of sizes in the range from min_width
 * to max_width and min_height to max_height. */
```

Errors

BadWindow

Related Commands

XAllocIconSize, XFetchName, XGetClassHint, XGetIconName, XGetNormal-
Hints, XGetSizeHints, XGetTransientForHint, XGetWMHints, XGetZoom-
Hints, XSetClassHint, XSetCommand, XSetIconSizes, XSetNormalHints,
XSetSizeHints, XSetTransientForHint, XSetWMHints, XSetZoomHints,
XStoreName.

Name

XGetImage — place contents of a rectangle from drawable into an image.

Synopsis

```
XImage *XGetImage(display, drawable, x, y, width, height,
        plane_mask, format)
    Display *display;
    Drawable drawable;
    int x, y;
    unsigned int width, height;
    unsigned long plane_mask;
    int format;
```

Arguments

display	Specifies a connection to an X server; returned from XOpenDisplay.
drawable	Specifies the drawable to get the data from.
x y	Specify the x and y coordinates of the upper-left corner of the rectangle, relative to the origin of the drawable.
width height	Specify the width and height in pixels of the image.
plane_mask	Specifies a plane mask that indicates which planes are represented in the image.
format	Specifies the format for the image. Pass either XYPixmap or ZPixmap.

Description

XGetImage dumps the contents of the specified rectangle, a drawable, into a client-side XImage structure, in the format you specify. Depending on which format you pass to the format argument, the function does the following:

- If the format is XYPixmap

  Gets only the bit planes you passed to the *plane_mask* argument.

- If the format is ZPixmap

  Sets to 0 the bits in all planes not specified in the *plane_mask* argument. The function performs no range checking on the values in *plane_mask*, and ignores extraneous bits.

XGetImage returns the depth of the image to the depth member of the XImage structure. This depth is as specified when the drawable was created.

If the drawable is a pixmap, the specified rectangle must be completely inside the pixmap, or a BadMatch error will occur, and the visual field in the image will be None. If XGetImage fails, it returns NULL. If the drawable is a window, the window must be viewable, and the specified rectangle must not go off the edge of the screen. Otherwise, a BadMatch error will occur. If the drawable is a window, the *visual* argument will return the visual specified when the drawable was created.

The returned image will include any visible portions of inferiors or overlapping windows contained in the rectangle. The image will not include the cursor. The specified area can include the borders. The returned contents of visible regions of inferiors of different depth than the specified window are undefined.

If the window has a backing-store, the backing-store contents are returned for regions of the window that are obscured by noninferior windows. Otherwise, the return contents of such obscured regions are undefined. Also undefined are the returned contents of visible regions of inferiors of different depth than the specified window.

The data in the image structure is stored in the server's natural byte- and bit-order.

For more information, see Volume One, Chapter 6, *Drawing Graphics and Text*.

Errors

```
BadDrawable
BadMatch        See Description above.
BadValue
```

Related Commands

```
ImageByteOrder, XAddPixel, XCreateImage, XDestroyImage, XGetPixel,
XGetSubImage, XPutImage, XPutPixel, XSubImage.
```

Name

XGetInputFocus — return the current keyboard focus window.

Synopsis

```
XGetInputFocus(display, focus, revert_to)
    Display *display;
    Window *focus;          /* RETURN */
    int *revert_to;         /* RETURN */
```

Arguments

display   Specifies a connection to an X server; returned from XOpenDisplay.

focus   Returns the ID of the focus window, or one of the constants PointerRoot or None.

revert_to   Returns the window to which the focus would revert if the focus window became invisible. This is one of these constants: RevertToParent, RevertToPointerRoot, or RevertToNone. Must not be a window ID.

Description

XGetInputFocus returns the current keyboard focus window and the window to which the focus would revert if the focus window became invisible.

XGetInputFocus does not report the last focus change time. This is available only from FocusIn and FocusOut events.

Related Commands

QLength, XAllowEvents, XCheckIfEvent, XCheckMaskEvent, XCheckTyped-Event, XCheckTypedWindowEvent, XCheckWindowEvent, XEventsQueued, XGetMotionEvents, XIfEvent, XMaskEvent, XNextEvent, XPeekEvent, XPeek-IfEvent, XPending, XPutBackEvent, XSelectInput, XSendEvent, XSetInput-Focus, XSynchronize, XWindowEvent.

Name

XGetKeyboardControl — obtain a list of the current keyboard preferences.

Synopsis

```
XGetKeyboardControl(display, values)
    Display *display;
    XKeyboardState *values;   /* RETURN */
```

Arguments

display   Specifies a connection to an X server; returned from XOpenDisplay.

values   Returns filled XKeyboardState structure.

Description

XGetKeyboardControl returns the current control values for the keyboard. For the LEDs (light emitting diodes), the least significant bit of led_mask corresponds to LED 1, and each bit that is set to 1 in led_mask indicates an LED that is lit. auto_repeats is a bit vector; each bit that is set to 1 indicates that auto-repeat is enabled for the corresponding key. The vector is represented as 32 bytes. Byte N (from 0) contains the bits for keys 8N to 8N+7, with the least significant bit in the byte representing key 8N. global_auto_repeat is either AutoRepeatModeOn or AutoRepeatModeOff.

For the ranges of each member of XKeyboardState, see the description of XChange-PointerControl.

For more information, see Volume One, Chapter 9, *The Keyboard and Pointer*.

Structures

```
typedef struct {
    int key_click_percent;
    int bell_percent;
    unsigned int bell_pitch, bell_duration;
    unsigned long led_mask;
    int global_auto_repeat;
    char auto_repeats[32];
} XKeyboardState;
```

Related Commands

XAutoRepeatOff, XAutoRepeatOn, XBell, XChangeKeyboardControl, XGet-Default, XGetPointerControl.

XGetKeyboardMapping

Name

XGetKeyboardMapping — return symbols for keycodes.

Synopsis

```
KeySym *XGetKeyboardMapping(display, first_keycode,
        keycode_count, keysyms_per_keycode)
    Display *display;
    KeyCode first_keycode;
    int keycode_count;
    int *keysyms_per_keycode; /* RETURN */
```

Arguments

display   Specifies a connection to an X server; returned from XOpenDisplay.

first_keycode
                 Specifies the first keycode that is to be returned.

keycode_count
                 Specifies the number of keycodes that are to be returned.

keysyms_per_keycode
                 Returns the number of keysyms per keycode.

Description

Starting with *first_keycode*, XGetKeyboardMapping returns the symbols for the specified number of keycodes. The specified *first_keycode* must be greater than or equal to min_keycode as returned by XDisplayKeycodes, otherwise a BadValue error occurs. In addition, the following expression must be less than or equal to max_keycode (also returned by XDisplayKeycodes) as returned in the Display structure, otherwise a BadValue error occurs:

```
first_keycode + keycode_count - 1
```

The number of elements in the keysyms list is:

```
keycode_count * keysyms_per_keycode
```

Then, keysym number *N* (counting from 0) for keycode *K* has an index (counting from 0) of the following (in keysyms):

```
(K - first_keycode) * keysyms_per_keycode + N
```

The keysyms_per_keycode value is chosen arbitrarily by the server to be large enough to report all requested symbols. A special KeySym value of NoSymbol is used to fill in unused elements for individual keycodes.

Use XFree to free the returned keysym list when you no longer need it.

For more information, see Volume One, Chapter 9, *The Keyboard and Pointer*.

Errors

BadValue   *first_keycode* less than *display*->min_keycode.

                  display->max_keycode exceeded.

Related Commands

XChangeKeyboardMapping, XDeleteModifiermapEntry, XFreeModifiermap,
XGetModifierMapping, XInsertModifiermapEntry, XKeycodeToKeysym,
XKeysymToKeycode, XKeysymToString, XLookupKeysym, XLookupString,
XNewModifierMap, XQueryKeymap, XRebindKeySym, XRefreshKeyboard-
Mapping, XSetModifierMapping, XStringToKeysym.

Name

XGetModifierMapping — obtain a mapping of modifier keys (Shift, Control, etc.).

Synopsis

```
XModifierKeymap *XGetModifierMapping(display)
    Display *display;
```

Arguments

display   Specifies a connection to an X server; returned from XOpenDisplay.

Description

XGetModifierMapping returns the keycodes of the keys being used as modifiers.

There are eight modifiers, represented by the symbols ShiftMapIndex, LockMapIndex, ControlMapIndex, Mod1MapIndex, Mod2MapIndex, Mod3MapIndex, Mod4Map-Index, and Mod5MapIndex. The modifiermap member of the XModifierKeymap structure contains eight sets of keycodes, each set containing max_keypermod keycodes. Zero keycodes are not meaningful. If an entire modifiermap is filled with zero's, the corresponding modifier is disabled. No keycode will appear twice anywhere in the map.

Structures

```
typedef struct {
    int max_keypermod;      /* server's max number of keys per modifier */
    KeyCode *modifiermap; /* an 8 by max_keypermod array of
                          * keycodes to be used as modifiers */
} XModifierKeymap;

/* modifier names.  Used to build a SetModifierMapping request or
   to read a GetModifierMapping request. */
#define ShiftMapIndex      0
#define LockMapIndex       1
#define ControlMapIndex    2
#define Mod1MapIndex       3
#define Mod2MapIndex       4
#define Mod3MapIndex       5
#define Mod4MapIndex       6
#define Mod5MapIndex       7
```

Related Commands

XChangeKeyboardMapping, XDeleteModifiermapEntry, XFreeModifiermap, XGetKeyboardMapping, XInsertModifiermapEntry, XKeycodeToKeysym, XKeysymToKeycode, XKeysymToString, XLookupKeysym, XLookupString, XNewModifierMap, XQueryKeymap, XRebindKeySym, XRefreshKeyboard-Mapping, XSetModifierMapping, XStringToKeysym.

Name

XGetMotionEvents — get events from pointer motion history buffer.

Synopsis

```
XTimeCoord *XGetMotionEvents(display, w, start, stop, nevents)
    Display *display;
    Window w;
    Time start, stop;
    int *nevents;               /* RETURN */
```

Arguments

display   Specifies a connection to an X server; returned from XOpenDisplay.

w   Specifies the ID of the window whose associated pointer motion events will be returned.

start   Specify the time interval for which the events are returned from the motion his-
stop   tory buffer. Pass a time stamp (in milliseconds) or CurrentTime.

nevents   Returns the number of events returned from the motion history buffer.

Description

XGetMotionEvents returns all events in the motion history buffer that fall between the specified start and stop times (inclusive) and that have coordinates that lie within (including borders) the specified window at its present placement. The x and y coordinates of the XTimeCoord return structure are reported relative to the origin of w.

XGetMotionEvent returns NULL if the server does not support a motion history buffer (which is common), or if the start time is after the stop time, or if the start time is in the future. A motion history buffer is supported if XDisplayMotionBufferSize (display) > 0. The pointer position at each pointer hardware interrupt is then stored for later retrieval.

If the start time is later than the stop time, or if the start time is in the future, no events are returned. If the stop time is in the future, it is equivalent to specifying the constant Current-Time, since the server does not wait to report future events.

Use XFree to free the returned XTimeCoord structures when they are no longer needed.

For more information, see Volume One, Chapter 9, *The Keyboard and Pointer*.

Structures

```
typedef struct _XTimeCoord {
    Time time;
    short x, y;
} XTimeCoord;
```

Errors

BadWindow

Related Commands

QLength, XAllowEvents, XCheckIfEvent, XCheckMaskEvent, XCheckTyped-
Event, XCheckTypedWindowEvent, XCheckWindowEvent, XEventsQueued,
XGetInputFocus, XIfEvent, XMaskEvent, XNextEvent, XPeekEvent, XPeek-
IfEvent, XPending, XPutBackEvent, XSelectInput, XSendEvent, XSetInput-
Focus, XSynchronize, XWindowEvent.

Name

XGetNormalHints — get the size hints property of a window in normal state (not zoomed or iconified).

Synopsis

```
Status XGetNormalHints(display, w, hints)
    Display *display;
    Window w;
    XSizeHints *hints;              /* RETURN */
```

Arguments

display	Specifies a connection to an X server; returned from XOpenDisplay.
w	Specifies the ID of the window to be queried.
hints	Returns the sizing hints for the window in its normal state.

Description

XGetNormalHints has been superseded by XGetWMNormalHints as of Release 4, because new interclient communication conventions are now standard.

XGetNormalHints returns the size hints for a window in its normal state by reading the XA_WM_NORMAL_HINTS property. This function is normally used only by a window manager. It returns a nonzero Status if it succeeds, and zero if it fails (e.g., the application specified no normal size hints for this window.)

For more information on using hints, see Volume One, Chapter 10, *Interclient Communication*.

Structures

```
typedef struct {
    long flags;     /* which fields in structure are defined */
    int x, y;
    int width, height;
    int min_width, min_height;
    int max_width, max_height;
    int width_inc, height_inc;
    struct {
        int x;      /* numerator */
        int y;      /* denominator */
    } min_aspect, max_aspect;
} XSizeHints;

/* flags argument in size hints */
#define USPosition (1L << 0)/* user specified x, y */
#define USSize     (1L << 1)/* user specified width, height */

#define PPosition  (1L << 2)/* program specified position */
#define PSize      (1L << 3)/* program specified size */
#define PMinSize   (1L << 4)/* program specified minimum size */
#define PMaxSize   (1L << 5)/* program specified maximum size */
```

```
#define PResizeInc (1L << 6)/* program specified resize increments */
#define PAspect    (1L << 7)/* program specified min/max aspect ratios */
#define PAllHints (PPosition|PSize|PMinSize|PMaxSize|PResizeInc|PAspect)
```

Errors
BadWindow

Related Commands
XFetchName, XGetClassHint, XGetIconName, XGetIconSizes, XGetSize-
Hints, XGetTransientForHint, XGetWMHints, XGetZoomHints, XSetClass-
Hint, XSetCommand, XSetIconName, XSetIconSizes, XSetNormalHints, XSet-
SizeHints, XSetTransientForHint, XSetWMHints, XSetZoomHints, XStore-
Name.

XGetPixel

XGetPixel

Name

XGetPixel — obtain a single pixel value from an image.

Synopsis

```
unsigned long XGetPixel(ximage, x, y)
    XImage *ximage;
    int x;
    int y;
```

Arguments

ximage   Specifies a pointer to the image.

x
            Specify the x and y coordinates of the pixel whose value is to be returned.
y

Description

XGetPixel returns the specified pixel from the named image. The *x* and *y* coordinates are relative to the origin (upper left [0,0]) of the image). The pixel value is returned in the clients bit- and byte-order. The x and y coordinates must be contained in the image.

For more information, see Volume One, Chapter 6, *Drawing Graphics and Text*.

Structures

```
typedef struct _XImage {
    int width, height;          /* size of image */
    int xoffset;                /* number of pixels offset in X direction */
    int format;                 /* XYBitmap, XYPixmap, ZPixmap */
    char *data;                 /* pointer to image data */
    int byte_order;             /* data byte order, LSBFirst, MSBFirst */
    int bitmap_unit;            /* quant. of scan line 8, 16, 32 */
    int bitmap_bit_order;       /* LSBFirst, MSBFirst */
    int bitmap_pad;             /* 8, 16, 32 either XY or ZPixmap */
    int depth;                  /* depth of image */
    int bytes_per_line;         /* accelerator to next line */
    int bits_per_pixel;         /* bits per pixel (ZPixmap) */
    unsigned long red_mask;     /* bits in z arrangment */
    unsigned long green_mask;
    unsigned long blue_mask;
    char *obdata;               /* hook for the object routines to hang on */
    struct funcs {              /* image manipulation routines */
        struct _XImage *(*create_image)();
        int (*destroy_image)();
        unsigned long (*get_pixel)();
        int (*put_pixel)();
        struct _XImage *(*sub_image)();
        int (*add_pixel)();
    } f;
} XImage;
```

Related Commands

ImageByteOrder, XAddPixel, XCreateImage, XDestroyImage, XGetImage,
XGetSubImage, XPutImage, XPutPixel, XSubImage.

XGetPointerControl

Name

XGetPointerControl — get the current pointer preferences.

Synopsis

```
XGetPointerControl(display, accel_numerator, accel_denominator,
        threshold)
    Display *display;
    int *accel_numerator, *accel_denominator;  /* RETURN */
    int *threshold;                             /* RETURN */
```

Arguments

display   Specifies a connection to an X server; returned from XOpenDisplay.

accel_numerator
        Returns the numerator for the acceleration multiplier.

accel_denominator
        Returns the denominator for the acceleration multiplier.

threshold   Returns the acceleration threshold in pixels. The pointer must move more than this amount before acceleration takes effect.

Description

XGetPointerControl gets the pointer acceleration parameters.

accel_numerator divided by *accel_denominator* is the number of pixels the cursor moves per unit of motion of the pointer, applied only to the amount of movement over *threshold*.

Related Commands

XChangeActivePointerGrab, XChangePointerControl, XGetPointer-Mapping, XGrabPointer, XQueryPointer, XSetPointerMapping, XUngrab-Pointer, XWarpPointer.

XGetPointerMapping

Name

XGetPointerMapping — get the pointer button mapping.

Synopsis

```
int XGetPointerMapping(display, map, nmap)
    Display *display;
    unsigned char map[];        /* RETURN */
    int nmap;
```

Arguments

display   Specifies a connection to an X server; returned from XOpenDisplay.

map   Returns the mapping list. Array begins with map[].

nmap   Specifies the number of items in mapping list.

Description

XGetPointerMapping returns the current mapping of the pointer buttons. Information is returned in both the arguments and the function's return value. map is an array of the numbers of the buttons as they are currently mapped. Elements of the list are indexed starting from 1. The nominal mapping for a pointer is the identity mapping: map[i]=i. If map[3]=2, it means that the third physical button triggers the second logical button.

nmap indicates the desired number of button mappings.

The return value of the function is the actual number of elements in the pointer list, which may be greater or less than nmap.

Related Commands

XChangeActivePointerGrab, XChangePointerControl, XGetPointer-Control, XGrabPointer, XQueryPointer, XSetPointerMapping, XUngrab-Pointer, XWarpPointer.

Name

XGetRGBColormaps — obtain the XStandardColormap structure associated with the specified property.

Synopsis

```
Status XGetRGBColormaps(display, w, std_colormap, count,
          property)
    Display *display;
    Window w;
    XStandardColormap **std_colormap;      /* RETURN */
    int *count;                            /* RETURN */
    Atom property;
```

Arguments

display   Specifies a connection to an X server; returned from XOpenDisplay.

w   Specifies the window.

std_colormap
                 Returns the XStandardColormap structure.

count   Returns the number of colormaps.

property   Specifies the property name.

Availability

Release 4 and later.

Description

XGetRGBColormaps returns the RGB colormap definitions stored in the specified property on the named window. If the property exists, is of type RGB_COLOR_MAP, is of format 32, and is long enough to contain a colormap definition, XGetRGBColormaps allocates and fills in space for the returned colormaps, and returns a non-zero status. Otherwise, none of the fields are set, and XGetRGBColormaps returns a zero status. If the visualid field is not present, XGetRGBColormaps assumes the default visual for the screen on which the window is located; if the killid field is not present, it is assumed to have a value of None, which indicates that the resources cannot be released. Note that it is the caller's responsibility to honor the ICCCM restriction that only RGB_DEFAULT_MAP contain more than one definition.

XGetRGBColormaps supersedes XGetStandardColormap.

For more information, see Volume One, Chapter 7, *Color*.

Structures

```
typedef struct {
    Colormap colormap;
    unsigned long red_max;
    unsigned long red_mult;
    unsigned long green_max;
```

```
        unsigned long green_mult;
        unsigned long blue_max;
        unsigned long blue_mult;
        unsigned long base_pixel;
        VisualID visualid;              /* added by ICCCM version 1 */
        XID killid;                     /* added by ICCCM version 1 */
    } XStandardColormap;
```

Errors

```
    BadAtom
    BadWindow
```

Related Commands

```
    XAllocStandardColormap, XSetRGBColormaps.
```

Name

XGetScreenSaver — get the current screen saver parameters.

Synopsis

```
XGetScreenSaver(display, timeout, interval, prefer_blanking,
        allow_exposures)
    Display *display;
    int *timeout, *interval;   /* RETURN */
    int *prefer_blanking;      /* RETURN */
    int *allow_exposures;      /* RETURN */
```

Arguments

display Specifies a connection to an X server; returned from XOpenDisplay.

timeout Returns the idle time, in seconds, until the screen saver turns on.

interval Returns the interval between screen changes, in seconds.

prefer_blanking
    Returns the current screen blanking preference, one of these constants: DontPreferBlanking, PreferBlanking, or DefaultBlanking.

allow_exposures
    Returns the current screen save control value, either DontAllowExposures, AllowExposures, or DefaultExposures.

Description

XGetScreenSaver returns the current settings of the screen saver, which may be set with XSetScreenSaver.

A positive *timeout* indicates that the screen saver is enabled. A *timeout* of zero indicates that the screen saver is disabled.

If the server-dependent screen saver method supports periodic change, *interval* serves as a hint about the length of the change period, and zero serves as a hint that no periodic change will be made. An *interval* of zero indicates that random pattern motion is disabled.

For more information on the screen saver, see Volume One, Chapter 13, *Other Programming Techniques*.

Related Commands

XActivateScreenSaver, XForceScreenSaver, XResetScreenSaver, XSetScreenSaver.

XGetSelectionOwner

Name
XGetSelectionOwner — return the owner of a selection.

Synopsis
```
Window XGetSelectionOwner(display, selection)
    Display *display;
    Atom selection;
```

Arguments
display   Specifies a connection to an X server; returned from XOpenDisplay.

selection   Specifies the selection atom whose owner you want returned.

Description
XGetSelectionOwner returns the window ID of the current owner of the specified selection. If no selection was specified, or there is no owner, the function returns the constant None.

For more information on selections, see Volume One, Chapter 10, *Interclient Communication*.

Errors
BadAtom

Related Commands
XConvertSelection, XSetSelectionOwner.

XGetSizeHints

Name

XGetSizeHints — read any property of type XA_SIZE_HINTS.

Synopsis

```
Status XGetSizeHints(display, w, hints, property)
    Display *display;
    Window w;
    XSizeHints *hints;          /* RETURN */
    Atom property;
```

Arguments

display   Specifies a connection to an X server; returned from XOpenDisplay.

w   Specifies the ID of the window for which size hints will be returned.

hints   Returns the size hints structure.

property   Specifies a property atom of type XA_WM_SIZE_HINTS. May be XA_WM_NORMAL_HINTS, XA_WM_ZOOM_HINTS (in Release 3), or a property defined by an application.

Description

XGetSizeHints has been superseded by XGetWMSizeHints as of Release 4, because the interclient communication conventions are now standard.

XGetSizeHints returns the XSizeHints structure for the named property and the specified window. This is used by XGetNormalHints and XGetZoomHints, and can be used to retrieve the value of any property of type XA_WM_SIZE_HINTS; thus, it is useful if other properties of that type get defined. This function is used almost exclusively by window managers.

XGetSizeHints returns a nonzero Status if a size hint was defined, and zero otherwise.

For more information on using hints, see Volume One, Chapter 10, *Interclient Communication*.

Structures

```
typedef struct {
    long flags;      /* which fields in structure are defined */
    int x, y;
    int width, height;
    int min_width, min_height;
    int max_width, max_height;
    int width_inc, height_inc;
    struct {
        int x;      /* numerator */
        int y;      /* denominator */
    } min_aspect, max_aspect;
} XSizeHints;

/* flags argument in size hints */
#define USPosition (1L << 0) /* user specified x, y */
#define USSize     (1L << 1) /* user specified width, height */
```

```
#define PPosition  (1L << 2) /* program specified position */
#define PSize      (1L << 3) /* program specified size */
#define PMinSize   (1L << 4) /* program specified minimum size */
#define PMaxSize   (1L << 5) /* program specified maximum size */
#define PResizeInc (1L << 6) /* program specified resize increments */
#define PAspect    (1L << 7) /* program specified min/max aspect ratios */
#define PAllHints (PPosition|PSize|PMinSize|PMaxSize|PResizeInc|PAspect)
```

Errors

```
BadAtom
BadWindow
```

Related Commands

XFetchName, XGetClassHint, XGetIconName, XGetIconSizes, XGetNormal-
Hints, XGetTransientForHint, XGetWMHints, XGetZoomHints, XSetClass-
Hint, XSetCommand, XSetIconName, XSetIconSizes, XSetNormalHints, XSet-
SizeHints, XSetTransientForHint, XSetWMHints, XSetZoomHints, XStore-
Name.

Name

XGetStandardColormap — get the standard colormap property.

Synopsis

```
Status XGetStandardColormap(display, w, cmap_info, property)
    Display *display;
    Window w;
    XStandardColormap *cmap_info;/* RETURN */
    Atom property;
```

Arguments

display   Specifies a connection to an X server; returned from XOpenDisplay.

w   Specifies the ID of the window on which the property is set. This is normally the root window.

cmap_info   Returns the filled colormap information structure.

property   Specifies the atom indicating the type of standard colormap desired. The predefined standard colormap atoms are XA_RGB_BEST_MAP, XA_RGB_RED_MAP, XA_RGB_GREEN_MAP, XA_RGB_BLUE_MAP, XA_RGB_DEFAULT_MAP, and XA_RGB_GRAY_MAP.

Description

XGetStandardColormap is superseded by XGetWMColormap in Release 4.

XGetStandardColormap gets a property on the root window that describes a standard colormap.

This call does not install the colormap into the hardware colormap, it does not allocate entries, and it does not even create a virtual colormap. It just provides information about one design of colormap and the ID of the colormap if some other client has already created it. The application can otherwise attempt to create a virtual colormap of the appropriate type, and allocate its entries according to the information in the XStandardColormap structure. Installing the colormap must then be done with XInstallColormap, in cooperation with the window manager. Any of these steps could fail, and the application should be prepared.

If the server or another client has already created a standard colormap of this type, then its ID will be returned in the colormap member of the XStandardColormap structure. Some servers and window managers, particular on high-performance workstations, will create some or all of the standard colormaps so they can be quickly installed when needed by applications.

An application should go through the standard colormap creation process only if it needs the special qualities of the standard colormaps. For one, they allow the application to convert RGB values into pixel values quickly because the mapping is predictable. Given an XStandard-Colormap structure for an XA_RGB_BEST_MAP colormap, and floating point RGB coefficients in the range 0.0 to 1.0, you can compose pixel values with the following C expression:

```
pixel = base_pixel
    + ((unsigned long) (0.5 + r * red_max)) * red_mult
    + ((unsigned long) (0.5 + g * green_max)) * green_mult
    + ((unsigned long) (0.5 + b * blue_max)) * blue_mult;
```

The use of addition rather than logical-OR for composing pixel values permits allocations where the RGB value is not aligned to bit boundaries.

XGetStandardColormap returns zero if it fails, or nonzero if it succeeds.

See Volume One, Chapter 7, *Color*, for a complete description of standard colormaps.

Structures

```
typedef struct {
    Colormap colormap;    /* ID of colormap created by XCreateColormap */
    unsigned long red_max;
    unsigned long red_mult;
    unsigned long green_max;
    unsigned long green_mult;
    unsigned long blue_max;
    unsigned long blue_mult;
    unsigned long base_pixel;
    /* new fields here in R4 */
} XStandardColormap;
```

Errors

```
BadAtom
BadWindow
```

Related Commands

DefaultColormap, DisplayCells, XCopyColormapAndFree, XCreate-
Colormap, XFreeColormap, XInstallColormap, XListInstalledColormaps,
XSetStandardColormap, XSetWindowColormap, XUninstallColormap.

Name

XGetSubImage — copy a rectangle in drawable to a location within the pre-existing image.

Synopsis

```
XImage *XGetSubImage(display, drawable, x, y, width, height,
        plane_mask, format, dest_image, dest_x, dest_y)
    Display *display;
    Drawable drawable;
    int x, y;
    unsigned int width, height;
    unsigned long plane_mask;
    int format;
    XImage *dest_image;
    int dest_x, dest_y;
```

Arguments

display	Specifies a connection to an X server; returned from XOpenDisplay.
drawable	Specifies the drawable from which the rectangle is to be copied.
x *y*	Specify the x and y coordinates of the upper-left corner of the rectangle, relative to the origin of the drawable.
width *height*	Specify the width and height in pixels of the subimage taken.
plane_mask	Specifies which planes of the drawable are transferred to the image.
format	Specifies the format for the image. Either XYPixmap or ZPixmap.
dest_image	Specifies the the destination image.
dest_x *dest_y*	Specify the x and y coordinates of the destination rectangle's upper left corner, relative to the image's origin.

Description

XGetSubImage updates the *dest_image* with the specified subimage in the same manner as XGetImage, except that it does not create the image or necessarily fill the entire image. If *format* is XYPixmap, the function transmits only the bit planes you specify in *plane_mask*. If *format* is ZPixmap, the function transmits as zero the bits in all planes not specified in *plane_mask*. The function performs no range checking on the values in *plane_mask* and ignores extraneous bits.

The depth of the destination XImage structure must be the same as that of the drawable. Otherwise, a BadMatch error is generated. If the specified subimage does not fit at the specified location on the destination image, the right and bottom edges are clipped. If the drawable is a window, the window must be mapped or held in backing store, and it must be the case that, if there were no inferiors or overlapping windows, the specified rectangle of the window would be fully visible on the screen. Otherwise, a BadMatch error is generated.

If the window has a backing store, the backing store contents are returned for regions of the window that are obscured by noninferior windows. Otherwise, the return contents of such obscured regions are undefined. Also undefined are the returned contents of visible regions of inferiors of different depth than the specified window.

XSubImage extracts a subimage from an image, instead of from a drawable like XGetSub-Image.

For more information on images, see Volume One, Chapter 6, *Drawing Graphics and Text*.

Errors
BadDrawable

BadMatch   Depth of *dest_image* is not the same as depth of *drawable*.

BadValue

Related Commands
ImageByteOrder, XAddPixel, XCreateImage, XDestroyImage, XGetImage, XGetPixel, XPutImage, XPutPixel, XSubImage.

Name

XGetTextProperty — read one of a window's text properties.

Synopsis

```
Status XGetTextProperty(display, w, text_prop, property)
      Display *display;
      Window w;
      XTextProperty *text_prop;        /* RETURN */
      Atom property;
```

Arguments

display	Specifies a connection to an X server; returned from XOpenDisplay.
w	Specifies the window.
text_prop	Returns the XTextProperty structure.
property	Specifies the property name.

Availability

Release 4 and later.

Description

XGetTextProperty reads the specified property from the window and stores the data in the returned XTextProperty structure. It stores the data in the value field, the type of the data in the encoding field, the format of the data in the format field, and the number of items of data in the nitems field. The particular interpretation of the property's encoding and data as "text" is left to the calling application. If the specified property does not exist on the window, XGetTextProperty sets the value field to NULL, the encoding field to None, the format field to zero, and the nitems field to zero.

If it was able to set these files in the XTextProperty structure, XGetTextProperty returns a non-zero status; otherwise, it returns a zero status.

For more information, see Volume One, Chapter 10, *Interclient Communication*.

Structures

```
typedef struct {
    unsigned char *value;        /* same as Property routines */
    Atom encoding;               /* prop type */
    int format;                  /* prop data format: 8, 16, or 32 */
    unsigned long nitems;        /* number of data items in value */
} XTextProperty;
```

Errors

```
BadAtom
BadWindow
```

Related Commands

`XFreeStringList`, `XSetTextProperty`, `XStringListToTextProperty`, `XTextPropertytoStringList`.

XGetTransientForHint

Name

XGetTransientForHint — get the XA_WM_TRANSIENT_FOR property of a window.

Synopsis

```
Status XGetTransientForHint(display, w, prop_window)
    Display *display;
    Window w;
    Window *prop_window;          /* RETURN */
```

Arguments

display   Specifies a connection to an X server; returned from XOpenDisplay.

w   Specifies the ID of the window to be queried.

prop_window Returns the window contained in the XA_WM_TRANSIENT_FOR property of the specified window.

Description

XGetTransientForHint obtains the XA_WM_TRANSIENT_FOR property for the specified window. This function is normally used by a window manager. This property should be set for windows that are to appear only temporarily on the screen, such as pop-up dialog boxes. The window returned is the main window to which this popup window is related. This lets the window manager decorate the popup window appropriately.

XGetTransientForHint returns a Status of zero on failure, and nonzero on success.

For more information on using hints, see Volume One, Chapter 10, *Interclient Communication*.

Errors

BadWindow

Related Commands

XFetchName, XGetClassHint, XGetIconName, XGetIconSizes, XGetNormal-
Hints, XGetSizeHints, XGetWMHints, XGetZoomHints, XSetClassHint, XSet-
Command, XSetIconName, XSetIconSizes, XSetNormalHints, XSetSizeHints,
XSetTransientForHint, XSetWMHints, XSetZoomHints, XStoreName.

Name

XGetVisualInfo — find the visual information structures that match the specified template.

Synopsis

```
XVisualInfo *XGetVisualInfo(display, vinfo_mask,
        vinfo_template, nitems)
    Display *display;
    long vinfo_mask;
    XVisualInfo *vinfo_template;
    int *nitems;                    /* RETURN */
```

Arguments

display   Specifies a connection to an X server; returned from XOpenDisplay.

vinfo_mask   Specifies the visual mask value. Indicates which elements in template are to be matched.

vinfo_template

        Specifies the visual attributes that are to be used in matching the visual structures.

nitems   Returns the number of matching visual structures.

Description

XGetVisualInfo returns a list of visual structures that describe visuals supported by the server and that match the attributes specified by the *vinfo_template* argument. If no visual structures match the template, XGetVisualInfo returns a NULL. To free the data returned by this function, use XFree.

For more information, see Volume One, Chapter 7, *Color*.

Structures

```
typedef struct {
    Visual *visual;
    VisualID visualid;
    int screen;
    unsigned int depth;
    int class;
    unsigned long red_mask;
    unsigned long green_mask;
    unsigned long blue_mask;
    int colormap_size;
    int bits_per_rgb;
} XVisualInfo;

/* The symbols for the vinfo_mask argument are: */

#define VisualNoMask                0x0
#define VisualIDMask                0x1
#define VisualScreenMask            0x2
```

```
#define VisualDepthMask        0x4
#define VisualClassMask        0x8
#define VisualRedMaskMask      0x10
#define VisualGreenMaskMask    0x20
#define VisualBlueMaskMask     0x40
#define VisualColormapSizeMask 0x80
#define VisualBitsPerRGBMask   0x100
#define VisualAllMask          0x1FF
```

Related Commands

`DefaultVisual, XVisualIDFromVisual, XMatchVisualInfo, XListDepths.`

Name

XGetWMIconName — read a window's XA_WM_ICON_NAME property.

Synopsis

```
Status XGetWMIconName(display, w, text_prop)
    Display *display;
    Window w;
    XTextProperty *text_prop;/* RETURN */
```

Arguments

display   Specifies a connection to an X server; returned from XOpenDisplay.

w   Specifies the window.

text_prop   Returns the XTextProperty structure.

Availability

Release 4 and later.

Description

XGetWMIconName performs an XGetTextProperty on the XA_WM_ICON_NAME property of the specified window. XGetWMIconName supersedes XGetIconName.

This function is primarily used by window managers to get the name to be written in a window's icon when they need to display that icon.

For more information, see Volume One, Chapter 10, *Interclient Communication*.

Structures

```
typedef struct {
    unsigned char *value;          /* same as Property routines */
    Atom encoding;                 /* prop type */
    int format;                    /* prop data format: 8, 16, or 32 */
    unsigned long nitems;          /* number of data items in value */
} XTextProperty;
```

Related Commands

XGetWMName, XSetWMIconName, XSetWMName, XSetWMProperties.

Name
XGetWMName — read a window's XA_WM_NAME property.

Synopsis
```
Status XGetWMName(display, w, text_prop)
      Display *display;
      Window w;
      XTextProperty *text_prop;/* RETURN */
```

Arguments
display   Specifies a connection to an X server; returned from XOpenDisplay.

w   Specifies the window.

text_prop Returns the XTextProperty structure.

Availability
Release 4 and later.

Description
XGetWMName performs an XGetTextProperty on the XA_WM_NAME property of the specified window. XGetWMName supersedes XFetchName.

XGetWMName returns nonzero if it succeeds, and zero if the property has not been set for the argument window.

For more information, see Volume One, Chapter 10, *Interclient Communication*.

Structures
```
typedef struct {
    unsigned char *value;          /* same as Property routines */
    Atom encoding;                 /* prop type */
    int format;                    /* prop data format: 8, 16, or 32 */
    unsigned long nitems;          /* number of data items in value */
} XTextProperty;
```

Related Commands
XGetWMIconName, XSetWMIconName, XSetWMName, XSetWMProperties.

Name

XGetWMNormalHints — read a window's XA_WM_NORMAL_HINTS property.

Synopsis

```
Status XGetWMNormalHints(display, w, hints, supplied)
    Display *display;
    Window w;
    XSizeHints *hints;/* RETURN */
    long *supplied;
```

Arguments

display	Specifies a connection to an X server; returned from XOpenDisplay.
w	Specifies the window.
hints	Returns the size hints for the window in its normal state.
supplied	Returns the hints that were supplied by the user.

Availability

Release 4 and later.

Description

XGetWMNormalHints returns the size hints stored in the XA_WM_NORMAL_HINTS property on the specified window. If the property is of type XA_WM_SIZE_HINTS, of format 32, and is long enough to contain either an old (pre-ICCCM) or new size hints structure, XGetWMNormal-Hints sets the various fields of the XSizeHints structure, sets the supplied argument to the list of fields that were supplied by the user (whether or not they contained defined values) and returns a non-zero status. XGetWMNormalHints returns a zero status if the application specified no normal size hints for this window.

XGetWMNormalHints supersedes XGetNormalHints.

If XGetWMNormalHints returns successfully and a pre-ICCCM size hints property is read, the supplied argument will contain the following bits:

(USPosition|USSize|PPosition|PSize|PMinSize| PMaxSize|PResizeInc|PAspect)

If the property is large enough to contain the base size and window gravity fields as well, the supplied argument will also contain the following bits:

(PBaseSize|PWinGravity)

This function is normally used only by a window manager.

For more information, see Volume One, Chapter 10, *Interclient Communication*.

Structures

```
typedef struct {
    long flags;    /* marks which fields in this structure are defined */
    int x, y;      /* obsolete for new window mgrs, but clients */
```

```
    int width, height;   /* should set so old wm's don't mess up */
    int min_width, min_height;
    int max_width, max_height;
    int width_inc, height_inc;
    struct {
            int x;   /* numerator */
            int y;   /* denominator */
    } min_aspect, max_aspect;
    int base_width, base_height;      /* added by ICCCM version 1 */
    int win_gravity;                  /* added by ICCCM
version 1 */
} XSizeHints;
```

Errors

BadWindow

Related Commands

XAllocSizeHints,   XGetWMSizeHints,   XSetWMNormalHints,   XSet-
WMProperties, XSetWMSizeHints.

XGetWMSizeHints

Name

XGetWMSizeHints — read a window's XA_WM_SIZE_HINTS property.

Synopsis

```
Status XGetWMSizeHints(display, w, hints, supplied, property)
      Display *display;
      Window w;
      XSizeHints *hints;            /* RETURN */
      long *supplied;               /*RETURN */
      Atom property;
```

Arguments

display	Specifies a connection to an X server; returned from XOpenDisplay.
w	Specifies the window.
hints	Returns the XSizeHints structure.
supplied	Returns the hints that were supplied by the user.
property	Specifies the property name.

Availability

Release 4 and later.

Description

XGetWMSizeHints returns the size hints stored in the specified property on the named window. If the property is of type XA_WM_SIZE_HINTS, of format 32, and is long enough to contain either an old (pre-ICCCM) or new size hints structure, XGetWMSizeHints sets the various fields of the XSizeHints structure, sets the *supplied* argument to the list of fields that were supplied by the user (whether or not they contained defined values), and returns a non-zero status. If the hint was not set, it returns a zero status. To get a window's normal size hints, you can use the XGetWMNormalHints function instead.

XGetWMSizeHints supersedes XGetSizeHints.

If XGetWMSizeHints returns successfully and a pre-ICCCM size hints property is read, the *supplied* argument will contain the following bits:

(USPosition|USSize|PPosition|PSize|PMinSize| PMaxSize|PResizeInc|PAspect)

If the property is large enough to contain the base size and window gravity fields as well, the supplied argument will also contain the following bits:

(PBaseSize|PWinGravity)

This function is used almost exclusively by window managers.

For more information, see Volume One, Chapter 10, *Interclient Communication*.

Structures

```
typedef struct {
    long flags;       /* marks which fields in this structure are defined */
    int x, y;         /* obsolete for new window mgrs, but clients */
    int width, height;    /* should set so old wm's don't mess up */
    int min_width, min_height;
    int max_width, max_height;
    int width_inc, height_inc;
    struct {
            int x;  /* numerator */
            int y;  /* denominator */
    } min_aspect, max_aspect;
    int base_width, base_height;            /* added by ICCCM version 1 */
    int win_gravity;                        /* added by ICCCM version 1 */
} XSizeHints;
```

Errors

BadAtom
BadWindow

Related Commands

XAllocSizeHints, XGetWMNormalHints, XSetWMNormalHints, XSetWMSize-
Hints.

XGetWindowAttributes

Name

XGetWindowAttributes — obtain the current attributes of window.

Synopsis

```
Status XGetWindowAttributes(display, w, window_attributes)
    Display *display;
    Window w;
    XWindowAttributes *window_attributes; /* RETURN */
```

Arguments

display   Specifies a connection to an X server; returned from XOpenDisplay.

w   Specifies the window whose current attributes you want.

window_attributes
               Returns a filled XWindowAttributes structure, containing the current attributes for the specified window.

Description

XGetWindowAttributes returns the XWindowAttributes structure containing the current window attributes.

While *w* is defined as type Window, a Pixmap can also be used, in which case all the returned members will be zero except width, height, depth, and screen.

XGetWindowAttributes returns a Status of zero on failure, or nonzero on success. However, it will only return zero if you have defined an error handler that does not exit, using XSetErrorHandler. The default error handler exits, and therefore XGetWindow-Attributes never gets a chance to return. (This is relevant only if you are writing a window manager or other application that deals with windows that might have been destroyed.)

The following list briefly describes each member of the XWindowAttributes structure. For more information, see Volume One, Chapter 4, *Window Attributes*.

x, y   The current position of the upper-left pixel of the window's border, relative to the origin of its parent.

width, height   The current dimensions in pixels of this window.

border_width   The current border width of the window.

depth   The number of bits per pixel in this window.

visual   The visual structure.

root   The root window ID of the screen containing the window.

class   The window class. One of these constants: InputOutput or Input-Only.

bit_gravity   The new position for existing contents after resize. One of the constants ForgetGravity, StaticGravity, or CenterGravity, or one of the compass constants (NorthWestGravity, NorthGravity, etc.).

`win_gravity` The new position for this window after its parent is resized. One of the constants `CenterGravity`, `UnmapGravity`, `StaticGravity`, or one of the compass constants.

`backing_store` When to maintain contents of the window. One of these constants: `Not-Useful`, `WhenMapped`, or `Always`.

`backing_planes`
The bit planes to be preserved in a backing store.

`backing_pixel` The pixel value used when restoring planes from a partial backing store.

`save_under` A boolean value, indicating whether saving bits under this window would be useful.

`colormap` The colormap ID being used in this window, or `None`.

`map_installed` A boolean value, indicating whether the colormap is currently installed. If `True`, the window is being displayed in its chosen colors.

`map_state` The window's map state. One of these constants: `IsUnmapped`, `Is-Unviewable`, or `IsViewable`. `IsUnviewable` indicates that the specified window is mapped but some ancestor is unmapped.

`all_event_masks`
The set of events any client have selected. This member is the bitwise inclusive OR of all event masks selected on the window by all clients.

`your_event_mask`
The bitwise inclusive OR of all event mask symbols selected by the querying client.

`do_not_propagate_mask`
The bitwise inclusive OR of the event mask symbols that specify the set of events that should not propagate. This is global across all clients.

`override_redirect`
A boolean value, indicating whether this window will override structure control facilities. This is usually only used for temporary pop-up windows such as menus. Either `True` or `False`.

`screen` A pointer to the `Screen` structure for the screen containing this window.

Errors
`BadWindow`

Structures
The `XWindowAttributes` structure contains:

```
typedef struct {
    int x, y;                   /* location of window */
    int width, height;          /* width and height of window */
    int border_width;           /* border width of window */
    int depth;                  /* depth of window */
```

```
        Visual *visual;                /* the associated visual structure */
        Window root;                   /* root of screen containing window */
        int class;                     /* InputOutput, InputOnly*/
        int bit_gravity;               /* one of bit gravity values */
        int win_gravity;               /* one of the window gravity values */
        int backing_store;             /* NotUseful, WhenMapped, Always */
        unsigned long backing_planes;  /* planes to be preserved if possible */
        unsigned long backing_pixel;   /* value to be used when restoring planes */
        Bool save_under;               /* boolean, should bits under be saved */
        Colormap colormap;             /* colormap to be associated with window */
        Bool map_installed;            /* boolean, is colormap currently installed*/
        int map_state;                 /* IsUnmapped, IsUnviewable, IsViewable */
        long all_event_masks;          /* set of events all people have interest in*/
        long your_event_mask;          /* my event mask */
        long do_not_propagate_mask;    /* set of events that should not propagate */
        Bool override_redirect;        /* boolean value for override-redirect */
        Screen *screen;                /* pointer to correct screen */
} XWindowAttributes;
```

Related Commands

XChangeWindowAttributes, XGetGeometry, XSetWindowBackground, XSet-
WindowBackgroundPixmap, XSetWindowBorder, XSetWindowBorderPixmap.

Name

XGetWindowProperty — obtain the atom type and property format for a window.

Synopsis

```
int XGetWindowProperty(display, w, property, long_offset,
        long_length, delete, req_type, actual_type, actual_for-
        mat, nitems, bytes_after, prop)
    Display *display;
    Window w;
    Atom property;
    long long_offset, long_length;
    Bool delete;
    Atom req_type;
    Atom *actual_type;              /* RETURN */
    int *actual_format;             /* RETURN */
    unsigned long *nitems;          /* RETURN */
    unsigned long *bytes_after;     /* RETURN */
    unsigned char **prop;           /* RETURN */
```

Arguments

display — Specifies a connection to an X server; returned from XOpenDisplay.

w — Specifies the ID of the window whose atom type and property format you want to obtain.

property — Specifies the atom of the desired property.

long_offset — Specifies the offset in 32-bit quantities where data will be retrieved.

long_length — Specifies the length in 32-bit multiples of the data to be retrieved.

delete — Specifies a boolean value of True or False. If you pass True and a property is returned, the property is deleted from the window after being read and a PropertyNotify event is generated on the window.

req_type — Specifies an atom describing the desired format of the data. If AnyPropertyType is specified, returns the property from the specified window regardless of its type. If a type is specified, the function returns the property only if its type equals the specified type.

actual_type — Returns the actual type of the property.

actual_format — Returns the actual data type of the returned data.

nitems — Returns the actual number of 8-, 16-, or 32-bit items returned in prop.

bytes_after — Returns the number of bytes remaining to be read in the property if a partial read was performed.

prop   Returns a pointer to the data actually returned, in the specified format. XGetWindowProperty always allocates one extra byte after the data and sets it to NULL. This byte is not counted in *nitems*.

Description

XGetWindowProperty gets the value of a property if it is the desired type. XGetWindow-Property sets the return arguments acccording to the following rules:

- If the specified property does not exist for the specified window, then: *actual_type* is None; *actual_format* = 0; and *bytes_after* = 0. *delete* is ignored in this case, and *nitems* is empty.

- If the specified property exists, but its type does not match *req_type*, then: *actual_type* is the actual property type; *actual_format* is the actual property format (never zero); and *bytes_after* is the property length in bytes (even if *actual_format* is 16 or 32). *delete* is ignored in this case, and *nitems* is empty.

- If the specified property exists, and either *req_type* is AnyPropertyType or the specified type matches the actual property type, then: *actual_type* is the actual property type; and *actual_format* is the actual property format (never zero). *bytes_after* and *nitems* are defined by combining the following values:

  N = actual length of stored property in bytes (even if *actual_format* is 16 or 32)
  I = 4 * *long_offset* (convert offset from *longs* into bytes)
  L = MINIMUM((N - I), 4 * *long_length*) (BadValue if L < 0)
  bytes_after = N - (I + L) (number of trailing unread bytes in stored property)

The returned data (in *prop*) starts at byte index I in the property (indexing from 0). The actual length of the returned data in bytes is *L*. *L* is converted into the number of 8-, 16-, or 32-bit items returned by dividing by 1, 2, or 4 respectively and this value is returned in *nitems*. The number of trailing unread bytes is returned in *bytes_after*.

If *delete* == True and *bytes_after* == 0 the function deletes the property from the window and generates a PropertyNotify event on the window.

When XGetWindowProperty executes successfully, it returns Success. The Success return value and the undocumented value returned on failure are the opposite of all other routines that return int or Status. The value of Success is undocumented, but is zero (0) in the current sample implementation from MIT. The failure value, also undocumented, is currently one (1). Therefore, comparing either value to True or False, or using the syntax "if (!XGetWindowProperty(...))" is not allowed.

To free the resulting data, use XFree.

For more information, see Volume One, Chapter 10, *Interclient Communication*.

Errors

`BadAtom`

`BadValue`   Value of *long_offset* caused *L* to be negative above.

`BadWindow`

Related Commands

`XChangeProperty`, `XGetAtomName`, `XGetFontProperty`, `XListProperties`,
`XRotateWindowProperties`, `XSetStandardProperties`.

Name

XGetWMHints — read the window manager hints property.

Synopsis

```
XWMHints *XGetWMHints(display, w)
    Display *display;
    Window w;
```

Arguments

display   Specifies a connection to an X server; returned from XOpenDisplay.

w   Specifies the ID of the window to be queried.

Description

This function is primarily for window managers. XGetWMHints returns NULL if no XA_WM_HINTS property was set on window *w*, and returns a pointer to an XWMHints structure if it succeeds. Programs must free the space used for that structure by calling XFree.

For more information on using hints, see Volume One, Chapter 10, *Interclient Communication*.

Structures

```
typedef struct {
    long flags;             /* marks which fields in this structure are defined */
    Bool input;             /* does application need window manager for input */
    int initial_state;      /* see below */
    Pixmap icon_pixmap;     /* pixmap to be used as icon */
    Window icon_window;     /* window to be used as icon */
    int icon_x, icon_y;     /* initial position of icon */
    Pixmap icon_mask;       /* icon mask bitmap */
    XID window_group;       /* ID of related window group */
    /* this structure may be extended in the future */
} XWMHints;

/* initial state flag: */
#define DontCareState      0
#define NormalState        1
#define ZoomState          2
#define IconicState        3
#define InactiveState      4
```

Errors

BadWindow

Related Commands

XAllocWMHints, XFetchName, XGetClassHint, XGetIconName, XGetIcon-Sizes, XGetNormalHints, XGetSizeHints, XGetTransientForHint, XGet-ZoomHints, XSetClassHint, XSetCommand, XSetIconName, XSetIconSizes, XSetNormalHints, XSetSizeHints, XSetTransientForHint, XSetWMHints, XSetZoomHints, XStoreName, XSetWMProperties.

Name

XGetZoomHints — read the size hints property of a zoomed window.

Synopsis

```
Status XGetZoomHints(display, w, zhints)
    Display *display;
    Window w;
    XSizeHints *zhints;          /* RETURN */
```

Arguments

display   Specifies a connection to an X server; returned from XOpenDisplay.

w   Specifies the ID of the window to be queried.

zhints   Returns a pointer to the zoom hints.

Description

XGetZoomHints is obsolete beginning in Release 4, because zoom hints are no longer defined in the ICCCM.

XGetZoomHints is primarily for window managers. XGetZoomHints returns the size hints for a window in its zoomed state (not normal or iconified) read from the XA_WM_ZOOM_HINTS property. It returns a nonzero Status if it succeeds, and zero if the application did not specify zoom size hints for this window.

For more information on using hints, see Volume One, Chapter 10, *Interclient Communication*.

Structures

```
typedef struct {
    long flags;     /* which fields in structure are defined */
    int x, y;
    int width, height;
    int min_width, min_height;
    int max_width, max_height;
    int width_inc, height_inc;
    struct {
        int x;      /* numerator */
        int y;      /* denominator */
    } min_aspect, max_aspect;
} XSizeHints;

/* flags argument in size hints */
#define USPosition (1L << 0) /* user specified x, y */
#define USSize     (1L << 1) /* user specified width, height */

#define PPosition  (1L << 2) /* program specified position */
#define PSize      (1L << 3) /* program specified size */
#define PMinSize   (1L << 4) /* program specified minimum size */
#define PMaxSize   (1L << 5) /* program specified maximum size */
#define PResizeInc (1L << 6) /* program specified resize increments */
```

```
#define PAspect     (1L << 7) /* program specified min/max aspect ratios */
#define PAllHints (PPosition|PSize|PMinSize|PMaxSize|PResizeInc|PAspect)
```

Errors
BadWindow

Related Commands
XFetchName, XGetClassHint, XGetIconName, XGetIconSizes, XGetNormal-
Hints, XGetSizeHints, XGetTransientForHint, XGetWMHints, XSetClass-
Hint, XSetCommand, XSetIconName, XSetIconSizes, XSetNormalHints, XSet-
SizeHints, XSetTransientForHint, XSetWMHints, XSetZoomHints, XStore-
Name.

XGrabButton

Name

XGrabButton — grab a pointer button.

Synopsis

```
XGrabButton(display, button, modifiers, grab_window,
        owner_events, event_mask, pointer_mode, keyboard_mode,
        confine_to, cursor)
    Display *display;
    unsigned int button;
    unsigned int modifiers;
    Window grab_window;
    Bool owner_events;
    unsigned int event_mask;
    int pointer_mode, keyboard_mode;
    Window confine_to;
    Cursor cursor;
```

Arguments

display   Specifies a connection to an X server; returned from `XOpenDisplay`.

button   Specifies the mouse button. May be `Button1`, `Button2`, `Button3`, `Button4`, `Button5`, or `AnyButton`. The constant `AnyButton` is equivalent to issuing the grab request for all possible buttons. The button symbols cannot be ORed.

modifiers   Specifies a set of keymasks. This is a bitwise OR of one or more of the following symbols: `ShiftMask`, `LockMask`, `ControlMask`, `Mod1Mask`, `Mod2Mask`, `Mod3Mask`, `Mod4Mask`, `Mod5Mask`, or `AnyModifier`. `AnyModifier` is equivalent to issuing the grab key request for all possible modifier combinations (including no modifiers).

grab_window   Specifies the ID of the window you want to the grab to occur in.

owner_events   Specifies a boolean value of either `True` or `False`. See Description below.

event_mask   Specifies the event mask to take effect during the grab. This mask is the bitwise OR of one or more of the event masks listed on the reference page for `XSelectInput`.

pointer_mode   Controls processing of pointer events during the grab. Pass one of these constants: `GrabModeSync` or `GrabModeAsync`.

keyboard_mode   Controls processing of keyboard events during the grab. Pass one of these constants: `GrabModeSync` or `GrabModeAsync`.

confine_to   Specifies the ID of the window to confine the pointer. One possible value is the constant `None`, in which case the pointer is not confined to any window.

cursor   Specifies the cursor to be displayed during the grab. One possible value you can pass is the constant None, in which case the existing cursor is used.

Description

XGrabButton establishes a passive grab, such that an active grab may take place when the specified key/button combination is pressed in the specified window. After this call, if

1) the specified button is pressed when the specified modifier keys are down (and no other buttons or modifier keys are down),

2) *grab_window* contains the pointer,

3) the *confine_to* window (if any) is viewable, and

4) these constraints are not satisfied for any ancestor,

then the pointer is actively grabbed as described in XGrabPointer, the last pointer grab time is set to the time at which the button was pressed, and the ButtonPress event is reported.

The interpretation of the remaining arguments is as for XGrabPointer. The active grab is terminated automatically when all buttons are released (independent of the state of modifier keys).

A modifier of AnyModifier is equivalent to issuing the grab request for all possible modifier combinations (including no modifiers). A button of AnyButton is equivalent to issuing the request for all possible buttons (but at least one).

XGrabButton overrides all previous passive grabs by the same client on the same key/button combination on the same window, but has no effect on an active grab. The request fails if some other client has already issued an XGrabButton with the same button/key combination on the same window. When using AnyModifier or AnyButton, the request fails completely (no grabs are established) if there is a conflicting grab for any combination.

The *owner_events* argument specifies whether the grab window should receive all events (False) or whether the grabbing application should receive all events normally (True).

The *pointer_mode* and *keyboard_mode* control the processing of events during the grab. If either is GrabModeSync, events for that device are not sent from the server to Xlib until XAllowEvents is called to release the events. If either is GrabModeAsync, events for that device are sent normally.

An automatic grab takes place between a ButtonPress event and the corresponding ButtonRelease event, so this call is not necessary in some of the most common situations. But this call is necessary for certain styles of menus.

For more information on grabbing, see Volume One, Chapter 9, *The Keyboard and Pointer*.

Errors

BadAccess   When using `AnyModifier` or `AnyButton` and there is a conflicting grab by another client. No grabs are established.

                      Another client has already issued an `XGrabButton` request with the same key/button combination on the same window.

BadCursor

BadValue

BadWindow

Related Commands

`XChangeActivePointerGrab`, `XGrabKey`, `XGrabKeyboard`, `XGrabPointer`, `XGrabServer`, `XUngrabButton`, `XUngrabKey`, `XUngrabKeyboard`, `XUngrab-Pointer`, `XUngrabServer`.

Name

XGrabKey — grab a key.

Synopsis

```
XGrabKey(display, keycode, modifiers, grab_window,
        owner_events, pointer_mode, keyboard_mode)
    Display *display;
    int keycode;
    unsigned int modifiers;
    Window grab_window;
    Bool owner_events;
    int pointer_mode, keyboard_mode;
```

Arguments

display   Specifies a connection to an X server; returned from `XOpenDisplay`.

keycode   Specifies the keycode to be grabbed. It may be a modifier key. Specifying `AnyKey` is equivalent to issuing the request for all key codes.

modifiers   Specifies a set of keymasks. This is a bitwise OR of one or more of the following symbols: `ShiftMask`, `LockMask`, `ControlMask`, `Mod1Mask`, `Mod2Mask`, `Mod3Mask`, `Mod4Mask`, `Mod5Mask`, or `AnyModifier`. `AnyModifier` is equivalent to issuing the grab key request for all possible modifier combinations (including no modifiers). All specified modifiers do not need to have currently assigned keycodes.

grab_window Specifies the window in which the specified key combination will initiate an active grab.

owner_events

      Specifies whether the grab window should receive all events (`True`) or whether the grabbing application should receive all events normally (`False`).

pointer_mode

      Controls processing of pointer events during the grab. Pass one of these constants: `GrabModeSync` or `GrabModeAsync`.

keyboard_mode

      Controls processing of keyboard events during the grab. Pass one of these constants: `GrabModeSync` or `GrabModeAsync`.

Description

`XGrabKey` establishes a passive grab on the specified keys, such that when the specified key/modifier combination is pressed, the keyboard may be grabbed, and all keyboard events sent to this application. More formally, once an `XGrabKey` call has been issued on a particular key/button combination:

- IF the keyboard is not already actively grabbed,

- AND the specified key, which itself can be a modifier key, is logically pressed when the specified modifier keys are logically down,

- AND no other keys or modifier keys are logically down,

- AND EITHER the grab window is an ancestor of (or is) the focus window OR the grab window is a descendent of the focus window and contains the pointer,

- AND a passive grab on the same key combination does not exist on any ancestor of the grab window,

- THEN the keyboard is actively grabbed, as for XGrabKeyboard, the last keyboard grab time is set to the time at which the key was pressed (as transmitted in the KeyPress event), and the KeyPress event is reported.

The active grab is terminated automatically when the specified key is released (independent of the state of the modifier keys).

The *pointer_mode* and *keyboard_mode* control the processing of events during the grab. If either is GrabModeSync, events for that device are not sent from the server to Xlib until XAllowEvents is called to send the events. If either is GrabModeAsync, events for that device are sent normally.

For more information on grabbing, see Volume One, Chapter 9, *The Keyboard and Pointer*.

Errors

BadAccess   When using AnyModifier or AnyKey and another client has grabbed any overlapping combinations. In this case, no grabs are established.

Another client has issued XGrabKey for the same key combination in *grab_window*.

BadValue   *keycode* is not in the range between min_keycode and max_keycode as returned by XDisplayKeycodes.

BadWindow

Related Commands

XChangeActivePointerGrab, XGrabButton, XGrabKeyboard, XGrabPointer, XGrabServer, XUngrabButton, XUngrabKey, XUngrabKeyboard, XUngrab-Pointer, XUngrabServer.

Name

XGrabKeyboard — grab the keyboard.

Synopsis

```
int XGrabKeyboard(display, grab_window, owner_events,
        pointer_mode, keyboard_mode, time)
    Display *display;
    Window grab_window;
    Bool owner_events;
    int pointer_mode, keyboard_mode;
    Time time;
```

Arguments

display   Specifies a connection to an X server; returned from XOpenDisplay.

grab_window   Specifies the ID of the window that requires continuous keyboard input.

owner_events
                 Specifies a boolean value of either True or False. See Description below.

pointer_mode
                 Controls processing of pointer events during the grab. Pass either Grab-ModeSync or GrabModeAsync.

keyboard_mode
                 Controls processing of keyboard events during the grab. Pass either Grab-ModeSync or GrabModeAsync.

time   Specifies the time when the grab should take place. Pass either a timestamp, expressed in milliseconds, or the constant CurrentTime.

Description

XGrabKeyboard actively grabs control of the main keyboard. Further key events are reported only to the grabbing client. This request generates FocusIn and FocusOut events.

XGrabKeyboard processing is controlled by the value in the *owner_events* argument:

- If *owner_events* is False, all generated key events are reported to *grab_window*.

- If *owner_events* is True, then if a generated key event would normally be reported to this client, it is reported normally. Otherwise the event is reported to *grab_window*.

    Both KeyPress and KeyRelease events are always reported, independent of any event selection made by the client.

XGrabKeyboard processing of pointer events and keyboard events are controlled by *pointer_mode* and *keyboard_mode*:

- If the *pointer_mode* or *keyboard_mode* is GrabModeAsync, event processing for the respective device continues normally.

- For *keyboard_mode* GrabModeAsync only: if the keyboard was currently frozen by this client, then processing of keyboard events is resumed.

- If the *pointer_mode* or *keyboard_mode* is GrabModeSync, events for the respective device are queued by the server until a releasing XAllowEvents request occurs or until the keyboard grab is released as described above.

If the grab is successful, XGrabKeyboard returns the constant GrabSuccess. XGrab-Keyboard fails under the following conditions and returns the following:

- If the keyboard is actively grabbed by some other client, it returns AlreadyGrabbed.

- If *grab_window* is not viewable, it returns GrabNotViewable.

- If *time* is earlier than the last keyboard grab time or later than the current server time, it returns GrabInvalidTime.

- If the pointer is frozen by an active grab of another client, the request fails with a status GrabFrozen.

If the grab succeeds, the last keyboard grab time is set to the specified time, with Current-Time replaced by the current X server time.

For more information on grabbing, see Volume One, Chapter 9, *The Keyboard and Pointer*.

Errors
BadValue
BadWindow

Related Commands
XChangeActivePointerGrab, XGrabButton, XGrabKey, XGrabPointer, XGrab-Server, XUngrabButton, XUngrabKey, XUngrabKeyboard, XUngrabPointer, XUngrabServer.

Name

XGrabPointer — grab the pointer.

Synopsis

```
int XGrabPointer(display, grab_window, owner_events,
        event_mask, pointer_mode, keyboard_mode, confine_to,
        cursor, time)
    Display *display;
    Window grab_window;
    Bool owner_events;
    unsigned int event_mask;
    int pointer_mode, keyboard_mode;
    Window confine_to;
    Cursor cursor;
    Time time;
```

Arguments

display   Specifies a connection to an X server; returned from XOpenDisplay.

grab_window   Specifies the ID of the window that should grab the pointer input independent of pointer location.

owner_events

Specifies if the pointer events are to be reported normally within this application (pass True) or only to the grab window (pass False).

event_mask   Specifies the event mask symbols that can be ORed together. Only events selected by this mask, plus ButtonPress and ButtonRelease, will be delivered during the grab. See XSelectInput for a complete list of event masks.

pointer_mode

Controls further processing of pointer events. Pass either GrabModeSync or GrabModeAsync.

keyboard_mode

Controls further processing of keyboard events. Pass either GrabModeSync or GrabModeAsync.

confine_to   Specifies the ID of the window to confine the pointer. One option is None, in which case the pointer is not confined to any window.

cursor   Specifies the ID of the cursor that is displayed with the pointer during the grab. One option is None, which causes the cursor to keep its current pattern.

time   Specifies the time when the grab request took place. Pass either a timestamp, expressed in milliseconds (from an event), or the constant CurrentTime.

Description

XGrabPointer actively grabs control of the pointer. Further pointer events are only reported to the grabbing client until XUngrabPointer is called.

event_mask is always augmented to include ButtonPressMask and ButtonRelease-Mask. If *owner_events* is False, all generated pointer events are reported to *grab_window*, and are only reported if selected by *event_mask*. If *owner_events* is True, then if a generated pointer event would normally be reported to this client, it is reported normally; otherwise the event is reported with respect to the *grab_window*, and is only reported if selected by *event_mask*. For either value of *owner_events*, unreported events are discarded.

pointer_mode controls processing of pointer events during the grab, and *keyboard_mode* controls further processing of main keyboard events. If the mode is GrabModeAsync, event processing continues normally. If the mode is GrabModeSync, events for the device are queued by the server but not sent to clients until the grabbing client issues a releasing XAllowEvents request or an XUngrabPointer request.

If a cursor is specified, then it is displayed regardless of which window the pointer is in. If no cursor is specified, then when the pointer is in *grab_window* or one of its subwindows, the normal cursor for that window is displayed. When the pointer is outside grab_window, the cursor for *grab_window* is displayed.

If a *confine_to* window is specified, then the pointer will be restricted to that window. The *confine_to* window need have no relationship to the *grab_window*. If the pointer is not initially in the *confine_to* window, then it is warped automatically to the closest edge (and enter/leave events generated normally) just before the grab activates. If the *confine_to* window is subsequently reconfigured, the pointer will be warped automatically as necessary to keep it contained in the window.

The *time* argument lets you avoid certain circumstances that come up if applications take a long while to respond or if there are long network delays. Consider a situation where you have two applications, both of which normally grab the pointer when clicked on. If both applications specify the timestamp from the ButtonPress event, the second application will successfully grab the pointer, while the first will get a return value of AlreadyGrabbed, indicating that the other application grabbed the pointer before its request was processed. This is the desired response because the latest user action is most important in this case.

XGrabPointer generates EnterNotify and LeaveNotify events.

If the grab is successful, it returns the constant GrabSuccess. The XGrabPointer function fails under the following conditions, with the following return values:

•   If *grab_window* or *confine_to* window is not viewable, or if the confine_to window is completely off the screen, GrabNotViewable is returned.

•   If the pointer is actively grabbed by some other client, the constant AlreadyGrabbed is returned.

•   If the pointer is frozen by an active grab of another client, GrabFrozen is returned.

• If the specified time is earlier than the last-pointer-grab time or later than the current X server time, `GrabInvalidTime` is returned. (If the call succeeds, the last pointer grab time is set to the specified time, with the constant `CurrentTime` replaced by the current X server time.)

For more information on grabbing, see Volume One, Chapter 9, *The Keyboard and Pointer*.

Errors

```
BadCursor
BadValue
BadWindow
```

Related Commands

`XChangeActivePointerGrab`, `XGrabButton`, `XGrabKey`, `XGrabKeyboard`, `XGrabServer`, `XUngrabButton`, `XUngrabKey`, `XUngrabKeyboard`, `XUngrabPointer`, `XUngrabServer`.

XGrabServer

Name

XGrabServer — grab the server.

Synopsis

```
XGrabServer (display)
    Display *display;
```

Arguments

display   Specifies a connection to an X server; returned from XOpenDisplay.

Description

Grabbing the server means that only requests by the calling client will be acted on. All others will be queued in the server until the next XUngrabServer call. The X server should not be grabbed any more than is absolutely necessary.

Related Commands

XChangeActivePointerGrab, XGrabButton, XGrabKey, XGrabKeyboard, XGrabPointer, XUngrabButton, XUngrabKey, XUngrabKeyboard, XUngrab-Pointer, XUngrabServer.

XIconifyWindow

Name

XIconifyWindow — request that a top-level window be iconified.

Synopsis

```
Status XIconifyWindow(display, w, screen_number)
        Display *display;
        Window w;
        int screen_number;
```

Arguments

display   Specifies a connection to an X server; returned from XOpenDisplay.

w   Specifies the window.

screen_number
                 Specifies the appropriate screen number on the server.

Availability

Release 4 and later.

Description

XIconifyWindow sends a WM_CHANGE_STATE ClientMessage event with a format of 32 and a first data element of IconicState (as described in Section 4.1.4 of the *Inter-Client Communication Conventions Manual* in Volume Zero, *X Protocol Reference Manual*), to the root window of the specified screen. Window managers may elect to receive this message and, if the window is in its normal state, may treat it as a request to change the window's state from normal to iconic. If the WM_CHANGE_STATE property cannot be interned, XIconifyWindow does not send a message and returns a zero status. It returns a nonzero status if the client message is sent successfully; otherwise, it returns a zero status.

For more information, see Volume One, Chapter 10, *Interclient Communication*.

Errors

BadWindow

Related Commands

XReconfigureWindow, XWithdrawWindow.

XIfEvent

Name

XIfEvent — wait for event matched in predicate procedure.

Synopsis

```
XIfEvent(display, event, predicate, args)
    Display *display;
    XEvent *event;                  /* RETURN */
    Bool (*predicate)();
    char *args;
```

Arguments

display   Specifies a connection to an X server; returned from XOpenDisplay.

event   Returns the matched event.

predicate   Specifies the procedure to be called to determine if the next event satisfies your criteria.

args   Specifies the user-specified arguments to be passed to the predicate procedure.

Description

XIfEvent checks the event queue for events, uses the user-supplied routine to check if one meets certain criteria, and removes the matching event from the input queue. XIfEvent returns only when the specified predicate procedure returns True for an event. The specified predicate is called once for each event on the queue until a match is made, and each time an event is added to the queue, with the arguments display, event, and arg.

If no matching events exist on the queue, XIfEvent flushes the request buffer and waits for an appropriate event to arrive. Use XCheckIfEvent if you don't want to wait for an event.

For more information, see Volume One, Chapter 8, *Events*.

Related Commands

QLength, XAllowEvents, XCheckIfEvent, XCheckMaskEvent, XCheckTyped-Event, XCheckTypedWindowEvent, XCheckWindowEvent, XEventsQueued, XGetInputFocus, XGetMotionEvents, XMaskEvent, XNextEvent, XPeekEvent, XPeekIfEvent, XPending, XPutBackEvent, XSelectInput, XSendEvent, XSet-InputFocus, XSynchronize, XWindowEvent.

XInsertModifiermapEntry

Name

XInsertModifiermapEntry — add a new entry to an XModifierKeymap structure.

Synopsis

```
XModifierKeymap *XInsertModifiermapEntry(modmap,
        keysym_entry, modifier)
    XModifierKeymap *modmap;
    KeyCode keysym_entry;
    int modifier;
```

Arguments

modmap   Specifies a pointer to an XModifierKeymap structure.

keysym_entry
                Specifies the keycode of the key to be added to modmap.

modifier   Specifies the modifier you want mapped to the keycode specified in
                keysym_entry. This should be one of the constants: ShiftMapIndex,
                LockMapIndex, ControlMapIndex, Mod1MapIndex, Mod2Map-
                Index, Mod3MapIndex, Mod4MapIndex, or Mod5MapIndex.

Description

XInsertModifiermapEntry returns an XModifierKeymap structure suitable for calling XSetModifierMapping, in which the specified keycode is deleted from the set of keycodes that is mapped to the specified modifier (like Shift or Control). XInsert-
ModifiermapEntry does not change the mapping itself.

This function is normally used by calling XGetModifierMapping to get a pointer to the
current XModifierKeymap structure for use as the modmap argument to XInsert-
ModifiermapEntry.

Note that the structure pointed to by modmap is freed by XInsertModifiermapEntry. It
should not be freed or otherwise used by applications.

For a description of the modifier map, see XSetModifierMapping.

Structures

```
typedef struct {
    int max_keypermod;      /* server's max number of keys per modifier */
    KeyCode *modifiermap;   /* an 8 by max_keypermod array of
                             * keycodes to be used as modifiers */
} XModifierKeymap;

#define ShiftMapIndex     0
#define LockMapIndex      1
#define ControlMapIndex   2
#define Mod1MapIndex      3
#define Mod2MapIndex      4
#define Mod3MapIndex      5
```

```
#define Mod4MapIndex      6
#define Mod5MapIndex      7
```

Related Commands

XDeleteModifiermapEntry, XFreeModifiermap, XGetKeyboardMapping,
XGetModifierMapping, XKeycodeToKeysym, XKeysymToKeycode, XKeysymTo-
String, XLookupKeysym, XLookupString, XNewModifierMap, XQueryKeymap,
XRebindKeySym, XRefreshKeyboardMapping, XSetModifierMapping,
XStringToKeysym.

XInstallColormap

Name

XInstallColormap — install a colormap.

Synopsis

```
XInstallColormap(display, cmap)
    Display *display;
    Colormap cmap;
```

Arguments

display   Specifies a connection to an X server; returned from XOpenDisplay.

cmap   Specifies the colormap to install.

Description

XInstallColormap installs a virtual colormap into a hardware company. If there is only one hardware colormap, XInstallColormap loads a virtual colormap into the hardware colormap. All windows associated with this colormap immediately display with their chosen colors. Other windows associated with the old colormap will display with false colors.

If additional hardware colormaps are possible, XInstallColormap loads the new hardware map and keeps the existing ones. Other windows will then remain in their true colors unless the limit for colormaps has been reached. If the maximum number of allowed hardware colormaps is already installed, an old colormap is swapped out. The MinCmapsOfScreen(screen) and MaxCmapsOfScreen(screen) macros can be used to determine how many hardware colormaps are supported.

If cmap is not already an installed map, a ColormapNotify event is generated on every window having cmap as an attribute. If a colormap is uninstalled as a result of the install, a ColormapNotify event is generated on every window having that colormap as an attribute.

Colormaps are usually installed and uninstalled by the window manager, not by clients.

At any time, there is a subset of the installed colormaps, viewed as an ordered list, called the "required list." The length of the required list is at most the min_maps specified for each screen in the Display structure. When a colormap is installed with XInstallColormap it is added to the head of the required list and the last colormap in the list is removed if necessary to keep the length of the list at mim_maps. When a colormap is uninstalled with XUninstallColormap and it is in the required list, it is removed from the list. No other actions by the server or the client change the required list. It is important to realize that on all but high-performance workstations, min_maps is likely to be 1.

If the hardware colormap is immutable, and therefore installing any colormap is impossible, XInstallColormap will work but not do anything.

For more information, see Volume One, Chapter 7, *Color*.

Errors

BadColormap

Related Commands

```
DefaultColormap, DisplayCells, XCopyColormapAndFree, XCreate-
Colormap, XFreeColormap, XGetStandardColormap, XListInstalled-
Colormaps, XSetStandardColormap, XSetWindowColormap, XUninstall-
Colormap.
```

XInternAtom

Name

XInternAtom — return an atom for a given property name string.

Synopsis

```
Atom XInternAtom(display, property_name, only_if_exists)
    Display *display;
    char *property_name;
    Bool only_if_exists;
```

Arguments

display   Specifies a connection to an X server; returned from XOpenDisplay.

property_name

Specifies the string name of the property for which you want the atom. Upper or lower case is important. The string should be in ISO LATIN-1 encoding, which means that the first 128 character codes are ASCII, and the second 128 character codes are for special characters needed in western languages other than English.

only_if_exists

Specifies a boolean value: if no such *property_name* exists XIntern-Atom will return None if this argument is set to True or will create the atom if it is set to False.

Description

XInternAtom returns the atom identifier corresponding to string *property_name*.

If the atom does not exist, then XInternAtom either returns None (if *only_if_exists* is True) or creates the atom and returns its ID (if *only_if_exists* is False).

The string name should be a null-terminated. Case matters: the strings "thing," "Thing," and "thinG" all designate different atoms.

The atom will remain defined even after the client that defined it has exited. It will become undefined only when the last connection to the X server closes. Therefore, the number of atoms interned should be kept to a minimum.

This function is the opposite of XGetAtomName, which returns the atom name when given an atom ID.

Predefined atoms require no call to XInternAtom. Predefined atoms are defined in *<X11/Xatom.h>* and begin with the prefix "XA_". Predefined atoms are the only ones that do not require a call to XInternAtom.

Errors

```
BadAlloc
BadValue
```

Related Commands

XChangeProperty, XDeleteProperty, XGetAtomName, XGetFontProperty,
XGetWindowProperty, XListProperties, XRotateWindowProperties, XSet-
StandardProperties.

XIntersectRegion

Name

XIntersectRegion — compute the intersection of two regions.

Synopsis

```
XIntersectRegion(sra, srb, dr)
    Region sra, srb;
    Region dr;                      /* RETURN */
```

Arguments

sra   Specify the two regions with which to perform the computation.
srb

dr   Returns the result of the computation.

Description

XIntersectRegion generates a region that is the intersection of two regions.

Structures

Region is a pointer to an opaque structure type.

Related Commands

XClipBox, XCreateRegion, XDestroyRegion, XEmptyRegion, XEqualRegion, XOffsetRegion, XPointInRegion, XPolygonRegion, XRectInRegion, XSetRegion, XShrinkRegion, XSubtractRegion, XUnionRectWithRegion, XUnionRegion, XXorRegion.

Name

XKeycodeToKeysym — convert a keycode to a keysym.

Synopsis

```
KeySym XKeycodeToKeysym(display, keycode, index)
    Display *display;
    KeyCode keycode;
    int index;
```

Arguments

display   Specifies a connection to an X server; returned from XOpenDisplay.

keycode   Specifies the keycode.

index   Specifies which keysym in the list for the keycode to return.

Description

XKeycodeToKeysym returns one of the keysyms defined for the specified keycode. XKeycodeToKeysym uses internal Xlib tables. index specifies which keysym in the array of keysyms corresponding to a keycode should be returned. If no symbol is defined, XKeycodeToKeysym returns NoSymbol.

Related Commands

IsCursorKey, IsFunctionKey, IsKeypadKey, IsMiscFunctionKey, Is-ModifierKey, IsPFKey, XChangeKeyboardMapping, XDeleteModifiermap-Entry, XDisplayKeycodes, XFreeModifiermap, XGetKeyboardMapping, XGet-ModifierMapping, XInsertModifiermapEntry, XKeysymToKeycode, XKeysym-ToString, XLookupKeysym, XLookupString, XNewModifierMap, XQuery-Keymap, XRebindKeySym, XRefreshKeyboardMapping, XSetModifierMapping, XStringToKeysym.

XKeysymToKeycode

Name

XKeysymToKeycode — convert a keysym to the appropriate keycode.

Synopsis

```
KeyCode XKeysymToKeycode(display, keysym)
    Display *display;
    Keysym keysym;
```

Arguments

display   Specifies a connection to an X server; returned from XOpenDisplay.

keysym   Specifies the keysym that is to be searched for.

Description

XKeysymToKeycode returns the keycode corresponding to the specified keysym in the current mapping. If the specified keysym is not defined for any keycode, XKeysymToKeycode returns zero.

Related Commands

IsCursorKey, IsFunctionKey, IsKeypadKey, IsMiscFunctionKey, Is-
ModifierKey, IsPFKey, XChangeKeyboardMapping, XDeleteModifiermap-
Entry, XDisplayKeycodes, XFreeModifiermap, XGetKeyboardMapping, XGet-
ModifierMapping, XInsertModifiermapEntry, XKeycodeToKeysym, XKeysym-
ToString, XLookupKeysym, XLookupString, XNewModifierMap, XQuery-
Keymap, XRebindKeySym, XRefreshKeyboardMapping, XSetModifierMapping,
XStringToKeysym.

Name

XKeysymToString — convert a keysym symbol to a string.

Synopsis

```
char *XKeysymToString(keysym)
    KeySym keysym;
```

Arguments

keysym   Specifies the keysym that is to be converted.

Description

`XKeysymToString` converts a keysym symbol (a number) into a character string. The returned string is in a static area and must not be modified. If the specified keysym is not defined, `XKeysymToString` returns `NULL`. For example, `XKeysymToString` converts `XK_Shift` to "Shift".

Note that `XKeysymString` does not return the string that is mapped to the keysym, but only a string version of the keysym itself. In other words, even if the F1 key is mapped to the string "-STOP" using `XRebindKeysym`, `XKeysymToString` still returns "F1". `XLookupString`, however, would return "STOP".

In Release 4, `XKeysymToString` can process keysyms that are not defined by the Xlib standard. Note that the set of keysyms that are available in this manner and the mechanisms by which Xlib obtains them is implementation dependent. (In the MIT sample implementation, the resource file */usr/lib/X11/XKeysymDB* is used starting in Release 4. The keysym name is used as the resource name, and the resource value is the keysym value in uppercase hexadecimal.)

Related Commands

`IsCursorKey`, `IsFunctionKey`, `IsKeypadKey`, `IsMiscFunctionKey`, `IsModifierKey`, `IsPFKey`, `XChangeKeyboardMapping`, `XDeleteModifiermapEntry`, `XFreeModifiermap`, `XGetKeyboardMapping`, `XGetModifierMapping`, `XInsertModifiermapEntry`, `XKeycodeToKeysym`, `XKeysymToKeycode`, `XLookupKeysym`, `XLookupString`, `XNewModifierMap`, `XQueryKeymap`, `XRebindKeysym`, `XRefreshKeyboardMapping`, `XSetModifierMapping`, `XStringToKeysym`.

Name

XKillClient — destroy a client or its remaining resources.

Synopsis

```
XKillClient (display, resource)
    Display *display;
    XID resource;
```

Arguments

display   Specifies a connection to an X server; returned from XOpenDisplay.

resource   Specifies any resource created by the client you want to destroy, or the constant AllTemporary.

Description

If a valid resource is specified, XKillClient forces a close-down of the client that created the resource. If the client has already terminated in either RetainPermanent or Retain-Temporary mode, all of the client's resources are destroyed. If AllTemporary is specified in the resource argument, then the resources of all clients that have terminated in Retain-Temporary are destroyed.

For more information, see Volume One, Chapter 13, *Other Programming Techniques*.

Errors

BadValue

Related Commands

XSetCloseDownMode.

XListDepths

Xlib – Window Manager Hints –

Name
XListDepths — determine the depths available on a given screen.

Synopsis
```
int *XListDepths(display, screen_number, count)
    Display *display;
    int screen_number;
    int *count;      /* RETURN */
```

Arguments
display Specifies a connection to an X server; returned from XOpenDisplay.

screen_number
        Specifies the appropriate screen number on the host server.

count   Returns the number of depths.

Availability
Release 4 and later.

Description
XListDepths returns the array of depths that are available on the specified screen. If the specified *screen_number* is valid and sufficient memory for the array can be allocated, XListDepths sets *count* to the number of available depths. Otherwise, it does not set *count* and returns NULL. To release the memory allocated for the array of depths, use XFree.

Related Commands
DefaultDepthOfScreen macro, DefaultDepth macro, XListPixmapFormats.

294   *Xlib Reference Manual*

Name

XListExtensions — return a list of all extensions to X supported by Xlib and the server.

Synopsis

```
char **XListExtensions(display, nextensions)
    Display *display;
    int *nextensions;              /* RETURN */
```

Arguments

display   Specifies a connection to an X server; returned from XOpenDisplay.

nextensions Returns the number of extensions in the returned list.

Description

XListExtensions lists all the X extensions supported by Xlib and the current server. The returned strings will be in ISO LATIN-1 encoding, which means that the first 128 character codes are ASCII, and the second 128 character codes are for special characters needed in western languages other than English.

For more information on extensions, see Volume One, Chapter 13, *Other Programming Techniques*.

Related Commands

XFreeExtensionList, XQueryExtension.

XListFonts

Name

XListFonts — return a list of the available font names.

Synopsis

```
char **XListFonts(display, pattern, maxnames, actual_count)
    Display *display;
    char *pattern;
    int maxnames;
    int *actual_count;          /* RETURN */
```

Arguments

display   Specifies a connection to an X server; returned from XOpenDisplay.

pattern   Specifies the string associated with the font names you want returned. You
can specify any string, including asterisks (*), and question marks. The asterisk indicates a wildcard for any number of characters and the question mark
indicates a wildcard for a single character. Upper or lower case is not important. The string should be in ISO LATIN-1 encoding, which means that the
first 128 character codes are ASCII, and the second 128 character codes are
for special characters needed in western languages other than English.

maxnames   Specifies the maximum number of names that are to be in the returned list.

actual_count
               Returns the actual number of font names in the list.

Description

XListFonts returns a list of font names that match the string *pattern*. Each returned font
name string is terminated by NULL and is lower case. The maximum number of names returned
in the list is the value you passed to *maxnames*. The function returns the actual number of
font names in *actual_count*.

If no fonts match the specified names, XListFonts returns NULL.

The client should call XFreeFontNames when done with the font name list.

The font search path (the order in which font names in various directories are compared to
pattern) is set by XSetFontPath.

For more information on fonts, see Volume One, Chapter 6, *Drawing Graphics and Text*.

Related Commands

XCreateFontCursor, XFreeFont, XFreeFontInfo, XFreeFontNames, XFree-
FontPath, XGetFontPath, XGetFontProperty, XListFontsWithInfo, XLoad-
Font, XLoadQueryFont, XQueryFont, XSetFont, XSetFontPath, XUnloadFont.

Name

XListFontsWithInfo — obtain the names and information about loaded fonts.

Synopsis

```
char **XListFontsWithInfo(display, pattern, maxnames,
        count, info)
    Display *display;
    char *pattern;              /* null-terminated */
    int maxnames;
    int *count;                 /* RETURN */
    XFontStruct **info;         /* RETURN */
```

Arguments

display   Specifies a connection to an X server; returned from XOpenDisplay.

pattern   Specifies the string associated with the font names you want returned. You can specify any string, including asterisks (*) and question marks. The asterisk indicates a wildcard on any number of characters and the question mark indicates a wildcard on a single character. Upper or lower case is not important. The string should be in ISO LATIN-1 encoding, which means that the first 128 character codes are ASCII, and the second 128 character codes are for special characters needed in western languages other than English.

maxnames   Specifies the maximum number of names that are to be in the returned list.

count   Returns the actual number of matched font names.

info   Returns a pointer to a list of font information structures. XListFontsWithInfo provides enough space for maxnames pointers.

Description

XListFontsWithInfo returns a list of font names that match the specified pattern and a also returns limited information about each font that matches. The list of names is limited to the size specified by the maxnames argument. The list of names is in lower case.

XListFontsWithInfo returns NULL if no matches were found.

To free the allocated name array, the client should call XFreeFontNames. To free the font information array, the client should call XFreeFontInfo.

The information returned for each font is identical to what XQueryFont would return, except that the per-character metrics (lbearing, rbearing, width, ascent, descent for single characters) are not returned.

The font search path (the order in which font names in various directories are compared to pattern) is set by XSetFontPath. XListFonts returns NULL if no matches were found.

For more information on fonts, see Volume One, Chapter 6, *Drawing Graphics and Text*.

Structures

```
typedef struct {
    XExtData *ext_data;          /* hook for extension to hang data */
    Font fid;                    /* Font ID for this font */
    unsigned direction;          /* hint about direction the font is painted */
    unsigned min_char_or_byte2; /* first character */
    unsigned max_char_or_byte2; /* last character */
    unsigned min_byte1;          /* first row that exists */
    unsigned max_byte1;          /* last row that exists */
    Bool all_chars_exist;        /* flag if all characters have nonzero size*/
    unsigned default_char;       /* char to print for undefined character */
    int n_properties;            /* how many properties there are */
    XFontProp *properties;       /* pointer to array of additional properties*/
    XCharStruct min_bounds;      /* minimum bounds over all existing char*/
    XCharStruct max_bounds;      /* minimum bounds over all existing char*/
    XCharStruct *per_char;       /* first_char to last_char information */
    int ascent;                  /* logical extent above baseline for spacing */
    int descent;                 /* logical descent below baseline for spacing */
} XFontStruct;
```

Related Commands

XCreateFontCursor, XFreeFont, XFreeFontInfo, XFreeFontNames, XFree-
FontPath, XGetFontPath, XGetFontProperty, XListFonts, XLoadFont,
XLoadQueryFont, XQueryFont, XSetFont, XSetFontPath, XUnloadFont.

XListHosts

Name

XListHosts — obtain a list of hosts having access to this display.

Synopsis

```
XHostAddress *XListHosts(display, nhosts, state)
    Display *display;
    int *nhosts;                /* RETURN */
    Bool *state;                /* RETURN */
```

Arguments

display   Specifies a connection to an X server; returned from XOpenDisplay.

nhosts   Returns the number of hosts currently in the access control list.

state   Returns whether the access control list is currently being used by the server to process new connection requests from clients. True if enabled, False if disabled.

Description

XListHosts returns the current access control list as well as whether the use of the list is enabled or disabled. XListHosts allows a program to find out what machines make connections, by looking at a list of host structures. This XHostAddress list should be freed when it is no longer needed. XListHosts returns NULL on failure.

For more information on access control lists, see Volume One, Chapter 13, *Other Programming Techniques*.

Structures

```
typedef struct {
    int family;
    int length;
    char *address;
} XHostAddress;
```

Related Commands

XAddHost, XAddHosts, XDisableAccessControl, XEnableAccessControl, XRemoveHost, XRemoveHosts, XSetAccessControl.

XListInstalledColormaps

Name

XListInstalledColormaps — get a list of installed colormaps.

Synopsis

```
Colormap *XListInstalledColormaps(display, w, num)
    display *display;
    Window w;
    int *num;                        /* RETURN */
```

Arguments

display	Specifies a connection to an X server; returned from XOpenDisplay.
w	Specifies the ID of the window for whose screen you want the list of currently installed colormaps.
num	Returns the number of currently installed colormaps in the returned list.

Description

XListInstalledColormaps returns a list of the currently installed colormaps for the screen containing the specified window. The order in the list is not significant. There is no distinction in the list between colormaps actually being used by windows and colormaps no longer in use which have not yet been freed or destroyed.

XListInstalledColormaps returns None and sets *num* to zero on failure.

The allocated list should be freed using XFree when it is no longer needed.

For more information on installing colormaps, see Volume One, Chapter 7, *Color*.

Errors

BadWindow

Related Commands

DefaultColormap, DisplayCells, XCopyColormapAndFree, XCreate-
Colormap, XFreeColormap, XGetStandardColormap, XInstallColormap,
XSetStandardColormap, XSetWindowColormap, XUninstallColormap.

XListPixmapFormats

Name

XListPixmapFormats — obtain the supported pixmap formats for a given server.

Synopsis

```
XPixmapFormatValues *XListPixmapFormats(display, count)
        Display *display;
        int *count;      /* RETURN */
```

Arguments

display   Specifies a connection to an X server; returned from XOpenDisplay.

count   Returns the number of pixmap formats that are supported by the server.

Availability

Release 4 and later.

Description

XListPixmapFormats returns an array of XPixmapFormatValues structures that describe the types of Z format images that are supported by the specified server. If insufficient memory is available, XListPixmapFormats returns NULL. To free the allocated storage for the XPixmapFormatValues structures, use XFree.

Structures

```
typedef struct {
    int depth;
    int bits_per_pixel;
    int scanline_pad;
} XPixmapFormatValues;
```

Related Commands

XListDepths.

XListProperties

Name

XListProperties — get the property list for a window.

Synopsis

```
Atom *XListProperties(display, w, num_prop)
    Display *display;
    Window w;
    int *num_prop;                /* RETURN */
```

Arguments

display   Specifies a connection to an X server; returned from XOpenDisplay.

w   Specifies the window whose property list you want.

num_prop   Returns the length of the properties array.

Description

XListProperties returns a pointer to an array of atoms for properties that are defined for the specified window. XListProperties returns NULL on failure (when window w is invalid).

To free the memory allocated by this function, use XFree.

For more information, see Volume One, Chapter 10, *Interclient Communication*.

Errors

BadWindow

Related Commands

XChangeProperty, XDeleteProperty, XGetAtomName, XGetFontProperty, XGetWindowProperty, XInternAtom, XRotateWindowProperties, XSet-StandardProperties.

Name

XLoadFont — load a font if not already loaded; get font ID.

Synopsis

```
Font XLoadFont (display, name)
    Display *display;
    char *name;
```

Arguments

display Specifies a connection to an X server; returned from XOpenDisplay.

name Specifies the name of the font in a null terminated string. As of Release 4, the * and ? wildcards are allowed and may be supported by the server. Upper or lower case is not important. The string should be in ISO LATIN-1 encoding, which means that the first 128 character codes are ASCII, and the second 128 character codes are for special characters needed in western languages other than English.

Description

XLoadFont loads a font into the server if it has not already been loaded by another client. XLoadFont returns the font ID or, if it was unsuccessful, generates a BadName error. When the font is no longer needed, the client should call XUnloadFont. Fonts are not associated with a particular screen. Once the font ID is available, it can be set in the font member of any GC, and thereby used in subsequent drawing requests.

Font information is usually necessary for locating the text. Call XLoadFontWithInfo to get the info at the time you load the font, or call XQueryFont if you used XLoadFont to load the font.

For more information on fonts, see Volume One, Chapter 6, *Drawing Graphics and Text*.

Errors

BadAlloc Server has insufficient memory to store font.

BadName *name* specifies an unavailable font.

Related Commands

XCreateFontCursor, XFreeFont, XFreeFontInfo, XFreeFontNames, XFree-FontPath, XGetFontPath, XGetFontProperty, XListFonts, XListFontsWith-Info, XLoadQueryFont, XQueryFont, XSetFont, XSetFontPath, XUnloadFont.

XLoadQueryFont

Name

XLoadQueryFont — load a font and fill information structure.

Synopsis

```
XFontStruct *XLoadQueryFont(display, name)
    Display *display;
    char *name;
```

Arguments

display   Specifies a connection to an X server; returned from XOpenDisplay.

name   Specifies the name of the font. This name is a null terminated string. As of Release 4, the * and ? wildcards are allowed and may be supported by the server. Upper or lower case is not important.

Description

XLoadQueryFont performs a XLoadFont and XQueryFont in a single operation. XLoadQueryFont provides the easiest way to get character-size tables for placing a proportional font. That is, XLoadQueryFont both opens (loads) the specified font and returns a pointer to the appropriate XFontStruct structure. If the font does not exist, XLoadQueryFont returns NULL.

The XFontStruct structure consists of the font-specific information and a pointer to an array of XCharStruct structures for each character in the font.

For more information on fonts, see Volume One, Chapter 6, *Drawing Graphics and Text*.

Errors

BadAlloc   server has insufficient memory to store font.

BadName   name specifies an unavailable font.

Structures

```
typedef struct {
    XExtData *ext_data;             /* hook for extension to hang data */
    Font fid;                       /* Font ID for this font */
    unsigned direction;             /* hint about direction the font is painted */
    unsigned min_char_or_byte2;     /* first character */
    unsigned max_char_or_byte2;     /* last character */
    unsigned min_byte1;             /* first row that exists */
    unsigned max_byte1;             /* last row that exists */
    Bool all_chars_exist;           /* flag if all characters have nonzero size*/
    unsigned default_char;          /* char to print for undefined character */
    int n_properties;               /* how many properties there are */
    XFontProp *properties;          /* pointer to array of additional properties*/
    XCharStruct min_bounds;         /* minimum bounds over all existing char*/
    XCharStruct max_bounds;         /* minimum bounds over all existing char*/
    XCharStruct *per_char;          /* first_char to last_char information */
    int ascent;                     /* logical extent above baseline for spacing */
    int descent;                    /* logical descent below baseline for spacing */
} XFontStruct;
```

```
typedef struct {
    short lbearing;              /* origin to left edge of character */
    short rbearing;              /* origin to right edge of character */
    short width;                 /* advance to next char's origin */
    short ascent;                /* baseline to top edge of character */
    short descent;               /* baseline to bottom edge of character */
    unsigned short attributes;   /* per char flags (not predefined) */
} XCharStruct;
```

Related Commands

XCreateFontCursor, XFreeFont, XFreeFontInfo, XFreeFontNames, XFree-
FontPath, XGetFontPath, XGetFontProperty, XListFonts, XListFontsWith-
Info, XLoadFont, XQueryFont, XSetFont, XSetFontPath, XUnloadFont.

Name
XLookUpAssoc — obtain data from an association table.

Synopsis
```
caddr_t XLookUpAssoc(display, table, x_id)
    Display *display;
    XAssocTable *table;
    XID x_id;
```

Arguments
display   Specifies a connection to an X server; returned from XOpenDisplay.

table   Specifies the association table.

x_id   Specifies the X resource ID.

Description
This function is provided for compatibility with X Version 10. To use it you must include the file *<X11/X10.h>* and link with the library *-loldX*.

Association tables provide a way of storing data locally and accessing by ID. XLookUp-Assoc retrieves the data stored in an XAssocTable by its XID. If the matching XID can be found in the table, the routine returns the data associated with it. If the *x_id* cannot be found in the table the routine returns NULL.

For more information on association tables, see Volume One, Appendix B, *X10 Compatibility*.

Structures
```
typedef struct {
    XAssoc *buckets;          /* pointer to first bucket in bucket array */
    int size;                 /* table size (number of buckets) */
} XAssocTable;

typedef struct _XAssoc {
    struct _XAssoc *next;     /* next object in this bucket */
    struct _XAssoc *prev;     /* previous object in this bucket */
    Display *display;         /* display which owns the ID */
    XID x_id;                 /* X Window System ID */
    char *data;               /* pointer to untyped memory */
} XAssoc;
```

Related Commands
XCreateAssocTable, XDeleteAssoc, XDestroyAssocTable, XMakeAssoc.

Name

XLookupColor — get database RGB values and closest hardware-supported RGB values from color name.

Synopsis

```
Status XLookupColor(display, cmap, colorname, rgb_db_def,
        hardware_def)
    Display *display;
    Colormap cmap;
    char *colorname;
    XColor *rgb_db_def, *hardware_def; /* RETURN */
```

Arguments

display   Specifies a connection to an X server; returned from XOpenDisplay.

cmap   Specifies the colormap.

colorname   Specifies a color name string (for example "red"). Upper or lower case does not matter. The string should be in ISO LATIN1 encoding, which means that the first 128 character codes are ASCII, and the second 128 character codes are for special characters needed in western languages other than English.

rgb_db_def   Returns the exact RGB values for the specified color name from the */usr/lib/X11/rgb* database.

hardware_def   Returns the closest RGB values possible on the hardware.

Description

XLookupColor looks up RGB values for a color given the colorname string. It returns both the exact color values and the closest values possible on tthe screen specified by *cmap*.

XLookupColor returns nonzero if *colorname* exists in the RGB database or zero if it does not exist.

To determine the exact RGB values, XLookupColor uses a database on the X server. On UNIX, this database is */usr/lib/X11/rgb*. To read the colors provided by the database on a UNIX-based system, see */usr/lib/X11/rgb.txt*. The location, name, and contents of this file are server-dependent.

For more information see Volume One, Chapter 7, *Color*, and Appendix D, *The Color Database*, in this volume.

Errors

BadName   Color name not in database.

BadColormap   Specified colormap invalid.

Structures

```
typedef struct {
    unsigned long pixel;
    unsigned short red, green, blue;
    char flags;                          /* DoRed, DoGreen, DoBlue */
    char pad;
} XColor;
```

Related Commands

BlackPixel, WhitePixel, XAllocColor, XAllocColorCells, XAllocColor-
Planes, XAllocNamedColor, XFreeColors, XParseColor, XQueryColor,
XQueryColors, XStoreColor, XStoreColors, XStoreNamedColor.

XLookupKeysym

Name

XLookupKeysym — get the keysym corresponding to a keycode in structure.

Synopsis

```
KeySym XLookupKeysym(event, index)
    XKeyEvent *event;
    int index;
```

Arguments

event   Specifies the KeyPress or KeyRelease event that is to be used.

index   Specifies which keysym from the list associated with the keycode in the event to
            return. These correspond to the modifier keys, and the symbols ShiftMap-
            Index, LockMapIndex, ControlMapIndex, Mod1MapIndex, Mod2-
            MapIndex, Mod3MapIndex, Mod4MapIndex, and Mod5MapIndex can be
            used.

Description

Given a keyboard event and the index into the list of keysyms for that keycode, XLookup-
Keysym returns the keysym from the list that corresponds to the keycode in the event. If no
keysym is defined for the keycode of the event, XLookupKeysym returns NoSymbol.

Each keycode may have a list of associated keysyms, which are portable symbols representing
the meanings of the key. The index specifies which keysym in the list is desired, indicating
the combination of modifier keys that are currently pressed. Therefore, the program must interpret the state member of the XKeyEvent structure to determine the index before calling
this function. The exact mapping of modifier keys into the list of keysyms for each keycode is
server-dependent beyond the fact that the first keysym corresponds to the keycode without
modifier keys, and the second corresponds to the keycode with Shift pressed.

XLookupKeysym simply calls XKeycodeToKeysym, using arguments taken from the specified event structure.

Structures

```
typedef struct {
    int type;                   /* of event */
    unsigned long serial;       /* # of last request processed by server */
    Bool send_event;            /* true if this came from a SendEvent request */
    Display *display;           /* display the event was read from */
    Window window;              /* "event" window it is reported relative to */
    Window root;                /* root window that the event occured on */
    Window subwindow;           /* child window */
    Time time;                  /* milliseconds */
    int x, y;                   /* pointer x, y coordinates in event window */
    int x_root, y_root;         /* coordinates relative to root */
    unsigned int state;         /* key or button mask */
    unsigned int keycode;       /* detail */
    Bool same_screen;           /* same screen flag */
} XKeyEvent;
```

Related Commands

XChangeKeyboardMapping, XDeleteModifiermapEntry, XFreeModifiermap,
XGetKeyboardMapping, XGetModifierMapping, XInsertModifiermapEntry,
XKeycodeToKeysym, XKeysymToKeycode, XKeysymToString, XLookupString,
XNewModifierMap, XQueryKeymap, XRebindKeysym, XRefreshKeyboard-
Mapping, XSetModifierMapping, XStringToKeysym.

Name

XLookupString — map a key event to ASCII string, keysym, and `ComposeStatus`.

Synopsis

```
int XLookupString(event, buffer, num_bytes, keysym, status)
    XKeyEvent *event;
    char *buffer;              /* RETURN */
    int num_bytes;
    KeySym *keysym;            /* RETURN */
    XComposeStatus *status;    /* not implemented */
```

Arguments

event	Specifies the key event to be used.
buffer	Returns the resulting string.
num_bytes	Specifies the length of the buffer. No more than *num_bytes* of translation are returned.
keysym	If this argument is not NULL, it specifies the keysym ID computed from the event.
status	Specifies the XCompose structure that contains compose key state information and that allows the compose key processing to take place. This can be NULL if the caller is not interested in seeing compose key sequences. Not implemented in X Consortium Xlib through Release 4.

Description

XLookupString gets an ASCII string and a keysym that are currently mapped to the keycode in a KeyPress or KeyRelease event, using the modifier bits in the key event to deal with shift, lock and control. The XLookupString return value is the length of the translated string and the string's bytes are copied into *buffer*. The length may be greater than 1 if the event's keycode translates into a keysym that was rebound with XRebindKeysym.

The compose *status* is not implemented in any release of the X Consortium version of Xlib through Release 4.

In Release 4, XLookupString implements the new concept of keyboard groups. Keyboard groups support having two complete sets of keysyms for a keyboard. Which set will be used can be toggled using a particular key. This is implemented by using the first two keysyms in the list for a key as one set, and the next two keysyms as the second set. For more information on keyboard groups, see Volume One, Appendix G, *Release Notes*.

For more information on using XLookupString in general, see Volume One, Chapter 9, *The Keyboard and Pointer*.

Structures

```
/*
 * Compose sequence status structure, used in calling XLookupString.
 */
```

```
typedef struct _XComposeStatus {
    char *compose_ptr;      /* state table pointer */
    int chars_matched;      /* match state */
} XComposeStatus;

typedef struct {
    int type;                    /* of event */
    unsigned long serial;        /* # of last request processed by server */
    Bool send_event;        /* true if this came from a SendEvent request */
    Display *display;       /* Display the event was read from */
    Window window;          /* "event" window it is reported relative to */
    Window root;            /* root window that the event occured on */
    Window subwindow;       /* child window */
    Time time;              /* milliseconds */
    int x, y;               /* pointer x, y coordinates in event window */
    int x_root, y_root;     /* coordinates relative to root */
    unsigned int state;     /* key or button mask */
    unsigned int keycode;   /* detail */
    Bool same_screen;       /* same screen flag */
} XKeyEvent;
```

Related Commands

XChangeKeyboardMapping, XDeleteModifiermapEntry, XFreeModifiermap,
XGetKeyboardMapping, XGetModifierMapping, XInsertModifiermapEntry,
XKeycodeToKeysym, XKeysymToKeycode, XKeysymToString, XLookupKeysym,
XNewModifierMap, XQueryKeymap, XRebindKeySym, XRefreshKeyboard-
Mapping, XSetModifierMapping, XStringToKeysym.

XLowerWindow

Name

XLowerWindow — lower a window in the stacking order.

Synopsis

```
XLowerWindow(display, w)
    Display *display;
    Window w;
```

Arguments

display   Specifies a connection to an X server; returned from XOpenDisplay.

w   Specifies the ID of the window to be lowered.

Description

XLowerWindow lowers a window in the stacking order of its siblings so that it does not obscure any sibling windows. If the windows are regarded as overlapping sheets of paper stacked on a desk, then lowering a window is analogous to moving the sheet to the bottom of the stack, while leaving its x and y location on the desk constant. Lowering a mapped window will generate exposure events on any windows it formerly obscured.

If the override_redirect attribute of the window (see Chapter 4, *Window Attributes*) is False and the window manager has selected SubstructureRedirectMask on the parent, then a ConfigureRequest event is sent to the window manager, and no further processing is performed. Otherwise, the window is lowered to the bottom of the stack.

LeaveNotify events are sent to the lowered window if the pointer was inside it, and EnterNotify events are sent to the window which was immediately below the lowered window at the pointer position.

For more information, see Volume One, Chapter 14, *Window Management*.

Errors

BadWindow

Related Commands

XCirculateSubwindows, XCirculateSubwindowsDown, XCirculate-
SubwindowsUp, XConfigureWindow, XMoveResizeWindow, XMoveWindow,
XQueryTree, XRaiseWindow, XReparentWindow, XResizeWindow, XRestack-
Windows.

XMakeAssoc

Name
XMakeAssoc — create an entry in an association table.

Synopsis
```
XMakeAssoc(display, table, x_id, data)
    Display *display;
    XAssocTable *table;
    XID x_id;
    caddr_t data;
```

Arguments
display   Specifies a connection to an X server; returned from XOpenDisplay.

table   Specifies the association table in which an entry is to be made.

x_id   Specifies the X resource ID.

data   Specifies the data to be associated with the X resource ID.

Description
XMakeAssoc inserts data into an XAssocTable keyed on an XID. Association tables allow you to easily associate data with resource ID's for later retrieval. Association tables are local, accessible only by this client.

This function is provided for compatibility with X Version 10. To use it you must include the file *<X11/X10.h>* and link with the library *-loldX*.

Data is inserted into the table only once. Redundant inserts are meaningless and cause no problems. The queue in each association bucket is sorted from the lowest XID to the highest XID.

For more information, see Volume One, Appendix B, *X10 Compatibility*.

Structure
```
typedef struct {
    XAssoc *buckets;            /* pointer to first bucket in bucket array */
    int size;                   /* table size (number of buckets) */
} XAssocTable;

typedef struct _XAssoc {
    struct _XAssoc *next;       /* next object in this bucket */
    struct _XAssoc *prev;       /* previous object in this bucket */
    Display *display;           /* display which owns the ID */
    XID x_id;                   /* X Window System ID */
    char *data;                 /* pointer to untyped memory */
} XAssoc;
```

Related Commands
XCreateAssocTable, XDeleteAssoc, XDestroyAssocTable, XLookUpAssoc.

XMapRaised

Name

XMapRaised — map a window on top of its siblings.

Synopsis

```
XMapRaised(display, w)
    Display *display;
    Window w;
```

Arguments

display   Specifies a connection to an X server; returned from XOpenDisplay.

w   Specifies the window ID of the window to be mapped and raised.

Description

XMapRaised marks a window as eligible to be displayed. It will actually be displayed if its ancestors are mapped, it is on top of sibling windows, and it is not obscured by unrelated windows. XMapRaised is similar to XMapWindow, except it additionally raises the specified window to the top of the stack among its siblings. Mapping an already mapped window with XMapRaised raises the window. See XMapWindow for further details.

For more information, see Volume One, Chapter 14, *Window Management*.

Errors

BadWindow

Related Commands

XMapSubwindows, XMapWindow, XUnmapSubwindows, XUnmapWindow.

XMapSubwindows

Name

XMapSubwindows — map all subwindows of window.

Synopsis

```
XMapSubwindows(display, w)
    Display *display;
    Window w;
```

Arguments

display   Specifies a connection to an X server; returned from `XOpenDisplay`.

w   Specifies the ID of the window whose subwindows are to be mapped.

Description

`XMapSubwindows` maps all subwindows of a window in top-to-bottom stacking order. `XMapSubwindows` also generates an `Expose` event on each newly displayed window. This is much more efficient than mapping many windows one at a time, as much of the work need only be performed once for all of the windows rather than for each window. `XMap-Subwindows` is not recursive — it does not map the subwindows of the subwindows.

For more information, see Volume One, Chapter 14, *Window Management*.

Errors

`BadWindow`

Related Commands

`XMapRaised, XMapWindow, XUnmapSubwindows, XUnmapWindow.`

XMapWindow

Name

XMapWindow — map a window.

Synopsis

```
XMapWindow(display, w)
    Display *display;
    Window w;
```

Arguments

display   Specifies a connection to an X server; returned from XOpenDisplay.

w   Specifies the ID of the window to be mapped.

Description

XMapWindow maps a window, making it eligible for display depending on its stacking order among its siblings, the mapping status of its ancestors, and the placement of other visible windows. If all the ancestors are mapped, and it is not obscured by siblings higher in the stacking order, the window and all of its mapped subwindows are displayed.

Mapping a window that has an unmapped ancestor does not display the window but marks it as eligible for display when its ancestors become mapped. Mapping an already mapped window has no effect (it does not raise the window).

Note that for a top-level window, the window manager may intervene and delay the mapping of the window. The application must not draw until it has received an Expose event on the window.

If the window is opaque, XMapWindow generates Expose events on each opaque window that it causes to become displayed. If the client first maps the window, then paints the window, then begins processing input events, the window is painted twice. To avoid this, the client should use either of two strategies:

1. Map the window, call XSelectInput for exposure events, wait for the first Expose event, and repaint each window explicitly.

2. Call XSelectInput for exposure events, map, and process input events normally. Exposure events are generated for each window that has appeared on the screen, and the client's normal response to an Expose event should be to repaint the window.

The latter method is preferred as it usually leads to simpler programs. If you fail to wait for the Expose event in the first method, it can cause incorrect behavior with certain window managers that intercept the request.

Errors

BadWindow

Related Commands

XMapRaised, XMapSubwindows, XUnmapSubwindows, XUnmapWindow.

Name

XMaskEvent — remove the next event that matches mask.

Synopsis

```
XMaskEvent (display, event_mask, rep)
    Display *display;
    long event_mask;
    XEvent *rep;                    /* RETURN */
```

Arguments

display   Specifies a connection to an X server; returned from XOpenDisplay.

event_mask   Specifies the event mask. See XSelectInput for a complete list of the
               event mask symbols that can be ORed together.

rep   Returns the event removed from the input queue.

Description

XMaskEvent removes the next event in the queue which matches the passed mask. The event
is copied into an XEvent supplied by the caller. Other events in the queue are not discarded.
If no such event has been queued, XMaskEvent flushes the request buffer and waits until one
is received. Use XCheckMaskEvent if you do not wish to wait.

XMaskEvent never returns MappingNotify, SelectionClear, SelectionNotify,
or SelectionRequest events. When you specify ExposureMask it will return
GraphicsExpose or NoExpose events if those occur.

Related Commands

QLength, XAllowEvents, XCheckIfEvent, XCheckMaskEvent, XCheckTyped-
Event, XCheckTypedWindowEvent, XCheckWindowEvent, XEventsQueued,
XGetInputFocus, XGetMotionEvents, XIfEvent, XNextEvent, XPeekEvent,
XPeekIfEvent, XPending, XPutBackEvent, XSelectInput, XSendEvent, XSet-
InputFocus, XSynchronize, XWindowEvent.

Name

XMatchVisualInfo — obtain the visual information that matches the desired depth and class.

Synopsis

```
Status XMatchVisualInfo(display, screen, depth, class, vinfo)
    Display *display;
    int screen;
    int depth;
    int class;
    XVisualInfo *vinfo;        /* RETURN */
```

Arguments

display   Specifies a connection to an X server; returned from XOpenDisplay.

screen   Specifies the screen.

depth   Specifies the desired depth of the visual.

class   Specifies the desired class of the visual, such as PseudoColor or True-Color.

vinfo   Returns the matched visual information.

Description

XMatchVisualInfo returns the visual information for a visual supported on the screen that matches the specified *depth* and *class*. Because multiple visuals that match the specified *depth* and *class* may be supported, the exact visual chosen is undefined.

If a visual is found, this function returns a nonzero value and the information on the visual is returned to *vinfo*. If a visual is not found, it returns zero.

For more information on visuals, see Volume One, Chapter 7, *Color*.

Structures

```
typedef struct {
    Visual *visual;
    VisualID visualid;
    int screen;
    unsigned int depth;
    int class;
    unsigned long red_mask;
    unsigned long green_mask;
    unsigned long blue_mask;
    int colormap_size;
    int bits_per_rgb;
} XVisualInfo;
```

Related Commands

DefaultVisual, XGetVisualInfo.

XMoveResizeWindow

Name

XMoveResizeWindow — change the size and position of a window.

Synopsis

```
XMoveResizeWindow(display, w, x, y, width, height)
    Display *display;
    Window w;
    int x, y;
    unsigned int width, height;
```

Arguments

display   Specifies a connection to an X server; returned from XOpenDisplay.

w   Specifies the ID of the window to be reconfigured.

x
y   Specify the new x and y coordinates of the upper-left pixel of the window's border, relative to the window's parent.

width
height   Specify the new width and height in pixels. These arguments define the interior size of the window.

Description

XMoveResizeWindow moves or resizes a window or both. XMoveResizeWindow does not raise the window. Resizing a mapped window may lose its contents and generate an Expose event on that window depending on the bit_gravity attribute. Configuring a window may generate exposure events on windows that the window formerly obscured, depending on the new size and location parameters.

If the override_redirect attribute of the window is False (see Volume One, Chapter 4, *Window Attributes*) and the window manager has selected SubstructureRedirectMask on the parent, then a ConfigureRequest event is sent to the window manager, and no further processing is performed.

If the client has selected StructureNotifyMask on the window, then a ConfigureNotify event is generated after the move and resize takes place, and the event will contain the final position and size of the window.

Errors

BadValue
BadWindow

Related Commands

XCirculateSubwindows, XCirculateSubwindowsDown, XCirculateSubwindowsUp, XConfigureWindow, XLowerWindow, XMoveWindow, XQueryTree, XRaiseWindow, XReparentWindow, XResizeWindow, XRestackWindows.

XMoveWindow

Name
XMoveWindow — move a window.

Synopsis
```
XMoveWindow(display, w, x, y)
    Display *display;
    Window w;
    int x, y;
```

Arguments

display   Specifies a connection to an X server; returned from XOpenDisplay.

w   Specifies the ID of the window to be moved.

x
y   Specify the new x and y coordinates of the upper-left pixel of the window's border (or of the window itself, if it has no border), relative to the window's parent.

Description
XMoveWindow changes the position of the origin of the specified window relative to its parent. XMoveWindow does not change the mapping state, size, or stacking order of the window, nor does it raise the window. Moving a mapped window will lose its contents if:

- Its background_pixmap attribute is ParentRelative.

- The window is obscured by nonchildren and no backing store exists.

If the contents are lost, exposure events will be generated for the window and any mapped subwindows. Moving a mapped window will generate exposure events on any formerly obscured windows.

If the override_redirect attribute of the window is False (see Volume One, Chapter 4, *Window Attributes*) and the window manager has selected SubstructureRedirectMask on the parent, then a ConfigureRequest event is sent to the window manager, and no further processing is performed.

If the client has selected StructureNotifyMask on the window, then a Configure-Notify event is generated after the move takes place, and the event will contain the final position of the window.

Errors
BadWindow

Related Commands
XCirculateSubwindows, XCirculateSubwindowsDown, XCirculate-SubwindowsUp, XConfigureWindow, XLowerWindow, XMoveResizeWindow, XQueryTree, XRaiseWindow, XReparentWindow, XResizeWindow, XRestack-Windows.

Name

XNewModifiermap — create a keyboard modifier mapping structure.

Synopsis

```
XModifierKeymap *XNewModifiermap(max_keys_per_mod)
    int max_keys_per_mod;
```

Arguments

max_keys_per_mod

      Specifies the maximum number of keycodes assigned to any of the modifiers in the map.

Description

XNewModifiermap returns a XModifierKeymap structure and allocates the needed space. This function is used when more than one XModifierKeymap structure is needed. *max_keys_per_mod* depends on the server and should be gotten from the XModifier-Keymap returned by XGetModifierMapping.

For more information on keyboard preferences, see Volume One, Chapter 9, *The Keyboard and Pointer*.

Structures

```
typedef struct {
    int max_keypermod;       /* server's max number of keys per modifier */
    KeyCode *modifiermap;    /* An 8 by max_keypermod array
                              * of the modifiers */
} XModifierKeymap;
```

Related Commands

XChangeKeyboardMapping, XDeleteModifiermapEntry, XFreeModifiermap, XGetKeyboardMapping, XGetModifierMapping, XInsertModifiermapEntry, XKeycodeToKeysym, XKeysymToKeycode, XKeysymToString, XLookupKeysym, XLookupString, XQueryKeymap, XRebindKeysym, XRefreshKeyboardMapping, XSetModifierMapping, XStringToKeysym.

Name

XNextEvent — get the next event of any type or window.

Synopsis

```
XNextEvent(display, report)
    Display *display;
    XEvent *report;                 /* RETURN */
```

Arguments

display   Specifies a connection to an X server; returned from `XOpenDisplay`.

report   Returns the event removed from the event queue.

Description

`XNextEvent` removes an event from the head of the event queue and copies it into an `XEvent` structure supplied by the caller. If the event queue is empty, `XNextEvent` flushes the request buffer and waits (blocks) until an event is received. Use `XCheckMaskEvent` or `XCheckIfEvent` if you do not want to wait.

For more information, see Volume One, Chapter 8, *Events*.

Related Commands

`QLength`, `XAllowEvents`, `XCheckIfEvent`, `XCheckMaskEvent`, `XCheckTyped-Event`, `XCheckTypedWindowEvent`, `XCheckWindowEvent`, `XEventsQueued`, `XGetInputFocus`, `XGetMotionEvents`, `XIfEvent`, `XMaskEvent`, `XPeekEvent`, `XPeekIfEvent`, `XPending`, `XPutBackEvent`, `XSelectInput`, `XSendEvent`, `XSet-InputFocus`, `XSynchronize`, `XWindowEvent`.

XNoOp

Name

XNoOp — send a NoOp to exercise connection with the server.

Synopsis

```
XNoOp(display)
    Display *display;
```

Arguments

display   Specifies a connection to an X server; returned from XOpenDisplay.

Description

XNoOp sends a NoOperation request to the X server, thereby exercising the connection. This request can be used to measure the response time of the network connection. XNoOp does not flush the request buffer.

Related Commands

DefaultScreen, XCloseDisplay, XFree, XOpenDisplay.

Xlib Reference Manual

Name

XOffsetRegion — change offset of a region.

Synopsis

```
XOffsetRegion(r, dx, dy)
    Region r;
    int dx, dy;
```

Arguments

r   Specifies the region.

dx   Specify the amount to move the specified region relative to the origin of all
dy   regions.

Description

XOffsetRegion changes the offset of the region the specified amounts in the x and y directions.

Regions are located using an offset from a point (the *region origin*) which is common to all regions. It is up to the application to interpret the location of the region relative to a drawable. If the region is to be used as a clip_mask by calling XSetRegion, the upper-left corner of the region relative to the drawable used in the graphics request will be at (xoffset + clip_x_origin, yoffset + clip_y_origin), where xoffset and yoffset are the offset of the region and clip_x_origin and clip_y_origin are components of the GC used in the graphics request.

Structures

Region is a pointer to an opaque structure type.

Related Commands

XClipBox, XCreateRegion, XDestroyRegion, XEmptyRegion, XEqualRegion, XIntersectRegion, XPointInRegion, XPolygonRegion, XRectInRegion, XSetRegion, XShrinkRegion, XSubtractRegion, XUnionRectWithRegion, XUnionRegion, XXorRegion.

XOpenDisplay

Name

XOpenDisplay — connect a client program to an X server.

Synopsis

```
Display *XOpenDisplay(display_name)
    char *display_name;
```

Arguments

display_name

Specifies the display name, which determines the server to connect to and the communications domain to be used. See Description below.

Description

The XOpenDisplay routine connects the client to the server controlling the hardware display through TCP, or UNIX or DECnet streams.

If *display_name* is NULL, the value defaults to the contents of the DISPLAY environment variable on UNIX-based systems. On non-UNIX-based systems, see that operating system's Xlib manual for the default *display_name*. The *display_name* or DISPLAY environment variable is a string that has the format *hostname:server* or *hostname:server.screen*. For example, frog:0.2 would specify screen 2 of server 0 on the machine frog.

hostname Specifies the name of the host machine on which the display is physically connected. You follow the hostname with either a single colon (:) or a double colon (::), which determines the communications domain to use. Any or all of the communication protocols can be used simultaneously on a server built to support them (but only one per client).

- If *hostname* is a host machine name and a single colon (:) separates the hostname and display number, XOpenDisplay connects the hardware display to TCP streams. In Release 4 and later, the string "unix" is no longer required and the string ":o" connects the local server.

- If *hostname* is "unix" and a single colon (:) separates it from the display number, XOpenDisplay connects the hardware display to UNIX domain IPC streams. In Release 4, the string "unix" should be omitted.

- If *hostname* is a host machine name and a double colon (::) separates the hostname and display number, XOpenDisplay connects with the server using DECnet streams. To use DECnet, however, you must build all software for DECnet. A single X server can accept both TCP and DECnet connections if it has been built for DECnet.

server   Specifies the number of the server on its host machine. This display number may be followed by a period (.). A single CPU can have more than one display; the displays are numbered starting from 0.

screen   Specifies the number of the default screen on `server`. Multiple screens can be
                connected to (controlled by) a single X server, but they are used as a single dis-
                play by a single user. `screen` merely sets an internal variable that is returned
                by the `DefaultScreen` macro. If `screen` is omitted, it defaults to 0.

If successful, `XOpenDisplay` returns a pointer to a `Display`. This structure provides many
of the specifications of the server and its screens. If `XOpenDisplay` does not succeed, it
returns a `NULL`.

After a successful call to `XOpenDisplay`, all of the screens on the server may be used by the
application. The screen number specified in the *display_name* argument serves only to
specify the value that will be returned by the `DefaultScreen` macro. After opening the display, you can use the `ScreenCount` macro to determine how many screens are available.
Then you can reference each screen with integer values between 0 and the value returned by
(`ScreenCount` -1).

For more information, see Volume One, Chapter 2, *X Concepts*, and Chapter 3, *Basic Window
Program*.

Related Commands

`DefaultScreen`, `XCloseDisplay`, `XFree`, `XNoOp`.

XParseColor

Name

XParseColor — look up RGB values from ASCII color name or translate hexadecimal value.

Synopsis

```
Status XParseColor(display, colormap, spec, rgb_db_def)
    Display *display;
    Colormap colormap;
    char *spec;
    XColor *rgb_db_def;          /* RETURN */
```

Arguments

display Specifies a connection to an X server; returned from XOpenDisplay.

colormap Specifies a colormap. This argument is required but is not used. The same code is used to process XParseColor and XLookupColor, but only XLookupColor returns the closest values physically possible on the screen specified by colormap.

spec Specifies the color specification, either as a color name or as hexadecimal coded in ASCII (see below). Upper or lower case does not matter. The string must be null-terminated, and should be in ISO LATIN-1 encoding, which means that the first 128 character codes are ASCII, and the second 128 character codes are for special characters needed in western languages other than English.

rgb_db_def Returns the RGB values corresponding to the specified color name or hexadecimal specification, and sets its DoRed, DoGreen and DoBlue flags.

Description

XParseColor returns the RGB values corresponding to the English color name or hexadecimal values specified, by looking up the color name in the color database, or translating the hexadecimal code into separate RGB values. It takes a string specification of a color, typically from a command line or XGetDefault option, and returns the corresponding red, green, and blue values, suitable for a subsequent call to XAllocColor or XStoreColor. spec can be given either as an English color name (as in XAllocNamedColor) or as an initial sharp sign character followed by a hexadecimal specification in one of the following formats:

```
#RGB              (one character per color)
#RRGGBB           (two characters per color)
#RRRGGGBBB        (three characters per color)
#RRRRGGGGBBBB     (four characters per color)
```

where R, G, and B represent single hexadecimal digits (upper or lower case).

The hexadecimal strings must be null-terminated so that XParseColor knows when it has reached the end. When fewer than 16 bits each are specified, they represent the most significant bits of the value. For example, #3a7 is the same as #3000a0007000.

This routine will fail and return a Status of zero if the initial character is a sharp sign but the string otherwise fails to fit one of the above formats, or if the initial character is not a sharp sign and the named color does not exist in the server's database.

Status is zero on failure, nonzero on success.

For more information, see Volume One, Chapter 7, *Color*.

Structures
```
typedef struct {
    unsigned long pixel;
    unsigned short red, green, blue;
    char flags;                        /* DoRed, DoGreen, DoBlue */
    char pad;
} XColor;
```

Errors
```
BadColormap
```

Related Commands
BlackPixel, WhitePixel, XAllocColor, XAllocColorCells, XAllocColor-
Planes, XAllocNamedColor, XFreeColors, XLookupColor, XQueryColor,
XQueryColors, XStoreColor, XStoreColors, XStoreNamedColor.

XParseGeometry

Name

XParseGeometry — generate position and size from standard window geometry string.

Synopsis

```
int XParseGeometry(parsestring, x, y, width, height)
    char *parsestring;
    int *x, *y;                              /* RETURN */
    unsigned int *width, *height;            /* RETURN */
```

Arguments

parsestring   Specifies the string you want to parse.

x   Return the x and y coordinates (offsets) from the string.

y

width   Return the width and height in pixels from the string.

height

Description

By convention, X applications provide a geometry command line option to indicate window size and placement. XParseGeometry makes it easy to conform to this standard because it allows you to parse the standard window geometry string. Specifically, this function lets you parse strings of the form:

```
=<width>x<height>{+-}<xoffset>{+-}<yoffset>
```

The items in this string map into the arguments associated with this function. (Items enclosed in <> are integers and items enclosed in { } are a set from which one item is allowed. Note that the brackets should not appear in the actual string.)

XParseGeometry returns a bitmask that indicates which of the four values (width, height, xoffset, and yoffset) were actually found in the string, and whether the x and y values are negative. The bits are represented by these constants: XValue, YValue, WidthValue, HeightValue, XNegative, and YNegative, and are defined in *<X11/Xutil.h>*. For each value found, the corresponding argument is updated and the corresponding bitmask element set; for each value not found, the argument is left unchanged, and the bitmask element is not set.

For more information, see Volume One, Chapter 11, *Managing User Preferences*.

Related Commands

XGeometry, XTranslateCoordinates, XWMGeometry.

XPeekEvent

Name

XPeekEvent — get an event without removing it from the queue.

Synopsis

```
XPeekEvent(display, report)
    Display *display;
    XEvent *report;                  /* RETURN */
```

Arguments

display   Specifies a connection to an X server; returned from XOpenDisplay.

report   Returns the event peeked from the input queue.

Description

XPeekEvent peeks at an input event from the head of the event queue and copies it into an XEvent supplied by the caller, without removing it from the input queue. If the queue is empty, XPeekEvent flushes the request buffer and waits (blocks) until an event is received. If you do not want to wait, use the QLength macro to determine if there are any events to peek at, or use XPeekIfEvent. XEventsQueued can perform the function of either QLength or XPending and more.

For more information, see Volume One, Chapter 8, *Events*.

Related Commands

QLength, XAllowEvents, XCheckIfEvent, XCheckMaskEvent, XCheckTyped-Event, XCheckTypedWindowEvent, XCheckWindowEvent, XEventsQueued, XGetInputFocus, XGetMotionEvents, XIfEvent, XMaskEvent, XNextEvent, XPeekIfEvent, XPending, XPutBackEvent, XSelectInput, XSendEvent, XSet-InputFocus, XSynchronize, XWindowEvent.

Name

XPeekIfEvent — get an event matched by predicate procedure without removing it from the queue.

Synopsis

```
XPeekIfEvent(display, event, predicate, args)
    Display *display;
    XEvent *event;                  /* RETURN */
    Bool (*predicate)();
    char *args;
```

Arguments

display   Specifies a connection to an X server; returned from XOpenDisplay.

event   Returns the matched event.

predicate Specifies the procedure to be called to determine if each event that arrives in the queue is the desired one.

args   Specifies the user-specified arguments that will be passed to the predicate procedure.

Description

XPeekIfEvent returns an event only when the specified predicate procedure returns True for the event. The event is copied into *event* but not removed from the queue. The specified predicate is called each time an event is added to the queue, with the arguments *display*, *event*, and *arg*.

XPeekIfEvent flushes the request buffer if no matching events could be found on the queue, and then waits for the next matching event.

For more information, see Volume One, Chapter 8, *Events*.

Related Commands

QLength, XAllowEvents, XCheckIfEvent, XCheckMaskEvent, XCheckTyped-Event, XCheckTypedWindowEvent, XCheckWindowEvent, XEventsQueued, XGetInputFocus, XGetMotionEvents, XIfEvent, XMaskEvent, XNextEvent, XPeekEvent, XPending, XPutBackEvent, XSelectInput, XSendEvent, XSet-InputFocus, XSynchronize, XWindowEvent.

Name

XPending — flush the request buffer and return the number of pending input events.

Synopsis

```
int XPending (display)
    Display *display;
```

Arguments

display   Specifies a connection to an X server; returned from XOpenDisplay.

Description

XPending returns the number of input events that have been received by Xlib from the server, but not yet removed from the queue. If there are no events on the queue, XPending flushes the request buffer, and returns the number of events transferred to the input queue as a result of the flush.

The QLength macro returns the number of events on the queue, but without flushing the request buffer first.

For more information, see Volume One, Chapter 8, *Events*.

Related Commands

QLength, XAllowEvents, XCheckIfEvent, XCheckMaskEvent, XCheckTyped-
Event, XCheckTypedWindowEvent, XCheckWindowEvent, XEventsQueued,
XGetInputFocus, XGetMotionEvents, XIfEvent, XMaskEvent, XNextEvent,
XPeekEvent, XPeekIfEvent, XPutBackEvent, XSelectInput, XSendEvent,
XSetInputFocus, XSynchronize, XWindowEvent.

Name

Xpermalloc — allocate memory never to be freed.

Synopsis

```
char *Xpermalloc(size)
    unsigned int size;
```

Arguments

size   Specifies the size in bytes of the space to be allocated. This specification is rounded to the nearest 4-byte boundary.

Description

Xpermalloc allocates some memory that will not be freed until the process exits. Xpermalloc is used by some toolkits for permanently allocated storage and allows some performance and space savings over the completely general memory allocator.

XPointInRegion

Name

XPointInRegion — determine if a point is inside a region.

Synopsis

```
Bool XPointInRegion(r, x, y)
    Region r;
    int x, y;
```

Arguments

r   Specifies the region.

x   Specify the x and y coordinates of the point relative to the region's origin.

y

Description

XPointInRegion returns True if the point x, y is contained in the region r. A point exactly on the boundary of the region is considered inside the region.

Regions are located using an offset from a point (the *region origin*) which is common to all regions. It is up to the application to interpret the location of the region relative to a drawable.

For more information on regions, see Volume One, Chapter 6, *Drawing Graphics and Text*.

Structures

Region is a pointer to an opaque structure type.

Related Commands

XClipBox, XCreateRegion, XDestroyRegion, XEmptyRegion, XEqualRegion, XIntersectRegion, XOffsetRegion, XPolygonRegion, XRectInRegion, XSetRegion, XShrinkRegion, XSubtractRegion, XUnionRectWithRegion, XUnionRegion, XXorRegion.

Name

XPolygonRegion — generate a region from points.

Synopsis

```
Region XPolygonRegion(points, n, fill_rule)
    XPoint points[];
    int n;
    int fill_rule;
```

Arguments

points   Specifies a pointer to an array of points.

n   Specifies the number of points in the polygon.

fill_rule   Specifies whether areas overlapping an odd number of times should be part of the region (WindingRule) or not part of the region (EvenOddRule). See Volume One, Chapter 5, *The Graphics Context*, for a description of the fill rule.

Description

XPolygonRegion creates a region defined by connecting the specified points, and returns a pointer to be used to refer to the region.

Regions are located relative to a point (the *region origin*) which is common to all regions. In XPolygonRegion, the coordinates specified in points are relative to the region origin. By specifying all points relative to the drawable in which they will be used, the region origin can be coincident with the drawable origin. It is up to the application whether to interpret the location of the region relative to a drawable or not.

If the region is to be used as a clip_mask by calling XSetRegion, the upper-left corner of the region relative to the drawable used in the graphics request will be at (xoffset + clip_x_origin, yoffset + clip_y_origin), where xoffset and yoffset are the offset of the region (if any) and clip_x_origin and clip_y_origin are elements of the GC used in the graphics request. The fill_rule can be either of these values:

- EvenOddRule   Areas overlapping an odd number of times are *not* part of the region.

- WindingRule   Overlapping areas are always filled.

For more information on structures, see Volume One, Chapter 6, *Drawing Graphics and Text*.

Structures

Region is a pointer to an opaque structure type.

Related Commands

XClipBox, XCreateRegion, XDestroyRegion, XEmptyRegion, XEqualRegion, XIntersectRegion, XOffsetRegion, XPointInRegion, XRectInRegion, XSetRegion, XShrinkRegion, XSubtractRegion, XUnionRectWithRegion, XUnionRegion, XXorRegion.

Name

XPutBackEvent — push an event back on the input queue.

Synopsis

```
XPutBackEvent(display, event)
    Display *display;
    XEvent *event;
```

Arguments

display   Specifies a connection to an X server; returned from XOpenDisplay.

event   Specifies a pointer to the event to be requeued.

Description

XPutBackEvent pushes an event back onto the head of the current display's input queue (so that it would become the one returned by the next XNextEvent call). This can be useful if you have read an event and then decide that you'd rather deal with it later. There is no limit to how many times you can call XPutBackEvent in succession.

For more information, see Volume One, Chapter 8, *Events*.

Related Commands

QLength, XAllowEvents, XCheckIfEvent, XCheckMaskEvent, XCheckTyped-Event, XCheckTypedWindowEvent, XCheckWindowEvent, XEventsQueued, XGetInputFocus, XGetMotionEvents, XIfEvent, XMaskEvent, XNextEvent, XPeekEvent, XPeekIfEvent, XPending, XSelectInput, XSendEvent, XSet-InputFocus, XSynchronize, XWindowEvent.

Name

XPutImage — draw an image on a window or pixmap.

Synopsis

```
XPutImage(display, drawable, gc, image, src_x, src_y,
        dst_x, dst_y, width, height)
    Display *display;
    Drawable drawable;
    GC gc;
    XImage *image;
    int src_x, src_y;
    int dst_x, dst_y;
    unsigned int width, height;
```

Arguments

display	Specifies a connection to an X server; returned from XOpenDisplay.
drawable	Specifies the drawable.
gc	Specifies the graphics context.
image	Specifies the image you want combined with the rectangle.
src_x src_y	Specify the coordinates of the upper-left corner of the rectangle to be copied, relative to the origin of the image.
dst_x dst_y	Specify the x and y coordinates, relative to the origin of the drawable, where the upper-left corner of the copied rectangle will be placed.
width height	Specify the width and height in pixels of the rectangular area to be copied.

Description

XPutImage draws a section of an image on a rectangle in a window or pixmap. The section of the image is defined by src_x, src_y, $width$ and $height$.

There is no limit to the size of image that can be sent to the server using XPutImage. XPutImage automatically decomposes the request to make sure that the maximum request size of the server is not exceeded.

XPutImage uses these graphics context components: function, plane_mask, subwindow_mode, clip_x_origin, clip_y_origin, and clip_mask. This function also uses these graphics context mode-dependent components: foreground and background.

If an XYBitmap format image is used, then the depth of $drawable$ must be 1, otherwise a BadMatch error is generated. The foreground pixel in gc defines the source for bits set to one in the image, and the background pixel defines the source for the bits set to zero.

For XYPixmap and ZPixmap format images, the depth of the image must match the depth of drawable.

Structures

```
typedef struct _XImage {
    int width, height;      /* size of image */
    int xoffset;            /* number of pixels offset in x direction */
    int format;             /* XYBitmap, XYPixmap, ZPixmap */
    char *data;             /* pointer to image data */
    int byte_order;         /* data byte order, LSBFirst, MSBFirst */
    int bitmap_unit;        /* quant. of scan line 8, 16, 32 */
    int bitmap_bit_order;   /* LSBFirst, MSBFirst */
    int bitmap_pad;         /* 8, 16, 32 either XY or ZPixmap */
    int depth;              /* depth of image */
    int bytes_per_line;     /* accelerator to next line */
    int bits_per_pixel;     /* bits per pixel (ZPixmap) */
    char *obdata;           /* hook for the object routines to hang on */
    struct funcs {          /* image manipulation routines */
        struct _XImage *(*create_image)();
        int (*destroy_image)();
        unsigned long (*get_pixel)();
        int (*put_pixel)();
        struct _XImage *(*sub_image)();
        int (*add_pixel)();
    } f;
} XImage;
```

Errors

BadDrawable

BadGC

BadMatch   See Description above.

BadValue

Related Commands

ImageByteOrder, XAddPixel, XCreateImage, XDestroyImage, XGetImage,
XGetPixel, XGetSubImage, XPutPixel, XSubImage.

XPutPixel

Name

XPutPixel — set a pixel value in an image.

Synopsis

```
int XPutPixel(ximage, x, y, pixel)
    XImage *ximage;
    int x;
    int y;
    unsigned long pixel;
```

Arguments

ximage   Specifies a pointer to the image to be modified.

x   Specify the x and y coordinates of the pixel to be set, relative to the origin of
y   the image.

pixel   Specifies the new pixel value.

Description

XPutPixel overwrites the pixel in the named image with the specified pixel value. The *x*
and *y* coordinates are relative to the origin of the image. The input pixel value must be in same
bit- and byte-order as the machine in which the client is running (that is, the Least Significant
Byte (LSB) of the long is the LSB of the pixel). The x and y coordinates must be contained in
the image.

Structures

```
typedef struct _XImage {
    int width, height;              /* size of image */
    int xoffset;                    /* number of pixels offset in x direction */
    int format;                     /* XYBitmap, XYPixmap, ZPixmap */
    char *data;                     /* pointer to image data */
    int byte_order;                 /* data byte order, LSBFirst, MSBFirst */
    int bitmap_unit;                /* quant. of scan line 8, 16, 32 */
    int bitmap_bit_order;           /* LSBFirst, MSBFirst */
    int bitmap_pad;                 /* 8, 16, 32 either XY or ZPixmap */
    int depth;                      /* depth of image */
    int bytes_per_line;             /* accelerator to next line */
    int bits_per_pixel;             /* bits per pixel (ZPixmap) */
    unsigned long red_mask;         /* bits in z arrangment */
    unsigned long green_mask;
    unsigned long blue_mask;
    char *obdata;                   /* hook for the object routines to hang on */
    struct funcs {                  /* image manipulation routines */
        struct _XImage *(*create_image)();
        int (*destroy_image)();
        unsigned long (*get_pixel)();
        int (*put_pixel)();
        struct _XImage *(*sub_image)();
        int (*add_pixel)();
    } f;
} XImage;
```

Related Commands

ImageByteOrder, XAddPixel, XCreateImage, XDestroyImage, XGetImage,
XGetPixel, XGetSubImage, XPutImage, XSubImage.

XQueryBestCursor

Name

XQueryBestCursor — get the closest supported cursor sizes.

Synopsis

```
Status XQueryBestCursor(display, drawable, width, height,
        rwidth, rheight)
    Display *display;
    Drawable drawable;
    unsigned int width, height;
    unsigned int *rwidth, *rheight; /* RETURN */
```

Arguments

display   Specifies a connection to an X server; returned from XOpenDisplay.

drawable   Specifies a drawable that indicates which screen the cursor is to be used on.
             The best cursor may be different on different screens.

width   Specify the preferred width and height, in pixels.
height

rwidth   Returns the closest supported cursor dimensions, in pixels, on the display
rheight   hardware.

Description

XQueryBestCursor returns the closest cursor dimensions actually supported by the display hardware to the dimensions you specify.

Call this function if you wish to use a cursor size other than 16 by 16. XQueryBestCursor provides a way to find out what size cursors are actually possible on the display. Applications should be prepared to use smaller cursors on displays which cannot support large ones.

XQueryBestCursor returns nonzero if the call succeeded in getting a supported size (which may be the same or different from the specified size), or zero if the call failed.

Errors

BadDrawable

Related Commands

XCreateFontCursor, XCreateGlyphCursor, XCreatePixmapCursor, XDefine-Cursor, XFreeCursor, XQueryBestSize, XRecolorCursor, XUndefineCursor.

XQueryBestSize

Name

XQueryBestSize — obtain the "best" supported cursor, tile, or stipple size.

Synopsis

```
Status XQueryBestSize(display, class, drawable, width,
        height, rwidth, rheight)
    Display *display;
    int class;
    Drawable drawable;
    unsigned int width, height;
    unsigned int *rwidth, *rheight; /* RETURN */
```

Arguments

display   Specifies a connection to an X server; returned from XOpenDisplay.

class   Specifies the class that you are interested in. Pass one of these constants: TileShape, CursorShape, or StippleShape.

drawable   Specifies a drawable ID that tells the server which screen you want the best size for.

width   Specify the preferred width and height in pixels.
height

rwidth   Return the closest supported width and height, in pixels, available for the
rheight   object on the display hardware.

Description

XQueryBestSize returns the "fastest" or "closest" size to the specified size. For class of CursorShape, this is the closest size that can be fully displayed on the screen. For Tile-Shape and StippleShape, this is the closest size that can be tiled or stippled "fastest."

For CursorShape, the drawable indicates the desired screen. For TileShape and StippleShape, the drawable indicates the screen and possibly the visual class and depth (server-dependent). An InputOnly window cannot be used as the drawable for TileShape or StippleShape (else a BadMatch error occurs).

XQueryBestSize returns nonzero if the call succeeded in getting a supported size (may be the same or different from the specified size), or zero if the call failed.

Errors

BadDrawable

BadMatch   InputOnly drawable for *class* TileShape or StippleShape.

BadValue

Related Commands

XCreateBitmapFromData, XCreatePixmap, XCreatePixmapFromBitmapData,
XFreePixmap, XQueryBestStipple, XQueryBestTile, XReadBitmapFile,
XSetTile, XSetWindowBackgroundPixmap, XSetWindowBorderPixmap,
XWriteBitmapFile.

XQueryBestStipple

Name

XQueryBestStipple — obtain the fastest supported stipple shape.

Synopsis

```
Status XQueryBestStipple(display, drawable, width, height,
        rwidth, rheight)
    Display *display;
    Drawable drawable;
    unsigned int width, height;
    unsigned int *rwidth, *rheight; /* RETURN */
```

Arguments

display Specifies a connection to an X server; returned from XOpenDisplay.

drawable Specifies a drawable that tells the server which screen you want the best size for.

width
height Specify the preferred width and height in pixels.

rwidth
rheight Return the width and height, in pixels, of the stipple best supported by the display hardware.

Description

XQueryBestStipple returns the closest stipple size that can be stippled fastest. The drawable indicates the screen and possibly the visual class and depth. An InputOnly window cannot be used as the drawable (else a BadMatch error occurs).

XQueryBestStipple returns nonzero if the call succeeded in getting a supported size (may be the same or different from the specified size), or zero if the call failed.

For more information on stipples, see Volume One, Chapter 5, *The Graphics Context*.

Errors

BadDrawable

BadMatch InputOnly window.

Related Commands

XCreateBitmapFromData, XCreatePixmap, XCreatePixmapFromBitmapData, XFreePixmap, XQueryBestSize, XQueryBestTile, XReadBitmapFile, XSetTile, XSetWindowBackgroundPixmap, XSetWindowBorderPixmap, XWriteBitmapFile.

Name

XQueryBestTile — obtain the fastest supported fill tile shape.

Synopsis

```
Status XQueryBestTile(display, drawable, width, height,
        rwidth, rheight)
    Display *display;
    Drawable drawable;
    unsigned int width, height;
    unsigned int *rwidth, *rheight; /* RETURN */
```

Arguments

display	Specifies a connection to an X server; returned from XOpenDisplay.
drawable	Specifies a drawable that tells the server which screen you want the best size for.
width height	Specify the preferred width and height in pixels.
rwidth rheight	Return the width and height, in pixels, of the tile best supported by the display hardware.

Description

XQueryBestTile returns the closest size that can be tiled fastest. The drawable indicates the screen and possibly the visual class and depth. An InputOnly window cannot be used as the drawable.

XQueryBestTile returns nonzero if the call succeeded in getting a supported size (may be the same or different from the specified size), or zero if the call failed.

For more information on tiles, see Volume One, Chapter 5, *The Graphics Context*.

Errors

BadDrawable

BadMatch   InputOnly drawable specified.

Related Commands

XCreateBitmapFromData, XCreatePixmap, XCreatePixmapFromBitmapData, XFreePixmap, XQueryBestSize, XQueryBestStipple, XReadBitmapFile, XSetTile, XSetWindowBackgroundPixmap, XSetWindowBorderPixmap, XWriteBitmapFile.

XQueryColor

Name

XQueryColor — obtain the RGB values and flags for a specified colorcell.

Synopsis

```
XQueryColor(display, cmap, colorcell_def)
    Display *display;
    Colormap cmap;
    XColor *colorcell_def;      /* SEND and RETURN */
```

Arguments

display Specifies a connection to an X server; returned from `XOpenDisplay`.

cmap Specifies the ID of the colormap from which RGB values will be retrieved.

colorcell_def
  Specifies the pixel value and returns the RGB contents of that colorcell.

Description

XQueryColor returns the RGB values in colormap *cmap* for the colorcell corresponding to the pixel value specified in the `pixel` member of the `XColor` structure `colorcell_def`. The RGB values are returned in the `red`, `green`, and `blue` members of that structure, and the `flags` member of that structure is set to (`DoRed` | `DoGreen` | `DoBlue`). The values returned for an unallocated entry are undefined.

For more information, see Volume One, Chapter 7, *Color*.

Structures

```
typedef struct {
    unsigned long pixel;
    unsigned short red, green, blue;
    char flags;                     /* DoRed, DoGreen, DoBlue */
    char pad;
} XColor;
```

Errors

```
BadColormap
```

`BadValue` Pixel not valid index into *cmap*.

Related Commands

`BlackPixel`, `WhitePixel`, `XAllocColor`, `XAllocColorCells`, `XAllocColor-Planes`, `XAllocNamedColor`, `XFreeColors`, `XLookupColor`, `XParseColor`, `XQueryColors`, `XStoreColor`, `XStoreColors`, `XStoreNamedColor`.

Name

XQueryColors — obtain RGB values for an array of colorcells.

Synopsis

```
XQueryColors(display, cmap, colorcell_defs, ncolors)
    Display *display;
    Colormap cmap;
    XColor colorcell_defs[ncolors];    /* SEND and RETURN */
    int ncolors;
```

Arguments

display   Specifies a connection to an X server; returned from XOpenDisplay.

cmap   Specifies the ID of the colormap from which RGB values will be retrieved.

colorcell_defs

Specifies an array of XColor structures. In each one, pixel is set to indicate which colorcell in the colormap to return, and the RGB values in that colorcell are returned in red, green, and blue.

ncolors   Specifies the number of XColor structures in the color definition array.

Description

XQueryColors is similar to XQueryColor, but it returns an array of RGB values. It returns the RGB values in colormap *cmap* for the colorcell corresponding to the pixel value specified in the pixel member of the XColor structure colorcell_def. The RGB values are returned in the red, green, and blue members of that same structure, and sets the flags member in each XColor structure to (DoRed | DoGreen | DoBlue).

For more information, see Volume One, Chapter 7, *Color*.

Structures

```
typedef struct {
    unsigned long pixel;
    unsigned short red, green, blue;
    char flags;                        /* DoRed, DoGreen, DoBlue */
    char pad;
} XColor;
```

Errors

BadColormap   Specified colormap does not exist.

BadValue   Pixel not valid index into *cmap*.

Note: if more than one pixel value is in error, the one reported is arbitrary.

Related Commands

BlackPixel, WhitePixel, XAllocColor, XAllocColorCells, XAllocColor-
Planes, XAllocNamedColor, XFreeColors, XLookupColor, XParseColor,
XQueryColor, XStoreColor, XStoreColors, XStoreNamedColor.

XQueryExtension

Name

XQueryExtension — get extension information.

Synopsis

```
Bool XQueryExtension(display, name, major_opcode,
        first_event, first_error)
    Display *display;
    char *name;
    int *major_opcode;          /* RETURN */
    int *first_event;           /* RETURN */
    int *first_error;           /* RETURN */
```

Arguments

display   Specifies a connection to an X server; returned from XOpenDisplay.

name   Specifies the name of the desired extension. Upper or lower case is important. The string should be in ISO LATIN-1 encoding, which means that the first 128 character codes are ASCII, and the second 128 character codes are for special characters needed in western languages other than English.

major_opcode
       Returns the major opcode of the extension, for use in error handling routines.

first_event   Returns the code of the first custom event type created by the extension.

first_error   Returns the code of the first custom error defined by the extension.

Description

XQueryExtension determines if the named extension is present, and returns True if it is. If so, the routines in the extension can be used just as if they were core Xlib requests, except that they may return new types of events or new error codes. The available extensions can be listed with XListExtensions.

The *major_opcode* for the extension is returned, if it has one. Otherwise, zero is returned. This opcode will appear in errors generated in the extension.

If the extension involves additional event types, the base event type code is returned in *first_event*. Otherwise, zero is returned in *first_event*. The format of the events is specific to the extension.

If the extension involves additional error codes, the base error code is returned in *first_error*. Otherwise, zero is returned. The format of additional data in the errors is specific to the extension.

See Volume One, Chapter 13, *Other Programming Techniques*, for more information on using extensions, and Volume One, Appendix C, *Writing Extensions to X*, for information on writing them.

Related Commands

XFreeExtensionList, XListExtensions.

XQueryFont

Name

XQueryFont — return information about a loaded font.

Synopsis

```
XFontStruct *XQueryFont(display, font_ID)
    Display *display;
    XID font_ID;
```

Arguments

display   Specifies a connection to an X server; returned from `XOpenDisplay`.

font_ID   Specifies either the font ID or the graphics context ID. You can declare the data type for this argument as either `Font` or `GContext` (both X IDs). If `GContext`, the font in that GC will be queried.

Description

`XQueryFont` returns a pointer to an `XFontStruct` structure containing information describing the specified font. This call is needed if you loaded the font with `XLoadFont`, but need the font information for multiple calls to determine the extent of text. `XLoadQueryFont` combines these two operations.

If the font hasn't been loaded (or the font ID passed is invalid), `XQueryFont` returns `NULL`.

If *font_ID* is declared as data type `GContext` (also a resource ID), this function queries the font specified by the font component of the GC specified by this ID. This is useful for getting information about the default font, whose ID is stored in the default GC. However, in this case the `GContext` ID will be the ID stored in the `fid` field of the returned `XFontStruct`, and you can't use that ID in `XSetFont` or `XUnloadFont`, since it is not itself the ID of the font.

Use `XFreeFont` to free this data.

For more information on fonts, see Volume One, Chapter 6, *Drawing Graphics and Text*.

Errors

`BadFont`

Structures

```
typedef struct {
    XExtData *ext_data;            /* hook for extension to hang data */
    Font fid;                      /* font ID for this font */
    unsigned direction;            /* hint about direction font is painted */
    unsigned min_char_or_byte2;    /* first character */
    unsigned max_char_or_byte2;    /* last character */
    unsigned min_byte1;            /* first row that exists */
    unsigned max_byte1;            /* last row that exists */
    Bool all_chars_exist;          /* flag if all characters have nonzero size*/
    unsigned default_char;         /* char to print for undefined character */
    int n_properties;              /* how many properties there are */
    XFontProp *properties;         /* pointer to array of additional properties*/
    XCharStruct min_bounds;        /* minimum bounds over all existing char*/
    XCharStruct max_bounds;        /* minimum bounds over all existing char*/
```

```
    XCharStruct *per_char;      /* first_char to last_char information */
    int ascent;                 /* logical extent above baseline for spacing */
    int descent;                /* logical descent below baseline for spacing */
} XFontStruct;
```

Related Commands

XCreateFontCursor, XFreeFont, XFreeFontInfo, XFreeFontNames, XFree-
FontPath, XGetFontPath, XGetFontProperty, XListFonts, XListFontsWith-
Info, XLoadFont, XLoadQueryFont, XSetFont, XSetFontPath, XUnloadFont.

Name

XQueryKeymap — obtain a bit vector for the current state of the keyboard.

Synopsis

```
XQueryKeymap(display, keys)
    Display *display;
    char keys[32];                /* RETURN */
```

Arguments

display   Specifies a connection to an X server; returned from XOpenDisplay.

keys   Returns an array of bytes that identifies which keys are pressed down. Each bit represents one key of the keyboard.

Description

XQueryKeymap returns a bit vector for the logical state of the keyboard, where each bit set to 1 indicates that the corresponding key is currently pressed down. The vector is represented as 32 bytes. Byte *N* (from 0) contains the bits for keys *8N* to *8N+7* with the least significant bit in the byte representing key *8N*. Note that the logical state may lag the physical state if device event processing is frozen due to a grab.

Related Commands

XChangeKeyboardMapping, XDeleteModifiermapEntry, XFreeModifiermap, XGetKeyboardMapping, XGetModifierMapping, XInsertModifiermapEntry, XKeycodeToKeysym, XKeysymToKeycode, XKeysymToString, XLookupKeysym, XLookupString, XNewModifierMap, XRebindKeysym, XRefreshKeyboard-Mapping, XSetModifierMapping, XStringToKeysym.

Name

XQueryPointer — get the current pointer location.

Synopsis

```
Bool XQueryPointer(display, w, root, child, root_x, root_y,
          win_x, win_y, keys_buttons)
    Display *display;
    Window w;
    Window *root, *child;        /* RETURN */
    int *root_x, *root_y;        /* RETURN */
    int *win_x, *win_y;          /* RETURN */
    unsigned int *keys_buttons;  /* RETURN */
```

Arguments

display   Specifies a connection to an X server; returned from XOpenDisplay.

w   Specifies a window which indicates which screen the pointer position is returned for, and child will be a child of this window if pointer is inside a child.

root   Returns the root window ID the pointer is currently on.

child   Returns the ID of the child of w the pointer is located in, or zero if it not in a child.

root_x
root_y   Return the x and y coordinates of the pointer relative to the root's origin.

win_x
win_y   Return the x and y coordinates of the pointer relative to the origin of window w.

keys_buttons
            Returns the current state of the modifier keys and pointer buttons. This is a mask composed of the OR of any number of the following symbols: Shift-Mask, LockMask, ControlMask, Mod1Mask, Mod2Mask, Mod3Mask, Mod4Mask, Mod5Mask, Button1Mask, Button2Mask, Button3Mask, Button4Mask, Button5Mask.

Description

XQueryPointer gets the pointer coordinates relative to a window and relative to the root window, the root window ID and the child window ID (if any) the pointer is currently in, and the current state of modifier keys and buttons.

If XQueryPointer returns False, then the pointer is not on the same screen as w, child is None, and win_x and win_y are zero. However, root, root_x, and root_y are still valid. If XQueryPointer returns True, then the pointer is on the same screen as the window w, and all return values are valid.

The logical state of the pointer buttons and modifier keys can lag behind their physical state if device event processing is frozen due to a grab.

Errors

    BadWindow

Related Commands

    XChangeActivePointerGrab, XChangePointerControl, XGetPointer-
    Control, XGetPointerMapping, XGrabPointer, XSetPointerMapping,
    XUngrabPointer, XWarpPointer.

Name

XQueryTextExtents — query the server for string and font metrics.

Synopsis

```
XQueryTextExtents(display, font_ID, string, nchars,
        direction, ascent, descent, overall)
    Display *display;
    XID font_ID;
    char *string;
    int nchars;
    int *direction;              /* RETURN */
    int *ascent, *descent;       /* RETURN */
    XCharStruct *overall;        /* RETURN */
```

Arguments

display   Specifies a connection to an X server; returned from XOpenDisplay.

font_ID   Specifies the appropriate font ID previously returned by XLoadFont, or the GContext that specifies the font.

string   Specifies the character string for which metrics are to be returned.

nchars   Specifies the number of characters in string.

direction   Returns the direction the string would be drawn using the specified font. Either FontLeftToRight or FontRightToLeft.

ascent   Returns the maximum ascent for the specified font.

descent   Returns the maximum descent for the specified font.

overall   Returns the overall characteristics of the string. These are the sum of the width measurements for each character, the maximum ascent and descent, the minimum lbearing added to the width of all characters up to the character with the smallest lbearing, and the maximum rbearing added to the width of all characters up to the character with the largest rbearing.

Description

XQueryTextExtents returns the dimensions in pixels that specify the bounding box of the specified string of characters in the named font, and the maximum ascent and descent for the entire font. This function queries the server and, therefore, suffers the round trip overhead that is avoided by XTextExtents, but XQueryTextExtents does not require a filled XFontInfo structure stored on the client side. Therefore, this would be used when memory is precious, or when just a small number of text width calculations are to be done.

The returned ascent and descent should usually be used to calculate the line spacing, while the width, rbearing, and lbearing members of overall should be used for horizontal measures. The total height of the bounding rectangle, good for any string in this font, is ascent + descent.

overall.ascent is the maximum of the ascent metrics of all characters in the string. The *overall.descent* is the maximum of the descent metrics. The *overall.width* is the sum of the character-width metrics of all characters in the string. The *overall.lbearing* is usually the lbearing of the first character in the string, and *overall.rbearing* is the rbearing of the last character in the string plus the sum of the widths of all the characters up to but not including the last character. More technically, here is the X protocol definition: *For each character in the string, let W be the sum of the character-width metrics of all characters preceding it in the string, let L be the lbearing metric of the character plus W, and let R be the rbearing metric of the character plus W. The* overall.lbearing *is the minimum L of all characters in the string, and the* overall.rbearing *is the maximum R.*

For more information on drawing text, see Volume One, Chapter 6, *Drawing Graphics and Text.*

Structures

```
typedef struct {
    short lbearing;            /* origin to left edge of character */
    short rbearing;            /* origin to right edge of character */
    short width;               /* advance to next char's origin */
    short ascent;              /* baseline to top edge of character */
    short descent;             /* baseline to bottom edge of character */
    unsigned short attributes; /* per char flags (not predefined) */
} XCharStruct;
```

Errors

BadFont

Related Commands

XDrawImageString, XDrawImageString16, XDrawString, XDrawString16, XDrawText, XDrawText16, XQueryTextExtents16, XTextExtents, XText-Extents16, XTextWidth, XTextWidth16.

Name

XQueryTextExtents16 — query the server for string and font metrics of a 16-bit character string.

Synopsis

```
XQueryTextExtents16(display, font_ID, string, nchars,
        direction, ascent, descent, overall)
    Display *display;
    XID font_ID;
    XChar2b *string;
    int nchars;
    int *direction;           /* RETURN */
    int *ascent, *descent;    /* RETURN */
    XCharStruct *overall;     /* RETURN */
```

Arguments

display   Specifies a connection to an X server; returned from XOpenDisplay.

font_ID   Specifies the appropriate font ID previously returned by XLoadFont, or the GContext that specifies the font.

string   Specifies the character string for which metrics are to be returned.

nchars   Specifies the number of characters in *string*.

direction   Returns the direction of painting in the specified font. Either FontLefttoRight or FontRighttoLeft.

ascent   Returns the maximum ascent in pixels for the specified font.

descent   Returns the maximum descent in pixels for the specified font.

overall   Returns the overall characteristics of the string. These are the sum of the width measurements for each character, the maximum ascent and descent, the minimum lbearing added to the width of all characters up to the character with the smallest lbearing, and the maximum rbearing added to the width of all characters up to the character with the largest rbearing.

Description

XQueryTextExtents16 returns the dimensions in pixels that specify the bounding box of the specified string of characters in the named font, and the maximum ascent and descent for the entire font. This function queries the server and, therefore, suffers the round trip overhead that is avoided by XTextExtents16, but XQueryTextExtents does not require a filled XFontInfo structure.

The returned *ascent* and *descent* should usually be used to calculate the line spacing, while the width, rbearing, and lbearing members of *overall* should be used for horizontal measures. The total height of the bounding rectangle, good for any string in this font, is *ascent + descent*.

overall.ascent is the maximum of the ascent metrics of all characters in the string. The *overall.descent* is the maximum of the descent metrics. The *overall.width* is the sum of the character-width metrics of all characters in the string. The *overall.lbearing* is usually the lbearing of the first character in the string, and *overall.rbearing* is the rbearing of the last character in the string plus the sum of the widths of all the characters up to but not including the last character. More technically, here is the X protocol definition: *For each character in the string, let W be the sum of the character-width metrics of all characters preceding it in the string, let L be the lbearing metric of the character plus W, and let R be the rbearing metric of the character plus W. The* overall.lbearing *is the minimum L of all characters in the string, and the* overall.rbearing *is the maximum R.*

For fonts defined with linear indexing rather than two-byte matrix indexing, the server interprets each XChar2b as a 16-bit number that has been transmitted with the most significant byte first. That is, byte one of the XChar2b is taken as the most significant byte.

If the font has no defined default character, then undefined characters in the string are taken to have all zero metrics.

Structures

```
typedef struct {              /* normal 16-bit characters are two bytes */
    unsigned char byte1;
    unsigned char byte2;
} XChar2b;

typedef struct {
    short lbearing;           /* origin to left edge of character */
    short rbearing;           /* origin to right edge of character */
    short width;              /* advance to next char's origin */
    short ascent;             /* baseline to top edge of character */
    short descent;            /* baseline to bottom edge of character */
    unsigned short attributes; /* per char flags (not predefined) */
} XCharStruct;
```

Errors

BadFont

Related Commands

XDrawImageString, XDrawImageString16, XDrawString, XDrawString16, XDrawText, XDrawText16, XQueryTextExtents, XTextExtents, XTextExtents16, XTextWidth, XTextWidth16.

XQueryTree

Name

XQueryTree — return a list of children, parent, and root.

Synopsis

```
Status XQueryTree(display, w, root, parent, children,
        nchildren)
    Display *display;
    Window w;
    Window *root;                   /* RETURN */
    Window *parent;                 /* RETURN */
    Window **children;              /* RETURN */
    unsigned int *nchildren;        /* RETURN */
```

Arguments

display	Specifies a connection to an X server; returned from XOpenDisplay.
w	Specifies the ID of the window to be queried. For this window, XQueryTree will list its children, its root, its parent, and the number of children.
root	Returns the root ID for the specified window.
parent	Returns the parent window of the specified window.
children	Returns the list of children associated with the specified window.
nchildren	Returns the number of children associated with the specified window.

Description

XQueryTree uses its last four arguments to return the root ID, the parent ID, a pointer to a list of children and the number of children in that list, all for the specified window w. The *children* are listed in current stacking order, from bottommost (first) to topmost (last). XQueryTree returns zero if it fails, nonzero if it succeeds.

You should deallocate the list of children with XFree when it is no longer needed.

Errors

BadWindow

Related Commands

XCirculateSubwindows, XCirculateSubwindowsDown, XCirculate-
SubwindowsUp, XConfigureWindow, XLowerWindow, XMoveResizeWindow,
XMoveWindow, XRaiseWindow, XReparentWindow, XResizeWindow, XRestack-
Windows.

XRaiseWindow

Name

XRaiseWindow — raise a window to the top of the stacking order.

Synopsis

```
XRaiseWindow(display, w)
    Display *display;
    Window w;
```

Arguments

display   Specifies a connection to an X server; returned from XOpenDisplay.

w   Specifies the ID of the window to be raised to the top of the stack.

Description

XRaiseWindow moves a window to the top of the stacking order among its siblings. If the windows are regarded as overlapping sheets of paper stacked on a desk, then raising a window is analogous to moving the sheet to the top of the stack, while leaving its x and y location on the desk constant.

Raising a mapped window may generate exposure events for that window and any mapped subwindows of that window that were formerly obscured.

If the override_redirect attribute of the window (see Volume One, Chapter 4, *Window Attributes*) is False and the window manager has selected SubstructureRedirectMask on the parent, then a ConfigureRequest event is sent to the window manager, and no further processing is performed.

Errors

BadWindow

Related Commands

XCirculateSubwindows, XCirculateSubwindowsDown, XCirculate-SubwindowsUp, XConfigureWindow, XLowerWindow, XMoveResizeWindow, XMoveWindow, XQueryTree, XReparentWindow, XResizeWindow, XRestack-Windows.

Name

XReadBitmapFile — read a bitmap from disk.

Synopsis

```
int XReadBitmapFile(display, drawable, filename, width,
        height, bitmap, x_hot, y_hot)
    Display *display;
    Drawable drawable;
    char *filename;
    unsigned int *width, *height;      /* RETURN */
    Pixmap *bitmap;                    /* RETURN */
    int *x_hot, *y_hot;                /* RETURN */
```

Arguments

display   Specifies a connection to an X server; returned from XOpenDisplay.

drawable   Specifies the drawable.

filename   Specifies the filename to use. The format of the filename is operating system specific.

width   Return the dimensions in pixels of the bitmap that is read.
height

bitmap   Returns the pixmap resource ID that is created.

x_hot   Return the hotspot coordinates in the file (or –1,–1 if none present).
y_hot

Description

XReadBitmapFile reads in a file containing a description of a pixmap of depth 1 (a bitmap) in X Version 11 bitmap format.

XReadBitmapFile creates a pixmap of the appropriate size and reads the bitmap data from the file into the pixmap. The caller should free the pixmap using XFreePixmap when finished with it.

If the file cannot be opened, XReadBitmapFile returns BitmapOpenFailed. If the file can be opened but does not contain valid bitmap data, XReadBitmapFile returns Bitmap-FileInvalid. If insufficient working storage is allocated, XReadBitmapFile returns BitmapNoMemory. If the file is readable and valid, XReadBitmapFile returns Bitmap-Success.

Here is an example X Version 11 bitmap file:

```
#define name_width 16
#define name_height 16
#define name_x_hot 8
#define name_y_hot 8
static char name_bits[] = {
  0xf8, 0x1f, 0xe3, 0xc7, 0xcf, 0xf3, 0x9f, 0xf9, 0xbf, 0xfd, 0x33, 0xcc,
  0x7f, 0xfe, 0x7f, 0xfe, 0x7e, 0x7e, 0x7f, 0xfe, 0x37, 0xec, 0xbb, 0xdd,
  0x9c, 0x39, 0xcf, 0xf3, 0xe3, 0xc7, 0xf8, 0x1f};
```

For more information, see Volume One, Chapter 6, *Drawing Graphics and Text.*

Errors

```
BadDrawable
```

Related Commands

XCreateBitmapFromData, XCreatePixmap, XCreatePixmapFromBitmapData, XFreePixmap, XQueryBestSize, XQueryBestStipple, XQueryBestTile, XSetTile, XSetWindowBackgroundPixmap, XSetWindowBorderPixmap, XWriteBitmapFile.

Name

XRebindKeysym — rebind a keysym to a string for client.

Synopsis

```
XRebindKeysym(display, keysym, mod_list, mod_count, string,
        num_bytes)
    Display *display;
    KeySym keysym;
    KeySym *mod_list;
    int mod_count;
    unsigned char *string;
    int num_bytes;
```

Arguments

display   Specifies a connection to an X server; returned from XOpenDisplay.

keysym   Specifies the keysym to be rebound.

mod_list   Specifies a pointer to an array of keysyms that are being used as modifiers.

mod_count   Specifies the number of modifiers in the modifier list.

string   Specifies a pointer to the string that is to be copied and returned by XLookupString in response to later events.

num_bytes   Specifies the length of the string.

Description

XRebindKeysym binds the ASCII *string* to the specified *keysym*, so that *string* and *keysym* are returned by XLookukpString when that key is pressed and the modifiers specified in *mod_list* are also being held down. This function rebinds the meaning of a keysym for a client. It does not redefine the keycode in the server but merely provides an easy way for long strings to be attached to keys. Note that you are allowed to rebind a keysym that may not exist.

See Volume One, Chapter 9, *The Keyboard and Pointer*, for a description of keysyms and keyboard mapping.

Related Commands

XChangeKeyboardMapping, XDeleteModifiermapEntry, XFreeModifiermap, XGetKeyboardMapping, XGetModifierMapping, XInsertModifiermapEntry, XKeycodeToKeysym, XKeysymToKeycode, XKeysymToString, XLookupKeysym, XLookupString, XNewModifierMap, XQueryKeymap, XRefreshKeyboard-Mapping, XSetModifierMapping, XStringToKeysym.

XRecolorCursor

Xlib – Cursors –

Name

XRecolorCursor — change the color of a cursor.

Synopsis

```
XRecolorCursor(display, cursor, foreground_color,
        background_color)
    Display *display;
    Cursor cursor;
    XColor *foreground_color, *background_color;
```

Arguments

display   Specifies a connection to an X server; returned from XOpenDisplay.

cursor   Specifies the cursor ID.

foreground_color
Specifies the red, green, and blue (RGB) values for the foreground.

background_color
Specifies the red, green, and blue (RGB) values for the background.

Description

XRecolorCursor applies a foreground and background color to a cursor. Cursors are normally created using a single plane pixmap, composed of 0's and 1's, with one pixel value assigned to 1's and another assigned to 0's. XRecolorCursor changes these pixel values. If the cursor is being displayed on a screen, the change is visible immediately. On some servers, these color selections are read/write cells from the colormap, and can't be shared by applications.

Structures

```
typedef struct {
    unsigned long pixel;
    unsigned short red, green, blue;
    char flags;                         /* DoRed, DoGreen, DoBlue */
    char pad;
} XColor;
```

Errors

BadCursor

Related Commands

XCreateFontCursor, XCreateGlyphCursor, XCreatePixmapCursor, XDefine-
Cursor, XFreeCursor, XQueryBestCursor, XQueryBestSize, XUndefine-
Cursor.

XReconfigureWMWindow

Name

XReconfigureWMWindow — request that a top-level window be reconfigured.

Synopsis

```
Status XReconfigureWMWindow(display, w, screen_number,
        value_mask, values)
    Display *display;
    Window w;
    int screen_number;
    unsigned int value_mask;
    XWindowChanges *values;
```

Arguments

display	Specifies a connection to an X server; returned from XOpenDisplay.
w	Specifies the window.
screen_number	
	Specifies the appropriate screen number on the host server.
value_mask	Specifies which values are to be set using information in the values structure. This mask is the bitwise inclusive OR of the valid configure window values bits.
values	Specifies a pointer to the XWindowChanges structure.

Availability

Release 4 and later.

Description

XReconfigureWMWindow issues a ConfigureWindow request on the specified top-level window. If the stacking mode is changed and the request fails with a BadMatch error, the error event is trapped and a synthetic ConfigureRequest event containing the same configuration parameters is sent to the root of the specified window. Window managers may elect to receive this event and treat it as a request to reconfigure the indicated window.

For more information, see Volume One, Chapter 10, *Interclient Communication*.

Structures

```
typedef struct {
    int x, y;
    int width, height;
    int border_width;
    Window sibling;
    int stack_mode;
} XWindowChanges;
```

Errors
    BadValue
    BadWindow

Related Commands
    XIconifyWindow, XWithdrawWindow.

XRectInRegion

Name

XRectInRegion — determine if a rectangle resides in a region.

Synopsis

```
int XRectInRegion(r, x, y, width, height)
    Region r;
    int x, y;
    unsigned int width, height;
```

Arguments

r   Specifies the region.

x   Specify the x and y coordinates of the upper-left corner of the rectangle, rela-
y   tive to the region's origin.

width   Specify the width and height in pixels of the rectangle.
height

Description

XRectInRegion returns RectangleIn if the rectangle is completely contained in the region r, RectangleOut if it is completely outside, and RectanglePart if it is partially inside.

Regions are located using an offset from a point (the *region origin*) which is common to all regions. It is up to the application to interpret the location of the region relative to a drawable. If the region is to be used as a clip_mask by calling XSetRegion, the upper-left corner of region relative to the drawable used in the graphics request will be at (xoffset + clip_x_origin, yoffset + clip_y_origin), where xoffset and yoffset are the offset of the region and clip_x_origin and clip_y_origin are the clip origin in the GC used.

For this function, the x and y arguments are interpreted relative to the region origin; no drawable is involved.

Structures

Region is a pointer to an opaque structure type.

Related Commands

XClipBox, XCreateRegion, XDestroyRegion, XEmptyRegion, XEqualRegion, XIntersectRegion, XOffsetRegion, XPointInRegion, XPolygonRegion, XSetRegion, XShrinkRegion, XSubtractRegion, XUnionRectWithRegion, XUnionRegion, XXorRegion.

XRefreshKeyboardMapping

Name

XRefreshKeyboardMapping — read keycode-keysym mapping from server into Xlib.

Synopsis

```
XRefreshKeyboardMapping(event)
    XMappingEvent *event;
```

Arguments

event   Specifies the mapping event that triggered this call.

Description

XRefreshKeyboardMapping causes Xlib to update its knowledge of the mapping between keycodes and keysyms. This updates the application's knowledge of the keyboard.

The application should call XRefreshKeyboardMapping when a MappingNotify event occurs. MappingNotify events occur when some client has called XChangeKeyboardMapping.

For more information, see Volume One, Chapter 9, *The Keyboard and Pointer*.

Structures

```
typedef struct {
    int type;
    unsigned long serial;   /* # of last request processed by server */
    Bool send_event;       /* true if this came from a SendEvent request */
    Display *display;      /* display the event was read from */
    Window window;         /* unused */
    int request;           /* one of MappingModifier, MappingKeyboard,
                              MappingPointer */
    int first_keycode;     /* first keycode */
    int count;             /* defines range of change with first_keycode*/
} XMappingEvent;
```

Related Commands

XChangeKeyboardMapping, XDeleteModifiermapEntry, XFreeModifiermap, XGetKeyboardMapping, XGetModifierMapping, XInsertModifiermapEntry, XKeycodeToKeysym, XKeysymToKeycode, XKeysymToString, XLookupKeysym, XLookupString, XNewModifierMap, XQueryKeymap, XRebindKeysym, XSetModifierMapping, XStringToKeysym.

XRemoveFromSaveSet

Name

XRemoveFromSaveSet — remove a window from the client's save-set.

Synopsis

```
XRemoveFromSaveSet(display, w)
    Display *display;
    Window w;
```

Arguments

display   Specifies a connection to an X server; returned from XOpenDisplay.

w   Specifies the window you want to remove from this client's save-set. This
                 window must have been created by a client other than the client making this
                 call.

Description

XRemoveFromSaveSet removes a window from the save-set of the calling application.

The save-set is a safety net for windows that have been reparented by the window manager,
usually to provide a shadow or other background for each window. When the window manager
dies unexpectedly, the windows in the save-set are reparented to their closest living ancestor, so
that they remain alive.

This call is not necessary when a window is destroyed since destroyed windows are automatically removed from the save-set. Therefore, many window managers get away without ever
calling XRemoveFromSaveSet. See Volume One, Chapter 14, *Window Management*, for
more information about save-sets.

Errors

BadMatch   *w* not created by some other client.

BadWindow

Related Commands

XAddToSaveSet, XChangeSaveSet.

XRemoveHost

Name

XRemoveHost — remove a host from the access control list.

Synopsis

```
XRemoveHost(display, host)
    Display *display;
    XHostAddress *host;
```

Arguments

display   Specifies a connection to an X server; returned from XOpenDisplay.

host   Specifies the network address of the machine to be removed.

Description

XRemoveHost removes the specified host from the access control list of the connected server. The server must be on the same host as the process that calls XRemoveHost in order to change the access control list.

If you remove your own machine from the access control list, you can no longer connect to that server, and there is no way back from this call other than to log out, edit the access control file, and reset the server.

The address data must be a valid address for the type of network in which the server operates, as specified in the family member.

For TCP/IP, the address should be in network byte order. For the DECnet family, the server performs no automatic swapping on the address bytes. A Phase IV address is two bytes long. The first byte contains the least significant eight bits of the node number. The second byte contains the most significant two bits of the node number in the least significant two bits of the byte, and the area in the most significant six bits of the byte.

For more information on access control lists, see Volume One, Chapter 13, *Other Programming Techniques*.

Structures

```
typedef struct {
    int family;          /* for example Family Internet */
    int length;          /* length of address, in bytes */
    char *address;       /* pointer to where to find the bytes */
} XHostAddress;

/* constants used for family member of XHostAddress */
#define FamilyInternet       0
#define FamilyDECnet         1
#define FamilyChaos          2
```

Errors

BadAccess
BadValue

Related Commands

XAddHost, XAddHosts, XDisableAccessControl, XEnableAccessControl,
XListHosts, XRemoveHosts, XSetAccessControl.

XRemoveHosts

Name

XRemoveHosts — remove multiple hosts from the access control list.

Synopsis

```
XRemoveHosts(display, hosts, num_hosts)
    Display *display;
    XHostAddress *hosts;
    int num_hosts;
```

Arguments

display   Specifies a connection to an X server; returned from XOpenDisplay.

hosts   Specifies the list of hosts that are to be removed.

num_hosts   Specifies the number of hosts that are to be removed.

Description

XRemoveHosts removes each specified host from the access control list of the connected server. The server must be on the same host as the process that call XRemoveHosts, in order to change the access control list.

If you remove your machine from the access control list, you can no longer connect to that server, and there is no way back from this call except to log out, edit the access control file, and reset the server.

The address data must be a valid address for the type of network in which the server operates, as specified in the family member.

For TCP/IP, the address should be in network byte order. For the DECnet family, the server performs no automatic swapping on the address bytes. A Phase IV address is two bytes long. The first byte contains the least significant eight bits of the node number. The second byte contains the most significant two bits of the node number in the least significant two bits of the byte, and the area in the most significant six bits of the byte.

For more information on access control lists, see Volume One, Chapter 13, *Other Programming Techniques*.

Structures

```
typedef struct {
    int family;            /* for example Family Internet */
    int length;            /* length of address, in bytes */
    char *address;         /* pointer to where to find the bytes */
} XHostAddress;

/* constants used for family member of XHostAddress */
#define FamilyInternet      0
#define FamilyDECnet        1
#define FamilyChaos         2
```

Errors
    BadAccess
    BadValue

Related Commands
    XAddHost, XAddHosts, XDisableAccessControl, XEnableAccessControl,
    XListHosts, XRemoveHost, XSetAccessControl.

XReparentWindow

Name

XReparentWindow — insert a window between another window and its parent.

Synopsis

```
XReparentWindow(display, win, parent, x, y)
    Display *display;
    Window win;
    Window parent;
    int x, y;
```

Arguments

display   Specifies a connection to an X server; returned from XOpenDisplay.

win   Specifies the ID of the window to be reparented.

parent   Specifies the window ID of the new parent window.

x   Specify the coordinates of the window relative to the new parent.
y

Description

XReparentWindow modifies the window hierarchy by placing window win as a child of window parent. This function is usually used by a window manager to put a decoration window behind each application window. In the case of the window manager, the new parent window must first be created as a child of the root window.

If win is mapped, an XUnmapWindow request is performed on it automatically. win is then removed from its current position in the hierarchy, and is inserted as a child of the specified parent. win is placed on top in the stacking order with respect to siblings.

A ReparentNotify event is then generated. The override_redirect member of the structure returned by this event is set to either True or False. Window manager clients normally should ignore this event if this member is set to True.

Finally, if the window was originally mapped, an XMapWindow request is performed automatically.

Descendants of win remain descendants of win; they are not reparented to the old parent of win.

Normal exposure processing on formerly obscured windows is performed. The server might not generate exposure events for regions from the initial unmap that are immediately obscured by the final map. The request fails if the new parent is not on the same screen as the old parent, or if the new parent is the window itself or an inferior of the window.

Errors

BadMatch   *parent* not on same screen as old parent of *win*.

win has a `ParentRelative` background and *parent* is not the same depth as *win*.

parent is *win* or an inferior of *win*.

BadWindow

Related Commands

XCirculateSubwindows, XCirculateSubwindowsDown, XCirculate-
SubwindowsUp, XConfigureWindow, XLowerWindow, XMoveResizeWindow,
XMoveWindow, XQueryTree, XRaiseWindow, XResizeWindow, XRestack-
Windows.

XResetScreenSaver

Name

XResetScreenSaver — reset the screen saver.

Synopsis

```
XResetScreenSaver(display)
    Display *display;
```

Arguments

display   Specifies a connection to an X server; returned from XOpenDisplay.

Description

XResetScreenSaver redisplays the screen if the screen saver was activated. This may result in exposure events to all visible windows if the server cannot save the screen contents. If the screen is already active, nothing happens.

For more information on the screen saver, see Volume One, Chapter 13, *Other Programming Techniques*.

Related Commands

XActivateScreenSaver, XForceScreenSaver, XGetScreenSaver, XSet-ScreenSaver.

Name

XResizeWindow — change a window's size.

Synopsis

```
XResizeWindow(display, w, width, height)
    Display *display;
    Window w;
    unsigned int width, height;
```

Arguments

display   Specifies a connection to an X server; returned from XOpenDisplay.

w   Specifies the ID of the window to be resized.

width   Specify the new dimensions of the window in pixels.
height

Description

XResizeWindow changes the inside dimensions of the window. The border is resized to match but its border width is not changed. XResizeWindow does not raise the window, or change its origin. Changing the size of a mapped window may lose its contents and generate an Expose event, depending on the bit_gravity attribute (see Volume One, Chapter 4, *Window Attributes*). If a mapped window is made smaller, exposure events will be generated on windows that it formerly obscured.

If the override_redirect attribute of the window is False and the window manager has selected SubstructureRedirectMask on the parent, then a ConfigureRequest event is sent to the window manager, and no further processing is performed.

If the client has selected StructureNotifyMask on the window, then a Configure-Notify event is generated after the move takes place, and the event will contain the final size of the window.

Errors

BadValue
BadWindow

Related Commands

XCirculateSubwindows, XCirculateSubwindowsDown, XCirculate-SubwindowsUp, XConfigureWindow, XLowerWindow, XMoveResizeWindow, XMoveWindow, XQueryTree, XRaiseWindow, XReparentWindow, XRestack-Windows.

XRestackWindows

Name

XRestackWindows — change the stacking order of siblings.

Synopsis

```
XRestackWindows(display, windows, nwindows);
    Display *display;
    Window windows[];
    int nwindows;
```

Arguments

display   Specifies a connection to an X server; returned from XOpenDisplay.

windows   Specifies an array containing the windows to be restacked. All the windows must have a common parent.

nwindows   Specifies the number of windows in the windows array.

Description

XRestackWindows restacks the windows in the order specified, from top to bottom. The stacking order of the first window in the windows array will be on top, and the other windows will be stacked underneath it in the order of the array. Note that you can exclude other siblings from the windows array so that the top window in the array will not move relative to these other siblings.

For each window in the window array that is not a child of the specified window, a BadMatch error will be generated. If the override_redirect attribute of the window is False and the window manager has selected SubstructureRedirectMask on the parent, then ConfigureRequest events are sent to the window manager for each window whose override_redirect is not set, and no further processing is performed. Otherwise, the windows will be restacked in top to bottom order.

Errors

BadMatch
BadWindow

Related Commands

XCirculateSubwindows, XCirculateSubwindowsDown, XCirculate-SubwindowsUp, XConfigureWindow, XLowerWindow, XMoveResizeWindow, XMoveWindow, XQueryTree, XRaiseWindow, XReparentWindow, XResize-Window.

XrmDestroyDatabase

Name
XrmDestroyDatabase — destroy a resource database.

Synopsis
```
void XrmDestroyDatabase(database)
    XrmDatabase database;
```

Arguments
database   Specifies the resource database.

Availability
Release 4 and later.

Description
XrmDestroyDatabase destroys a resource database and frees its allocated memory. The destroyed resource database should not be referenced again. If database is NULL, Xrm-DestroyDatabase returns immediately.

For more information, see Volume One, Chapter 11, *Managing User Preferences*.

Related Commands
XrmMergeDatabases.

Name
XrmGetFileDatabase — retrieve a database from a file.

Synopsis
```
XrmDatabase XrmGetFileDatabase(filename)
    char *filename;
```

Arguments
filename   Specifies the resource database filename.

Description
XrmGetFileDatabase opens the specified file, creates a new resource database, and loads the database with the data read in from the file. The return value of the function is as a pointer to the created database.

The specified file must contain lines in the format accepted by XrmPutLineResource. If XrmGetFileDatabase cannot open the specified file, it returns NULL.

For more information, see Volume One, Chapter 11, *Managing User Preferences*.

Structures
XrmDatabase is a pointer to an opaque data type.

Related Commands
XrmDestroyDatabase, XrmGetResource, XrmGetStringDatabase, Xrm-
Initialize, XrmMergeDatabases, XrmParseCommand, XrmPutFileDatabase,
XrmPutLineResource, XrmPutResource, XrmPutStringResource, XrmQGet-
Resource, XrmQGetSearchList, XrmQGetSearchResource, XrmQPutResource,
XrmQPutStringResource, XrmQuarkToString, XrmStringToBindingQuark-
List, XrmStringToQuarkList, XrmStringToQuark, XrmUniqueQuark.

Name

XrmGetResource — get a resource from name and class as strings.

Synopsis

```
Bool XrmGetResource(database, str_name, str_class,
        str_type, value)
    XrmDatabase database;
    char *str_name;
    char *str_class;
    char **str_type;          /* RETURN */
    XrmValue *value;          /* RETURN */
```

Arguments

database   Specifies the database that is to be used.

str_name   Specifies the fully specified name of the value being retrieved.

str_class Specifies the fully specified class of the value being retrieved.

str_type   Returns a pointer to the representation type of the destination. In this func-
           tion, the representation type is represented as a string, not as an Xrm-
           Representation.

value   Returns the value in the database. Do not modify or free this data.

Description

The resource manager manages databases of resource specifications consisting of lines containing resource name/class strings followed by a colon and the value of the resource. XrmGet-
Resource retrieves a resource from the specified database. It takes fully specified name and
class strings, and returns the representation and value of the matching resource. The value
returned points into database memory; you must not modify that data. If a resource was found,
XrmGetResource returns True. Otherwise, it returns False.

Currently, the database only frees or overwrites entries when new data is stored with Xrm-
MergeDatabases, or XrmPutResource and related routines. A client that avoids these
functions should be safe using the address passed back at any time until it exits.

XrmGetResource is very similar to XrmQGetResource, except that in XrmQGet-
Resource, the equivalent arguments to str_name, str_class, and str_type are
quarks instead of strings.

To understand how data is stored and retrieved from the database, you must understand:

1)   The basic components that make up the storage key and retrieval keys.

2)   How keys are made up from components.

3)   The two ways that components can be bound together.

4)   What sort of keys are used to store and retrieve data.

5)   How the storage key and retrieval keys are compared to determine whether they match.

6)   If there are multiple matches, how the best match is chosen so only one value is returned.

Each will be covered in turn.

1)   The storage key and retrieval keys are composed of a variable number of components, bound together. There are two types of components: names and classes. By convention, names begin with a lower case character and classes begin with an upper case character. Therefore, xmh, `background`, and `toc` are examples of names, while Xmh, Box, and Command are examples of classes. A name key (like *str_name*) consists purely of name components. A class key (like *str_class*) consists purely of class components. The retrieval keys are a pair of keys, one composed of purely name components, the other of purely class components. A storage key (like *specifier* in XrmPut-Resource) consists of a mixture of name and class components.

2)   A key is composed of multiple components bound together in sequence. This allows you to build logical keys for your application. For example, at the top level, the application might consist of a paned window (that is, a window divided into several sections) named `toc`. One pane of the paned window is a button box window named `buttons` filled with command buttons. One of these command buttons is used to retrieve (`include`) new mail and has the name `include`. This window has a fully qualified name xmh.toc.buttons.include and a fully qualified class Xmh.VPaned.Box.Command. Its fully qualified name is the name of its parent, xmh.toc.buttons, followed by its name `include`. Its class is the class of its parent, Xmh.VPaned.Box, followed by its particular class, Command.

3)   The components in a key can be bound together in two ways: by a tight binding (a dot "."). or by a loose binding (an asterisk "*"). Thus xmhtoc.background has three name components tightly bound together, while Xmh*Command.foreground uses both a loose and a tight binding. Bindings can also precede the first component (but may not follow the last component). By convention, if no binding is specified before the first component, a tight binding is assumed. For example, xmh.background and .xmh.background both begin with tight bindings before the xmh, while *xmh.background begins with a loose binding.

        The difference between tight and loose bindings comes when comparing two keys. A tight binding means that the components on either side of the binding must be sequential. A loose binding is a sort of wildcard, meaning that there may be unspecified components between the two components that are loosely bound togehter. For example, xmh.toc.background would match xmh*background and *background but not xmh.background or background.

4)   A key used to store data into the database can use both loose and tight bindings. This allows you to specify a data value which can match to many different retrieval keys. In contrast, keys used to retrieve data from the database can use only tight bindings. You can only look up one item in the database at a time. Remember also that a storage key

can mix name and class components, while the retrieval keys are a pair of keys, one consisting purely of name (first character lower case) components and one consisting purely of class (capitalized) components.

5) The resource manager must solve the problem of how to compare the pair of retrieval keys to a single storage key. (Actually, to many single storage keys, since the resource manager will compare the retrieval keys against every key in the database, but one at a time.) The solution of comparing a pair of keys to a single key is simple. The resource manager compares component by component, comparing a component from the storage key against both the corresponding component from the name retrieval key, and the corresponding component from the class retrieval key. If the storage key component matches either retrieval key component, then that component is considered to match. For example, the storage key `xmh.toc.Foreground` matches the name key `xmh.toc.foreground` with the class key `Xmh.Box.Foreground`. This is why storage keys can mix name and class components, while retrieval keys cannot.

6) Because the resource manager allows loose bindings (wildcards) and mixing names and classes in the storage key, it is possible for many storage keys to match a single name/class retrieval key pair. To solve this problem, the resource manager uses the following precedence rules to determine which is the best match (and only the value from that match will be returned). The precedence rules are, in order of preference:

1. The attribute of the name and class must match. For example, queries for

   ```
   xterm.scrollbar.background     (name)
   XTerm.Scrollbar.Background     (class)
   ```

   will not match the following database entry:

   ```
   xterm.scrollbar:      on
   ```

   because background does not appear in the database entry.

2. Database entries with name or class prefixed by a dot (.) are more specific than those prefixed by an asterisk (*). For example, the entry `xterm.geometry` is more specific than the entry `xterm*geometry`.

3. Names are more specific than classes. For example, the entry `*scrollbar.-background` is more specific than the entry `*Scrollbar.Background`.

4. A name or class is more specific than omission. For example, the entry `Scrollbar*Background` is more specific than the entry `*Background`.

5. Left components are more specific than right components. For example, to query for `.xterm.scrollbar.background`, the entry `xterm*background` is more specific than the entry `scrollbar*background`.

Names and classes can be mixed. As an example of these rules, assume the following user preference specification:

```
xmh*background:                    red
*command.font:                     8x13
*command.background:               blue
*Command.Foreground:               green
xmh.toc*Command.activeForeground:  black
```

A query for the name xmh.toc.messagefunctions.include.activeForeground and class Xmh.VPaned.Box.Command.Foreground would match xmh.toc*-Command.activeForeground and return black. However, it also matches *Command.Foreground but with lower preference, so it would not return green.

For more information, see Volume One, Chapter 11, *Managing User Preferences*, and Volume Four, *X Toolkit Intrinsics Programming Manual*, Chapter 9, *Resource Management and Type Conversion*.

Structures

XrmDatabase is a pointer to an opaque data type.

```
typedef struct {
    unsigned int    size;
    caddr_t         addr;
} XrmValue;
```

Related Commands

XrmDestroyDatabase, XrmGetFileDatabase, XrmGetStringDatabase, Xrm-Initialize, XrmMergeDatabases, XrmParseCommand, XrmPutFileDatabase, XrmPutLineResource, XrmPutResource, XrmPutStringResource, XrmQGet-Resource, XrmQGetSearchList, XrmQGetSearchResource, XrmQPutResource, XrmQPutStringResource, XrmQuarkToString, XrmStringToBindingQuark-List, XrmStringToQuarkList, XrmStringToQuark, XrmUniqueQuark.

XrmGetStringDatabase

Name

XrmGetStringDatabase — create a database from a string.

Synopsis

```
XrmDatabase XrmGetStringDatabase(data)
      char *data;
```

Arguments

data   Specifies the database contents using a string.

Description

XrmGetStringDatabase creates a new database and stores in it the resources specified in data. The return value is subsequently used to refer to the created database. XrmGet-StringDatabase is similar to XrmGetFileDatabase, except that it reads the information out of a string instead of a file. Each line in the string is separated by a new line character in the format accepted by XrmPutLineResource.

For more information, see Volume One, Chapter 11, *Managing User Preferences*.

Structures

XrmDatabase is a pointer to an opaque data type.

Related Commands

XrmDestroyDatabase, XrmGetFileDatabase, XrmGetResource, Xrm-Initialize, XrmMergeDatabases, XrmParseCommand, XrmPutFileDatabase, XrmPutLineResource, XrmPutResource, XrmPutStringResource, XrmQGet-Resource, XrmQGetSearchList, XrmQGetSearchResource, XrmQPutResource, XrmQPutStringResource, XrmQuarkToString, XrmStringToBindingQuark-List, XrmStringToQuarkList, XrmStringToQuark, XrmUniqueQuark.

Name

XrmInitialize — initialize the resource manager.

Synopsis

```
void XrmInitialize();
```

Description

XrmInitialize initializes the resource manager, and should be called once before using any other resource manager functions. It just creates a representation type of "String" for values defined as strings. This representation type is used by XrmPutStringResource and XrmQPutStringResource, which require a value as a string. See XrmQPutResource for a description of representation types.

For more information, see Volume One, Chapter 11, *Managing User Preferences*.

Related Commands

XrmDestroyDatabase, XrmGetFileDatabase, XrmGetResource, XrmGetStringDatabase, XrmMergeDatabases, XrmParseCommand, XrmPutFileDatabase, XrmPutLineResource, XrmPutResource, XrmPutStringResource, XrmQGetResource, XrmQGetSearchList, XrmQGetSearchResource, XrmQPutResource, XrmQPutStringResource, XrmQuarkToString, XrmStringToBindingQuarkList, XrmStringToQuarkList, XrmStringToQuark, XrmUniqueQuark.

XrmMergeDatabases

Name
XrmMergeDatabases — merge the contents of one database into another.

Synopsis
```
void XrmMergeDatabases(source_db, target_db)
    XrmDatabase source_db, *target_db;
```

Arguments
source_db   Specifies the resource database to be merged into the existing database.

target_db   Specifies a pointer to the resource database into which the *source_db* database will be merged.

Description
XrmMergeDatabases merges *source_db* into *target_db*. This procedure is used to combine databases, for example, an application specific database of defaults and a database of user preferences. The merge is destructive; it destroys the original *source_db* database and modifies the original *target_db*.

For more information, see Volume One, Chapter 11, *Managing User Preferences*.

Structures
XrmDatabase is a pointer to an opaque data type.

Related Commands
XrmDestroyDatabase, XrmGetFileDatabase, XrmGetResource, XrmGet-
StringDatabase, XrmInitialize, XrmParseCommand, XrmPutFileDatabase,
XrmPutLineResource, XrmPutResource, XrmPutStringResource, XrmQGet-
Resource, XrmQGetSearchList, XrmQGetSearchResource, XrmQPutResource,
XrmQPutStringResource, XrmQuarkToString, XrmStringToBindingQuark-
List, XrmStringToQuarkList, XrmStringToQuark, XrmUniqueQuark.

Name

XrmParseCommand — load a resource database from command line arguments.

Synopsis

```
void XrmParseCommand(db, table, table_count, name, argc,
      argv)
    XrmDatabase *db;              /* SEND and if NULL, RETURN */
    XrmOptionDescList table;
    int table_count;
    char *name;
    int *argc;                    /* SEND and RETURN */
    char **argv;                  /* SEND and RETURN */
```

Arguments

database	Specifies a pointer to the resource database. If `database` contains NULL, a new resource database is created and a pointer to it is returned in `database`.
table	Specifies table of command line arguments to be parsed.
table_count	Specifies the number of entries in the table.
name	Specifies the application name.
argc	Before the call, specifies the number of arguments. After the call, returns the number of arguments not parsed.
argv	Before the call, specifies a pointer to the command line arguments. After the call, returns a pointer to a string containing the command line arguments that could not be parsed.

Description

XrmParseCommand parses an (`argc`, `argv`) pair according to the specified option table, loads recognized options into the specified database, and modifies the (`argc`, `argv`) pair to remove all recognized options.

The specified table is used to parse the command line. Recognized entries in the table are removed from `argv`, and entries are made in the specified resource database. The table entries contain information on the option string, the option name, which style of option and a value to provide if the option kind is XrmoptionNoArg. See the example table below.

`argc` specifies the number of arguments in `argv` and is set to the remaining number of arguments that were not parsed. `name` should be the name of your application for use in building the database entry. `name` is prepended to the resourceName in the option table before storing the specification. No separating (binding) character is inserted. The table must contain either a dot (".") or an asterisk ("*") as the first character in each resourceName entry. The resourceName entry can contain multiple components.

The following is a typical options table:

```
static XrmOptionDescRec opTable[ ] = {
{"-background",  "*background",              XrmoptionSepArg, (caddr_t) NULL},
```

```
{"-bd",           "*borderColor",          XrmoptionSepArg, (caddr_t) NULL},
{"-bg",           "*background",           XrmoptionSepArg, (caddr_t) NULL},
{"-borderwidth",  "*TopLevelShell.borderWidth", XrmoptionSepArg, (caddr_t) NULL},
{"-bordercolor",  "*borderColor",          XrmoptionSepArg, (caddr_t) NULL},
{"-bw",           "*TopLevelShell.borderWidth", XrmoptionSepArg, (caddr_t) NULL},
{"-display",      ".display",              XrmoptionSepArg, (caddr_t) NULL},
{"-fg",           "*foreground",           XrmoptionSepArg, (caddr_t) NULL},
{"-fn",           "*font",                 XrmoptionSepArg, (caddr_t) NULL},
{"-font",         "*font",                 XrmoptionSepArg, (caddr_t) NULL},
{"-foreground",   "*foreground",           XrmoptionSepArg, (caddr_t) NULL},
{"-geometry",     ".TopLevelShell.geometry", XrmoptionSepArg, (caddr_t) NULL},
{"-iconic",       ".TopLevelShell.iconic", XrmoptionNoArg,  (caddr_t) "on"},
{"-name",         ".name",                 XrmoptionSepArg, (caddr_t) NULL},
{"-reverse",      "*reverseVideo",         XrmoptionNoArg,  (caddr_t) "on"},
{"-rv",           "*reverseVideo",         XrmoptionNoArg,  (caddr_t) "on"},
{"-synchronous",  ".synchronous",          XrmoptionNoArg,  (caddr_t) "on"},
{"-title",        ".TopLevelShell.title",  XrmoptionSepArg, (caddr_t) NULL},
{"-xrm",          NULL,                    XrmoptionResArg, (caddr_t) NULL},
};
```

In this table, if the *-background* (or *-bg*) option is used to set background colors, the stored
resource specifier will match all resources of attribute background. If the *-borderwidth* option
is used, the stored resource specifier applies only to border width attributes of class Top-
LevelShell (that is, outermost windows, including pop-up windows). If the *-title* option is
used to set a window name, only the topmost application windows receive the resource.

When parsing the command line, any unique unambiguous abbreviation for an option name in
the table is considered a match for the option. Note that upper case and lower case matter.

For more information, see Volume One, Chapter 11, *Managing User Preferences*.

Structures

XrmDatabase is a pointer to an opaque data type.

```
typedef enum {
    XrmoptionNoArg,        /* value is specified in OptionDescRec.value */
    XrmoptionIsArg,        /* value is the option string itself */
    XrmoptionStickyArg,    /* value is chars immediately following option */
    XrmoptionSepArg,       /* value is next argument in argv */
    XrmoptionResArg,       /* resource and value in next argument in argv */
    XrmoptionSkipArg,      /* ignore this option and next argument in argv */
    XrmoptionSkipLine,     /* ignore this option and the rest of argv */
    XrmoptionSkipNArgs     /* new in R4: ignore this option, skip
                              number specified in next argument */
} XrmOptionKind;

typedef struct {
    char *option;          /* option specification string in argv */
    char *resourceName;    /* binding & resource name (w/out application name) */
    XrmOptionKind argKind; /* which style of option it is */
    caddr_t value;         /* value to provide if XrmoptionNoArg */
} XrmOptionDescRec, *XrmOptionDescList;
```

Related Commands

XrmDestroyDatabase, XrmGetFileDatabase, XrmGetResource, XrmGet-
StringDatabase, XrmInitialize, XrmMergeDatabases, XrmPutFile-
Database, XrmPutLineResource, XrmPutResource, XrmPutStringResource,
XrmQGetResource, XrmQGetSearchList, XrmQGetSearchResource, XrmQPut-
Resource, XrmQPutStringResource, XrmQuarkToString, XrmString-
ToBindingQuarkList, XrmStringToQuarkList, XrmStringToQuark, Xrm-
UniqueQuark.

Name

XrmPutFileDatabase — store a resource database in a file.

Synopsis

```
void XrmPutFileDatabase(database, stored_db)
    XrmDatabase database;
    char *stored_db;
```

Arguments

database   Specifies the resource database that is to be saved.

stored_db   Specifies the filename for the stored database.

Description

XrmPutFileDatabase stores a copy of the application's current database in the specified file. The file is an ASCII text file that contains lines in the format that is accepted by XrmPut-LineResource.

For more information, see Volume One, Chapter 11, *Managing User Preferences*.

Structures

XrmDatabase is a pointer to an opaque data type.

Related Commands

XrmDestroyDatabase, XrmGetFileDatabase, XrmGetResource, XrmGet-StringDatabase, XrmInitialize, XrmMergeDatabases, XrmParseCommand, XrmPutLineResource, XrmPutResource, XrmPutStringResource, XrmQGet-Resource, XrmQGetSearchList, XrmQGetSearchResource, XrmQPutResource, XrmQPutStringResource, XrmQuarkToString, XrmStringToBindingQuark-List, XrmStringToQuarkList, XrmStringToQuark, XrmUniqueQuark.

Name

XrmPutLineResource — add a resource specification to a resource database.

Synopsis

```
void XrmPutLineResource(database, line)
    XrmDatabase *database; /* SEND, and if NULL, RETURN */
    char *line;
```

Arguments

database   Specifies a pointer to the resource database. If `database` contains NULL, a new resource database is created and a pointer to it is returned in `database`.

line   Specifies the resource name (possibly with multiple components) and value pair as a single string, in the format `resource:value`.

Description

XrmPutLineResource adds a single resource entry to the specified database.

XrmPutLineResource is similar to XrmPutStringResource, except that instead of having separate string arguments for the resource and its value, XrmPutLineResource takes a single string argument (`line`) which consists of the resource name, a colon, then the value. Since the value is a string, it is stored into the database with representation type String.

Any whitespace before or after the name or colon in the `line` argument is ignored. The value is terminated by a new-line or a NULL character. The value may contain embedded new-line characters represented by the "\" and "n" two character pair (not the single "\n" character), which are converted into a single linefeed character. In addition, the value may run over onto the next line, this is indicated by a "\" character at the end of each line to be continued.

Null-terminated strings without a new line are also permitted. XrmPutResource, XrmQPutResource, XrmPutStringResource, XrmQPutStringResource and XrmPutLineResource all store data into a database. See XrmQPutResource for the most complete description of this process.

For more information, see Volume One, Chapter 11, *Managing User Preferences*.

Structures

XrmDatabase is a pointer to an opaque data type.

Related Commands

XrmDestroyDatabase, XrmGetFileDatabase, XrmGetResource, XrmGet-
StringDatabase, XrmInitialize, XrmMergeDatabases, XrmParseCommand,
XrmPutFileDatabase, XrmPutResource, XrmPutStringResource, XrmQGet-
Resource, XrmQGetSearchList, XrmQGetSearchResource, XrmQPutResource,
XrmQPutStringResource, XrmQuarkToString, XrmStringToBindingQuark-
List, XrmStringToQuarkList, XrmStringToQuark, XrmUniqueQuark.

Name

XrmPutResource — store a resource specification into a resource database.

Synopsis

```
void XrmPutResource(database, specifier, type, value)
    XrmDatabase *database; /* SEND, and if NULL, RETURN */
    char *specifier;
    char *type;
    XrmValue *value;
```

Arguments

database   Specifies a pointer to the resource database. If database contains NULL, a new
            resource database is created and a pointer to it is returned in _database_.

specifier   Specifies a complete or partial specification of the resource.

type   Specifies the type of the resource.

value   Specifies the value of the resource.

Description

XrmPutResource is one of several functions which store data into a database.

XrmQPutResource first converts _specifier_ into a binding list and a quark list by calling
XrmStringToBindingQuarkList, and converts _type_ into an XrmRepresentation
by calling XrmStringToRepresentation. Finally, it puts the data into the database.

XrmPutResource, XrmQPutResource, XrmPutStringResource, XrmQPut-
StringResource and XrmPutLineResource all store data into a database. See the
description of XrmQPutResource for the most complete description of this process.

For more information, see Volume One, Chapter 11, _Managing User Preferences_.

Structures

XrmDatabase is a pointer to an opaque data type.

```
typedef struct {
    unsigned int    size;
    caddr_t         addr;
} XrmValue, *XrmValuePtr;
```

Related Commands

XrmDestroyDatabase, XrmGetFileDatabase, XrmGetResource, XrmGet-
StringDatabase, XrmInitialize, XrmMergeDatabases, XrmParseCommand,
XrmPutFileDatabase, XrmPutLineResource, XrmPutStringResource, Xrm-
QGetResource, XrmQGetSearchList, XrmQGetSearchResource, XrmQPut-
Resource, XrmQPutStringResource, XrmQuarkToString, XrmString-
ToBindingQuarkList, XrmStringToQuarkList, XrmStringToQuark, Xrm-
UniqueQuark.

XrmPutStringResource

Name

XrmPutStringResource — add a resource specification with separate resource name and value.

Synopsis

```
void XrmPutStringResource(database, resource, value)
    XrmDatabase *database; /* SEND, and if NULL, RETURN */
    char *resource;
    char *value;
```

Arguments

database   Specifies a pointer to the resource database. If database contains NULL, a
            new resource database is created and a pointer to it is returned in database.

resource   Specifies the resource, as a string.

value   Specifies the value of the resource, as a string.

Description

XrmPutStringResource adds a resource specification with the specified resource and
value to the specified database. The resource string may contain both names and classes,
bound with either loose (*) or tight (.) bindings. See the description of XrmGetResource for
more information about bindings.

The representation type used in the database is String.

XrmPutResource, XrmQPutResource, XrmPutStringResource, XrmQPut-
StringResource and XrmPutLineResource all store data into a database. See Xrm-
QPutResource for the most complete description of this process.

For more information, see Volume One, Chapter 11, *Managing User Preferences*.

Structures

XrmDatabase is a pointer to an opaque data type.

Related Commands

XrmDestroyDatabase, XrmGetFileDatabase, XrmGetResource, XrmGet-
StringDatabase, XrmInitialize, XrmMergeDatabases, XrmParseCommand,
XrmPutFileDatabase, XrmPutLineResource, XrmPutResource, XrmQGet-
Resource, XrmQGetSearchList, XrmQGetSearchResource, XrmQPutResource,
XrmQPutStringResource, XrmQuarkToString, XrmStringToBindingQuark-
List, XrmStringToQuarkList, XrmStringToQuark, XrmUniqueQuark.

Name

XrmQGetResource — get a resource value using name and class as quarks.

Synopsis

```
Bool XrmQGetResource(database, quark_name, quark_class,
        quark_type, value)
    XrmDatabase database;
    XrmNameList quark_name;
    XrmClassList quark_class;
    XrmRepresentation *quark_type; /* RETURN */
    XrmValue *value;                /* RETURN */
```

Arguments

database   Specifies the database that is to be used.

quark_name   Specifies the fully qualified name of the value being retrieved (as a list of quarks).

quark_class   Specifies the fully qualified class of the value being retrieved (as a list of quarks).

quark_type   Returns a pointer to the representation type of the value. In this function, the representation type is represented as a quark.

value   Returns a pointer to the value in the database. Do not modify or free this data.

Description

XrmQGetResource retrieves a resource from the specified database. It takes fully qualified name and class strings, and returns the representation and value of the matching resource. The value returned points into database memory; you must not modify that data. If a resource was found, XrmQGetResource returns True. Otherwise, it returns False.

Currently, the database only frees or overwrites entries when new data is stored with Xrm-MergeDatabases, or XrmPutResource and related routines. A client that avoids these functions should be safe using the address passed back at any time until it exits.

XrmQGetResource is very similar to XrmGetResource, except that in XrmGet-Resource, the equivalent arguments to quark_name, quark_class, and quark_type arguments are strings instead of quarks.

See XrmGetResource for a full description of how data is looked up in the database.

For more information, see Volume One, Chapter 11, *Managing User Preferences*.

Structures

XrmDatabase is a pointer to an opaque data type.

```
typedef XrmQuarkList XrmNameList;
typedef XrmQuarkList XrmClassList;
typedef XrmQuark     XrmRepresentation;

typedef struct {
    unsigned int    size;
    caddr_t         addr;
} XrmValue, *XrmValuePtr;
```

Related Commands

XrmDestroyDatabase, XrmGetFileDatabase, XrmGetResource, XrmGet-
StringDatabase, XrmInitialize, XrmMergeDatabases, XrmParseCommand,
XrmPutFileDatabase, XrmPutLineResource, XrmPutResource, XrmPut-
StringResource, XrmQGetSearchList, XrmQGetSearchResource, XrmQPut-
Resource, XrmQPutStringResource, XrmQuarkToString, XrmString-
ToBindingQuarkList, XrmStringToQuarkList, XrmStringToQuark, Xrm-
UniqueQuark.

Name

XrmQGetSearchList — return a list of database levels.

Synopsis

```
Bool XrmQGetSearchList(database, names, classes,
        search_list, list_length)
    XrmDatabase database;
    XrmNameList names;
    XrmClassList classes;
    XrmSearchList search_list; /* RETURN */
    int list_length;
```

Arguments

database   Specifies the database to be searched.

names   Specifies a list of resource names.

classes   Specifies a list of resource classes.

search_list   Returns a search list for further use. The caller must allocate sufficient space for the list before calling XrmQGetSearchList.

list_length   Specifies the number of entries (not the byte size) allocated for search_list.

Description

XrmQGetSearchList is a tool for searching the database more efficiently. It is used in combination with XrmQGetSearchResource. Often, one searches the database for many similar resources which differ only in their final component (e.g., xmh.toc.foreground, xmh.toc.background, etc). Rather than looking for each resource in its entirety, Xrm-GetSearchList searches the database for the common part of the resource name, returning a whole list of items in the database that match it. This list is called the *search list*. This search list is then used by XrmQGetSearchList, which searches for the last components one at a time. In this way, the common work of searching for similar resources is done only once, and the specific part of the search is done on the much shorter search list.

XrmQGetSearchList takes a list of names and classes and returns a list of database levels where a match might occur. The returned list is in best-to-worst order and uses the same algorithm as XrmGetResource for determining precedence. If search_list was large enough for the search list, XrmQGetSearchList returns True. Otherwise, it returns False.

The size of the search list that must be allocated by the caller is dependent upon the number of levels and wildcards in the resource specifiers that are stored in the database. The worst case length is 3^n, where n is the number of name or class components in names or classes.

Only the common prefix of a resource name should be specified in the name and class list to XrmQGetSearchList. In the example above, the common prefix would be xmh.toc. However, note that XrmQGetSearchResource requires that name represent a single component only. Therefore, the common prefix must be all but the last component of the name and class.

For more information, see Volume One, Chapter 11, *Managing User Preferences*.

Structures

XrmDatabase is a pointer to an opaque data type.

```
typedef XrmQuarkList XrmNameList;
typedef XrmQuarkList XrmClassList;
typedef XrmQuark     XrmRepresentation;
```

XrmSearchList is a pointer to an opaque data type.

Related Commands

XrmDestroyDatabase, XrmGetFileDatabase, XrmGetResource, XrmGet-
StringDatabase, XrmInitialize, XrmMergeDatabases, XrmParseCommand,
XrmPutFileDatabase, XrmPutLineResource, XrmPutResource, XrmPut-
StringResource, XrmQGetResource, XrmQGetSearchResource, XrmQPut-
Resource, XrmQPutStringResource, XrmQuarkToString, XrmString-
ToBindingQuarkList, XrmStringToQuarkList, XrmStringToQuark, Xrm-
UniqueQuark.

XrmQGetSearchResource

Name

XrmQGetSearchResource — search prepared list for a given resource.

Synopsis

```
Bool XrmQGetSearchResource(search_list, name, class,
        type, value)
    XrmSearchList search_list;
    XrmName name;
    XrmClass class;
    XrmRepresentation *type; /* RETURN */
    XrmValue *value;         /* RETURN */
```

Arguments

search_list   Specifies the search list returned by XrmQGetSearchList.

name   Specifies the resource name.

class   Specifies the resource class.

type   Returns the data representation type.

value   Returns the value from the database.

Description

XrmQGetSearchResource is a tool for searching the database more efficiently. It is used in combination with XrmQGetSearchList. Often, one searches the database for many similar resources which differ only in their final component (e.g., xmh.toc.foreground, xmh.toc.background, etc). Rather than looking for each resource in its entirety, XrmQGetSearchList searches the database for the common part of the resource name, returning a whole list of items in the database that match it. This list is called the *search list*. XrmQGetSearchResource searches the search list for the resource that is fully identified by *name* and *class*. The search stops with the first match. XrmQGetSearchResource returns True if the resource was found; otherwise, it returns False.

A call to XrmQGetSearchList with a name and class list containing all but the last component of a resource name followed by a call to XrmQGetSearchResource with the last component name and class returns the same database entry as XrmQGetResource or XrmQGetResource would with the fully qualified name and class.

For more information, see Volume One, Chapter 11, *Managing User Preferences*.

Structures

XrmDatabase is a pointer to an opaque data type.

```
typedef XrmQuark XrmName;
typedef XrmQuark XrmClass;
typedef XrmQuark XrmRepresentation;

typedef struct {
    unsigned int    size;
    caddr_t         addr;
} XrmValue, *XrmValuePtr;
```

XrmSearchList is a pointer to an opaque data type.

Related Commands

XrmDestroyDatabase, XrmGetFileDatabase, XrmGetResource, XrmGet-
StringDatabase, XrmInitialize, XrmMergeDatabases, XrmParseCommand,
XrmPutFileDatabase, XrmPutLineResource, XrmPutResource, XrmPut-
StringResource, XrmQGetResource, XrmQGetSearchList, XrmQPutResource,
XrmQPutStringResource, XrmQuarkToString, XrmStringToBindingQuark-
List, XrmStringToQuarkList, XrmStringToQuark, XrmUniqueQuark.

Name

XrmQPutResource — store a resource specification into a database using quarks.

Synopsis

```
void XrmQPutResource(database, bindings, quarks, type, value)
    XrmDatabase *database;  /* SEND, and if NULL, RETURN */
    XrmBindingList bindings;
    XrmQuarkList quarks;
    XrmRepresentation type;
    XrmValue *value;
```

Arguments

database   Specifies a pointer to the resource database. If database contains NULL, a new resource database is created and a pointer to it is returned in *database*.

bindings   Specifies a list of bindings for binding together the `quarks` argument.

quarks   Specifies the complete or partial name or class list of the resource to be stored.

type   Specifies the type of the resource.

value   Specifies the value of the resource.

Description

XrmQPutResource stores a resource specification into the database.

database can be a previously defined database, as returned by XrmGetStringDatabase, XrmGetFileDatabase, or from XrmMergeDatabases. If *database* is NULL, a new database is created and a pointer to it returned in *database*.

bindings and *quarks* together specify where the value should be stored in the database. See XrmStringToBindingQuarkList for a brief description of binding and quark lists. See XrmGetResource for a description of the resource manager naming conventions and lookup rules.

type is the representation type of *value*. This provides a way to distinguish between different representations of the same information. Representation types are user defined character strings describing the way the data is represented. For example, a color may be specified by a color name ("red"), or be coded in a hexadecimal string ("#4f6c84") (if it is to be used as an argument to XParseColor.) The representation type would distinguish between these two. Representation types are created from simple character strings by using the macro Xrm-StringToRepresentation. The type XrmRepresentation is actually the same type as XrmQuark, since it is an ID for a string. The representation is stored along with the value in the database, and is returned when the database is accessed.

value returns the value of the resource, specified as an XrmValue.

XrmGetResource contains the complete description of how data is accessed from the database, and so provides a good perspective on how it is stored.

For more information, see Volume One, Chapter 11, *Managing User Preferences*.

Structures

`XrmDatabase` is a pointer to an opaque data type.

```
typedef enum {
    XrmBindTightly, XrmBindLoosely
} XrmBinding, *XrmBindingList;

typedef int XrmQuark, *XrmQuarkList;
typedef XrmQuarkList XrmNameList;
typedef XrmQuark XrmRepresentation;

typedef struct {
    unsigned int size;
    caddr_t addr;
} XrmValue, *XrmValuePtr;
```

Related Commands

XrmDestroyDatabase, XrmGetFileDatabase, XrmGetResource, XrmGet-
StringDatabase, XrmInitialize, XrmMergeDatabases, XrmParseCommand,
XrmPutFileDatabase, XrmPutLineResource, XrmPutResource, XrmPut-
StringResource, XrmQGetResource, XrmQGetSearchList, XrmQGetSearch-
Resource, XrmQPutStringResource, XrmQuarkToString, XrmString-
ToBindingQuarkList, XrmStringToQuarkList, XrmStringToQuark, Xrm-
UniqueQuark.

Name

XrmQPutStringResource — add a resource specification to a database using a quark resource name and string value.

Synopsis

```
void XrmQPutStringResource(database, bindings, quarks, value)
    XrmDatabase *database; /* SEND, and if NULL, RETURN */
    XrmBindingList bindings;
    XrmQuarkList quarks;
    char *value;
```

Arguments

database   Specifies a pointer to the resource database. If database contains NULL, a new resource database is created and a pointer to it is returned in *database*.

bindings   Specifies a list of bindings for binding together the *quarks* argument.

quarks   Specifies the complete or partial name or class list of the resource to be stored.

value   Specifies the value of the resource as a string.

Description

XrmQPutStringResource stores a resource specification into the specified database.

XrmQPutStringResource is a cross between XrmQPutResource and XrmPutStringResource. Like XrmQPutResource, it specifies the resource by *quarks* and *bindings*, two lists that together make a name/class list with loose and tight bindings. Like XrmPutStringResource, it specifies the value to be stored as a string, that value is converted into an XrmValue, and the default representation type String is used.

XrmPutResource, XrmQPutResource, XrmPutStringResource, XrmQPutStringResource and XrmPutLineResource all store data into a database. See XrmQPutResource for the most complete description of this process.

For more information, see Volume One, Chapter 11, *Managing User Preferences*.

Structures

XrmDatabase is a pointer to an opaque data type.

```
typedef enum {
    XrmBindTightly, XrmBindLoosely
} XrmBinding, *XrmBindingList;

typedef int XrmQuark, *XrmQuarkList;
```

Related Commands

XrmDestroyDatabase, XrmGetFileDatabase, XrmGetResource, XrmGetStringDatabase, XrmInitialize, XrmMergeDatabases, XrmParseCommand, XrmPutFileDatabase, XrmPutLineResource, XrmPutResource, XrmPutStringResource, XrmQGetResource, XrmQGetSearchList, XrmQGetSearch-

Resource, XrmQPutResource, XrmQuarkToString, XrmStringToBinding-
QuarkList, XrmStringToQuarkList, XrmStringToQuark, XrmUniqueQuark.

Name

XrmQuarkToString — convert a quark to a string.

Synopsis

```
char *XrmQuarkToString(quark)
    XrmQuark quark;
```

Arguments

quark   Specifies the quark for which the equivalent string is desired.

Description

XrmQuarkToString returns the string for which the specified quark is serving as a short-hand symbol. The quark was earlier set to represent the string by XrmStringToQuark. The string pointed to by the return value must not be modified or freed, because that string is in the data structure used by the resource manager for assigning quarks. If no string exists for that quark, XrmQuarkToString returns NULL.

Since the resource manager needs to make many comparisons of strings when it gets data from the database, it is more efficient to convert these strings into quarks, and to compare quarks instead. Since quarks are represented by integers, comparing quarks is trivial.

The three #define statements in the Structures section provide an extra level of abstraction. They define macros so that names, classes and representations can also be represented as quarks.

For more information, see Volume One, Chapter 11, *Managing User Preferences*.

Structures

```
typedef int XrmQuark;

/* macro definitions from <X11/Xresource.h> */

#define XrmNameToString(name) XrmQuarkToString(name)
#define XrmClassToString(class) XrmQuarkToString(class)
#define XrmRepresentationToString(type) XrmQuarkToString(type)
```

Related Commands

XrmDestroyDatabase, XrmGetFileDatabase, XrmGetResource, XrmGet-
StringDatabase, XrmInitialize, XrmMergeDatabases, XrmParseCommand,
XrmPutFileDatabase, XrmPutLineResource, XrmPutResource, XrmPut-
StringResource, XrmQGetResource, XrmQGetSearchList, XrmQGetSearch-
Resource, XrmQPutResource, XrmQPutStringResource, XrmString-
ToBindingQuarkList, XrmStringToQuarkList, XrmStringToQuark, Xrm-
UniqueQuark.

Name

XrmStringToBindingQuarkList — convert a key string to a binding list and a quark list.

Synopsis

```
XrmStringToBindingQuarkList (string, bindings, quarks)
    char *string;
    XrmBindingList bindings; /* RETURN */
    XrmQuarkList quarks;     /* RETURN */
```

Arguments

string   Specifies the string for which the list of quarks and list of bindings are to be generated. Must be NULL terminated.

bindings   Returns the binding list. The caller must allocate sufficient space for the binding list before the call.

quark   Returns the list of quarks. The caller must allocate sufficient space for the quarks list before the call.

Description

XrmStringToBindingQuarkList converts a resource specification string into two lists— one of quarks and one of bindings. Component names in the list are separated by a dot (".") indicating a tight binding or an asterisk ("*") indicating a loose binding. If the string does not start with dot or asterisk, a dot (".") is assumed.

A tight binding means that the quarks on either side of the binding are consecutive in the key. A loose binding, on the other hand, is a wildcard that can match any number of unspecified components in between the two quarks separated by the binding. Tight and loose bindings are used in the match rules, which compare multicomponent strings to find matches and determine the best match. See XrmGetResource for a full description of lookup rules.

For example, *a.b*c becomes:

quarks	bindings
"a"	XrmBindLoosely
"b"	XrmBindTightly
"c"	XrmBindLoosely

For more information, see Volume One, Chapter 11, *Managing User Preferences*.

Structures

```
typedef int XrmQuark, *XrmQuarkList;
typedef enum (
    XrmBindLoosely, XrmBindTightly
) XrmBinding, *XrmBindingList;
```

Related Commands

XrmDestroyDatabase, XrmGetFileDatabase, XrmGetResource, XrmGet-
StringDatabase, XrmInitialize, XrmMergeDatabases, XrmParseCommand,
XrmPutFileDatabase, XrmPutLineResource, XrmPutResource, XrmPut-
StringResource, XrmQGetResource, XrmQGetSearchList, XrmQGetSearch-
Resource, XrmQPutResource, XrmQPutStringResource, XrmQuarkToString,
XrmStringToQuarkList, XrmStringToQuark, XrmUniqueQuark.

XrmStringToQuark

Name

XrmStringToQuark — convert a string to a quark.

Synopsis

```
XrmQuark XrmStringToQuark(string)
    char *string;
```

Arguments

string   Specifies the string for which a quark is to be allocated.

Description

XrmStringToQuark returns a quark that will represent the specified string. If a quark already exists for the string, that previously existing quark is returned. If no quark exists for the string, then a new quark is created, assigned to the string, and *string* is copied into the quark table. (Since *string* is copied, it may be freed. However, the copy of the string in the quark table must not be modified or freed.) XrmQuarkToString performs the inverse function.

Since the resource manager needs to make many comparisons of strings when it gets data from the database, it is more efficient to convert these strings into quarks, and to compare quarks instead. Since quarks are presently represented by integers, comparing quarks is trivial.

The three #define statements in the Structures section provide an extra level of abstraction. They define macros so that names, classes, and representations can also be represented as quarks.

For more information, see Volume One, Chapter 11, *Managing User Preferences*.

Structures

```
typedef int XrmQuark;

/* macro definitions from <X11/Xresource.h> */

#define XrmStringToName(string) XrmStringToQuark(string)
#define XrmStringToClass(string) XrmStringToQuark(string)
#define XrmStringToRepresentation(string) XrmStringToQuark(string)
```

Related Commands

XrmDestroyDatabase, XrmGetFileDatabase, XrmGetResource, XrmGet-StringDatabase, XrmInitialize, XrmMergeDatabases, XrmParseCommand, XrmPutFileDatabase, XrmPutLineResource, XrmPutResource, XrmPut-StringResource, XrmQGetResource, XrmQGetSearchList, XrmQGetSearch-Resource, XrmQPutResource, XrmQPutStringResource, XrmQuarkToString, XrmStringToBindingQuarkList, XrmStringToQuarkList, XrmUniqueQuark.

Name

XrmStringToQuarkList — convert a key string to a quark list.

Synopsis

```
void XrmStringToQuarkList(string, quarks)
    char *string;
    XrmQuarkList quarks;        /* RETURN */
```

Arguments

string   Specifies the string for which a list of quarks is to be generated. Must be null-terminated. The components may be separated by the "." character (tight binding) or the "*" character (loose binding).

quarks   Returns the list of quarks.

Description

`XrmStringToQuarkList` converts *string* (generally a fully qualified name/class string) to a list of quarks. Components of the string may be separated by a tight binding (the "." character) or a loose binding ("*"). Use `XrmStringToBindingQuarkList` for lists which contain both tight and loose bindings. See `XrmGetResource` for a description of tight and loose binding.

Each component of the string is individually converted into a quark. See `XrmString-ToQuark` for information about quarks and converting strings to quarks. *quarks* is a null-terminated list of quarks.

For example, `xmh.toc.command.background` is converted into a list of four quarks: the quarks for `xmh`, `toc`, `command`, and `background`, in that order. A `NULLQUARK` is appended to the end of the list.

Note that `XrmStringToNameList` and `XrmStringToClassList` are macros that perform exactly the same function as `XrmStringToQuarkList`. These may be used in cases where they clarify the code.

For more information, see Volume One, Chapter 11, *Managing User Preferences*.

Structures

```
typedef int XrmQuark *XrmQuarkList;

#define XrmStringToNameList(str, name)  XrmStringToQuarkList((str), (name))
#define XrmStringToClassList(str,class) XrmStringToQuarkList((str), (class))
```

Related Commands

XrmDestroyDatabase, XrmGetFileDatabase, XrmGetResource, XrmGet-
StringDatabase, XrmInitialize, XrmMergeDatabases, XrmParseCommand,
XrmPutFileDatabase, XrmPutLineResource, XrmPutResource, XrmPut-
StringResource, XrmQGetResource, XrmQGetSearchList, XrmQGetSearch-
Resource, XrmQPutResource, XrmQPutStringResource, XrmQuarkToString,
XrmStringToBindingQuarkList, XrmStringToQuark, XrmUniqueQuark.

Name

XrmUniqueQuark — allocate a new quark.

Synopsis

```
XrmQuark XrmUniqueQuark()
```

Description

XrmUniqueQuark allocates a quark that is guaranteed not to represent any existing string. For most applications, XrmStringToQuark is more useful, as it binds a quark to a string. However, on some occasions, you may want to allocate a quark that has no string equivalent.

The shorthand name for a string is called a *quark* and is the type XrmQuark. Quarks are used to improve performance of the resource manager, which must make many string comparisons. Quarks are presently represented as integers. Simple comparisons of quarks can be performed rather than lengthy string comparisons.

A quark is to a string what an atom is to a property name in the server, but its use is entirely local to your application.

For more information, see Volume One, Chapter 11, *Managing User Preferences*.

Structures

```
typedef int XrmQuark;
```

Related Commands

XrmDestroyDatabase, XrmGetFileDatabase, XrmGetResource, XrmGet-StringDatabase, XrmInitialize, XrmMergeDatabases, XrmParseCommand, XrmPutFileDatabase, XrmPutLineResource, XrmPutResource, XrmPut-StringResource, XrmQGetResource, XrmQGetSearchList, XrmQGetSearch-Resource, XrmQPutResource, XrmQPutStringResource, XrmQuarkToString, XrmStringToBindingQuarkList, XrmStringToQuarkList, XrmStringTo-Quark.

XRotateBuffers

Name

XRotateBuffers — rotate the cut buffers.

Synopsis

```
XRotateBuffers(display, rotate)
    Display *display;
    int rotate;
```

Arguments

display   Specifies a connection to an X server; returned from XOpenDisplay.

rotate   Specifies how many positions to rotate the cut buffers.

Description

XRotateBuffers rotates the 8 cut buffers the amount specified by rotate. The contents of buffer 0 moves to buffer rotate, contents of buffer 1 moves to buffer (rotate+1) mod 8, contents of buffer 2 moves to buffer (rotate+2) mod 8, and so on.

This routine will not work if any of the buffers have not been stored into with XStoreBuffer or XStoreBytes.

This cut buffer numbering is global to the display.

See the description of cut buffers in Volume One, Chapter 13, *Other Programming Techniques*.

Related Commands

XFetchBuffer, XFetchBytes, XStoreBuffer, XStoreBytes.

XRotateWindowProperties

Name

XRotateWindowProperties — rotate properties in the properties array.

Synopsis

```
XRotateWindowProperties(display, w, properties, num_prop,
        npositions)
    Display *display;
    Window w;
    Atom properties[];
    int num_prop;
    int npositions;
```

Arguments

display	Specifies a connection to an X server; returned from XOpenDisplay.
w	Specifies the ID of the window whose properties are to be rearranged.
properties	Specifies the list of properties to be rotated.
num_prop	Specifies the length of the properties array.
npositions	Specifies the number of positions to rotate the property list. The sign controls the direction of rotation.

Description

XRotateWindowProperties rotates the contents of an array of properties on a window. If the property names in the *properties* array are viewed as if they were numbered starting from 0 and if there are *num_prop* property names in the list, then the value associated with property name *I* becomes the value associated with property name (*I* + *npositions*) mod *num_prop*, for all *I* from 0 to *num_prop* – 1. Therefore, the sign of *npositions* controls the direction of rotation. The effect is to rotate the states by *npositions* places around the virtual ring of property names (right for positive *npositions*, left for negative *nposition*).

If *npositions* mod *num_prop* is nonzero, a PropertyNotify event is generated for each property, in the order listed.

If a BadAtom, BadMatch, or BadWindow error is generated, no properties are changed.

Error

BadAtom	Atom occurs more than once in list for the window. No property with that name for the window.
BadMatch	An atom appears more that once in the list or no property with that name is defined for the window.
BadWindow	

Related Commands

XChangeProperty, XDeleteProperty, XGetAtomName, XGetFontProperty,
XGetWindowProperty, XInternAtom, XListProperties, XSetStandard-
Properties.

XSaveContext

Name

XSaveContext — save a data value corresponding to a window and context type (not graphics context).

Synopsis

```
int XSaveContext(display, w, context, data)
    Display *display;
    Window w;
    XContext context;
    caddr_t data;
```

Arguments

display   Specifies a connection to an X server; returned from XOpenDisplay.

w   Specifies the ID of the window with which the data is associated.

context   Specifies the context type to which the data corresponds.

data   Specifies the data to be associated with the window and context.

Description

XSaveContext saves *data* to the context manager database, according to the specified window and *context* ID. The context manager is used for associating data with windows within an application. The client must have called XUniqueContext to get the *context* ID before calling this function. The meaning of the *data* is indicated by the *context* ID, but is completely up to the client.

If an entry with the specified window and *context* ID already exists, XSaveContext writes over it with the specified data.

The XSaveContext function returns XCNOMEM (a nonzero error code) if an error has occurred and zero (0) otherwise. For more information, see the description of the context manager in Volume One, Chapter 13, *Other Programming Techniques*.

Structures

```
typedef int XContext;
```

Related Commands

XDeleteContext, XFindContext, XUniqueContext.

Name

XSelectInput — select the event types to be sent to a window.

Synopsis

```
XSelectInput(display, w, event_mask)
    Display *display;
    Window w;
    long event_mask;
```

Arguments

display   Specifies a connection to an X server; returned from XOpenDisplay.

w   Specifies the ID of the window interested in the events.

event_mask   Specifies the event mask. This mask is the bitwise OR of one or more of the
              valid event mask bits (see below).

Description

XSelectInput defines which input events the window is interested in. If a window is not
interested in a device event (button, key, motion, or border crossing), it propagates up to the
closest ancestor unless otherwise specified in the do_not_propagate_mask attribute.

The bits of the mask are defined in *<X11/X.h>* :

ButtonPressMask	NoEventMask
ButtonReleaseMask	KeyPressMask
EnterWindowMask	KeyReleaseMask
LeaveWindowMask	ExposureMask
PointerMotionMask	VisibilityChangeMask
PointerMotionHintMask	StructureNotifyMask
Button1MotionMask	ResizeRedirectMask
Button2MotionMask	SubstructureNotifyMask
Button3MotionMask	SubstructureRedirectMask
Button4MotionMask	FocusChangeMask
Button5MotionMask	PropertyChangeMask
ButtonMotionMask	ColormapChangeMask
KeymapStateMask	OwnerGrabButtonMask

A call on XSelectInput overrides any previous call on XSelectInput for the same window from the same client but not for other clients. Multiple clients can select input on the same
window; their event_mask window attributes are disjoint. When an event is generated it will
be reported to all interested clients. However, only one client at a time can select for each of
SubstructureRedirectMask, ResizeRedirectMask, and ButtonPress.

If a window has both ButtonPressMask and ButtonReleaseMask selected, then a
ButtonPress event in that window will automatically grab the mouse until all buttons are
released, with events sent to windows as described for XGrabPointer. This ensures that a

window will see the `ButtonRelease` event corresponding to the `ButtonPress` event, even though the mouse may have exited the window in the meantime.

If `PointerMotionMask` is selected, events will be sent independent of the state of the mouse buttons. If instead, one or more of `Button1MotionMask`, `Button2MotionMask`, `Button3MotionMask`, `Button4MotionMask`, `Button5MotionMask` is selected, `MotionNotify` events will be generated only when one or more of the specified buttons is depressed.

`XCreateWindow` and `XChangeWindowAttributes` can also set the *event_mask* attribute.

For more information, see Volume One, Chapter 8, *Events*.

Errors
`BadValue`   Specified event mask invalid.

`BadWindow`

Related Commands
`QLength`, `XAllowEvents`, `XCheckIfEvent`, `XCheckMaskEvent`, `XCheckTyped-Event`, `XCheckTypedWindowEvent`, `XCheckWindowEvent`, `XEventsQueued`, `XGetInputFocus`, `XGetMotionEvents`, `XIfEvent`, `XMaskEvent`, `XNextEvent`, `XPeekEvent`, `XPeekIfEvent`, `XPending`, `XPutBackEvent`, `XSendEvent`, `XSet-InputFocus`, `XSynchronize`, `XWindowEvent`.

Name

XSendEvent — send an event.

Synopsis

```
Status XSendEvent(display, w, propagate, event_mask, event)
    Display *display;
    Window w;
    Bool propagate;
    long event_mask;
    XEvent *event;
```

Arguments

display   Specifies a connection to an X server; returned from XOpenDisplay.

w   Specifies the ID of the window where you want to send the event. Pass the window resource ID, PointerWindow, or InputFocus.

propagate   Specifies how the sent event should propagate depending on *event_mask*. See description below. May be True or False.

event_mask   Specifies the event mask. See XSelectInput for a detailed list of the event masks.

event   Specifies a pointer to the event to be sent.

Errors

BadValue   Specified event is not a valid core or extension event type, or event mask is invalid.

BadWindow

Description

XSendEvent sends an event from one client to another (or conceivably to itself). This function is used for communication between clients using selections, for simulating user actions in demos, and for other purposes.

The specified event is sent to the window indicated by *w* regardless of active grabs.

If *w* is set to PointerWindow, the destination of the event will be the window that the pointer is in. If *w* is InputFocus is specified, then the destination is the focus window, regardless of pointer position.

If *propagate* is False, then the event is sent to every client selecting on the window specified by *w* any of the event types in *event_mask*. If *propagate* is True and no clients have been selected on *w* any of the event types in *event_mask*, then the event propagates like any other event.

The event code must be one of the core events, or one of the events defined by a loaded extension, so that the server can correctly byte swap the contents as necessary. The contents of the event are otherwise unaltered and unchecked by the server. The send_event field in every event type, which if True indicates that the event was sent with XSendEvent.

This function is often used in selection processing. For example, the owner of a selection should use XSendEvent to send a SelectionNotify event to a requestor when a selection has been converted and stored as a property. See Volume One, Chapter 10, *Interclient Communication* for more information.

The status returned by XSendEvent indicates whether or not the given XEvent structure was successfully converted into a wire event. This value is zero on failure, or nonzero on success. Along with changes in the extensions mechanism, this makes merging of two wire events into a single user-visible event possible.

Structures

See Appendix E, *Event Reference*, for the contents of each event structure.

Related Commands

QLength, XAllowEvents, XCheckIfEvent, XCheckMaskEvent, XCheckTyped-
Event, XCheckTypedWindowEvent, XCheckWindowEvent, XEventsQueued,
XGetInputFocus, XGetMotionEvents, XIfEvent, XMaskEvent, XNextEvent,
XPeekEvent, XPeekIfEvent, XPending, XPutBackEvent, XSelectInput, XSet-
InputFocus, XSynchronize, XWindowEvent.

Name

XSetAccessControl — disable or enable access control.

Synopsis

```
XSetAccessControl(display, mode)
    Display *display;
    int mode;
```

Arguments

display   Specifies a connection to an X server; returned from XOpenDisplay.

mode   Specifies whether you want to enable or disable the access control. Pass one of these constants: EnableAccess or DisableAccess.

Description

XSetAccessControl specifies whether the server should check the host access list before allowing access to clients running on remote hosts. If the constant used is DisableAccess, clients from any host have access unchallenged.

This routine can only be called from a client running on the same host as the server.

For more information on access control lists, see Volume One, Chapter 13, *Other Programming Techniques*.

Errors

BadAccess
BadValue

Related Commands

XAddHost, XAddHosts, XDisableAccessControl, XEnableAccessControl, XListHosts, XRemoveHost, XRemoveHosts.

XSetAfterFunction

Name

XSetAfterFunction — set a function called after all Xlib functions.

Synopsis

```
int (*XSetAfterFunction(display, func))()
    Display *display;
    int (*func)();
```

Arguments

display   Specifies a connection to an X server; returned from XOpenDisplay.

func   Specifies the user-defined function to be called after each Xlib function. This function is called with one argument, the *display* pointer.

Description

All Xlib functions that generate protocol requests can call what is known as an *after function* after completing their work (normally, they don't). XSetAfterFunction allows you to write a function to be called.

XSynchronize sets an after function to make sure that the input and request buffers are flushed after every Xlib routine.

For more information, see Volume One, Chapter 13, *Other Programming Techniques*.

Related Commands

XDisplayName, XGetErrorDatabaseText, XGetErrorText, XSetError-Handler, XSetIOErrorHandler, XSynchronize.

XSetArcMode

Name

XSetArcMode — set the arc mode in a graphics context.

Synopsis

```
XSetArcMode(display, gc, arc_mode)
    Display *display;
    GC gc;
    int arc_mode;
```

Arguments

display   Specifies a connection to an X server; returned from XOpenDisplay.

gc   Specifies the graphics context.

arc_mode   Specifies the arc mode for the specified graphics context. Possible values are
             ArcChord or ArcPieSlice.

Description

XSetArcMode sets the arc_mode component of a GC, which controls filling in the XFill-
Arcs function. ArcChord specifies that the area between the arc and a line segment joining
the endpoints of the arc is filled. ArcPieSlice specifies that the area filled is delimited by
the arc and two line segments connecting the ends of the arc to the center point of the rectangle
defining the arc.

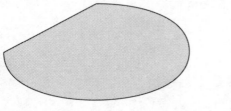

ArcChord

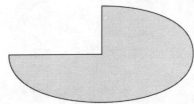

ArcPieSlice

Errors
    BadGC
    BadValue

Related Commands
    DefaultGC, XChangeGC, XCopyGC, XCreateGC, XFreeGC, XGContextFromGC,
    XSetBackground, XSetClipMask, XSetClipOrigin, XSetClipRectangles,
    XSetDashes, XSetFillRule, XSetFillStyle, XSetForeground, XSet-
    Function, XSetGraphicsExposures, XSetLineAttributes, XSetPlaneMask,
    XSetState, XSetStipple, XSetSubwindowMode, XSetTSOrigin.

XSetBackground

Name

XSetBackground — set the background pixel value in a graphics context.

Synopsis

```
XSetBackground(display, gc, background)
    Display *display;
    GC gc;
    unsigned long background;
```

Arguments

display   Specifies a connection to an X server; returned from XOpenDisplay.

gc   Specifies the graphics context.

background   Specifies the *background* component of the GC.

Description

XSetBackground sets the *background* pixel value component of a GC. Note that this is different from the background of a window, which can be set with either XSetWindowBackground or XSetWindowBackgroundPixmap.

The specified pixel value must be returned by BlackPixel, WhitePixel, or one of the routines that allocate colors.

Errors

BadGC

Related Commands

DefaultGC, XChangeGC, XCopyGC, XCreateGC, XFreeGC, XGContextFromGC, XSetArcMode, XSetClipMask, XSetClipOrigin, XSetClipRectangles, XSetDashes, XSetFillRule, XSetFillStyle, XSetForeground, XSetFunction, XSetGraphicsExposures, XSetLineAttributes, XSetPlaneMask, XSetState, XSetStipple, XSetSubwindowMode, XSetTSOrigin.

Name

XSetClassHint — set the XA_WM_CLASS property of a window.

Synopsis

```
XSetClassHint(display, w, class_hints)
    Display *display;
    Window w;
    XClassHint *class_hints;
```

Arguments

display   Specifies a connection to an X server; returned from XOpenDisplay.

w   Specifies the ID of the window for which the class hint is to be set.

class_hints   Specifies the XClassHint structure that is to be used.

Description

XSetClassHint sets the XA_WM_CLASS property for the specified window. The window manager may (or may not) read this property, and use it to get resource defaults that apply to the window manager's handling of this application.

The XClassHint structure set contains res_class, which is the name of the client such as "emacs", and res_name, which is the first of the following that applies:

• command line option (*–rn name*)

• a specific environment variable (e.g., RESOURCE_NAME)

• the trailing component of argv[0] (after the last /)

For more information, see Volume One, Chapter 10, *Interclient Communication*.

Errors

```
BadAlloc
BadWindow
```

Structures

```
typedef struct {
    char *res_name;
    char *res_class;
} XClassHint;
```

Related Commands

XAllocClassHint, XFetchName, XGetClassHint, XGetIconName, XGetIcon-Sizes, XGetNormalHints, XGetSizeHints, XGetTransientForHint, XGet-WMHints, XGetZoomHints, XSetCommand, XSetIconName, XSetIconSizes, XSetNormalHints, XSetSizeHints, XSetTransientForHint, XSetWMHints, XSetZoomHints, XStoreName, XSetWMProperties.

Name

XSetClipMask — set clip_mask pixmap in a graphics context.

Synopsis

```
XSetClipMask(display, gc, clip_mask)
    Display *display;
    GC gc;
    Pixmap clip_mask;
```

Arguments

display   Specifies a connection to an X server; returned from XOpenDisplay.

gc   Specifies the graphics context.

clip_mask Specifies a pixmap of depth 1 to be used as the clip mask. Pass the constant
           None if no clipping is desired.

Description

XSetClipMask sets the clip_mask component of a GC to a pixmap. The clip_mask filters which pixels in the destination are drawn. If clip_mask is set to None, the pixels are
always drawn, regardless of the clip origin. Use XSetClipRectangles to set clip_mask
to a set of rectangles, or XSetRegion to set clip_mask to a region.

For more information, see Volume One, Chapter 5, *The Graphics Context*.

Errors

BadGC
BadMatch
BadPixmap

Related Commands

DefaultGC, XChangeGC, XCopyGC, XCreateGC, XFreeGC, XGContextFromGC,
XSetArcMode, XSetBackground, XSetClipOrigin, XSetClipRectangles,
XSetDashes, XSetFillRule, XSetFillStyle, XSetForeground, XSet-
Function, XSetGraphicsExposures, XSetLineAttributes, XSetPlaneMask,
XSetState, XSetStipple, XSetSubwindowMode, XSetTSOrigin.

Name

XSetClipOrigin — set the clip origin in a graphics context.

Synopsis

```
XSetClipOrigin(display, gc, clip_x_origin, clip_y_origin)
    Display *display;
    GC gc;
    int clip_x_origin, clip_y_origin;
```

Arguments

display	Specifies a connection to an X server; returned from XOpenDisplay.
gc	Specifies the graphics context.
clip_x_origin *clip_y_origin*	Specify the coordinates of the clip origin (interpreted later relative to the window drawn into with this GC).

Description

XSetClipOrigin sets the *clip_x_origin* and *clip_y_origin* components of a GC. The clip origin controls the position of the clip_mask in the GC, which filters which pixels are drawn in the destination of a drawing request using this GC.

For more information, see Volume One, Chapter 5, *The Graphics Context*.

Errors

BadGC

Related Commands

DefaultGC, XChangeGC, XCopyGC, XCreateGC, XFreeGC, XGContextFromGC, XSetArcMode, XSetBackground, XSetClipMask, XSetClipRectangles, XSet-Dashes, XSetFillRule, XSetFillStyle, XSetForeground, XSetFunction, XSetGraphicsExposures, XSetLineAttributes, XSetPlaneMask, XSetState, XSetStipple, XSetSubwindowMode, XSetTSOrigin.

Name

XSetClipRectangles — change `clip_mask` in a graphics context to a list of rectangles.

Synopsis

```
XSetClipRectangles(display, gc, clip_x_origin,
        clip_y_origin, rectangles, nrects, ordering)
    Display *display;
    GC gc;
    int clip_x_origin, clip_y_origin;
    XRectangle rectangles[];
    int nrects;
    int ordering;
```

Arguments

display	Specifies a connection to an X server; returned from `XOpenDisplay`.
gc	Specifies the graphics context.
clip_x_origin clip_y_origin	Specify the x and y coordinates of the clip origin (interpreted later relative to the window drawn into with this GC).
rectangles	Specifies an array of rectangles. These are the rectangles you want drawing clipped to.
nrects	Specifies the number of rectangles.
ordering	Specifies the ordering relations of the rectangles. Possible values are `Unsorted`, `YSorted`, `YXSorted`, or `YXBanded`.

Description

`XSetClipRectangles` changes the `clip_mask` component in the specified GC to the specified list of rectangles and sets the clip origin to `clip_x_origin` and `clip_y_origin`. The rectangle coordinates are interpreted relative to the clip origin. The output from drawing requests using that GC are henceforth clipped to remain contained within the rectangles. The rectangles should be nonintersecting, or the graphics results will be undefined. If the list of rectangles is empty, output is effectively disabled as all space is clipped in that GC. This is the opposite of a `clip_mask` of `None` in `XCreateGC`, `XChangeGC`, or `XSetClipMask`.

If known by the client, ordering relations on the rectangles can be specified with the `ordering` argument. This may provide faster operation by the server. If an incorrect ordering is specified, the X server may generate a `BadMatch` error, but it is not required to do so. If no error is generated, the graphics results are undefined. `Unsorted` means the rectangles are in arbitrary order. `YSorted` means that the rectangles are nondecreasing in their y origin. `YXSorted` additionally constrains `YSorted` order in that all rectangles with an equal y origin are nondecreasing in their x origin. `YXBanded` additionally constrains `YXSorted` by requiring that, for every possible horizontal y scan line, all rectangles that include that scan line have identical y origins and y extents.

To cancel the effect of this command, so that there is no clipping, pass None as the clip_mask in XChangeGC or XSetClipMask.

For more information, see Volume One, Chapter 5, *The Graphics Context*.

Structures

```
typedef struct {
    short x,y;
    unsigned short width, height;
} XRectangle;
```

Errors

BadAlloc

BadGC

BadMatch   Incorrect *ordering* (error message server-dependent).

BadValue

Related Commands

DefaultGC, XChangeGC, XCopyGC, XCreateGC, XFreeGC, XGContextFromGC, XSetArcMode, XSetBackground, XSetClipMask, XSetClipOrigin, XSet-Dashes, XSetFillRule, XSetFillStyle, XSetForeground, XSetFunction, XSetGraphicsExposures, XSetLineAttributes, XSetPlaneMask, XSetState, XSetStipple, XSetSubwindowMode, XSetTSOrigin.

XSetCloseDownMode

Name
XSetCloseDownMode — change the close down mode of a client.

Synopsis
```
XSetCloseDownMode(display, close_mode)
    Display *display;
    int close_mode;
```

Arguments

display   Specifies a connection to an X server; returned from XOpenDisplay.

close_mode   Specifies the client close down mode you want. Pass one of these constants: DestroyAll, RetainPermanent, or RetainTemporary.

Description

XSetCloseDownMode defines what will happen to the client's resources at connection close. A connection between a client and the server starts in DestroyAll mode, and all resources associated with that connection will be freed when the client process dies. If the close down mode is RetainTemporary or RetainPermanent when the client dies, its resources live on until a call to XKillClient. The *resource* argument of XKillClient can be used to specify which client to kill, or it may be the constant AllTemporary, in which case XKill-Client kills all resources of all clients that have terminated in RetainTemporary mode.

One use of RetainTemporary or RetainPermanent might be to allow an application to recover from a failure of the network connection to the display server. After restarting, the application would need to be able to identify its own resources and reclaim control of them.

Errors
BadValue

Related Commands
XKillClient.

XSetCommand

Name

XSetCommand — set the XA_WM_COMMAND atom (command line arguments).

Synopsis

```
XSetCommand(display, w, argv, argc)
    Display *display;
    Window w;
    char **argv;
    int argc;
```

Arguments

display   Specifies a connection to an X server; returned from XOpenDisplay.

w   Specifies the ID of the window whose atom is to be set.

argv   Specifies a pointer to the command and arguments used to start the application.

argc   Specifies the number of arguments.

Description

XSetCommand is superseded by XSetWMCommand in Release 4.

XSetCommand is used by the application to set the XA_WM_COMMAND property for the window manager with the command and its arguments used to invoke the application.

XSetCommand creates a zero-length property if argc is zero.

Use this command only if not calling XSetStandardProperties or XSet-WMProperties.

Errors

```
BadAlloc
BadWindow
```

Related Commands

XFetchName, XGetClassHint, XGetIconName, XGetIconSizes, XGetNormal-Hints, XGetSizeHints, XGetTransientForHint, XGetWMHints, XGetZoom-Hints, XSetClassHint, XSetIconName, XSetIconSizes, XSetNormalHints, XSetSizeHints, XSetTransientForHint, XSetWMHints, XSetZoomHints, XStoreName.

Name

XSetDashes — set a pattern of line dashes in a graphics context.

Synopsis

```
XSetDashes(display, gc, dash_offset, dash_list, n)
    Display *display;
    GC gc;
    int dash_offset;
    char dash_list[];
    int n;
```

Arguments

display   Specifies a connection to an X server; returned from XOpenDisplay.

gc   Specifies the graphics context.

dash_offset   Specifies the phase of the pattern for the dashed line style.

dash_list   Specifies the dash list for the dashed line style. An odd-length list is equivalent to the same list concatenated with itself to produce an even-length list.

n   Specifies the length of the dash list argument.

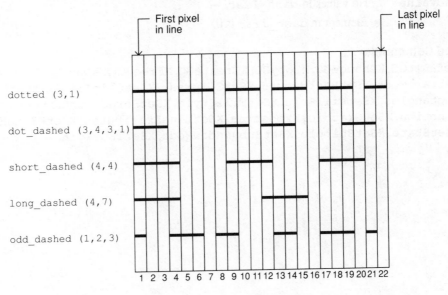

Pixels

Description

XSetDashes sets the dashes component of a GC. The initial and alternating elements of the *dash_list* argument are the dashes, the others are the gaps. All of the elements must be nonzero, with lengths measured in pixels. The *dash_offset* argument defines the phase of the pattern, specifying how many pixels into the *dash_list* the pattern should actually begin in the line drawn by the request.

n specifies the length of *dash_list*. An odd value for *n* is interpreted as specifying the *dash_list* concatenated with itself to produce twice as long a list.

Ideally, a dash length is measured along the slope of the line, but server implementors are only required to match this ideal for horizontal and vertical lines. Failing the ideal semantics, it is suggested that the length be measured along the major axis of the line. The major axis is defined as the x axis for lines drawn at an angle of between –45 and +45 degrees or between 315 and 225 degrees from the x axis. For all other lines, the major axis is the y axis.

See Volume One, Chapter 5, *The Graphics Context*, for further information.

Errors

BadAlloc

BadGC

BadValue   No values in *dash_list*.

Element in *dash_list* is 0.

Related Commands

DefaultGC, XChangeGC, XCopyGC, XCreateGC, XFreeGC, XGContextFromGC, XSetArcMode, XSetBackground, XSetClipMask, XSetClipOrigin, XSetClip-Rectangles, XSetFillRule, XSetFillStyle, XSetForeground, XSet-Function, XSetGraphicsExposures, XSetLineAttributes, XSetPlaneMask, XSetState, XSetStipple, XSetSubwindowMode, XSetTSOrigin.

XSetErrorHandler

Name

XSetErrorHandler — set a nonfatal error event handler.

Synopsis

In Release 3:

```
XSetErrorHandler (handler)
    int (* handler) (Display *, XErrorEvent *)
```

In Release 4: `int (*XSetErrorHandler (handler)) ()`

```
    int (* handler) (Display *, XErrorEvent *)
```

Arguments

handler   The user-defined function to be called to handle error events. If a NULL pointer, reinvoke the default handler, which prints a message and exits.

Description

The error handler function specified in *handler* will be called by Xlib whenever an XError event is received. These are nonfatal conditions, such as unexpected values for arguments, or a failure in server memory allocation. It is acceptable for this procedure to return, though the default handler simply prints a message and exits. However, the error handler should NOT perform any operations (directly or indirectly) on the server.

In Release 4, XSetErrorHandler returns a pointer to the previous error handler.

The function is called with two arguments, the display variable and a pointer to the XError-Event structure. Here is a trivial example of a user-defined error handler:

```
int myhandler (display, myerr)
Display *display;
XErrorEvent *myerr;
{
    char msg[80];
    XGetErrorText(display, myerr->error_code, msg, 80);
    fprintf(stderr, "Error code %s\n", msg);
}
```

This is how the example routine would be used in XSetErrorHandler.

```
XSetErrorHandler(myhandler);
```

Note that XSetErrorHandler is one of the few routines that does not require a display argument. The routine that calls the error handler gets the display variable from the XError-Event structure.

The error handler is not called on BadName errors from OpenFont, LookupColor, and AllocNamedColor protocol requests, on BadFont errors from a QueryFont protocol request, or on BadAlloc or BadAccess errors. These errors are all indicated by Status return value of zero in the corresponding Xlib routines, which must be caught and handled by the application.

Use XIOErrorHandler to provide a handler for I/O errors such as network failures or server host crashes.

In the XErrorEvent structure shown below, the serial member is the number of requests (starting from 1) sent over the network connection since it was opened. It is the number that was the value of the request sequence number immediately after the failing call was made. The request_code member is a protocol representation of the name of the procedure that failed and is defined in *<X11/X.h>*.

For more information, see Volume One, Chapter 3, *Basic Window Program*.

Structures

```
typedef struct {
    int type
    Display *display;      /* display the event was read from */
    XID resourceid;        /* resource ID */
    unsigned long serial;  /* serial number of failed request */
    unsigned char error_code;/* error code of failed request */
    unsigned char request_code;/* major opcode of failed request */
    unsigned char minor_code;/* minor opcode of failed request */
} XErrorEvent;
```

Related Commands

XDisplayName, XGetErrorDatabaseText, XGetErrorText, XSetAfter-Function, XSetIOErrorHandler, XSynchronize.

Name

XSetFillRule — set the fill rule in a graphics context.

Synopsis

```
XSetFillRule(display, gc, fill_rule)
    Display *display;
    GC gc;
    int fill_rule;
```

Arguments

display   Specifies a connection to an X server; returned from XOpenDisplay.

gc   Specifies the graphics context.

fill_rule   Specifies the fill rule you want to set for the specified graphics context. Possible values are EvenOddRule or WindingRule.

Description

XSetFillRule sets the *fill_rule* component of a GC. The *fill_rule* member of the GC determines what pixels are drawn in XFillPolygon requests. Simply put, WindingRule fills overlapping areas of the polygon, while EvenOddRule does not fill areas that overlap an odd number of times. Technically, EvenOddRule means that the point is drawn if an arbitrary ray drawn from the point would cross the path determined by the request an odd number of times. WindingRule indicates that a point is drawn if a point crosses an unequal number of clockwise and counterclockwise path segments, as seen from the point.

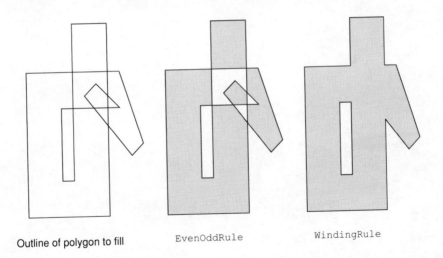

Outline of polygon to fill   EvenOddRule   WindingRule

A clockwise-directed path segment is one which crosses the ray from left to right as observed from the point. A counterclockwise segment is one which crosses the ray from right to left as observed from the point. The case where a directed line segment is coincident with the ray is uninteresting because you can simply choose a different ray that is not coincident with a segment.

All calculations are performed on infinitely small points, so that if any point within a pixel is considered inside, the entire pixel is drawn. Pixels with centers exactly on boundaries are considered inside only if the filled area is to the right, except that on horizontal boundaries, the pixel is considered inside only if the filled area is below the pixel.

See Volume One, Chapter 5, *The Graphics Context*, for more information.

Errors
    BadGC
    BadValue

Related Commands
    DefaultGC, XChangeGC, XCopyGC, XCreateGC, XFreeGC, XGContextFromGC,
    XSetArcMode, XSetBackground, XSetClipMask, XSetClipOrigin, XSetClip-
    Rectangles, XSetDashes, XSetFillStyle, XSetForeground, XSetFunction,
    XSetGraphicsExposures, XSetLineAttributes, XSetPlaneMask, XSetState,
    XSetStipple, XSetSubwindowMode, XSetTSOrigin.

XSetFillStyle

Name
XSetFillStyle — set the fill style in a graphics context.

Synopsis
```
XSetFillStyle(display, gc, fill_style)
    Display *display;
    GC gc;
    int fill_style;
```

Arguments

display   Specifies a connection to an X server; returned from XOpenDisplay.

gc   Specifies the graphics context.

fill_style   Specifies the fill style for the specified graphics context. Possible values are FillSolid, FillTiled, FillStippled, or FillOpaque-Stippled.

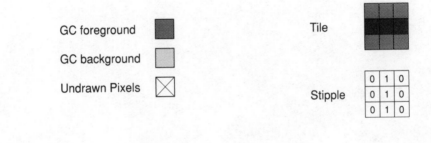

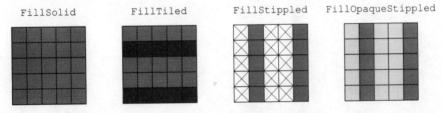

Description
XSetFillStyle sets the *fill_style* component of a GC. The *fill_style* defines the contents of the source for line, text, and fill requests. FillSolid indicates that the pixels represented by set bits in the source are drawn in the foreground pixel value, and unset bits in the source are not drawn. FillTiled uses the tile specified in the GC to determine the pixel values for set bits in the source. FillOpaqueStippled specifies that bits set in the stipple are drawn in the foreground pixel value and unset bits are drawn in the background. FillStippled draws bits set in the source and set in the stipple in the foreground color, and leaves unset bits alone.

For more information, see Volume One, Chapter 5, *The Graphics Context*.

Errors
    BadGC
    BadValue

Related Commands

    DefaultGC, XChangeGC, XCopyGC, XCreateGC, XFreeGC, XGContextFromGC,
    XSetArcMode, XSetBackground, XSetClipMask, XSetClipOrigin, XSetClip-
    Rectangles, XSetDashes, XSetFillRule, XSetForeground, XSetFunction,
    XSetGraphicsExposures, XSetLineAttributes, XSetPlaneMask, XSetState,
    XSetStipple, XSetSubwindowMode, XSetTSOrigin.

XSetFont

Name

XSetFont — set the current font in a graphics context.

Synopsis

```
XSetFont(display, gc, font)
    Display *display;
    GC gc;
    Font font;
```

Arguments

display   Specifies a connection to an X server; returned from XOpenDisplay.

gc   Specifies the graphics context.

font   Specifies the ID of the font to be used.

Description

XSetFont sets the font in the GC. Text drawing requests using this GC will use this font only if the font is loaded. Otherwise, the text will not be drawn.

For more information, see Volume One, Chapter 5, *The Graphics Context*.

Errors

BadFont
BadGC

Related Commands

XCreateFontCursor, XFreeFont, XFreeFontInfo, XFreeFontNames, XFree-FontPath, XGetFontPath, XGetFontProperty, XListFonts, XListFontsWith-Info, XLoadFont, XLoadQueryFont, XQueryFont, XSetFontPath, XUnloadFont.

XSetFontPath

Name

XSetFontPath — set the font search path.

Synopsis

```
XSetFontPath(display, directories, ndirs)
    Display *display;
    char **directories;
    int ndirs;
```

Arguments

display   Specifies a connection to an X server; returned from XOpenDisplay.

directories Specifies the directory path used to look for the font. Setting the path to the empty list restores the default path defined for the X server.

ndirs   Specifies the number of directories in the path.

Description

XSetFontPath defines the directory search path for font lookup for all clients. Therefore the user should construct a new directory search path carefully by adding to the old directory search path obtained by XGetFontPath. Passing an invalid path can result in preventing the server from accessing any fonts. Also avoid restoring the default path, since some other client may have changed the path on purpose.

The interpretation of the strings is operating system dependent, but they are intended to specify directories to be searched in the order listed. Also, the contents of these strings are operating system specific and are not intended to be used by client applications.

The meaning of errors from this request is system specific.

Errors

BadValue

Related Commands

XCreateFontCursor, XFreeFont, XFreeFontInfo, XFreeFontNames, XFree-FontPath, XGetFontPath, XGetFontProperty, XListFonts, XListFontsWith-Info, XLoadFont, XLoadQueryFont, XQueryFont, XSetFont, XUnloadFont.

XSetForeground

Name

XSetForeground — set the foreground pixel value in a graphics context.

Synopsis

```
XSetForeground(display, gc, foreground)
    Display *display;
    GC gc;
    unsigned long foreground;
```

Arguments

display	Specifies a connection to an X server; returned from XOpenDisplay.
gc	Specifies the graphics context.
foreground	Specifies the foreground pixel value you want for the specified graphics context.

Description

XSetForeground sets the *foreground* component in a GC. This pixel value is used for set bits in the source according to the fill_style. This pixel value must be returned by BlackPixel, WhitePixel, or a routine that allocates colors.

See Volume One, Chapter 5, *The Graphics Context*, for more information on the GC.

Errors

BadGC

Related Commands

DefaultGC, XChangeGC, XCopyGC, XCreateGC, XFreeGC, XGContextFromGC, XSetArcMode, XSetBackground, XSetClipMask, XSetClipOrigin, XSetClipRectangles, XSetDashes, XSetFillRule, XSetFillStyle, XSetFunction, XSetGraphicsExposures, XSetLineAttributes, XSetPlaneMask, XSetState, XSetStipple, XSetSubwindowMode, XSetTSOrigin.

XSetFunction

Name

XSetFunction — set the bitwise logical operation in a graphics context.

Synopsis

```
XSetFunction(display, gc, function)
    Display *display;
    GC gc;
    int function;
```

Arguments

display   Specifies a connection to an X server; returned from XOpenDisplay.

gc   Specifies the graphics context.

function   Specifies the logical operation you want for the specified graphics context. See Description for the choices and their meanings.

Description

XSetFunction sets the logical operation applied between the source pixel values (generated by the drawing request) and existing destination pixel values (already in the window or pixmap) to generate the final destination pixel values in a drawing request (what is actually drawn to the window or pixmap). Of course, the plane_mask and clip_mask in the GC also affect this operation by preventing drawing to planes and pixels respectively. GXcopy, GXinvert, and GXxor are the only logical operations that are commonly used.

See Volume One, Chapter 5, *The Graphics Context*, for more information about the logical function.

The *function* symbols and their logical definitions are:

Symbol	Bit	Meaning
GXclear	0x0	0
GXand	0x1	src AND dst
GXandReverse	0x2	src AND (NOT dst)
GXcopy	0x3	src
GXandInverted	0x4	(NOT src) AND dst
GXnoop	0x5	dst
GXxor	0x6	src XOR dst
GXor	0x7	src OR dst
GXnor	0x8	(NOT src) AND (NOT dst)
GXequiv	0x9	(NOT src) XOR dst
GXinvert	0xa	(NOT dst)
GXorReverse	0xb	src OR (NOT dst)
GXcopyInverted	0xc	(NOT src)
GXorInverted	0xd	(NOT src) OR dst
GXnand	0xe	(NOT src) OR (NOT dst)
GXset	0xf	1

Errors
BadGC
BadValue

Related Commands
DefaultGC, XChangeGC, XCopyGC, XCreateGC, XFreeGC, XGContextFromGC,
XSetArcMode, XSetBackground, XSetClipMask, XSetClipOrigin, XSetClip-
Rectangles, XSetDashes, XSetFillRule, XSetFillStyle, XSetForeground,
XSetGraphicsExposures, XSetLineAttributes, XSetPlaneMask, XSetState,
XSetStipple, XSetSubwindowMode, XSetTSOrigin.

XSetGraphicsExposures

Name

XSetGraphicsExposures — set the `graphics_exposures` component in a graphics context.

Synopsis

```
XSetGraphicsExposures(display, gc, graphics_exposures)
    Display *display;
    GC gc;
    Bool graphics_exposures;
```

Arguments

display   Specifies a connection to an X server; returned from `XOpenDisplay`.

gc   Specifies the graphics context.

graphics_exposures

Specifies whether you want `GraphicsExpose` and `NoExpose` events when calling `XCopyArea` and `XCopyPlane` with this graphics context.

Description

`XSetGraphicsExposure` sets the *graphics_exposures* member of a GC. If *graphics_exposures* is `True`, `GraphicsExpose` events will be generated when `XCopyArea` and `XCopyPlane` requests cannot be completely satisfied because a source region is obscured, and `NoExpose` events are generated when they can be completely satisfied. If *graphics_exposures* is `False`, these events are not generated.

These events are not selected in the normal way with `XSelectInput`. Setting the *graphics_exposures* member of the GC used in the `CopyArea` or `CopyPlane` request is the only way to select these events.

For more information, see Volume One, Chapter 5, *The Graphics Context*.

Errors

BadGC
BadValue

Related Commands

DefaultGC, XChangeGC, XCopyGC, XCreateGC, XFreeGC, XGContextFromGC, XSetArcMode, XSetBackground, XSetClipMask, XSetClipOrigin, XSetClip-Rectangles, XSetDashes, XSetFillRule, XSetFillStyle, XSetForeground, XSetFunction, XSetLineAttributes, XSetPlaneMask, XSetState, XSet-Stipple, XSetSubwindowMode, XSetTSOrigin.

XSetIconName

Name

XSetIconName — set the name to be displayed in a window's icon.

Synopsis

```
XSetIconName(display, w, icon_name)
    Display *display;
    Window w;
    char *icon_name;
```

Arguments

display	Specifies a connection to an X server; returned from XOpenDisplay.
w	Specifies the ID of the window whose icon name is being set.
icon_name	Specifies the name to be displayed in the window's icon. The name should be a null-terminated string. This name is returned by any subsequent call to XGetIconName.

Description

XSetIconName is superseded by XSetWMIconName in Release 4.

XSetIconName sets the XA_WM_ICON_NAME property for a window. This is usually set by an application for the window manager. The name should be short, since it is to be displayed in association with an icon.

XSetStandardProperties (in Release 4) or XSetWMProperties (in Release 4) also set this property.

For more information, see Volume One, Chapter 10, *Interclient Communication*.

Errors

```
BadAlloc
BadWindow
```

Related Commands

XFetchName, XGetClassHint, XGetIconName, XGetIconSizes, XGetNormal-
Hints, XGetSizeHints, XGetTransientForHint, XGetWMHints, XGetZoom-
Hints, XSetClassHint, XSetCommand, XSetIconSizes, XSetNormalHints,
XSetSizeHints, XSetTransientForHint, XSetWMHints, XSetZoomHints,
XStoreName.

XSetIconSizes

Name

XSetIconSizes — set the value of the XA_WM_ICON_SIZE property.

Synopsis

```
XSetIconSizes(display, w, size_list, count)
    Display *display;
    Window w;
    XIconSize *size_list;
    int count;
```

Arguments

display   Specifies a connection to an X server; returned from XOpenDisplay.

w   Specifies the ID of the window whose icon size property is to be set. Normally the root window.

size_list Specifies a pointer to the size list.

count   Specifies the number of items in the size list.

Description

XSetIconSizes is normally used by a window manager to set the range of preferred icon sizes in the XA_WM_ICON_SIZE property of the root window.

Applications can then read the property with XGetIconSizes.

Structures

```
typedef struct {
    int min_width, min_height;
    int max_width, max_height;
    int width_inc, height_inc;
} XIconSize;
```

Errors

```
BadAlloc
BadWindow
```

Related Commands

XAllocIconSize, XFetchName, XGetClassHint, XGetIconName, XGetIcon-Sizes, XGetNormalHints, XGetSizeHints, XGetTransientForHint, XGet-WMHints, XGetZoomHints, XSetClassHint, XSetCommand, XSetIconName, XSetNormalHints, XSetSizeHints, XSetTransientForHint, XSetWMHints, XSetZoomHints, XStoreName.

XSetInputFocus

Name

XSetInputFocus — set the keyboard focus window.

Synopsis

```
XSetInputFocus(display, focus, revert_to, time)
    Display *display;
    Window focus;
    int revert_to;
    Time time;
```

Arguments

display	Specifies a connection to an X server; returned from XOpenDisplay.
focus	Specifies the ID of the window you want to be the keyboard focus. Pass the window ID, PointerRoot, or None.
revert_to	Specifies which window the keyboard focus reverts to if the focus window becomes not viewable. Pass one of these constants: RevertToParent, RevertToPointerRoot, or RevertToNone. Must not be a window ID.
time	Specifies the time when the focus change should take place. Pass either a timestamp, expressed in milliseconds, or the constant CurrentTime. Also returns the time of the focus change when CurrentTime is specified.

Description

XSetInputFocus changes the keyboard focus and the last-focus-change time. The function has no effect if *time* is earlier than the current last-focus-change time or later than the current X server time. Otherwise, the last-focus-change time is set to the specified time, with CurrentTime replaced by the current X server time.

XSetInputFocus generates FocusIn and FocusOut events if *focus* is different from the current focus.

XSetInputFocus executes as follows, depending on what value you assign to the *focus* argument:

- If you assign None, all keyboard events are discarded until you set a new focus window. In this case, *revert_to* is ignored.

- If you assign a window ID, it becomes the main keyboard's focus window. If a generated keyboard event would normally be reported to this window or one of its inferiors, the event is reported normally; otherwise, the event is reported to the focus window. The specified focus window must be viewable at the time of the request (else a BadMatch error). If the focus window later becomes not viewable, the focus window will change to the *revert_to* argument.

- If you assign PointerRoot, the focus window is dynamically taken to be the root window of whatever screen the pointer is on at each keyboard event. In this case, *revert_to* is ignored. This is the default keyboard focus setting.

If the focus window later becomes not viewable, XSetInputFocus evaluates the *revert_to* argument to determine the new focus window:

- If you assign RevertToParent, the focus reverts to the parent (or the closest viewable ancestor) automatically with a new *revert_to* argument of RevertToName.

- If you assign RevertToPointerRoot or RevertToNone, the focus reverts to that value automatically. FocusIn and FocusOut events are generated when the focus reverts, but the last focus change time is not affected.

Errors
BadMatch   *focus* window not viewable when XSetInputFocus called.

BadValue

BadWindow

Related Commands
QLength, XAllowEvents, XCheckIfEvent, XCheckMaskEvent, XCheckTyped-
Event, XCheckTypedWindowEvent, XCheckWindowEvent, XEventsQueued,
XGetInputFocus, XGetMotionEvents, XIfEvent, XMaskEvent, XNextEvent,
XPeekEvent, XPeekIfEvent, XPending, XPutBackEvent, XSelectInput,
XSendEvent, XSynchronize, XWindowEvent.

Name

XSetErrorHandler — set a nonfatal error event handler.

Synopsis

In Release 3:
```
XSetIOErrorHandler(handler)
    int (* handler)(Display *, XErrorEvent *)
```
In Release 4:
```
int (*XSetIOErrorHandler(handler))()
    int (* handler)(Display *, XErrorEvent *)
```

Arguments

handler   Specifies user-defined fatal error handling routine. If NULL, reinvoke the default fatal error handler.

Description

XSetIOErrorHandler specifies a user-defined error handling routine for fatal errors. This error handler will be called by Xlib if any sort of system call error occurs, such as the connection to the server being lost. The called routine should not return. If the I/O error handler does return, the client process will exit.

If *handler* is a NULL pointer, the default error handler is reinstated. The default I/O error handler prints an error message and exits.

In Release 4, XSetIOErrorHandler returns a pointer to the previous error handler.

For more information, see Volume One, Chapter 3, *Basic Window Program.*

Related Commands

XDisplayName, XGetErrorDatabaseText, XGetErrorText, XSetAfter-Function, XSetErrorHandler, XSynchronize.

XSetLineAttributes

Name

XSetLineAttributes — set the line drawing components in a graphics context.

Synopsis

```
XSetLineAttributes(display, gc, line_width, line_style,
        cap_style, join_style)
    Display *display;
    GC gc;
    unsigned int line_width;
    int line_style;
    int cap_style;
    int join_style;
```

Arguments

display   Specifies a connection to an X server; returned from XOpenDisplay.

gc   Specifies the graphics context.

line_style

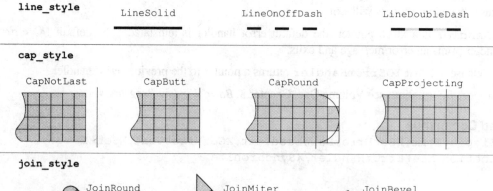

LineSolid   LineOnOffDash   LineDoubleDash

cap_style

CapNotLast   CapButt   CapRound   CapProjecting

join_style

JoinRound   JoinMiter   JoinBevel

fill_style

Tile   GC foreground ▓   GC background ░   Undrawn Pixels ⊠

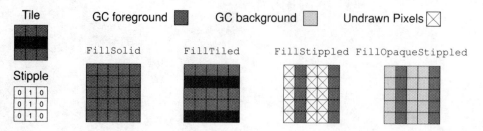

FillSolid   FillTiled   FillStippled FillOpaqueStippled

Stipple

0	1	0
0	1	0
0	1	0

line_width   Specifies the line width in the specified graphics context.

line_style   Specifies the line style in the specified graphics context. Possible values are LineSolid, LineOnOffDash, or LineDoubleDash.

cap_style   Specifies the line and cap style in the specified graphics context. Possible values are CapNotLast, CapButt, CapRound, or CapProjecting.

join_style   Specifies the line-join style in the specified graphics context. Possible values are JoinMiter, JoinRound, or JoinBevel. If you specify Join-Mitre, JoinBevel is used instead if the angle separating the two lines is less than 11 degrees.

Description

XSetLineAttributes sets four types of line characteristics in the GC: *line_width*, *line_style*, *cap_style*, and *join_style*.

See the description of line and join styles in Volume One, Chapter 5, *The Graphics Context*. See also XSetDashes.

A *line_width* of zero (0) means to use the fastest algorithm for drawing a line of one pixel width. These lines may not meet properly with lines specified as width one or more.

Errors

BadGC
BadValue

Related Commands

DefaultGC, XChangeGC, XCopyGC, XCreateGC, XFreeGC, XGContextFromGC, XSetArcMode, XSetBackground, XSetClipMask, XSetClipOrigin, XSetClip-Rectangles, XSetDashes, XSetFillRule, XSetFillStyle, XSetForeground, XSetFunction, XSetGraphicsExposures, XSetPlaneMask, XSetState, XSet-Stipple, XSetSubwindowMode, XSetTSOrigin.

XSetModifierMapping

Name

XSetModifierMapping — set keycodes to be used as modifiers (Shift, Control, etc.).

Synopsis

```
int XSetModifierMapping(display, mod_map)
    Display *display;
    XModifierKeymap *mod_map;
```

Arguments

display   Specifies a connection to an X server; returned from XOpenDisplay.

mod_map   Specifies the XModifierKeymap structure containing the desired modifier key codes.

Description

XSetModifierMapping is one of two ways to specify the keycodes of the keys that are to be used as modifiers (like Shift, Control, etc.). XSetModifierMapping specifies all the keycodes for all the modifiers at once. The other, easier, way is to use XInsert-ModifiermapEntry and XDeleteModifiermapEntry, which add or delete a single keycode for a single modifier key. XSetModifierMapping does the work in a single call, but the price of this call is that you need to manually set up the XModifierKeymap structure pointed to by mod_map. This requires you to know how the XModifierKeymap structure is defined and organized, as described in the next three paragraphs.

The XModifierKeymap structure for the mod_map argument should be created using XNewModifierMap or XGetModifierMapping. The Max_keypermod element of the structure specifies the maximum number of keycodes that can be mapped to each modifier. You define this number but there may be an upper limit on a particular server.

The modifiermap element of the structure is an array of keycodes. There are eight by max_keypermod keycodes in this array: eight because there are eight modifiers, and max_keypermod because that is the number of keycodes that must be reserved for each modifier.

The eight modifiers are represented by the constants ShiftMapIndex, LockMapIndex, ControlMapIndex, Mod1MapIndex, Mod2MapIndex, Mod3MapIndex, Mod4Map-Index, and Mod5MapIndex. These are not actually used as arguments, but they are convenient for referring to each row in the modifiermap structure while filling it. The definitions of these constants are shown in the Structures section below.

Now you can interpret the modifiermap array. For each modifier in a given modifier-map, the keycodes which correspond are from modifiermap[index * max_keypermod] to modifiermap[((index + 1) * max_keyspermod) -1] where index is the appropriate modifier index definition (ShiftMapIndex, LockMap-Index, etc.). You must set the mod_map array up properly before calling XSetModifier-Mapping. Now you know why XInsertModifierMapEntry and XDeleteModifier-MapEntry were created!

Zero keycodes are ignored. No keycode may appear twice anywhere in the map (otherwise, a BadValue error is generated). In addition, all of the nonzero keycodes must be in the range specified by `min_keycode` and `max_keycode` in the `Display` structure (otherwise a `BadValue` error occurs).

A server can impose restrictions on how modifiers can be changed. For example, certain keys may not generate up transitions in hardware, certain keys may always auto-repeat and therefore be unsuitable for use as modifiers, or multiple modifier keys may not be supported. If a restriction is violated, then the status reply is `MappingFailed`, and none of the modifiers are changed.

`XSetModifierMapping` returns `MappingSuccess` or `MappingBusy`. The server generates a `MappingNotify` event on a `MappingSuccess` status. If the new keycodes specified for a modifier differ from those currently defined and any (current or new) keys for that modifier are in the down state, then the status reply is `MappingBusy`, and none of the modifiers are changed.

A value of zero for `modifiermap` indicates that no keys are valid as any modifier.

Structures

```
typedef struct {
    int max_keypermod;       /* server's max # of keys per modifier */
    KeyCode *modifiermap;    /* an 8 by max_keypermod array */
} XModifierKeymap;

/* Modifier name symbols.  Used to build a SetModifierMapping request or
   to read a GetModifierMapping request. */
#define ShiftMapIndex      0
#define LockMapIndex       1
#define ControlMapIndex    2
#define Mod1MapIndex       3
#define Mod2MapIndex       4
#define Mod3MapIndex       5
#define Mod4MapIndex       6
#define Mod5MapIndex       7
```

Errors

`BadAlloc`

`BadValue`   Keycode appears twice in the map.

Keycode < *display*->min_keycode or
keycode > *display*->max_keycode.

Related Commands

`XChangeKeyboardMapping`, `XDeleteModifiermapEntry`, `XDelete-`
`ModifiermapEntry`, `XFreeModifiermap`, `XGetKeyboardMapping`, `XGet-`
`ModifierMapping`, `XInsertModifiermapEntry`, `XInsertModifiermapEntry`,
`XKeycodeToKeysym`, `XKeysymToKeycode`, `XKeysymToString`, `XLookupKeysym`,
`XLookupString`, `XNewModifierMap`, `XQueryKeymap`, `XRebindKeysym`,
`XRefreshKeyboardMapping`, `XStringToKeysym`.

Name

XSetNormalHints — set the size hints property of a window in normal state (not zoomed or iconified).

Synopsis

```
void XSetNormalHints(display, w, hints)
    Display *display;
    Window w;
    XSizeHints *hints;
```

Arguments

display   Specifies a connection to an X server; returned from XOpenDisplay.

w   Specifies the window ID.

hints   Specifies a pointer to the sizing hints for the window in its normal state.

Description

XSetNormalHints has been superseded by XSetWMNormalHints as of Release 4.

XSetNormalHints sets the XA_WM_NORMAL_HINTS property for the specified window. Applications use XSetNormalHints to inform the window manager of the size or position desirable for that window. In addition, an application wanting to move or resize itself should call XSetNormalHints specifying its new desired location and size, in addition to making direct X calls to move or resize. This is because some window managers may redirect window configuration requests, but ignore the resulting events and pay attention to property changes instead.

To set size hints, an application must assign values to the appropriate elements in the hints structure, and also set the flags field of the structure to indicate which members have assigned values and the source of the assignment. These flags are listed in the Structures section below.

For more information on using hints, see Volume One, Chapter 10, *Interclient Communication*.

Structures

```
typedef struct {
    long flags;      /* which fields in structure are defined */
    int x, y;
    int width, height;
    int min_width, min_height;
    int max_width, max_height;
    int width_inc, height_inc;
    struct {
        int x;      /* numerator */
        int y;      /* denominator */
    } min_aspect, max_aspect;
} XSizeHints;         /* new fields in R4 here */
```

```
#define USPosition (1L << 0) /* user specified x, y */
#define USSize     (1L << 1) /* user specified width, height */

#define PPosition  (1L << 2) /* program specified position */
#define PSize      (1L << 3) /* program specified size */
#define PMinSize   (1L << 4) /* program specified minimum size */
#define PMaxSize   (1L << 5) /* program specified maximum size */
#define PResizeInc (1L << 6) /* program specified resize increments */
#define PAspect    (1L << 7) /* program specified min/max aspect ratios */
#define PAllHints (PPosition|PSize|PMinSize|PMaxSize|PResizeInc|PAspect)
```

Errors

BadAlloc
BadWindow

Related Commands

XFetchName, XGetClassHint, XGetIconName, XGetIconSizes, XGetNormal-
Hints, XGetSizeHints, XGetTransientForHint, XGetWMHints, XGetZoom-
Hints, XSetClassHint, XSetCommand, XSetIconName, XSetIconSizes, XSet-
SizeHints, XSetTransientForHint, XSetWMHints, XSetZoomHints, XStore-
Name.

Name

XSetPlaneMask — set the plane mask in a graphics context.

Synopsis

```
XSetPlaneMask(display, gc, plane_mask)
    Display *display;
    GC gc;
    unsigned long plane_mask;
```

Arguments

display   Specifies a connection to an X server; returned from XOpenDisplay.

gc   Specifies the graphics context.

plane_mask   Specifies the plane mask. You can use the macro AllPlanes if desired.

Description

XSetPlaneMask sets the plane_mask component of the specified GC. The plane_mask determines which planes of the destination drawable are affected by a graphics request.

For more information, see Volume One, Chapter 5, *The Graphics Context*.

Errors

BadGC

Related Commands

DefaultGC, XChangeGC, XCopyGC, XCreateGC, XFreeGC, XGContextFromGC,
XSetArcMode, XSetBackground, XSetClipMask, XSetClipOrigin, XSetClip-
Rectangles, XSetDashes, XSetFillRule, XSetFillStyle, XSetForeground,
XSetFunction, XSetGraphicsExposures, XSetLineAttributes, XSetState,
XSetStipple, XSetSubwindowMode, XSetTSOrigin.

XSetPointerMapping

Name

XSetPointerMapping — set the pointer button mapping.

Synopsis

```
int XSetPointerMapping(display, map, nmap)
    Display *display;
    unsigned char map[];
    int nmap;
```

Arguments

display   Specifies a connection to an X server; returned from XOpenDisplay.

map   Specifies the mapping list.

nmap   Specifies the number of items in the mapping list.

Description

XSetPointerMapping sets the mapping of the pointer buttons. Elements of the map list are indexed starting from 1. The length of the list nmap must be the same as XGetPointer-Mapping returns (you must call that first). The index is a physical button number, and the element of the list defines the effective button number. In other words, if map[2] is set to 1, when the second physical button is pressed, a ButtonPress event will be generated if Button1Mask was selected but not if Button2Mask was selected. The button member in the event will read Button1.

No two elements can have the same nonzero value (else a BadValue error). A value of zero for an element of map disables a button, and values for elements are not restricted in value by the number of physical buttons. If any of the buttons to be altered are currently in the down state, the returned value is MappingBusy and the mapping is not changed.

This function returns either MappingSuccess or MappingBusy. XSetPointer-Mapping generates a MappingNotify event when it returns MappingSuccess.

Errors

BadValue   Two elements of map[] have same nonzero value.

nmap not equal to XGetPointerMapping return value.

Related Commands

XChangeActivePointerGrab, XChangePointerControl, XGetPointer-Control, XGetPointerMapping, XGrabPointer, XQueryPointer, XUngrab-Pointer, XWarpPointer.

Name

XSetRGBColormaps — set an XStandardColormap structure.

Synopsis

```
void XSetRGBColormaps(display, w, std_colormap, count, prop-
        erty)
    Display *display;
    Window w;
    XStandardColormap *std_colormap;
    int count;
    Atom property;
```

Arguments

display   Specifies a connection to an X server; returned from XOpenDisplay.

w   Specifies the window.

std_colormap
                Specifies the XStandardColormap structure to be used.

count   Specifies the number of colormaps.

property   Specifies the property name.

Availability

Release 4 and later.

Description

XSetRGBColormaps replaces the RGB colormap definition in the specified property on the named window. If the property does not already exist, XSetRGBColormaps sets the RGB colormap definition in the specified property on the named window. The property is stored with a type of RGB_COLOR_MAP and a format of 32. Note that it is the caller's responsibility to honor the ICCCM restriction that only RGB_DEFAULT_MAP contain more than one definition.

XSetRGBColormaps supersedes XSetStandardColormap.

For more information, see Volume One, Chapter 7, *Color*.

Structures

```
typedef struct {
    Colormap colormap;
    unsigned long red_max;
    unsigned long red_mult;
    unsigned long green_max;
    unsigned long green_mult;
    unsigned long blue_max;
    unsigned long blue_mult;
```

```
    unsigned long base_pixel;
    VisualID visualid;              /* added by ICCCM version 1 */
    XID killid;                     /* added by ICCCM version 1 */
} XStandardColormap;
```

Errors
```
BadAlloc
BadAtom
BadWindow
```

Related Commands
XAllocStandardColormap, XGetRGBColormaps, XVisualIDFromVisual.

XSetRegion

Name

XSetRegion — set `clip_mask` of the graphics context to the specified region.

Synopsis

```
XSetRegion(display, gc, r)
    Display *display;
    GC gc;
    Region r;
```

Arguments

display   Specifies a connection to an X server; returned from XOpenDisplay.

gc   Specifies the graphics context.

r   Specifies the region.

Description

XSetRegion sets the *clip_mask* component of a GC to the specified region. Thereafter, all drawing made with gc will be confined to the the area of intersection of the region and the drawable.

Regions are located using an offset from a point (the *region origin*) which is common to all regions. It is up to the application to interpret the location of the region relative to a drawable. When the region is to be used as a clip_mask by calling XSetRegion, the upper-left corner of region relative to the drawable used in the graphics request will be at (xoffset + clip_x_origin, yoffset + clip_y_origin), where xoffset and yoffset are the offset of the region and clip_x_origin and clip_y_origin are elements of the GC used in the graphics request.

For more information on regions, see Volume One, Chapter 5, *The Graphics Context*, and Chapter 6, *Drawing Graphics and Text*.

Structures

Region is a pointer to an opaque structure type.

Related Commands

XClipBox, XCreateRegion, XDestroyRegion, XEmptyRegion, XEqualRegion, XIntersectRegion, XOffsetRegion, XPointInRegion, XPolygonRegion, XRectInRegion, XShrinkRegion, XSubtractRegion, XUnionRectWithRegion, XUnionRegion, XXorRegion.

XSetScreenSaver

Name

XSetScreenSaver — set the parameters of the screen saver.

Synopsis

```
XSetScreenSaver(display, timeout, interval,
        prefer_blanking, allow_exposures)
    Display *display;
    int timeout, interval;
    int prefer_blanking;
    int allow_exposures;
```

Arguments

display   Specifies a connection to an X server; returned from XOpenDisplay.

timeout   Specifies the time of inactivity, in seconds, before the screen saver turns on.

interval   Specifies the interval, in seconds, between screen saver invocations. This is for intermittent changes to the display, not blanking.

prefer_blanking
                Specifies whether to enable screen blanking. Possible values are Dont-PreferBlanking, PreferBlanking, or DefaultBlanking.

allow_exposures
                Specifies the current screen saver control values. Possible values are Dont-AllowExposures, AllowExposures, or DefaultExposures.

Description

XSetScreenSaver sets the parameters that control the screen saver. *timeout* and *interval* are specified in seconds. A positive *timeout* enables the screen saver. A *timeout* of zero (0) disables the screen saver, while a timeout of −1 restores the default. An *interval* of zero (0) disables the random pattern motion. If no input from devices (keyboard, mouse, etc.) is generated for the specified number of timeout seconds, the screen saver is activated.

For each screen, if blanking is preferred and the hardware supports video blanking, the screen will simply go blank. Otherwise, if either exposures are allowed or the screen can be regenerated without sending exposure events to clients, the screen is tiled with the root window background tile, with a random origin, each *interval* seconds. Otherwise, the state of the screen does not change. All screen states are restored at the next input from a device.

If the server-dependent screen saver method supports periodic change, *interval* serves as a hint about how long the change period should be, and a value of zero (0) hints that no periodic change should be made. Examples of ways to change the screen include scrambling the color map periodically, moving an icon image about the screen periodically, or tiling the screen with the root window background tile, randomly reoriginated periodically.

For more information on the screen saver, see Volume One, Chapter 13, *Other Programming Techniques*.

Errors

BadValue   *timeout* < –1.

Related Commands

XActivateScreenSaver, XForceScreenSaver, XGetScreenSaver, XReset-
ScreenSaver.

XSetSelectionOwner

Name
XSetSelectionOwner — set the owner of a selection.

Synopsis
```
XSetSelectionOwner(display, selection, owner, time)
    Display *display;
    Atom selection;
    Window owner;
    Time time;
```

Arguments

display   Specifies a connection to an X server; returned from XOpenDisplay.

selection   Specifies the selection atom. Predefined atoms are XA_PRIMARY and XA_SECONDARY.

owner   Specifies the desired owner of the specified selection atom. This value is either a window ID or None.

time   Specifies the time when the grab should take place. Pass either a timestamp, expressed in milliseconds, or the constant CurrentTime.

Description

XSetSelectionOwner sets the owner and last-change time of a selection property. This should be called by an application that supports cutting and pasting between windows (or at least cutting), when the user has made a selection of any kind of text, graphics, or data. This makes the information available so that other applications can request the data from the new selection owner using XConvertSelection, which generates a SelectionRequest event specifying the desired type and format of the data. Then the selection owner sends a SelectionNotify using XSendEvent, which notes that the information is stored in the selection property in the desired format or indicates that it couldn't do the conversion to the desired type.

If owner is specified as None, then this client is giving up ownership voluntarily. Otherwise, the new owner is the client executing the request.

If the new owner is not the same as the current owner of the selection, and the current owner is a window, then the current owner is sent a SelectionClear event. This indicates to the old owner that the selection should be unhighlighted.

If the selection owner window is later destroyed, the owner of the selection automatically reverts to None.

The value you pass to the time argument must be no earlier than the last-change time of the specified selection, and no later than the current time, or the selection is not affected. The new last-change time recorded is the specified time, with CurrentTime replaced by the current server time. If the X server reverts a selection owner to None, the last-change time is not affected.

For more information on selections, see Volume One, Chapter 10, *Interclient Communication*.

Errors
    `BadAtom`
    `BadWindow`

Related Commands
    `XConvertSelection, XGetSelectionOwner.`

Name

XSetSizeHints — set the value of any property of type XA_SIZE_HINTS.

Synopsis

```
XSetSizeHints(display, w, hints, property)
    Display *display;
    Window w;
    XSizeHints *hints;
    Atom property;
```

Arguments

display   Specifies a connection to an X server; returned from XOpenDisplay.

w   Specifies the window ID.

hints   Specifies a pointer to the size hints.

property   Specifies the property atom.

Description

XSetSizeHints has been superseded by XSetWMSizeHints as of Release 4.

XSetSizeHints sets the named property on the specified window to the specified XSize-Hints structure. This routine is useful if new properties of type XA_WM_SIZE_HINTS are defined. The predefined properties of that type have their own set and get functions, XSet-NormalHints and XSetZoomHints (XSetWMHints in Release 4—zoom hints are obsolete).

The flags member of XSizeHints must be set to the OR of the symbols representing each member to be set.

For more information on using hints, see Volume One, Chapter 10, *Interclient Communication*.

Structures

```
typedef struct {
    long flags;    /* which fields in structure are defined */
    int x, y;
    int width, height;
    int min_width, min_height;
    int max_width, max_height;
    int width_inc, height_inc;
    struct {
        int x;    /* numerator */
        int y;    /* denominator */
    } min_aspect, max_aspect;
} XSizeHints;

/* flags argument in size hints */
#define USPosition (1L << 0) /* user specified x, y */
#define USSize     (1L << 1) /* user specified width, height */
#define PPosition  (1L << 2) /* program specified position */
#define PSize      (1L << 3) /* program specified size */
```

```
#define PMinSize   (1L << 4) /* program specified minimum size */
#define PMaxSize   (1L << 5) /* program specified maximum size */
#define PResizeInc (1L << 6) /* program specified resize increments */
#define PAspect    (1L << 7) /* program specified min/max aspect ratios */
#define PAllHints (PPosition|PSize|PMinSize|PMaxSize|PResizeInc|PAspect)
```

Errors
BadAlloc
BadAtom
BadWindow

Related Commands
XFetchName, XGetClassHint, XGetIconName, XGetIconSizes, XGetNormal-
Hints, XGetSizeHints, XGetTransientForHint, XGetWMHints, XGetZoom-
Hints, XSetClassHint, XSetCommand, XSetIconName, XSetIconSizes, XSet-
NormalHints, XSetTransientForHint, XSetWMHints, XSetZoomHints,
XStoreName.

Name
XSetStandardColormap — change the standard colormap property.

Synopsis
```
void XSetStandardColormap(display, w, cmap_info, property)
    Display *display;
    Window w;
    XStandardColormap *cmap_info;
    Atom property;
```

Arguments
display   Specifies a connection to an X server; returned from XOpenDisplay.

w   Specifies the ID of the window with which this colormap will be associated.

cmap_info   Specifies the filled colormap information structure.

property   Specifies the standard colormap property to set. The predefined standard colormaps are: XA_RGB_BEST_MAP, XA_RGB_RED_MAP, XA_RGB_GREEN_MAP, XA_RGB_BLUE_MAP, XA_RGB_DEFAULT_MAP, and XA_RGB_GRAY_MAP.

Description
XSetStandardColormap has been superseded by XSetRGBColormap as of Release 4.

XSetStandardColormap defines a standard colormap property. To create a standard colormap, follow this procedure:

1. Open a new connection to the same server.

2. Grab the server.

3. See if property is on the property list of the root window for the display, using XGetStandardColormap. If so, see if the colormap field is nonzero. If it is, the colormap already exists.

4. If the desired property is not present, do the following:

   - Determine the color capabilities of the display. Choose a visual.

   - Create a colormap (not required for XA_RGB_DEFAULT_MAP).

   - Call XAllocColorPlanes or XAllocColorCells to allocate cells in the colormap.

   - Call XStoreColors to store appropriate color values in the colormap.

   - Fill in the descriptive fields in the structure.

   - Call XSetStandardColormap to set the property on the root window.

   - Use XSetCloseDownMode to make the resource permanent.

   - Close the new connection to the server.

5.   Ungrab the server.

6.   Close the new connection to the server.

See description of standard colormaps in Volume One, Chapter 7, *Color*.

Errors

```
BadAlloc
BadAtom
BadWindow
```

Structures

```
typedef struct {
    Colormap colormap;          /* ID of colormap made by XCreateColormap */
    unsigned long red_max;
    unsigned long red_mult;
    unsigned long green_max;
    unsigned long green_mult;
    unsigned long blue_max;
    unsigned long blue_mult;
    unsigned long base_pixel;
} XStandardColormap;            /* new fields in R4 */
```

Related Commands

DefaultColormap, DisplayCells, XCopyColormapAndFree, XCreate-
Colormap, XFreeColormap, XGetStandardColormap, XInstallColormap,
XListInstalledColormaps, XSetWindowColormap, XUninstallColormap.

XSetStandardProperties

Name
XSetStandardProperties — set the minimum set of properties for the window manager.

Synopsis
```
XSetStandardProperties(display, w, window_name, icon_name,
        icon_pixmap, argv, argc, hints)
    Display *display;
    Window w;
    char *window_name;
    char *icon_name;
    Pixmap icon_pixmap;
    char **argv;
    int argc;
    XSizeHints *hints
```

Arguments

display   Specifies a connection to an X server; returned from XOpenDisplay.

w   Specifies the window ID.

window_name Specifies the name of the window.

icon_name Specifies the name to be displayed in the window's icon.

icon_pixmap Specifies the pixmap that is to be used for the icon, or None. This pixmap must be of depth 1.

argv   Specifies a pointer to the command and arguments used to start the application.

argc   Specifies the number of arguments.

hints   Specifies a pointer to the size hints for the window in its normal state.

Description

XSetStandardProperties is superceded by XSetWMProperties in Release 4.

XSetStandardProperties sets in a single call the most essential properties for a quickie application. XSetStandardProperties gives a window manager some information about your program's preferences; it probably will not be sufficient for complex programs.

See Volume One, Chapter 10, *Interclient Communication* for a description of standard properties.

Structures

```
typedef struct {
    long flags;                 /* which fields in structure are defined */
    int x, y;
    int width, height;
    int min_width, min_height;
    int max_width, max_height;
    int width_inc, height_inc;
```

```
        struct {
            int x;      /* numerator */
            int y;      /* denominator */
        } min_aspect, max_aspect;      /* new fields in R4 */
    } XSizeHints;

    /* flags argument in size hints */
    #define USPosition  (1L << 0)/* user specified x, y */
    #define USSize      (1L << 1)/* user specified width, height */

    #define PPosition   (1L << 2)/* program specified position */
    #define PSize       (1L << 3)/* program specified size */
    #define PMinSize    (1L << 4)/* program specified minimum size */
    #define PMaxSize    (1L << 5)/* program specified maximum size */
    #define PResizeInc  (1L << 6)/* program specified resize increments */
    #define PAspect     (1L << 7)/* program specified min and max aspect ratios */
    #define PAllHints   (PPosition|PSize|PMinSize|PMaxSize|PResizeInc|PAspect)
```

Errors

BadAlloc
BadWindow

Related Commands

XChangeProperty, XDeleteProperty, XGetAtomName, XGetFontProperty,
XGetWindowProperty, XInternAtom, XListProperties, XRotateWindow-
Properties.

XSetState

Name

XSetState — set the foreground, background, logical function, and plane mask in a graphics context.

Synopsis

```
XSetState(display, gc, foreground, background, function,
        plane_mask)
    Display *display;
    GC gc;
    unsigned long foreground, background;
    int function;
    unsigned long plane_mask;
```

Arguments

display   Specifies a connection to an X server; returned from XOpenDisplay.

gc   Specifies the graphics context.

foreground   Specifies the foreground for the specified graphics context.

background   Specifies the background for the specified graphics context.

function   Specifies the logical function for the specified graphics context.

plane_mask   Specifies the plane mask for the specified graphics context.

Description

XSetState sets the foreground and background pixel values, the logical function, and the plane_mask in a GC. See XSetForeground, XSetBackground, XSet-Function, and XSetPlaneMask for what these members do and appropriate values.

See Volume One, Chapter 5, *The Graphics Context*, for more information.

Errors

BadGC
BadValue

Related Commands

DefaultGC, XChangeGC, XCopyGC, XCreateGC, XFreeGC, XGContextFromGC, XSetArcMode, XSetBackground, XSetClipMask, XSetClipOrigin, XSetClip-Rectangles, XSetDashes, XSetFillRule, XSetFillStyle, XSetForeground, XSetFunction, XSetGraphicsExposures, XSetLineAttributes, XSetPlane-Mask, XSetStipple, XSetSubwindowMode, XSetTSOrigin.

XSetStipple

Name

XSetStipple — set the stipple in a graphics context.

Synopsis

```
XSetStipple(display, gc, stipple)
    Display *display;
    GC gc;
    Pixmap stipple;
```

Arguments

display   Specifies a connection to an X server; returned from XOpenDisplay.

gc   Specifies the graphics context.

stipple   Specifies the stipple for the specified graphics context.

Description

XSetStipple sets the stipple component of a GC. The stipple is a pixmap of depth one. It is laid out like a tile. Set bits in the stipple determine which pixels in an area are drawn in the foreground pixel value. Unset bits in the stipple determine which pixels are drawn in the background pixel value if the fill_style is FillOpaqueStippled. If fill_style is FillStippled, pixels overlayed with unset bits in the stipple are not drawn. If fill_style is FillTiled or FillSolid, the stipple is not used.

For more information, see Volume One, Chapter 5, *The Graphics Context*.

Errors

BadGC
BadMatch
BadPixmap

Related Commands

DefaultGC, XChangeGC, XCopyGC, XCreateGC, XFreeGC, XGContextFromGC, XSetArcMode, XSetBackground, XSetClipMask, XSetClipOrigin, XSetClip-Rectangles, XSetDashes, XSetFillRule, XSetFillStyle, XSetForeground, XSetFunction, XSetGraphicsExposures, XSetLineAttributes, XSetPlane-Mask, XSetState, XSetSubwindowMode, XSetTSOrigin.

XSetSubwindowMode

Name
XSetSubwindowMode — set the subwindow mode in a graphics context.

Synopsis
```
XSetSubwindowMode(display, gc, subwindow_mode)
    Display *display;
    GC gc;
    int subwindow_mode;
```

Arguments

display   Specifies a connection to an X server; returned from XOpenDisplay.

gc   Specifies the graphics context.

subwindow_mode
    Specifies the subwindow mode you want to set for the specified graphics context. Possible values are ClipByChildren or IncludeInferiors.

Description

XSetSubwindowMode sets the subwindow_mode component of a GC. ClipByChildren means that graphics requests will be clipped by all viewable children. IncludeInferiors means draw through all subwindows.

For more information, see Volume One, Chapter 5, *The Graphics Context*.

Errors
BadGC
BadValue

Related Commands

DefaultGC, XChangeGC, XCopyGC, XCreateGC, XFreeGC, XGContextFromGC, XSetArcMode, XSetBackground, XSetClipMask, XSetClipOrigin, XSetClipRectangles, XSetDashes, XSetFillRule, XSetFillStyle, XSetForeground, XSetFunction, XSetGraphicsExposures, XSetLineAttributes, XSetPlaneMask, XSetState, XSetStipple, XSetTSOrigin.

XSetTextProperty

Name

XSetTextProperty — set one of a window's text properties.

Synopsis

```
void XSetTextProperty(display, w, text_prop, property)
    Display *display;
    Window w;
    XTextProperty *text_prop;
    Atom property;
```

Arguments

display	Specifies a connection to an X server; returned from XOpenDisplay.
w	Specifies the window.
text_prop	Specifies the XTextProperty structure to be used.
property	Specifies the property name.

Availability

Release 4 and later.

Description

XSetTextProperty sets the specified property for the named window with the data, type, format, and number of items determined by the *value* field, the *encoding* field, the *format* field, and the *nitems* field, respectively, of the specified XTextProperty structure.

Structures

```
typedef struct {
    unsigned char *value;          /* same as Property routines */
    Atom encoding;                 /* prop type */
    int format;                    /* prop data format: 8, 16, or 32 */
    unsigned long nitems;          /* number of data items in value */
} XTextProperty;
```

Errors

```
BadAlloc
BadAtom
BadValue
BadWindow
```

Related Commands

XFreeStringList, XGetTextProperty, XStringListToTextProperty, XTextPropertytoStringList.

Name

XSetTile — set the fill tile in a graphics context.

Synopsis

```
XSetTile(display, gc, tile)
    Display *display;
    GC gc;
    Pixmap tile;
```

Arguments

display   Specifies a connection to an X server; returned from XOpenDisplay.

gc   Specifies the graphics context.

tile   Specifies the desired tile for the specified graphics context.

Description

XSetTile sets the tile member of the GC. This member of the GC determines the pixmap used to tile areas. The tile must have the same depth as the destination drawable. This tile will only be used in drawing if the fill-style is *FillTiled*.

For more information, see Volume One, Chapter 5, *The Graphics Context*.

Errors

```
BadGC
BadMatch
BadPixmap
```

Related Commands

XCreateBitmapFromData, XCreatePixmap, XCreatePixmapFromBitmapData, XFreePixmap, XQueryBestSize, XQueryBestStipple, XQueryBestTile, XReadBitmapFile, XSetWindowBackgroundPixmap, XSetWindowBorder-Pixmap, XWriteBitmapFile.

Name

XSetTransientForHint — set the XA_WM_TRANSIENT_FOR property for a window.

Synopsis

```
XSetTransientForHint(display, w, prop_window)
    Display *display;
    Window w;
    Window prop_window;
```

Arguments

display   Specifies a connection to an X server; returned from XOpenDisplay.

w   Specifies the window ID, normally of a dialog box popup.

prop_window Specifies the window ID that the XA_WM_TRANSIENT_FOR property is to be set to. This is usually the main window of the application.

Description

XSetTransientForHint sets the XA_WM_TRANSIENT_FOR property of the specified window. This should be done when the window *w* is a temporary child (for example, a dialog box) and the main top-level window of its application is *prop_window*. Some window managers may use this information to unmap an application's dialog boxes (for example, when the main application window gets iconified).

For more information, see Volume One, Chapter 10, *Interclient Communication*.

Errors

```
BadAlloc
BadWindow
```

Related Commands

XFetchName, XGetClassHint, XGetIconName, XGetIconSizes, XGetNormal-
Hints, XGetSizeHints, XGetTransientForHint, XGetWMHints, XGetZoom-
Hints, XSetClassHint, XSetCommand, XSetIconName, XSetIconSizes, XSet-
NormalHints, XSetSizeHints, XSetWMHints, XSetZoomHints, XStoreName.

Name

XSetTSOrigin — set the tile/stipple origin in a graphics context.

Synopsis

```
XSetTSOrigin(display, gc, ts_x_origin, ts_y_origin)
    Display *display;
    GC gc;
    int ts_x_origin, ts_y_origin;
```

Arguments

display   Specifies a connection to an X server; returned from XOpenDisplay.

gc   Specifies the graphics context.

ts_x_origin   Specify the x and y coordinates of the tile/stipple origin.
ts_y_origin

Description

XSetTSOrigin sets the *ts_x_origin* and *ts_y_origin* components in a GC, which are measured relative to the origin of the drawable specified in the drawing request that uses the GC. This controls the placement of the tile or the stipple pattern that patterns an area. To tile or stipple a child so that the pattern matches the parent, you need to subtract the current position of the child window from *ts_x_origin* and *ts_y_origin*.

For more information, see Volume One, Chapter 5, *The Graphics Context*.

Errors

BadGC

Related Commands

DefaultGC, XChangeGC, XCopyGC, XCreateGC, XFreeGC, XGContextFromGC, XSetArcMode, XSetBackground, XSetClipMask, XSetClipOrigin, XSetClip-Rectangles, XSetDashes, XSetFillRule, XSetFillStyle, XSetForeground, XSetFunction, XSetGraphicsExposures, XSetLineAttributes, XSetPlane-Mask, XSetState, XSetStipple, XSetSubwindowMode.

Name

XSetWMClientMachine — set a window's WM_CLIENT_MACHINE property.

Synopsis

```
void XSetWMClientMachine(display, w, text_prop)
    Display *display;
    Window w;
    XTextProperty *text_prop;
```

Arguments

display   Specifies a connection to an X server; returned from XOpenDisplay.

w   Specifies the window.

text_prop   Specifies the XTextProperty structure to be used.

Availability

Release 4 and later.

Description

XSetWMClientMachine performs an XSetTextProperty to set the WM_CLIENT_MACHINE property of the specified window. This property should contain the name of the host machine on which this client is being run, as seen from the server.

For more information, see Volume One, Chapter 10, *Interclient Communication*.

Structures

```
typedef struct {
    unsigned char *value;          /* same as Property routines */
    Atom encoding;                 /* prop type */
    int format;                    /* prop data format: 8, 16, or 32 */
    unsigned long nitems;          /* number of data items in value */
} XTextProperty;
```

Related Commands

XGetWMClientMachine.

XSetWMColormapWindows

Name

XSetWMColormapWindows — set a window's WM_COLORMAP_WINDOWS property.

Synopsis

```
Status XSetWMColormapWindows(display, w, colormap_windows,
        count)
    Display *display;
    Window w;
    Window *colormap_windows;
    int count;
```

Arguments

display   Specifies a connection to an X server; returned from XOpenDisplay.

w   Specifies the window.

colormap_windows
               Specifies the list of windows.

count   Specifies the number of windows in the list.

Availability

Release 4 and later.

Description

XSetWMColormapWindows sets the WM_COLORMAP_WINDOWS property on the specified window to the list of windows specified by the colormap_windows argument. The property is stored with a type of WINDOW and a format of 32. If it cannot intern the WM_COLORMAP_WINDOWS atom, XSetWMColormapWindows returns a zero status. Otherwise, it returns a non-zero status.

This property tells the window manager that subwindows of this application need to have their own colormaps installed.

For more information, see Volume One, Chapter 10, *Interclient Communication*.

Errors

BadAlloc
BadWindow

Related Commands

XGetWMColormapWindows.

Name

XSetWMIconName — set a window's XA_WM_ICON_NAME property.

Synopsis

```
void XSetWMIconName(display, w, text_prop)
    Display *display;
    Window w;
    XTextProperty *text_prop;
```

Arguments

display   Specifies a connection to an X server; returned from XOpenDisplay.

w   Specifies the window.

text_prop   Specifies the XTextProperty structure to be used.

Availability

Release 4 and later.

Description

XSetWMIconName performs an XSetTextProperty to set the XA_WM_ICON_NAME property of the specified window. XSetWMIconName supersedes XSetIconName.

This is usually called by an application to set the property for the window manager. The name should be short, since it is to be displayed in association with an icon.

XSetStandardProperties (in Release 4) or XSetWMProperties (in Release 4) also set this property.

For more information, see Volume One, Chapter 10, *Interclient Communication*.

Structures

```
typedef struct {
    unsigned char *value;          /* same as Property routines */
    Atom encoding;                 /* prop type */
    int format;                    /* prop data format: 8, 16, or 32 */
    unsigned long nitems;          /* number of data items in value */
} XTextProperty;
```

Related Commands

XGetWMIconName, XGetWMName, XSetWMName, XSetWMProperties.

XSetWMName

Name

XSetWMName — set a window's XA_WM_NAME property.

Synopsis

```
void XSetWMName(display, w, text_prop)
    Display *display;
    Window w;
    XTextProperty *text_prop;
```

Arguments

display   Specifies a connection to an X server; returned from XOpenDisplay.

w   Specifies the window.

text_prop   Specifies the XTextProperty structure to be used.

Availability

Release 4 and later.

Description

XSetWMName performs a XSetTextProperty to set the XA_WM_NAME property on the specified window. XSetWMName supersedes XStoreName. This property can also be set with XSetWMProperties.

XSetWMName be used by the application to communicate a string to the window manager. According to current conventions, this string should either:

- permit the user to identify one of a number of instances of the same client, or

- provide the user with noncritical state information.

Clients can assume that at least the beginning of this string is visible to the user.

The XA_WM_CLASS property, on the other hand, has two members which should be used to identify the application's instance and class name, for the lookup of resources. See XSetClassHint for details.

For more information, see Volume One, Chapter 10, *Interclient Communication*.

Structures

```
typedef struct {
    unsigned char *value;           /* same as Property routines */
    Atom encoding;                  /* prop type */
    int format;                     /* prop data format: 8, 16, or 32 */
    unsigned long nitems;           /* number of data items in value */
} XTextProperty;
```

Related Commands

XGetWMIconName, XGetWMName, XSetWMIconName, XSetWMProperties.

Name

XSetWMNormalHints — set a window's XA_WM_NORMAL_HINTS property.

Synopsis

```
void XSetWMNormalHints(display, w, hints)
    Display *display;
    Window w;
    XSizeHints *hints;
```

Arguments

display   Specifies a connection to an X server; returned from XOpenDisplay.

w   Specifies the window.

hints   Specifies the size hints for the window in its normal state.

Availability

Release 4 and later.

Description

XSetWMNormalHints sets the size hints in the XA_WM_NORMAL_HINTS property on the specified window. The property is stored with a type of WM_SIZE_HINTS and a format of 32. XSetWMNormalHints supersedes XSetNormalHints. This property can also be set with XSetWMProperties.

Applications use XSetNormalHints to inform the window manager of the sizes desirable for that window.

To set size hints, an application must assign values to the appropriate elements in the hints structure, and also set the flags field of the structure to indicate which members have assigned values and the source of the assignment. These flags are listed in the Structures section below.

For more information, see Volume One, Chapter 10, *Interclient Communication*.

Structures

```
typedef struct {
    long flags;          /* marks which fields in this structure */
                         /* are defined */
    int x, y;            /* obsolete for new window mgrs, but clients */
    int width, height;   /* should set so old wm's don't mess up */
    int min_width, min_height;
    int max_width, max_height;
    int width_inc, height_inc;
    struct {
            int x;   /* numerator */
            int y;   /* denominator */
    } min_aspect, max_aspect;
    int base_width, base_height;      /* added by ICCCM version 1 */
    int win_gravity;                  /* added by ICCCM version 1 */
```

```
} XSizeHints;

#define USPosition (1L << 0) /* user specified x, y */
#define USSize     (1L << 1) /* user specified width, height */

#define PPosition (1L << 2) /* program specified position
*/
#define PSize     (1L << 3) /* program specified size */
#define PMinSize   (1L << 4) /* program specified minimum size */
#define PMaxSize   (1L << 5) /* program specified maximum size */
#define PResizeInc (1L << 6) /* program specified resize increments *
/
#define PAspect   (1L << 7) /* program specified min/max aspect
ratios */
#define PAllHints (PPosition|PSize|PMinSize|PMaxSize|PResizeInc|PAspect)
#define PBaseSize  (1L << 8) /* program specified base
                            for incrementing */
#define PWinGravity (1L << 9)/* program specified window
                            gravity */
```

Errors

```
BadAlloc
BadWindow
```

Related Commands

XGetWMNormalHints, XSetWMProperties, XSetWMSizeHints, XGetWMSize-
Hints.

Name

XSetWMProperties — set a window's standard window manager properties.

Synopsis

```
void XSetWMProperties(display, w, window_name, icon_name, argv,
        argc, normal_hints, wm_hints, class_hints)
    Display *display;
    Window w;
    XTextProperty *window_name;
    XTextProperty *icon_name;
    char **argv;
    int argc;
    XSizeHints *normal_hints;
    XWMHints *wm_hints;
    XClassHint *class_hints;
```

Arguments

display   Specifies a connection to an X server; returned from XOpenDisplay.

w   Specifies the window.

window_name   Specifies the window name, which should be a null-terminated string.

icon_name   Specifies the icon name, which should be a null-terminated string.

argv   Specifies the application's argument list.

argc   Specifies the number of arguments.

normal_hints
                 Specifies the size hints for the window in its normal state.

wm_hints   Specifies the XWMHints structure to be used.

class_hints   Specifies the XClassHint structure to be used.

Availability

Release 4 and later.

Description

XSetWMProperties provides a single programming interface for setting the essential window properties that communicate with window and session managers. XSetWMProperties supersedes XSetStandardProperties.

If the window_name argument is non-null, XSetWMProperties calls XSetWMName, which, in turn, sets the WM_NAME property. If the icon_name argument is non-null, XSetWMProperties calls XSetWMIconName, which sets the WM_ICON_NAME property. If the argv argument is non-null, XSetWMProperties calls XSetCommand, which sets the WM_COMMAND property. Note that an argc of 0 is allowed to indicate a zero-length command. XSetWMProperties stores the hostname of this machine using XSetWMClientMachine.

If the *normal_hints* argument is non-null, XSetWMProperties calls XSetWMNormal-Hints, which sets the WM_NORMAL_HINTS property. If the *wm_hints* argument is non-null, XSetWMProperties calls XSetWMHints, which sets the WM_HINTS property.

If the *class_hints* argument is non-null, XSetWMProperties calls XSetClassHint, which sets the WM_CLASS property. If the res_name member in the XClassHint structure is set to the null pointer and the RESOURCE_NAME environment variable is set, then value of the environment variable is substituted for res_name. If the res_name member is NULL, and if the environment variable is not set, and if *argv* and *argv[0]* are set, then the value of *argv[0]*, stripped of any directory prefixes, is substituted for res_name.

For more information, see Volume One, Chapter 10, *Interclient Communication*.

Structures

```
typedef struct {
    unsigned char *value;            /* same as Property routines */
    Atom encoding;                   /* prop type */
    int format;                      /* prop data format: 8, 16, or 32 */
    unsigned long nitems;            /* number of data items in value */
} XTextProperty;


typedef struct {
    long flags;        /* marks which fields in this structure */
                       /* are defined */
    int x, y;          /* obsolete for new window mgrs, but clients */
    int width, height;         /* should set so old wm's don't mess up */
    int min_width, min_height;
    int max_width, max_height;
    int width_inc, height_inc;
    struct {
            int x;   /* numerator */
            int y;   /* denominator */
    } min_aspect, max_aspect;
    int base_width, base_height;      /* added by ICCCM version 1 */
    int win_gravity;                  /* added by ICCCM version 1 */
} XSizeHints;


typedef struct {
    long flags;        /* marks which fields in this structure */
                       /* are defined */
    Bool input;        /* does this application rely on the window */
                       /* manager to get keyboard input? */
    int initial_state;        /* see below */
    Pixmap icon_pixmap;       /* pixmap to be used as icon */
    Window icon_window;       /* window to be used as icon */
    int icon_x, icon_y;       /* initial position of icon */
    Pixmap icon_mask;         /* icon mask bitmap */
```

```
    XID window_group;        /* id of related window group */
    /* this structure may be extended in the future */
} XWMHints;

typedef struct {
    char *res_name;
    char *res_class;
} XClassHint;
```

Errors

```
BadAlloc
BadWindow
```

Related Commands

XGetClassHints, XGetCommand, XGetWMHints, XGetWMIconName, XGetWMName,
XGetWMNormalHints, XSetWMClientMachine, XSetWMColormapWindows, XSet-
WMProtocols.

XSetWMProtocols

Name

XSetWMProtocols — set a window's WM_PROTOCOLS property.

Synopsis

```
Status XSetWMProtocols(display, w, protocols, count)
    Display *display;
    Window w;
    Atom *protocols;
    int count;
```

Arguments

display   Specifies a connection to an X server; returned from XOpenDisplay.

w   Specifies the window.

protocols   Specifies the list of protocols.

count   Specifies the number of protocols in the list.

Availability

Release 4 and later.

Description

XSetWMProtocols sets the WM_PROTOCOLS property on the specified window to the list of atoms specified by the protocols argument. The property is stored with a type of ATOM and a format of 32. If it cannot intern the WM_PROTOCOLS atom, XSetWMProtocols returns a zero status. Otherwise, it returns a non-zero status.

The list of standard protocols at present is as follows:

WM_TAKE_FOCUS   Assignment of keyboard focus

WM_SAVE_YOURSELF   Save client state warning

WM_DELETE_UNKNOWN   Request to delete top-level window

For more information, see Volume One, Chapter 10, *Interclient Communication*.

Errors

BadAlloc
BadWindow

Related Commands

XGetWMProtocols.

Name

XSetWMSizeHints — set a window's `WM_SIZE_HINTS` property.

Synopsis

```
void XSetWMSizeHints(display, w, hints, property)
    Display *display;
    Window w;
    XSizeHints *hints;
    Atom property;
```

Arguments

display   Specifies a connection to an X server; returned from `XOpenDisplay`.

w   Specifies the window.

hints   Specifies the `XSizeHints` structure to be used.

property   Specifies the property name.

Availability

Release 4 and later.

Description

`XSetWMSizeHints` sets the size hints for the specified property on the named window. The property is stored with a type of `WM_SIZE_HINTS` and a format of 32. To set a window's normal size hints, you can use the `XSetWMNormalHints` function instead. `XSetWMSizeHints` supersedes `XSetSizeHints`.

This routine is useful if new properties of type `XA_WM_SIZE_HINTS` are defined.

The `flags` member of `XSizeHints` must be set to the OR of the symbols representing each member to be set.

For more information, see Volume One, Chapter 10, *Interclient Communication*.

Structures

```
typedef struct {
    long flags;      /* marks which fields in this structure are */
                     /* defined as */
    int x, y;        /* obsolete for new window mgrs, but clients */
    int width, height;  /* should set so old wm's don't mess up */
    int min_width, min_height;
    int max_width, max_height;
    int width_inc, height_inc;
    struct {
            int x;   /* numerator */
            int y;   /* denominator */
    } min_aspect, max_aspect;
    int base_width, base_height;    /* added by ICCCM version 1 */
    int win_gravity;                /* added by ICCCM version 1 */
```

```
} XSizeHints;

#define USPosition (1L << 0) /* user specified x, y */
#define USSize     (1L << 1) /* user specified width, height */

#define PPosition  (1L << 2) /* program specified position
*/
#define PSize      (1L << 3) /* program specified size */
#define PMinSize   (1L << 4) /* program specified minimum size */
#define PMaxSize   (1L << 5) /* program specified maximum size */
#define PResizeInc (1L << 6) /* program specified resize increments *
/
#define PAspect    (1L << 7) /* program specified min/max aspect
ratios */
#define PAllHints (PPosition|PSize|PMinSize|PMaxSize|PResizeInc|PAspect)
#define PBaseSize  (1L << 8) /* program specified base
                                for incrementing */
#define PWinGravity (1L << 9)/* program specified window
                                gravity */
```

Errors

BadAlloc
BadAtom
BadWindow

Related Commands

XAllocSizeHints, XGetWMNormalHints, XGetWMSizeHints, XSetWMNormal-
Hints.

XSetWindowBackground

Xlib – Window Attributes

Name

XSetWindowBackground — set the background pixel value attribute of a window.

Synopsis

```
XSetWindowBackground(display, w, background_pixel)
    Display *display;
    Window w;
    unsigned long background_pixel;
```

Arguments

display   Specifies a connection to an X server; returned from XOpenDisplay.

w   Specifies the window ID. Must be an InputOutput window.

background_pixel

          Specifies which entry in the colormap is used as the background color. The constant CopyFromParent is NOT valid.

Description

XSetWindowBackground sets the background attribute of a window, setting the pixel value to be used to fill the background. This overrides any previous call to XSetWindowBackground or XSetWindowBackgroundPixmap on the same window.

XSetWindowBackground does not change the current window contents immediately. The background is automatically repainted after Expose events. You can also redraw the background without Expose events by calling XClearWindow immediately after.

For more information, see Volume One, Chapter 4, *Window Attributes*.

Errors

BadMatch   Setting background of InputOnly window.

BadWindow

Related Commands

XChangeWindowAttributes, XGetGeometry, XGetWindowAttributes, XSetWindowBackgroundPixmap, XSetWindowBorder, XSetWindowBorderPixmap.

492   *Xlib Reference Manual*

XSetWindowBackgroundPixmap

Name

XSetWindowBackgroundPixmap — change the background tile attribute of a window.

Synopsis

```
XSetWindowBackgroundPixmap(display, w, background_tile)
    Display *display;
    Window w;
    Pixmap background_tile;
```

Arguments

display Specifies a connection to an X server; returned from XOpenDisplay.

w   Specifies the window ID. Must be an InputOutput class window.

background_tile
    Specifies a pixmap ID, None or ParentRelative, to be used as a background.

Description

XSetWindowBackgroundPixmap sets the background_pixmap attribute of a window. This overrides any previous background_pixel or background_pixmap attribute setting set with XSetWindowBackgroundPixmap, XSetWindowBackground, or XChangeWindowAttributes. Drawing into the pixmap that was set as the background pixmap attribute has an undefined effect on the window background. The server may or may not make a copy of the pixmap.

If the background is set to a pixmap, the background is tiled with the pixmap. If the pixmap is not explicitly referenced again, it can be freed, since a copy is maintained in the server. The background of the window will not be redrawn with the new tile until the next Expose event or XClearWindow call.

If the background is set to None, The window background initially will be invisible and will share the bits of its parent, but only if the background_pixel attribute is not set. When anything is drawn by any client into the area enclosed by the window, the contents will remain until the area is explicitly cleared with XClearWindow. The background is not automatically refreshed after exposure.

If the background is set to ParentRelative, the parent's background is used, and the origin for tiling is the parent's origin (or the parent's parent if the parent's background_pixmap attribute is also ParentRelative, and so on). The difference between setting Parent-Relative and explicitly setting the same pixmap as the parent is the origin of the tiling. The difference between ParentRelative and None is that for ParentRelative the background is automatically repainted on exposure.

For ParentRelative, the window must have the same depth as the parent, or a BadMatch error will occur. If the parent has background None, then the window will also have background None. The parent's background is re-examined each time the window background is required (when it needs to be redrawn due to mapping or exposure). The window's contents will be lost when the window is moved relative to its parent, and the contents will have to be redrawn.

Changing the `background_pixmap` attribute of the root window to `None` or `Parent-Relative` restores the default.

`XSetWindowBackgroundPixmap` can only be performed on an `InputOutput` window. A `BadMatch` error will result otherwise.

`XSetWindowBackground` may be used if a solid color instead of a tile is desired.

For more information, see Volume One, Chapter 4, *Window Attributes*.

Errors
    BadMatch
    BadPixmap
    BadWindow

Related Commands
    XCreateBitmapFromData, XCreatePixmap, XCreatePixmapFromBitmapData,
    XFreePixmap, XQueryBestSize, XQueryBestStipple, XQueryBestTile,
    XReadBitmapFile, XSetTile, XSetWindowBorderPixmap, XWriteBitmapFile.

XSetWindowBorder

Name

XSetWindowBorder — change a window border pixel value attribute and repaint the border.

Synopsis

```
XSetWindowBorder(display, w, border_pixel)
    Display *display;
    Window w;
    unsigned long border_pixel;
```

Arguments

display   Specifies a connection to an X server; returned from XOpenDisplay.

w   Specifies the window ID. Must be an InputOutput window.

border_pixel
              Specifies the colormap entry with which the server will paint the border.

Description

XSetWindowBorder sets the border_pixel attribute of window w to a pixel value, and repaints the border. The border is also automatically repainted after Expose events.

Use XSetWindowBorderPixmap to create a tiled border. On top-level windows, the window manager often resets the border, so applications should not depend on their settings.

For more information, see Volume One, Chapter 4, *Window Attributes*.

Errors

BadMatch   Setting border of InputOnly window.

BadWindow

Related Commands

XChangeWindowAttributes, XGetGeometry, XGetWindowAttributes, XSet-
WindowBackground, XSetWindowBackgroundPixmap, XSetWindowBorder-
Pixmap.

Name

XSetWindowBorderPixmap — change a window border tile attribute and repaint the border.

Synopsis

```
XSetWindowBorderPixmap(display, w, border_tile)
    Display *display;
    Window w;
    Pixmap border_tile;
```

Arguments

display   Specifies a connection to an X server; returned from XOpenDisplay.

w   Specifies the ID of an InputOutput window whose border is to be to a file.

border_tile Specifies any pixmap or None.

Description

XSetWindowBorderPixmap sets the border_pixmap attribute of a window and repaints the border. The border_tile can be freed immediately after the call if no further explicit references to it are to be made.

This function can only be performed on an InputOutput window. On top-level windows, the window manager often resets the border, so applications should not depend on their settings.

Errors

```
BadMatch
BadPixmap
BadWindow
```

Related Commands

XCreateBitmapFromData, XCreatePixmap, XCreatePixmapFromBitmapData, XFreePixmap, XQueryBestSize, XQueryBestStipple, XQueryBestTile, XReadBitmapFile, XSetTile, XSetWindowBackgroundPixmap, XWriteBitmapFile.

XSetWindowBorderWidth

Name

XSetWindowBorderWidth — change the border width of a window.

Synopsis

```
XSetWindowBorderWidth(display, w, width)
    Display *display;
    Window w;
    unsigned int width;
```

Arguments

display   Specifies a connection to an X server; returned from XOpenDisplay.

w   Specifies the ID of the window whose border is to be changed.

width   Specifies the width of the window border.

Description

XSetWindowBorderWidth changes the border width of a window. This request is often used on top-level windows by the window manager as an indication of the current keyboard focus window, so other clients should not depend on the border width of top-level windows.

Errors

BadMatch   Setting border width of an InputOnly window.

BadWindow

Related Commands

XCirculateSubwindows, XCirculateSubwindowsDown, XCirculate-SubwindowsUp, XConfigureWindow, XLowerWindow, XMoveResizeWindow, XMoveWindow, XQueryTree, XRaiseWindow, XReparentWindow, XResize-Window, XRestackWindows.

XSetWindowColormap

Name

XSetWindowColormap — set the colormap attribute for a window.

Synopsis

```
XSetWindowColormap(display, w, cmap)
    Display *display;
    Window w;
    Colormap cmap;
```

Arguments

display   Specifies a connection to an X server; returned from XOpenDisplay.

w   Specifies the ID of the window for which you want to set the colormap.

cmap   Specifies the colormap.

Description

XSetWindowColormap sets the colormap attribute of the specified window. The colormap need not be installed to be set as an attribute. cmap will be used to translate pixel values drawn into this window when cmap is installed in the hardware, which will be taken care of by the window manager.

In Release 3, applications must install their own colormaps if they cannot use the default colormap. In Release 4, they should never do so.

The colormap must have the same visual as the window.

Errors

```
BadColormap
BadMatch
BadWindow
```

Related Commands

XChangeWindowAttributes, XGetGeometry, XGetWindowAttributes, XSet-WindowBackground, XSetWindowBackgroundPixmap, XSetWindowBorder, XSetWindowBorderPixmap, XSetWMColormapWindows.

XSetWMHints

Name
XSetWMHints — set a window manager hints property.

Synopsis
```
XSetWMHints(display, w, wmhints)
    Display *display;
    Window w;
    XWMHints *wmhints;
```

Arguments
display   Specifies a connection to an X server; returned from XOpenDisplay.

w   Specifies the ID for which window manager hints are to be set.

wmhints   Specifies a pointer to the window manager hints.

Description
XSetWMHints sets the window manager hints that include icon information and location, the initial state of the window, and whether the application relies on the window manager to get keyboard input.

This function is unnecessary in Release 4 if you call XSetWMProperties.

See Volume One, Chapter 10, *Interclient Communication*, for a description of each XWMHints structure member.

Structures
```
typedef struct {
    long flags;             /* marks defined fields in structure */
    Bool input;             /* does application need window manager for
                             * keyboard input */
    int initial_state;      /* see below */
    Pixmap icon_pixmap;     /* pixmap to be used as icon */
    Window icon_window;     /* window to be used as icon */
    int icon_x, icon_y;     /* initial position of icon */
    Pixmap icon_mask;       /* icon mask bitmap */
    XID window_group;       /* ID of related window group */
    /* this structure may be extended in the future */
} XWMHints;

/* definitions for the flags field: */
#define InputHint           (1L << 0)
#define StateHint           (1L << 1)
#define IconPixmapHint      (1L << 2)
#define IconWindowHint      (1L << 3)
#define IconPositionHint    (1L << 4)
#define IconMaskHint        (1L << 5)
#define WindowGroupHint     (1L << 6)
#define AllHints (InputHint|StateHint|IconPixmapHint|IconWindowHint| \
    IconPositionHint|IconMaskHint|WindowGroupHint)
```

```
/* definitions for the initial state flag: */
#define DontCareState   0     /* don't know or care */
#define NormalState     1     /* most applications want to start this way */
#define ZoomState       2     /* application wants to start zoomed */
#define IconicState     3     /* application wants to start as an icon */
#define InactiveState   4     /* application believes it is seldom used;
                                 some wm's may put it on inactive menu */
```

Errors

```
BadAlloc
BadWindow
```

Related Commands

XAllocWMHints, XFetchName, XGetClassHint, XGetIconName, XGetIcon-
Sizes, XGetNormalHints, XGetSizeHints, XGetTransientForHint, XGet-
WMHints, XGetZoomHints, XSetClassHint, XSetCommand. XSetIconName,
XSetIconSizes, XSetNormalHints, XSetSizeHints, XSetTransientForHint,
XSetZoomHints, XStoreName, XSetWMProperties.

Name

XSetZoomHints — set the size hints property of a zoomed window.

Synopsis

```
XSetZoomHints(display, w, zhints)
    Display *display;
    Window w;
    XSizeHints *zhints;
```

Arguments

display   Specifies a connection to an X server; returned from XOpenDisplay.

w   Specifies the ID of the window for which zoom hints are to be set.

zhints   Specifies a pointer to the zoom hints.

Description

XSetZoomHints is no longer used as of Release 3.

XSetZoomHints sets the XA_WM_ZOOM_HINTS property for an application's top-level window in its zoomed state. Many window managers think of windows in three states: iconified, normal, or zoomed, corresponding to small, medium, and large. Applications use XSetZoom-Hints to inform the window manager of the size or position desirable for the zoomed window.

In addition, an application wanting to move or resize its zoomed window should call XSet-ZoomHints specifying its new desired location and size, in addition to making direct X calls to move or resize. This is because some window managers may redirect window configuration requests, but ignore the resulting events and pay attention to property changes instead.

To set size hints, an application must assign values to the appropriate elements in the hints structure, and set the flags field of the structure to indicate which members have assigned values and the source of the assignment. These flags are listed in the Structures section below.

For more information on using hints, see Volume One, Chapter 10, *Interclient Communication*.

Structures

```
typedef struct {
    long flags;                    /* marks defined fields in structure */
    int x, y;
    int width, height;
    int min_width, min_height;
    int max_width, max_height;
    int width_inc, height_inc;
    struct {
        int x;                     /* numerator */
        int y;                     /* denominator */
    } min_aspect, max_aspect;
    /* new fields in R4 */
} XSizeHints;
```

```
/* flags argument in size hints */
#define USPosition (1L << 0)   /* user specified x, y */
#define USSize     (1L << 1)   /* user specified width, height */

#define PPosition  (1L << 2)   /* program specified position */
#define PSize      (1L << 3)   /* program specified size */
#define PMinSize   (1L << 4)   /* program specified minimum size */
#define PMaxSize   (1L << 5)   /* program specified maximum size */
#define PResizeInc (1L << 6)   /* program specified resize increments */
#define PAspect    (1L << 7)   /* program specified min/max aspect ratios */
#define PAllHints (PPosition|PSize|PMinSize|PMaxSize|PResizeInc|PAspect)
```

Errors

BadAlloc
BadWindow

Related Commands

XFetchName, XGetClassHint, XGetIconName, XGetIconSizes, XGetNormal-
Hints, XGetSizeHints, XGetTransientForHint, XGetWMHints, XGetZoom-
Hints, XSetClassHint, XSetCommand, XSetIconName, XSetIconSizes, XSet-
NormalHints, XSetSizeHints, XSetTransientForHint, XSetWMHints,
XStoreName.

Name

XShrinkRegion — reduce or expand the size of a region.

Synopsis

```
XShrinkRegion(r, dx, dy)
    Region r;
    int dx, dy;
```

Arguments

r   Specifies the region.

dx   Specify the amounts by which you want to shrink or expand the specified

dy   region. Positive values shrink the region while negative values expand the region.

Description

XShrinkRegion changes the width and/or height of the specified region. Positive values shrink the region; negative values expand the region. It is legal to expand the region in one dimension at the same time as shrinking it in the other dimension. The offset of the region is changed to keep the center of the resized region near its original position.

The exact amount of shrinkage for a given value for dx or dy is not specified by Xlib.

Structures

Region is a pointer to an opaque structure type.

Related Commands

XClipBox, XCreateRegion, XDestroyRegion, XEmptyRegion, XEqualRegion, XIntersectRegion, XOffsetRegion, XPointInRegion, XPolygonRegion, XRectInRegion, XSetRegion, XSubtractRegion, XUnionRectWithRegion, XUnionRegion, XXorRegion.

XStoreBuffer

Name

XStoreBuffer — store data in a cut buffer.

Synopsis

```
XStoreBuffer(display, bytes, nbytes, buffer)
    Display *display;
    char bytes[];
    int nbytes;
    int buffer;
```

Arguments

display   Specifies a connection to an X server; returned from XOpenDisplay.

bytes   Specifies the string of bytes you want stored. The byte string is not necessarily ASCII or null-terminated.

nbytes   Specifies the number of bytes in the string.

buffer   Specifies the cut buffer in which to store the byte string. Must be in the range 0-7.

Description

XStoreBuffer stores the specified data into any one of the eight cut buffers. All eight buffers must be stored into before they can be circulated with XRotateBuffers. The cut buffers are numbered 0 through 7. Use XFetchBuffer to recover data from any cut buffer.

Note that selections are the preferred method of transferring data between applications.

For more information on cut buffers, see Volume One, Chapter 13, *Other Programming Techniques*. For more information on selections, see Volume One, Chapter 10, *Interclient Communication*.

Errors

BadAlloc
BadAtom

Related Commands

XFetchBuffer, XFetchBytes, XRotateBuffers, XStoreBytes.

XStoreBytes

Name
XStoreBytes — store data in cut buffer 0.

Synopsis
```
XStoreBytes(display, bytes, nbytes)
    Display *display;
    char bytes[];
    int nbytes;
```

Arguments

display   Specifies a connection to an X server; returned from XOpenDisplay.

bytes   Specifies the string of bytes to store. The byte string is not necessarily ASCII or null-terminated.

nbytes   Specifies the number of bytes to store.

Description

XStoreBytes stores data in cut buffer 0, usually for reading by another client that already knows the meaning of the contents. Note that the cut buffer's contents need not be text, so null bytes are not special.

The cut buffer's contents may be retrieved later by any client calling XFetchBytes.

Use XStoreBuffer to store data in buffers 1-7. Note that selections are the preferred method of transferring data between applications.

For more information on cut buffers, see Volume One, Chapter 13, *Other Programming Techniques*. For more information on selections, see Volume One, Chapter 10, *Interclient Communication*.

Errors
BadAlloc

Related Commands

XFetchBuffer, XFetchBytes, XRotateBuffers, XStoreBuffer.

Name

XStoreColor — set or change the RGB values of a read/write colormap entry to the closest possible hardware color.

Synopsis

```
XStoreColor(display, cmap, colorcell_def)
    Display *display;
    Colormap cmap;
    XColor *colorcell_def;
```

Arguments

display   Specifies a connection to an X server; returned from XOpenDisplay.

cmap   Specifies the colormap.

colorcell_def   Specifies a pixel value and the desired RGB values.

Description

XStoreColor changes the RGB values of a colormap entry specified by colorcell_def.pixel to the closest values possible on the hardware. This pixel value must be a read/write cell and a valid index into cmap. XStoreColor changes the red, green, and/or blue color components in the cell according to the colorcell_def.flags member, which you set by ORing the constants DoRed, DoGreen, and/or DoBlue.

If the colormap is an installed map for its screen, the changes are visible immediately.

For more information, see Volume One, Chapter 7, *Color*.

Structures

```
typedef struct {
    unsigned long pixel;
    unsigned short red, green, blue;
    char flags;                        /* DoRed, DoGreen, DoBlue */
    char pad;
} XColor;
```

Errors

BadAccess   A specified pixel is unallocated or read-only.

BadColormap

BadValue   pixel not valid index into cmap.

Related Commands

BlackPixel, WhitePixel, XAllocColor, XAllocColorCells, XAllocColor-
Planes, XAllocNamedColor, XFreeColors, XLookupColor, XParseColor,
XQueryColor, XQueryColors, XStoreColors, XStoreNamedColor.

Name

XStoreColors — set or change the RGB values of read/write colorcells to the closest possible hardware colors.

Synopsis

```
XStoreColors(display, cmap, colorcell_defs, ncolors)
    Display *display;
    Colormap cmap;
    XColor colorcell_defs[ncolors];
    int ncolors;
```

Arguments

display   Specifies a connection to an X server; returned from XOpenDisplay.

cmap   Specifies the colormap.

colorcell_defs
      Specifies an array of color definition structures.

ncolors   Specifies the number of XColor structures in colorcell_defs.

Description

XStoreColors changes the RGB values of each colormap entry specified by color-cell_defs[].pixel to the closest possible hardware colors. Each pixel value must be a read/write cell and a valid index into cmap. XStoreColors changes the red, green, and/or blue color components in each cell according to the colorcell_defs[].flags member, which you set by ORing the constants DoRed, DoGreen, and/or DoBlue. The specified pixels are changed if they are writable by any client, even if one or more pixels generates an error.

If the colormap is an installed map for its screen, the changes are visible immediately. For more information, see Volume One, Chapter 7, *Color*.

Structures

```
typedef struct {
    unsigned long pixel;
    unsigned short red, green, blue;
    char flags;                        /* DoRed, DoGreen, DoBlue */
    char pad;
} XColor;
```

Errors

BadAccess   A specified pixel is unallocated or read-only.

BadColormap

BadValue   A specified pixel is not a valid entry into cmap.

Related Commands

BlackPixel, WhitePixel, XAllocColor, XAllocColorCells, XAllocColor-Planes, XAllocNamedColor, XFreeColors, XLookupColor, XParseColor, XQueryColor, XQueryColors, XStoreColor, XStoreNamedColor.

XStoreName

Xlib – Window Manager Hints –

Name

XStoreName — assign a name to a window for the window manager.

Synopsis

```
XStoreName(display, w, window_name)
    Display *display;
    Window w;
    char *window_name;
```

Arguments

display   Specifies a connection to an X server; returned from XOpenDisplay.

w   Specifies the ID of the window to which you want to assign a name.

window_name Specifies the name of the window. The name should be a null-terminated string. This name is returned by any subsequent call to XFetchName.

Description

XStoreName is superceded in Release 4 by XSetWMName.

XStoreName sets the XA_WM_NAME property, which should be used by the application to communicate the following information to the window manager, according to current conventions:

• To permit the user to identify one of a number of instances of the same client.

• To provide the user with noncritical state information.

Clients can assume that at least the beginning of this string is visible to the user.

The XA_WM_CLASS property, on the other hand, has two members which should be used to identify the application's instance and class name, for the lookup of resources. See XSetClassHint for details.

For more information, see Volume One, Chapter 10, *Interclient Communication*.

Errors

```
BadAlloc
BadWindow
```

Related Commands

XFetchName, XGetClassHint, XGetIconName, XGetIconSizes, XGetNormalHints, XGetSizeHints, XGetTransientForHint, XGetWMHints, XGetZoomHints, XSetClassHint, XSetCommand, XSetIconName, XSetIconSizes, XSetNormalHints, XSetSizeHints, XSetTransientForHint, XSetWMHints, XSetZoomHints.

508   Xlib Reference Manual

Name

XStoreNamedColor — set RGB values of a read/write colorcell by color name.

Synopsis

```
XStoreNamedColor(display, cmap, colorname, pixel, flags)
    Display *display;
    Colormap cmap;
    char *colorname;
    unsigned long pixel;
    int flags;
```

Arguments

display   Specifies a connection to an X server; returned from XOpenDisplay.

cmap   Specifies the colormap.

colorname   Specifies the color name string (for example, "red"). This cannot be in hex format (as used in XParseColor). Upper or lower case is not important. The string should be in ISO LATIN-1 encoding, which means that the first 128 character codes are ASCII, and the second 128 character codes are for special characters needed in western languages other than English.

pixel   Specifies the entry in the colormap to store color in.

flags   Specifies which red, green, and blue indexes are set.

Description

XStoreNamedColor looks up the named *color* in the database, with respect to the screen associated with *cmap*, then stores the result in the read/write colorcell of *cmap* specified by *pixel*. Upper or lower case in name does not matter. The *flags* argument, a bitwise OR of the constants DoRed, DoGreen, and DoBlue, determines which subfields within the pixel value in the cell are written.

For more information, see Volume One, Chapter 7, *Color*.

Errors

BadAccess   *pixel* is unallocated or read-only.

BadColormap

BadName   *colorname* is not in server's color database.

BadValue   *pixel* is not a valid index into *cmap*.

Related Commands

DefaultColormap, DisplayCells, XCopyColormapAndFree, XCreate-
Colormap, XFreeColormap, XGetStandardColormap, XInstallColormap,
XListInstalledColormaps, XSetStandardColormap, XSetWindowColormap,
XUninstallColormap.

Name

XStringListToTextProperty — set the specified list of strings to an XTextProperty structure.

Synopsis

```
Status XStringListToTextProperty(list, count, text_prop)
    char **list;
    int count;
    XTextProperty *text_prop;     /* RETURN */
```

Arguments

list   Specifies a list of null-terminated character strings.

count   Specifies the number of strings.

text_prop   Returns the XTextProperty structure.

Availability

Release 4 and later.

Description

XStringListToTextProperty fills the specified XTextProperty structure so that it represents a property of type STRING (format 8) with a value representing the concatenation of the specified list of null-separated character strings. An extra byte containing NULL (which is not included in the nitems member) is stored at the end of the value field of text_prop. If insufficient memory is available for the new value string, XStringListToTextProperty does not set any fields in the XTextProperty structure and returns a zero status. Otherwise, it returns a non-zero status. To free the storage for the value field, use XFree.

For more information, see Volume One, Chapter 10, *Interclient Communication*.

Structures

```
typedef struct {
    unsigned char *value;           /* same as Property routines */
    Atom encoding;                  /* prop type */
    int format;                     /* prop data format: 8, 16, or 32 */
    unsigned long nitems;           /* number of data items in value */
} XTextProperty;
```

Related Commands

XSetTextProperty,   XGetTextProperty,   XTextPropertyToStringList,
XFreeStringList.

XStringToKeysym

Name

XStringToKeysym — convert a keysym name string to a keysym.

Synopsis

```
KeySym XStringToKeysym(string)
    char *string;
```

Arguments

string   Specifies the name of the keysym that is to be converted.

Description

XStringToKeysym translates the character string version of a keysym name ("Shift") to the matching keysym which is a constant (XK_Shift). Valid keysym names are listed in *<X11/keysymdef.h>*. If the specified string does not match a valid keysym, XString-ToKeysym returns NoSymbol.

This string is not the string returned in the *buffer* argument of XLookupString, which can be set with XRebindKeysym. If that string is used, XStringToKeysym will return No-Symbol except by coincidence.

In Release 4, XStringToKeysym can return keysyms that are not defined by the Xlib standard. Note that the set of keysyms that are available in this manner and the mechanisms by which Xlib obtains them is implementation dependent. (In the MIT sample implementation, the resource file */usr/lib/X11/XKeysymDB* is used starting in Release 4. The keysym name is used as the resource name, and the resource value is the keysym value in uppercase hexadecimal.)

For more information, see Volume One, Chapter 9, *The Keyboard and Pointer*.

Related Commands

XChangeKeyboardMapping, XDeleteModifiermapEntry, XFreeModifiermap, XGetKeyboardMapping, XGetModifierMapping, XInsertModifiermapEntry, XKeycodeToKeysym, XKeysymToKeycode, XKeysymToString, XLookupKeysym, XLookupString, XNewModifierMap, XQueryKeymap, XRebindKeysym, XRefreshKeyboardMapping, XSetModifierMapping.

Name

XSubImage — create a subimage from part of an image.

Synopsis

```
XImage *XSubImage(ximage, x, y, subimage_width, subimage_height)
    XImage *ximage;
    int x;y;
    unsigned int subimage_width;subimage_height;
```

Arguments

ximage   Specifies a pointer to the image.

x   Specify the x and y coordinates in the existing image where the subimage will be
y   extracted.

subimage_width
subimage_height
        Specify the width and height (in pixels) of the new subimage.

Description

XSubImage creates a new image that is a subsection of an existing one. It allocates the memory necessary for the new XImage structure and returns a pointer to the new image. The data is copied from the source image, and the rectangle defined by x, y, subimage_width, and subimage_height must by contained in the image.

XSubImage extracts a subimage from an image, while XGetSubImage extracts an image from a drawable.

For more information on images, see Volume One, Chapter 6, *Drawing Graphics and Text*.

Related Commands

ImageByteOrder, XAddPixel, XCreateImage, XDestroyImage, XGetImage, XGetPixel, XGetSubImage, XPutImage, XPutPixel.

Name

XSubtractRegion — subtract one region from another.

Synopsis

```
XSubtractRegion(sra, srb, dr)
    Region sra, srb;
    Region dr;                      /* RETURN */
```

Arguments

sra   Specify the two regions in which you want to perform the computation.

srb

dr   Returns the result of the computation.

Description

XSubtractRegion calculates the difference between the two regions specified (*sra* – *srb*) and puts the result in *dr*.

This function returns a region which contains all parts of *sra* that are not also in *srb*.

For more information on regions, see Volume One, Chapter 6, *Drawing Graphics and Text*.

Structures

Region is a pointer to an opaque structure type.

Related Commands

XClipBox, XCreateRegion, XDestroyRegion, XEmptyRegion, XEqualRegion, XIntersectRegion, XOffsetRegion, XPointInRegion, XPolygonRegion, XRectInRegion, XSetRegion, XShrinkRegion, XUnionRectWithRegion, XUnionRegion, XXorRegion.

XSync

Name

XSync — flush the request buffer and wait for all events and errors to be processed by the server.

Synopsis

```
XSync(display, discard)
    Display *display;
    int discard;
```

Arguments

display   Specifies a connection to an X server; returned from XOpenDisplay.

discard   Specifies whether XSync discards all events on the input queue. This argument is either True or False.

Description

XSync flushes the request buffer, then waits until all events and errors resulting from previous calls have been received and processed by the X server. Events are placed on the input queue. The client's XError routine is called once for each error received.

If discard is True, XSync discards all events on the input queue (including those events that were on the queue before XSync was called).

XSync is sometimes used with window manipulation functions (by the window manager) to wait for all resulting exposure events. Very few clients need to use this function.

Related Commands

XFlush.

XSynchronize

Name

XSynchronize — enable or disable synchronization for debugging.

Synopsis

```
int (*XSynchronize(display, onoff))()
    Display *display;
    Bool onoff;
```

Arguments

display Specifies a connection to an X server; returned from XOpenDisplay.

onoff   Specifies whether to enable or disable synchronization. You can pass False (normal asynchronous mode) or True (enable synchronization for debugging).

Description

XSynchronize turns on or off synchronous mode for debugging. If onoff is True, it turns on synchronous behavior; False resets the state to normal mode.

When events are synchronized, they are reported as they occur instead of at some later time, but server performance is many times slower. This can be useful for debugging complex event handling routines. Under UNIX, the same result can be achieved without hardcoding by setting the global variable _Xdebug to True from within a debugger.

XSynchronize returns the previous after function.

For more information, see Volume One, Chapter 3, *Basic Window Program*.

Related Commands

QLength, XAllowEvents, XCheckIfEvent, XCheckMaskEvent, XCheckTyped-
Event, XCheckTypedWindowEvent, XCheckWindowEvent, XEventsQueued,
XGetInputFocus, XGetMotionEvents, XIfEvent, XMaskEvent, XNextEvent,
XPeekEvent, XPeekIfEvent, XPending, XPutBackEvent, XSelectInput,
XSendEvent, XSetInputFocus, XWindowEvent.

Name

XTextExtents — get string and font metrics locally.

Synopsis

```
XTextExtents(font_struct, string, nchars, direction,
        ascent, descent, overall)
    XFontStruct *font_struct;
    char *string;
    int nchars;
    int *direction;                 /* RETURN */
    int *ascent, *descent;          /* RETURN */
    XCharStruct *overall;           /* RETURN */
```

Arguments

font_struct   Specifies a connection to an XFontStruct structure.

string   Specifies the character string for which metrics are to be returned.

nchars   Specifies the number of characters in the character string.

direction   Returns the value of the direction element of the XFontStruct. Either FontRightToLeft or FontLeftToRight.

ascent   Returns the font ascent element of the XFontStruct. This is the overall maximum ascent for the font.

descent   Returns the font descent element of the XFontStruct. This is the overall maximum descent for the font.

overall   Returns the overall characteristics of the string. These are the sum of the width measurements for each character, the maximum ascent and descent, the minimum lbearing added to the width of all characters up to the character with the smallest lbearing, and the maximum rbearing added to the width of all characters up to the character with the largest rbearing.

Description

XTextExtents returns the dimensions in pixels that specify the bounding box of the specified string of characters in the named font, and the maximum ascent and descent for the entire font. This function performs the size computation locally and, thereby, avoids the roundtrip overhead of XQueryTextExtents, but it requires a filled XFontStruct.

ascent and descent return information about the font, while overall returns information about the given string. The returned ascent and descent should usually be used to calculate the line spacing, while the width, rbearing, and lbearing members of overall should be used for horizontal measures. The total height of the bounding rectangle, good for any string in this font, is ascent + descent.

overall.ascent is the maximum of the ascent metrics of all characters in the string. The overall.descent is the maximum of the descent metrics. The overall.width is the sum of the character-width metrics of all characters in the string. The overall.lbearing is the lbearing of the character in the string with the smallest lbearing plus the width of all the characters up to but not including that character. The *overall.rbearing* is the rbearing of the character in the string with the largest rbearing plus the width of all the characters up to but not including that character.

For more information on drawing text, see Volume One, Chapter 6, *Drawing Graphics and Text*.

Structures

```
typedef struct {
    XExtData *ext_data;         /* hook for extension to hang data */
    Font fid;                   /* font ID for this font */
    unsigned direction;         /* hint about direction the font is painted */
    unsigned min_char_or_byte2;/* first character */
    unsigned max_char_or_byte2;/* last character */
    unsigned min_byte1;         /* first row that exists */
    unsigned max_byte1;         /* last row that exists */
    Bool all_chars_exist;       /* flag if all characters have nonzero size*/
    unsigned default_char;      /* char to print for undefined character */
    int n_properties;           /* how many properties there are */
    XFontProp *properties;      /* pointer to array of additional properties*/
    XCharStruct min_bounds;     /* minimum bounds over all existing char*/
    XCharStruct max_bounds;     /* minimum bounds over all existing char*/
    XCharStruct *per_char;      /* first_char to last_char information */
    int ascent;                 /* logical extent above baseline for spacing */
    int descent;                /* logical descent below baseline for spacing */
} XFontStruct;

typedef struct {
    short lbearing;             /* origin to left edge of character */
    short rbearing;             /* origin to right edge of character */
    short width;                /* advance to next char's origin */
    short ascent;               /* baseline to top edge of character */
    short descent;              /* baseline to bottom edge of character */
    unsigned short attributes;  /* per char flags (not predefined) */
} XCharStruct;
```

Related Commands

XDrawImageString, XDrawImageString16, XDrawString, XDrawString16, XDrawText, XDrawText16, XQueryTextExtents, XQueryTextExtents16, XTextExtents16, XTextWidth, XTextWidth16.

Name

XTextExtents16 — get string and font metrics of a 16-bit character string, locally.

Synopsis

```
XTextExtents16(font_struct, string, nchars, direction,
        ascent, descent, overall)
    XFontStruct *font_struct;
    XChar2b *string;
    int nchars;
    int *direction;            /* RETURN */
    int *ascent, *descent;     /* RETURN */
    XCharStruct *overall;      /* RETURN */
```

Arguments

font_struct   Specifies a connection to an XFontStruct structure.

string   Specifies the character string made up of XChar26 structures.

nchars   Specifies the number of characters in the character string.

direction   Returns the value of the direction element of the XFontStruct. Font-RightToLeft of FontLeftToRight.

ascent   Returns the font ascent element of the XFontStruct. This is the overall maximum ascent for the font.

descent   Returns the font descent element of the XFontStruct. This is the overall maximum descent for the font.

overall   Returns the overall characteristics of the string. These are the sum of the width measurements for each character, the maximum ascent and descent, the minimum lbearing added to the width of all characters up to the character with the smallest lbearing, and the maximum rbearing added to the width of all characters up to the character with the largest rbearing.

Description

XTextExtents16 returns the dimensions in pixels that specify the bounding box of the specified string of characters in the named font, and the maximum ascent and descent for the entire font. This function performs the size computation locally and, thereby, avoids the roundtrip overhead of XQueryTextExtents16, but it requires a filled XFontStruct.

ascent and descent return information about the font, while overall returns information about the given string. The returned ascent and descent should usually be used to calculate the line spacing, while the width, rbearing, and lbearing members of overall should be used for horizontal measures. The total height of the bounding rectangle, good for any string in this font, is ascent + descent.

overall.ascent is the maximum of the ascent metrics of all characters in the string. The overall.descent is the maximum of the descent metrics. The overall.width is the sum of the character-width metrics of all characters in the string. The overall.lbearing is the `lbearing` of the character in the string with the smallest `lbearing` plus the width of all the characters up to but not including that character. The *overall.rbearing* is the `rbearing` of the character in the string with the largest `rbearing` plus the width of all the characters up to but not including that character.

For more information on drawing text, see Volume One, Chapter 6, *Drawing Graphics and Text*.

Structures

```
typedef struct {
    short lbearing;              /* origin to left edge of character */
    short rbearing;              /* origin to right edge of character */
    short width;                 /* advance to next char's origin */
    short ascent;                /* baseline to top edge of character */
    short descent;               /* baseline to bottom edge of character */
    unsigned short attributes;   /* per char flags (not predefined) */
} XCharStruct;

typedef struct {
    XExtData *ext_data;          /* hook for extension to hang data */
    Font fid;                    /* font ID for this font */
    unsigned direction;          /* hint about direction the font is painted */
    unsigned min_char_or_byte2;  /* first character */
    unsigned max_char_or_byte2;  /* last character */
    unsigned min_byte1;          /* first row that exists */
    unsigned max_byte1;          /* last row that exists */
    Bool all_chars_exist;        /* flag if all characters have nonzero size*/
    unsigned default_char;       /* char to print for undefined character */
    int n_properties;            /* how many properties there are */
    XFontProp *properties;       /* pointer to array of additional properties*/
    XCharStruct min_bounds;      /* minimum bounds over all existing char*/
    XCharStruct max_bounds;      /* minimum bounds over all existing char*/
    XCharStruct *per_char;       /* first_char to last_char information */
    int ascent;                  /* logical extent above baseline for spacing */
    int descent;                 /* logical descent below baseline for spacing */
} XFontStruct;

typedef struct {                 /* normal 16 bit characters are two bytes */
    unsigned char byte1;
    unsigned char byte2;
} XChar2b;
```

Related Commands

`XDrawImageString`, `XDrawImageString16`, `XDrawString`, `XDrawString16`, `XDrawText`, `XDrawText16`, `XQueryTextExtents`, `XQueryTextExtents16`, `XTextExtents`, `XTextWidth`, `XTextWidth16`.

XTextPropertyToStringList

Name

XTextPropertyToStringList — obtain a list of strings from a specified XTextProperty structure.

Synopsis

```
Status XTextPropertyToStringList(text_prop, list, count)
    XTextProperty *text_prop;
    char ***list;      /* RETURN */
    int *count;        /* RETURN */
```

Arguments

text_prop   Specifies the XTextProperty structure to be used.

list   Returns a list of null-terminated character strings.

count   Returns the number of strings.

Availability

Release 4 and later.

Description

XTextPropertyToStringList returns a list of strings representing the null-separated elements of the specified XTextProperty structure. The data in text_prop must be of type STRING and format 8. Multiple elements of the property (for example, the strings in a disjoint text selection) are separated by a NULL (encoding 0). The contents of the property are not null-terminated. If insufficient memory is available for the list and its elements, XTextPropertyToStringList sets no return values and returns a zero status. Otherwise, it returns a non-zero status. To free the storage for the list and its contents, use XFreeStringList.

For more information, see Volume One, Chapter 10, *Interclient Communication*.

Structures

```
typedef struct {
    unsigned char *value;        /* same as Property routines */
    Atom encoding;               /* prop type */
    int format;                  /* prop data format: 8, 16, or 32 */
    unsigned long nitems;        /* number of data items in value */
} XTextProperty;
```

Related Commands

XFreeStringList. XGetTextProperty, XSetTextProperty, XStringListToTextProperty.

XTextWidth

Name

XTextWidth — get the width in pixels of an 8-bit character string, locally.

Synopsis

```
int XTextWidth(font_struct, string, count)
    XFontStruct *font_struct;
    char *string;
    int count;
```

Arguments

font_struct   Specifies the font description structure of the font in which you want to draw
               the string.

string   Specifies the character string whose width is to be returned.

count   Specifies the character count in string.

Description

XTextWidth returns the width in pixels of the specified string using the specified font. This
is the sum of the XCharStruct.width for each character in the string. This is also equivalent to the value of overall.width returned by XQueryTextExtents or XText-
Extents. The calculation is done assuming 8-bit font indexing.

For more information on drawing text, see Volume One, Chapter 6, *Drawing Graphics and
Text*.

Structures

```
typedef struct {
    XExtData *ext_data;          /* hook for extension to hang data */
    Font fid;                    /* font ID for this font */
    unsigned direction;          /* hint about direction the font is painted */
    unsigned min_char_or_byte2;  /* first character */
    unsigned max_char_or_byte2;  /* last character */
    unsigned min_byte1;          /* first row that exists */
    unsigned max_byte1;          /* last row that exists */
    Bool all_chars_exist;        /* flag if all characters have nonzero size*/
    unsigned default_char;       /* char to print for undefined character */
    int n_properties;            /* how many properties there are */
    XFontProp *properties;       /* pointer to array of additional properties*/
    XCharStruct min_bounds;      /* minimum bounds over all existing char*/
    XCharStruct max_bounds;      /* minimum bounds over all existing char*/
    XCharStruct *per_char;       /* first_char to last_char information */
    int ascent;                  /* logical extent above baseline for spacing */
    int descent;                 /* logical descent below baseline for spacing */
} XFontStruct;
```

Related Commands

XDrawImageString, XDrawImageString16, XDrawString, XDrawString16,
XDrawText, XDrawText16, XQueryTextExtents, XQueryTextExtents16,
XTextExtents, XTextExtents16, XTextWidth16.

XTextWidth16

Name

XTextWidth16 — get the width in pixels of a 16-bit character string, locally.

Synopsis

```
int XTextWidth16(font_struct, string, count)
    XFontStruct *font_struct;
    XChar2b *string;
    int count;
```

Arguments

font_struct Specifies the font description structure of the font in which you want to draw the string.

string   Specifies a character string made up of XChar2b structures.

count   Specifies the character count in *string*.

Description

XTextWidth16 returns the width in pixels of the specified string using the specified font. This is the sum of the XCharStruct.width for each character in the string. This is also equivalent to the value of *overall.width* returned by XQueryTextExtents16 or XTextExtents16.

The calculation is done assuming 16-bit font indexing.

For more information on drawing text, see Volume One, Chapter 6, *Drawing Graphics and Text*.

Structures

```
typedef struct {
    XExtData *ext_data;          /* hook for extension to hang data */
    Font fid;                    /* font ID for this font */
    unsigned direction;          /* hint about direction the font is painted */
    unsigned min_char_or_byte2;  /* first character */
    unsigned max_char_or_byte2;  /* last character */
    unsigned min_byte1;          /* first row that exists */
    unsigned max_byte1;          /* last row that exists */
    Bool all_chars_exist;        /* flag if all characters have nonzero size*/
    unsigned default_char;       /* char to print for undefined character */
    int n_properties;            /* how many properties there are */
    XFontProp *properties;       /* pointer to array of additional properties*/
    XCharStruct min_bounds;      /* minimum bounds over all existing char*/
    XCharStruct max_bounds;      /* minimum bounds over all existing char*/
    XCharStruct *per_char;       /* first_char to last_char information */
    int ascent;                  /* logical extent above baseline for spacing */
    int descent;                 /* logical descent below baseline for spacing */
} XFontStruct;
```

Related Commands

XDrawImageString, XDrawImageString16, XDrawString, XDrawString16, XDrawText, XDrawText16, XQueryTextExtents, XQueryTextExtents16, XTextExtents, XTextExtents16, XTextWidth.

522   Xlib Reference Manual

XTranslateCoordinates

Name

XTranslateCoordinates — change the coordinate system from one window to another.

Synopsis

```
Bool XTranslateCoordinates(display, src_w, frame_w, src_x,
        src_y, new_x, new_y, child)
    Display *display;
    Window src_w, frame_w;
    int src_x, src_y;
    int *new_x, *new_y;          /* RETURN */
    Window *child;               /* RETURN */
```

Arguments

display   Specifies a connection to an X server; returned from XOpenDisplay.

src_w   Specifies the ID of the source window.

frame_w   Specifies the ID of the frame of reference window.

src_x
src_y   Specify the x and y coordinates within the source window.

new_x
new_y   Return the translated x and y coordinates within the frame of reference window.

child   If the point is contained in a mapped child of the destination window, then that child ID is returned in *child*.

Description

XTranslateCoordinates translates coordinates from the frame of reference of one window to another.

XTranslateCoordinates returns False and *new_x* and *new_y* are set to zero if *src_w* and *frame_w* are on different screens. In addition, if the coordinates are contained in a mapped child of *frame_w*, then that child is returned in the *child* argument. When src_w and frame_y are on the same screen, XTranslateCoordinates returns True, sets *new_x* and *new_y* to the location of the point relative to *frame_w*, and sets *child* to None.

This should be avoided in most applications since it requires a roundtrip request to the server. Most applications benefit from the window-based coordinate system anyway and don't need global coordinates. Window managers often need to perform a coordinate transformation from the coordinate space of one window to another, or unambiguously determine which subwindow a coordinate lies in. XTranslateCoordinates fulfills this need, while avoiding any race conditions by asking the server to perform this operation.

Errors

BadWindow

Related Commands

XGeometry, XParseGeometry.

XUndefineCursor

Name

XUndefineCursor — disassociate a cursor from a window.

Synopsis

```
XUndefineCursor(display, w)
    Display *display;
    Window w;
```

Arguments

display   Specifies a connection to an X server; returned from XOpenDisplay.

w   Specifies the ID of the window whose cursor is to be undefined.

Description

XUndefineCursor sets the cursor attribute for a window to its parent's cursor, undoing the effect of a previous XDefineCursor for this window. On the root window the default cursor is restored.

Errors

BadWindow

Related Commands

XCreateFontCursor, XCreateGlyphCursor, XCreatePixmapCursor, XDefine-Cursor, XFreeCursor, XQueryBestCursor, XQueryBestSize, XRecolor-Cursor.

Name

XUngrabButton — release a button from a passive grab.

Synopsis

```
XUngrabButton(display, button, modifiers, w)
    Display *display;
    unsigned int button;
    unsigned int modifiers;
    Window w;
```

Arguments

display   Specifies a connection to an X server; returned from XOpenDisplay.

button   Specifies the mouse button to be released from grab. Specify Button1, Button2, Button3, Button4, Button5, or the constant AnyButton, which is equivalent to issuing the ungrab request for all possible buttons.

modifiers   Specifies a set of keymasks. This is a bitwise OR of one or more of the following symbols: ShiftMask, LockMask, ControlMask, Mod1Mask, Mod2Mask, Mod3Mask, Mod4Mask, Mod5Mask, or AnyModifier. AnyModifier is equivalent to issuing the ungrab button request for all possible modifier combinations (including no modifiers).

w   Specifies the ID of the window you want to release the button grab.

Description

XUngrabButton cancels the passive grab on a button/key combination on the specified window if it was grabbed by this client. A *modifiers* of AnyModifier is equivalent to issuing the ungrab request for all possible modifier combinations (including the combination of no modifiers). A *button* of AnyButton is equivalent to issuing the request for all possible buttons. This call has no effect on an active grab.

For more information, see Volume One, Chapter 9, *The Keyboard and Pointer*.

Errors

BadWindow

BadValue   Invalid *button* or *modifiers* mask.

Related Commands

XChangeActivePointerGrab, XGrabButton, XGrabKey, XGrabKeyboard, XGrabPointer, XGrabServer, XUngrabKey, XUngrabKeyboard, XUngrabPointer, XUngrabServer.

Name

XUngrabKey — release a key from a passive grab.

Synopsis

```
XUngrabKey(display, keycode, modifiers, w)
    Display *display;
    int keycode;
    unsigned int modifiers;
    Window w;
```

Arguments

display	Specifies a connection to an X server; returned from XOpenDisplay.
keycode	Specifies the keycode. This keycode maps to the specific key you want to ungrab. Pass either a keycode or AnyKey.
modifiers	Specifies a set of keymasks. This is a bitwise OR of one or more of the following symbols: ShiftMask, LockMask, ControlMask, Mod1Mask, Mod2Mask, Mod3Mask, Mod4Mask, Mod5Mask, or AnyModifier. AnyModifier is equivalent to issuing the ungrab key request for all possible modifier combinations (including no modifiers).
w	Specifies the ID of the window for which you want to ungrab the specified keys.

Description

XUngrabKey cancels the passive grab on the key combination on the specified window if it was grabbed by this client. A modifiers of AnyModifier is equivalent to issuing the request for all possible modifier combinations (including the combination of no modifiers). A keycode of AnyKey is equivalent to issuing the request for all possible nonmodifier key codes. This call has no effect on an active grab.

For more information, see Volume One, Chapter 9, *The Keyboard and Pointer*.

Errors

BadWindow
BadValue Invalid keycode or modifiers mask.

Related Commands

XChangeActivePointerGrab, XGrabButton, XGrabKey, XGrabKeyboard, XGrabPointer, XGrabServer, XUngrabButton, XUngrabKeyboard, XUngrab-Pointer, XUngrabServer.

XUngrabKeyboard

Name

XUngrabKeyboard — release the keyboard from an active grab.

Synopsis

```
XUngrabKeyboard(display, time)
    Display *display;
    Time time;
```

Arguments

display   Specifies a connection to an X server; returned from XOpenDisplay.

time   Specifies the time. Pass either a timestamp, expressed in milliseconds, or the constant CurrentTime. If this time is earlier than the last-keyboard-grab time or later than the current server time, the keyboard will not be ungrabbed.

Description

XUngrabKeyboard releases any active grab on the keyboard by this client. It executes as follows:

- Releases the keyboard and any queued events if this client has it actively grabbed from either XGrabKeyboard or XGrabKey.

- Does not release the keyboard and any queued events if *time* is earlier than the last-keyboard-grab time or is later than the current X server time.

- Generates FocusIn and FocusOut events.

The X server automatically performs an UngrabKeyboard if the *grab_window* (argument to XGrabkey and XGrabkeyboard) that becomes unviewable.

For more information, see Volume One, Chapter 9, *The Keyboard and Pointer*.

Related Commands

XChangeActivePointerGrab, XGrabButton, XGrabKey, XGrabKeyboard, XGrabPointer, XGrabServer, XUngrabButton, XUngrabKey, XUngrabPointer, XUngrabServer.

XUngrabPointer

Name

XUngrabPointer — release the pointer from an active grab.

Synopsis

```
XUngrabPointer(display, time)
    Display *display;
    Time time;
```

Arguments

display   Specifies a connection to an X server; returned from XOpenDisplay.

time   Specifies the time when the grab should take place. Pass either a timestamp,
             expressed in milliseconds, or the constant CurrentTime. If this time is
             earlier than the last-pointer-grab time or later than current server time, the
             pointer will not be grabbed.

Description

XUngrabPointer releases an active grab on the pointer by the calling client. It executes as
follows:

- Releases the pointer and any queued events, if this client has actively grabbed the pointer
  from XGrabPointer, XGrabButton, or from a normal button press.

- Does not release the pointer if the specified time is earlier than the last-pointer-grab time
  or is later than the current X server time.

- Generates EnterNotify and LeaveNotify events.

The X server performs an XUngrabPointer automatically if the event_window or
confine_to window (arguments of XGrabButton and XGrabPointer) becomes not
viewable, or if the confine_to window is moved, completely outside the root window.

For more information, see Volume One, Chapter 9, *The Keyboard and Pointer*.

Related Commands

XChangeActivePointerGrab, XChangePointerControl, XGetPointer-
Control, XGetPointerMapping, XGrabPointer, XQueryPointer, XSet-
PointerMapping, XWarpPointer.

XUngrabServer

Name

XUngrabServer — release the server from grab.

Synopsis

```
XUngrabServer(display)
    Display *display;
```

Arguments

display   Specifies a connection to an X server; returned from XOpenDisplay.

Description

XUngrabServer releases the grabbed server, and begins execution of all the requests queued during the grab. XUngrabServer is called automatically when a client closes its connection.

For more information, see Volume One, Chapter 9, *The Keyboard and Pointer*.

Related Commands

XChangeActivePointerGrab, XGrabButton, XGrabKey, XGrabKeyboard, XGrabPointer, XGrabServer, XUngrabButton, XUngrabKey, XUngrab-Keyboard, XUngrabPointer.

XUninstallColormap

Name

XUninstallColormap — uninstall a colormap; install default if not already installed.

Synopsis

```
XUninstallColormap(display, cmap)
    Display *display;
    Colormap cmap;
```

Arguments

display   Specifies a connection to an X server; returned from XOpenDisplay.

cmap   Specifies the colormap to be uninstalled.

Description

If cmap is an installed map for its screen, it is uninstalled. If the screen's default colormap is not installed, it is installed.

If cmap is an installed map, a ColormapNotify event is generated on every window having this colormap as an attribute. If a colormap is installed as a result of the uninstall, a ColormapNotify event is generated on every window having that colormap as an attribute.

At any time, there is a subset of the installed colormaps, viewed as an ordered list, called the *required list*. The length of the required list is at most the min_maps specified for each screen in the Display structure. When a colormap is installed with XInstallColormap it is added to the head of the required list and the last colormap in the list is removed if necessary to keep the length of the list at min_maps. When a colormap is uninstalled with XUninstall-Colormap and it is in the required list, it is removed from the list. No other actions by the server or the client change the required list. It is important to realize that on all but high-performance workstations, min_maps is likely to be one.

For more information on installing and uninstalling colormaps, see Volume One, Chapter 7, *Color*.

Errors

BadColormap

Related Commands

DefaultColormap, DisplayCells, XCopyColormapAndFree, XCreate-Colormap, XFreeColormap, XGetStandardColormap, XInstallColormap, XListInstalledColormaps, XSetStandardColormap, XSetWindowColormap.

Name

XUnionRectWithRegion — add a rectangle to a region.

Synopsis

```
XUnionRectWithRegion(rectangle, src_region, dest_region)
    XRectangle *rectangle;
    Region src_region;
    Region dest_region;
```

Arguments

rectangle   Specifies the rectangle to add to the region.

src_region   Specifies the source region to be used.

dest_region   Specifies the resulting region. May be the same as *src_region*.

Description

XUnionRectWithRegion computes the destination region from a union of the specified rectangle and the specified source region. The source and destination regions may be the same.

One common application of this function is to simplify the combining of the rectangles specified in contiguous Expose events into a clip_mask in the GC, thus restricting the redrawn areas to the exposed rectangles. Use XUnionRectWithRegion to combine the rectangle in each Expose event into a region, then call XSetRegion. XSetRegion sets the clip_mask in a GC to the region. In this case, *src_region* and *dest_region* would be the same region.

If *src_region* and *dest_region* are not the same region, *src_region* is copied to *dest_region* before the rectangle is added to *dest_region*.

For more information on regions, see Volume One, Chapter 6, *Drawing Graphics and Text*.

Structures

```
typedef struct {
    short x, y;
    unsigned short width, height;
} XRectangle;
```

Region is a pointer to an opaque data type.

Related Commands

XClipBox, XDestroyRegion, XEmptyRegion, XEqualRegion, XIntersect-Region, XOffsetRegion, XPointInRegion, XPolygonRegion, XRectInRegion, XSetRegion, XShrinkRegion, XSubtractRegion, XUnionRegion, XXorRegion.

Name

XUnionRegion — compute the union of two regions.

Synopsis

```
XUnionRegion(sra, srb, dr)
    Region sra, srb;
    Region dr;
```

Arguments

sra
srb
Specify the two regions in which you want to perform the computation.

dr
Returns the result of the computation.

Description

XUnionRegion computes the union of two regions and places the result in *dr*. The resulting region will contain all the area of both the source regions.

For more information on regions, see Volume One, Chapter 6, *Drawing Graphics and Text*.

Structures

Region is a pointer to an opaque structure type.

Related Commands

XClipBox, XCreateRegion, XDestroyRegion, XEmptyRegion, XEqualRegion, XIntersectRegion, XOffsetRegion, XPointInRegion, XPolygonRegion, XRectInRegion, XSetRegion, XShrinkRegion, XSubtractRegion, XUnion-RectWithRegion, XXorRegion.

Name

XUniqueContext — create a new context ID (not graphics context).

Synopsis

```
XContext XUniqueContext()
```

Description

The context manager allows association of arbitrary data with a resource ID. This call creates a unique ID that can be used in subsequent calls to XFindContext, XDeleteContext, and XSaveContext.

For more information on the context manager, see Volume One, Chapter 13, *Other Programming Techniques*.

Structures

```
typedef int XContext;
```

Related Commands

XDeleteContext, XFindContext, XSaveContext.

XUnloadFont

Name

XUnloadFont — unload a font.

Synopsis

```
XUnloadFont(display, font)
    Display *display;
    Font font;
```

Arguments

display   Specifies a connection to an X server; returned from XOpenDisplay.

font   Specifies the ID of the font to be unloaded.

Description

XUnloadFont indicates to the server that this client no longer needs the specified font. The font may be unloaded on the X server if this is the last client that needs the font. In any case, the font should never again be referenced by this client because Xlib destroys the resource ID.

For more information on loading and unloading fonts, see Volume One, Chapter 6, *Drawing Graphics and Text*.

Errors

BadFont

Related Commands

XCreateFontCursor, XFreeFont, XFreeFontInfo, XFreeFontNames, XFree-
FontPath, XGetFontPath, XGetFontProperty, XListFonts, XListFontsWith-
Info, XLoadFont, XLoadQueryFont, XQueryFont, XSetFont, XSetFontPath.

Name

XUnmapSubwindows — unmap all subwindows of a given window.

Synopsis

```
XUnmapSubwindows(display, w)
    Display *display;
    Window w;
```

Arguments

display   Specifies a connection to an X server; returned from `XOpenDisplay`.

w   Specifies the ID of the window whose subwindows are to be unmapped.

Description

XUnmapSubwindows performs an `XUnmapWindow` on all mapped children of *w*, in bottom to top stacking order. (It does not unmap subwindows of subwindows.)

XUnmapSubwindows also generates an `UnmapNotify` event on each subwindow and generates exposure events on formerly obscured windows. This is much more efficient than unmapping many subwindows one at a time, since much of the work need only be performed once for all of the subwindows rather than for each subwindow.

For more information on window mapping, see Volume One, Chapter 2, *X Concepts*.

Errors

`BadWindow`

Related Commands

`XMapRaised`, `XMapSubwindows`, `XMapWindow`, `XUnmapWindow`.

XUnmapWindow

Name

XUnmapWindow — unmap a window.

Synopsis

```
XUnmapWindow (display, w)
    Display *display;
    Window w;
```

Arguments

display   Specifies a connection to an X server; returned from XOpenDisplay.

w   Specifies the window ID.

Description

XUnmapWindow removes *w* and all its descendants from the screen (but does not unmap the descendents). If *w* is already unmapped, XUnmapWindow has no effect. Otherwise, *w* is unmapped and an UnmapNotify event is generated. Normal exposure processing on formerly obscured windows is performed.

Descendants of *w* will not be visible until *w* is mapped again. In other words, the subwindows are still mapped, but are not visible because *w* is unmapped. Unmapping a window will generate exposure events on windows that were formerly obscured by *w*.

For more information on window mapping, see Volume One, Chapter 2, *X Concepts*.

Errors

BadWindow

Related Commands

XMapRaised, XMapSubwindows, XMapWindow, XUnmapSubwindows.

Name

XVisualIDFromVisual — obtain the visual ID from a `Visual`.

Synopsis

```
VisualID XVisualIDFromVisual(visual)
    Visual *visual;
```

Arguments

visual   Specifies the visual type.

Description

`XVisualIDFromVisual` returns the visual ID for the specified visual. This is needed when filling an `XVisualInfo` structure template before calling `XGetVisualInfo`.

For more information, see Volume One, Chapter 10, *Interclient Communication*.

Related Commands

XGetVisualInfo.

Name

XWMGeometry — obtain a window's geometry information.

Synopsis

```
int XWMGeometry(display, screen, user_geom, def_geom, bwidth,
        hints, x, y, width, height, gravity)
    Display *display;
    int screen;
    char *user_geom;
    char *def_geom;
    unsigned int bwidth;
    XSizeHints *hints;
    int *x, *y;          /* RETURN */
    int *width, *height;    /* RETURN */
    int *gravity;           /* RETURN */
```

Arguments

display	Specifies a connection to an X server; returned from XOpenDisplay.
screen	Specifies the screen.
user_geom	Specifies the user-specified geometry or NULL.
def_geom	Specifies the application's default geometry or NULL.
bwidth	Specifies the border width.
hints	Specifies the size hints for the window in its normal state.
x	
y	Return the x and y offsets.
width	
height	Return the width and height determined.
gravity	Returns the window gravity.

Availability

Release 4 and later.

Description

XWMGeometry combines possibly incomplete or nonexistent geometry information (given in the format used by XParseGeometry) specified by the user and by the calling program with complete program-supplied default size hints (usually the ones to be stored in WM_NORMAL_HINTS) and returns the position, size, and gravity (NorthWestGravity, NorthEastGravity, SouthEastGravity or SouthWestGravity) that describe the window. If the base size is not set in the XSizeHints structure, the minimum size is used if set. Otherwise, a base size of zero is assumed. If no minimum size is set in the hints structure, the base size is used. A mask (in the form returned by XParseGeometry) that describes which values came from the user and whether or not the position coordinates are relative to the right and bottom edges is returned (which will have already been accounted for in the x and y values).

Note that invalid user geometry specifications can cause a width or height of zero to be returned. The caller may pass the address of the win_gravity field of the *hints* argument as the *gravity* argument.

For more information, see Volume One, Chapter 10, *Interclient Communication*.

Structures

```
typedef struct {
        long flags;      /* marks which fields in this structure are
                          /* defined */
        int x, y;        /* obsolete for new window mgrs, but clients */
        int width, height;  /* should set so old wm's don't mess up */
        int min_width, min_height;
        int max_width, max_height;
        int width_inc, height_inc;
        struct {
                int x;  /* numerator */
                int y;  /* denominator */
        } min_aspect, max_aspect;
        int base_width, base_height;    /* added by ICCCM version 1 */
        int win_gravity;                /* added by ICCCM version 1 */
} XSizeHints
```

Related Commands

XChangeWindowAttributes, XParseGeometry, XSetWMProperties.

XWarpPointer

Xlib – Pointer –

Name

XWarpPointer — move the pointer to another point on the screen.

Synopsis

```
XWarpPointer(display, src_w, dest_w, src_x, src_y,
        src_width, src_height, dest_x, dest_y)
    Display *display;
    Window src_w, dest_w;
    int src_x, src_y;
    unsigned int src_width, src_height;
    int dest_x, dest_y;
```

Arguments

display	Specifies a connection to an X server; returned from XOpenDisplay.
src_w	Specifies the ID of the source window. You can also pass None.
dest_w	Specifies the ID of the destination window. You can also pass None.
src_x *src_y*	Specify the x and y coordinates within the source window. These are used with *src_width* and *src_height* to determine the rectangle the pointer must be in order to be moved. They are not the present pointer position. If *src_y* is None, these coordinates are relative to the root window of *src_w*.
src_width *src_height*	Specify the width and height in pixels of the source area. Used with *src_x* and *src_y*.
dest_x *dest_y*	Specify the destination x and y coordinates within the destination window. If *dest_y* is None, these coordinates are relative to the root window of *dest_w*.

Description

XWarpPointer moves the pointer suddenly from one point on the screen to another.

If *dest_w* is a window, XWarpPointer moves the pointer to [*dest_x*, *dest_y*] relative to the destination window's origin. If *dest_w* is None, XWarpPointer moves the pointer according to the offsets [*dest_x*, *dest_y*] relative to the current position of the pointer.

If *src_window* is None, the move is independent of the current cursor position (*dest_x* and *dest_y* use global coordinates). If the source window is not None, the move only takes place if the pointer is currently contained in a visible portion of the rectangle of the source window (including its inferiors) specified by *src_x*, *src_y*, *src_width* and *src_height*. If *src_width* is zero (0), the pointer must be between *src_x* and the right edge of the window to be moved. If *src_height* is zero (0), the pointer must be between *src_y* and the bottom edge of the window to be moved.

XWarpPointer cannot be used to move the pointer outside the confine_to window of an active pointer grab. If this is attempted the pointer will be moved to the point on the border of the confine_to window nearest the requested destination.

540   Xlib Reference Manual

`XWarpPointer` generates events as if the user had (instantaneously) moved the pointer.

This function should not be used unless absolutely necessary, and then only in tightly controlled, predictable situations. It has the potential to confuse the user.

Errors
`BadWindow`

Related Commands

`XChangeActivePointerGrab`, `XChangePointerControl`, `XGetPointer-Control`, `XGetPointerMapping`, `XGrabPointer`, `XQueryPointer`, `XSet-PointerMapping`, `XUngrabPointer`.

Name

XWindowEvent — remove the next event that matches the specified mask and window.

Synopsis

```
XWindowEvent(display, w, event_mask, rep)
    Display *display;
    Window w;
    long event_mask;
    XEvent *rep;                    /* RETURN */
```

Arguments

display   Specifies a connection to an X server; returned from XOpenDisplay.

w   Specifies the ID of the window whose next matching event you want.

event_mask   Specifies the event mask. See XSelectInput for a complete list of event masks.

rep   Returns the event removed from the input queue.

Description

XWindowEvent removes the next event in the queue which matches both the passed window and the passed mask. The event is copied into an XEvent structure supplied by the caller. Other events in the queue are not discarded. If no such event has been queued, XWindow-Event flushes the request buffer and waits until one is received.

Structures

See individual event structures described in Volume One, Chapter 8, *Events*, and Appendix F, *Structure Reference* in this volume.

Related Commands

QLength, XAllowEvents, XCheckIfEvent, XCheckMaskEvent, XCheckTyped-Event, XCheckTypedWindowEvent, XCheckWindowEvent, XEventsQueued, XGetInputFocus, XGetMotionEvents, XIfEvent, XMaskEvent, XNextEvent, XPeekEvent, XPeekIfEvent, XPending, XPutBackEvent, XSelectInput, XSendEvent, XSetInputFocus, XSynchronize.

Name

XWithdrawWindow — request that a top-level window be withdrawn.

Synopsis

```
Status XWithdrawWindow(display, w, screen_number)
    Display *display;
    Window w;
    int screen_number;
```

Arguments

display   Specifies a connection to an X server; returned from XOpenDisplay.

w   Specifies the window.

screen_number
               Specifies the appropriate screen number on the server.

Availability

Release 4 and later.

Description

XWithdrawWindow informs the window manager that the specified window and its icon should be unmapped. It unmaps the specified window and sends a synthetic UnmapNotify event to the root window of the specified screen. Window managers may elect to receive this message and may treat it as a request to change the window's state to withdrawn. When a window is in the withdrawn state, neither its normal nor its iconic representation is visible. XWithdrawWindow returns a nonzero status if the UnmapNotify event is successfully sent; otherwise, it returns a zero status.

For more information, see Volume One, Chapter 10, *Interclient Communication*.

Errors

BadWindow

Related Commands

XIconifyWindow, XReconfigureWindow.

XWriteBitmapFile

Name

XWriteBitmapFile — write a bitmap to a file.

Synopsis

```
int XWriteBitmapFile(display, filename, bitmap, width,
        height, x_hot, y_hot)
    Display *display;
    char *filename;
    Pixmap bitmap;
    unsigned int width, height;
    int x_hot, y_hot;
```

Arguments

display	Specifies a connection to an X server; returned from XOpenDisplay.
filename	Specifies the filename to use. The format of the filename is operating system specific.
bitmap	Specifies the bitmap to be written.
width height	Specify the width and height in pixels of the bitmap to be written.
x_hot y_hot	Specify where to place the hotspot coordinates (or –1,–1 if none present) in the file.

Description

XWriteBitmapFile writes a bitmap to a file. The file is written out in X version 11 bitmap file format, shown below.

If the file cannot be opened for writing, XWriteBitmapFile returns BitmapOpen-Failed. If insufficient memory is allocated XWriteBitmapFile returns Bitmap-NoMemory. Otherwise, on no error, XWriteBitmapFile returns BitmapSuccess.

If x_hot and y_hot are not –1, –1, then XWriteBitmapFile writes them out as the hotspot coordinates for the bitmap.

The following is an example of the contents of a bitmap file created. The name used ("gray" in this example) is the portion of filename after the last "/".

```
#define gray_width 16
#define gray_height 16
#define gray_x_hot 8
#define gray_y_hot 8
static char gray_bits[] = {
    0xf8, 0x1f, 0xe3, 0xc7, 0xcf, 0xf3, 0x9f, 0xf9, 0xbf, 0xfd, 0x33, 0xcc,
    0x7f, 0xfe, 0x7f, 0xfe, 0x7e, 0x7e, 0x7f, 0xfe, 0x37, 0xec, 0xbb, 0xdd,
    0x9c, 0x39, 0xcf, 0xf3, 0xe3, 0xc7, 0xf8, 0x1f};
```

For more information on bitmaps, see Volume One, Chapter 6, *Drawing Graphics and Text*.

Errors

BadAlloc

BadDrawable

BadMatch   The specified *width* and *height* did not match dimensions of the specified *bitmap*.

Related Commands

XCreateBitmapFromData, XCreatePixmap, XCreatePixmapFromBitmapData,
XFreePixmap, XQueryBestSize, XQueryBestStipple, XQueryBestTile,
XReadBitmapFile, XSetTile, XSetWindowBackgroundPixmap, XSetWindow-
BorderPixmap.

Name

XXorRegion — calculate the difference between the union and intersection of two regions.

Synopsis

```
XXorRegion(sra, srb, dr)
    Region sra, srb;
    Region dr;                      /* RETURN */
```

Arguments

sra   Specify the two regions on which you want to perform the computation.
srb

dr   Returns the result of the computation.

Description

XXorRegion calculates the union minus the intersection of two regions, and places it in *dr*. Xor is short for "Exclusive OR", meaning that a pixel is included in *dr* if it is set in either *sra* or *srb* but not in both.

For more information on regions, see Volume One, Chapter 6, *Drawing Graphics and Text*.

Structures

Region is a pointer to an opaque structure type.

Related Commands

XClipBox, XCreateRegion, XDestroyRegion, XEmptyRegion, XEqualRegion, XIntersectRegion, XOffsetRegion, XPointInRegion, XPolygonRegion, XRectInRegion, XSetRegion, XShrinkRegion, XSubtractRegion, XUnionRectWithRegion, XUnionRegion.

A
Function Group Summary

This quick reference is intended to help you find and use the right function for a particular task. It supplies two lists:

- Listing of Functions by Groups
- Alphabetical Listing of Functions

Both functions and macros are listed in all the groups in which they belong. Therefore, several of them are listed more than once.

Remember that Xlib functions begin with the letter "X"; macros do not.

A.1 Group Listing with Brief Descriptions

Association Tables

XCreateAssocTable	Create a new association table (X10).
XDeleteAssoc	Delete an entry from an association table.
XDestroyAssocTable	Free the memory allocated for an association table.
XLookUpAssoc	Obtain data from an association table.
XMakeAssoc	Create an entry in an association table.

Buffers

XStoreBuffer	Store data in a cut buffer.
XStoreBytes	Store data in cut buffer 0.
XFetchBuffer	Return data from a cut buffer.
XFetchBytes	Return data from cut buffer 0.
XRotateBuffers	Rotate the cut buffers.

Client Connections

XKillClient	Destroy a client or its remaining resources.
XSetCloseDownMode	Change the close down mode of a client.

Colorcells

XAllocColor	Allocate a read-only colormap cell with closest hardware-supported color.
XAllocColorCells	Allocate read/write (nonshared) colorcells.
XAllocColorPlanes	Allocate read/write (nonshareable) color planes.
XAllocNamedColor	Allocate a read-only colorcell from color name.
XLookupColor	Get database RGB values and closest hardware-supported RGB values from color name.
XParseColor	Look up or translate RGB values from color name or hexadecimal value.
XQueryColor	Obtain the RGB values for a specified pixel value.
XQueryColors	Obtain RGB values and flags for each specified pixel value.
XStoreColor	Set or change a read/write entry of a colormap to the closest available hardware color.
XStoreColors	Set or change read/write colorcells to the closest available hardware colors.
XStoreNamedColor	Allocate a read/write colorcell by English color name.
XFreeColors	Free colormap cells or planes.
BlackPixel	Return a black pixel value on the default colormap of screen.
WhitePixel	Return a pixel value representing white in default colormap.

Colormaps

XCopyColormapAndFree	Copy a colormap and return a new colormap ID.
XCreateColormap	Create a colormap.
XFreeColormap	Delete a colormap and install the default colormap.
XGetStandardColormap	Get the standard colormap property.
XSetStandardColormap	Change the standard colormap property.
XSetWindowColormap	Set the colormap for a specified window.
XInstallColormap	Install a colormap.
XUninstallColormap	Uninstall a colormap; install default if not already installed.
XListInstalledColormaps	Get a list of installed colormaps.
DefaultColormap	Return the default colormap on the default screen.
DefaultColormapOfScreen	Return the default colormap on the specified screen.
DisplayCells	Return the maximum number of colormap cells on the connected display.

Context Manager

XDeleteContext	Delete a context entry for a given window and type.
XFindContext	Get data from the context manager (not graphics context).

Context Manager (continued)

XSaveContext	Save a data value corresponding to a window and context type (not graphics context).
XUniqueContext	Create a new context ID (not graphics context).

Cursors

XDefineCursor	Assign a cursor to a window.
XUndefineCursor	Disassociate a cursor from a window.
XCreateFontCursor	Create a cursor from the standard cursor font.
XCreateGlyphCursor	Create a cursor from font glyphs.
XCreatePixmapCursor	Create a cursor from two bitmaps.
XFreeCursor	Destroy a cursor.
XRecolorCursor	Change the color of a cursor.
XQueryBestCursor	Get the closest supported cursor sizes.
XQueryBestSize	Obtain the "best" supported cursor, tile, or stipple size.

Display Specifications

DefaultColormap	Return the default colormap on the specified screen.
DefaultDepth	Return the depth of the default root window for a screen.
DefaultGC	Return the default graphics context for the root window of a screen.
DefaultScreen	Return the screen integer; the last segment of a string passed to XOpenDisplay, or the DISPLAY environment variable if NULL was used.
DefaultVisual	Return the default visual structure for a screen.
DisplayCells	Return the maximum number of colormap cells on the connected display.
DisplayHeight	Return an integer that describes the height of the screen in pixels.
DisplayHeightMM	Return the height of the specified screen in millimeters.
DisplayPlanes	Return the number of planes on the connected display.
DisplayString	Return the string that was passed to XOpenDisplay or if that was NULL, the DISPLAY variable.
DisplayWidth	Return the width of the screen in pixels.
DisplayWidthMM	Return the width of the specified screen in millimeters.
RootWindow	Return the ID of the root window.
ScreenCount	Return the number of available screens.
XDisplayMotionBufferSize	Return size of server's motion history buffer.
XListDepths	Return a list of the depths supported on this server.
XListPixmapFormats	Return a list of the pixmap formats supported on this server.
XMaxRequestSize	Return maximum request size allowed on this server.
XResourceManagerString	Return string containing user's resource database.

Drawing Primitives

XDraw	Draw a polyline or curve between vertex list (from X10).
XDrawArc	Draw an arc fitting inside a rectangle.
XDrawArcs	Draw multiple arcs.
XDrawFilled	Draw a filled polygon or curve from vertex list (from X10).
XDrawLine	Draw a line between two points.
XDrawLines	Draw multiple connected lines.
XDrawPoint	Draw a point.
XDrawPoints	Draw multiple points.
XDrawRectangle	Draw an outline of a rectangle.
XDrawRectangles	Draw the outlines of multiple rectangles.
XDrawSegments	Draw multiple disjoint lines.
XCopyArea	Copy an area of a drawable.
XCopyPlane	Copy a single plane of a drawable into a drawable with depth, applying pixel values.
XFillArc	Fill an arc.
XFillArcs	Fill multiple arcs.
XFillPolygon	Fill a polygon.
XFillRectangle	Fill a rectangular area.
XFillRectangles	Fill multiple rectangular areas.
XClearArea	Clear a rectangular area in a window.
XClearWindow	Clear an entire window.

Errors

XGetErrorDatabaseText	Obtain error messages from the error database.
XGetErrorText	Obtain a description of error code.
XSetErrorHandler	Set a nonfatal error event handler.
XSetIOErrorHandler	Handle fatal I/O errors.
XDisplayName	Report the display name when connection to a display fails.
XSetAfterFunction	Set a function called after all Xlib functions.
XSynchronize	Enable or disable synchronization for debugging.

Events

XSelectInput	Select the event types to be sent to a window.
XSendEvent	Send an event.
XSetInputFocus	Set the keyboard focus window.
XGetInputFocus	Return the current keyboard focus window.
XWindowEvent	Remove the next event matching mask and window.
XCheckWindowEvent	Remove the next event matching both passed window and passed mask; don't wait.
XCheckTypedEvent	Return the next event in queue that matches event type; don't wait.
XCheckTypedWindowEvent	Return the next event in queue matching type and window.
XMaskEvent	Remove the next event that matches mask.
XCheckMaskEvent	Remove the next event that matches mask; don't wait.

Events (continued)

XIfEvent	Wait for matching event.
XCheckIfEvent	Check the event queue for a matching event.
XPeekEvent	Get an event without removing it from the queue.
XPeekIfEvent	Get an event without recovering it from the queue; don't wait.
XAllowEvents	Control the behavior of keyboard and pointer events when these resources are grabbed.
XGetMotionEvents	Get pointer motion events.
XNextEvent	Get the next event of any type or window.
XPutBackEvent	Push an event back on the input queue.
XEventsQueued	Check the number of events in the event queue.
XPending	Flush the request buffer and return the number of pending input events.
XSynchronize	Enable or disable synchronization for debugging.
QLength	Return the current length of the input queue on the connected display.

Extensions

XFreeExtensionList	Free memory allocated for a list of installed extensions to X.
XListExtensions	Return a list of all extensions to X supported by the server.
XQueryExtension	Get extension information.

Fonts

XLoadFont	Load a font if not already loaded; get font ID.
XUnloadFont	Unload a font.
XFreeFont	Unload a font and free storage for the font structure.
XFreeFontInfo	Free multiple font information arrays.
XFreeFontNames	Free the font name array.
XFreeFontPath	Free the memory allocated by XGetFontPath.
XListFonts	Return a list of the available font names.
XListFontsWithInfo	Obtain the names and information about loaded fonts.
XQueryFont	Return information about a loaded font.
XSetFont	Set the current font in a graphics context.
XSetFontPath	Set the font search path.
XGetFontPath	Get the current font search path.
XGetFontProperty	Get a font property given its atom.
XCreateFontCursor	Create a cursor from the standard cursor font.

Grabbing

XGrabKey	Grab a key.
XUngrabKey	Release a key from grab.
XGrabKeyboard	Grab the keyboard.
XUngrabKeyboard	Release the keyboard from grab.
XGrabButton	Grab a pointer button.

Grabbing (continued)

XUngrabButton	Release a button from grab.
XGrabPointer	Grab the pointer.
XUngrabPointer	Release the pointer from grab.
XGrabServer	Grab the server grab.
XUngrabServer	Release the server from grab.
XChangeActivePointerGrab	Change the parameters of an active pointer grab.

Graphics Context

XCreateGC	Create a new graphics context for a given screen with the depth of the specified drawable.
XChangeGC	Change the components of a given graphics context.
XCopyGC	Copy a graphics context.
XFreeGC	Free a graphics context.
XGContextFromGC	Obtain the GContext (resource ID) associated with the specified graphics context.
XGetGCValues	Get GC component values from Xlib's GC cache.
XSetArcMode	Set the arc mode in a graphics context.
XSetClipMask	Set clip_mask pixmap in a graphics context.
XSetClipOrigin	Set the clip origin in a graphics context.
XSetClipRectangles	Set clip_mask in a graphics context to the list of rectangles.
XSetRegion	Set clip_mask of the graphics context to the specified region.
XSetDashes	Set dash_offset and dashes (for lines) in a graphics context.
XSetLineAttributes	Set the line drawing components in a graphics context.
XSetFillRule	Set the fill rule in a graphics context.
XSetFillStyle	Set the fill style in a graphics context.
XSetTile	Set the fill tile in a graphics context.
XSetStipple	Set the stipple in a graphics context.
XSetTSOrigin	Set the tile/stipple origin in a graphics context.
XSetGraphicsExposures	Set graphics_exposures in a graphics context.
XSetForeground	Set the foreground pixel value in a graphics context.
XSetBackground	Set the background pixel value in a graphics context.
XSetFunction	Set the bitwise logical operation in a graphics context.
XSetPlaneMask	Set the plane mask in a graphics context.
XSetState	Set the foreground, background, logical function and plane mask in a graphics context.
XSetSubwindowMode	Set the subwindow mode in a graphics context.
DefaultGC	Return the default graphics context for the root window of a screen.

Host Access

XAddHost	Add a host to the access control list.
XAddHosts	Add multiple hosts to the access control list.
XListHosts	Obtain a list of hosts having access to this display.
XRemoveHost	Remove a host from the access control list.
XRemoveHosts	Remove multiple hosts from the access control list.
XDisableAccessControl	Allow access from any host.
XEnableAccessControl	Use access control list to allow or deny connection requests.
XSetAccessControl	Disable or enable access control.

HouseKeeping

XFree	Free specified in-memory data created by an Xlib function.
XOpenDisplay	Connect a client program to an X server.
XCloseDisplay	Disconnect a client program from an X server and display.
XNoOp	Send a NoOp to exercise connection with the server.

Images

XCreateImage	Allocate memory for an XImage structure.
XDestroyImage	Deallocate memory associated with an image.
XPutImage	Draw a rectangular image on a window or pixmap.
XSubImage	Create a subimage from part of an image.
XGetImage	Place contents of a rectangle from drawable into an image.
XGetSubImage	Copy a rectangle in drawable to a location within the pre-existing image.
XAddPixel	Add a constant value to every pixel value in an image.
XPutPixel	Set a pixel value in an image.
XGetPixel	Obtain a single pixel value from an image.
ImageByteOrder	Specify the required byte order for images for each scan line unit in XYFormat (bitmap) or for each pixel value in ZFormat. Returns either LSBFirst or MSBFirst.

Interclient Communication

(*see Window Manager Hints, Selections, and Cut Buffers*)

Keyboard

XKeycodeToKeysym	Convert a keycode to a keysym.
XKeysymToKeycode	Convert a keysym to the appropriate keycode.
XKeysymToString	Convert a keysym symbol to a string.
XStringToKeysym	Convert a keysym name string to a keysym.
XLookupKeysym	Get the keysym corresponding to a keycode in a structure.
XRebindKeysym	Rebind a keysym to a string for client.

Keyboard (continued)

XLookupString	Map a key event to ASCII string, keysym, and Compose-Status.
XQueryKeymap	Obtain a bit vector for the current state of the keyboard.
XGetKeyboardMapping	Return symbols for keycodes.
XChangeKeyboardMapping	Change the keyboard mapping.
XRefreshKeyboardMapping	Update the stored modifier and keymap information.
XSetModifierMapping	Set keycodes to be used as modifiers (Shift, Control, etc.).
XGetModifierMapping	Obtain modifier key mapping (Shift, Control, etc.).
XDeleteModifiermapEntry	Delete an entry from an XModifierKeymap structure.
XInsertModifiermapEntry	Add a new entry to an XModifierKeymap structure.
XNewModifiermap	Create a keyboard modifier mapping structure.
XFreeModifiermap	Destroy and free a keyboard modifier mapping structure.
XDisplayKeycodes	Returns range of keycodes used by server.

Macros, Display

AllPlanes	Return an unsigned long value with all bits set.
BlackPixel	Return a black pixel value on the default colormap of screen.
BlackPixelOfScreen	Return the black pixel value in the default colormap of the specified screen.
CellsOfScreen	Return the number of colormap cells of the specified screen.
ConnectionNumber	Return the connection number (file descriptor on UNIX system).
DefaultColormap	Return the default colormap on the specified screen.
DefaultColormapOfScreen	Return the default colormap of the specified screen.
DefaultDepth	Return the depth of the default root window for a screen.
DefaultDepthOfScreen	Return the default depth of the specified screen.
DefaultGC	Return the default graphics context for the root window of a screen.
DefaultGCOfScreen	Return the default graphics context (GC) of the specified screen.
DefaultRootWindow	Return the root window for the default screen.
DefaultScreen	Return the screen integer; the last segment of a string passed to XOpenDisplay, or the DISPLAY environment variable if NULL was used.
DefaultScreenOfDisplay	Return the default screen of the specified display.
DefaultVisual	Return the default visual structure for a screen.
DefaultVisualOfScreen	Return the default visual of the specified screen.
DisplayCells	Return the maximum number of colormap cells on the connected display.
DisplayHeight	Return an integer that describes the height of the screen in pixels.
DisplayHeightMM	Return the height of the specified screen in millimeters.
DisplayOfScreen	Return the display of the specified screen.
DisplayPlanes	Return the number of planes on the connected display.

DisplayString	Return the string that was passed to XOpenDisplay or if that was NULL, the DISPLAY variable.
DisplayType	Return the connected display manufacturer, as defined in *<X11/Xvendors.h>*.
DisplayWidth	Return the width of the screen in pixels.
DisplayWidthMM	Return the width of the specified screen in millimeters.
DoesBackingStore	Return a value indicating whether the screen supports backing stores. Return one of WhenMapped, NotUseful, or Always.
DoesSaveUnders	Return whether the screen supports save unders. True or False.
dpyno	Return the file descriptor of the connected display.
EventMaskOfScreen	Return the initial root event mask for the specified screen.
HeightOfScreen	Return the height of the specified screen.
HeightMMOfScreen	Return the height of the specified screen in millimeters.
Keyboard	Return the device ID for the main keyboard connected to the display.
LastKnownRequest-Processed	Return the serial ID of the last known protocol request to have been issued.
MaxCmapsOfScreen	Return the maximum number of colormaps supported by a screen.
MinCmapsOfScreen	Return the minimum number of colormaps supported by a screen.
NextRequest	Return the serial ID of the next protocol request to be issued.
PlanesOfScreen	Return the number of planes in a screen.
ProtocolRevision	Return the minor protocol revision number of the X server.
ProtocolVersion	Return the version number of the X protocol on the connected display.
QLength	Return the current length of the input queue on the connected display.
RootWindow	Return the ID of the root window.
RootWindowOfScreen	Return the root window of the specified screen.
ScreenCount	Return the number of available screens.
XScreenNumberOfScreen	Return the integer corresponding to the specified pointer to a Screen structure.
ScreenOfDisplay	Return the specified screen of the specified display.
ServerVendor	Return a pointer to a null-terminated string giving some identification of the maker of the X server implementation.
VendorRelease	Return a number related to the release of the X server by the vendor.
WhitePixel	Return a pixel value representing white in default colormap.
WhitePixelOfScreen	Return the white pixel value in the default colormap of the specified screen.
WidthOfScreen	Return the width of the specified screen.
WidthMMOfScreen	Return the width of the specified screen in millimeters.
XDisplayMotionBufferSize	Return size of server's motion history buffer.

Macros, Display (continued)

XListDepths	Return a list of the depths supported on this server.
XListPixmapFormats	Return a list of the pixmap formats supported on this server.
XMaxRequestSize	Return maximum request size allowed on this server.
XResourceManagerString	Return string containing user's resource database.

Macros, Image Format

BitmapBitOrder	Return `LeastSignificant` or `MostSignificant`. Indicates the bit order in `BitmapUnit`.
BitmapPad	Each scan line is padded to a multiple of bits specified by the value returned by this macro.
BitmapUnit	The scan line is quantized (calculated) in multiples of this value.
ByteOrder	Specifies the required byte order for images for each scan line unit in `XYFormat` (bitmap) or for each pixel value in `ZFormat`. Possible values are `LSBFirst` or `MSBFirst`.
ImageByteOrder	Specifies the required byte order for images for each scan line unit in `XYFormat` (bitmap) or for each pixel value in `ZFormat`. Return either `LSBFirst` or `MSBFirst`.

Macros, Keysym Classification

IsCursorKey	Return `True` if the keysym is on the cursor key.
IsFunctionKey	Return `True` if the keysym is on the function keys.
IsKeypadKey	Return `True` if the keysym is on the key pad.
IsMiscFunctionKey	Return `True` if the keysym is on the miscellaneous function keys.
IsModifierKey	Return `True` if the keysym is on the modifier keys.
IsPFKey	Return `True` if the keysym is on the PF keys.

Mapping

(see Window Mapping, Keyboard, or Pointer)

Output Buffer

XFlush	Flush the request buffer.
XSync	Flush the request buffer and wait for all events to be processed by the server.

Pointers

XQueryPointer	Get the current pointer location.
XWarpPointer	Move the pointer to another point on the screen.
XGrabPointer	Grab the pointer.
XUngrabPointer	Release the pointer from grab.

Pointers (continued)

XGetPointerMapping	Get the pointer button mapping.
XSetPointerMapping	Set the pointer button mapping.
XGetPointerControl	Get the current pointer preferences.
XChangePointerControl	Change the pointer preferences.
XChangeActivePointerGrab	Change the parameters of an active pointer grab.

Properties

XListProperties	Get the property list for a window.
XDeleteProperty	Delete a window property.
XChangeProperty	Change a property associated with a window.
XSetStandardProperties	Set the minimum set of properties for the window manager.
XRotateWindowProperties	Rotate properties in the properties array.
XGetAtomName	Get a name for a given atom.
XGetFontProperty	Get a font property given its atom.
XGetWindowProperty	Obtain the atom type and property format for a window.
XInternAtom	Return an atom for a given name string.
XGetTextProperty	Read a TEXT property.
XSetTextProperty	Write a TEXT property.
XStringListToTextProperty	Convert a list of strings to an XTextProperty structure.
XTextPropertyToStringList	Convert an XTextProperty to a list of strings.
XFreeStringList	Free memory allocated by XTextPropertyToStringList.

Regions

XCreateRegion	Create a new empty region.
XDestroyRegion	Deallocate storage associated with a region.
XEmptyRegion	Determine if a region is empty.
XPolygonRegion	Generate a region from points.
XPointInRegion	Determine if a point resides in a region.
XRectInRegion	Determine if a rectangle resides in a region.
XUnionRectWithRegion	Add a rectangle to a region.
XClipBox	Generate the smallest rectangle enclosing a region.
XOffsetRegion	Change offset of a region.
XShrinkRegion	Reduce the size of a region.
XEqualRegion	Determine if two regions have the same size, offset, and space.
XSetRegion	Set clip_mask of the graphics context to the specified region.
XSubtractRegion	Subtract one region from another.
XIntersectRegion	Compute the intersection of two regions.
XUnionRegion	Compute the union of two regions.
XXorRegion	Calculate the difference between the union and intersection of 2 regions.

Resource Manager

XrmDestroyDatabase	Destroy a resource database.
XrmGetFileDatabase	Retrieve a database from a file.
XrmGetResource	Get a resource from name and class as strings.
XrmGetStringDatabase	Create a database from a string.
XrmInitialize	Initialize the resource manager.
XrmMergeDatabases	Merge the contents of one database with another.
XrmParseCommand	Load a resource database from command line arguments.
XrmPutFileDatabase	Store a database in a file.
XrmPutLineResource	Add a resource entry given as a string of name and value.
XrmPutResource	Store a resource into a database.
XrmPutStringResource	Add a resource that is specified as a string.
XrmQGetResource	Get a resource from name and class as quarks.
XrmQGetSearchList	Return a list of database levels.
XrmQGetSearchResource	Search resource database levels for a given resource.
XrmQPutResource	Store a resource into a database using quarks.
XrmQPutStringResource	Add a string resource value to a database using quarks.
XrmQuarkToString	Convert a quark to a string.
XrmStringToBinding-QuarkList	Convert a key string to a binding list and a quark list.
XrmStringToQuarkList	Convert a key string to a quark list.
XrmStringToQuark	Convert a string to a quark.
XrmUniqueQuark	Allocate a new quark.
Xpermalloc	Allocate memory never to be freed.
XResourceManagerString	Get user's database set with *xrdb* from Display structure.

Save Set

XAddToSaveSet	Add a window to the client's save-set.
XRemoveFromSaveSet	Remove a window from the client's save-set.
XChangeSaveSet	Add or remove a window to or from the client's save-set.

Screen Saver

XActivateScreenSaver	Activate screen blanking.
XForceScreenSaver	Turn the screen saver on or off.
XResetScreenSaver	Reset the screen saver.
XGetScreenSaver	Get the current screen saver parameters.
XSetScreenSaver	Set the parameters of the screen saver.

Selections

XGetSelectionOwner	Return the owner of a selection.
XSetSelectionOwner	Set the owner of a selection.
XConvertSelection	Use the value of a selection.

Server Specifications

(see Display Specifications)

Standard Geometry

XGeometry	Calculate window geometry given user geometry string and default geometry. Superceded in R4 by XWMGeometry.
XWMGeometry	Calculate window geometry given user geometry string and default geometry.
XParseGeometry	Generate position and size from standard window geometry string.
XTranslateCoordinates	Change the coordinate system from one window to another.

Text

XDrawImageString	Draw 8-bit image text characters.
XDrawImageString16	Draw 16-bit image text characters.
XDrawString	Draw an 8-bit text string, foreground only.
XDrawString16	Draw two-byte text strings.
XDrawText	Draw 8-bit polytext strings.
XDrawText16	Draw 16-bit polytext strings.
XQueryTextExtents	Query the server for string and font metrics.
XQueryTextExtents16	Query the server for string and font metrics of a 16-bit character string.
XTextExtents	Get string and font metrics.
XTextExtents16	Get string and font metrics of a 16-bit character string.
XTextWidth	Get the width in pixels of an 8-bit character string.
XTextWidth16	Get the width in pixels of a 16-bit character string.

Tile, Pixmap, Stipple and Bitmap

XCreatePixmap	Create a pixmap.
XFreePixmap	Free a pixmap ID.
XQueryBestSize	Obtain the "best" supported cursor, tile, or stipple size.
XQueryBestStipple	Obtain the best supported stipple shape.
XQueryBestTile	Obtain the best supported fill tile shape.
XSetTile	Set the fill tile in a graphics context.
XSetWindowBorderPixmap	Change a window border tile attribute and repaint the border.
XSetWindowBackgroundPixmap	Change the background tile attribute of a window.
XReadBitmapFile	Read a bitmap from disk.
XWriteBitmapFile	Write a bitmap to a file.
XCreateBitmapFromData	Create a bitmap from X11 bitmap format data.
XCreatePixmapFromBitmapData	Create a pixmap with depth from bitmap data.
XListPixmapFormats	Read supported pixmap formats from Display structure.

User Preferences

XAutoRepeatOff	Turn off the keyboard auto-repeat keys.
XAutoRepeatOn	Turn on the keyboard auto-repeat keys.
XBell	Ring the bell (Control G).
XGetDefault	Scan the user preferences for program name and options.
XGetPointerControl	Get the current pointer preferences.
XGetKeyboardControl	Obtain a list of the current keyboard preferences.
XChangeKeyboardControl	Change the keyboard preferences.

Visuals

XGetVisualInfo	Find a visual information structure that matches the specified template.
XMatchVisualInfo	Obtain the visual information that matches the desired depth and class.
DefaultVisual	Return the default visual structure for a screen.
XVisualIDFromVisual	Get resource ID from a visual structure.

Window Attributes

XGetWindowAttributes	Obtain the current attributes of window.
XChangeWindowAttributes	Set window attributes.
XSetWindowBackground	Set the background pixel attribute of a window.
XSetWindowBackgroundPixmap	Change the background tile attribute of a window.
XSetWindowBorder	Change a window border attribute to the specified pixel value and repaint the border.
XSetWindowBorderPixmap	Change a window border tile attribute and repaint the border.
XSetWindowColormap	Set the colormap for a specified window.
XDefineCursor	Assign a cursor to a window.
XGetGeometry	Obtain the current geometry of drawable.
XSelectInput	Select the event types to be sent to a window.

Window Configuration

XMoveWindow	Move a window.
XResizeWindow	Change a window's size.
XMoveResizeWindow	Change the size and position of a window.
XSetWindowBorderWidth	Change the border width of a window.
XRestackWindows	Change the stacking order of siblings.
XConfigureWindow	Change the window position, size, border width, or stacking order.
XGetGeometry	Obtain the current geometry of drawable.
XReconfigureWMWindow	Change top-level window position, size, border width, or stacking order.

Window Existence

XCreateSimpleWindow	Create an unmapped InputOutput subwindow.
XCreateWindow	Create a window and set attributes.
XDestroySubwindows	Destroy all subwindows of a window.
XDestroyWindow	Unmap and destroy a window and all subwindows.

Window Manager Hints

XGetClassHint	Get the XA_WM_CLASS property of a window. Obsolete in R4.
XSetClassHint	Set the XA_WM_CLASS property of a window. Obsolete in R4.
XGetNormalHints	Get the size hints property of a window in normal state (not zoomed or iconified). Obsolete in R4.
XSetNormalHints	Set the size hints property of a window in normal state (not zoomed or iconified). Obsolete in R4.
XGetSizeHints	Read any property of type XA_WM_SIZE_HINTS. Obsolete in R4.
XSetSizeHints	Set the value of any property of type XA_WM_-SIZE_HINTS. Obsolete in R4.
XGetTransientForHint	Get the XA_WM_TRANSIENT_FOR property of a window.
XSetTransientForHint	Set the XA_WM_TRANSIENT_FOR property of a window.
XGetWMHints	Read a window manager hints property.
XSetWMHints	Set a window manager hints property.
XGetZoomHints	Read the size hints property of a zoomed window. Obsolete in R4.
XSetZoomHints	Set the size hints property of a zoomed window. Obsolete in R4.
XFetchName	Get a window's name (XA_WM_NAME property). Obsolete in R4.
XStoreName	Assign a name to a window for the window manager. Obsolete in R4.
XGetIconName	Get the name to be displayed in an icon. Obsolete in R4.
XSetIconName	Set the name to be displayed in a window's icon. Obsolete in R4.
XGetIconSizes	Get preferred icon sizes.
XSetIconSizes	Set the value of the XA_WM_ICON_SIZE property.
XSetCommand	Set the XA_WM_COMMAND property (command line arguments). Obsolete in R4.
XAllocClassHint	Allocate and zero fields in XClassHint structure.
XAllocIconSize	Allocate and zero fields in XIconSize structure.
XAllocSizeHints	Allocate and zero fields in XSizeHints structure.
XAllocStandardColormap	Allocate and zero fields in XStandardColormap structure.
XAllocWMHints	Allocate and zero fields in XWMHints structure.

Window Manager Hints (continued)

`XGetRGBColormaps`	Read standard colormap property. Replaces `XGetStandardColormap`.
`XSetRGBColormaps`	Write standard colormap property. Replaces `XSetStandardColormap`.
`XGetWMClientMachine`	Read `WM_CLIENT_MACHINE` property.
`XSetWMClientMachine`	Write `WM_CLIENT_MACHINE` property.
`XGetWMIconName`	Read `XA_WM_ICON_NAME` property. Replaces `XGetIconName`.
`XSetWMIconName`	Write `XA_WM_ICON_NAME` property. Replaces `XSetIconName`.
`XGetWMProtocols`	Read `WM_PROTOCOLS` property.
`XSetWMProtocols`	Write `WM_PROTOCOLS` property.
`XGetWMNormalHints`	Read `XA_WM_NORMAL_HINTS` property. Replaces `XGetNormalHints`.
`XSetWMNormalHints`	Write `XA_WM_NORMAL_HINTS` property. Replaces `XSetNormalHints`.
`XSetWMSizeHints`	Write `XA_WM_SIZE_HINTS` property. Replaces `XSetSizeHints`.
`XSetWMColormapWindows`	Write `WM_COLORMAP_WINDOWS` property.
`XGetWMColormapWindows`	Read `WM_COLORMAP_WINDOWS` property.
`XSetWMProperties`	Write all standard properties. Replaces `XSetStandardProperties`.
`XSetWMName`	Write `XA_WM_NAME` property. Replaces `XStoreName`.
`XGetWMName`	Read `XA_WM_NAME` property. Replaces `XFetchName`.

Window Manipulation

`XLowerWindow`	Lower a window in the stacking order.
`XRaiseWindow`	Raise a window to the top of the stacking order.
`XCirculateSubwindows`	Circulate the stacking order of children up or down.
`XCirculateSubwindowsDown`	Circulate the bottom child to the top of the stacking order.
`XCirculateSubwindowsUp`	Circulate the top child to the bottom of the stacking order.
`XQueryTree`	Return a list of children, parent, and root.
`XReparentWindow`	Change a window's parent.
`XMoveWindow`	Move a window.
`XResizeWindow`	Change a window's size.
`XMoveResizeWindow`	Change the size and position of a window.
`XSetWindowBorderWidth`	Change the border width of a window.
`XRestackWindows`	Change the stacking order of siblings.
`XConfigureWindow`	Change the window position, size, border width, or stacking order.
`XIconifyWindow`	Inform window manager that a top-level window should be iconified.
`XWithdrawWindow`	Inform window manager that a top-level window should be unmapped.
`XReconfigureWMWindow`	Reconfigure a top-level window.

Window Mapping

XMapRaised	Map a window on top of its siblings.
XMapSubwindows	Map all subwindows.
XMapWindow	Map a window.
XUnmapSubwindows	Unmap all subwindows of a given window.
XUnmapWindow	Unmap a window.
XIconifyWindow	Inform window manager that a top-level window should be iconified.
XWithdrawWindow	Inform window manager that a top-level window should be unmapped.

A.2 Alphabetical Listing of Routines

Table A-1. Alphabetical Listing of Routines

Routine	Description
XActivateScreenSaver	Activate screen blanking.
XAddHost	Add a host to the access control list.
XAddHosts	Add multiple hosts to the access control list.
XAddPixel	Add a constant value to every pixel value in an image.
XAddToSaveSet	Add a window to the client's save-set.
XAllocClassHint	Allocate and zero fields in XClassHint structure.
XAllocIconSize	Allocate and zero fields in XIconSize structure.
XAllocSizeHints	Allocate and zero fields in XSizeHints structure.
XAllocStandardColormap	Allocate and zero fields in XStandardColormap structure.
XAllocWMHints	Allocate and zero fields in XWMHints structure.
XAllocColor	Allocate a read-only colormap cell with closest hardware-supported color.
XAllocColorCells	Allocate read/write (nonshared) colorcells.
XAllocColorPlanes	Allocate read/write (nonshareable) color planes.
XAllocNamedColor	Allocate a read-only colorcell from color name.
XAllowEvents	Control the behavior of keyboard and pointer events when these resources are grabbed.
XAutoRepeatOff	Turn off the keyboard auto-repeat keys.
XAutoRepeatOn	Turn on the keyboard auto-repeat keys.
XBell	Ring the bell (Control G).
XChangeActivePointerGrab	Change the parameters of an active pointer grab.
XChangeGC	Change the components of a given graphics context.
XChangeKeyboardControl	Change the keyboard preferences such as key click.
XChangeKeyboardMapping	Change the keyboard mapping.
XChangePointerControl	Change the pointer preferences.
XChangeProperty	Change a property associated with a window.
XChangeSaveSet	Add or remove a window to or from the client's save-set.
XChangeWindowAttributes	Set window attributes.
XCheckIfEvent	Check the event queue for a matching event.
XCheckMaskEvent	Remove the next event that matches mask; don't wait.

Table A-1. Alphabetical Listing of Routines (continued)

Routine	Description
XCheckTypedEvent	Return the next event in queue that matches event type;
XCheckTypedWindowEvent	Return the next event in queue matching type and window.
XCheckWindowEvent	Remove the next event matching both passed window and passed mask; don't wait.
XCirculateSubwindows	Circulate the stacking order of children up or down.
XCirculateSubwindowsDown	Circulate the bottom child to the top of the stacking order.
XCirculateSubwindowsUp	Circulate the top child to the bottom of the stacking order.
XClearArea	Clear a rectangular area in a window.
XClearWindow	Clear an entire window.
XClipBox	Generate the smallest rectangle enclosing a region.
XCloseDisplay	Disconnect a client program from an X server and display.
XConfigureWindow	Change the window position, size, border width, or stacking order.
XConvertSelection	Use the value of a selection.
XCopyArea	Copy an area of a drawable.
XCopyColormapAndFree	Copy a colormap and return a new colormap ID.
XCopyGC	Copy a graphics context.
XCopyPlane	Copy a single plane of a drawable into a drawable with depth, applying pixel values.
XCreateAssocTable	Create a new association table (X10).
XCreateBitmapFromData	Create a bitmap from X11 bitmap format data.
XCreateColormap	Create a colormap.
XCreateFontCursor	Create a cursor from the standard cursor font.
XCreateGC	Create a new graphics context for a given screen with the depth of the specified drawable.
XCreateGlyphCursor	Create a cursor from font glyphs.
XCreateImage	Allocate memory for an XImage structure.
XCreatePixmap	Create a pixmap.
XCreatePixmapCursor	Create a cursor from two bitmaps.
XCreatePixmapFrom-BitmapData	Create a pixmap with depth from bitmap data.
XCreateRegion	Create a new empty region.
XCreateSimpleWindow	Create an unmapped InputOutput window.
XCreateWindow	Create a window and set attributes.
XDefineCursor	Assign a cursor to a window.
XDeleteAssoc	Delete an entry from an association table.
XDeleteContext	Delete a context entry for a given window and type.
XDeleteModifiermapEntry	Delete an entry from an XModifierKeymap structure.
XDeleteProperty	Delete a window property.
XDestroyAssocTable	Free the memory allocated for an association table.
XDestroyImage	Deallocate memory associated with an image.
XDestroyRegion	Deallocate storage associated with a region.

Routine	Description
XDestroySubwindows	Destroy all subwindows of a window.
XDestroyWindow	Unmap and destroy a window and all subwindows.
XDisableAccessControl	Allow access from any host.
XDisplayKeycodes	Returns range of keycodes used by server.
XDisplayMotionBufferSize	Return size of server's motion history buffer.
XDisplayName	Report the display name when connection to a display fails.
XDraw	Draw a polyline or curve between vertex list (from X10).
XDrawArc	Draw an arc fitting inside a rectangle.
XDrawArcs	Draw multiple arcs.
XDrawFilled	Draw a filled polygon or curve from vertex list (from X10).
XDrawImageString	Draw 8-bit image text characters.
XDrawImageString16	Draw 16-bit image text characters.
XDrawLine	Draw a line between two points.
XDrawLines	Draw multiple connected lines.
XDrawPoint	Draw a point.
XDrawPoints	Draw multiple points.
XDrawRectangle	Draw an outline of a rectangle.
XDrawRectangles	Draw the outlines of multiple rectangles.
XDrawSegments	Draw multiple disjoint lines.
XDrawString	Draw an 8-bit text string, foreground only.
XDrawString16	Draw two-byte text strings.
XDrawText	Draw 8-bit polytext strings.
XDrawText16	Draw 16-bit polytext strings.
XEmptyRegion	Determine if a region is empty.
XEnableAccessControl	Use access control list to allow or deny connection requests.
XEqualRegion	Determine if two regions have the same size, offset, and shape.
XEventsQueued	Check the number of events in the event queue.
XFetchBuffer	Return data from a cut buffer.
XFetchBytes	Return data from cut buffer 0.
XFetchName	Get a window's name (XA_WM_NAME property).
XFillArc	Fill an arc.
XFillArcs	Fill multiple arcs.
XFillPolygon	Fill a polygon.
XFillRectangle	Fill a rectangular area.
XFillRectangles	Fill multiple rectangular areas.
XFindContext	Get data from the context manager (not graphics context).
XFlush	Flush the request buffer (display all queued requests).
XForceScreenSaver	Turn the screen saver on or off.
XFree	Free specified in-memory data created by an Xlib function.
XFreeColormap	Delete a colormap and install the default colormap.
XFreeColors	Free colormap cells or planes.
XFreeCursor	Destroy a cursor.

Routine	Description
XFreeExtensionList	Free memory allocated for a list of installed extensions to X.
XFreeFont	Unload a font and free storage for the font structure.
XFreeFontInfo	Free multiple font information arrays.
XFreeFontNames	Free the font name array.
XFreeFontPath	Free the memory allocated by XGetFontPath.
XFreeGC	Free a graphics context.
XFreeModifiermap	Destroy and free a keyboard modifier mapping structure.
XFreePixmap	Free a pixmap ID.
XFreeStringList	Free memory allocated by XTextProperty-ToStringList.
XGContextFromGC	Obtain the GContext (resource ID) associated with the specified graphics context.
XGeometry	Calculate window geometry given user geometry string and default geometry.
XGetAtomName	Get a name for a given atom.
XGetClassHint	Get the XA_WM_CLASS property of a window.
XGetDefault	Scan the user preferences for program name and options.
XGetErrorDatabaseText	Obtain error messages from the error database.
XGetErrorText	Obtain a description of error code.
XGetFontPath	Get the current font search path.
XGetFontProperty	Get a font property given its atom.
XGetGeometry	Obtain the current geometry of drawable.
XGetGCValues	Get GC component values from Xlib's GC cache.
XGetIconName	Get the name to be displayed in an icon.
XGetIconSizes	Get preferred icon sizes.
XGetImage	Place contents of a rectangle from drawable into an image.
XGetInputFocus	Return the current keyboard focus window.
XGetKeyboardControl	Obtain a list of the current keyboard preferences.
XGetKeyboardMapping	Return symbols for keycodes.
XGetModifierMapping	Obtain a mapping of modifier keys (Shift, Control, etc.).
XGetMotionEvents	Get pointer motion events.
XGetNormalHints	Get the size hints property of a window in normal state (not zoomed or iconified).
XGetPixel	Obtain a single pixel value from an image.
XGetPointerControl	Get the current pointer preferences.
XGetPointerMapping	Get the pointer button mapping.
XGetRGBColormaps	Read standard colormap property. Replaces XGetStandardColormap.
XGetScreenSaver	Get the current screen saver parameters.
XGetSelectionOwner	Return the owner of a selection.
XGetSizeHints	Read any property of type XA_WM_SIZE_HINTS.
XGetStandardColormap	Get the standard colormap property.

Routine	Description
XGetSubImage	Copy a rectangle in drawable to a location within the pre-existing image.
XGetTextProperty	Read a TEXT property.
XGetTransientForHint	Get the XA_WM_TRANSIENT_FOR property of a window.
XGetVisualInfo	Find a visual information structure that matches the specified template.
XGetWindowAttributes	Obtain the current attributes of window.
XGetWindowProperty	Obtain the atom type and property format for a window.
XGetWMClientMachine	Read WM_CLIENT_MACHINE property.
XGetWMColormapWindows	Read WM_COLORMAP_WINDOWS property.
XGetWMHints	Read a window manager hints property.
XGetWMIconName	Read XA_WM_ICON_NAME property. Replaces XGetIconName.
XGetWMName	Read XA_WM_NAME property. Replaces XFetchName.
XGetWMNormalHints	Read XA_WM_NORMAL_HINTS property. Replaces XGetNormalHints.
XGetWMProtocols	Read WM_PROTOCOLS property.
XGetWMSizeHints	Read XA_WM_SIZE_HINTS property. Replaces XGetSizeHints.
XGetZoomHints	Read the size hints property of a zoomed window.
XGrabButton	Grab a pointer button.
XGrabKey	Grab a key.
XGrabKeyboard	Grab the keyboard.
XGrabPointer	Grab the pointer.
XGrabServer	Grab the server.
XIconifyWindow	Inform window manager that a top-level window should be iconified.
XIfEvent	Wait for matching event.
XInsertModifiermapEntry	Add a new entry to an XModifierKeymap structure.
XInstallColormap	Install a colormap.
XInternAtom	Return an atom for a given name string.
XIntersectRegion	Compute the intersection of two regions.
XKeycodeToKeysym	Convert a keycode to a keysym.
XKeysymToKeycode	Convert a keysym to the appropriate keycode.
XKeysymToString	Convert a keysym symbol to a string.
XKillClient	Destroy a client or its remaining resources.
XListDepths	Return a list of the depths supported on this server.
XListExtensions	Return a list of all extensions to X supported by the server.
XListFonts	Return a list of the available font names.
XListFontsWithInfo	Obtain the names and information about loaded fonts.
XListHosts	Obtain a list of hosts having access to this display.
XListInstalledColormaps	Get a list of installed colormaps.
XListPixmapFormats	Return a list of the pixmap formats supported on this server.

Function Group

Routine	Description
XListProperties	Get the property list for a window.
XLoadFont	Load a font if not already loaded; get font ID.
XLoadQueryFont	Load a font and fill information structure.
XLookUpAssoc	Obtain data from an association table.
XLookupColor	Get database RGB values and closest hardware-supported RGB values from color name.
XLookupKeysym	Get the keysym corresponding to a keycode in structure.
XLookupString	Map a key event to ASCII string, keysym, and ComposeStatus.
XLowerWindow	Lower a window in the stacking order.
XMakeAssoc	Create an entry in an association table.
XMapRaised	Map a window on top of its siblings.
XMapSubwindows	Map all subwindows.
XMapWindow	Map a window.
XMaskEvent	Remove the next event that matches mask.
XMatchVisualInfo	Obtain the visual information that matches the desired depth and class.
XMaxRequestSize	Return maximum request size allowed on this server.
XMoveResizeWindow	Change the size and position of a window.
XMoveWindow	Move a window.
XNewModifiermap	Create a keyboard modifier mapping structure.
XNextEvent	Get the next event of any type or window.
XNoOp	Send a NoOp to exercise connection with the server.
XOffsetRegion	Change offset of a region.
XOpenDisplay	Connect a client program to an X server.
XParseColor	Look up or translate RGB values from ASCII color name or hexadecimal value.
XParseGeometry	Generate position and size from standard window geometry string.
XPeekEvent	Get an event without removing it from the queue.
XPeekIfEvent	Get an event without removing it from the queue; do not wait.
XPending	Flush the request buffer and return the number of pending input events.
Xpermalloc	Allocate memory never to be freed.
XPointInRegion	Determine if a point is inside a region.
XPolygonRegion	Generate a region from points.
XPutBackEvent	Push an event back on the input queue.
XPutImage	Draw a rectangular image on a window or pixmap.
XPutPixel	Set a pixel value in an image.
XQueryBestCursor	Get the closest supported cursor sizes.
XQueryBestSize	Obtain the "best" supported cursor, tile, or stipple size.
XQueryBestStipple	Obtain the best supported stipple shape.
XQueryBestTile	Obtain the best supported fill tile shape.

Routine	Description
XQueryColor	Obtain the RGB values and flags for a specified pixel value.
XQueryColors	Obtain RGB values for an array of pixel values.
XQueryExtension	Get extension information.
XQueryFont	Return information about a loaded font.
XQueryKeymap	Obtain a bit vector for the current state of the keyboard.
XQueryPointer	Get the current pointer location.
XQueryTextExtents	Query the server for string and font metrics.
XQueryTextExtents16	Query the server for string and font metrics of a 16-bit character string.
XQueryTree	Return a list of children, parent, and root.
XRaiseWindow	Raise a window to the top of the stacking order.
XReadBitmapFile	Read a bitmap from disk.
XRebindKeysym	Rebind a keysym to a string for client.
XRecolorCursor	Change the color of a cursor.
XReconfigureWMWindow	Change top-level window position, size, border width, or stacking order.
XRectInRegion	Determine if a rectangle resides in a region.
XRefreshKeyboardMapping	Update the stored modifier and keymap information.
XRemoveFromSaveSet	Remove a window from the client's save-set.
XRemoveHost	Remove a host from the access control list.
XRemoveHosts	Remove multiple hosts from the access control list.
XReparentWindow	Change a window's parent.
XResetScreenSaver	Reset the screen saver.
XResizeWindow	Change a window's size.
XResourceManagerString	Return string containing user's resource database.
XRestackWindows	Change the stacking order of siblings.
XrmDestroyDatabase	Destroy a resource database.
XrmGetFileDatabase	Retrieve a database from a file.
XrmGetResource	Get a resource from name and class as strings.
XrmGetStringDatabase	Create a database from a string.
XrmInitialize	Initialize the resource manager.
XrmMergeDatabases	Merge the contents of one database with another.
XrmParseCommand	Load a resource database from command line arguments.
XrmPutFileDatabase	Store a database in a file.
XrmPutLineResource	Add a resource entry given as a string of name and value.
XrmPutResource	Store a resource into a database.
XrmPutStringResource	Add a resource that is specified as a string.
XrmQGetResource	Get a resource from name and class as quarks.
XrmQGetSearchList	Return a list of database levels.
XrmQGetSearchResource	Search resource database levels for a given resource.
XrmQPutResource	Store a resource into a database using quarks.
XrmQPutStringResource	Add a string resource value to a database using quarks.

Function Group

Routine	Description
XrmQuarkToString	Convert a quark to a string.
XrmStringToBinding- QuarkList	Convert a key string to a binding list and a quark list.
XrmStringToQuark	Convert a string to a quark.
XrmStringToQuarkList	Convert a key string to a quark list.
XrmUniqueQuark	Allocate a new quark.
XRotateBuffers	Rotate the cut buffers.
XRotateWindowProperties	Rotate properties in the properties array.
XSaveContext	Save a data value corresponding to a window and context type (not graphics context).
XSelectInput	Select the event types to be sent to a window.
XSendEvent	Send an event.
XSetAccessControl	Disable or enable access control.
XSetAfterFunction	Set a function called after all Xlib functions.
XSetArcMode	Set the arc mode in a graphics context.
XSetBackground	Set the background pixel value in a graphics context.
XSetClassHint	Set the XA_WM_CLASS property of a window.
XSetClipMask	Set clip_mask pixmap in a graphics context.
XSetClipOrigin	Set the clip origin in a graphics context.
XSetClipRectangles	Change clip_mask in a graphics context to the list of rectangles.
XSetCloseDownMode	Change the close down mode of a client.
XSetCommand	Set the XA_WM_COMMAND atom (command line arguments).
XSetDashes	Set dash_offset and dashes (for lines) in a graphics context.
XSetErrorHandler	Set a nonfatal error event handler.
XSetFillRule	Set the fill rule in a graphics context.
XSetFillStyle	Set the fill style in a graphics context.
XSetFont	Set the current font in a graphics context.
XSetFontPath	Set the font search path.
XSetForeground	Set the foreground pixel value in a graphics context.
XSetFunction	Set the bitwise logical operation in a graphics context.
XSetGraphicsExposures	Set graphics_exposures in a graphics context.
XSetIconName	Set the name to be displayed in a window's icon.
XSetIconSizes	Set the value of the XA_WM_ICON_SIZE property.
XSetInputFocus	Set the keyboard focus window.
XSetIOErrorHandler	Handle fatal I/O errors.
XSetLineAttributes	Set the line drawing components in a graphics context.
XSetModifierMapping	Set keycodes to be used as modifiers (Shift, Control, etc.).
XSetNormalHints	Set the size hints property of a window in normal state (not zoomed or iconified).
XSetPlaneMask	Set the plane mask in a graphics context.
XSetPointerMapping	Set the pointer button mapping.

Routine	Description
XSetRegion	Set `clip_mask` of the graphics context to the specified region.
XSetRGBColormaps	Write standard colormap property. Replaces `XSetStandardColormap`.
XSetScreenSaver	Set the parameters of the screen saver.
XSetSelectionOwner	Set the owner of a selection.
XSetSizeHints	Set the value of any property of type `XA_WM_SIZE_HINTS`.
XSetStandardColormap	Change the standard colormap property.
XSetStandardProperties	Set the minimum set of properties for the window manager.
XSetState	Set the foreground, background, logical function, and plane mask in a graphics context.
XSetStipple	Set the stipple in a graphics context.
XSetSubwindowMode	Set the subwindow mode in a graphics context.
XSetTextProperty	Write a TEXT property using `XTextProperty` structure.
XSetTile	Set the fill tile in a graphics context.
XSetTransientForHint	Set the `XA_WM_TRANSIENT_FOR` property of a window.
XSetTSOrigin	Set the tile/stipple origin in a graphics context.
XSetWindowBackground	Set the background pixel attribute of a window.
XSetWindowBackground-Pixmap	Change the background tile attribute of a window.
XSetWindowBorder	Change a window border attribute to the specified pixel value and repaint the border.
XSetWindowBorderPixmap	Change a window border tile attribute and repaint the border.
XSetWindowBorderWidth	Change the border width of a window.
XSetWindowColormap	Set the colormap for a specified window.
XSetWMClientMachine	Write `WM_CLIENT_MACHINE` property.
XSetWMColormapWindows	Write `WM_COLORMAP_WINDOWS` property.
XSetWMHints	Set a window manager hints property.
XSetWMIconName	Write `XA_WM_ICON_NAME` property. Replaces `XSetIconName`.
XSetWMName	Write `XA_WM_NAME` property. Replaces `XStoreName`.
XSetWMNormalHints	Write `XA_WM_NORMAL_HINTS` property. Replaces `XSetNormalHints`.
XSetWMProperties	Write all standard properties. Replaces `XSetStandardProperties`.
XSetWMProtocols	Write `WM_PROTOCOLS` property.
XSetWMSizeHints	Write `XA_WM_SIZE_HINTS` property. Replaces `XSetSizeHints`.
XSetZoomHints	Set the size hints property of a zoomed window.
XShrinkRegion	Reduce or expand the size of a region.
XStoreBuffer	Store data in a cut buffer.

Routine	Description
XStoreBytes	Store data in cut buffer 0.
XStoreColor	Set or change a read/write entry of a colormap to the closest available hardware color.
XStoreColors	Set or change read/write colorcells to the closest available hardware colors.
XStoreName	Assign a name to a window for the window manager.
XStoreNamedColor	Allocate a read/write colorcell by English color name.
XStringListToTextProperty	Convert a list of strings to an XTextProperty structure.
XStringToKeysym	Convert a keysym name string to a keysym.
XSubImage	Create a subimage from part of an image.
XSubtractRegion	Subtract one region from another.
XSync	Flush the request buffer and wait for all events and errors to be processed by the server.
XSynchronize	Enable or disable synchronization for debugging.
XTextExtents	Get string and font metrics.
XTextExtents16	Get string and font metrics of a 16-bit character string.
XTextWidth	Get the width in pixels of an 8-bit character string.
XTextWidth16	Get the width in pixels of a 16-bit character string.
XTranslateCoordinates	Change the coordinate system from one window to another.
XUndefineCursor	Disassociate a cursor from a window.
XUngrabButton	Release a button from grab.
XUngrabKey	Release a key from grab.
XUngrabKeyboard	Release the keyboard from grab.
XUngrabPointer	Release the pointer from grab.
XUngrabServer	Release the server from grab.
XUninstallColormap	Uninstall a colormap; install default if not already installed.
XUnionRectWithRegion	Add a rectangle to a region.
XUnionRegion	Compute the union of two regions.
XUniqueContext	Create a new context ID (not graphics context).
XUnloadFont	Unload a font.
XUnmapSubwindows	Unmap all subwindows of a given window.
XUnmapWindow	Unmap a window.
XWarpPointer	Move the pointer to another point on the screen.
XWindowEvent	Remove the next event matching mask and window.
XWMGeometry	Calculate window geometry given user geometry string and default geometry.
XWriteBitmapFile	Write a bitmap to a file.
XXorRegion	Calculate the difference between the union and intersection of two regions.

B

Error Messages and Protocol Requests

This appendix contains two tables: Table B-1 describes the standard error codes (the `error_code` member of `XErrorEvent`) and what causes them, and Table B-2 describes the mapping between protocol requests and Xlib functions. Each reference page in this volume describes in more detail the errors that may occur because of that Xlib routine. Volume One, Chapter 3, *Basic Window Program*, describes the handling of errors in general.

A protocol request is the actual network message that is sent from Xlib to the server. Many convenience functions are provided in Xlib to make programs easier to write and more readable. When any one of several convenience routines is called it will be translated into one type of protocol request. For example, `XMoveWindow` and `XResizeWindow` are convenience routines for the more general `XConfigureWindow`. Both of these Xlib routines use the protocol request ConfigureWindow. The protocol request that causes an error, along with other information about the error is printed to the standard error output by the default error handlers. In order to find out where in your code the error occurred, you will need to know what Xlib function to look for. Use Table B-2 to find this function.

Xlib functions that do not appear in Table B-2 do not generate protocol requests. They perform their function without affecting the display and without requiring information from the server. If errors can occur in them, the errors are reported in the returned value.

Table B-1. Error Messages

Error Codes:	Possible Cause
BadAccess	Specifies that the client attempted to grab a key/button combination that is already grabbed by another client; free a colormap entry that is not allocated by the client; store into a read-only colormap entry; modify the access control list from other than the local (or otherwise authorized) host; or select an event type that only one client can select at a time, when another client has already selected it.
BadAlloc	Specifies that the server failed to allocate the requested resource.
BadAtom	Specifies that a value for an `Atom` argument does not name a defined `Atom`.

Error Codes:	Possible Cause
BadColor	Specifies that a value for a Colormap argument does not name a defined Colormap.
BadCursor	Specifies that a value for a Cursor argument does not name a defined Cursor.
BadDrawable	Specifies that a value for a Drawable argument does not name a defined Window or Pixmap.
BadFont	Specifies that a value for a Font or GContext argument does not name a defined Font.
BadGC	Specifies that a value for a GContext argument does not name a defined GContext.
BadIDChoice	Specifies that the value chosen for a resource identifier either is not included in the range assigned to the client or is already in use.
BadImplement-ation	Specifies that the server does not implement some aspect of the request. A server that generates this error for a core request is deficient. Clients should be prepared to receive such errors and either handle or discard them.
BadLength	Specifies that the length of a request is shorter or longer than that required to minimally contain the arguments. This usually indicates an internal Xlib error.
BadMatch	Specifies that an InputOnly window is used as a Drawable.
	Some argument (or pair of arguments) has the correct type and range but fails to "match" in some other way required by the request.
BadName	Specifies that a font or color of the specified name does not exist.
BadPixmap	Specifies that a value for a Pixmap argument does not name a defined Pixmap.
BadRequest	Specifies that the major or minor opcode does not specify a valid request.
BadValue	Specifies that some numeric value falls outside the range of values accepted by the request. Unless a specific range is specified for an argument, the full range defined by the argument's type is accepted. Any argument defined as a set of alternatives can generate this error.
BadWindow	Specifies that a value for a Window argument does not name a defined Window.

The BadAtom, BadColor, BadCursor, BadDrawable, BadFont, BadGC, Bad-Pixmap, and BadWindow errors are also used when the argument type should be among a set of fixed alternatives (for example, a window ID, `PointerRoot`, or `None`) and some other constant or variable is used.

Table B-2. Xlib Functions and Protocol Requests

Protocol Request	Xlib Function
AllocColor	`XAllocColor`
AllocColorCells	`XAllocColorCells`
AllocColorPlanes	`XAllocColorPlanes`
AllocNamedColor	`XAllocNamedColor`
AllowEvents	`XAllowEvents`
Bell	`XBell`
ChangeActivePointerGrab	`XChangeActivePointerGrab`

ChangeGC	`XChangeGC`
	`XSetArcMode`
	`XSetBackground`
	`XSetClipMask`
	`XSetClipOrigin`
	`XSetFillRule`
	`XSetFillStyle`
	`XSetFont`
	`XSetForeground`
	`XSetFunction`
	`XSetGraphicsExposures`
	`XSetLineAttributes`
	`XSetPlaneMask`
	`XSetState`
	`XSetStipple`
	`XSetSubwindowMode`
	`XSetTile`
	`XSetTSOrigin`

ChangeHosts	`XAddHost`
	`XAddHosts`
	`XRemoveHost`
	`XRemoveHosts`

ChangeKeyboardControl	`XAutoRepeatOff`
	`XAutoRepeatOn`
	`XChangeKeyboardControl`

ChangeKeyboardMapping	`XChangeKeyboardMapping`
ChangePointerControl	`XChangePointerControl`

ChangeProperty	`XChangeProperty`
	`XSetCommand`
	`XSetIconName`
	`XSetIconSizes`
	`XSetNormalHints`

Protocol Request	Xlib Function
	`XSetWMProperties`
	`XSetSizeHints`
	`XSetStandardProperties`
	`XSetWMHints`
	`XSetZoomHints`
	`XStoreBuffer`
	`XStoreBytes`
	`XStoreName`
ChangeSaveSet	`XAddToSaveSet`
	`XChangeSaveSet`
	`XRemoveFromSaveSet`
ChangeWindowAttributes	`XChangeWindowAttributes`
	`XDefineCursor`
	`XSelectInput`
	`XSetWindowBackground`
	`XSetWindowBackgroundPixmap`
	`XSetWindowBorder`
	`XSetWindowBorderPixmap`
	`XSetWindowColormap`
	`XUndefineCursor`
CirculateWindow	`XCirculateSubwindows`
	`XCirculateSubwindowsDown`
	`XCirculateSubwindowsUp`
ClearArea	`XClearArea`
	`XClearWindow`
CloseFont	`XFreeFont`
	`XUnloadFont`
ConfigureWindow	`XConfigureWindow`
	`XLowerWindow`
	`XMapRaised`
	`XMoveResizeWindow`
	`XMoveWindow`
	`XRaiseWindow`
	`XReconfigureWMWindow`
	`XResizeWindow`
	`XRestackWindows`
	`XSetWindowBorderWidth`
ConvertSelection	`XConvertSelection`
CopyArea	`XCopyArea`
CopyColormapAndFree	`XCopyColormapAndFree`
CopyGC	`XCopyGC`
CopyPlane	`XCopyPlane`

Protocol Request	Xlib Function
CreateColormap	`XCreateColormap`
CreateCursor	`XCreatePixmapCursor`
CreateGC	`XCreateGC` `XOpenDisplay`
CreateGlyphCursor	`XCreateFontCursor` `XCreateGlyphCursor`
CreatePixmap	`XCreatePixmap`
CreateWindow	`XCreateSimpleWindow` `XCreateWindow`
DeleteProperty	`XDeleteProperty`
DestroySubwindows	`XDestroySubwindows`
DestroyWindow	`XDestroyWindow`
FillPoly	`XFillPolygon`

ForceScreenSaver	`XActivateScreenSaver`
	`XForceScreenSaver`
	`XResetScreenSaver`

FreeColormap	`XFreeColormap`
FreeColors	`XFreeColors`
FreeCursor	`XFreeCursor`
FreeGC	`XFreeGC`
FreePixmap	`XFreePixmap`
GetAtomName	`XGetAtomName`
GetFontPath	`XGetFontPath`
GetGeometry	`XGetGeometry` `XGetWindowAttributes`
GetImage	`XGetImage`
GetInputFocus	`XGetInputFocus` `XSync`
GetKeyboardControl	`XGetKeyboardControl`
GetKeyboardMapping	`XGetKeyboardMapping`
GetModifierMapping	`XGetModifierMapping`
GetMotionEvents	`XGetMotionEvents`
GetPointerControl	`XGetPointerControl`
GetPointerMapping	`XGetPonterMapping`

Errors

Protocol Request	Xlib Function

GetProperty	`XFetchBytes`
	`XFetchName`
	`XGetIconSizes`
	`XGetIconName`
	`XGetNormalHints`
	`XGetSizeHints`
	`XGetWindowProperty`
	`XGetWMProperties`
	`XGetWMHints`
	`XGetZoomHints`

GetScreenSaver	`XGetScreenSaver`
GetSelectionOwner	`XGetSelectionOwner`
GetWindowAttributes	`XGetWindowAttributes`
GrabButton	`XGrabButton`
GrabKey	`XGrabKey`
GrabKeyboard	`XGrabKeyboard`
GrabPointer	`XGrabPointer`
GrabServer	`XGrabServer`
ImageText8	`XDrawImageString`
ImageText16	`XDrawImageString16`
InstallColormap	`XInstallColormap`
InternAtom	`XInternAtom`
KillClient	`XKillClient`
ListExtensions	`XListExtensions`
ListFonts	`XListFonts`
ListFontsWithInfo	`XListFontsWithInfo`
ListHosts	`XListHosts`
ListInstalledColormaps	`XListInstalledColormaps`
ListProperties	`XListProperties`
LookupColor	`XLookupColor` `XParseColor`
MapSubwindows	`XMapSubwindows`
MapWindow	`XMapRaised` `XMapWindow`
NoOperation	`XNoOp`

Protocol Request	Xlib Function
OpenFont	`XLoadFont` `XLoadQueryFont`
PolyArc	`XDrawArc` `XDrawArcs`
PolyFillArc	`XFillArc` `XFillArcs`
PolyFillRectangle	`XFillRectangle` `XFillRectangles`
PolyLine	`XDrawLines`
PolyPoint	`XDrawPoint` `XDrawPoints`
PolyRectangle	`XDrawRectangle` `XDrawRectangles`
PolySegment	`XDrawLine` `XDrawSegments`
PolyText8	`XDrawString` `XDrawText`
PolyText16	`XDrawString16` `XDrawText16`
PutImage	`XPutImage`

QueryBestSize	`XQueryBestCursor`
	`XQueryBestSize`
	`XQueryBestStipple`
	`XQueryBestTile`

QueryColors	`XQueryColor` `XQueryColors`
QueryExtension	`XInitExtension` `XQueryExtension`
QueryFont	`XLoadQueryFont`
QueryKeymap	`XQueryKeymap`
QueryPointer	`XQueryPointer`
QueryTextExtents	`XQueryTextExtents` `XQueryTextExtents16`
QueryTree	`XQueryTree`
RecolorCursor	`XRecolorCursor`
ReparentWindow	`XReparentWindow`
RotateProperties	`XRotateBuffers`

Errors

Protocol Request	Xlib Function
	`XRotateWindowProperties`
SendEvent	`XSendEvent`
SetAccessControl	`XDisableAccessControl`
	`XEnableAccessControl`
	`XSetAccessControl`
SetClipRectangles	`XSetClipRectangles`
SetCloseDownMode	`XSetCloseDownMode`
SetDashes	`XSetDashes`
SetFontPath	`XSetFontPath`
SetInputFocus	`XSetInputFocus`
SetModifierMapping	`XSetModifierMapping`
SetPointerMapping	`XSetPointerMapping`
SetScreenSaver	`XSetScreenSaver`
SetSelectionOwner	`XSetSelectionOwner`
StoreColors	`XStoreColor`
	`XStoreColors`
StoreNamedColor	`XStoreNamedColor`
TranslateCoords	`XTranslateCoordinates`
UngrabButton	`XUngrabButton`
UngrabKey	`XUngrabKey`
UngrabKeyboard	`XUngrabKeyboard`
UngrabPointer	`XUngrabPointer`
UngrabServer	`XUngrabServer`
UninstallColormap	`XUninstallColormap`
UnmapSubwindows	`XUnmapSubWindows`
UnmapWindow	`XUnmapWindow`
WarpPointer	`XWarpPointer`

C
Macros

Once you have successfully connected your application to an X server, you can obtain data from the `Display` structure associated with that display. The Xlib interface provides a number of useful C language macros and corresponding functions for other language bindings which return data from the `Display` structure.

The function versions of these macros have the same names as the macros except that the function forms begin with the letter "X." They use the same arguments. Using the macro versions is slightly more efficient in C because it eliminates function call overhead.

In R3 and R4, a few new functions were added that access members of the `Display` structure. These are `XDisplayMotionBufferSize`, `XResourceManagerString`, `XDisplayKeycodes`, and `XMaxRequestSize` in R3 and `XScreenNumber-OfScreen`, `XListDepths`, and `XListPixmapFormats` in R4. Also, `XVisual-IDFromVisual` was added in R3 to extract the resource ID from a visual structure. `XDisplayMotionBufferSize`, `XResourceManagerString`, `XMaxRequest-Size`, `XScreenNumberOfScreen`, and `XVisualIDFromVisual` are simple enough to have macro versions, but these were not provided. Nevertheless, we have chosen to cover them in this macro appendix instead of devoting a reference page to each. `XDisplay-Keycodes`, `XListDepths`, and `XListPixmapFormats` are more complicated and therefore have their own reference pages; they are not covered here.

For the purposes of this appendix, the macros are divided into four categories: Display macros, Image Format macros, Keysym Classification macros, and Resource Manager macros. The macros are listed alphabetically within each category.

Note that some macros take as arguments an integer screen (*scr_num*) while others take a pointer to a `Screen` structure (*scr_ptr*). *scr_num* is returned by the `Default-Screen` macro and *scr_ptr* is returned by the `DefaultScreenOfDisplay` macro.

Macros

C.1 Display Macros

AllPlanes	Return a value with all bits set suitable for use as a plane mask argument.
BlackPixel(*display*,*scr_num*)	Return the black pixel value in the default colormap that is created by XOpenDisplay.
BlackPixelOfScreen(*scr_ptr*)	Return the black pixel value in the default colormap of the specified screen.
CellsOfScreen(*scr_ptr*)	Return the number of colormap cells in the default colormap of the specified screen.
ConnectionNumber(*display*)	Return a connection number for the specified display. On a UNIX system, this is the file descriptor of the connection.
DefaultColormap(*display*,*scr_num*)	Return the default colormap for the specified screen. Most routine allocations of color should be made out of this colormap.
DefaultColormapOfScreen(*scr_ptr*)	Return the default colormap of the specified screen.
DefaultDepth(*display*,*scr_num*)	Return the depth (number of planes) of the root window for the specified screen. Other depths may also be supported on this screen. See Volume One, Chapter 7, *Color*, or the reference pages for XMatchVisualInfo and XGet-VisualInfo to find out how to determine what depths are available.
DefaultDepthOfScreen(*scr_ptr*)	Return the default depth of the specified screen.
DefaultGC(*display*,*scr_num*)	Return the default graphics context for the specified screen.
DefaultGCOfScreen(*scr_ptr*)	Return the default graphics context (GC) of the specified screen.
DefaultRootWindow(*display*)	Return the ID of the root window on the default screen. Most applications should use Root-Window instead so that screen selection is supported.
DefaultScreen(*display*)	Return the integer that was specified in the last segment of the string passed to XOpen-Display or from the DISPLAY environment variable if NULL was used. For example, if the DISPLAY environment were Ogre:0.1, then DefaultScreen would return 1.

`DefaultScreenOfDisplay(display)`	Return the default screen of the specified display.
`DefaultVisual(display,scr_num)`	Return a pointer to the default visual structure for the specified screen.
`DefaultVisualOfScreen(scr_ptr)`	Return the default visual of the specified screen.
`DisplayCells(display,scr_num)`	Return the maximum possible number of colormap cells on the specified screen. This macro is misnamed: it should have been `Screen-Cells`.
`DisplayHeight(display,scr_num)`	Return the height in pixels of the screen. This macro is misnamed: it should have been `ScreenHeight`.
`DisplayHeightMM(display,scr_num)`	Return the height in millimeters of the specified screen. This macro is misnamed: it should have been `ScreenHeightMM`.
`DisplayOfScreen(scr_ptr)`	Return the display associated with the specified screen.
`DisplayPlanes(display,scr_num)`	Return the number of planes on the specified screen. This macro is misnamed: it should have been `ScreenPlanes`.
`DisplayString(display)`	Return the string that was passed to `XOpen-Display` when the current display was opened (or, if that was `NULL`, the value of the DISPLAY environment variable). This macro is useful in applications which invoke the fork system call and want to open a new connection to the same display from the child process.
`DisplayWidth(display,scr_num)`	Return the width in pixels of the screen. This macro is misnamed: it should have been `ScreenWidth`.
`DisplayWidthMM(display,scr_num)`	Return the width in millimeters of the specified screen. This macro is misnamed: it should have been `ScreenWidthMM`.
`DoesBackingStore(scr_ptr)`	Return a value indicating whether the screen supports backing stores. Values are `When-Mapped`, `NotUseful`, or `Always`. See Volume One, Section 4.3.5 for a discussion of the backing store.
`DoesSaveUnders(scr_ptr)`	Return a Boolean value indicating whether the screen supports save unders. If `True`, the screen supports save unders. If `False`, the screen does not support save unders. See

Macros

Volume One, Section 4.3.6 for a discussion of the save under.

dpyno(*display*)	Return the file descriptor of the connected display. On a UNIX system, you can then pass this returned file descriptor to the *select*(3) system call when your application program is driving more than one display at a time.
EventMaskOfScreen(*scr_ptr*)	Return the initial event mask for the root window of the specified screen.
HeightOfScreen(*scr_ptr*)	Return the height in pixels of the specified screen.
HeightMMOfScreen(*scr_ptr*)	Return the height in millimeters of the specified screen.
Keyboard(*display*)	Return the device ID for the main keyboard connected to the display.
LastKnownRequestProcessed (*display*)	Return the serial ID of the last known protocol request to have been issued. This can be useful in processing errors, since the serial number of failing requests are provided in the XError-Event structure.
MaxCmapsOfScreen(*scr_ptr*)	Return the maximum number of installed (hardware) colormaps supported by the specified screen.
MinCmapsOfScreen(*scr_ptr*)	Return the minimum number of installed (hardware) colormaps supported by the specified screen.
NextRequest(*display*)	Return the serial ID of the next protocol request to be issued. This can be useful in processing errors, since the serial number of failing requests are provided in the XErrorEvent structure.
PlanesOfScreen(*scr_ptr*)	Return the number of planes in the specified screen.
ProtocolRevision(*display*)	Return the minor protocol revision number of the X server.
ProtocolVersion(*display*)	Return the version number of the X protocol associated with the connected display. This is currently 11.
QLength(*display*)	Return the number of events that can be queued by the specified display.
RootWindow(*display*,*scr_num*)	Return the ID of the root window. This macro is necessary for routines that reference the root

	window or create a top-level window for an application.
RootWindowOfScreen(*scr_ptr*)	Return the ID of the root window of the specified screen.
ScreenCount(*display*)	Return the number of available screens on a specified display.
ScreenOfDisplay(*display,scr_num*)	Return the specified screen of the specified display.
ServerVendor(*display*)	Return a pointer to a null terminated string giving some identification of the owner of the X server implementation.
VendorRelease(*display*)	Return a number related to the release of the X server by the vendor.
WhitePixel(*display,scr_num*)	Return the white pixel value in the default colormap that is created by XOpenDisplay.
WhitePixelOfScreen(*scr_ptr*)	Return the white pixel value in the default colormap of the specified screen.
WidthOfScreen(*scr_ptr*)	Return the width of the specified screen.
WidthMMOfScreen(*scr_ptr*)	Return the width of the specified screen in millimeters.
XDisplayMotionBufferSize(*display*)	
	Return an unsigned long value containing the size of the motion buffer on the server. If this function returns zero, the server has no motion history buffer.
XMaxRequestSize(*display*)	Return a long value containing the maximum size of a protocol request for the specified server, in units of four bytes.
XScreenNumberOfScreen(*scr_ptr*)	Return the integer screen number corresponding to the specified pointer to a Screen structure.
XVisualIDFromVisual(*visual*)	Returns the ID of the server resource associated with a visual structure. This is useful when storing standard colormap properties.

C.2 Image Format Macros

BitmapBitOrder(*display*)   Within each `BitmapUnit`, the leftmost bit in the bit-map as displayed on the screen is either the least or the most significant bit in the unit. Returns `LSBFirst` or `MSBFirst`.

BitmapPad(*display*)   Each scan line must be padded to a multiple of bits speci-fied by the value returned by this macro.

BitmapUnit(*display*)   Returns the size of a bitmap's unit. The scan line is quan-tized (calculated) in multiples of this value.

ImageByteOrder(*display*)   Returns the byte order for images required by the server for each scan line unit in XY format (bitmap) or for each pixel value in Z format. Values are `LSBFirst` or `MSBFirst`.

C.3 Keysym Classification Macros

You may want to test if a keysym of the defined set (XK_MISCELLANY) is, for example, on the key pad or the function keys. You can use the keysym macros to perform the following tests:

IsCursorKey(*keysym*)   Return `True` if the keysym represents a cursor key.

IsFunctionKey(*keysym*)   Return `True` if the keysym represents a function key.

IsKeypadKey(*keysym*)   Return `True` if the keysym represents a key pad.

IsMiscFunctionKey(*keysym*)   Return `True` if the keysym represents a miscellaneous function key.

IsModifierKey(*keysym*)   Return `True` if the keysym represents a modifier key.

IsPFKey(*keysym*)   Return `True` if the keysym represents a PF key.

C.4 Resource Manager Macros

These macros convert from strings to quarks and quarks to strings. They are used by the resource manager. Note that they do not follow the normal naming conventions for macros, since they begin with an X.

XrmStringToName(*string*)   Convert string to `XrmName`. Same as `XString-ToQuark`.

XrmStringToClass(*string*)   Convert string to `XrmClass`. Same as `XString-ToQuark`.

XrmStringToRepresentation (*string*)	Convert string to XrmRepresentation. Same as XStringToQuark.
XrmNameToString(*name*)	Convert XrmName to string. Same as XrmQuark-ToString.
XrmClassToString(*class*)	Convert XrmClass to string. Same as XrmQuark-ToString.
XrmRepresentationToString (*type*)	Convert XrmRepresentation to string. Same as XrmQuarkToString.
XResourceManagerString(*display*)	
	Return a pointer to the resource database string stored in the Display structure. This string is read from the RESOURCE_MANAGER property on the root window; this property is normally set by the *xrdb* client.

Macros

D
The Color Database

The color database translates color name strings into RGB values. It is used by XParse-Color, XLookupColor, and XStoreNamedColor. These routines make it easier to allow the user to specify color names. Use of these names for routine color allocation of read-only colorcells is encouraged since this increases the chance of sharing colorcells and thereby makes the colormap go further before running out of colorcells. The location in the file system of the text version of the color database is an implementation detail, but by default on a UNIX system it is */usr/lib/X11/rgb.txt*.

It should be noted that while a sample color database is provided with the standard X11 distribution, it is not specified as an X Consortium standard and is not part of the X Protocol or Xlib. Therefore, it is permissible for server vendors to change the color names, although they will probably only add color names. Furthermore, hardware vendors can change the RGB values for each display hardware to achieve the proper "gamma correction" so that the colors described by the name really generate that color.

The RGB values in the R3 database were originally tuned for the DEC VT240 display. The color that appears on a Sun system given these RGB values for "pink," for example, looks more like light burgundy. In R4 a new RGB color database is provided, which provides many more color names and provides values that generate colors that match their names on more monitors.

Each color name in the database may be used in the form shown or in mixed case, with initial capitals and all spaces eliminated. Table D-1 (see next page) shows the R3 database, and Table D-2 shows the R4 database.

Table D-1. The R3 Color Database*

English Words	Red	Green	Blue	English Words	Red	Green	Blue
English Words	Red	Green	Blue	medium aquamarine	50	204	153
aquamarine	112	219	147	English Words	Red	Green	Blue
black	0	0	0	medium blue	50	50	204
blue	0	0	255	medium forest green	107	142	35
blue violet	159	95	159	medium goldenrod	234	234	173
brown	165	42	42	medium orchid	147	112	219
cadet blue	95	159	159	medium sea green	66	111	66
coral	255	127	0	medium slate blue	127	0	255
cornflower blue	66	66	111	medium spring green	127	255	0
cyan	0	255	255	medium turquoise	112	219	219
dark green	47	79	47	medium violet red	219	112	147
dark olive green	79	79	47	midnight blue	47	47	79
dark orchid	153	50	204	navy	35	35	142
dark slate blue	107	35	142	navy blue	35	35	142
dark slate gray	47	79	79	orange	204	50	50
dark slate grey	47	79	79	orange red	255	0	127
dark turquoise	112	147	219	orchid	219	112	219
dim gray	84	84	84	pale green	143	188	143
dim grey	84	84	84	pink	188	143	143
firebrick	142	35	35	plum	234	173	234
forest green	35	142	35	purple	176	0	255
gold	204	127	50	red	255	0	0
goldenrod	219	219	112	salmon	111	66	66
gray	192	192	192	sea green	35	142	107
green	0	255	0	sienna	142	107	35
green yellow	147	219	112	sky blue	50	153	204
grey	192	192	192	slate blue	0	127	255
indian red	79	47	47	spring green	0	255	127
khaki	159	159	95	steel blue	35	107	142
light blue	191	216	216	tan	219	147	112
light gray	168	168	168	thistle	216	191	216
light grey	168	168	168	turquoise	173	234	234
light steel blue	143	143	188	violet	79	47	79
lime green	50	204	50	violet red	204	50	153
magenta	255	0	255	wheat	216	216	191
maroon	142	35	107	white	252	252	252
yellow	255	255	0	yellow green	153	204	50

*Also defined are the color names "gray0" through "gray100", spelled with an "e" or an "a". "gray0" is black and "gray100" is white.

Table D-2. The R4 Color Database

English Words	Red	Green	Blue	English Words	Red	Green	Blue
snow	255	250	250	black	0	0	0
ghost white	248	248	255	dark slate gray	47	79	79
GhostWhite	248	248	255	DarkSlateGray	47	79	79
white smoke	245	245	245	dark slate grey	47	79	79
WhiteSmoke	245	245	245	DarkSlateGrey	47	79	79
gainsboro	220	220	220	dim gray	105	105	105
floral white	255	250	240	DimGray	105	105	105
FloralWhite	255	250	240	dim grey	105	105	105
old lace	253	245	230	DimGrey	105	105	105
OldLace	253	245	230	slate gray	112	128	144
linen	250	240	230	SlateGray	112	128	144
antique white	250	235	215	slate grey	112	128	144
AntiqueWhite	250	235	215	SlateGrey	112	128	144
papaya whip	255	239	213	light slate gray	119	136	153
PapayaWhip	255	239	213	LightSlateGray	119	136	153
blanched almond	255	235	205	light slate grey	119	136	153
BlanchedAlmond	255	235	205	LightSlateGrey	119	136	153
bisque	255	228	196	gray	192	192	192
peach puff	255	218	185	grey	192	192	192
PeachPuff	255	218	185	light grey	211	211	211
navajo white	255	222	173	LightGrey	211	211	211
NavajoWhite	255	222	173	light gray	211	211	211
moccasin	255	228	181	LightGray	211	211	211
cornsilk	255	248	220	midnight blue	25	25	112
ivory	255	255	240	MidnightBlue	25	25	112
lemon chiffon	255	250	205	navy	0	0	128
LemonChiffon	255	250	205	navy blue	0	0	128
seashell	255	245	238	NavyBlue	0	0	128
honeydew	240	255	240	cornflower blue	100	149	237
mint cream	245	255	250	CornflowerBlue	100	149	237
MintCream	245	255	250	dark slate blue	72	61	139
azure	240	255	255	DarkSlateBlue	72	61	139
alice blue	240	248	255	slate blue	106	90	205
AliceBlue	240	248	255	SlateBlue	106	90	205
lavender	230	230	250	medium slate blue	123	104	238
lavender blush	255	240	245	MediumSlateBlue	123	104	238
LavenderBlush	255	240	245	light slate blue	132	112	255
misty rose	255	228	225	LightSlateBlue	132	112	255
MistyRose	255	228	225	medium blue	0	0	205
white	255	255	255	MediumBlue	0	0	205

Color
Database

English Words	Red	Green	Blue	English Words	Red	Green	Blue
royal blue	65	105	225	sea green	46	139	87
RoyalBlue	65	105	225	SeaGreen	46	139	87
blue	0	0	255	medium sea green	60	179	113
dodger blue	30	144	255	MediumSeaGreen	60	179	113
DodgerBlue	30	144	255	light sea green	32	178	170
deep sky blue	0	191	255	LightSeaGreen	32	178	170
DeepSkyBlue	0	191	255	pale green	152	251	152
sky blue	135	206	235	PaleGreen	152	251	152
SkyBlue	135	206	235	spring green	0	255	127
light sky blue	135	206	250	SpringGreen	0	255	127
LightSkyBlue	135	206	250	lawn green	124	252	0
steel blue	70	130	180	LawnGreen	124	252	0
SteelBlue	70	130	180	green	0	255	0
light steel blue	176	196	222	chartreuse	127	255	0
LightSteelBlue	176	196	222	medium spring green	0	250	154
light blue	173	216	230	MediumSpringGreen	0	250	154
LightBlue	173	216	230	green yellow	173	255	47
powder blue	176	224	230	GreenYellow	173	255	47
PowderBlue	176	224	230	lime green	50	205	50
pale turquoise	175	238	238	LimeGreen	50	205	50
PaleTurquoise	175	238	238	yellow green	154	205	50
dark turquoise	0	206	209	YellowGreen	154	205	50
DarkTurquoise	0	206	209	forest green	34	139	34
medium turquoise	72	209	204	ForestGreen	34	139	34
MediumTurquoise	72	209	204	olive drab	107	142	35
turquoise	64	224	208	OliveDrab	107	142	35
cyan	0	255	255	dark khaki	189	183	107
light cyan	224	255	255	DarkKhaki	189	183	107
LightCyan	224	255	255	khaki	240	230	140
cadet blue	95	158	160	pale goldenrod	238	232	170
CadetBlue	95	158	160	PaleGoldenrod	238	232	170
medium aquamarine	102	205	170	light goldenrod yellow	250	250	210
MediumAquamarine	102	205	170	LightGoldenrodYellow	250	250	210
aquamarine	127	255	212	light yellow	255	255	224
dark green	0	100	0	LightYellow	255	255	224
DarkGreen	0	100	0	yellow	255	255	0
dark olive green	85	107	47	gold	255	215	0
DarkOliveGreen	85	107	47	light goldenrod	238	221	130
dark sea green	143	188	143	LightGoldenrod	238	221	130
DarkSeaGreen	143	188	143	goldenrod	218	165	32

English Words	Red	Green	Blue	English Words	Red	Green	Blue
dark goldenrod	184	134	11	LightPink	255	182	193
DarkGoldenrod	184	134	11	pale violet red	219	112	147
rosy brown	188	143	143	PaleVioletRed	219	112	147
RosyBrown	188	143	143	maroon	176	48	96
indian red	205	92	92	medium violet red	199	21	133
IndianRed	205	92	92	MediumVioletRed	199	21	133
saddle brown	139	69	19	violet red	208	32	144
SaddleBrown	139	69	19	VioletRed	208	32	144
sienna	160	82	45	magenta	255	0	255
peru	205	133	63	violet	238	130	238
burlywood	222	184	135	plum	221	160	221
beige	245	245	220	orchid	218	112	214
wheat	245	222	179	medium orchid	186	85	211
sandy brown	244	164	96	MediumOrchid	186	85	211
SandyBrown	244	164	96	dark orchid	153	50	204
tan	210	180	140	DarkOrchid	153	50	204
chocolate	210	105	30	dark violet	148	0	211
firebrick	178	34	34	DarkViolet	148	0	211
brown	165	42	42	blue violet	138	43	226
dark salmon	233	150	122	BlueViolet	138	43	226
DarkSalmon	233	150	122	purple	160	32	240
salmon	250	128	114	medium purple	147	112	219
light salmon	255	160	122	MediumPurple	147	112	219
LightSalmon	255	160	122	thistle	216	191	216
orange	255	165	0	snow1	255	250	250
dark orange	255	140	0	snow2	238	233	233
DarkOrange	255	140	0	snow3	205	201	201
coral	255	127	80	snow4	139	137	137
light coral	240	128	128	seashell1	255	245	238
LightCoral	240	128	128	seashell2	238	229	222
tomato	255	99	71	seashell3	205	197	191
orange red	255	69	0	seashell4	139	134	130
OrangeRed	255	69	0	AntiqueWhite1	255	239	219
red	255	0	0	AntiqueWhite2	238	223	204
hot pink	255	105	180	AntiqueWhite3	205	192	176
HotPink	255	105	180	AntiqueWhite4	139	131	120
deep pink	255	20	147	bisque1	255	228	196
DeepPink	255	20	147	bisque2	238	213	183
pink	255	192	203	bisque3	205	183	158
light pink	255	182	193	bisque4	139	125	107

English Words	Red	Green	Blue	English Words	Red	Green	Blue
PeachPuff1	255	218	185	LightPink	255	182	193
PeachPuff2	238	203	173	pale violet red	219	112	147
PeachPuff3	205	175	149	PaleVioletRed	219	112	147
PeachPuff4	139	119	101	maroon	176	48	96
NavajoWhite1	255	222	173	medium violet red	199	21	133
NavajoWhite2	238	207	161	MediumVioletRed	199	21	133
NavajoWhite3	205	179	139	violet red	208	32	144
NavajoWhite4	139	121	94	VioletRed	208	32	144
LemonChiffon1	255	250	205	magenta	255	0	255
LemonChiffon2	238	233	191	violet	238	130	238
LemonChiffon3	205	201	165	plum	221	160	221
LemonChiffon4	139	137	112	orchid	218	112	214
cornsilk1	255	248	220	medium orchid	186	85	211
cornsilk2	238	232	205	MediumOrchid	186	85	211
cornsilk3	205	200	177	dark orchid	153	50	204
cornsilk4	139	136	120	DarkOrchid	153	50	204
ivory1	255	255	240	dark violet	148	0	211
ivory2	238	238	224	DarkViolet	148	0	211
ivory3	205	205	193	blue violet	138	43	226
ivory4	139	139	131	BlueViolet	138	43	226
honeydew1	240	255	240	purple	160	32	240
honeydew2	224	238	224	medium purple	147	112	219
honeydew3	193	205	193	MediumPurple	147	112	219
honeydew4	131	139	131	thistle	216	191	216
LavenderBlush1	255	240	245	snow1	255	250	250
LavenderBlush2	238	224	229	snow2	238	233	233
LavenderBlush3	205	193	197	snow3	205	201	201
LavenderBlush4	139	131	134	snow4	139	137	137
MistyRose1	255	228	225	seashell1	255	245	238
MistyRose2	238	213	210	seashell2	238	229	222
MistyRose3	205	183	181	seashell3	205	197	191
MistyRose4	139	125	123	seashell4	139	134	130
azure1	240	255	255	AntiqueWhite1	255	239	219
azure2	224	238	238	AntiqueWhite2	238	223	204
azure3	193	205	205	AntiqueWhite3	205	192	176
azure4	131	139	139	AntiqueWhite4	139	131	120
SlateBlue1	131	111	255	bisque1	255	228	196
SlateBlue2	122	103	238	bisque2	238	213	183
SlateBlue3	105	89	205	bisque3	205	183	158
SlateBlue4	71	60	139	bisque4	139	125	107

English Words	Red	Green	Blue	English Words	Red	Green	Blue
RoyalBlue1	72	118	255	LightCyan1	224	255	255
RoyalBlue2	67	110	238	LightCyan2	209	238	238
RoyalBlue3	58	95	205	LightCyan3	180	205	205
RoyalBlue4	39	64	139	LightCyan4	122	139	139
blue1	0	0	255	PaleTurquoise1	187	255	255
blue2	0	0	238	PaleTurquoise2	174	238	238
blue3	0	0	205	PaleTurquoise3	150	205	205
blue4	0	0	139	PaleTurquoise4	102	139	139
DodgerBlue1	30	144	255	CadetBlue1	152	245	255
DodgerBlue2	28	134	238	CadetBlue2	142	229	238
DodgerBlue3	24	116	205	CadetBlue3	122	197	205
DodgerBlue4	16	78	139	CadetBlue4	83	134	139
SteelBlue1	99	184	255	turquoise1	0	245	255
SteelBlue2	92	172	238	turquoise2	0	229	238
SteelBlue3	79	148	205	turquoise3	0	197	205
SteelBlue4	54	100	139	turquoise4	0	134	139
DeepSkyBlue1	0	191	255	cyan1	0	255	255
DeepSkyBlue2	0	178	238	cyan2	0	238	238
DeepSkyBlue3	0	154	205	cyan3	0	205	205
DeepSkyBlue4	0	104	139	cyan4	0	139	139
SkyBlue1	135	206	255	DarkSlateGray1	151	255	255
SkyBlue2	126	192	238	DarkSlateGray2	141	238	238
SkyBlue3	108	166	205	DarkSlateGray3	121	205	205
SkyBlue4	74	112	139	DarkSlateGray4	82	139	139
LightSkyBlue1	176	226	255	aquamarine1	127	255	212
LightSkyBlue2	164	211	238	aquamarine2	118	238	198
LightSkyBlue3	141	182	205	aquamarine3	102	205	170
LightSkyBlue4	96	123	139	aquamarine4	69	139	116
SlateGray1	198	226	255	DarkSeaGreen1	193	255	193
SlateGray2	185	211	238	DarkSeaGreen2	180	238	180
SlateGray3	159	182	205	DarkSeaGreen3	155	205	155
SlateGray4	108	123	139	DarkSeaGreen4	105	139	105
LightSteelBlue1	202	225	255	SeaGreen1	84	255	159
LightSteelBlue2	188	210	238	SeaGreen2	78	238	148
LightSteelBlue3	162	181	205	SeaGreen3	67	205	128
LightSteelBlue4	110	123	139	SeaGreen4	46	139	87
LightBlue1	191	239	255	PaleGreen1	154	255	154
LightBlue2	178	223	238	PaleGreen2	144	238	144
LightBlue3	154	192	205	PaleGreen3	124	205	124
LightBlue4	104	131	139	PaleGreen4	84	139	84

Color
Database

English Words	Red	Green	Blue	English Words	Red	Green	Blue
SpringGreen1	0	255	127	goldenrod1	255	193	37
SpringGreen2	0	238	118	goldenrod2	238	180	34
SpringGreen3	0	205	102	goldenrod3	205	155	29
SpringGreen4	0	139	69	goldenrod4	139	105	20
green1	0	255	0	DarkGoldenrod1	255	185	15
green2	0	238	0	DarkGoldenrod2	238	173	14
green3	0	205	0	DarkGoldenrod3	205	149	12
green4	0	139	0	DarkGoldenrod4	139	101	8
chartreuse1	127	255	0	RosyBrown1	255	193	193
chartreuse2	118	238	0	RosyBrown2	238	180	180
chartreuse3	102	205	0	RosyBrown3	205	155	155
chartreuse4	69	139	0	RosyBrown4	139	105	105
OliveDrab1	192	255	62	IndianRed1	255	106	106
OliveDrab2	179	238	58	IndianRed2	238	99	99
OliveDrab3	154	205	50	IndianRed3	205	85	85
OliveDrab4	105	139	34	IndianRed4	139	58	58
DarkOliveGreen1	202	255	112	sienna1	255	130	71
DarkOliveGreen2	188	238	104	sienna2	238	121	66
DarkOliveGreen3	162	205	90	sienna3	205	104	57
DarkOliveGreen4	110	139	61	sienna4	139	71	38
khaki1	255	246	143	burlywood1	255	211	155
khaki2	238	230	133	burlywood2	238	197	145
khaki3	205	198	115	burlywood3	205	170	125
khaki4	139	134	78	burlywood4	139	115	85
LightGoldenrod1	255	236	139	wheat1	255	231	186
LightGoldenrod2	238	220	130	wheat2	238	216	174
LightGoldenrod3	205	190	112	wheat3	205	186	150
LightGoldenrod4	139	129	76	wheat4	139	126	102
LightYellow1	255	255	224	tan1	255	165	79
LightYellow2	238	238	209	tan2	238	154	73
LightYellow3	205	205	180	tan3	205	133	63
LightYellow4	139	139	122	tan4	139	90	43
yellow1	255	255	0	chocolate1	255	127	36
yellow2	238	238	0	chocolate2	238	118	33
yellow3	205	205	0	chocolate3	205	102	29
yellow4	139	139	0	chocolate4	139	69	19
gold1	255	215	0	firebrick1	255	48	48
gold2	238	201	0	firebrick2	238	44	44
gold3	205	173	0	firebrick3	205	38	38
gold4	139	117	0	firebrick4	139	26	26

English Words	Red	Green	Blue	English Words	Red	Green	Blue
brown1	255	64	64	HotPink1	255	110	180
brown2	238	59	59	HotPink2	238	106	167
brown3	205	51	51	HotPink3	205	96	144
brown4	139	35	35	HotPink4	139	58	98
salmon1	255	140	105	pink1	255	181	197
salmon2	238	130	98	pink2	238	169	184
salmon3	205	112	84	pink3	205	145	158
salmon4	139	76	57	pink4	139	99	108
LightSalmon1	255	160	122	LightPink1	255	174	185
LightSalmon2	238	149	114	LightPink2	238	162	173
LightSalmon3	205	129	98	LightPink3	205	140	149
LightSalmon4	139	87	66	LightPink4	139	95	101
orange1	255	165	0	PaleVioletRed1	255	130	171
orange2	238	154	0	PaleVioletRed2	238	121	159
orange3	205	133	0	PaleVioletRed3	205	104	137
orange4	139	90	0	PaleVioletRed4	139	71	93
DarkOrange1	255	127	0	maroon1	255	52	179
DarkOrange2	238	118	0	maroon2	238	48	167
DarkOrange3	205	102	0	maroon3	205	41	144
DarkOrange4	139	69	0	maroon4	139	28	98
coral1	255	114	86	VioletRed1	255	62	150
coral2	238	106	80	VioletRed2	238	58	140
coral3	205	91	69	VioletRed3	205	50	120
coral4	139	62	47	VioletRed4	139	34	82
tomato1	255	99	71	magenta1	255	0	255
tomato2	238	92	66	magenta2	238	0	238
tomato3	205	79	57	magenta3	205	0	205
tomato4	139	54	38	magenta4	139	0	139
OrangeRed1	255	69	0	orchid1	255	131	250
OrangeRed2	238	64	0	orchid2	238	122	233
OrangeRed3	205	55	0	orchid3	205	105	201
OrangeRed4	139	37	0	orchid4	139	71	137
red1	255	0	0	plum1	255	187	255
red2	238	0	0	plum2	238	174	238
red3	205	0	0	plum3	205	150	205
red4	139	0	0	plum4	139	102	139
DeepPink1	255	20	147	MediumOrchid1	224	102	255
DeepPink2	238	18	137	MediumOrchid2	209	95	238
DeepPink3	205	16	118	MediumOrchid3	180	82	205
DeepPink4	139	10	80	MediumOrchid4	122	55	139

Color Database

English Words	Red	Green	Blue
DarkOrchid1	191	62	255
DarkOrchid2	178	58	238
DarkOrchid3	154	50	205
DarkOrchid4	104	34	139
purple1	155	48	255
purple2	145	44	238
purple3	125	38	205
purple4	85	26	139
MediumPurple1	171	130	255
MediumPurple2	159	121	238
MediumPurple3	137	104	205
MediumPurple4	93	71	139
thistle1	255	225	255
thistle2	238	210	238
thistle3	205	181	205
thistle4	139	123	139

*Also defined are the color names "gray0" through "gray 100", spelled with and "e" or an "a". "gray0" is black and "gray100" is white.

This appendix describes each event structure in detail and briefly shows how each event type is used. It covers the most common uses of each event type, the information contained in each event structure, how the event is selected, and the side effects of the event, if any. Each event is described on a separate reference page.

Table E-1 lists each event mask, its associated event types, and the associated structure definition. See Chapter 8, *Events*, of Volume One, *Xlib Programming Manual*, for more information on events.

Table E-1. Event Masks, Event Types, and Event Structures

Event Mask	Event Type	Structure
KeyPressMask	KeyPress	XKeyPressedEvent
KeyReleaseMask	KeyRelease	XKeyReleasedEvent
ButtonPressMask	ButtonPress	XButtonPressedEvent
ButtonReleaseMask	ButtonRelease	XButtonReleasedEvent
OwnerGrabButtonMask	n/a	n/a
KeymapStateMask	KeymapNotify	XKeymapEvent
PointerMotionMask PointerMotionHintMask ButtonMotionMask Button1MotionMask Button2MotionMask Button3MotionMask Button4MotionMask Button5MotionMask	MotionNotify	XPointerMovedEvent
EnterWindowMask	EnterNotify	XEnterWindowEvent
LeaveWindowMask	LeaveNotify	XLeaveWindowEvent
FocusChangeMask	FocusIn FocusOut	XFocusInEvent XFocusOutEvent

Event Mask	Event Type	Structure
ExposureMask	Expose	XExposeEvent
selected in GC by graphics_expose member	GraphicsExpose NoExpose	XGraphicsExposeEvent XNoExposeEvent
ColormapChangeMask	ColormapNotify	XColormapEvent
PropertyChangeMask	PropertyNotify	XPropertyEvent
VisibilityChangeMask	VisibilityNotify	XVisibilityEvent
ResizeRedirectMask	ResizeRequest	XResizeRequestEvent
StructureNotifyMask	CirculateNotify ConfigureNotify DestroyNotify GravityNotify MapNotify ReparentNotify UnmapNotify	XCirculateEvent XConfigureEvent XDestroyWindowEvent XGravityEvent XMapEvent XReparentEvent XUnmapEvent
SubstructureNotifyMask	CirculateNotify ConfigureNotify CreateNotify DestroyNotify GravityNotify MapNotify ReparentNotify UnmapNotify	XCirculateEvent XConfigureEvent XCreateWindowEvent XDestroyWindowEvent XGravityEvent XMapEvent XReparentEvent XUnmapEvent
SubstructureRedirectMask	CirculateRequest ConfigureRequest MapRequest	XCirculateRequestEvent XConfigureRequestEvent XMapRequestEvent
(always selected)	MappingNotify	XMappingEvent
(always selected)	ClientMessage	XClientMessageEvent
(always selected)	SelectionClear	XSetSelectClearEvent
(always selected)	SelectionNotify	XSelectionEvent
(always selected)	SelectionRequest	XSelectionRequestEvent

E.1 Meaning of Common Structure Elements

Example E-1 shows the XEvent union and a simple event structure that is one member of the union. Several of the members of this structure are present in nearly every event structure. They are described here before we go into the event-specific members (see also Section 8.2.2 of Volume One, *Xlib Programming Manual*).

Example E-1. XEvent union and XAnyEvent structure

```
typedef union _XEvent {
    int type;               /* Must not be changed; first member */
    XAnyEvent xany;
    XButtonEvent xbutton;
    XCirculateEvent xcirculate;
    XCirculateRequestEvent xcirculaterequest;
    XClientMessageEvent xclient;
    XColormapEvent xcolormap;
    XConfigureEvent xconfigure;
    XConfigureRequestEvent xconfigurerequest;
    XCreateWindowEvent xcreatewindow;
    XDestroyWindowEvent xdestroywindow;
    XCrossingEvent xcrossing;
    XExposeEvent xexpose;
    XFocusChangeEvent xfocus;
    XNoExposeEvent xnoexpose;
    XGraphicsExposeEvent xgraphicsexpose;
    XGravityEvent xgravity;
    XKeymapEvent xkeymap;
    XKeyEvent xkey;
    XMapEvent xmap;
    XUnmapEvent xunmap;
    XMappingEvent xmapping;
    XMapRequestEvent xmaprequest;
    XMotionEvent xmotion;
    XPropertyEvent xproperty;
    XReparentEvent xreparent;
    XResizeRequestEvent xresizerequest;
    XSelectionClearEvent xselectionclear;
    XSelectionEvent xselection;
    XSelectionRequestEvent xselectionrequest;
    XVisibilityEvent xvisibility;
} XEvent;

typedef struct {
    int type;
    unsigned long serial;   /* # of last request processed by server */
    Bool send_event;        /* True if this came from SendEvent
                             * request */
    Display *display;       /* Display the event was read from */
    Window window;          /* window on which event was requested
                             * in event mask */
} XAnyEvent;
```

The first member of the XEvent union is the type of event. When an event is received (with XNextEvent, for example), the application checks the type member in the XEvent union. Then the specific event type is known and the specific event structure (such as xbutton) is used to access information specific to that event type.

Before the branching depending on the event type, only the XEvent union is used. After the branching, only the event structure which contains the specific information for each event type should be used in each branch. For example, if the XEvent union were called report, the report.xexpose structure should be used within the branch for Expose events.

You will notice that each event structure also begins with a type member. This member is rarely used, since it is an identical copy of the type member in the XEvent union.

Most event structures also have a window member. The only ones that do not are selection events (SelectionClear, SelectionNotify, and SelectionRequest) and events selected by the graphics_exposures member of the GC (GraphicsExpose and NoExpose). The window member indicates the event window that selected and received the event. This is the window where the event arrives if it has propagated through the hierarchy as described in Section 8.3.2, of Volume One, *Xlib Programming Manual*. One event type may have two different meanings to an application, depending on which window it appears in.

Many of the event structures also have a display and/or root member. The display member identifies the connection to the server that is active. The root member indicates which screen the window that received the event is linked to in the hierarchy. Most programs only use a single screen and therefore do not need to worry about the root member. The display member can be useful, since you can pass the display variable into routines by simply passing a pointer to the event structure, eliminating the need for a separate display argument.

All event structures include a serial member that gives the number of the last protocol request processed by the server. This is useful in debugging, since an error can be detected by the server but not reported to the user (or programmer) until the next routine that gets an event. That means several routines may execute successfully after the error occurs. The last request processed will often indicate the request that contained the error.

All event structures also include a send_event flag, which, if True, indicates that the event was sent by XSendEvent (i.e., by another client rather than by the server).

The following pages describe each event type in detail. The events are presented in alphabetical order, each on a separate page. Each page describes the circumstances under which the event is generated, the mask used to select it, the structure itself, its members, and useful programming notes. Note that the description of the structure members does not include those members common to many structures. If you need more information on these members, please refer to this introductory section.

When Generated

There are two types of pointer button events: ButtonPress and ButtonRelease. Both contain the same information.

Select With

May be selected separately, using ButtonPressMask and ButtonReleaseMask.

XEvent Structure Name

```
typedef union _XEvent {
    . . .
    XButtonEvent xbutton;
    . . .
} XEvent;
```

Event Structure

```
typedef struct {
int type;                    /* of event */
unsigned long serial;        /* # of last request processed by server */
Bool send_event;             /* True if this came from a SendEvent request */
Display *display;            /* Display the event was read from */
Window window;               /* event window it is reported relative to */
Window root;                 /* root window that the event occurred under */
Window subwindow;            /* child window */
Time time;                   /* when event occurred, in milliseconds */
int x, y;                    /* pointer coordinates relative to receiving
                              * window */
int x_root, y_root;          /* coordinates relative to root */
unsigned int state;          /* mask of all buttons and modifier keys */
unsigned int button;         /* button that triggered event */
Bool same_screen;            /* same screen flag */
} XButtonEvent;
typedef XButtonEvent XButtonPressedEvent;
typedef XButtonEvent XButtonReleasedEvent;
```

Event Structure Members

subwindow   If the source window is the child of the receiving window, then the subwindow member is set to the ID of that child.

time   The server time when the button event occurred, in milliseconds. Time is declared as unsigned long, so it wraps around when it reaches the maximum value of a 32-bit number (every 49.7 days).

x, y   If the receiving window is on the same screen as the root window specified by root, then x and y are the pointer coordinates relative to the receiving window's origin. Otherwise, x and y are zero.

Event
Reference

When active button grabs and pointer grabs are in effect (see Section 9.4 of Volume One, *Xlib Programming Manual*), the coordinates relative to the receiving window may not be within the window (they may be negative or greater than window height or width).

x_root, y_root The pointer coordinates relative to the root window which is an ancestor of the event window. If the pointer was on a different screen, these are zero.

state The state of all the buttons and modifier keys just before the event, represented by a mask of the button and modifier key symbols: Button1Mask, Button2Mask, Button3Mask, Button4Mask, Button5Mask, ControlMask, LockMask, Mod1Mask, Mod2-Mask, Mod3Mask, Mod4Mask, Mod5Mask, and ShiftMask. If a modifier key is pressed and released when no other modifier keys are held, the ButtonPress will have a state member of 0 and the ButtonRelease will have a nonzero state member indicating that itself was held just before the event.

button A value indicating which button changed state to trigger this event. One of the constants: Button1, Button2, Button3, Button4, or Button5.

same_screen Indicates whether the pointer is currently on the same screen as this window. This is always True unless the pointer was actively grabbed before the automatic grab could take place.

Notes

Unless an active grab already exists or a passive grab on the button combination that was pressed already exists at a higher level in the hierarchy than where the ButtonPress occurred, an automatic active grab of the pointer takes place when a ButtonPress occurs. Because of the automatic grab, the matching ButtonRelease is sent to the same application that received the ButtonPress event. If OwnerGrabButtonMask has been selected, the ButtonRelease event is delivered to the window which contained the pointer when the button was released, as long as that window belongs to the same client as the window in which the ButtonPress event occurred. If the ButtonRelease occurs outside of the client's windows or OwnerGrabButtonMask was not selected, the ButtonRelease is delivered to the window in which the ButtonPress occurred. The grab is terminated when all buttons are released. During the grab, the cursor associated with the grabbing window will track the pointer anywhere on the screen.

If the application has invoked a passive button grab on an ancestor of the window in which the ButtonPress event occurs, then that grab takes precedence over the automatic grab, and the ButtonRelease will go to that window, or it will be handled normally by that client depending on the owner_events flag in the XGrabButton call.

When Generated

A `CirculateNotify` event reports a call to change the stacking order, and it includes whether the final position is on the top or on the bottom. This event is generated by `XCirculateSubwindows`, `XCirculateSubwindowsDown`, or `XCirculate-SubwindowsUp`. See also the `CirculateRequest` and `ConfigureNotify` reference pages.

Select With

This event is selected with `StructureNotifyMask` in the `XSelectInput` call for the window to be moved or with `SubstructureNotifyMask` for the parent of the window to be moved.

XEvent Structure Name

```
typedef union _XEvent {
    . . .
    XCirculateEvent xcirculate;
    . . .
} XEvent;
```

Event Structure

```
typedef struct {
    int type;
    unsigned long serial;   /* # of last request processed by server */
    Bool send_event;        /* True if this came from SendEvent request */
    Display *display;       /* Display the event was read from */
    Window event;
    Window window;
    int place;              /* PlaceOnTop, PlaceOnBottom */
} XCirculateEvent;
```

Event Structure Members

event   The window receiving the event. If the event was selected by `Structure-NotifyMask`, event will be the same as window. If the event was selected by `SubstructureNotifyMask`, event will be the parent of window.

window   The window that was restacked.

place   Either `PlaceOnTop` or `PlaceOnBottom`. Indicates whether the window was raised to the top or bottom of the stack.

Event Reference

CirculateRequest

When Generated

A `CirculateRequest` event reports when `XCirculateSubwindows`, `XCirculate-SubwindowsDown`, `XCirculateSubwindowsUp`, or `XRestackWindows` is called to change the stacking order of a group of children.

This event differs from `CirculateNotify` in that it delivers the parameters of the request before it is carried out. This gives the client that selects this event (usually the window manager) the opportunity to review the request in the light of its window management policy before executing the circulate request itself or to deny the request. (`CirculateNotify` indicates the final outcome of the request.)

Select With

This event is selected for the parent window with `SubstructureRedirectMask`.

XEvent Structure Name

```
typedef union _XEvent {
    . . .
    XCirculateRequestEvent xcirculaterequest;
    . . .
} XEvent;
```

Event Structure

```
typedef struct {
    int type;
    unsigned long serial;  /* # of last request processed by server */
    Bool send_event;       /* True if this came from SendEvent request */
    Display *display;      /* Display the event was read from */
    Window parent;
    Window window;
    int place;             /* PlaceOnTop, PlaceOnBottom */
} XCirculateRequestEvent;
```

Event Structure Members

parent   The parent of the window that was restacked. This is the window that selected the event.

window   The window being restacked.

place   `PlaceOnTop` or `PlaceOnBottom`. Indicates whether the window was to be placed on the top or on the bottom of the stacking order.

When Generated

A `ClientMessage` event is sent as a result of a call to `XSendEvent` by a client to a particular window. Any type of event can be sent with `XSendEvent`, but it will be distinguished from normal events by the `send_event` member being set to `True`. If your program wants to be able to treat events sent with `XSendEvent` as different from normal events, you can read this member.

Select With

There is no event mask for `ClientMessage` events, and they are not selected with `XSelectInput`. Instead `XSendEvent` directs them to a specific window, which is given as a window ID: the `PointerWindow` or the `InputFocus`.

XEvent Structure Name

```
typedef union _XEvent {
    ...
    XClientMessageEvent xclient;
    ...
} XEvent;
```

Event Structure

```
typedef struct {
    int type;
    unsigned long serial; /* # of last request processed by server */
    Bool send_event;      /* True if this came from SendEvent request */
    Display *display;     /* Display the event was read from */
    Window window;
    Atom message_type;
    int format;
    union {
        char b[20];
        short s[10];
        long l[5];
    } data;
} XClientMessageEvent;
```

Event Structure Members

message_type   An atom that specifies how the data is to be interpreted by the receiving client. The X server places no interpretation on the type or the data, but it must be a list of 8-bit, 16-bit, or 32-bit quantities, so that the X server can correctly swap bytes as necessary. The data always consists of twenty 8-bit values, ten 16-bit values, or five 32-bit values, although each particular message might not make use of all of these values.

format   Specifies the format of the property specified by message_type. This will be on of the values 8, 16, or 32.

ColormapNotify

When Generated

A `ColormapNotify` event reports when the colormap attribute of a window changes or when the colormap specified by the attribute is installed, uninstalled, or freed. This event is generated by `XChangeWindowAttributes`, `XFreeColormap`, `XInstallColormap`, and `XUninstallColormap`.

Select With

This event is selected with `ColormapChangeMask`.

XEvent Structure Name

```
typedef union _XEvent {
    . . .
    XColormapEvent xcolormap;
    . . .
} XEvent;
```

Event Structure

```
typedef struct {
    int type;
    unsigned long serial;   /* # of last request processed by server */
    Bool send_event;        /* True if this came from SendEvent request */
    Display *display;       /* Display the event was read from */
    Window window;
    Colormap colormap;      /* a colormap or None */
    Bool new;
    int state;              /* ColormapInstalled, ColormapUninstalled */
} XColormapEvent;
```

Event Structure Members

window   The window whose associated colormap or attribute changes.

colormap   The colormap associated with the window, either a colormap ID or the constant None. It will be `None` only if this event was generated due to an `XFree-Colormap` call.

new   `True` when the colormap attribute has been changed, or `False` when the colormap is installed or uninstalled.

state   Either `ColormapInstalled` or `ColormapUninstalled`; it indicates whether the colormap is installed or uninstalled.

When Generated

A `ConfigureNotify` event announces actual changes to a window's configuration (size, position, border, and stacking order). See also the `CirculateRequest` reference page.

Select With

This event is selected for a single window by specifying the window ID of that window with `StructureNotifyMask`. To receive this event for all children of a window, specify the parent window ID with `SubstructureNotifyMask`.

XEvent Structure Name

```
typedef union _XEvent {
    ...
    XConfigureEvent xconfigure;
    ...
} XEvent;
```

Event Structure

```
typedef struct {
    int type;
    unsigned long serial;   /* # of last request processed by server */
    Bool send_event;        /* True if this came from SendEvent request */
    Display *display;       /* Display the event was read from */
    Window event;
    Window window;
    int x, y;
    int width, height;
    int border_width;
    Window above;
    Bool override_redirect;
} XConfigureEvent;
```

Event Structure Members

`event`	The window that selected the event. The event and window members are identical if the event was selected with `Structure-NotifyMask`.
`window`	The window whose configuration was changed.
`x, y`	The final coordinates of the reconfigured window relative to its parent.
`width, height`	The width and height in pixels of the window after reconfiguration.
`border_width`	The width in pixels of the border after reconfiguration.
`above`	If this member is `None`, then the window is on the bottom of the stack with respect to its siblings. Otherwise, the window is immediately on top of the specified sibling window.

override_redirect   The `override_redirect` attribute of the reconfigured window. If `True`, it indicates that the client wants this window to be immune to interception by the window manager of configuration requests. Window managers normally should ignore this event if `override_redirect` is `True`.

When Generated

A `ConfigureRequest` event reports when another client attempts to change a window's size, position, border, and/or stacking order.

This event differs from `ConfigureNotify` in that it delivers the parameters of the request before it is carried out. This gives the client that selects this event (usually the window manager) the opportunity to revise the requested configuration before executing the `XConfigureWindow` request itself or to deny the request. (`ConfigureNotify` indicates the final outcome of the request.)

Select With

This event is selected for any window in a group of children by specifying the parent window with `SubstructureRedirectMask`.

XEvent Structure Name

```
typedef union _XEvent {
    ...
    XConfigureRequestEvent xconfigurerequest;
    ...
} XEvent;
```

Event Structure

```
typedef struct {
    int type;
    unsigned long serial; /* # of last request processed by server */
    Bool send_event;      /* True if this came from SendEvent request */
    Display *display;     /* Display the event was read from */
    Window parent;
    Window window;
    int x, y;
    int width, height;
    int border_width;
    Window above;
    int detail;           /* Above, Below, BottomIf, TopIf, Opposite */
    unsigned long value_mask;
} XConfigureRequestEvent;
```

Event Structure Members

parent   The window that selected the event. This is the parent of the window being configured.

window   The window that is being configured.

x, y   The requested position for the upper-left pixel of the window's border relative to the origin of the parent window.

width, height   The requested width and height in pixels for the window.

Event
Reference

border_width   The requested border width for the window.

above   None, Above, Below, TopIf, BottomIf, or Opposite. Specifies
                the sibling window on top of which the specified window should be
                placed. If this member has the constant None, then the specified win-
                dow should be placed on the bottom.

Notes

The geometry is derived from the XConfigureWindow request that triggered the event.

When Generated

A `CreateNotify` event reports when a window is created.

Select With

This event is selected on children of a window by specifying the parent window ID with `SubstructureNotifyMask`. (Note that this event type cannot be selected by `StructureNotifyMask`.)

XEvent Structure Name

```
typedef union _XEvent {
    ...
    XCreateWindowEvent xcreatewindow;
    ...
} XEvent;
```

Event Structure

```
typedef struct {
    int type;
    unsigned long serial;      /* # of last request processed by server */
    Bool send_event;           /* True if this came from SendEvent
                                * request */
    Display *display;          /* Display the event was read from */
    Window parent;             /* parent of the window */
    Window window;             /* window ID of window created */
    int x, y;                  /* window location */
    int width, height;         /* size of window */
    int border_width;          /* border width */
    Bool override_redirect;    /* creation should be overridden */
} XCreateWindowEvent;
```

Event Structure Members

parent	The ID of the created window's parent.
window	The ID of the created window.
x, y	The coordinates of the created window relative to its parent.
width, height	The width and height in pixels of the created window.
border_width	The width in pixels of the border of the created window.
override_redirect	The `override_redirect` attribute of the created window. If `True`, it indicates that the client wants this window to be immune to interception by the window manager of configuration requests. Window managers normally should ignore this event if `override_redirect` is `True`.

Event
Reference

Notes

For descriptions of these members, see the XCreateWindow function and the XSet-WindowAttributes structure.

When Generated

A DestroyNotify event reports that a window has been destroyed.

Select With

To receive this event type on children of a window, specify the parent window ID and pass SubstructureNotifyMask as part of the event_mask argument to XSelectInput. This event type cannot be selected with StructureNotifyMask.

XEvent Structure Name

```
typedef union _XEvent {
    ...
    XDestroyWindowEvent xdestroywindow;
    ...
} XEvent;
```

Event Structure

```
typedef struct {
    int type;
    unsigned long serial; /* # of last request processed by server */
    Bool send_event;      /* True if this came from SendEvent request */
    Display *display;      /* Display the event was read from */
    Window event;
    Window window;
} XDestroyWindowEvent;
```

Event Structure Members

event   The window that selected the event.

window   The window that was destroyed.

EnterNotify, LeaveNotify

When Generated

`EnterNotify` and `LeaveNotify` events occur when the pointer enters or leaves a window.

When the pointer crosses a window border, a `LeaveNotify` event occurs in the window being left and an `EnterNotify` event occurs in the window being entered. Whether or not each event is queued for any application depends on whether any application selected the right event on the window in which it occurred.

In addition, `EnterNotify` and `LeaveNotify` events are delivered to windows that are *virtually crossed*. These are windows that are between the origin and destination windows in the hierarchy but not necessarily on the screen. Further explanation of virtual crossing is provided two pages following.

Select With

Each of these events can be selected separately with `XEnterWindowMask` and `XLeave-WindowMask`.

XEvent Structure Name

```
typedef union _XEvent {
    . . .
    XCrossingEvent xcrossing;
    . . .
} XEvent;
```

Event Structure

```
typedef struct {
    int type;                 /* of event */
    unsigned long serial;     /* # of last request processed by server */
    Bool send_event;          /* True if this came from SendEvent request */
    Display *display;         /* Display the event was read from */
    Window window;            /* event window it is reported relative to */
    Window root;              /* root window that the event occurred on */
    Window subwindow;         /* child window */
    Time time;                /* milliseconds */
    int x, y;                 /* pointer x,y coordinates in receiving
                               * window */
    int x_root, y_root;       /* coordinates relative to root */
    int mode;                 /* NotifyNormal, NotifyGrab, NotifyUngrab */
    int detail;               /* NotifyAncestor, NotifyInferior,
                               * NotifyNonLinear, NotifyNonLinearVirtual,
                               * NotifyVirtual */
    Bool same_screen;         /* same screen flag */
    Bool focus;               /* boolean focus */
    unsigned int state;       /* key or button mask */
} XCrossingEvent;
typedef XCrossingEvent XEnterWindowEvent;
typedef XCrossingEvent XLeaveWindowEvent;
```

Event Structure Members

The following list describes the members of the XCrossingEvent structure.

subwindow
: In a LeaveNotify event, if the pointer began in a child of the receiving window, then the child member is set to the window ID of the child. Otherwise, it is set to None. For an EnterNotify event, if the pointer ends up in a child of the receiving window, then the child member is set to the window ID of the child. Otherwise, it is set to None.

time
: The server time when the crossing event occurred, in milliseconds. Time is declared as unsigned long, so it wraps around when it reaches the maximum value of a 32-bit number (every 49.7 days).

x, y
: The point of entry or exit of the pointer relative to the event window.

x_root, y_root
: The point of entry or exit of the pointer relative to the root window.

mode
: Normal crossing events or those caused by pointer warps have mode NotifyNormal, events caused by a grab have mode NotifyGrab, and events caused by a released grab have mode NotifyUngrab.

detail
: The value of the detail member depends on the hierarchical relationship between the origin and destination windows and the direction of pointer transfer. Determining which windows receive events and with which detail members is quite complicated. This topic is described in the next section.

same_screen
: Indicates whether the pointer is currently on the same screen as this window. This is always True unless the pointer was actively grabbed before the automatic grab could take place.

focus
: If the receiving window is the focus window or a descendant of the focus window, the focus member is True; otherwise, it is False.

state
: The state of all the buttons and modifier keys just before the event, represented by a mask of the button and modifier key symbols: Button1Mask, Button2Mask, Button3Mask, Button4Mask, Button5Mask, ControlMask, LockMask, Mod1Mask, Mod2-Mask, Mod3Mask, Mod4Mask, Mod5Mask, and ShiftMask.

Virtual Crossing and the detail Member

Virtual crossing occurs when the pointer moves between two windows that do not have a parent-child relationship. Windows between the origin and destination windows in the hierarchy receive EnterNotify and LeaveNotify events. The detail member of each of these events depends on the hierarchical relationship of the origin and destination windows and the direction of pointer transfer.

Event
Reference

Virtual crossing is an advanced topic that you should not spend time figuring out unless you have an important reason to use it. We have never seen an application that uses this feature, and we know of no reason for its extreme complexity. With that word of warning, proceed.

Let's say the pointer has moved from one window, the origin, to another, the destination. First, we'll specify what types of events each window gets and then the detail member of each of those events.

The window of origin receives a `LeaveNotify` event and the destination window receives an `EnterNotify` event, if they have requested this type of event. If one is an inferior of the other, the `detail` member of the event received by the inferior is `NotifyAncestor` and the detail of the event received by the superior is `NotifyInferior`. If the crossing is between parent and child, these are the only events generated.

However, if the origin and destination windows are not parent and child, other windows are *virtually crossed* and also receive events. If neither window is an ancestor of the other, ancestors of each window, up to but not including the least common ancestor, receive `Leave-Notify` events, if they are in the same branch of the hierarchy as the origin, and `Enter-Notify` events, if they are in the same branch as the destination. These events can be used to track the motion of the pointer through the hierarchy.

- In the case of a crossing between a parent and a child of a child, the middle child receives a `LeaveNotify` with detail `NotifyVirtual`.

- In the case of a crossing between a child and the parent of its parent, the middle child receives an `EnterNotify` with detail `NotifyVirtual`.

- In a crossing between windows whose least common ancestor is two or more windows away, both the origin and destination windows receive events with detail `Notify-Nonlinear`. The windows between the origin and the destination in the hierarchy, up to but not including their least common ancestor, receive events with detail `Notify-NonlinearVirtual`. The least common ancestor is the lowest window from which both are descendants.

- If the origin and destination windows are on separate screens, the events and details generated are the same as for two windows not parent and child, except that the root windows of the two screens are considered the least common ancestor. Both root windows also receive events.

Table E-1 shows the event types generated by a pointer crossing from window *A* to window *B* when window *C* is the least common ancestor of *A* and *B*.

Table E-1. Border Crossing Events and Window Relationship

LeaveNotify	EnterNotify
Origin window (*A*)	Destination window (*B*)
Windows between *A* and *B*, exclusive, if *A* is inferior	Windows between *A* and *B*, exclusive, if *B* is inferior
Windows between *A* and *C*, exclusive	Windows between *B* and *C*, exclusive,
Root window on screen of origin if different from screen of destination	Root window on screen of destination if different from screen of origin

Table E-2 lists the detail members in events generated by a pointer crossing from window *A* to window *B*.

Table E-2. Event detail Member and Window Relationship

detail Flag	Window Delivered To
NotifyAncestor	Origin or destination when either is descendant
NotifyInferior	Origin or destination when either is ancestor
NotifyVirtual	Windows between *A* and *B*, exclusive, if either is descendant
NotifyNonlinear	Origin and destination when *A* and *B* are two or more windows distant from least common ancestor *C*
NotifyNonlinearVirtual	Windows between *A* and *C*, exclusive, and between *B* and *C*, exclusive, when *A* and *B* have least common ancestor *C*; also on both root windows if *A* and *B* are on different screens

For example, Figure E-1 shows the events that are generated by a movement from a window (window *A*) to a child (window *B1*) of a sibling (window *B*). This would generate three events: a LeaveNotify with detail NotifyNonlinear for the window *A*, an EnterNotify with detail NotifyNonlinearVirtual for its sibling window *B*, and an EnterNotify with detail NotifyNonlinear for the child (window *B1*).

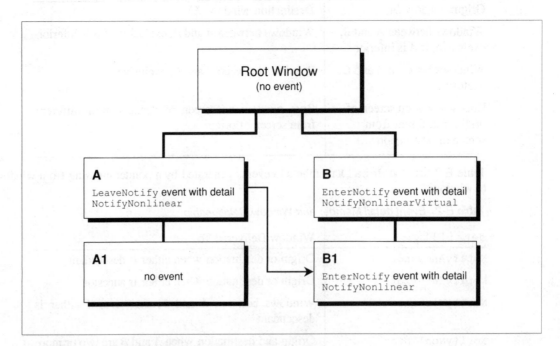

Figure E-1. Events generated by a move between windows

EnterNotify and LeaveNotify events are also generated when the pointer is grabbed, if the pointer was not already inside the grabbing window. In this case, the grabbing window receives an EnterNotify and the window containing the pointer receives a LeaveNotify event, both with mode NotifyUngrab. The pointer position in both events is the position before the grab. The result when the grab is released is exactly the same, except that the two windows receive EnterNotify instead of LeaveNotify and vice versa.

Figure E-2 demonstrates the events and details caused by various pointer transitions, indicated by heavy arrows.

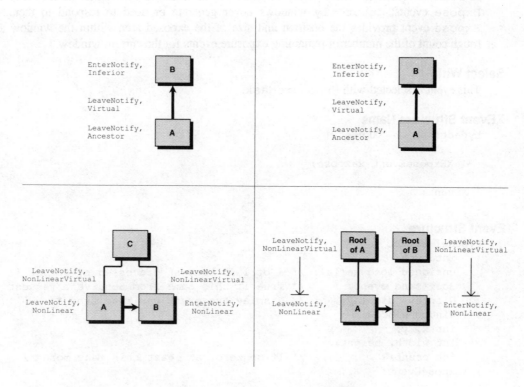

Figure E-2. Border crossing events and detail member for pointer movement from window A to window B, for various window relationships

When Generated

An `Expose` event is generated when a window becomes visible or a previously invisible part of a window becomes visible. Only `InputOutput` windows generate or need to respond to `Expose` events; `InputOnly` windows never generate or need to respond to them. The `Expose` event provides the position and size of the exposed area within the window and a rough count of the number of remaining exposure events for the current window.

Select With

This event is selected with `ExposureMask`.

XEvent Structure Name

```
typedef union _XEvent {
    . . .
    XExposeEvent xexpose;
    . . .
} XEvent;
```

Event Structure

```
typedef struct {
    int type;
    unsigned long serial;    /* # of last request processed by server */
    Bool send_event;         /* True if this came from SendEvent request */
    Display *display;        /* Display the event was read from */
    Window window;
    int x, y;
    int width, height;
    int count;               /* If nonzero, at least this many more */
} XExposeEvent;
```

Event Structure Members

x, y   The coordinates of the upper-left corner of the exposed region relative to the origin of the window.

width, height   The width and height in pixels of the exposed region.

count   The approximate number of remaining contiguous `Expose` events that were generated as a result of a single function call.

Notes

A single action such as a window movement or a function call can generate several exposure events on one window or on several windows. The server guarantees that all exposure events generated from a single action will be sent contiguously, so that they can all be handled before moving on to other event types. This allows an application to keep track of the rectangles specified in contiguous `Expose` events, set the `clip_mask` in a GC to the areas specified in the rectangle using XSetRegion or XSetClipRectangles, and then finally redraw the window clipped with the GC in a single operation after all the Expose events have arrived. The last event to arrive is indicated by a count of 0. In Release 2, XUnionRectWith-Region can be used to add the rectangle in Expose events to a region before calling XSet-Region.

If your application is able to redraw partial windows, you can also read each exposure event in turn and redraw each area.

FocusIn, FocusOut

When Generated

FocusIn and FocusOut events occur when the keyboard focus window changes as a result of an XSetInputFocus call. They are much like EnterNotify and LeaveNotify events except that they track the focus rather than the pointer.

When a focus change occurs, a FocusOut event is delivered to the old focus window and a FocusIn event to the window which receives the focus. In addition, windows in between these two windows in the window hierarchy are virtually crossed and receive focus change events, as described below. Some or all of the windows between the window containing the pointer at the time of the focus change and the root window also receive focus change events, as described below.

Select With

FocusIn and FocusOut events are selected with FocusChangeMask. They cannot be selected separately.

XEvent Structure Name

```
typedef union _XEvent {
    . . .
    XFocusChangeEvent xfocus;
    (. . .
} XEvent;
```

Event Structure

```
typedef struct {
    int type;              /* FocusIn or FocusOut */
    unsigned long serial;  /* # of last request processed by server */
    Bool send_event;       /* True if this came from SendEvent request */
    Display *display;       /* Display the event was read from */
    Window window;         /* Window of event */
    int mode;              /* NotifyNormal, NotifyGrab, NotifyUngrab */
    int detail;            /* NotifyAncestor, NotifyDetailNone,
                            * NotifyInferior, NotifyNonLinear,
                            * NotifyNonLinearVirtual, NotifyPointer,
                            * NotifyPointerRoot, NotifyVirtual*/
} XFocusChangeEvent;
typedef XFocusChangeEvent XFocusInEvent;
typedef XFocusChangeEvent XFocusOutEvent;
```

Event Structure Members

mode   For events generated when the keyboard is not grabbed, mode is Notify-Normal; when the keyboard is grabbed, mode is NotifyGrab; and when a keyboard is ungrabbed, mode is NotifyUngrab.

detail The detail member identifies the relationship between the window that receives the event and the origin and destination windows. It will be described in detail after the description of which windows get what types of events.

Notes

The *keyboard focus* is a window that has been designated as the one to receive all keyboard input irrespective of the pointer position. Only the keyboard focus window and its descendants receive keyboard events. By default, the focus window is the root window. Since all windows are descendants of the root, the pointer controls the window that receives input.

Most window managers allow the user to set a focus window to avoid the problem where the pointer sometimes gets bumped into the wrong window and your typing does not go to the intended window. If the pointer is pointing at the root window, all typing is usually lost, since there is no application for this input to propagate to. Some applications may set the keyboard focus so that they can get all keyboard input for a given period of time, but this practice is not encouraged.

Focus events are used when an application wants to act differently when the keyboard focus is set to another window or to itself. FocusChangeMask is used to select FocusIn and FocusOut events.

When a focus change occurs, a FocusOut event is delivered to the old focus window and a FocusIn event is delivered to the window which receives the focus. Windows in between in the hierarchy are virtually crossed and receive one focus change event each depending on the relationship and direction of transfer between the origin and destination windows. Some or all of the windows between the window containing the pointer at the time of the focus change and that window's root window can also receive focus change events. By checking the detail member of FocusIn and FocusOut events, an application can tell which of its windows can receive input.

The detail member gives clues about the relationship of the event receiving window to the origin and destination of the focus. The detail member of FocusIn and FocusOut events is analogous to the detail member of EnterNotify and LeaveNotify events but with even more permutations to make life complicated.

Virtual Focus Crossing and the detail Member

We will now embark on specifying the types of events sent to each window and the detail member in each event, depending on the relative position in the hierarchy of the origin window (old focus), destination window (new focus), and the pointer window (window containing pointer at time of focus change). Don't even try to figure this out unless you have to.

Table E-3 shows the event types generated by a focus transition from window *A* to window *B* when window *C* is the least common ancestor of *A* and *B*. This table includes most of the events generated, but not all of them. It is quite possible for a single window to receive more than one focus change event from a single focus change.

Table E-3. FocusIn and FocusOut Events and Window Relationship

FocusOut	FocusIn
Origin window (*A*)	Destination window (*B*)
Windows between *A* and *B*, exclusive, if *A* is inferior	Windows between *A* and *B*, exclusive, if *B* is inferior
Windows between *A* and *C*, exclusive	Windows between *B* and *C*, exclusive
Root window on screen of origin if different from screen of destination	Root window on screen of destination if different from screen of origin
Pointer window up to but not including origin window if pointer window is descendant of origin	Pointer window up to but not including destination window if pointer window is descendant of destination
Pointer window up to and including pointer window's root if transfer was from `PointerRoot`	Pointer window up to and including pointer window's root if transfer was to `PointerRoot`

Table E-4 lists the detail members in events generated by a focus transition from window *A* to window *B* when window *C* is the least common ancestor of *A* and *B*, with *P* being the window containing the pointer.

Table E-4. Event detail Member and Window Relationship

detail Flag	Window Delivered To
NotifyAncestor	Origin or destination when either is descendant
NotifyInferior	Origin or destination when either is ancestor
NotifyVirtual	Windows between *A* and *B*, exclusive, if either is descendant
NotifyNonlinear	Origin and destination when *A* and *B* are two or more windows distant from least common ancestor *C*
NotifyNonlinearVirtual	Windows between *A* and *C*, exclusive, and between *B* and *C*, exclusive, when *A* and *B* have least common ancestor *C*; also on both root windows if *A* and *B* are on different screens
NotifyPointer	Window *P* and windows up to but not including the origin or destination windows
NotifyPointerRoot	Window *P* and all windows up to its root, and all other roots, when focus is set to or from Pointer-Root
NotifyDetailNone	All roots, when focus is set to or from None

Figure E-3 shows all the possible combinations of focus transitions and of origin, destination, and pointer windows and shows the types of events that are generated and their detail member. Solid lines indicate branches of the hierarchy. Dotted arrows indicate the direction of transition of the focus. At each end of this arrow are the origin and destination windows, windows *A* to *B*. Arrows ending in a bar indicate that the event type and detail described are delivered to all windows up to the bar.

In any branch, there may be windows that are not shown. Windows in a single branch between two boxes shown will get the event types and details shown beside the branch.

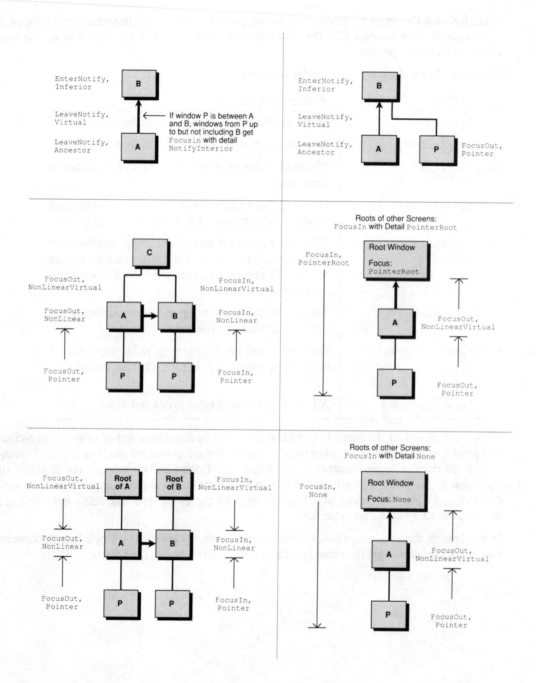

Figure E-3. FocusIn and FocusOut event schematics

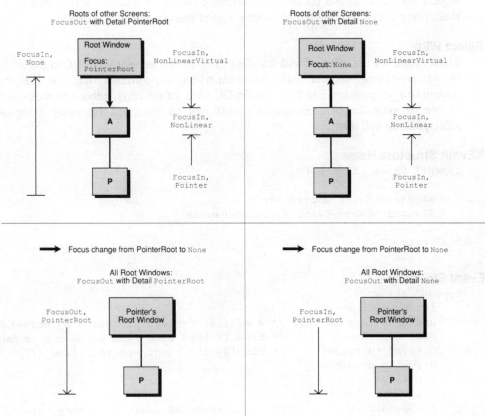

Figure E-3. FocusIn and FocusOut event schematics (cont.)

FocusIn and FocusOut events are also generated when the keyboard is grabbed, if the focus was not already assigned to the grabbing window. In this case, all windows receive events as if the focus was set from the current focus to the grab window. When the grab is released, the events generated are just as if the focus was set back.

GraphicsExpose, NoExpose

When Generated

GraphicsExpose events indicate that the source area for a XCopyArea or XCopyPlane request was not available because it was outside the source window or obscured by a window. NoExpose events indicate that the source region was completely available.

Select With

These events are not selected with XSelectInput but are sent if the GC in the XCopyArea or XCopyPlane request had its graphics_exposures flag set to True. If graphics_exposures is True in the GC used for the copy, either one NoExpose event or one or more GraphicsExpose events will be generated for every XCopyArea or XCopyPlane call made.

XEvent Structure Name

```
typedef union _XEvent {
    . . .
    XNoExposeEvent xnoexpose;
    XGraphicsExposeEvent xgraphicsexpose;
    . . .
} XEvent;
```

Event Structure

```
typedef struct {
    int type;
    unsigned long serial;  /* # of last request processed by server */
    Bool send_event;       /* True if this came from SendEvent request */
    Display *display;      /* Display the event was read from */
    Drawable drawable;
    int x, y;
    int width, height;
    int count;             /* if nonzero, at least this many more */
    int major_code;        /* core is CopyArea or CopyPlane */
    int minor_code;        /* not defined in the core */
} XGraphicsExposeEvent;

typedef struct {
    int type;
    unsigned long serial;  /* # of last request processed by server */
    Bool send_event;       /* True if this came from SendEvent request */
    Display *display;      /* Display the event was read from */
    Drawable drawable;
    int major_code;        /* core is CopyArea or CopyPlane */
    int minor_code;        /* not defined in the core */
} XNoExposeEvent;
```

Event Structure Members

drawable	A window or an off-screen pixmap. This specifies the destination of the graphics request that generated the event.
x, y	The coordinates of the upper-left corner of the exposed region relative to the origin of the window.
width, height	The width and height in pixels of the exposed region.
count	The approximate number of remaining contiguous GraphicsExpose events that were generated as a result of the XCopyArea or XCopy-Plane call.
major_code	The graphics request used. This may be one of the symbols CopyArea or CopyPlane or a symbol defined by a loaded extension.
minor_code	Zero unless the request is part of an extension.

Notes

Expose events and GraphicsExpose events both indicate the region of a window that was actually exposed (x, y, width, and height). Therefore, they can often be handled similarly.

GravityNotify

When Generated

A GravityNotify event reports when a window is moved because of a change in the size of its parent. This happens when the win_gravity attribute of the child window is something other than StaticGravity or UnmapGravity.

Select With

This event is selected for a single window by specifying the window ID of that window with StructureNotifyMask. To receive notification of movement due to gravity for a group of siblings, specify the parent window ID with SubstructureNotifyMask.

XEvent Structure Name

```
typedef union _XEvent {
    . . .
    XGravityEvent xgravity;
    . . .
} XEvent;
```

Event Structure

```
typedef struct {
    int type;
    unsigned long serial;   /* # of last request processed by server */
    Bool send_event;        /* True if this came from SendEvent request */
    Display *display;       /* Display the event was read from */
    Window event;
    Window window;
    int x, y;
} XGravityEvent;
```

Event Structure Members

event   The window that selected the event.

window   The window that was moved.

x, y   The new coordinates of the window relative to its parent.

KeymapNotify

When Generated

A `KeymapNotify` event reports the state of the keyboard and occurs when the pointer or keyboard focus enters a window. `KeymapNotify` events are reported immediately after `EnterNotify` or `FocusIn` events. This is a way for the application to read the keyboard state as the application is "woken up," since the two triggering events usually indicate that the application is about to receive user input.

Select With

This event is selected with `KeymapStateMask`.

XEvent Structure Name

```
typedef union _XEvent {
    . . .
    XKeymapEvent xkeymap;
    . . .
} XEvent;
```

Event Structure

```
typedef struct {
    int type;
    unsigned long serial;   /* # of last request processed by server */
    Bool send_event;        /* True if this came from SendEvent request */
    Display *display;       /* Display the event was read from */
    Window window;
    char key_vector[32];
} XKeymapEvent;
```

Event Structure Members

window   Reports the window which was reported in the `window` member of the preceding `EnterNotify` or `FocusIn` event.

key_vector A bit vector or mask, each bit representing one physical key, with a total of 256 bits. For a given key, its keycode is its position in the keyboard vector. You can also get this bit vector by calling `XQueryKeymap`.

Notes

The `serial` member of `KeymapNotify` does not contain the serial number of the most recent protocol request processed, because this event always follows immediately after `EnterNotify` or `FocusIn` events in which the `serial` member is valid.

KeyPress, KeyRelease

When Generated

`KeyPress` and `KeyRelease` events are generated for all keys, even those mapped to modifier keys such as Shift or Control.

Select With

Each type of keyboard event may be selected separately with `KeyPressMask` and `KeyReleaseMask`.

XEvent Structure Name

```
typedef union _XEvent {
    ...
    XKeyEvent xkey;
    ...
} XEvent;
```

Event Structure

```
typedef struct {
    int type;                 /* of event */
    unsigned long serial;     /* # of last request processed by server */
    Bool send_event;          /* True if this came from SendEvent request */
    Display *display;         /* Display the event was read from */
    Window window;            /* event window it is reported relative to */
    Window root;              /* root window that the event occurred on */
    Window subwindow;         /* child window */
    Time time;                /* milliseconds */
    int x, y;                 /* pointer coordinates relative to receiving
                               * window */
    int x_root, y_root;       /* coordinates relative to root */
    unsigned int state;       /* modifier key and button mask */
    unsigned int keycode;     /* server-dependent code for key */
    Bool same_screen;         /* same screen flag */
} XKeyEvent;
typedef XKeyEvent XKeyPressedEvent;
typedef XKeyEvent XKeyReleasedEvent;
```

Event Structure Members

subwindow   If the source window is the child of the receiving window, then the `subwindow` member is set to the ID of that child.

time   The server time when the button event occurred, in milliseconds. `Time` is declared as `unsigned long`, so it wraps around when it reaches the maximum value of a 32-bit number (every 49.7 days).

x, y   If the receiving window is on the same screen as the root window specified by `root`, then x and y are the pointer coordinates relative to the receiving window's origin. Otherwise, x and y are zero.

	When active button grabs and pointer grabs are in effect (see Section 9.4 of Volume One, *Xlib Programming Manual*), the coordinates relative to the receiving window may not be within the window (they may be negative or greater than window height or width).
x_root, y_root	The pointer coordinates relative to the root window which is an ancestor of the event window. If the pointer was on a different screen, these are zero.
state	The state of all the buttons and modifier keys just before the event, represented by a mask of the button and modifier key symbols: Button1Mask, Button2Mask, Button3Mask, Button4Mask, Button5Mask, ControlMask, LockMask, Mod1Mask, Mod2-Mask, Mod3Mask, Mod4Mask, Mod5Mask, and ShiftMask.
keycode	The keycode member contains a server-dependent code for the key that changed state. As such, it should be translated into the portable symbol called a keysym before being used. It can also be converted directly into ASCII with XLookupString. For a description and examples of how to translate keycodes, see Volume One, Section 9.1.1.

Notes

Remember that not all hardware is capable of generating release events and that only the main keyboard (a-z, A-Z, 0-9), Shift, and Control keys are always found.

Keyboard events are analogous to button events, though, of course, there are many more keys than buttons and the keyboard is not automatically grabbed between press and release.

All the structure members have the same meaning as described for ButtonPress and ButtonRelease events, except that button is replaced by keycode.

When Generated

The X server generates `MapNotify` and `UnmapNotify` events when a window changes state from unmapped to mapped or vice versa.

Select With

To receive these events on a single window, use `StructureNotifyMask` in the call to `XSelectInput` for the window. To receive these events for all children of a particular parent, specify the parent window ID and use `SubstructureNotifyMask`.

XEvent Structure Name

```
typedef union _XEvent {
    . . .
    XMapEvent xmap;
    XUnmapEvent xunmap;
    . . .
} XEvent;
```

Event Structure

```
typedef struct {
    int type;
    unsigned long serial;      /* # of last request processed by server */
    Bool send_event;           /* True if this came from SendEvent request */
    Display *display;          /* Display the event was read from */
    Window event;
    Window window;
    Bool override_redirect;    /* boolean, is override set */
} XMapEvent;

typedef struct {
    int type;
    unsigned long serial;      /* # of last request processed by server */
    Bool send_event;           /* True if this came from SendEvent request */
    Display *display;          /* Display the event was read from */
    Window event;
    Window window;
    Bool from_configure;
} XUnmapEvent;
```

Event Structure Members

event   The window that selected this event.

window   The window that was just mapped or unmapped.

override_redirect (XMapEvent only)
            `True` or `False`. The value of the `override_redirect` attribute of the window that was just mapped.

`from_configure` (XUnmapEvent only)

> `True` if the event was generated as a result of a resizing of the window's parent when the window itself had a `win_gravity` of UnmapGravity. See the description of the `win_gravity` attribute in Section 4.3.4 of Volume One, *Xlib Programming Manual.* `False` otherwise.

MappingNotify

When Generated

A MappingNotify event is sent when any of the following is changed by another client: the mapping between physical keyboard keys (keycodes) and keysyms, the mapping between modifier keys and logical modifiers, or the mapping between physical and logical pointer buttons. These events are triggered by a call to XSetModifierMapping or XSet-PointerMapping, if the return status is MappingSuccess, or by any call to XChange-KeyboardMapping.

This event type should not be confused with the event that occurs when a window is mapped; that is a MapNotify event. Nor should it be confused with the KeymapNotify event, which reports the state of the keyboard as a mask instead of as a keycode.

Select With

The X server sends MappingNotify events to all clients. It is never selected and cannot be masked with the window attributes.

XEvent Structure Name

```
typedef union _XEvent {
    . . .
    XMappingEvent xmapping;
    . . .
} XEvent;
```

Event Structure

```
typedef struct {
    int type;
    unsigned long serial;   /* # of last request processed by server */
    Bool send_event;        /* True if this came from SendEvent request */
    Display *display;       /* Display the event was read from */
    Window window;          /* unused */
    int request;            /* one of MappingMapping, MappingKeyboard,
                             * MappingPointer */
    int first_keycode;      /* first keycode */
    int count;              /* range of change with first_keycode*/
} XMappingEvent;
```

Event Structure Members

request   The kind of mapping change that occurred: MappingModifier for a successful XSetModifierMapping (keyboard Shift, Lock, Control, Meta keys), MappingKeyboard for a successful XChange-KeyboardMapping (other keys), and MappingPointer for a successful XSetPointerMapping (pointer button numbers).

first_keycode   If the request member is MappingKeyboard or Mapping-Modifier, then first_keycode indicates the first in a range of keycodes with altered mappings. Otherwise, it is not set.

count   If the request member is MappingKeyboard or Mapping-
Modifier, then count indicates the number of keycodes with altered
mappings. Otherwise, it is not set.

Notes

If the request member is MappingKeyboard, clients should call XRefreshKeyboard-
Mapping.

The normal response to a request member of MappingPointer or MappingModifier
is no action. This is because the clients should use the logical mapping of the buttons and
modifiers to allow the user to customize the keyboard if desired. If the application requires a
particular mapping regardless of the user's preferences, it should call XGetModifier-
Mapping or XGetPointerMapping to find out about the new mapping.

Event
Reference

MapRequest

When Generated

A MapRequest event occurs when the functions XMapRaised and XMapWindow are called.

This event differs from MapNotify in that it delivers the parameters of the request before it is carried out. This gives the client that selects this event (usually the window manager) the opportunity to revise the size or position of the window before executing the map request itself or to deny the request. (MapNotify indicates the final outcome of the request.)

Select With

This event is selected by specifying the window ID of the parent of the receiving window with SubstructureRedirectMask. (In addition, the override_redirect member of the XSetWindowAttributes structure for the specified window must be False.)

XEvent Structure Name

```
typedef union _XEvent {
    ...
    XMapRequestEvent xmaprequest;
    ...
} XEvent;
```

Event Structure

```
typedef struct {
    int type;
    unsigned long serial;   /* # of last request processed by server */
    Bool send_event;        /* True if this came from SendEvent request */
    Display *display;       /* Display the event was read from */
    Window parent;
    Window window;
} XMapRequestEvent;
```

Event Structure Members

parent   The ID of the parent of the window being mapped.

window   The ID of the window being mapped.

When Generated

A `MotionNotify` event reports that the user moved the pointer or that a program warped the pointer to a new position within a single window.

Select With

This event is selected with `ButtonMotionMask`, `Button1MotionMask`, `Button2-MotionMask`, `Button3MotionMask`, `Button4MotionMask`, `Button5MotionMask`, `PointerMotionHintMask`, and `PointerMotionMask`. These masks determine the specific conditions under which the event is generated.

See Section 8.3.3.3 of Volume One, *Xlib Programming Manual*, for a description of selecting button events.

XEvent Structure Name

```
typedef union _XEvent {
    . . .
    XMotionEvent xmotion;
    . . .
} XEvent;
```

Event Structure

```
typedef struct {
    int type;                /* of event */
    unsigned long serial;    /* # of last request processed by server */
    Bool send_event;         /* True if this came from SendEvent request */
    Display *display;        /* Display the event was read from */
    Window window;           /* event window it is reported relative to */
    Window root;             /* root window that the event occurred on */
    Window subwindow;        /* child window */
    Time time;               /* milliseconds */
    int x, y;                /* pointer coordinates relative to receiving
                              * window */
    int x_root, y_root;      /* coordinates relative to root */
    unsigned int state;      /* button and modifier key mask */
    char is_hint;            /* is this a motion hint */
    Bool same_screen;        /* same screen flag */
} XMotionEvent;
typedef XMotionEvent XPointerMovedEvent;
```

Event Structure Members

subwindow   If the source window is the child of the receiving window, then the `subwindow` member is set to the ID of that child.

time   The server time when the button event occurred, in milliseconds. `Time` is declared as `unsigned long`, so it wraps around when it reaches the maximum value of a 32-bit number (every 49.7 days).

Event Reference

x, y
If the receiving window is on the same screen as the root window specified by root, then x and y are the pointer coordinates relative to the receiving window's origin. Otherwise, x and y are zero.

When active button grabs and pointer grabs are in effect (see Volume One, Section 9.4), the coordinates relative to the receiving window may not be within the window (they may be negative or greater than window height or width).

x_root, y_root
The pointer coordinates relative to the root window which is an ancestor of the event window. If the pointer was on a different screen, these are zero.

state
The state of all the buttons and modifier keys just before the event, represented by a mask of the button and modifier key symbols: Button1Mask, Button2Mask, Button3Mask, Button4Mask, Button5Mask, ControlMask, LockMask, Mod1Mask, Mod2-Mask, Mod3Mask, Mod4Mask, Mod5Mask, and ShiftMask.

is_hint
Either the constant NotifyNormal or NotifyHint. NotifyHint indicates that the PointerMotionHintMask was selected. In this case, just one event is sent when the mouse moves, and the current position can be found by calling XQueryPointer or by examining the motion history buffer with XGetMotionEvents, if a motion history buffer is available on the server. NotifyNormal indicates that the event is real, but it may not be up to date, since there may be many more later motion events on the queue.

same_screen
Indicates whether the pointer is currently on the same screen as this window. This is always True unless the pointer was actively grabbed before the automatic grab could take place.

Notes

If the processing you have to do for every motion event is fast, you can probably handle all of them without requiring motion hints. However, if you have extensive processing to do for each one, you might be better off using the hints and calling XQueryPointer or using the history buffer if it exists. XQueryPointer is a round-trip request, so it can be slow.

EnterNotify and LeaveNotify events are generated instead of MotionEvents if the pointer starts and stops in different windows.

When Generated

A `PropertyNotify` event indicates that a property of a window has changed or been deleted. This event can also be used to get the current server time (by appending zero-length data to a property). `PropertyNotify` events are generated by `XChangeProperty`, `XDeleteProperty`, `XGetWindowProperty`, or `XRotateWindowProperties`.

Select With

This event is selected with `PropertyChangeMask`.

XEvent Structure Name

```
typedef union _XEvent {
    ...
    XPropertyEvent xproperty;
    ...
} XEvent;
```

Event Structure

```
typedef struct {
    int type;
    unsigned long serial; /* # of last request processed by server */
    Bool send_event;      /* True if this came from SendEvent request */
    Display *display;     /* Display the event was read from */
    Window window;
    Atom atom;
    Time time;
    int state;            /* property NewValue, property Deleted */
} XPropertyEvent;
```

Event Structure Members

window	The window whose property was changed, not the window that selected the event.
atom	The property that was changed.
state	Either `PropertyNewValue` or `PropertyDelete`. Whether the property was changed to a new value or deleted.
time	The `time` member specifies the server time when the property was changed.

When Generated

A ReparentNotify event reports when a client successfully reparents a window.

Select With

This event is selected with SubstructureNotifyMask by specifying the window ID of the old or the new parent window or with StructureNotifyMask by specifying the window ID.

XEvent Structure Name

```
typedef union _XEvent {
    . . .
    XReparentEvent xreparent;
    . . .
} XEvent;
```

Event Structure

```
typedef struct {
    int type;
    unsigned long serial; /* # of last request processed by server */
    Bool send_event;      /* True if this came from SendEvent request */
    Display *display;     /* Display the event was read from */
    Window event;
    Window window;
    Window parent;
    int x, y;
    Bool override_redirect;
} XReparentEvent;
```

Event Structure Members

window	The window whose parent window was changed.
parent	The new parent of the window.
x, y	The coordinates of the upper-left pixel of the window's border relative to the new parent window's origin.
override_redirect	The override_redirect attribute of the reparented window. If True, it indicates that the client wants this window to be immune to meddling by the window manager. Window managers normally should not have reparented this window to begin with.

When Generated

A `ResizeRequest` event reports another client's attempt to change the size of a window. The X server generates this event type when another client calls `XConfigureWindow`, `XMoveResizeWindow`, or `XResizeWindow`. If this event type is selected, the window is not resized. This gives the client that selects this event (usually the window manager) the opportunity to revise the new size of the window before executing the resize request or to deny the request itself.

Select With

To receive this event type, specify a window ID and pass `ResizeRedirectMask` as part of the `event_mask` argument to `XSelectInput`. Only one client can select this event on a particular window. When selected, this event is triggered instead of resizing the window.

XEvent Structure Name

```
typedef union _XEvent {
    . . .
    XResizeRequestEvent xresizerequest;
    . . .
} XEvent;
```

Event Structure

```
typedef struct {
    int type;
    unsigned long serial; /* # of last request processed by server */
    Bool send_event;      /* True if this came from SendEvent request */
    Display *display;     /* Display the event was read from */
    Window window;
    int width, height;
} XResizeRequestEvent;
```

Event Structure Members

window   The window whose size another client attempted to change.

width, height   The requested size of the window, not including its border.

SelectionClear

When Generated

A SelectionClear event reports to the current owner of a selection that a new owner is being defined.

Select With

This event is not selected. It is sent to the previous selection owner when another client calls XSetSelectionOwner for the same selection.

XEvent Structure Name

```
typedef union _XEvent {
    ...
    XSelectionClearEvent xselectionclear;
    ...
} XEvent;
```

Event Structure

```
typedef struct {
    int type;
    unsigned long serial;  /* # of last request processed by server */
    Bool send_event;       /* True if this came from SendEvent request */
    Display *display;       /* Display the event was read from */
    Window window;
    Atom selection;
    Time time;
} XSelectionClearEvent;
```

Event Structure Members

window   The window that is receiving the event and losing the selection.

selection   The selection atom specifying the selection that is changing ownership.

time   The last-change time recorded for the selection.

SelectionNotify

When Generated

A `SelectionNotify` event is sent only by clients, not by the server, by calling `XSend-Event`. The owner of a selection sends this event to a requestor (a client that calls `XConvertSelection` for a given property) when a selection has been converted and stored as a property or when a selection conversion could not be performed (indicated with property `None`).

Select With

There is no event mask for `SelectionNotify` events, and they are not selected with `XSelectInput`. Instead `XSendEvent` directs the event to a specific window, which is given as a window ID: `PointerWindow`, which identifies the window the pointer is in, or `InputFocus`, which identifies the focus window.

XEvent Structure Name

```
typedef union _XEvent {
    ...
    XSelectionEvent xselection;
    ...
} XEvent;
```

Event Structure

```
typedef struct {
    int type;
    unsigned long serial;   /* # of last request processed by server */
    Bool send_event;        /* True if this came from SendEvent request */
    Display *display;       /* Display the event was read from */
    Window requestor;
    Atom selection;
    Atom target;
    Atom property;          /* Atom or None */
    Time time;
} XSelectionEvent;
```

Event Structure Members

The members of this structure have the values specified in the `XConvertSelection` call that triggers the selection owner to send this event, except that the `property` member either will return the atom specifying a property on the requestor window with the data type specified in `target` or will return `None`, which indicates that the data could not be converted into the target type.

Event
Reference

SelectionRequest

When Generated

A SelectionRequest event is sent to the owner of a selection when another client requests the selection by calling XConvertSelection.

Select With

There is no event mask for SelectionRequest events, and they are not selected with XSelectInput.

XEvent Structure Name

```
typedef union _XEvent {
    ...
    XSelectionRequestEvent xselectionrequest;
    ...
} XEvent;
```

Event Structure

```
typedef struct {
    int type;
    unsigned long serial;  /* # of last request processed by server */
    Bool send_event;       /* True if this came from SendEvent request */
    Display *display;      /* Display the event was read from */
    Window owner;
    Window requestor;
    Atom selection;
    Atom target;
    Atom property;
    Time time;
} XSelectionRequestEvent;
```

Event Structure Members

The members of this structure have the values specified in the XConvertSelection call that triggers this event.

The owner should convert the selection based on the specified target type, if possible. If a property is specified, the owner should store the result as that property on the requestor window and then send a SelectionNotify event to the requestor by calling XSendEvent. If the selection cannot be converted as requested, the owner should send a SelectionNotify event with property set to the constant None.

When Generated

A VisibilityNotify event reports any change in the visibility of the specified window. This event type is never generated on windows whose class is InputOnly. All of the window's subwindows are ignored when calculating the visibility of the window.

Select With

This event is selected with VisibilityChangeMask.

XEvent Structure Name

```
typedef union _XEvent {
    ...
    XVisibilityEvent xvisibility;
    ...
} XEvent;
```

Event Structure

```
typedef struct {
    int type;
    unsigned long serial; /* # of last request processed by server */
    Bool send_event;      /* True if this came from SendEvent request */
    Display *display;      /* Display the event was read from */
    Window window;
    int state;            /* VisibilityObscured,
                           * VisibilityPartiallyObscured,
                           * VisibilityUnobscured*/
} XVisibilityEvent;
```

Event Structure Members

state   A symbol indicating the final visibility status of the window: Visibility-Obscured, VisibilityPartiallyObscured, or Visibility-Unobscured.

Notes

Table E-5 lists the transitions that generate VisibilityNotify events and the corresponding state member of the XVisibilityEvent structure.

Table E-5. State Element of the XVisibilityEvent Structure

Visibility Status Before	Visibility Status After	State Member
Partially obscured, fully obscured, or not viewable	Viewable and completely unobscured	`VisibilityUnobscured`
Viewable and completely unobscured, or not viewable	Viewable and partially obscured	`VisibilityPartially-Obscured`
Viewable and completely unobscured, or viewable and partially obscured, or not viewable	Viewable and partially obscured	`VisibilityPartially-Obscured`

F

Structure Reference

This appendix summarizes the contents of the include files for Xlib, and presents each structure in alphabetical order.

F.1 Description of Header Files

All include files are normally located in */usr/include/X11*. All Xlib programs require *<X11/Xlib.h>*, which includes *<X11/X.h>*. *<X11/Xlib.h>* contains most of the structure declarations, while *<X11/X.h>* contains most of the defined constants. Virtually all programs will also require *<X11/Xutil.h>*, which include structure types and declarations applicable to window manager hints, colors, visuals, regions, standard geometry strings, and images.

Here is a summary of the contents of the include files:

<X11/Xlib.h>	structure declarations for core Xlib functions.
<X11/X.h>	constant definitions for Xlib functions.
<X11/Xutil.h>	additional structure types and constant definitions for miscellaneous Xlib functions.
<X11/Xatom.h>	the predefined atoms for properties, types, and font characteristics.
<X11/cursorfont.h>	the constants used to select a cursor shape from the standard cursor font.
<X11/keysym.h>	predefined key symbols corresponding to keycodes. It includes *<X11/keysymdef.h>*.
<X11/Xresource.h>	resource manager structure definitions and function declarations.

F.2 Resource Types

The following types are defined in *<X11/X.h>*:

```
unsigned long XID
XID Colormap
XID Cursor
XID Drawable
XID Font
XID GContext
XID KeySym
XID Pixmap
XID Window
unsigned long Atom
unsigned char KeyCode
unsigned long Mask
unsigned long Time
unsigned long VisualID
```

F.3 Structure Definitions

This section lists all public Xlib structure definitions in `Xlib.h` and `Xutil.h`, in alphabetical order, except the event structures, which are listed on the reference page for each event in Appendix E, *Event Reference*.

Before each structure is a description of what the structure is used for and a list of the Xlib routines that use the structure.

F.3.1 XArc

XArc specifies the bounding box for an arc and two angles indicating the extent of the arc within the box. A list of these structures is used in `XDrawArcs` and `XFillArcs`.

```
typedef struct {
    short x, y;
    unsigned short width, height;
    short angle1, angle2;
} XArc;
```

F.3.2 XChar2b

XChar2b specifies a character in a two-byte font. A list of structures of this type is an argument to XDrawImageString16, XDrawString16, XDrawText16, XQueryText-Extents16, XTextExtents16, and XTextWidth16. The only two-byte font currently available is Kanji (Japanese).

```
typedef struct {                        /* normal 16 bit characters are two bytes */
    unsigned char byte1;
    unsigned char byte2;
} XChar2b;
```

F.3.3 XCharStruct

XCharStruct describes the metrics of a single character in a font or the overall characteristics of a font. This structure is the type of several of members of XFontStruct and is used to return the overall characteristics of a string in XQueryTextExtents* and XTextExtents*.

```
typedef struct {
    short lbearing;                  /* origin to left edge of raster */
    short rbearing;                  /* origin to right edge of raster */
    short width;                     /* advance to next char's origin */
    short ascent;                    /* baseline to top edge of raster */
    short descent;                   /* baseline to bottom edge of raster */
    unsigned short attributes;       /* per char flags (not predefined) */
} XCharStruct;
```

F.3.4 XClassHint

XClassHint is used to set or get the XA_WM_CLASS_HINT property for an application's top-level window, as arguments to XSetClassHint or XGetClassHint.

```
typedef struct {
    char *res_name;
    char *res_class;
} XClassHint;
```

F.3.5 XColor

XColor describes a single colorcell. This structure is used to specify and return the pixel value and RGB values for a colorcell. The flags indicate which of the RGB values should be changed when used in XStoreColors, XAllocNamedColor, or XAllocColor. Also used in XCreateGlyphCursor, XCreatePixmapCursor, XLookupColor, XParseColor, XQueryColor, XQueryColors, and XRecolorCursor.

```
typedef struct {
    unsigned long pixel;
    unsigned short red, green, blue;
    char flags;                                 /* DoRed, DoGreen, DoBlue */
    char pad;
} XColor;
```

F.3.6 XComposeStatus

XComposeStatus describes the current state of a multikey character sequence. Used in calling `XLookupString`. This processing is not implemented in the MIT sample servers.

```
typedef struct _XComposeStatus {
    char *compose_ptr;                          /* state table pointer */
    int chars_matched;                          /* match state */
} XComposeStatus;
```

F.3.7 XExtCodes

XExtCodes is a structure used by the extension mechanism. This structure is returned by `XInitExtension` which is not a standard Xlib routine but should be called within the extension code. Its contents are not normally accessible to the application.

```
typedef struct {                                /* public to extension, cannot be changed */
    int extension;                              /* extension number */
    int major_opcode;                           /* major opcode assigned by server */
    int first_event;                            /* first event number for the extension */
    int first_error;                            /* first error number for the extension */
} XExtCodes;
```

F.3.8 XExtData

XExtData provides a way for extensions to attach private data to the existing structure types GC, `Visual`, `Screen`, `Display`, and `XFontStruct`. This structure is not used in normal Xlib programming.

```
typedef struct _XExtData {
    int number;                                 /* number returned by XRegisterExtension */
    struct _XExtData *next;                     /* next item on list of data for structure */
    int (*free_private)();                      /* called to free private storage */
    char *private_data;                         /* data private to this extension */
} XExtData;
```

F.3.9 XFontProp

XFontProp is used in XFontStruct. This structure allows the application to find out the names of additional font properties beyond the predefined set, so that they too can be accessed with XGetFontProperty. This structure is not used as an argument or return value for any core Xlib function.

```
typedef struct {
    Atom name;
    unsigned long card32;
} XFontProp;
```

F.3.10 XFontStruct

XFontStruct specifies metric information for an entire font. This structure is filled with the XLoadQueryFont and XQueryFont routines. ListFontsWithInfo also fills it but with metric information for the entire font only, not for each character. A pointer to this structure is used in the routines XFreeFont, XFreeFontInfo, XGetFontProp, XTextExtents*, and XTextWidth*.

```
typedef struct {
    XExtData *ext_data;              /* hook for extension to hang data */
    Font fid;                        /* font ID for this font */
    unsigned direction;              /* direction the font is painted */
    unsigned min_char_or_byte2;      /* first character */
    unsigned max_char_or_byte2;      /* last character */
    unsigned min_byte1;              /* first row that exists */
    unsigned max_byte1;              /* last row that exists */
    Bool all_chars_exist;            /* flag if all characters have nonzero size*/
    unsigned default_char;           /* char to print for undefined character */
    int n_properties;                /* how many properties there are */
    XFontProp *properties;           /* pointer to array of additional properties*/
    XCharStruct min_bounds;          /* minimum bounds over all existing char*/
    XCharStruct max_bounds;          /* maximum bounds over all existing char*/
    XCharStruct *per_char;           /* first_char to last_char information */
    int ascent;                      /* logical extent above baseline for spacing */
    int descent;                     /* logical descent below baseline for spacing */
} XFontStruct;
```

F.3.11 XGCValues

XGCValues is used to set or change members of the GC by the routines XCreateGC and XChangeGC.

```
typedef struct {
    int function;                    /* logical operation */
    unsigned long plane_mask;        /* plane mask */
    unsigned long foreground;        /* foreground pixel */
```

```
        unsigned long background;           /* background pixel */
        int line_width;                     /* line width */
        int line_style;                     /* LineSolid, LineOnOffDash, LineDoubleDash */
        int cap_style;                      /* CapNotLast, CapButt, CapRound, CapProjecting */
        int join_style;                     /* JoinMiter, JoinRound, JoinBevel */
        int fill_style;                     /* FillSolid, FillTiled, FillStippled */
        int fill_rule;                      /* EvenOddRule, WindingRule */
        int arc_mode;                       /* ArcPieSlice, ArcChord */
        Pixmap tile;                        /* tile pixmap for tiling operations */
        Pixmap stipple;                     /* stipple 1 plane pixmap for stippling */
        int ts_x_origin;                    /* offset for tile or stipple operations */
        int ts_y_origin;
        Font font;                          /* default text font for text operations */
        int subwindow_mode;                 /* ClipByChildren, IncludeInferiors */
        Bool graphics_exposures;            /* Boolean, should exposures be generated */
        int clip_x_origin;                  /* origin for clipping */
        int clip_y_origin;
        Pixmap clip_mask;                   /* bitmap clipping; other calls for rects */
        int dash_offset;                    /* patterned/dashed line information */
        char dashes;
} XGCValues;
```

F.3.12 XHostAddress

XHostAddress specifies the address of a host machine that is to be added or removed from the host access list for a server. Used in XAddHost, XAddHosts, XListHosts, XRemoveHost, and XRemoveHosts.

```
typedef struct {
        int family;                         /* for example FAMILY_INTERNET */
        int length;                         /* length of address, in bytes */
        char *address;                      /* pointer to where to find the bytes */
} XHostAddress;
```

F.3.13 XIconSize

XIconSize is Used to set or read the XA_WM_ICON_SIZE property. This is normally set by the window manager with XSetIconSizes and read by each application with XGet-IconSizes.

```
typedef struct {
        int min_width, min_height;
        int max_width, max_height;
        int width_inc, height_inc;
} XIconSize;
```

F.3.14 XImage

XImage describes an area of the screen; is used in XCreateImage, XDestroyImage, XGetPixel, XPutPixel, XSubImage, XAddPixel, XGetImage, XGetSub- Image, and XPutImage.

```
typedef struct _XImage {
    int width, height;                    /* size of image */
    int xoffset;                          /* number of pixels offset in X direction */
    int format;                           /* XYBitmap, XYPixmap, ZPixmap */
    char *data;                           /* pointer to image data */
    int byte_order;                       /* data byte order, LSBFirst, MSBFirst */
    int bitmap_unit;                      /* quant. of scan line 8, 16, 32 */
    int bitmap_bit_order;                 /* LSBFirst, MSBFirst */
    int bitmap_pad;                       /* 8, 16, 32 either XY or ZPixmap */
    int depth;                            /* depth of image */
    int bytes_per_line;                   /* accelerator to next line */
    int bits_per_pixel;                   /* bits per pixel (ZPixmap) */
    unsigned long red_mask;               /* bits in z arrangement */
    unsigned long green_mask;
    unsigned long blue_mask;
    char *obdata;                         /* hook for the object routines to hang on */
    struct funcs {                        /* image manipulation routines */
    struct _XImage *(*create_image)();
    int (*destroy_image)();
    unsigned long (*get_pixel)();
    int (*put_pixel)();
    struct _XImage *(*sub_image)();
    int (*add_pixel)();
    } f;
} XImage;
```

F.3.15 XKeyboardControl

XKeyboardControl is used to set user preferences with XChangeKeyboard- Control.

```
typedef struct {
    int key_click_percent;
    int bell_percent;
    int bell_pitch;
    int bell_duration;
    int led;
    int led_mode;
    int key;
    int auto_repeat_mode;     /* AutoRepeatModeOn, AutoRepeatModeOff,
                               * AutoRepeatModeDefault */
} XKeyboardControl;
```

F.3.16 XKeyboardState

XKeyboardState is used to return the current settings of user preferences with XGet-KeyboardControl.

```
typedef struct {
    int key_click_percent;
    int bell_percent;
    unsigned int bell_pitch, bell_duration;
    unsigned long led_mask;
    int global_auto_repeat;
    char auto_repeats[32];
} XKeyboardState;
```

F.3.17 XModifierKeymap

XModifierKeymap specifies which physical keys are mapped to modifier functions. This structure is returned by XGetModifierMapping and is an argument to XDeleteModifiermapEntry, XFreeModifiermap, XInsertModifiermapEntry, XNewModifiermap, and XSetModifierMapping.

```
typedef struct {
    int max_keypermod;          /* server's max # of keys per modifier */
    KeyCode *modifiermap;       /* an 8 by max_keypermod array of modifiers */
} XModifierKeymap;
```

F.3.18 XPixmapFormatValues

XPixmapFormatValues describes one pixmap format that is supported on the server. A list of these structures is returned by XListPixmapFormats.

```
typedef struct {
    int depth;
    int bits_per_pixel;
    int scanline_pad;
} XPixmapFormatValues;
```

F.3.19 XPoint

XPoint specifies the coordinates of a point. Used in XDrawPoints, XDrawLines, XFillPolygon, and XPolygonRegion.

```
typedef struct {
    short x, y;
} XPoint;
```

F.3.20 XRectangle

XRectangle specifies a rectangle. Used in `XClipBox`, `XDrawRectangles`, `XFill-Rectangles`, `XSetClipRectangles`, and `XUnionRectWithRegion`.

```
typedef struct {
    short x, y;
    unsigned short width, height;
} XRectangle;
```

F.3.21 XSegment

XSegment specifies two points. Used in `XDrawSegments`.

```
typedef struct {
    short x1, y1, x2, y2;
} XSegment;
```

F.3.22 XSetWindowAttributes

XSetWindowAttributes contains all the attributes that can be set without window manager intervention. Used in `XChangeWindowAttributes` and `XCreateWindow`.

```
typedef struct {
    Pixmap background_pixmap;       /* background or None or ParentRelative */
    unsigned long background_pixel; /* background pixel */
    Pixmap border_pixmap;           /* border of the window */
    unsigned long border_pixel;     /* border pixel value */
    int bit_gravity;                /* one of bit gravity values */
    int win_gravity;                /* one of the window gravity values */
    int backing_store;              /* NotUseful, WhenMapped, Always */
    unsigned long backing_planes;   /* planes to be preserved if possible */
    unsigned long backing_pixel;    /* value to use in restoring planes */
    Bool save_under;                /* should bits under be saved? (popups) */
    long event_mask;                /* set of events that should be saved */
    long do_not_propagate_mask;     /* set of events that should not */
                                    /* propagate */
    Bool override_redirect;         /* Boolean value for override-redirect */
    Colormap colormap;              /* colormap to be associated with window */
    Cursor cursor;                  /* cursor to be displayed (or None) */
} XSetWindowAttributes;
```

Appendix F: Structure Reference

659

F.3.23 XSizeHints

XSizeHints describes a range of preferred sizes and aspect ratios. Used to set the
XA_WM_NORMAL_HINTS and XA_WM_ZOOM_HINTS properties for the window manager with
XSetStandardProperties, XSetNormalHints, XSetSizeHints, or XSet-
ZoomHints in R3, and XSetWMProperties, XSetWMNormalHints, and XSet-
WMSizeHints in R4. Also used in reading these properties with XGetNormalHints,
XGetSizeHints, or XGetZoomHints in R3, and XGetWMNormalHints and
XGetWMSizeHints.

```
typedef struct {
    long flags;                      /* marks defined fields in structure */
    int x, y;                        /* obsolete in R4 */
    int width, height;               /* obsolete in R4 */
    int min_width, min_height;
    int max_width, max_height;
    int width_inc, height_inc;
    struct {
        int x;                       /* numerator */
        int y;                       /* denominator */
    } min_aspect, max_aspect;
    int base_width, base_height;     /* Added in R4 */
    int win_gravity;                 /* Added in R4 */
} XSizeHints;
```

F.3.24 XStandardColormap

XStandardColormap describes a standard colormap, giving its ID and its color characteristics. This is the format of the standard colormap properties set on the root window, which
can be changed with XSetRGBColormaps (XSetStandardProperties in R3) and
read with XGetRGBColormaps (XGetStandardProperties in R3).

```
typedef struct {
    Colormap colormap;
    unsigned long red_max;
    unsigned long red_mult;
    unsigned long green_max;
    unsigned long green_mult;
    unsigned long blue_max;
    unsigned long blue_mult;
    unsigned long base_pixel;
    VisualID visualid;               /* added in R4 */
    XID killid;                      /* added in R4 */
} XStandardColormap;
```

F.3.25 XTextItem

XTextItem describes a string, the font to print it in, and the horizontal offset from the previous string drawn or from the location specified by the drawing command. Used in XDrawText.

```
typedef struct {
    char *chars;              /* pointer to string */
    int nchars;              /* number of characters */
    int delta;               /* delta between strings */
    Font font;               /* font to print it in, None don't change */
} XTextItem;
```

F.3.26 XTextItem16

XTextItem16 describes a string in a two-byte font, the font to print it in, and the horizontal offset from the previous string drawn or from the location specified by the drawing command. Used in XDrawText16.

```
typedef struct {
    XChar2b *chars;          /* two-byte characters */
    int nchars;              /* number of characters */
    int delta;               /* delta between strings */
    Font font;               /* font to print it in, None don't change */
} XTextItem16;
```

F.3.27 XTextProperty

XTextProperty holds the information necessary to write or read a TEXT property, which contains a list of strings. This structure is used by many of the R4 routines that write and read window manager hints that are in string format. The purpose of this structure is to allow these properties to be processed in non-european languages where more than 8 bits might be needed. These structures are also used in XGetTextProperty, XSetTextProperty, XStringListToTextProperty, and XTextPropertyToStringList.

```
typedef struct {
    unsigned char *value;      /* same as Property routines */
    Atom encoding;             /* prop type */
    int format;                /* prop data format: 8, 16, or 32 */
    unsigned long nitems;      /* number of data items in value */
} XTextProperty;
```

F.3.28 XTimeCoord

XTimeCoord specifies a time and position pair, for use in tracking the pointer with XGet-MotionEvents. This routine is not supported on all systems.

```
typedef struct {
    Time time;
    short x, y;
} XTimeCoord;
```

F.3.29 XVisualInfo

XVisualInfo contains all the information about a particular visual. It is used in XGet-VisualInfo and XMatchVisualInfo to specify the desired visual type. The visual member of XVisualInfo is used for the *visual* argument of XCreate-Colormap or XCreateWindow.

```
typedef struct {
    Visual *visual;
    VisualID visualid;
    int screen;
    unsigned int depth;
    int class;
    unsigned long red_mask;
    unsigned long green_mask;
    unsigned long blue_mask;
    int colormap_size;
    int bits_per_rgb;
} XVisualInfo;
```

F.3.30 XWindowAttributes

XWindowAttributes describes the complete set of window attributes, including those that cannot be set without window manager interaction. This structure is returned by XGet-WindowAttributes. It is *not* used by XChangeWindowAttributes or XCreateWindow.

```
typedef struct {
    int x, y;                   /* location of window */
    int width, height;          /* width and height of window */
    int border_width;           /* border width of window */
    int depth;                  /* depth of window */
    Visual *visual;             /* the associated visual structure */
    Window root;                /* root of screen containing window */
    int class;                  /* InputOutput, InputOnly*/
    int bit_gravity;            /* one of bit gravity values */
    int win_gravity;            /* one of the window gravity values */
    int backing_store;          /* NotUseful, WhenMapped, Always */
```

```
    unsigned long backing_planes; /* planes to be preserved if possible */
    unsigned long backing_pixel;  /* value to be used when restoring planes */
    Bool save_under;              /* Boolean, should bits under be saved */
    Colormap colormap;            /* colormap to be associated with window */
    Bool map_installed;           /* Boolean, is colormap currently installed*/
    int map_state;                /* IsUnmapped, IsUnviewable, IsViewable */
    long all_event_masks;         /* events all people have interest in*/
    long your_event_mask;         /* my event mask */
    long do_not_propagate_mask;   /* set of events that should not propagate */
    Bool override_redirect;       /* Boolean value for override-redirect */
    Screen *screen;
} XWindowAttributes;
```

F.3.31 XWindowChanges

XWindowChanges describes a configuration for a window. Used in XConfigure-Window, which can change the screen layout and therefore can be intercepted by the window manager. This sets some of the remaining members of XWindowAttributes that cannot be set with XChangeWindowAttributes or XCreateWindow.

```
typedef struct {
    int x, y;
    int width, height;
    int border_width;
    Window sibling;
    int stack_mode;
} XWindowChanges;
```

F.3.32 XWMHints

XWMHints describes various application preferences for communication to the window manager via the XA_WM_HINTS property. Used in XSetWMHints and XGetWMHints.

```
typedef struct {
    long flags;              /* marks defined fields in structure */
    Bool input;             /* does application need window manager for
                             * keyboard input */

    int initial_state;      /* see below */
    Pixmap icon_pixmap;     /* pixmap to be used as icon */
    Window icon_window;     /* window to be used as icon */
    int icon_x, icon_y;     /* initial position of icon */
    Pixmap icon_mask;       /* icon mask bitmap */
    XID window_group;        /* ID of related window group */
    /* this structure may be extended in the future */
} XWMHints;
```

This appendix presents an alphabetical listing of the symbols used in Xlib. The routines in parentheses following the descriptions indicate the routines associated with those symbols.

A

Above	Specifies that the indicated window is placed above the indicated sibling window. (XConfigureWindow)
AllHints	XA_WM_HINTS property, stores optional information for the window manager. If AllHints is set, all members of XA_WM_HINTS are set. (XGetWMHints, XSetWMHints)
AllocAll	Creates a colormap and allocates all of its entries. Available for the DirectColor, GrayScale, and PseudoColor visual classes only. (XCreateColormap)
AllocNone	Creates a colormap and allocates none of its entries. (XCreateColormap)
AllowExposures	Specifies that exposures are generated when the screen is restored after blanking. (XGetScreenSaver, XSetScreen-Saver)
AllTemporary	Specifies that the resources of all clients that have terminated in RetainTemporary (see XSetCloseDownMode) should be killed. (XKillClient)
AllValues	Mask used by XParseGeometry; returns those set by user.
AlreadyGrabbed	Specifies that the pointer or keyboard is actively grabbed by another client. (XGrabKeyboard, XGrabPointer)
Always	Advises the server to maintain contents even when the window is unmapped. (XChangeWindowAttributes, XCreate-Window)
AnyButton	Specifies that any button is to be grabbed (XGrabButton) or ungrabbed (XUngrabButton) or that any button will trigger a ButtonPress or ButtonRelease event.
AnyKey	Specifies that any key is to be grabbed or ungrabbed. (XGrab-Key, XUngrabKey)
AnyModifier	Specifies a modifier keymask for XGrabButton, XGrabKey, and XUngrabKey, and for the results of XQueryPointer.

AnyPropertyType	Specifies that the property from a specified window should be returned regardless of its type. (XGetWindowProperty)
ArcChord	Value of the `arc_mode` member of the GC: specifies that the area between the arc and a line segment joining the endpoints of the arc is filled. (XSetArcMode)
ArcPieSlice	Value of the `arc_mode` member of the GC: specifies that the area filled is delineated by the arc and two line segments connecting the ends of the arc to the center point of the rectangle defining the arc. (XSetArcMode)
AsyncBoth	Specifies that pointer and keyboard event processing resume normally if both the pointer and the keyboard are frozen by the client when XAllowEvents is called with AsyncBoth. (XAllowEvents)
AsyncKeyboard	Specifies that keyboard event processing resumes normally if the keyboard is frozen by the client when XAllowEvents is called with AsyncPointer. (XAllowEvents)
AsyncPointer	Specifies that pointer event processing resumes normally if the pointer is frozen by the client when XAllowEvents is called with AsyncPointer. (XAllowEvents)
AutoRepeatModeDefault	Value of `auto_repeat_mode`: specifies that the key or keyboard is set to the default setting for the server. (XChangeKeyboardControl, XGetKeyboardControl)
AutoRepeatModeOff	Value of `auto_repeat_mode`: specifies that no keys will repeat. (XChangeKeyboardControl, XGetKeyboardControl)
AutoRepeatModeOn	Value of `auto_repeat_mode`: specifies that keys that are set to `auto_repeat` will do so. (XChangeKeyboardControl, XGetKeyboardControl)

B

BadAccess	Used by non-fatal error handlers only, meaning depends on context.
BadAlloc	Used by non-fatal error handlers only, insufficient resources.
BadAtom	Used by non-fatal error handlers only, parameter not an Atom.
BadColor	Used by non-fatal error handlers only, no such colormap.
BadCursor	Used by non-fatal error handlers only, parameter not a Cursor.
BadDrawable	Used by non-fatal error handlers only, parameter not a Pixmap or Window.
BadFont	Used by non-fatal error handlers only, parameter not a Font.
BadGC	Used by non-fatal error handlers only, parameter not a GC.
BadIDChoice	Used by non-fatal error handlers only, choice not in range or already used.
BadImplementation	Used by non-fatal error handlers only, server is defective.
BadLength	Used by non-fatal error handlers only, request length incorrect.
BadMatch	Used by non-fatal error handlers only, parameter mismatch.

BadName	Used by non-fatal error handlers only, font or color name does not exist.
BadPixmap	Used by non-fatal error handlers only, parameter not a Pixmap.
BadRequest	Used by non-fatal error handlers only, bad request code.
BadValue	Used by non-fatal error handlers only, integer parameter out of range.
BadWindow	Used by non-fatal error handlers only, parameter not a Window.
Below	Specifies that the indicated window is placed below the indicated sibling window. (XConfigureWindow)
BitmapFileInvalid	Specifies that a file does not contain valid bitmap data. (XReadBitmapFile, XWriteBitmapFile)
BitmapNoMemory	Specifies that insufficient working storage is allocated. (XReadBitmapFile, XWriteBitmapFile)
BitmapOpenFailed	Specifies that a file cannot be opened. (XReadBitmapFile, XWriteBitmapFile)
BitmapSuccess	Specifies that a file is readable and valid. (XReadBitmapFile, XWriteBitmapFile)
BottomIf	Specifies that the indicated window is placed at the bottom of the stack if it is obscured by the indicated sibling window. (XConfigureWindow)
Button1	Specifies that button1 is to be grabbed (XGrabButton) or ungrabbed (XUngrabButton).
Button1Mask	Returns the current state of button1. (XQueryPointer)
Button1MotionMask	Specifies that any button1 MotionNotify events are to be selected for this window. A MotionNotify event reports pointer movement. (XSelectInput)
Button2	Specifies that button2 is to be grabbed (XGrabButton) or ungrabbed (XUngrabButton).
Button2Mask	Returns the current state of button2. (XQueryPointer)
Button2MotionMask	Specifies that any button2 MotionNotify events are to be selected for this window. A MotionNotify event reports pointer movement. (XSelectInput)
Button3	Specifies that button3 is to be grabbed (XGrabButton) or ungrabbed (XUngrabButton).
Button3Mask	Returns the current state of button3. (XQueryPointer)
Button3MotionMask	Specifies that any button3 MotionNotify events are to be selected for this window. A MotionNotify event reports pointer movement. (XSelectInput)
Button4	Specifies that button4 is to be grabbed (XGrabButton) or ungrabbed (XUngrabButton).
Button4Mask	Returns the current state of button4. (XQueryPointer)

Button4MotionMask	Specifies that any button4 MotionNotify events are to be selected for this window. A MotionNotify event reports pointer movement. (XSelectInput)
Button5	Specifies that button5 is to be grabbed (XGrabButton) or ungrabbed (XUngrabButton).
Button5Mask	Returns the current state of button5. (XQueryPointer)
Button5MotionMask	Specifies that any button5 MotionNotify events are to be selected for this window. A MotionNotify event reports pointer movement. (XSelectInput)
ButtonMotionMask	Specifies that any button MotionNotify events are to be selected for this window. A MotionNotify event reports pointer movement. (XSelectInput)
ButtonPress	Event type.
ButtonPressMask	Specifies that any ButtonPress events are to be selected for this window. A ButtonPress event reports that a pointing device button has been pressed. (XSelectInput)
ButtonRelease	Event type.
ButtonReleaseMask	Specifies that any ButtonRelease events are to be selected for this window. A ButtonRelease event reports that a pointing device button has been released. (XSelectInput)

C

CapButt	Value of the cap_style member of a GC: specifies that lines will be square at the endpoint with no projection beyond. (XSetLineAttributes)
CapNotLast	Value of the cap_style member of a GC: equivalent to CapButt except that, for a line_width of 0 or 1, the final endpoint is not drawn. (XSetLineAttributes)
CapProjecting	Value of the cap_style member of a GC: specifies that lines will be square at the end but with the path continuing beyond the endpoint for a distance equal to half the line_width. (XSetLineAttributes)
CapRound	Value of the cap_style member of a GC: specifies that lines will be terminated by a circular arc. (XSetLineAttributes)
CenterGravity	When a window is resized, specifies the new location of the contents or the children of the window. (XChangeWindow-Attributes, XCreateWindow)
CirculateNotify	Event type.
CirculateRequest	Event type.
ClientIconState	Indicates that the client wants its icon_window to be visible. If an icon_window is not available, it wants its top-level window visible. (Value for initial_state member of XWMHints.)
ClientMessage	Event type.
ClipByChildren	Value of the subwindow_mode member of the GC: specifies that graphics requests will not draw through viewable children. (XSetSubwindowMode)

ColormapChangeMask	Specifies that ColormapNotify events are to be selected for the window. A ColormapNotify event reports colormap changes. (XSelectInput)
ColormapInstalled	In a ColormapNotify event, specifies that the colormap is installed.
ColormapNotify	Event type.
ColormapUninstalled	In a ColormapNotify event, specifies that the colormap is uninstalled.
Complex	Specifies that paths may self-intersect in polygon shapes. (XFillPolygon)
ConfigureNotify	Event type.
ConfigureRequest	Event type.
ControlMapIndex	Identifies one of eight modifiers to which keycodes can be mapped. (XDeleteModifiermapEntry, XGetModifier-Mapping, XInsertModifiermapEntry, XLookupKeysym, XSetModifierMapping)
ControlMask	Specifies a modifier keymask for XGrabButton, XGrabKey, XUngrabButton, and XUngrabKey, and for the results of XQueryPointer.
Convex	Specifies that a polygon's path is wholly convex. (XFill-Polygon)
CoordModeOrigin	Specifies that all coordinates are relative to the origin of the drawable. (XDrawLines, XDrawPoints, XFillPolygon)
CoordModePrevious	Specifies that all coordinates are relative to the previous point (the first point is relative to the origin). (XDrawLines, XDrawPoints, XFillPolygon)
CopyFromParent	Specifies that a window's border pixmap, visual ID, or class should be copied from the window's parent. (XChange-WindowAttributes, XCreateWindow)
CreateNotify	Event type.
CurrentTime	Specifies time in most time arguments.
CursorShape	Specifies the "best" supported cursor size available on the display hardware. (XQueryBestSize)
CWBackingPixel	Mask to set the backing_pixel window attribute. (XChangeWindowAttributes, XCreateWindow)
CWBackingPlanes	Mask to set the backing_planes window attribute. (XChangeWindowAttributes, XCreateWindow)
CWBackingStore	Mask to set the backing_store window attribute. (XChangeWindowAttributes, XCreateWindow)
CWBackPixel	Mask to set the background_pixel window attribute. (XChangeWindowAttributes, XCreateWindow)
CWBackPixmap	Mask to set the background_pixmap window attribute. (XChangeWindowAttributes, XCreateWindow)
CWBitGravity	Mask to set the bit_gravity window attribute.
CWBorderPixel	Mask to set the border_pixel window attribute.

CWBorderPixmap	Mask to set the `border_pixmap` window attribute.
CWBorderWidth	Mask to set a new width for the window's border. (`XConfigureWindow`)
CWColormap	Mask to set the `colormap` window attribute. (`XChangeWindowAttributes`, `XCreateWindow`)
CWCursor	Mask to set the `cursor` window attribute. (`XChangeWindowAttributes`, `XCreateWindow`)
CWDontPropagate	Mask to set the `do_not_propagate_mask` window attribute. (`XChangeWindowAttributes`, `XCreateWindow`)
CWEventMask	Mask to set the `event_mask` window attribute. (`XChangeWindowAttributes`, `XCreateWindow`)
CWHeight	Mask to set a new height for the window. (`XConfigureWindow`)
CWOverrideRedirect	Mask to set the `override_redirect` window attribute. (`XChangeWindowAttributes`, `XCreateWindow`)
CWSaveUnder	Mask to set the `save_under` window attribute. (`XChangeWindowAttributes`, `XCreateWindow`)
CWSibling	Mask to specify a sibling of the window, used in stacking operations. (`XConfigureWindow`)
CWStackMode	Mask to set a new stack mode for the window. (`XConfigureWindow`)
CWWidth	Mask to set a new width for the window. (`XConfigureWindow`)
CWWinGravity	Mask to set the `win_gravity` window attribute. (`XChangeWindowAttributes`, `XCreateWindow`)
CWX	Mask to set a new X value for the window's position. (`XConfigureWindow`)
CWY	Mask to set a new Y value for the window's position. (`XConfigureWindow`)

DEF

DefaultBlanking	Specifies default screen saver screen blanking. (`XGetScreenSaver`, `XSetScreenSaver`)
DefaultExposures	Specifies that the default <??what default??> will govern whether or not exposures are generated when the screen is restored after blanking. (`XGetScreenSaver`, `XSetScreenSaver`)
DestroyAll	Specifies that all resources associated with a client/server connection will be freed when the client process dies. (`XSetCloseDownMode`)
DestroyNotify	Event type.
DirectColor	Visual class, read/write. (`XGetVisualInfo`, `XMatchVisualInfo`)
DisableAccess	Specifies that clients from any host have access unchallenged (access control is disabled). (`XSetAccessControl`)
DisableScreenInterval	Internal to Xlib.

`DisableScreenSaver`	Internal to Xlib.
`DoBlue`	Sets or changes the read/write colormap cell that corresponds to the specified pixel value to the hardware color that most closely matches the specified blue value. (`XStoreColor`, `XStoreColors`, `XStoreNamedColor`)
`DoGreen`	Sets or changes the read/write colormap cell that corresponds to the specified pixel value to the hardware color that most closely matches the specified green value. (`XStoreColor`, `XStoreColors`, `XStoreNamedColor`)
`DontAllowExposures`	Specifies that exposures are not generated when the screen is restored after blanking. (`XGetScreenSaver`, `XSetScreenSaver`)
`DontCareState`	Indicates that the client does not know or care what the initial state of the client is when the top-level window is mapped. Obsolete in R4. (Value for `initial_state` member of `XWMHints`.)
`DontPreferBlanking`	Specifies no screen saver screen blanking. (`XGetScreenSaver`, `XSetScreenSaver`)
`DoRed`	Sets or changes the read/write colormap cell that corresponds to the specified pixel value to the hardware color that most closely matches the specified red value. (`XStoreColor`, `XStoreColors`, `XStoreNamedColor`)
`EastGravity`	When a window is resized, specifies the new location of the contents or the children of the window. (`XChangeWindowAttributes`, `XCreateWindow`)
`EnableAccess`	Specifies that the host access list should be checked before allowing access to clients running on remote hosts (access control is enabled). (`XSetAccessControl`)
`EnterNotify`	Event type.
`EnterWindowMask`	Specifies that any `EnterNotify` events are to be selected for this window. An `EnterNotify` event reports pointer window entry. (`XSelectInput`)
`EvenOddRule`	Value of the `fill_rule` member of a GC: specifies that areas overlapping an odd number of times should not be part of the region. (`XPolygonRegion`, `XSetFillRule`)
`Expose`	Event type.
`ExposureMask`	Specifies that any exposure event except `GraphicsExpose` or `NoExpose` is to be selected for the window. An `Expose` event reports when a window or a previously invisible part of a window becomes visible. (`XSelectInput`)
`FamilyChaos`	Specifies an address in the ChaosNet network. (`XAddHost`)
`FamilyDECnet`	Specifies an address in the DECnet network. (`XAddHost`)
`FamilyInternet`	Specifies an address in the Internet network. (`XAddHost`)
`FillOpaqueStippled`	Value of the `fill_style` member of a GC: specifies that graphics should be drawn using `stipple`, using the foreground pixel value for set bits in stipple and the `background` pixel value for unset bits in pixel. (`XSetFillStyle`)

FillSolid	Value of the `fill_style` member of a GC: specifies that graphics should be drawn using the `foreground` pixel value. (XSetFillStyle)
FillStippled	Value of the `fill_style` member of a GC: specifies that graphics should be drawn using the `foreground` pixel value masked by `stipple`. (XSetFillStyle)
FillTiled	Value of the `fill_style` member of a GC: specifies that graphics should be drawn using the `tile` pixmap. (XSet-FillStyle)
FirstExtensionError	Use if writing extension.
FocusChangeMask	Specifies that any FocusIn and FocusOut events are to be selected for this window. FocusIn and FocusOut events report changes in keyboard focus. (XSelectInput)
FocusIn	Event type.
FocusOut	Event type.
FontChange	Internal to Xlib.
FontLeftToRight	Reports that, using the specified font, the string would be drawn left to right. (XQueryFont, XQueryTextExtents, XQueryTextExtents16, XTextExtents, XText-Extents16)
FontRightToLeft	Reports that, using the specified font, the string would be drawn right to left. (XQueryFont, XQueryTextExtents, XQueryTextExtents16, XTextExtents, XText-Extents16)
ForgetGravity	Specifies that window contents should always be discarded after a size change. (XChangeWindowAttributes, XCreateWindow)

G

GCArcMode	Mask to set the `arc_mode` component of a GC. (XChangeGC, XCopyGC, XCreateGC)
GCBackground	Mask to set the `background` component of a GC. (XChange-GC, XCopyGC, XCreateGC)
GCCapStyle	Mask to set the `cap_style` component of a GC. (XChange-GC, XCopyGC, XCreateGC)
GCClipMask	Mask to set the `clip_mask` component of a GC. (XChange-GC, XCopyGC, XCreateGC)
GCClipXOrigin	Mask to set the `clip_x_origin` of the `clip_mask`. (XChangeGC, XCopyGC, XCreateGC)
GCClipYOrigin	Mask to set the `clip_y_origin` of the `clip_mask`. (XChangeGC, XCopyGC, XCreateGC)
GCDashList	Mask to set the `dashes` component of a GC. (XChangeGC, XCopyGC, XCreateGC)

GCDashOffset	Mask to set the dash_offset component of a GC. (XChangeGC, XCopyGC, XCreateGC)
GCFillRule	Mask to set the fill_rule component of a GC. (XChangeGC, XCopyGC, XCreateGC)
GCFillStyle	Mask to set the fill_style component of a GC. (XChangeGC, XCopyGC, XCreateGC)
GCFont	Mask to set the font component of a GC. (XChangeGC, XCopyGC, XCreateGC)
GCForeground	Mask to set the foreground component of a GC. (XChangeGC, XCopyGC, XCreateGC)
GCFunction	Mask to set the function component of a GC. (XChangeGC, XCopyGC, XCreateGC)
GCGraphicsExposures	Mask to set the graphics_exposures component of a GC. (XChangeGC, XCopyGC, XCreateGC)
GCJoinStyle	Mask to set the join_style component of a GC. (XChangeGC, XCopyGC, XCreateGC)
GCLastBit	Higher than last GC mask value.
GCLineStyle	Mask to set the line_style component of a GC. (XChangeGC, XCopyGC, XCreateGC)
GCLineWidth	Mask to set the line_width component of a GC. (XChangeGC, XCopyGC, XCreateGC)
GCPlaneMask	Mask to set the plane_mask component of a GC. (XChangeGC, XCopyGC, XCreateGC)
GCStipple	Mask to set the stipple component of a GC. (XChangeGC, XCopyGC, XCreateGC)
GCSubwindowMode	Mask to set the subwindow_mode component of a GC. (XChangeGC, XCopyGC, XCreateGC)
GCTile	Mask to set the tile component of a GC. (XChangeGC, XCopyGC, XCreateGC)
GCTileStipXOrigin	Mask to set the ts_x_origin component of a GC. (XChangeGC, XCopyGC, XCreateGC)
GCTileStipYOrigin	Mask to set the ts_y_origin component of a GC. (XChangeGC, XCopyGC, XCreateGC)
GrabFrozen	Specifies that the pointer is frozen by an active grab of another client. (XGrabKeyboard, XGrabPointer)
GrabInvalidTime	Specifies that the indicated grab time is involved (earlier than the last keyboard grab time or later than the current server time). (XGrabKeyboard, XGrabPointer)
GrabModeAsync	Specifies the pointer or keyboard mode. (XGrabButton, XGrabKey, XGrabKeyboard, XGrabPointer)
GrabModeSync	Specifies the pointer or keyboard mode. (XGrabButton, XGrabKey, XGrabKeyboard, XGrabPointer)
GrabNotViewable	Specifies that the grab_window is not viewable. (XGrabKeyboard, XGrabPointer)

GrabSuccess	Specifies a successful pointer or keyboard grab. (XGrab-Keyboard, XGrabPointer)
GraphicsExpose	Event type.
GravityNotify	Event type.
GrayScale	Visual class, read/write. (XGetVisualInfo, XMatch-VisualInfo)
GXand	Value of the function member of the GC: used with source and destination pixels to generate final destination pixel values: src AND dst. (XChangeGC, XCreateGC, XSetFunction)
GXandInverted	(NOT src) AND dst. (XChangeGC, XCreateGC, XSetFunction)
GXandReverse	src AND (NOT dst). (XChangeGC, XCreateGC, XSetFunction)
GXclear	Set dst to 0. (XChangeGC, XCreateGC, XSetFunction)
GXcopy	src. (XChangeGC, XCreateGC, XSetFunction)
GXcopyInverted	(NOT src). (XChangeGC, XCreateGC, XSetFunction)
GXequiv	(NOT src) XOR dst. (XChangeGC, XCreateGC, XSetFunction)
GXinvert	(NOT dst). (XChangeGC, XCreateGC, XSetFunction)
GXnand	(NOT src) OR (NOT dst). (XChangeGC, XCreateGC, XSetFunction)
GXnoop	dst. (XChangeGC, XCreateGC, XSetFunction)
GXnor	(NOT src) AND (NOT dst). (XChangeGC, XCreateGC, XSetFunction)
GXor	src OR dst. (XChangeGC, XCreateGC, XSetFunction)
GXorInverted	(NOT src) OR dst. (XChangeGC, XCreateGC, XSetFunction)
GXorReverse	src OR (NOT dst). (XChangeGC, XCreateGC, XSetFunction)
GXset	set pixel. (XChangeGC, XCreateGC, XSetFunction)
GXxor	src XOR dst. (XChangeGC, XCreateGC, XSetFunction)

HIJ

HeightValue	Represents a user-specified window height in the standard window geometry string. (XParseGeometry)
HostDelete	Used internally to distinguish XAddHost and XRemoveHost.
HostInsert	Used internally to distinguish XAddHost and XRemoveHost.
IconicState	Indicates that the client wants to be iconified when the top-level window is mapped. (Value for initial_state member of XWMHints.)
IconMaskHint	In the XA_WM_HINTS property, the icon pixmap mask mask communicates to the window manager a bitmap that determines which pixels in icon_pixmap are drawn on the icon window. (XGetWMHints, XSetWMHints)

IconPixmapHint	In the XA_WM_HINTS property, the icon pixmap mask communicates to the window manager the pattern used to distinguish this icon from other clients. (XGetWMHints, XSetWMHints)
IconPositionHint	In the XA_WM_HINTS property, the position mask communicates to the window manager the preferred initial position of the icon. (XGetWMHints, XSetWMHints)
IconWindowHint	In the XA_WM_HINTS property, the icon window mask communicates to the window manager that icon_window contains a window that should be used instead of creating a new one. (XGetWMHints, XSetWMHints)
IgnoreState	Indicates that the client wants the window manager to ignore this window. (Value for initial_state member of XWMHints.)
InactiveState	Indicates that the client wants to be inactive when the top-level window is mapped. Obsolete in R4. (Value for initial_state member of XWMHints.)
IncludeInferiors	Value of the subwindow_mode member of the GC: specifies that graphics requests will draw through viewable children. (XSetSubwindowMode)
InputFocus	Specifies that the event will be sent to the focus window, regardless of the position of the pointer. (XSendEvent)
InputHint	In the XA_WM_HINTS property, the input member mask communicates to the window manager the keyboard focus model used by the application. (XGetWMHints, XSetWMHints)
InputOnly	InputOnly is a window class in which windows may receive input but may not be used to display output. (XCreateWindow)
InputOutput	InputOutput is a window class in which windows may receive input and may be used to display output. (XCreateWindow)
IsCursorKey	Keysym class macro.
IsFunctionKey	Keysym class macro.
IsKeypadKey	Keysym class macro.
IsMiscFunctionKey	Keysym class macro.
IsModifierKey	Keysym class macro.
IsPFKey	Keysym class macro.
IsUnmapped	Means that the window is unmapped. (XGetWindowAttributes)
IsUnviewable	Means that the window is mapped but is unviewable because some ancestor is unmapped. (XGetWindowAttributes)
IsViewable	Means that the window is currently viewable. (XGetWindowAttributes)
JoinBevel	Value of the join_style member of a GC: specifies CapButt enpoint styles, with the triangular notch filled. (XSetLineAttributes)

JoinMiter	Value of the `join_style` member of a GC: specifies that the outer edges of the two lines should extend to meet at an angle. (`XSetLineAttributes`)
JoinRound	Value of the `join_style` member of a GC: specifies that the lines should be joined by a circular arc with diameter equal to the `line_width`, centered on the join point. (`XSetLine-Attributes`)

KL

KBAutoRepeatMode	Mask to specify keyboard auto-repeat preferences. (`XChangeKeyboardControl`, `XGetKeyboardControl`)
KBBellDuration	Mask to specify keyboard bell-duration preferences. (`XChangeKeyboardControl`, `XGetKeyboardControl`)
KBBellPercent	Mask to specify keyboard base-volume preferences. (`XChangeKeyboardControl`, `XGetKeyboardControl`)
KBBellPitch	Mask to specify keyboard bell-pitch preferences. (`XChange-KeyboardControl`, `XGetKeyboardControl`)
KBKey	Mask to specify the keycode of the key whose auto-repeat status will be changed to the setting specified by `auto_repeat_mode`. (`XChangeKeyboardControl`, `XGet-KeyboardControl`)
KBKeyClickPercent	Mask to set keyboard key click-volume preferences. (`XChangeKeyboardControl`, `XGetKeyboardControl`)
KBLed	Mask to specify keyboard led preferences. (`XChange-KeyboardControl`, `XGetKeyboardControl`)
KBLedMode	Mask to specify keyboard led_mode preferences. (`XChange-KeyboardControl`, `XGetKeyboardControl`)
KeymapNotify	Event type.
KeymapStateMask	Specifies that any `KeymapNotify` events are to be selected for this window. A `KeymapNotify` event notifies the client about the state of the keyboard when the pointer or keyboard focus enters a window. (`XSelectInput`)
KeyPress	Event type.
KeyPressMask	Specifies that any `KeyPress` events are to be selected for this window. A `KeyPress` event reports that a keyboard key has been pressed. (`XSelectInput`)
KeyRelease	Event type.
KeyReleaseMask	Specifies that any `KeyRelease` events are to be selected for this window. A `KeyRelease` event reports that a keyboard key has been released. (`XSelectInput`)
LASTEvent	Bigger than any event type value. For extensions.
LastExtensionError	Use if writing extension.
LeaveNotify	Event type.
LeaveWindowMask	Specifies that any `LeaveNotify` events are to be selected for this window. A `LeaveNotify` event reports when the pointer leaves the window. (`XSelectInput`)

LedModeOff	Value of `led_mode`: specifies that the states of all the lights are not changed. (`XChangeKeyboardControl`, `XGet-KeyboardControl`)
LedModeOn	Value of `led_mode`: specifies that the states of all the lights are changed. (`XChangeKeyboardControl`, `XGet-KeyboardControl`)
LineDoubleDash	Value of the `line_style` member of a GC: specifies that dashes are drawn with the foreground pixel value and gaps with the background pixel value. (`XSetLineAttributes`)
LineOnOffDash	Value of the `line_style` member of a GC: specifies that only the dashes are drawn with the foreground pixel value, and `cap_style` applies to each dash. (`XSetLineAttributes`)
LineSolid	Value of the `line_style` member of a GC: specifies that the full path of the line is drawn using the foreground pixel value. (`XSetLineAttributes`)
LockMapIndex	Identifies one of eight modifiers to which keycodes can be mapped. (`XDeleteModifiermapEntry`, `XGetModifier-Mapping`, `XInsertModifiermapEntry`, `XLookupKeysym`, `XSetModifierMapping`)
LockMask	Specifies a modifier keymask for `XGrabButton`, `XGrabKey`, `XUngrabButton`, and `XUngrabKey`, and for the results of `XQueryPointer`.
LowerHighest	Specifies that the stacking order of children should be circulated down. (`XCirculateSubwindows`)
LSBFirst	In image structure, specifies the byte order used by VAXes. (`XCreateImage`)

M

MapNotify	Event type.
MappingBusy	Specifies that, in pointer or modifier mapping, no modifiers were changed because new keycodes for a modifier differ from those currently defined and any (current or new) keys for that modifier are in a down state. (`XSetModifierMapping`, `XSetPointerMapping`)
MappingFailed	Specifies that pointer or modifier mapping failed. (`XSet-ModifierMapping`, `XSetPointerMapping`)
MappingKeyboard	In a `MappingNotify` event, reports that keyboard mapping was changed.
MappingModifier	In a `MappingNotify` event, reports that keycodes were set to be used as modifiers.
MappingNotify	Event type.
MappingPointer	In a `MappingNotify` event, reports that pointer button mapping was set.
MappingSuccess	Specifies that pointer or modifier mapping succeeded. (`XSet-ModifierMapping`, `XSetPointerMapping`)
MapRequest	Event type.

`MessageHint`	In the `XA_WM_HINTS` property, the message member mask communicates to the window manager the <??what??>. (`XGetWMHints`, `XSetWMHints`)
`Mod1MapIndex`	Identifies one of eight modifiers to which keycodes can be mapped. (`XDeleteModifiermapEntry`, `XGetModifier-Mapping`, `XInsertModifiermapEntry`, `XLookupKeysym`, `XSetModifierMapping`)
`Mod1Mask`	Specifies a modifier keymask for `XGrabButton`, `XGrabKey`, `XUngrabButton`, and `XUngrabKey`, and for the results of `XQueryPointer`.
`Mod2MapIndex`	Identifies one of eight modifiers to which keycodes can be mapped. (`XDeleteModifiermapEntry`, `XGetModifier-Mapping`, `XInsertModifiermapEntry`, `XLookupKeysym`, `XSetModifierMapping`)
`Mod2Mask`	Specifies a modifier keymask for `XGrabButton`, `XGrabKey`, `XUngrabButton`, and `XUngrabKey`, and for the results of `XQueryPointer`.
`Mod3MapIndex`	Identifies one of eight modifiers to which keycodes can be mapped. (`XDeleteModifiermapEntry`, `XGetModifier-Mapping`, `XInsertModifiermapEntry`, `XLookupKeysym`, `XSetModifierMapping`)
`Mod3Mask`	Specifies a modifier keymask for `XGrabButton`, `XGrabKey`, `XUngrabButton`, and `XUngrabKey`, and for the results of `XQueryPointer`.
`Mod4MapIndex`	Identifies one of eight modifiers to which keycodes can be mapped. (`XDeleteModifiermapEntry`, `XGetModifier-Mapping`, `XInsertModifiermapEntry`, `XLookupKeysym`, `XSetModifierMapping`)
`Mod4Mask`	Specifies a modifier keymask for `XGrabButton`, `XGrabKey`, `XUngrabButton`, and `XUngrabKey`, and for the results of `XQueryPointer`.
`Mod5MapIndex`	Identifies one of eight modifiers to which keycodes can be mapped. (`XDeleteModifiermapEntry`, `XGetModifier-Mapping`, `XInsertModifiermapEntry`, `XLookupKeysym`, `XSetModifierMapping`)
`Mod5Mask`	Specifies a modifier keymask for `XGrabButton`, `XGrabKey`, `XUngrabButton`, and `XUngrabKey`, and for the results of `XQueryPointer`.
`MotionNotify`	Event type.
`MSBFirst`	In image structure, specifies the byte order used by 68000-family systems. (`XCreateImage`)

N

`NoEventMask`	Specifies that no events are to be selected for this window. (`XSelectInput`)
`NoExpose`	Event type.
`Nonconvex`	Specifies that a polygon's path does not self-intersect but that the polygon is not wholly convex. (`XFillPolygon`)

None	Specifies a universal null resource or null atom.
NormalState	Indicates that the client wants its top-level window visible. (Value for `initial_state` member of `XWMHints`.)
NorthEastGravity	When a window is resized, specifies the new location of the contents or the children of the window. (`XChangeWindow-Attributes`, `XCreateWindow`)
NorthGravity	When a window is resized, specifies the new location of the contents or the children of the window. (`XChangeWindow-Attributes`, `XCreateWindow`)
NorthWestGravity	When a window is resized, specifies the new location of the contents or the children of the window. (`XChangeWindow-Attributes`, `XCreateWindow`)
NoSymbol	Specifies the keysym for no symbol.
NotifyAncestor	In `EnterNotify`, `FocusIn`, `FocusOut`, and `LeaveNotify` events, specifies the hierarchical relationship of the origin and destination windows.
NotifyDetailNone	In `EnterNotify`, `FocusIn`, `FocusOut`, and `LeaveNotify` events, specifies the hierarchical relationship of the origin and destination windows.
NotifyGrab	In `EnterNotify`, `FocusIn`, `FocusOut`, and `LeaveNotify` events, specifies that the keyboard or pointer was grabbed.
NotifyHint	In a `MotionNotify` event, a hint that specifies that `PointerMotionHintMask` was selected.
NotifyInferior	In `EnterNotify`, `FocusIn`, `FocusOut`, and `LeaveNotify` events, specifies the hierarchical relationship of the origin and destination windows.
NotifyNone	In `EnterNotify`, `FocusIn`, `FocusOut`, and `LeaveNotify` events, specifies the hierarchical relationship of the origin and destination windows.
NotifyNonlinear	In `EnterNotify`, `FocusIn`, `FocusOut`, and `LeaveNotify` events, specifies the hierarchical relationship of the origin and destination windows.
NotifyNonlinear-Virtual	In `EnterNotify`, `FocusIn`, `FocusOut`, and `LeaveNotify` events, specifies the hierarchical relationship of the origin and destination windows.
NotifyNormal	In a `MotionNotify` event, a hint that specifies that the event is real but may not be up to date since there may be many more later motion events on the queue. In `EnterNotify`, `Focus-In`, `FocusOut`, and `LeaveNotify` events, specifies that the keyboard was not grabbed at the time the event was generated.
NotifyPointer	In `FocusIn` and `FocusOut` events, specifies the hierarchical relationship of the origin and destination windows.
NotifyPointerRoot	In `FocusIn` and `FocusOut` events, specifies the hierarchical relationship of the origin and destination windows.
NotifyUngrab	In `EnterNotify`, `FocusIn`, `FocusOut`, and `LeaveNotify` events, specifies that the keyboard or pointer was ungrabbed.

NotifyVirtual	In `EnterNotify`, `FocusIn`, `FocusOut`, and `LeaveNotify` events, specifies the hierarchical relationship of the origin and destination windows.
NotifyWhileGrabbed	`EnterNotify`, `FocusIn`, `FocusOut`, `LeaveNotify` mode.
NotUseful	Specifies that maintaining the contents of an unmapped window is unnecessary. (`XChangeWindowAttributes`, `XCreateWindow`)
NoValue	Mask used by `XParseGeometry`; returns those set by user.

OP

Opposite	Specifies that, if the indicated sibling occludes the indicated window, the window is placed at the top of the stack; if the window occludes the sibling, the window is placed at the bottom of the stack. (`XConfigureWindow`)
OwnerGrabButtonMask	Controls the distribution of button events to a client between `ButtonPress` and `ButtonRelease` events. (`XSelectInput`)
PAllHints	Specifies that the program determined the window hints. (`XGetNormalHints`, `XSetNormalHints`)
ParentRelative	Specifies that a window's background will be repainted when it is moved. (`XSetWindowBackgroundPixmap`)
PAspect	Specifies that the program determined the min and max aspect ratio. (`XGetNormalHints`, `XSetNormalHints`)
PBaseSize	Specifies that the program determined the base window size. (`XGetNormalHints`, `XSetNormalHints`)
PlaceOnBottom	In a `CirculateNotify` event, specifies that the window will be placed on the bottom of the stack.
PlaceOnTop	In a `CirculateNotify` event, specifies that the window will be placed on the top of the stack.
PMaxSize	Specifies that the program determined the maximum desired window size. (`XGetNormalHints`, `XSetNormalHints`)
PMinSize	Specifies that the program determined the minimum desired window size. (`XGetNormalHints`, `XSetNormalHints`)
PointerMotionHintMask	Specifies that the server should send only one `MotionNotify` event when the pointer moves. Used in concert with other pointer motion masks to reduce the number of events generated. (`XSelectInput`)
PointerMotionMask	Specifies that any pointer `MotionNotify` events are to be selected for this window. A `MotionNotify` event reports pointer movement. (`XSelectInput`)
PointerRoot	Specifies the ID of the window that is the current keyboard focus. (`XGetInputFocus`, `XSetInputFocus`)
PointerWindow	Specifies that the event will be sent to the window that the pointer is in. (`XSendEvent`)
PPosition	Specifies that the program determined the window position. (`XGetNormalHints`, `XSetNormalHints`)

PreferBlanking	Specifies screen saver screen blanking. (XGetScreenSaver, XSetScreenSaver)
PResizeInc	Specifies that the program determined the window resize increments. (XGetNormalHints, XSetNormalHints)
PropertyChangeMask	Specifies that any PropertyNotify events are to be selected for this window. A PropertyNotify event indicates that a property of a certain window was changed or deleted. (XSelectInput)
PropertyDelete	In a PropertyNotify event, specifies that a property of a window was deleted.
PropertyNewValue	In a PropertyNotify event, specifies that a property of a window was changed.
PropertyNotify	Event type.
PropModeAppend	Appends the data onto the end of the existing data. (XChangeProperty)
PropModePrepend	Inserts the data before the beginning of the existing data. (XChangeProperty)
PropModeReplace	Discards the previous property and stores the new data. (XChangeProperty)
PseudoColor	Visual class, read/write. (XGetVisualInfo, XMatch-VisualInfo)
PSize	Specifies that the program determined the window size. (XGetNormalHints, XSetNormalHints)
PWinGravity	Specifies that the program determined the window gravity. (XGetNormalHints, XSetNormalHints)

R

RaiseLowest	Specifies that the stacking order of children should be circulated up. (XCirculateSubwindows)
RectangleIn	Specifies that the rectangle is inside the region. (XRect-InRegion)
RectangleOut	Specifies that the rectangle is completely outside the region. (XRectInRegion)
RectanglePart	Specifies that the rectangle is partly inside the region. (XRectInRegion)
ReleaseByFreeing Colormap	Value for the killid field of XStandardColormap. (XSetRGBColormap and XGetRGBColormap)
ReparentNotify	Event type.
ReplayKeyboard	Specifies the conditions under which queued events are released: ReplayKeyboard has an effect only if the keyboard is grabbed by the client and thereby frozen as the result of an event. (XAllowEvents)
ReplayPointer	Specifies the conditions under which queued events are released: ReplayPointer has an effect only if the pointer is grabbed by the client and thereby frozen as the result of an event. (XAllowEvents)

ResizeRedirectMask	Specifies that any ResizeRequest events should be selected for this window when some other client (usually the window manager) attempts to resize the window on which this mask is selected. (XSelectInput)
ResizeRequest	Event type.
RetainPermanent	Specifies that resources associated with a client/server connection live on until a call to XKillClient. If AllTemporary is specified in XKillClient, the resources of all clients that have terminated in RetainTemporary are destroyed. <??vol2 unclear — XKillClient doc??> (XSetClose-DownMode)
RetainTemporary	Specifies that resources associated with a client/server connection live on until a call to XKillClient. If AllTemporary is specified in XKillClient, the resources of all clients that have terminated in RetainTemporary are destroyed. (XSet-CloseDownMode)
RevertToNone	Specifies that there is no backup keyboard focus window. (XGetInputFocus, XSetInputFocus)
RevertToParent	Specifies that the backup keyboard focus window is the parent window. (XGetInputFocus, XSetInputFocus)
RevertToPointerRoot	Specifies that the backup keyboard focus window is the pointer root window. (XGetInputFocus, XSetInputFocus)

S

ScreenSaverActive	Specifies that the screen saver is to be activated. (XForce-ScreenSaver)
ScreenSaverReset	Specifies that the screen saver is to be turned off. (XForce-ScreenSaver)
SelectionClear	Event type.
SelectionNotify	Event type.
SelectionRequest	Event type.
SetModeDelete	Specifies that a subwindow is to be deleted from the client's save-set. (XChangeSaveSet)
SetModeInsert	Specifies that a subwindow is to be added to the client's save-set. (XChangeSaveSet)
ShiftMapIndex	Identifies one of eight modifiers to which keycodes can be mapped. (XDeleteModifiermapEntry, XGetModifier-Mapping, XInsertModifiermapEntry, XLookupKeysym, XSetModifierMapping)
ShiftMask	Specifies a modifier keymask for XGrabButton, XGrabKey, XUngrabButton, and XUngrabKey, and for the results of XQueryPointer.
SouthEastGravity	When a window is resized, specifies the new location of the contents or the children of the window. (XChangeWindow-Attributes, XCreateWindow)

SouthGravity	When a window is resized, specifies the new location of the contents or the children of the window. (XChangeWindow-Attributes, XCreateWindow)
SouthWestGravity	When a window is resized, specifies the new location of the contents or the children of the window. (XChangeWindow-Attributes, XCreateWindow)
StateHint	In the XA_WM_HINTS property, the window state mask communicates to the window manager whether the client prefers to be in iconified, zoomed, normal, or inactive state. (XGet-WMHints, XSetWMHints)
StaticColor	Visual class, read-only. (XGetVisualInfo, XMatch-VisualInfo)
StaticGravity	Specifies that window contents should not move relative to the origin of the root window. (XChangeWindowAttribute, XCreateWindow)
StaticGray	Visual class, read-only. (XGetVisualInfo, XMatch-VisualInfo)
StippleShape	Specifies the "best" supported stipple size available on the display hardware. (XQueryBestSize)
StructureNotifyMask	Selects a group of event types (CirculateNotify, ConfigureNotify, DestroyNotify, GravityNotify, MapNotify, ReparentNotify, UnmapNotify) that report when the state of a window has changed. (XSelectInput)
SubstructureNotify-Mask	Selects a group of event types (CirculateNotify, ConfigureNotify, DestroyNotify, GravityNotify, MapNotify, ReparentNotify, UnmapNotify) that report when the state of a window has changed, plus an event that indicates that a window has been created. It monitors all the subwindows of the window specified in the XSelectInput call that used this mask.
SubstructureRedirect-Mask	The three event types selected by this mask (Circulate-Request, ConfigureRequest, and MapRequest) can be used by the window manager to intercept and cancel window-configuration-changing requests made by other clients. (XSelectInput)
Success	Indicates that everything is okay.
SyncBoth	Specifies that pointer and keyboard event processing resumes normally, until the next ButtonPress, ButtonRelease, KeyPress, or KeyRelease event, if the pointer and the keyboard are both frozen by the client when XAllowEvents is called with SyncBoth. (XAllowEvents)
SyncKeyboard	Specifies that key event processing resumes normally, until the next ButtonPress or ButtonRelease event, if the keyboard is frozen by the client when XAllowEvents is called with SyncPointer. (XAllowEvents)
SyncPointer	Specifies that pointer event processing resumes normally, until the next ButtonPress or ButtonRelease event, if the

pointer is frozen by the client when XAllowEvents is called with SyncPointer. (XAllowEvents)

TU

TileShape	Specifies the "best" supported tile size available on the display hardware. (XQueryBestSize)
TopIf	Specifies that the indicated window is placed on top of the stack if it is obscured by the indicated sibling window. (XConfigureWindow)
TrueColor	Visual class, read-only. (XGetVisualInfo, XMatch-VisualInfo)
UnmapGravity	Specifies that the child is unmapped when the parent is resized and an UnmapNotify event is generated. (XChangeWindow-Attributes, XCreateWindow)
UnmapNotify	Event type.
Unsorted	Specifies that the ordering of rectangles specified for a particular GC is arbitrary. (XSetClipRectangles)
USPosition	Specifies that the user provided a position value for the window. (XGetNormalHints, XSetNormalHints)
USSize	Specifies that the user provided a size value for the window. (XGetNormalHints, XSetNormalHints)

VW

VisibilityChangeMask	Specifies that any VisibilityNotify events are to be selected for this window, except when the window becomes not viewable. A VisibilityNotify event reports any changes in the window's visibility. (XSelectInput)
VisibilityFully-Obscured	In a VisibilityNotify event, specifies that the window is fully obscured.
VisibilityNotify	Event type.
VisibilityPartially-Obscured	In a VisibilityNotify event, specifies that the window is partially obscured.
VisibilityUnobscured	In a VisibilityNotify event, specifies that the window is unobscured.
VisualAllMask	Determines which elements in a template are to be matched. (XGetVisualInfo, XMatchVisualInfo)
VisualBitsPerRGBMask	Determines which elements in a template are to be matched. (XGetVisualInfo, XMatchVisualInfo)
VisualBlueMaskMask	Determines which elements in a template are to be matched. (XGetVisualInfo, XMatchVisualInfo)
VisualClassMask	Determines which elements in a template are to be matched. (XGetVisualInfo, XMatchVisualInfo)

VisualColormapSize-Mask	Determines which elements in a template are to be matched. (XGetVisualInfo, XMatchVisualInfo)
VisualDepthMask	Determines which elements in a template are to be matched. (XGetVisualInfo, XMatchVisualInfo)
VisualGreenMaskMask	Determines which elements in a template are to be matched. (XGetVisualInfo, XMatchVisualInfo)
VisualIDMask	Determines which elements in a template are to be matched. (XGetVisualInfo, XMatchVisualInfo)
VisualNoMask	Determines which elements in a template are to be matched. (XGetVisualInfo, XMatchVisualInfo)
VisualRedMaskMask	Determines which elements in a template are to be matched. (XGetVisualInfo, XMatchVisualInfo)
VisualScreenMask	Determines which elements in a template are to be matched. (XGetVisualInfo, XMatchVisualInfo)
WestGravity	When a window is resized, specifies the new location of the contents or the children of the window. (XChangeWindow-Attributes, XCreateWindow)
WhenMapped	Advises the server to maintain contents of obscured regions when the window is unmapped. (XChangeWindow-Attributes, XCreateWindow)
WidthValue	Represents a user-specified window width in the standard window geometry string. (XParseGeometry)
WindingRule	Value of the fill_rule member of a GC: specifies that areas overlapping an odd number of times should be part of the region. (XPolygonRegion, XSetFillRule)
WindowGroupHint	In the XA_WM_HINTS property, the group property mask communicates to the window manager that the client has multiple top-level windows. (XGetWMHints, XSetWMHints)
WithdrawnState	Indicates that the client wants neither its top-level nor its icon visible. (Value for initial_state member of XWMHints.)

X

XA_ARC	Specifies the atom of the type property that specifies the desired format for the data. (XConvertSelection)
XA_ATOM	Specifies the atom of the type property that specifies the desired format for the data. (XConvertSelection)
XA_BITMAP	Specifies the atom of the type property that specifies the desired format for the data. (XConvertSelection)
XA_CAP_HEIGHT	Predefined type atom.
XA_CARDINAL	Specifies the atom of the type property that specifies the desired format for the data. (XConvertSelection)
XA_COLORMAP	Specifies the atom of the type property that specifies the desired format for the data. (XConvertSelection)
XA_COPYRIGHT	Predefined font atom.
XA_CURSOR	Specifies the atom of the type property that specifies the desired format for the data. (XConvertSelection)

`XA_CUT_BUFFER0`	Represents a predefined cut buffer atom.
`XA_CUT_BUFFER1`	Represents a predefined cut buffer atom.
`XA_CUT_BUFFER2`	Represents a predefined cut buffer atom.
`XA_CUT_BUFFER3`	Represents a predefined cut buffer atom.
`XA_CUT_BUFFER4`	Represents a predefined cut buffer atom.
`XA_CUT_BUFFER5`	Represents a predefined cut buffer atom.
`XA_CUT_BUFFER6`	Represents a predefined cut buffer atom.
`XA_CUT_BUFFER7`	Represents a predefined cut buffer atom.
`XA_DRAWABLE`	Specifies the atom of the type property that specifies the desired format for the data. (`XConvertSelection`)
`XA_END_SPACE`	Specifies the additional spacing at the end of sentences.
`XA_FAMILY_NAME`	Predefined font atom.
`XA_FONT`	Specifies the atom of the type property that specifies the desired format for the data. (`XConvertSelection`)
`XA_FONT_NAME`	Predefined font atom.
`XA_FULL_NAME`	Predefined font atom.
`XA_INTEGER`	Specifies the atom of the type property that specifies the desired format for the data. (`XConvertSelection`)
`XA_ITALIC_ANGLE`	Specifies the angle of the dominant staffs of characters in the font.
`XA_LAST_PREDEFINED`	Predefined font atom.
`XA_MAX_SPACE`	Specifies the maximum interword spacing.
`XA_MIN_SPACE`	Specifies the minimum interword spacing.
`XA_NORM_SPACE`	Specifies the normal interword spacing.
`XA_NOTICE`	Predefined font atom.
`XA_PIXMAP`	Specifies the atom of the type property that specifies the desired format for the data. (`XConvertSelection`)
`XA_POINT`	Specifies the atom of the type property that specifies the desired format for the data. (`XConvertSelection`)
`XA_POINT_SIZE`	Specifies the point size of this font at the ideal resolution, expressed in tenths of a point.
`XA_PRIMARY`	Specifies the primary built-in selection atom used in transferring data between clients.
`XA_QUAD_WIDTH`	"1 em" as in TeX but expressed in units of pixels. The width of an m in the current font and point size.
`XA_RECTANGLE`	Specifies the atom of the type property that specifies the desired format for the data. (`XConvertSelection`)
`XA_RESOLUTION`	Specifies the number of pixels per point at which this font was created.
`XA_RESOURCE_MANAGER`	Specifies a predefined resource manager property containing default values for user preferences.

`XA_RGB_BEST_MAP`	Specifies a predefined colormap atom that defines the "best" RGB colormap available on the display.
`XA_RGB_BLUE_MAP`	Specifies a predefined colormap atom that defines an all-blue colormap.
`XA_RGB_COLOR_MAP`	Specifies the atom of the type property that specifies the desired format for the data. (`XConvertSelection`)
`XA_RGB_DEFAULT_MAP`	Specifies a predefined colormap atom that defines part of the system default colormap.
`XA_RGB_GRAY_MAP`	Specifies a predefined colormap atom that defines the "best" gray-scale colormap available on the display.
`XA_RGB_GREEN_MAP`	Specifies a predefined colormap atom that defines an all-green colormap.
`XA_RGB_RED_MAP`	Specifies a predefined colormap atom that defines an all-red colormap.
`XA_SECONDARY`	Specifies the secondary built-in selection atom used in transferring data between clients.
`XA_STRIKEOUT_ASCENT`	Specifies the vertical extents (in pixels) for boxing or voiding characters.
`XA_STRIKEOUT_DESCENT`	Specifies the vertical extents (in pixels) for boxing or voiding characters.
`XA_STRING`	Specifies the atom of the type property that specifies the desired format for the data. (`XConvertSelection`)
`XA_SUBSCRIPT_X`	Specifies the X offset (in pixels) from the character origin where subscripts should begin.
`XA_SUBSCRIPT_Y`	Specifies the Y offset (in pixels) from the character origin where subscripts should begin.
`XA_SUPERSCRIPT_X`	Specifies the X offset (in pixels) from the character origin where superscripts should begin.
`XA_SUPERSCRIPT_Y`	Specifies the Y offset (in pixels) from the character origin where superscripts should begin.
`XA_UNDERLINE_POSITION`	Specifies the Y offset (in pixels) from the baseline to the top of the underline.
`XA_UNDERLINE_THICKNESS`	Specifies the thickness (in pixels) from the baseline to the top of the underline.
`XA_VISUALID`	Specifies the atom of the type property that specifies the desired format for the data. (`XConvertSelection`)
`XA_WEIGHT`	Specifies the weight or boldness of the font, expressed as a value between 0 and 1000.
`XA_WINDOW`	Specifies the atom of the type property that specifies the desired format for the data. (`XConvertSelection`)
`XA_WM_CLASS`	The `XA_WM_CLASS` property is a string containing two null-separated elements, `res_class` and `res_name`, that are meant to be used by clients both as a means of permanent identification and as the handles by which both the client and the window manager obtain resources related to the window.

`XA_WM_CLIENT_MACHINE`	The `XA_WM_CLIENT_MACHINE` property is a string forming the name of the machine running the client, as seen from the machine running the server.
`XA_WM_COMMAND`	The `XA_WM_COMMAND` property stores the shell command and arguments used to invoke the application.
`XA_WM_HINTS`	The `XA_WM_HINTS` property contains hints stored by the window manager that provide a means of communicating optional information from the client to the window manager.
`XA_WM_ICON_NAME`	The `XA_WM_ICON_NAME` property is an uninterpreted string that the client wishes displayed in association with the window when it is iconified (for example, in an icon label).
`XA_WM_ICON_SIZE`	The window manager may set the `XA_WM_ICON_SIZE` property on the root window to specify the icon sizes it allows.
`XA_WM_NAME`	The `XA_WM_NAME` property is an uninterpreted string that the client wishes displayed in association with the window (for example, a window headline bar).
`XA_WM_NORMAL_HINTS`	The `XA_WM_NORMAL_HINTS` property is an `XSizeHints` structure describing the desired position and range of sizes that are preferable for each top-level window in normal state.
`XA_WM_SIZE_HINTS`	The `XA_WM_SIZE_HINTS` property contains hints stored..
`XA_WM_TRANSIENT_FOR`	The `XA_WM_TRANSIENT_FOR` property is the ID of another top-level window.
`XA_WM_ZOOM_HINTS`	The `XA_WM_ZOOM_HINTS` property is an `XSizeHints` structure describing the desired position and range of sizes that are preferable for each top-level window in a zoomed state.
`XA_X_HEIGHT`	"1 ex" as in TeX but expressed in units of pixels, often the height of lower case x.
`XCNOENT`	Association table lookup return codes, No entry in table.
`XCNOMEM`	Association table lookup return codes, Out of memory.
`XCSUCCESS`	Association table lookup return codes, No error.
`XK_*`	Keysyms, see Appendix H, *Keysym Reference*.
`XNegative`	Represents a user-specified negative X offset in the standard window geometry string. (`XParseGeometry`)
`XValue`	Represents a user-specified positive X offset in the standard window geometry string. (`XParseGeometry`)
`XYBitmap`	`XYBitmap` specified the format for an image. The data for an image is said to be in `XYBitmap` format if the bitmap is represented in scan line order, with each scan line made up of multiples of the `bitmap_unit` and padded with meaningless bits. (`XGetImage`, `XPutImage`)
`XYPixmap`	Depth == drawable depth. (`XGetImage`, `XPutImage`)
`X_PROTOCOL`	Current protocol version.
`X_PROTOCOL_REVISION`	Current minor revision.

YZ

YNegative
Represents a user-specified negative Y offset in the standard window geometry string. (XParseGeometry)

YSorted
Specifies that rectangles specified for a particular GC are non-decreasing in their Y origin. (XSetClipRectangles)

YValue
Represents a user-specified positive Y offset in the standard window geometry string. (XParseGeometry)

YXBanded
Specifies that, in addition to the constraints of YXSorted, for every possible horizontal Y scan line, all rectangles that include that scan line have identical Y origins and X extents. (XSetClipRectangles)

YXSorted
Specifies that rectangles specified for a particular GC are non-decreasing in their Y origin and that all rectangles with an equal Y origin are nondecreasing in their X origin. (XSet-ClipRectangles)

ZoomState
Indicates that the client wants to be in zoomed state when the top-level window is mapped. Obsolete in R4. (Value for initial_state member of XWMHints.)

ZPixmap
Depth == drawable depth. (XGetImage, XPutImage)

Symbol
Reference

H
Keysyms

This appendix provides a list of keysyms and a brief description of each keysym. Keysyms, as you may remember, are the portable representation of the symbols on the caps of keys.

The normal way to process a keyboard event is to use `XLookupKeysym` to determine the keysym or, if the application allows remapping of keys to strings, it may use `XLookup-String` to get the ASCII string mapped to the key or keys pressed. This allows the application to treat keys in a simple and portable manner, and places the responsibility of tailoring the mapping between keys and keysyms on the server vendor.*

Many keysyms do not have obvious counterparts on the keyboard, but may be generated with certain key combinations. You will need a table for each particular model of hardware you intend the program to work on, to tell you what key combination results in each keysym that is not present on the caps of the keyboard. For real portability, you will want to use only the keysyms that are supported on all vendors equipment you intend the program to be displayed on.

The keysyms are defined in two standard include files: *<X11/keysym.h>* and *<X11/keysym-def.h>*. There are several families of keysyms defined in *<X11/keysymdef.h>*; LATIN1, LATIN2, LATIN3, LATIN4, KATAKANA, ARABIC, CYRILLIC, GREEK, TECHNICAL, SPECIAL, PUBLISHING, APL, HEBREW, and MISCELLANY. The *<X11/keysym.h>* file specifies which families are enabled. Only the LATIN1, LATIN2, LATIN3, LATIN4, GREEK, and MISCELLANY families are enabled in the standard *<X11/keysym.h>* file, probably because some compilers have an upper limit on the number of defined symbols that are allowed.

The developers of X at MIT say that to the best of their knowledge the Latin, Kana, Arabic, Cyrillic, Greek, Technical, APL, and Hebrew keysym sets are from the appropriate ISO (International Standards Organization) and/or ECMA international standards. There are no Technical, Special nor Publishing international standards, so these sets are based on Digital Equipment Corporation standards.

---

* While keycode information is not necessary for normal application programming, it may be necessary for writing certain programs that change the keycode to keysym mapping. If you are writing such an application, you will need to obtain a list of keycodes and their normal mappings from the system manufacturer. Any program that uses this mapping is not fully portable.

Keysyms are four byte long values. In the standard keysyms, the least significant 8 bits indicate a particular character within a set. and the next 8 bits indicate a particular keysym set. The order of the sets is important since not all the sets are complete. Each character set contains gaps where codes have been removed that were duplicates with codes in previous (that is, with lesser keysym set) character sets.

The 94 and 96 character code sets have been moved to occupy the right hand quadrant (decimal 129 - 256), so the ASCII subset has a unique encoding across the least significant byte which corresponds to the ASCII character code. However, this cannot be guaranteed in the keysym sets of future releases and does not apply to all of the MISCELLANY set.

As far as possible, keysym codes are the same as the character code. In the LATIN1 to LATIN4 sets, all duplicate glyphs occupy the same position. However, duplicates between GREEK and TECHNICAL do not occupy the same code position. Thus, applications wishing to use the TECHNICAL character set must transform the keysym using an array.

The MISCELLANY set is a miscellaneous collection of commonly occurring keys on keyboards. Within this set, the keypad symbols are generally duplicates of symbols found on keys on the alphanumeric part of the keyboard but are distinguished here because they often have distinguishable keycodes associated with them.

There is a difference between European and US usage of the names Pilcrow, Paragraph, and Section, as shown in Table H-1.

Table H-1. European vs. US usage of Pilcrow, Paragraph, and Section symbol names

US name	European name	Keysym in LATIN1	Symbol
Section sign	Paragraph sign	`XK_section`	§
Paragraph sign	Pilcrow sign	`XK_paragraph`	¶

X has adopted the names used by both the ISO and ECMA standards. Thus, `XK_paragraph` is what Europeans call the pilcrow sign, and `XK_section` is what they would call the paragraph sign. This favors the US usage.

H.1 Keysyms and Description

Tables H-2 through H-7 list the six commonly available sets of keysyms (MISCELLANY, LATIN1 through LATIN4, and GREEK) and describe each keysym briefly. When necessary and possible, these tables show a representative character or characters that might appear on the cap of the key or on the screen when the key or keys corresponding to the keysym were typed.

Keysym	Description
XK_BackSpace	Backspace, Back Space, Back Char
XK_Tab	Tab
XK_Linefeed	Linefeed, LF
XK_Clear	Clear
XK_Return	Return, Enter
XK_Pause	Pause, Hold, Scroll Lock
XK_Escape	Escape
XK_Delete	Delete, Rubout
XK_Multi_key	Multi-key character preface
XK_Kanji	Kanji, Kanji convert
XK_Home	Home
XK_Left	Left, move left, left arrow
XK_Up	Up, move up, up arrow
XK_Right	Right, move right, right arrow
XK_Down	Down, move down, down arrow
XK_Prior	Prior, previous
XK_Next	Next
XK_End	End, EOL
XK_Begin	Begin, BOL
XK_Select	Select, mark
XK_Print	Print
XK_Execute	Execute, run, do
XK_Insert	Insert, insert here
XK_Undo	Undo, oops
XK_Redo	Redo, again
XK_Menu	Menu
XK_Find	Find, search
XK_Cancel	Cancel, stop, abort, exit
XK_Help	Help, question mark
XK_Break	Break
XK_Mode_switch	Mode switch, script switch, character set switch
XK_script_switch	Alias for mode switch, script switch, character set switch
XK_Num_Lock	Num Lock
XK_KP_Space	Keypad Space
XK_KP_Tab	Keypad Tab
XK_KP_Enter	Keypad Enter
XK_KP_F1	Keypad F1, PF1, a
XK_KP_F2	Keypad F2, PF2, b
XK_KP_F3	Keypad F3, PF3, c
XK_KP_F4	Keypad F4, PF4, d
XK_KP_Equal	Keypad equals sign
XK_KP_Multiply	Keypad multiplication sign, asterisk
XK_KP_Add	Keypad plus sign

Keysum
Reference

Keysym	Description
XK_KP_Separator	Keypad separator, comma
XK_KP_Subtract	Keypad minus sign, hyphen
XK_KP_Decimal	Keypad decimal point, full stop
XK_KP_Divide	Keypad division sign, solidus
XK_KP_0	Keypad digit zero
XK_KP_1	Keypad digit one
XK_KP_2	Keypad digit two
XK_KP_3	Keypad digit three
XK_KP_4	Keypad digit four
XK_KP_5	Keypad digit five
XK_KP_6	Keypad digit six
XK_KP_7	Keypad digit seven
XK_KP_8	Keypad digit eight
XK_KP_9	Keypad digit nine
XK_F1	F1 function key
XK_F2	F2 function key
XK_F3	F3 function key
XK_F4	F4 function key
XK_F5	F5 function key
XK_F6	F6 function key
XK_F7	F7 function key
XK_F8	F8 function key
XK_F9	F9 function key
XK_F10	F10 function key
XK_F11	F11 function key
XK_L1	L1 function key
XK_F12	F12 function key
XK_L2	L2 function key
XK_F13	F13 function key
XK_L3	L3 function key
XK_F14	F14 function key
XK_L4	L4 function key
XK_F15	F15 function key
XK_L5	L5 function key
XK_F16	F16 function key
XK_L6	L6 function key
XK_F17	F17 function key
XK_L7	L7 function key
XK_F18	F18 function key
XK_L8	L8 function key
XK_F19	F19 function key
XK_L9	L9 function key
XK_F20	F20 function key
XK_L10	L10 function key
XK_F21	F21 function key

Keysym	Description
XK_R1	R1 function key
XK_F22	F22 function key
XK_R2	R2 function key
XK_F23	F23 function key
XK_R3	R3 function key
XK_F24	F24 function key
XK_R4	R4 function key
XK_F25	F25 function key
XK_R5	R5 function key
XK_F26	F26 function key
XK_R6	R6 function key
XK_F27	F27 function key
XK_R7	R7 function key
XK_F28	F28 function key
XK_R8	R8 function key
XK_F29	F29 function key
XK_R9	R9 function key
XK_F30	F30 function key
XK_R10	R10 function key
XK_F31	F31 function key
XK_R11	R11 function key
XK_F32	F32 function key
XK_R12	R12 function key
XK_R13	F33 function key
XK_F33	R13 function key
XK_F34	F34 function key
XK_R14	R14 function key
XK_F35	F35 function key
XK_R15	R15 function key
XK_Shift_L	Left Shift
XK_Shift_R	Right Shift
XK_Control_L	Left Control
XK_Control_R	Right Control
XK_Caps_Lock	Caps Lock
XK_Shift_Lock	Shift Lock
XK_Meta_L	Left Meta
XK_Meta_R	Right Meta
XK_Alt_L	Left Alt
XK_Alt_R	Right Alt
XK_Super_L	Left Super
XK_Super_R	Right Super
XK_Hyper_L	Left Hyper
XK_Hyper_R	Right Hyper

Keysym	Description	Character
XK_space	Space	
XK_exclam	Exclamation point	!
XK_quotedbl	Quotation mark	,,
XK_numbersign	Number sign	#
XK_dollar	Dollar sign	$
XK_percent	Percent sign	%
XK_ampersand	Ampersand	&
XK_quoteright	Apostrophe	'
XK_parenleft	Left parenthesis	(
XK_parenright	Right parenthesis	)
XK_asterisk	Asterisk	*
XK_plus	Plus sign	+
XK_comma	Comma	,
XK_minus	Hyphen, minus sign	−
XK_period	Full stop	.
XK_slash	Solidus	/
XK_0	Digit zero	0
XK_1	Digit one	1
XK_2	Digit two	2
XK_3	Digit three	3
XK_4	Digit four	4
XK_5	Digit five	5
XK_6	Digit six	6
XK_7	Digit seven	7
XK_8	Digit eight	8
XK_9	Digit nine	9
XK_colon	Colon	:
XK_semicolon	Semicolon	;
XK_less	Less than sign	<
XK_equal	Equals sign	=
XK_greater	Greater than sign	>
XK_question	Question mark	?
XK_at	Commercial at	@
XK_A	Latin capital A	A
XK_B	Latin capital B	B
XK_C	Latin capital C	C

Keysym	Description	Character
XK_D	Latin capital D	D
XK_E	Latin capital E	E
XK_F	Latin capital F	F
XK_G	Latin capital G	G
XK_H	Latin capital H	H
XK_I	Latin capital I	I
XK_J	Latin capital J	J
XK_K	Latin capital K	K
XK_L	Latin capital L	L
XK_M	Latin capital M	M
XK_N	Latin capital N	N
XK_O	Latin capital O	O
XK_P	Latin capital P	P
XK_Q	Latin capital Q	Q
XK_R	Latin capital R	R
XK_S	Latin capital S	S
XK_T	Latin capital T	T
XK_U	Latin capital U	U
XK_V	Latin capital V	V
XK_W	Latin capital W	W
XK_X	Latin capital X	X
XK_Y	Latin capital Y	Y
XK_Z	Latin capital Z	Z
XK_bracketleft	Left square bracket	[
XK_backslash	Reverse solidus	\
XK_bracketright	Right square bracket	]
XK_asciicircum	Circumflex accent	^
XK_underscore	Low line	_
XK_quoteleft	Grave accent	`
XK_a	Latin small a	a
XK_b	Latin small b	b
XK_c	Latin small c	c
XK_d	Latin small d	d
XK_e	Latin small e	e
XK_f	Latin small f	f
XK_g	Latin small g	g
XK_h	Latin small h	h
XK_i	Latin small i	i

Keysym	Description	Character
XK_j	Latin small j	j
XK_k	Latin small k	k
XK_l	Latin small l	l
XK_m	Latin small m	m
XK_n	Latin small n	n
XK_o	Latin small o	o
XK_p	Latin small p	p
XK_q	Latin small q	q
XK_r	Latin small r	r
XK_s	Latin small s	s
XK_t	Latin small t	t
XK_u	Latin small u	u
XK_v	Latin small v	v
XK_w	Latin small w	w
XK_x	Latin small x	x
XK_y	Latin small y	y
XK_z	Latin small z	z
XK_braceleft	Left brace	{
XK_bar	Vertical line	|
XK_braceright	Right brace	}
XK_asciitilde	Tilde	~
XK_nobreakspace	No-break space	
XK_exclamdown	Inverted exclamation mark	¡
XK_cent	Cent sign	¢
XK_sterling	Pound sign	£
XK_currency	Currency sign	¤
XK_yen	Yen sign	¥
XK_brokenbar	Broken vertical bar	¦
XK_section	Paragraph sign, section sign	§
XK_diaeresis	Diaeresis	¨
XK_copyright	Copyright sign	©
XK_ordfeminine	Feminine ordinal indicator	ª
XK_guillemotleft	Left angle quotation mark	«
XK_notsign	Not sign	¬
XK_hyphen	Short horizontal hyphen	-
XK_registered	Registered trade mark sign	®
XK_macron	Macron	¯
XK_degree	Degree sign, ring above	°

Keysym	Description	Character
XK_plusminus	Plus-minus sign	±
XK_twosuperior	Superscript two	²
XK_threesuperior	Superscript three	³
XK_acute	Acute accent	´
XK_mu	Micro sign	μ
XK_paragraph	Pilcrow sign	¶
XK_periodcentered	Middle dot	·
XK_cedilla	Cedilla	¸
XK_onesuperior	Superscript one	¹
XK_masculine	Masculine ordinal indicator	º
XK_guillemotright	Right angle quotation mark	»
XK_onequarter	Vulgar fraction one quarter	¼
XK_onehalf	Vulgar fraction one half	½
XK_threequarters	Vulgar fraction three quarters	¾
XK_questiondown	Inverted question mark	¿
XK_Agrave	Latin capital A with grave accent	À
XK_Aacute	Latin capital A with acute accent	Á
XK_Acircumflex	Latin capital A with circumflex accent	Â
XK_Atilde	Latin capital A with tilde	Ã
XK_Adiaeresis	Latin capital A with diaeresis	Ä
XK_Aring	Latin capital A with ring above	Å
XK_AE	Latin capital diphthong AE	Æ
XK_Ccedilla	Latin capital C with cedilla	Ç
XK_Egrave	Latin capital E with grave accent	È
XK_Eacute	Latin capital E with acute accent	É
XK_Ecircumflex	Latin capital E with circumflex accent	Ê
XK_Ediaeresis	Latin capital E with diaeresis	Ë
XK_Igrave	Latin capital I with grave accent	Ì
XK_Iacute	Latin capital I with acute accent	Í
XK_Icircumflex	Latin capital I with circumflex accent	Î
XK_Idiaeresis	Latin capital I with diaeresis	Ï
XK_Eth	Icelandic capital ETH	
XK_Ntilde	Latin capital N with tilde	Ñ
XK_Ograve	Latin capital O with grave accent	Ò
XK_Oacute	Latin capital O with acute accent	Ó
XK_Ocircumflex	Latin capital O with circumflex accent	Ô
XK_Otilde	Latin capital O with tilde	Õ
XK_Odiaeresis	Latin capital O with diaeresis	Ö

Keysym	Description	Character
XK_multiply	Multiplication sign	×
XK_Ooblique	Latin capital O with oblique stroke	Ø
XK_Ugrave	Latin capital U with grave accent	Ù
XK_Uacute	Latin capital U with acute accent	Ú
XK_Ucircumflex	Latin capital U with circumflex accent	Û
XK_Udiaeresis	Latin capital U with diaeresis	Ü
XK_Yacute	Latin capital Y with acute accent	Ý
XK_Thorn	Icelandic capital THORN	
XK_ssharp	German small sharp s	
XK_agrave	Latin small a with grave accent	à
XK_aacute	Latin small a with acute accent	á
XK_acircumflex	Latin small a with circumflex accent	â
XK_atilde	Latin small a with tilde	ã
XK_adiaeresis	Latin small a with diaeresis	ä
XK_aring	Latin small a with ring above	å
XK_ae	Latin small diphthong ae	æ
XK_ccedilla	Latin small c with cedilla	ç
XK_egrave	Latin small e with grave accent	è
XK_eacute	Latin small e with acute accent	é
XK_ecircumflex	Latin small e with circumflex accent	ê
XK_ediaeresis	Latin small e with diaeresis	ë
XK_igrave	Latin small i with grave accent	ì
XK_iacute	Latin small i with acute accent	í
XK_icircumflex	Latin small i with circumflex accent	î
XK_idiaeresis	Latin small i with diaeresis	ï
XK_eth	Icelandic small eth	
XK_ntilde	Latin small n with tilde	ñ
XK_ograve	Latin small o with grave accent	ò
XK_oacute	Latin small o with acute accent	ó
XK_ocircumflex	Latin small o with circumflex accent	ô
XK_otilde	Latin small o with tilde	õ
XK_odiaeresis	Latin small o with diaeresis	ö
XK_division	Division sign	÷
XK_oslash	Latin small o with oblique stroke	ø
XK_ugrave	Latin small u with grave accent	ù
XK_uacute	Latin small u with acute accent	ú
XK_ucircumflex	Latin small u with circumflex accent	û
XK_udiaeresis	Latin small u with diaeresis	ü

Keysym	Description	Character
XK_yacute	Latin small y with acute accent	ý
XK_thorn	Icelandic small thorn	
XK_ydiaeresis	Latin small y with diaeresis	ÿ

Keysym	Description	Character
XK_Aogonek	Latin capital A with ogonek	Ą
XK_breve	Breve	˘
XK_Lstroke	Latin capital L with stroke	Ł
XK_Lcaron	Latin capital L with caron	Ľ
XK_Sacute	Latin capital S with acute accent	Ś
XK_Scaron	Latin capital S with caron	Š
XK_Scedilla	Latin capital S with cedilla	Ş
XK_Tcaron	Latin capital T with caron	Ť
XK_Zacute	Latin capital Z with acute accent	Ź
XK_Zcaron	Latin capital Z with caron	Ž
XK_Zabovedot	Latin capital Z with dot above	Ż
XK_aogonek	Latin small a with ogonek	ą
XK_ogonek	Ogonek	˛
XK_lstroke	Latin small l with stroke	ł
XK_lcaron	Latin small l with caron	ľ
XK_sacute	Latin small s with acute accent	ś
XK_caron	Caron	ˇ
XK_scaron	Latin small s with caron	š
XK_scedilla	Latin small s with cedilla	ş
XK_tcaron	Latin small t with caron	ť
XK_zacute	Latin small z with acute accent	ź
XK_doubleacute	Double acute accent	˝
XK_zcaron	Latin small z with caron	ž
XK_zabovedot	Latin small z with dot above	ż
XK_Racute	Latin capital R with acute accent	Ŕ
XK_Abreve	Latin capital A with breve	Ă
XK_Cacute	Latin capital C with acute accent	Ć
XK_Ccaron	Latin capital C with caron	Č
XK_Eogonek	Latin capital E with ogonek	Ę
XK_Ecaron	Latin capital E with caron	Ě
XK_Dcaron	Latin capital D with caron	Ď
XK_Nacute	Latin capital N with acute accent	Ń
XK_Ncaron	Latin capital N with caron	Ň
XK_Odoubleacute	Latin capital O with double acute accent	Ő
XK_Rcaron	Latin capital R with caron	Ř
XK_Uring	Latin capital U with ring above	Ů
XK_Udoubleacute	Latin capital U with double acute accent	Ű
XK_Tcedilla	Latin capital T with cedilla	Ţ

Keysym	Description	Character
XK_racute	Latin small r with acute accent	ŕ
XK_abreve	Latin small a with breve	ă
XK_cacute	Latin small c with acute accent	ć
XK_ccaron	Latin small c with caron	č
XK_eogonek	Latin small e with ogonek	ę
XK_ecaron	Latin small e with caron	ě
XK_dcaron	Latin small d with caron	ď
XK_nacute	Latin small n with acute accent	ń
XK_ncaron	Latin small n with caron	ň
XK_odoubleacute	Latin small o with double acute accent	ő
XK_rcaron	Latin small r with caron	ř
XK_uring	Latin small u with ring above	ů
XK_udoubleacute	Latin small u with double acute accent	ű
XK_tcedilla	Latin small t with cedilla	ţ
XK_abovedot	Dot above	˙

Table H-5. LATIN3

Keysym	Description	Character
XK_Hstroke	Latin capital H with stroke	
XK_Hcircumflex	Latin capital H with circumflex accent	Ĥ
XK_Iabovedot	Latin capital I with dot above	İ
XK_Gbreve	Latin capital G with breve	Ğ
XK_Jcircumflex	Latin capital J with circumflex accent	Ĵ
XK_hstroke	Latin small h with stroke	
XK_hcircumflex	Latin small h with circumflex accent	ĥ
XK_idotless	Small dotless i	ı
XK_gbreve	Latin small g with breve	ğ
XK_jcircumflex	Latin small j with circumflex accent	ĵ
XK_Cabovedot	Latin capital C with dot above	Ċ
XK_Ccircumflex	Latin capital C with circumflex accent	Ĉ
XK_Gabovedot	Latin capital G with dot above	Ġ
XK_Gcircumflex	Latin capital G with circumflex accent	Ĝ
XK_Ubreve	Latin capital U with breve	Ŭ
XK_Scircumflex	Latin capital S with circumflex accent	Ŝ
XK_cabovedot	Latin small c with dot above	ċ
XK_ccircumflex	Latin small c with circumflex accent	ĉ
XK_gabovedot	Latin small g with dot above	ġ
XK_gcircumflex	Latin small g with circumflex accent	ĝ
XK_ubreve	Latin small u with breve	ŭ
XK_scircumflex	Latin small s with circumflex accent	ŝ

Table H-6. LATIN4

Keysym	Description	Character
XK_kappa	Latin small kappa	
XK_Rcedilla	Latin capital R with cedilla	Ŗ
XK_Itilde	Latin capital I with tilde	Ĩ
XK_Lcedilla	Latin capital L with cedilla	Ļ
XK_Emacron	Latin capital E with macron	Ē
XK_Gcedilla	Latin capital G with cedilla	Ģ
XK_Tslash	Latin capital T with oblique stroke	
XK_rcedilla	Latin small r with cedilla	ŗ
XK_itilde	Latin small i with tilde	ĩ
XK_lcedilla	Latin small l with cedilla	ļ
XK_emacron	Latin small e with macron	ē
XK_gacute	Latin small g with acute accent	ģ
XK_tslash	Latin small t with oblique stroke	
XK_ENG	Lappish capital ENG	
XK_eng	Lappish small eng	
XK_Amacron	Latin capital A with macron	Ā
XK_Iogonek	Latin capital I with ogonek	Į
XK_Eabovedot	Latin capital E with dot above	Ė
XK_Imacron	Latin capital I with macron	Ī
XK_Ncedilla	Latin capital N with cedilla	Ņ
XK_Omacron	Latin capital O with macron	Ō
XK_Kcedilla	Latin capital K with cedilla	Ķ
XK_Uogonek	Latin capital U with ogonek	Ų
XK_Utilde	Latin capital U with tilde	Ũ
XK_Umacron	Latin capital U with macron	Ū
XK_amacron	Latin small a with macron	ā
XK_iogonek	Latin small i with ogonek	į
XK_eabovedot	Latin small e with dot above	ė
XK_imacron	Latin small i with macron	ī
XK_ncedilla	Latin small n with cedilla	ņ
XK_omacron	Latin small o with macron	ō
XK_kcedilla	Latin small k with cedilla	ķ
XK_uogonek	Latin small u with ogonek	ų
XK_utilde	Latin small u with tilde	ũ
XK_umacron	Latin small u with macron	ū

Table H-7. GREEK

Keysym	Description	Character
XK_Greek_ALPHAaccent	Greek capital alpha with accent	
XK_Greek_EPSILONaccent	Greek capital epsilon with accent	
XK_Greek_ETAaccent	Greek capital eta with accent	
XK_Greek_IOTAaccent	Greek capital iota with accent	
XK_Greek_IOTAdiaeresis	Greek capital iota with diaeresis	
XK_Greek_IOTAaccentdiaeresis	Greek capital iota with accent+dieresis	
XK_Greek_OMICRONaccent	Greek capital omicron with accent	
XK_Greek_UPSILONaccent	Greek capital upsilon with accent	
XK_Greek_UPSILONdieresis	Greek capital upsilon with dieresis	
XK_Greek_UPSILONaccentdieresis	Greek capital upsilon with accent+dieresis	
XK_Greek_OMEGAaccent	Greek capital omega with accent	
XK_Greek_alphaaccent	Greek small alpha with accent	
XK_Greek_epsilonaccent	Greek small epsilon with accent	
XK_Greek_etaaccent	Greek small eta with accent	
XK_Greek_iotaaccent	Greek small iota with accent	
XK_Greek_iotadieresis	Greek small iota with dieresis	
XK_Greek_iotaaccentdieresis	Greek small iota with accent+dieresis	
XK_Greek_omicronaccent	Greek small omicron with accent	
XK_Greek_upsilonaccent	Greek small upsilon with accent	
XK_Greek_upsilondieresis	Greek small upsilon with dieresis	
XK_Greek_upsilonaccentdieresis	Greek small upsilon with accent+dieresis	
XK_Greek_omegaaccent	Greek small omega with accent	
XK_Greek_ALPHA	Greek capital alpha	A
XK_Greek_BETA	Greek capital beta	B
XK_Greek_GAMMA	Greek capital gamma	Γ
XK_Greek_DELTA	Greek capital delta	Δ
XK_Greek_EPSILON	Greek capital epsilon	E
XK_Greek_ZETA	Greek capital zeta	Z
XK_Greek_ETA	Greek capital eta	H
XK_Greek_THETA	Greek capital theta	Θ
XK_Greek_IOTA	Greek capital iota	I
XK_Greek_KAPPA	Greek capital kappa	K
XK_Greek_LAMBDA	Greek capital lambda	Λ
XK_Greek_MU	Greek capital mu	M
XK_Greek_NU	Greek capital nu	N
XK_Greek_XI	Greek capital xi	Ξ
XK_Greek_OMICRON	Greek capital omicron	O
XK_Greek_PI	Greek capital pi	Π

Keysym	Description	Character
XK_Greek_RHO	Greek capital rho	Ρ
XK_Greek_SIGMA	Greek capital sigma	Σ
XK_Greek_TAU	Greek capital tau	Τ
XK_Greek_UPSILON	Greek capital upsilon	Υ
XK_Greek_PHI	Greek capital phi	Φ
XK_Greek_CHI	Greek capital chi	Χ
XK_Greek_PSI	Greek capital psi	Ψ
XK_Greek_OMEGA	Greek capital omega	Ω
XK_Greek_alpha	Greek small alpha	α
XK_Greek_beta	Greek small beta	β
XK_Greek_gamma	Greek small gamma	γ
XK_Greek_delta	Greek small delta	δ
XK_Greek_epsilon	Greek small epsilon	ε
XK_Greek_zeta	Greek small zeta	ζ
XK_Greek_eta	Greek small eta	η
XK_Greek_theta	Greek small theta	θ
XK_Greek_iota	Greek small iota	ι
XK_Greek_kappa	Greek small kappa	κ
XK_Greek_lambda	Greek small lambda	λ
XK_Greek_mu	Greek small mu	μ
XK_Greek_nu	Greek small nu	ν
XK_Greek_xi	Greek small xi	ξ
XK_Greek_omicron	Greek small omicron	ο
XK_Greek_pi	Greek small pi	π
XK_Greek_rho	Greek small rho	ρ
XK_Greek_sigma	Greek small sigma	σ
XK_Greek_finalsmallsigma	Greek small final small sigma	ς
XK_Greek_tau	Greek small tau	τ
XK_Greek_upsilon	Greek small upsilon	υ
XK_Greek_phi	Greek small phi	φ
XK_Greek_chi	Greek small chi	χ
XK_Greek_psi	Greek small psi	ψ
XK_Greek_omega	Greek small omega	ω
XK_Greek_switch	Switch to Greek set	

Keysum
Reference

The Cursor Font

A standard font consisting of a number of cursor shapes is available. This font is loaded automatically when XCreateFontCursor, the routine used to create a standard cursor, is called. To specify a cursor shape from the standard font, use one of the symbols defined in the file *<X11/cursorfont.h>*, by including it in your source code. The symbols for the available cursors and an illustration of their shapes is provided here. The technique used for creating a cursor is described in Volume One, Section 6.6.

You may notice that the symbol values skip the odd numbers; there are really two font characters for each shape but we are only showing you one. Each odd-numbered character (not shown) is a mask that selects which pixels in the screen around the cursor are modified.

The standard cursor shapes are shown in Figure I-1. The mask shapes have been removed. Each row in Figure I-1 contains twelve cursor shapes (except the last one). Table I-1 shows the symbol definitions from *<X11/cursorfont.h>* grouped by rows corresponding to the rows in Figure I-1.

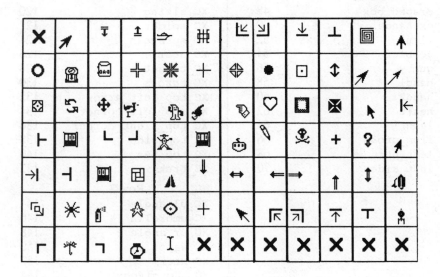

Figure I-1. The Standard Cursors

Table I-1. Standard Cursor Symbols

Symbol	Value	Symbol	Value
Row 1		**Row 4**	
XC_X_cursor	0	XC_left_tee	72
XC_arrow	2	XC_left_button	74
XC_based_arrow_down	4	XC_ll_angle	76
XC_based_arrow_up	6	XC_lr_angle	78
XC_boat	8	XC_man	80
XC_bogosity	10	XC_middlebutton	82
XC_bottom_left_corner	12	XC_mouse	84
XC_bottom_right_corner	14	XC_pencil	86
XC_bottom_side	16	XC_pirate	88
XC_bottom_tee	18	XC_plus	90
XC_box_spiral	20	XC_question_arrow	92
XC_center_ptr	22	XC_right_ptr	94
Row 2		**Row 5**	
XC_circle	24	XC_right_side	96
XC_clock	26	XC_right_tee	98
XC_coffee_mug	28	XC_rightbutton	100
XC_cross	30	XC_rtl_logo	102
XC_cross_reverse	32	XC_sailboat	104
XC_crosshair	34	XC_sb_down_arrow	106
XC_diamond_cross	36	XC_sb_h_double_arrow	108
XC_dot	38	XC_sb_left_arrow	110
XC_dotbox	40	XC_sb_right_arrow	112
XC_double_arrow	42	XC_sb_up_arrow	114
XC_draft_large	44	XC_sb_v_double_arrow	116
XC_draft_small	46	XC_shuttle	118
Row 3		**Row 6**	
XC_draped_box	48	XC_sizing	120
XC_exchange	50	XC_spider	122
XC_fleur	52	XC_spraycan	124
XC_gobbler	54	XC_star	126
XC_gumby	56	XC_target	128
XC_hand1	58	XC_tcross	130
XC_hand2	60	XC_top_left_arrow	132
XC_heart	62	XC_top_left_corner	134
XC_icon	64	XC_top_right_corner	136
XC_iron_cross	66	XC_top_side	138
XC_left_ptr	68	XC_top_tee	140
XC_left_side	70	XC_trek	142
		Row 7	
		XC_ul_angle	144
		XC_umbrella	146
		XC_ur_angle	148
		XC_watch	150
		XC_xterm	152
		XC_num_glyphs	154

J
The Xmu Library

The Xmu Library is a collection of miscellaneous utility functions that have been useful in building various applications and Xt toolkit widgets. Though not defined by any X consortium standard, this library is written and supported by MIT in the core distribution, and therefore should be available on virtually all machines.

This appendix presents reference pages for each Xmu function available in R4. For a summary of the contents of Xmu, see Volume One, Appendix H, *The Xmu Library*. For a list of which functions are available in R3, see Volume One, Appendix G, *Release Notes*. At each release the number and variety of functions in this library has increased dramatically. It is worthwhile skimming this appendix to see what is available in R4, even if you are familiar with the R3 Xmu library.

Each group of Xmu functions designed around a particular task has its own header file, listed in the Synopsis section of each reference page. Note that the location of the header files of Xmu has changed in R4. In R3 and earlier, the header files for all X libraries were stored in */usr/include/X11*. In R4, the header files for Xmu and Xaw are located in subdirectories of this directory, named after each library. In other words, the Xmu header files are now located (by default, on UNIX-based systems) in */usr/include/X11/Xmu*.

XctCreate

Name

XctCreate — create a `XctData` structure for parsing a Compound Text string.

Synopsis

```
#include <X11/Xmu/Xct.h>
XctData XctCreate(string, length, flags)
    XctString string;
    int length;
    XctFlags flags;
```

Arguments

string	Specifies the Compound Text string.
length	Specifies the number of bytes in *string*.
flags	Specifies parsing control flags.

Description

`XctCreate` creates an `XctData` structure for parsing a Compound Text string. The string need not be null terminated. The following flags are defined to control parsing of the string:

`XctSingleSetSegments`

This means that returned segments should contain characters from only one set (C0, C1, GL, GR). When this is requested, `XctSegment` is never returned by `XctNextItem`, instead `XctC0Segment`, `XctC1Segment`, `XctG1Segment`, and `XctGRSegment` are returned. C0 and C1 segments are always returned as singleton characters.

`XctProvideExtensions`

This means that if the Compound Text string is from a higher version than this code is implemented to, then syntactically correct but unknown control sequences should be returned as `XctExtension` items by `XctNextItem`. If this flag is not set, and the Compound Text string version indicates that extensions cannot be ignored, then each unknown control sequence will be reported as an `XctError`.

`XctAcceptC0Extensions`

This means that if the Compound Text string is from a higher version than this code is implemented to, then unknown C0 characters should be treated as if they were legal, and returned as C0 characters (regardless of how `XctProvideExtensions` is set) by `Xct-NextItem`. If this flag is not set, then all unknown C0 characters are treated according to `XctProvideExtensions`.

`XctAcceptC1Extensions`

This means that if the Compound Text string is from a higher version than this code is implemented to, then unknown C1 characters should be treated as if they were legal, and returned as C1 characters (regardless of how `XctProvideExtensions` is set) by `Xct-NextItem`. If this flag is not set, then all unknown C1 characters are treated according to `XctProvideExtensions`.

XctHideDirection

This means that horizontal direction changes should be reported as XctHorizontal items by XctNextItem. If this flag is not set, then direction changes are not returned as items, but the current direction is still maintained and reported for other items. The current direction is given as an enumeration, with the values XctUnspecified, XctLeft-ToRight, and XctRightToLeft.

XctFreeString

This means that XctFree should free the Compound Text string that is passed to Xct-Create. If this flag is not set, the string is not freed.

XctShiftMultiGRToGL

This means that XctNextItem should translate GR segments on-the-fly into GL segments for the GR sets: GB2312.1980-1, JISX0208.1983-1, and KSC5601.1987-1.

Related Commands

XctFree, XctNextItem, XctReset.

Name
XctFree — free an XctData structure.

Synopsis
```
#include <X11/Xmu/Xct.h>
void XctFree(data)
    XctData data;
```

Arguments
data   Specifies the Compound Text structure.

Description
XctFree frees all data associated with the XctData structure.

Related Commands
XctNextItem, XctReset.

XctNextItem

Name

XctNextItem — parse the next item in a Compound Text string.

Synopsis

```
#include <X11/Xmu/Xct.h>
XctResult XctNextItem(data)
    XctData data;
```

Arguments

data   Specifies the Compound Text structure.

Description

XctNextItem parses the next item in the Compound Text string. The return value indicates what kind of item is returned. The item itself, it's length, and the current contextual state, are reported as components of the XctData structure. XctResult is an enumeration, with the following values:

XctSegment
> The item contains some mixture of C0, GL, GR, and C1 characters.

XctC0Segment
> The item contains only C0 characters.

XctGLSegment
> The item contains only GL characters.

XctC1Segment
> the item contains only C1 characters.

XctGRSegment
> the item contains only GR characters.

XctExtendedSegment
> The item contains an extended segment.

XctExtension
> The item is an unknown extension control sequence.

XctHorizontal
> The item indicates a change in horizontal direction or depth. The new direction and depth are recorded in the XctData structure.

XctEndOfText
> The end of the Compound Text string has been reached.

XctError
> The string contains a syntactic or semantic error; no further parsing should be performed.

Structures

```
typedef struct {
    XctString item;                    /* the action item */
```

```
    int item_length;              /* the length of item in bytes */
    int char_size;                /* the number of bytes per character in
                                   * item, with zero meaning variable */

    char *encoding;               /* the XLFD encoding name for item */
    XctHDirection horizontal;     /* the direction of item */
    int horz_depth;               /* the current direction nesting depth */
    char *GL;                     /* the "{I} F" string for the current GL */
    char *GL_encoding;            /* the XLFD encoding name for the current GL *
    int GL_set_size;              /* 94 or 96 */
    int GL_char_size;             /* the number of bytes per GL character */
    char *GR;                     /* the "{I} F" string for the current GR */
    char *GR_encoding;            /* the XLFD encoding name the for current GR *
    int GR_set_size;              /* 94 or 96 */
    int GR_char_size;             /* the number of bytes per GR character */
    char *GLGR_encoding;          /* the XLFD encoding name for the current
                                   * GL+GR, if known */

        .
        .
        .

} XctData;
```

Related Commands

`XctCreate, XctFree, XctReset.`

Name

XctReset — reset an XctData structure for reparsing a Compound Text string.

Synopsis

```
#include <X11/Xmu/Xct.h>
void XctReset(data)
    XctData data;
```

Arguments

data   Specifies the Compound Text structure.

Description

XctReset resets the XctData structure to reparse the Compound Text string from the beginning.

Related Commands

XctCreate, XctFree, XctNextItem.

XmuAddCloseDisplayHook

Name

XmuAddCloseDisplayHook — add callback function to be called when display connection is closed.

Synopsis

```
#include <X11/Xmu/CloseHook.h>
CloseHook XmuAddCloseDisplayHook(display, func, arg)
   Display *display;
   int (*func)();
   caddr_t arg;
```

Arguments

display   Specifies a connection to an X server; returned from XOpenDisplay.

func   Specifies the function to call at display close.

arg   Specifies arbitrary data to pass to func.

Description

XmuAddCloseDisplayHook registers a callback for the given display. When the display is closed, the given function will be called with the given display and argument as:

```
(*func)(display, arg)
```

The function is declared to return int even though the value is ignored, because some compilers have problems with functions returning void.

This routine returns NULL if it was unable to add the callback, otherwise it returns an opaque handle that can be used to remove or lookup the callback.

Related Commands

XmuAddCloseDisplayHook, XmuLookupCloseDisplayHook, XmuRemoveClose-DisplayHook.

XmuAllStandardColormaps

Name

XmuAllStandardColormaps — create all supported standard colormaps and set standard color-map properties.

Synopsis

```
#include <X11/Xmu/StdCmap.h>
Status XmuAllStandardColormaps(display)
    Display *display;
```

Arguments

display   Specifies a connection to an X server; returned from XOpenDisplay.

Description

XmuAllStandardColormaps creates all of the appropriate standard colormaps for every visual of every screen on a given display.

XmuAllStandardColormaps defines and retains as permanent resources all these standard colormaps. It returns zero on failure, non-zero on success. If the property of any standard colormap is already defined, this function will redefine it.

This function is intended to be used by window managers or a special client at the start of a session.

The standard colormaps of a screen are defined by properties associated with the screen's root window. The property names of standard colormaps are predefined, and each property name except RGB_DEFAULT_MAP may describe at most one colormap.

The standard colormaps are: RGB_BEST_MAP, RGB_RED_MAP, RGB_GREEN_MAP, RGB_BLUE_MAP, RGB_DEFAULT_MAP, and RGB_GRAY_MAP. Therefore a screen may have at most 6 standard colormap properties defined.

A standard colormap is associated with a particular visual of the screen. A screen may have multiple visuals defined, including visuals of the same class at different depths. Note that a visual ID might be repeated for more than one depth, so the visual ID and the depth of a visual identify the visual. The characteristics of the visual will determine which standard colormaps are meaningful under that visual, and will determine how the standard colormap is defined. Because a standard colormap is associated with a specific visual, there must be a method of determining which visuals take precedence in defining standard colormaps.

The method used here is: for the visual of greatest depth, define all standard colormaps meaningful to that visual class, according to this order of (descending) precedence: DirectColor; PseudoColor; TrueColor; and GrayScale; and finally StaticColor and Static-Gray.

This function allows success on a per screen basis. For example, if a map on screen 1 fails, the maps on screen 0, created earlier, will remain. However, none on screen 1 will remain. If a map on screen 0 fails, none will remain.

Related Commands

`XmuCreateColormap`, `XmuDeleteStandardColormap`, `XmuGetColormap-`
`Allocation`, `XmuLookupStdCmp`, `XmuStandardColormap`, `XmuVisualStandard-`
`Colormaps`.

XmuClientWindow

Name

XmuClientWindow — find a window which has a WM_STATE property.

Synopsis

```
#include <X11/Xmu/WinUtil.h>
Window XmuClientWindow(display, win)
    Display *display;
    Window win;
```

Arguments

display   Specifies a connection to an X server; returned from XOpenDisplay.

win   Specifies the window.

Description

XmuClientWindow finds a window, at or below the specified window, which has a WM_STATE property. If such a window is found, it is returned, otherwise the argument window is returned.

Related Commands

XmuScreenOfWindow, XmuUpdateMapHints.

Xmu
Library

XmuCompareISOLatin1

Name

XmuCompareISOLatin1 — compare and determine order of two strings, ignoring case.

Synopsis

```
#include <X11/Xmu/CharSet.h>
int XmuCompareISOLatin1(first, second)
   char *first, *second;
```

Arguments

first   Specifies a string to compare.

second   Specifies a string to compare.

Description

XmuCompareISOLatin1 compares two NULL terminated Latin-1 strings, ignoring case differences, and returns an integer greater than, equal to, or less than zero, according to whether first is lexicographically greater than, equal to, or less than second. The two strings are assumed to be encoded using ISO 8859-1 (Latin-1).

Related Commands

XmuCopyISOLatin1Lowered, XmuCopyISOLatin1Uppered, XmuLookup.

XmuCopyISOLatin1Lowered

Name

XmuCopyISOLatin1Lowered — copy string, changing upper case to lower case.

Synopsis

```
#include <X11/Xmu/CharSet.h>
void XmuCopyISOLatin1Lowered(dst, src)
    char *dst, *src;
```

Arguments

dst	Returns the string copy.
src	Specifies the string to copy.

Description

XmuCopyISOLatin1Lowered copies a null terminated string from *src* to *dst* (including the NULL), changing all Latin-1 upper-case letters to lower-case. The string is assumed to be encoded using ISO 8859-1 (Latin-1).

Related Commands

XmuCompareISOLatin1, XmuCopyISOLatin1Uppered, XmuLookup.

Xmu
Library

XmuCopyISOLatin1Uppered

Name

XmuCopyISOLatin1Uppered — copy string, changing lower case to upper case.

Synopsis

```
#include <X11/Xmu/CharSet.h>
void XmuCopyISOLatin1Uppered(dst, src)
    char *dst, *src;
```

Arguments

dst   Returns the string copy.

src   Specifies the string to copy.

Description

XmuCopyISOLatin1Uppered copies a null terminated string from *src* to *dst* (including the NULL), changing all Latin-1 lower-case letters to upper-case. The string is assumed to be encoded using ISO 8859-1 (Latin-1).

Related Commands

XmuCompareISOLatin1, XmuCopyISOLatin1Lowered, XmuLookup.

XmuCreateColormap

Name

XmuCreateColormap — create a standard colormap from information in an XStandard-Colormap structure.

Synopsis

```
#include <X11/Xmu/StdCmap.h>
Status XmuCreateColormap(display, colormap)
    Display *display;
    XStandardColormap *colormap;
```

Arguments

display   Specifies the connection under which the map is created.

colormap   Specifies the map to be created.

Description

XmuCreateColormap creates any one colormap which is described by an XStandard-Colormap structure.

XmuCreateColormap returns zero on failure, and non-zero on success. The base_pixel field of the XStandardColormap structure is set on success. Resources created by this function are not made permanent. No argument error checking is provided; use at your own risk.

All colormaps are created with read-only allocations, with the exception of read-only allocations of colors which fail to return the expected pixel value, and these are individually defined as read/write allocations. This is done so that all the cells defined in the colormap are contiguous, for use in image processing. This typically happens with White and Black in the default map.

Colormaps of static visuals are considered to be successfully created if the map of the static visual matches the definition given in the standard colormap structure.

Related Commands

XmuAllStandardColormaps, XmuDeleteStandardColormap, XmuGet-ColormapAllocation, XmuLookupStdCmp, XmuStandardColormap, XmuVisual-StandardColormaps.

Xmu
Library

Name

XmuCreatePixmapFromBitmap — create multi-plane pixmap and copy data from one-plane pixmap.

Synopsis

```
#include <X11/Xmu/Drawing.h>
Pixmap XmuCreatePixmapFromBitmap(display, d, bitmap, width,
        height, depth, fore, back)
    Display *display;
    Drawable d;
    Pixmap bitmap;
    unsigned int width, height;
    unsigned int depth;
    unsigned long fore, back;
```

Arguments

display	Specifies a connection to an X server; returned from XOpenDisplay.
d	Specifies the screen the pixmap is created on.
bitmap	Specifies the bitmap source.
width	Specifies the width of the pixmap.
height	Specifies the height of the pixmap.
depth	Specifies the depth of the pixmap.
fore	Specifies the foreground pixel value.
back	Specifies the background pixel value.

Description

XmuCreatePixmapFromBitmap creates a pixmap of the specified width, height, and depth, on the same screen as the specified drawable, and then performs an XCopyPlane from the specified bitmap to the pixmap, using the specified foreground and background pixel values. The created pixmap is returned. The original bitmap is not destroyed.

Related Commands

XmuCreateStippledPixmap, XmuDrawLogo, XmuDrawRoundedRectangle, Xmu-FillRoundedRectangle, XmuLocateBitmapFile, XmuReadBitmapData, XmuReadBitmapDataFromFile, XmuReleaseStippledPixmap.

XmuCreateStippledPixmap

Name

XmuCreateStippledPixmap — create two pixel by two pixel gray pixmap.

Synopsis

```
#include <X11/Xmu/Drawing.h>
Pixmap XmuCreateStippledPixmap(screen, fore, back, depth)
    Screen *screen;
    Pixel fore, back;
    unsigned int depth;
```

Arguments

screen	Specifies the screen the pixmap is created on.
fore	Specifies the foreground pixel value.
back	Specifies the background pixel value.
depth	Specifies the depth of the pixmap.

Description

XmuCreateStippledPixmap creates a two pixel by two pixel stippled pixmap of specified
depth on the specified screen. The pixmap is cached so that multiple requests share the same
pixmap. The pixmap should be freed with XmuReleaseStippledPixmap to maintain correct reference counts.

Related Commands

XmuCreatePixmapFromBitmap, XmuDrawLogo, XmuDrawRoundedRectangle,
XmuFillRoundedRectangle, XmuLocateBitmapFile, XmuReadBitmapData,
XmuReadBitmapDataFromFile, XmuReleaseStippledPixmap.

XmuCursorNameToIndex

Name

XmuCursorNameToIndex — return index in cursor font given string name.

Synopsis

```
#include <X11/Xmu/CurUtil.h>
int XmuCursorNameToIndex(name)
    char *name;
```

Arguments

name   Specifies the name of the cursor.

Description

XmuCursorNameToIndex takes the name of a standard cursor and returns its index in the standard cursor font. The cursor names are formed by removing the XC_ prefix from the cursor defines listed in Appendix I, *The Cursor Font*.

Name

XmuDQAddDisplay — add a display connection to a display queue.

Synopsis

```
#include <X11/Xmu/DisplayQue.h>
XmuDisplayQueueEntry *XmuDQAddDisplay(q, display, data)
    XmuDisplayQueue *q;
    Display *display;
    caddr_t data;
```

Arguments

q	Specifies the queue.
display	Specifies the display connection to add.
data	Specifies private data for the free callback function.

Description

XmuDQAddDisplay adds the specified display to the queue. If successful, the queue entry is returned, otherwise NULL is returned. The data value is simply stored in the queue entry for use by the queue's free callback. This function does not attempt to prevent duplicate entries in the queue; the caller should use XmuDQLookupDisplay to determine if a display has already been added to a queue.

Related Commands

XmuDQCreate, XmuDQDestroy, XmuDQLookupDisplay, XmuDQNDisplays, Xmu-DQRemoveDisplay.

Xmu
Library

XmuDQCreate

Name

XmuDQCreate — creates an empty display queue.

Synopsis

```
#include <X11/Xmu/DisplayQue.h>
XmuDisplayQueue *XmuDQCreate(closefunc, freefunc, data)
    int (*closefunc)();
    int (*freefunc)();
    caddr_t data;
```

Arguments

closefunc   Specifies the close function.

freefunc   Specifies the free function.

data   Specifies private data for the functions.

Description

XmuDQCreate creates and returns an empty XmuDisplayQueue (which is really just a set of displays, but is called a queue for historical reasons). The queue is initially empty, but displays can be added using XmuAddDisplay. The data value is simply stored in the queue for use by the display close and free callbacks. Whenever a display in the queue is closed using XCloseDisplay, the display close callback (if non-NULL) is called with the queue and the display's XmuDisplayQueueEntry as follows:

```
(*closefunc)(queue, entry)
```

The free callback (if non-NULL) is called whenever the last display in the queue is closed, as follows:

```
(*freefunc)(queue)
```

The application is responsible for actually freeing the queue, by calling XmuDQDestroy.

Related Commands

XmuDQAddDisplay, XmuDQDestroy, XmuDQLookupDisplay, XmuDQNDisplays, XmuDQRemoveDisplay.

XmuDQDestroy

Name

XmuDQDestroy — destroy a display queue, and optionally call callbacks.

Synopsis

```
#include <X11/Xmu/DisplayQue.h>
Bool XmuDQDestroy(q, docallbacks)
    XmuDisplayQueue *q;
    Bool docallbacks;
```

Arguments

q Specifies the queue to destroy.

docallbacks Specifies whether the close callback functions should be called.

Description

XmuDQDestroy releases all memory associated with the specified queue. If *docallbacks* is True, then the queue's close callback (if non-NULL) is first called for each display in the queue, even though XCloseDisplay is not called on the display.

Related Commands

XmuDQAddDisplay, XmuDQCreate, XmuDQLookupDisplay, XmuDQNDisplays, XmuDQRemoveDisplay.

Xmu Library

Name

XmuDQLookupDisplay — determine display queue entry for specified display connection.

Synopsis

```
#include <X11/Xmu/DisplayQue.h>
XmuDisplayQueueEntry *XmuDQLookupDisplay(q, display)
    XmuDisplayQueue *q;
    Display *display;
```

Arguments

q   Specifies the queue.

display   Specifies the display to lookup.

Description

XmuDQLookupDisplay returns the queue entry for the specified display, or NULL if the display is not in the queue.

Related Commands

XmuDQAddDisplay, XmuDQCreate, XmuDQDestroy, XmuDQNDisplays, XmuDQRemoveDisplay.

XmuDQNDisplays

Name

XmuDQNDisplays — return the number of display connections in a display queue.

Synopsis

```
#include <X11/Xmu/DisplayQue.h>
XmuDQNDisplays(q)
```

Description

XmuDQNDisplays returns the number of displays in the specified queue.

Related Commands

XmuDQAddDisplay, XmuDQCreate, XmuDQDestroy, XmuDQLookupDisplay, Xmu-
DQRemoveDisplay.

Xmu
Library

XmuDQRemoveDisplay

Name

XmuDQRemoveDisplay — remove a display connection from a display queue.

Synopsis

```
#include <X11/Xmu/DisplayQue.h>
Bool XmuDQRemoveDisplay(q, display)
    XmuDisplayQueue *q;
    Display *display;
```

Arguments

q   Specifies the queue.

display   Specifies the display to remove.

Description

XmuDQNDisplays removes the specified display connection from the specified queue. No callbacks are performed. If the display is not found in the queue, False is returned, otherwise True is returned.

Related Commands

XmuDQAddDisplay, XmuDQCreate, XmuDQDestroy, XmuDQLookupDisplay, XmuDQNDisplays.

XmuDeleteStandardColormap

Name
XmuDeleteStandardColormap — remove any standard colormap property.

Synopsis
```
void XmuDeleteStandardColormap(display, screen, property)
    Display *display;
    int screen;
    Atom property;
```

Arguments
display   Specifies a connection to an X server; returned from XOpenDisplay.

screen   Specifies the screen of the display.

property   Specifies the standard colormap property.

Description
XmuDeleteStandardColormap will remove the specified property from the specified screen, releasing any resources used by the colormap(s) of the property, if possible.

Related Commands
XmuAllStandardColormaps, XmuCreateColormap, XmuGetColormap-Allocation, XmuLookupStdCmp, XmuStandardColormap, XmuVisualStandard-Colormaps.

Xmu Library

Name

XmuDrawLogo — draws the standard X logo.

Synopsis

```
#include <X11/Xmu/Drawing.h>
XmuDrawLogo(display, drawable, gcFore, gcBack, x, y, width,
        height)
    Display *display;
    Drawable drawable;
    GC gcFore, gcBack;
    int x, y;
    unsigned int width, height;
```

Arguments

display	Specifies a connection to an X server; returned from XOpenDisplay.
drawable	Specifies the drawable.
gcFore	Specifies the foreground GC.
gcBack	Specifies the background GC.
x	Specifies the upper left x coordinate.
y	Specifies the upper left y coordinate.
width	Specifies the logo width.
height	Specifies the logo height.

Description

XmuDrawLogo draws the "official" X Window System logo. The bounding box of the logo in the drawable is given by x, y, width, and height . The logo itself is filled using gcFore, and the rest of the rectangle is filled using gcBack.

Related Commands

XmuCreatePixmapFromBitmap, XmuCreateStippledPixmap, XmuDraw-RoundedRectangle, XmuFillRoundedRectangle, XmuLocateBitmapFile, Xmu-ReadBitmapData, XmuReadBitmapDataFromFile, XmuReleaseStippled-Pixmap.

XmuDrawRoundedRectangle

Name

XmuDrawRoundedRectangle — draws a rectangle with rounded corners.

Synopsis

```
#include <X11/Xmu/Drawing.h>
void XmuDrawRoundedRectangle(display, draw, gc, x, y, w, h, ew,
        eh)
    Display *display;
    Drawable draw;
    GC gc;
    int x, y, w, h, ew, eh;
```

Arguments

display	Specifies a connection to an X server; returned from XOpenDisplay.
draw	Specifies the drawable.
gc	Specifies the GC.
x	Specifies the upper left x coordinate.
y	Specifies the upper left y coordinate.
w	Specifies the rectangle width.
h	Specifies the rectangle height.
ew	Specifies the corner width.
eh	Specifies the corner height.

Description

XmuDrawRoundedRectangle draws a rounded rectangle, where x, y, w, h are the dimensions of the overall rectangle, and ew and eh are the sizes of a bounding box that the corners are drawn inside of; ew should be no more than half of w, and eh should be no more than half of h. The current GC line attributes control all attributes of the line.

Related Commands

XmuCreatePixmapFromBitmap, XmuCreateStippledPixmap, XmuDrawLogo, XmuFillRoundedRectangle, XmuLocateBitmapFile, XmuReadBitmapData, XmuReadBitmapDataFromFile, XmuReleaseStippledPixmap.

Xmu
Library

Name
XmuFillRoundedRectangle — fill a rectangle with rounded corners.

Synopsis
```
#include <X11/Xmu/Drawing.h>
void XmuFillRoundedRectangle(display, draw, gc, x, y, w, h, ew,
        eh)
    Display *display;
    Drawable draw;
    GC gc;
    int x, y, w, h, ew, eh;
```

Arguments

display	Specifies a connection to an X server; returned from XOpenDisplay.
draw	Specifies the drawable.
gc	Specifies the GC.
x	Specifies the upper left x coordinate.
y	Specifies the upper left y coordinate.
w	Specifies the rectangle width.
h	Specifies the rectangle height.
ew	Specifies the corner width.
eh	Specifies the corner height.

Description
XmuFillRoundedRectangle draws a filled rounded rectangle, where x, y, w, h are the dimensions of the overall rectangle, and ew and eh are the sizes of a bounding box that the corners are drawn inside of; ew should be no more than half of w, and eh should be no more than half of h. The current GC fill settings control all attributes of the fill contents.

Related Commands
XmuCreatePixmapFromBitmap, XmuCreateStippledPixmap, XmuDrawLogo, XmuDrawRoundedRectangle, XmuLocateBitmapFile, XmuReadBitmapData, XmuReadBitmapDataFromFile, XmuReleaseStippledPixmap.

XmuGetAtomName

Name

XmuGetAtomName — returns the property name string corresponding to the specified atom.

Synopsis

```
#include <X11/Xmu/Atoms.h>
char *XmuGetAtomName(d, atom)
    Display *d;
    Atom atom;
```

Arguments

d   Specifies a connection to an X server; returned from XOpenDisplay.

atom   Specifies the atom whose name is desired.

Description

XmuGetAtomName returns the property name string corresponding to the specified atom. The result is cached, such that subsequent requests do not cause another round-trip to the server. If the atom is zero, XmuGetAtomName returns "(BadAtom)".

Related Commands

XmuInternAtom, XmuInternStrings, XmuMakeAtom, XmuNameofAtom.

Name

XmuGetColormapAllocation — determine best allocation of reds, greens, and blues in a standard colormap.

Synopsis

```
#include <X11/Xmu/StdCmap.h>
Status XmuGetColormapAllocation(vinfo, property, red_max,
        green_max, blue_max)
    XVisualInfo *vinfo;
    Atom property;
    unsigned long *red_max, *green_max, *blue_max;
```

Arguments

vinfo   Specifies visual information for a chosen visual.

property   Specifies one of the standard colormap property names.

red_max   Returns maximum red value.

green_max   Returns maximum green value.

blue_max   Returns maximum blue value.

Description

XmuGetColormapAllocation determines the best allocation of reds, greens, and blues in a standard colormap.

XmuGetColormapAllocation returns zero on failure, non-zero on success. It is assumed that the visual is appropriate for the colormap property.

Related Commands

XmuAllStandardColormaps, XmuCreateColormap, XmuDeleteStandard-Colormap, XmuLookupStdCmp, XmuStandardColormap, XmuVisualStandard-Colormaps.

XmuGetHostname

Name

XmuGetHostname — operating system independent routine to get machine name.

Synopsis

```
#include <X11/Xmu/SysUtil.h>
int XmuGetHostname(buf, maxlen)
    char *buf;
    int maxlen;
```

Arguments

buf   Returns the host name.

maxlen   Specifies the length of *buf*.

Description

XmuGetHostname stores the null terminated name of the local host in *buf*, and returns the length of the name. This function hides operating system differences, such as whether to call gethostname or uname.

Xmu
Library

XmuInternAtom

Name

XmuInternAtom — get an atom from the server and load it into an `AtomPtr`.

Synopsis

```
Atom XmuInternAtom(d, atom_ptr)
      Display *d;
      AtomPtr atom_ptr;
```

Arguments

d   Specifies a connection to an X server; returned from `XOpenDisplay`.

atom_ptr   Specifies the `AtomPtr`.

Description

`XmuInternAtom` gets an atom from the server (for the string stored in `AtomPtr`) and stores the atom in the specified `AtomPtr`. The atom is cached such that subsequent requests do not cause another round-trip to the server.

Related Commands

`XmuGetAtomName`, `XmuInternStrings`, `XmuMakeAtom`, `XmuNameofAtom`.

XmuInternStrings

Name

XmuInternStrings — get the atoms for several property name strings.

Synopsis

```
#include <X11/Xmu/Atoms.h>
void XmuInternStrings(d, names, count, atoms)
    Display *d;
    String *names;
    Cardinal count;
    Atom *atoms;
```

Arguments

d	Specifies a connection to an X server; returned from XOpenDisplay.
names	Specifies the strings to intern.
count	Specifies the number of strings.
atoms	Returns the list of Atoms value.

Description

XmuInternStrings converts a list of property name strings into a list of atoms, possibly by querying the server. The results are cached, such that subsequent requests do not cause further round-trips to the server. The caller is responsible for preallocating the array of atoms.

Related Commands

XmuGetAtomName, XmuInternAtom, XmuMakeAtom, XmuNameofAtom.

Name

XmuLocateBitmapFile — creates a one-plane pixmap from a bitmap file in a standard location.

Synopsis

```
#include <X11/Xmu/Drawing.h>
XmuLocateBitmapFile(screen, name, srcname, srcnamelen, widthp,
        heightp, xhotp, yhotp)
 Screen *screen;
 char *name;
 char *srcname;
 int srcnamelen;
 int *widthp, *heightp, *xhotp, *yhotp;
```

Arguments

name	Specifies the file to read from.
srcname	Returns the full filename of the bitmap.
srcnamelen	Specifies the length of the srcname buffer.
width	Returns the width of the bitmap.
height	Returns the height of the bitmap.
xhotp	Returns the x coordinate of the hotspot.
yhotp	Returns the y coordinate of the hotspot.

Description

XmuLocateBitmapFile reads a file in standard bitmap file format, using XReadBitmap-
File, and returns the created bitmap. The filename may be absolute, or relative to the global
resource named *bitmapFilePath* with class *BitmapFilePath*. If the resource is not
defined, the default value is the build symbol BITMAPDIR, which is typically
/usr/include/X11/bitmaps. If *srcnamelen* is greater than zero and *srcname* is not NULL, the
null terminated filename will be copied into *srcname*. The size and hotspot of the bitmap are
also returned.

Related Commands

XmuCreatePixmapFromBitmap, XmuCreateStippledPixmap, XmuDrawLogo,
XmuDrawRoundedRectangle, XmuFillRoundedRectangle, XmuReadBitmap-
Data, XmuReadBitmapDataFromFile, XmuReleaseStippledPixmap.

Name

XmuLookup* — translate a key event into a keysym and string, using various keysym sets.

Synopsis

```
#include <X11/Xmu/CharSet.h>
int XmuLookupLatin1(event, buffer, nbytes, keysym, status)
int XmuLookupLatin2(event, buffer, nbytes, keysym, status)
int XmuLookupLatin3(event, buffer, nbytes, keysym, status)
int XmuLookupLatin4(event, buffer, nbytes, keysym, status)
int XmuLookupKana(event, buffer, nbytes, keysym, status)
int XmuLookupJISX0201(event, buffer, nbytes, keysym, status)
int XmuLookupArabic(event, buffer, nbytes, keysym, status)
int XmuLookupCyrillic(event, buffer, nbytes, keysym, status)
int XmuLookupGreek(event, buffer, nbytes, keysym, status)
int XmuLookupHebrew(event, buffer, nbytes, keysym, status)
int XmuLookupAPL(event, buffer, nbytes, keysym, status)
    XKeyEvent *event;
    char *buffer;
    int nbytes;
    KeySym *keysym;
    XComposeStatus *status;
```

Arguments

event   Specifies the key event.

buffer   Returns the translated characters.

nbytes   Specifies the length of the buffer.

keysym   Returns the computed KeySym, or None.

status   Specifies or returns the compose state.

Description

These functions translate a key event into a keysym and string, using a keysym set other than Latin-1, as shown in the following table.

Function	Converts To
XmuLookupLatin1	Latin-1 (ISO 8859-1), or ASCII control (Synonym for XLookupString)
XmuLookupLatin2	Latin-2 (ISO 8859-2), or ASCII control.
XmuLookupLatin3	Latin-3 (ISO 8859-3), or ASCII control.
XmuLookupLatin4	Latin-4 (ISO 8859-4), or ASCII control.
XmuLookupKana	Latin-1 (ISO 8859-1) and ASCII control in the Graphics Left half (values 0 to 127), and Katakana in the Graphics Right half (values 128 to 255), using the values from JIS X201-1976.
XmuLookupJISX0201	JIS X0201-1976 encoding, including ASCII control.
XmuLookupArabic	Latin/Arabic (ISO 8859-6), or ASCII control.
XmuLookupCyrillic	Latin/Cyrillic (ISO 8859-5), or ASCII control.
XmuLookupGreek	Latin/Greek (ISO 8859-7), or ASCII control.
XmuLookupHebrew	Latin/Hebrew (ISO 8859-8), or ASCII control string.
XmuLookupAPL	APL string

XmuLookupLatin1 is identical to XLookupString, and exists only for naming symmetry with other functions covered on this page.

Related Commands

XmuCompareISOLatin1, XmuCopyISOLatin1Lowered, XmuCopyISOLatin1-Uppered.

XmuLookupCloseDisplayHook

Name

XmuLookupCloseDisplayHook — get currently registered close display callback function.

Synopsis

```
#include <X11/Xmu/CloseHook.h>
Bool XmuLookupCloseDisplayHook(display, handle, func, arg)
    Display *display;
    CloseHook handle;
    int (*func)();
    caddr_t arg;
```

Arguments

isplay	Specifies a connection to an X server; returned from XOpenDisplay.
handle	Specifies the callback by ID, or NULL.
func	Specifies the callback by function.
arg	Specifies the function data to match.

Description

XmuLookupCloseDisplayHook determines if a callback is registered. If *handle* is not NULL, it specifies the callback to look for, and the *func* and *arg* parameters are ignored. If handle is NULL, the function will look for any callback that matches the specified *func* and *arg*. This function returns True if a matching callback exists, or otherwise False.

Related Commands

XmuAddCloseDisplayHook, XmuRemoveCloseDisplayHook.

Name

XmuLookupStandardColormap — create a standard colormap if not already created.

Synopsis

```
#include <X11/Xmu/StdCmap.h>
XmuLookupStandardColormap(display, screen, visualid, depth,
        property, replace, retain)
    Display *display;
    int screen;
    VisualID visualid;
    unsigned int depth;
    Atom property;
    Bool replace;
    Bool retain;
```

Arguments

display   Specifies a connection to an X server; returned from XOpenDisplay.

screen   Specifies the screen of the display.

visualid   Specifies the visual type.

depth   Specifies the visual depth.

property   Specifies the standard colormap property.

replace   Specifies whether or not to replace.

retain   Specifies whether or not to retain.

Description

XmuLookupStandardColormap creates a standard colormap if one does not currently exist, or replaces the currently existing standard colormap.

Given a screen, a visual, and a property, this function will determine the best allocation for the property under the specified visual, and determine whether to create a new colormap or to use the default colormap of the screen.

If replace is True, any previous definition of the property will be replaced. If retain is True, the property and the colormap will be made permanent for the duration of the server session. However, pre-existing property definitions which are not replaced cannot be made permanent by a call to this function; a request to retain resources pertains to newly created resources.

XmuLookupStandardColormap returns zero on failure, non-zero on success. A request to create a standard colormap upon a visual which cannot support such a map is considered a failure. An example of this would be requesting any standard colormap property on a monochrome visual, or, requesting an RGB_BEST_MAP on a display whose colormap size is 16.

Related Commands

XmuAllStandardColormaps,   XmuCreateColormap,   XmuDeleteStandard-
Colormap, XmuGetColormapAllocation, XmuStandardColormap, XmuVisual-
StandardColormaps.

Name

XmuMakeAtom — create `AtomPtr` to hold atom list for a property name string.

Synopsis

```
#include <X11/Xmu/Atoms.h>
AtomPtr XmuMakeAtom(name)
    char* name;
```

Arguments

name   Specifies the atom name.

Description

`XmuMakeAtom` creates and initializes an `AtomPtr`, which is an opaque object that contains a property name string and a list of atoms for that string—one for each display. `XmuIntern-Atom` is used to fill in the atom for each display.

Related Commands

`XmuGetAtomName`, `XmuInternAtom`, `XmuInternStrings`, `XmuNameofAtom`.

XmuNameOfAtom

Name

XmuNameOfAtom — return property name string represented by an `AtomPtr`.

Synopsis

```
#include <X11/Xmu/Atoms.h>
char *XmuNameOfAtom(atom_ptr)
    AtomPtr atom_ptr;
```

Arguments

atom_ptr   Specifies the `AtomPtr`.

Description

`XmuNameOfAtom` returns the property name string represented by the specified `AtomPtr`.

Related Commands

`XmuGetAtomName`, `XmuInternAtom`, `XmuInternStrings`, `XmuMakeAtom`.

Xmu
Library

XmuPrintDefaultErrorMessage

Name

XmuPrintDefaultErrorMessage — print the standard protocol error message.

Synopsis

```
#include <X11/Xmu/Error.h>
int XmuPrintDefaultErrorMessage(display, event, fp)
    Display *display;
    XErrorEvent *event;
    FILE *fp;
```

Arguments

display   Specifies a connection to an X server; returned from XOpenDisplay.

event   Specifies the error event whose contents will be printed.

fp   Specifies where to print the error message.

Description

XmuPrintDefaultErrorMessage prints an error message, equivalent to Xlib's default error message for protocol errors. It returns a non-zero value if the caller should consider exiting, otherwise it returns zero. This function can be used when you need to write your own error handler, but need to print out an error from within that handler.

Related Commands

XmuSimpleErrorHandler.

XmuReadBitmapData

Name

XmuReadBitmapData — read and check bitmap data from any stream source.

Synopsis

```
#include <X11/Xmu/Drawing.h>
int XmuReadBitmapData(fstream, width, height, datap, x_hot,
        y_hot)
  FILE *fstream;
  unsigned int *width, *height;
  unsigned char **datap;
  int *x_hot, *y_hot;
```

Arguments

stream	Specifies the stream to read from.
width	Returns the width of the bitmap.
height	Returns the height of the bitmap.
datap	Returns the parsed bitmap data.
x_hot	Returns the x coordinate of the hotspot.
y_hot	Returns the y coordinate of the hotspot.

Description

XmuReadBitmapData reads a standard bitmap file description from the specified stream, and returns the parsed data in a format suitable for passing to XCreatePixmapFromBitmapData. The return value of the function has the same meaning as the return value for XReadBitmapFile.

XmuReadBitmapData is equivalent to XReadBitmapFile, except that this routine processes any type of stream input, and it does not create a pixmap containing the resulting data. This is useful when you want to create a multi-plane pixmap from the data, and don't want to create an intermediate one-plane pixmap.

Related Commands

XmuCreatePixmapFromBitmap, XmuCreateStippledPixmap, XmuDrawLogo, XmuDrawRoundedRectangle, XmuFillRoundedRectangle, XmuLocateBitmapFile, XmuReadBitmapDataFromFile, XmuReleaseStippledPixmap.

Xmu
Library

XmuReadBitmapDataFromFile

Name
XmuReadBitmapDataFromFile — read and check bitmap data from a file.

Synopsis
```
#include <X11/Xmu/Drawing.h>
int XmuReadBitmapDataFromFile(filename, width, height, datap,
        x_hot, y_hot)
  char *filename;
  unsigned int *width, *height;
  unsigned char **datap;
  int *x_hot, *y_hot;
```

Arguments
filename	Specifies the file to read from.
width	Returns the width of the bitmap.
height	Returns the height of the bitmap.
datap	Returns the parsed bitmap data.
x_hot	Returns the x coordinate of the hotspot.
y_hot	Returns the y coordinate of the hotspot.

Description
XmuReadBitmapDataFromFile reads a standard bitmap file description from the specified file, and returns the parsed data in a format suitable for passing to XCreatePixmapFrom-BitmapData. The return value of the function has the same meaning as the return value for XReadBitmapFile.

Unlike XReadBitmapFile, this function does not create a pixmap. This function is useful when you want to create a multi-plane pixmap without creating an intermediate one-plane pixmap.

Related Commands
XmuCreatePixmapFromBitmap, XmuCreateStippledPixmap, XmuDrawLogo, XmuDrawRoundedRectangle, XmuFillRoundedRectangle, XmuLocateBitmap-File, XmuReadBitmapData, XmuReleaseStippledPixmap.

Name

XmuReleaseStippledPixmap — release pixmap created with `XmuCreateStippled-Pixmap`.

Synopsis

```
#include <X11/Xmu/Drawing.h>
void XmuReleaseStippledPixmap(screen, pixmap)
    Screen *screen;
    Pixmap pixmap;
```

Arguments

screen   Specifies the screen the pixmap was created on.

pixmap   Specifies the pixmap to free.

Description

`XmuReleaseStippledPixmap` frees a pixmap created with `XmuCreateStippled-Pixmap`, to maintain correct cache reference counts.

Related Commands

`XmuCreatePixmapFromBitmap`, `XmuCreateStippledPixmap`, `XmuDrawLogo`, `XmuDrawRoundedRectangle`, `XmuFillRoundedRectangle`, `XmuLocateBitmap-File`, `XmuReadBitmapData`, `XmuReadBitmapDataFromFile`.

XmuRemoveCloseDisplayHook

Name
XmuRemoveCloseDisplayHook — remove registered close display callback function.

Synopsis
```
#include <X11/Xmu/CloseHook.h>
Bool XmuRemoveCloseDisplayHook(display, handle, func, arg)
    Display *display;
    CloseHook handle;
    int (*func)();
    caddr_t arg;
```

Arguments

display   Specifies a connection to an X server; returned from XOpenDisplay.

handle   Specifies the callback by ID, or NULL.

func   Specifies the callback by function.

arg   Specifies the function data to match.

Description
XmuRemoveCloseDisplayHook unregisters a callback that has been registered with Xmu-AddCloseDisplayHook. If handle is not NULL, it specifies the ID of the callback to remove, and the *func* and *arg* parameters are ignored. If handle is NULL, the first callback found to match the specified *func* and *arg* will be removed. Returns True if a callback was removed, else returns False.

Related Commands
XmuAddCloseDisplayHook, XmuLookupCloseDisplayHook.

XmuScreenOfWindow

Name
XmuScreenOfWindow — returns a pointer to the Screen structure for the specified window.

Synopsis
```
#include <X11/Xmu/WinUtil.h>
Screen *XmuScreenOfWindow(display, w)
    Display *display;
    Window w;
```

Arguments
display   Specifies a connection to an X server; returned from XOpenDisplay.

w   Specifies the window.

Description
XmuScreenOfWindow returns a pointer to the Screen structure that describes the screen on which the specified window was created.

Related Commands
XmuClientWindow, XmuUpdateMapHints.

Xmu
Library

Name

XmuSimpleErrorHandler — an error handler that ignores certain errors.

Synopsis

```
#include <X11/Xmu/Error.h>
int XmuSimpleErrorHandler(display, error)
    Display *display;
    XErrorEvent *error;
```

Arguments

display   Specifies a connection to an X server; returned from XOpenDisplay.

error   Specifies the error event.

Description

XmuSimpleErrorHandler ignores BadWindow errors for XQueryTree and XGet-WindowAttributes, and ignores BadDrawable errors for XGetGeometry; it returns zero in those cases. Otherwise, it prints the default error message, and returns a non-zero value if the caller should consider exiting, and zero if the caller should not exit.

Related Commands

XmuPrintDefaultErrorMessage.

XmuStandardColormap

Name

XmuStandardColormap — create one standard colormap.

Synopsis

```
#include <X11/Xmu/StdCmap.h>
XmuStandardColormap(display, screen, visualid, depth, property,
        cmap, red_max, green_max, blue_max)
    Display display;
    int screen;
    VisualID visualid;
    unsigned int depth;
    Atom property;
    Colormap cmap;
    unsigned long red_max, green_max, blue_max;
```

Arguments

display	Specifies a connection to an X server; returned from XOpenDisplay.
screen	Specifies the screen of the display.
visualid	Specifies the visual type.
depth	Specifies the visual depth.
property	Specifies the standard colormap property.
cmap	Specifies the colormap ID, or None.
red_max	Specifies the red allocation.
green_max	Specifies the green allocation.
blue_max	Specifies the blue allocation.

Description

XmuStandardColormap creates one standard colormap for the given screen, visualid, and visual depth, with the given red, green, and blue maximum values, with the given standard property name. Upon success, it returns a pointer to an XStandardColormap structure which describes the newly created colormap. Upon failure, it returns NULL. If *cmap* is the default colormap of the screen, the standard colormap will be defined on the default colormap; otherwise a new colormap is created.

Resources created by this function are not made permanent; that is the caller's responsibility.

Related Commands

XmuAllStandardColormaps, XmuCreateColormap, XmuDeleteStandard-Colormap, XmuGetColormapAllocation, XmuLookupStdCmp, XmuVisual-StandardColormaps.

Xmu
Library

Name

XmuUpdateMapHints — set WM_HINTS flags to USSize and USPosition.

Synopsis

```
#include <X11/Xmu/WinUtil.h>
Bool XmuUpdateMapHints(display, w, hints)
    Display *display;
    Window w;
    XSizeHints *hints;
```

Arguments

display	Specifies a connection to an X server; returned from XOpenDisplay.
win	Specifies the window.
hints	Specifies the new hints, or NULL.

Description

XmuUpdateMapHints clears the PPosition and PSize flags and sets the USPosition and USSize flags in the hints structure, and then stores the hints for the window using XSet-WMNormalHints and returns True. If NULL is passed for the hints structure, then the current hints are read back from the window using XGetWMNormalHints the flags are set as described above, the property is reset, and True is returned. XmuUpdateMapHints returns False if it was unable to allocate memory or, when NULL is passed, if the existing hints could not be read.

Related Commands

XmuClientWindow, XmuScreenOfWindow.

XmuVisualStandardColormaps

Name

XmuVisualStandardColormaps — create all standard colormaps for given visual and screen.

Synopsis

```
#include <X11/Xmu/StdCmap.h>
XmuVisualStandardColormaps(display, screen, visualid, depth,
        replace, retain)
    Display *display;
    int screen;
    VisualID visualid;
    unsigned int depth;
    Bool replace;
    Bool retain;
```

Arguments

display   Specifies a connection to an X server; returned from XOpenDisplay.

screen   Specifies the screen of the display.

visualid   Specifies the visual type.

depth   Specifies the visual depth.

replace   Specifies whether or not to replace the standard colormap property.

retain   Specifies whether or not to retain the colormap resource permanently.

Description

XmuVisualStandardColormaps creates all of the appropriate standard colormaps for a given visual on a given screen, and optionally redefines the corresponding standard colormap properties.

If replace is True, any previous definition will be removed. If retain is True, new properties will be retained for the duration of the server session. This function returns zero on failure, non-zero on success. On failure, no new properties will be defined, but old ones may have been removed if replace was True.

Not all standard colormaps are meaningful to all visual classes. This routine will check and define the following properties for the following classes, provided that the size of the colormap is not too small. For DirectColor and PseudoColor: RGB_DEFAULT_MAP, RGB_BEST_MAP, RGB_RED_MAP, RGB_GREEN_MAP, RGB_BLUE_MAP, and RGB_GRAY_MAP. For TrueColor and StaticColor: RGB_BEST_MAP. For GrayScale and StaticGray: RGB_GRAY_MAP.

Related Commands

XmuAllStandardColormaps, XmuCreateColormap, XmuDeleteStandard-Colormap, XmuGetColormapAllocation, XmuLookupStdCmp, XmuStandard-Colormap.

Window Attributes at a Glance

Member	Values / Default	Mask	Convenience Function
Pixmap background_pixmap;	pixmap (depth of window), ParentRelative / **None**	CWBackPixmap	XSetWindowBackgroundPixmap
unsigned long background_pixel;	pixel value / **undefined**	CWBackPixel	XSetWindowBackground
Pixmap border_pixmap;	pixmap (depth of window), None / **CopyFromParent**	CWBorderPixmap	XSetWindowBorderPixmap
unsigned long border_pixel;	pixel value / **undefined**	CWBorderPixel	XSetWindowBorder
int bit_gravity;	StaticGravity, NorthWestGravity, NorthGravity, NorthEastGravity, WestGravity, CenterGravity, SouthWestGravity, SouthGravity, EastGravity, SouthEastGravity / **ForgetGravity**	CWBitGravity	none
int win_gravity;	same as above, UnmapGravity / **NorthWestGravity**	CWWinGravity	none
int backing_store;	WhenMapped, Always / **NotUseful**	CWBackingStore	none
unsigned long backing_planes;	bit mask / **AllPlanes**	CWBackingPlanes	none
unsigned long backing_pixel;	pixel value / **0**	CWBackingPixel	none
Bool save_under;	True / **False**	CWSaveUnder	none
long event_mask;	OR of event mask symbols * / **0**	CWEventMask	XSelectInput
long do_not_propagate_mask;	OR of event mask symbols * / **0**	CWDontPropagate	none
Bool override_redirect;	True / **False**,	CWOverrideRedirect	none
Colormap colormap;	colormap ID, None / **CopyFromParent**	CWColormap	XSetWindowColormap
Cursor cursor;	cursor ID / **None** (copy from parent)	CWCursor	XDefineCursor, XUndefineCursor

All attributes can be set with XCreateWindow or XChangeWindowAttributes.

* The event_mask **symbols are:**
NoEventMask, KeyPressMask, KeyReleaseMask, ButtonPressMask, ButtonReleaseMask, EnterWindowMask, LeaveWindowMask, PointerMotionMask, PointerMotionHintMask, Button1MotionMask, Button2MotionMask, Button3MotionMask, Button4MotionMask, Button5MotionMask, ButtonMotionMask, KeymapStateMask, ExposureMask, VisibilityChangeMask, StructureNotifyMask, ResizeRedirectMask, SubstructureNotifyMask, SubstructureRedirectMask, FocusChangeMask, PropertyChangeMask, ColormapChangeMask, OwnerGrabButtonMask.

line_style LineSolid LineOnOffDash LineDoubleDash

cap_style

CapNotLast CapButt CapRound CapProjecting

join_style

JoinRound JoinMiter JoinBevel

fill_style

Tile   GC foreground ▓   GC background ░   Undrawn Pixels ⊠

FillSolid FillTiled FillStippled FillOpaqueStippled

Stipple

0	1	0
0	1	0
0	1	0

fill_rule

Outline of polygon to fill   EvenOddRule   WindingRule

arc_mode

ArcChord   ArcPieSlice

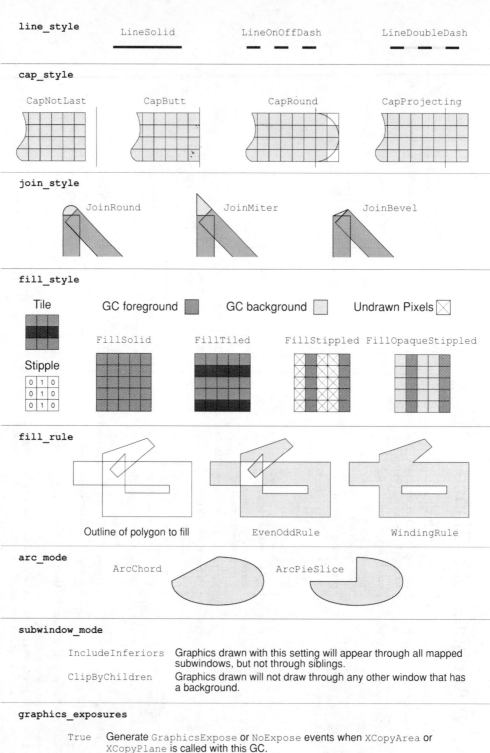

subwindow_mode

IncludeInferiors   Graphics drawn with this setting will appear through all mapped
subwindows, but not through siblings.

ClipByChildren   Graphics drawn will not draw through any other window that has
a background.

graphics_exposures

True   Generate GraphicsExpose or NoExpose events when XCopyArea or
XCopyPlane is called with this GC.

False   Don't generate GraphicsExpose or NoExpose events.